The Routledge Handbook of Language and Digital Communication

The Routledge Handbook of Language and Digital Communication provides a comprehensive, state-of-the-art overview of language-focused research on digital communication, taking stock and registering the latest trends that set the agenda for future developments in this thriving and fast-moving field. The contributors are all leading figures or established authorities in their areas, covering a wide range of topics and concerns in the following seven sections:

- Methods and perspectives
- Language resources, genres, and discourses
- Digital literacies
- Digital communication in public
- Digital selves and online–offline lives
- Communities, networks, relationships
- New debates and further directions.

This volume showcases critical syntheses of the established literature on key topics and issues and, at the same time, reflects upon and engages with cutting-edge research and new directions for study (as emerging within social media). A wide range of languages are represented, from Japanese, Greek, German, and Scandinavian languages, to computer-mediated Arabic, Chinese, and African languages.

The Routledge Handbook of Language and Digital Communication is an essential resource for advanced undergraduates, postgraduates, and researchers within English language and linguistics, applied linguistics, and media and communication studies.

Alexandra Georgakopoulou is Professor of Discourse Analysis and Sociolinguistics, King's College London, UK.

Tereza Spilioti is Senior Lecturer in Language and Communication at Cardiff University, UK.

Routledge Handbooks in Applied Linguistics

Routledge Handbooks in Applied Linguistics provide comprehensive overviews of the key topics in applied linguistics. All entries for the handbooks are specially commissioned and written by leading scholars in the field. Clear, accessible and carefully edited, *Routledge Handbooks in Applied Linguistics* are the ideal resource for both advanced undergraduates and postgraduate students.

The Routledge Handbook of Literacy Studies
Edited by Jennifer Rowsell and Kate Pahl

The Routledge Handbook of Interpreting
Edited by Holly Mikkelson and Renée Jourdenais

The Routledge Handbook of Hispanic Applied Linguistics
Edited by Manel Lacorte

The Routledge Handbook of Educational Linguistics
Edited by Martha Bigelow and Johanna Ennser-Kananen

The Routledge Handbook of Forensic Linguistics
Edited by Malcolm Coulthard and Alison Johnson

The Routledge Handbook of Corpus Linguistics
Edited by Anne O'Keeffe and Mike McCarthy

The Routledge Handbook of World Englishes
Edited by Andy Kirkpatrick

The Routledge Handbook of Applied Linguistics
Edited by James Simpson

The Routledge Handbook of Discourse Analysis
Edited by James Paul Gee and Michael Handford

The Routledge Handbook of Second Language Acquisition
Edited by Susan Gass and Alison Mackey

The Routledge Handbook of Language and Intercultural Communication
Edited by Jane Jackson

The Routledge Handbook of Language Testing
Edited by Glenn Fulcher and Fred Davidson

The Routledge Handbook of Multilingualism
Edited by Marilyn Martin-Jones, Adrian Blackledge and Angela Creese

The Routledge Handbook of Translation Studies
Edited by Carmen Millán-Varela and Francesca Bartrina

The Routledge Handbook of Language and Health Communication
Edited by Heidi E. Hamilton and Wen-ying Sylvia Chou

The Routledge Handbook of Language and Professional Communication
Edited by Stephen Bremner and Vijay Bhatia

The Routledge Handbook of Language and Digital Communication

*Edited by Alexandra Georgakopoulou
and Tereza Spilioti*

Routledge
Taylor & Francis Group

LONDON AND NEW YORK

First published in paperback 2020

First published 2016
by Routledge
2 Park Square, Milton Park, Abingdon, Oxon OX14 4RN

and by Routledge
52 Vanderbilt Avenue, New York, NY 10017

Routledge is an imprint of the Taylor & Francis Group, an informa business

British Library Cataloguing-in-Publication Data
A catalogue record for this book is available from the British Library

Library of Congress Cataloging-in-Publication Data
The Routledge handbook of language and digital communication / Edited by Alexandra Georgakopoulou and Tereza Spilioti.
pages cm
Includes bibliographical references and index.
1. Language and languages—Computer network resources—Handbooks, manuals, etc. 2. Digital communication—Handbooks, manuals, etc. I. Georgakopoulou, Alexandra, editor. II. Spilioti, Tereza, editor. III. Title: Handbook of language and digital communication.
P53.285.R68 2015
418.00285—dc23
2014049461

ISBN: 978-0-415-64249-1 (hbk)
ISBN: 978-0-367-46645-9 (pbk)
ISBN: 978-1-31569-434-4 (ebk)

Typeset in Bembo
by Swales & Willis Ltd, Exeter, Devon, UK

Contents

Contents

Figures

Tables

Contributors

Ashraf R. Abdullah is a recent PhD graduate of the School of English at the University of Leeds, UK, and now teaches at the University of Mosul, Iraq. His research focuses on sociolinguistics, corpus linguistics, digital communication, language and social media, language and identity, and virtual identity.

Jannis Androutsopoulos is Professor of German and Media Linguistics at the University of Hamburg, Germany. His research examines relations between language, media and society. He has published on youth language, hip-hop, style, computer-mediated communication, multilingualism, and language ideologies in media discourse.

Jo Angouri is an associate professor at The University of Warwick, UK, where she conducts research in sociolinguistics, pragmatics and discourse analysis in a range of corporate and institutional contexts. Her work addresses online and face-to-face interaction, language and identity, teamwork and leadership in medical settings, and comparative analyses of business discourse.

Naomi S. Baron is Professor of Linguistics and Executive Director of the Center for Teaching, Research and Learning at American University in Washington DC, USA. A Guggenheim Fellow and Swedish Fulbright Fellow, her most recent book is *Words Onscreen: The Fate of Reading in a Digital World* (Oxford).

Erika Darics (@LinguaDigitalis) holds a PhD from Loughborough University, UK. Her research has examined the linguistic and discursive features of digital discourse, with particular emphasis on professional and workplace settings. She is interested in digitally mediated business communication, and currently works for the Centre of Interdisciplinary Research into Language and Diversity at Aston University, UK.

Charles M. Ess is Professor of Media Studies, Department of Media and Communication, University of Oslo. Ess has published extensively in information and computing ethics and in internet studies. His work emphasizes cross–cultural approaches to media, communication, and ethics.

Alexandra Georgakopoulou is Professor of Discourse Analysis and Sociolinguistics, King's College London. She has researched the role of everyday life stories (both face-to-face and on new/social media) in the (re)formation of social relations. Her books include include *Small Stories, Interaction and Identities* (2007) and *Analyzing Narrative* (with Anna De Fina, 2012). Her current research project is entitled: 'Life-writing of the moment. The sharing and updating self on social media' and is part of an ERC funded project: www.ego-media.org.

Sage Lambert Graham completed her PhD in Linguistics at Georgetown University in 2003 and is currently an associate professor of linguistics at the University of Memphis. Using language as an analytical lens, she explores causes of misunderstanding and conflict in computer-mediated communication, impoliteness, and patterns of identity construction through language choices.

Rebecca Hagelmoser is founder of NarraTool, a company for strategic consulting in storytelling. She is currently writing her dissertation on 'Corporate storytelling: Forms and functions of narrative self-representation of the automotive industry' at the GCSC, Justus-Liebig University Giessen. Her research interests are transmedial storytelling, storytelling in organizations, and narration in computer games.

Susan C. Herring is Professor of Information Science and Linguistics at Indiana University, Bloomington. She has been researching computer-mediated communication since 1991, with a focus on language and discourse. She previously edited the *Journal of Computer-Mediated Communication* and currently edits *Language@Internet*.

Theresa Heyd is a researcher at the English Department of Freiburg University. Her current work is focused on the sociolinguistics of globalization and the emergence of globalized vernaculars. She has published on aspects of mediated discourse, including the pragmatics of CMC and digital genre theory.

Lars Hinrichs is Associate Professor of English Language and Linguistics at the University of Texas at Austin. He obtained his doctorate from the University of Freiburg, Germany with a dissertation on linguistic code-switching in online contexts among Jamaican writers of Creole and English. His current interests include spoken language among members of the Jamaican diaspora, as well as dialects of English in Texas. He also conducts corpus-linguistic research on variation in written Standard English.

Josh Iorio is a researcher in the department of Civil and Environmental Engineering at Virginia Tech. A trained linguist and a specialist in virtual world interactions, his current work focuses on conflict management in multilingual global virtual engineering project networks.

Carey Jewitt is Professor of Learning and Technology and Head of the Culture, Communication and Media Department at the Institute of Education, University of London. Her interests concern the development of visual and multimodal research methods, video-based research, and technology-mediated interaction in learning contexts. She is Director of the 'Multimodal Methods for Researching Digital Data and Environments', a NCRM Node funded by the ESRC (Mode.ioe.ac.uk). Carey's recent publications include *The Sage Handbook of Researching Digital Technologies* (2013) with Sara Price and Barry Brown; *The Routledge Handbook of Multimodal Analysis* (2013), and *Technology, Literacy and Learning: A Multimodal Approach* (Routledge, 2008).

Rodney H. Jones is Professor of Applied Linguistics at City University of Hong Kong. He is author, along with Christoph Hafner, of *Understanding Digital Literacies: A Practical Introduction* (Routledge 2012). His most recent monograph is *Health and Risk Communication: An Applied Linguistic Perspective* (Routledge 2013).

Elizabeth Keating is Professor of Anthropology at the University of Texas, Austin. Her research interests include technologically mediated communication, discourse and culture, language and social inequality, multimodality, American Sign Language, and online gaming. She has been editor of the *Journal of Linguistic Anthropology* and Director of the UT Austin Science, Technology and Society Program.

Contributors

Helen Kelly-Holmes is Senior Lecturer in Sociolinguistics and New Media at the University of Limerick, Ireland. She has published widely in a range of journals on the economic aspects of multilingualism, particularly in relation to marketing and advertising.

Nenagh Kemp received her doctorate from the University of Oxford and is now a Senior Lecturer in Psychology at the University of Tasmania, Australia. She is interested in spelling development and spelling in digital communication.

Michele Knobel is a professor of education at Montclair State University (USA). She is especially interested in young people's everyday literacy practices and what it means to 'be literate' in current times. Her books include (co-edited with Colin Lankshear) *A New Literacies Reader* (Peter Lang 2013).

Samu Kytölä is a postdoctoral researcher at the Department of Languages, University of Jyväskylä. His research interests include sociolinguistic diversity in Finland, non-native/non-Standard Englishes, metapragmatics of language ideologies, the sociolinguistics of inequalities, transcultural and multilingual football (soccer) discourses, and ethnographies of (digital) writing.

Colin Lankshear is an independent researcher and writer living in Mexico, and an adjunct professor in the College of Arts, Society and Education at James Cook University (Australia) and at Mount St Vincent University (Canada). His books include (with Michele Knobel) *New Literacies: Everyday Practices and Social Learning* (Peter Lang 2011, 3rd edition).

Carmen Lee is Associate Professor in the Department of English at the Chinese University of Hong Kong. She has published and carried out projects on social aspects of language and literacy, linguistic practices on the internet, and multilingual literacy practices. She is co-author (with David Barton) of *Language Online* (Routledge 2013).

Lisa Newon earned her PhD from the Department of Anthropology at UCLA in 2014. Her dissertation, 'Discourses of connectedness: Globalization, digital media, and the language of community', is an ethnographic study of how game developers and players build networked, global communities through language, technology, and interaction.

Yukiko Nishimura is Professor in the Faculty of Global Communication at Toyo Gakuen University, Tokyo. Her articles have appeared in *The Journal of Computer-Mediated Communication*, *Berkeley Linguistics Society Proceedings*, *Language@Internet*, and *The Journal of Politeness Research*, as well as in the volumes *The Multilingual Internet* and *Digital Discourse* (both from Oxford University Press).

Ruth Page is a reader at the University of Leicester. Her research spans literary-critical and discourse-analytic research narrative traditions, with a special focus on language and gender and narratives told in new media.

John C. Paolillo holds a BA in Linguistics from Cornell University (1986) and a PhD in Linguistics from Stanford University (1992). He is an associate professor of informatics and computing at Indiana University, Bloomington, where he teaches and conducts research in the area of Social Informatics, with an emphasis on quantitative methods.

Cornelius Puschmann is Acting Professor of Communication Science at Zeppelin University, Friedrichshafen and Research Associate at the Humboldt Institute for Internet and Society in Berlin. Prior to this, he was a visiting fellow at the Oxford Internet Institute and Visiting Assistant Professor at the University of Amsterdam. His interests include computer-mediated communication, science communication, and organisational communication.

Philip Seargeant is Senior Lecturer in Applied Linguistics at the Open University. He is author of *The Idea of English in Japan* (Multilingual Matters 2009) and *Exploring World Englishes* (Routledge 2012), and editor of *English in Japan in the Era of Globalization* (Palgrave Macmillan 2011), *English in the World* (with Joan Swann, Routledge 2012), *English and Development* (with Elizabeth J. Erling, Multilingual Matters 2013), and *The Language of Social Media* (with Caroline Tagg, Palgrave Macmillan 2014).

Tereza Spilioti is Senior Lecturer in Language and Communication at Cardiff University. Her research interests focus on the intersections of language and digital media and, particularly, issues of social presence online, multilingualism and language ideologies. Her publications include articles in journals (e.g. *Discourse, Context & Media* and *Language@Internet*), chapters in edited volumes, and a special issue on 'Online research ethics in applied linguistics' (with Caroline Tagg, *Applied Linguistics Review*, 2017).

Lauren Squires is Assistant Professor in the Department of English at The Ohio State University, USA. She conducts research on language and mass media, computer-mediated communication, language ideologies, and sociolinguistic perception.

Caroline Tagg is Lecturer in English Language and Applied Linguistics, University of Birmingham. Her research interests are in the language of social media, including language creativity and play, and the role of language in negotiating online privacy and intimacy. Her publications include *Exploring Digital Communication* (Routledge 2015), *The Language of Social Media: Identity and Community on the Internet* (with Philip Seargeant, Palgrave 2014), and *The Discourse of Text Messaging* (Continuum 2012).

Jana Tereick is Interim Full Professor of German Language Didactics at the University of Vechta, Germany. She has worked and published on corpus-assisted multimodal discourse analysis, language ideology, critical language use, and multilingualism and linguistic diversity in teaching environments.

Piia Varis is Assistant Professor at the Department of Culture Studies and Deputy Director of the Babylon Centre for the Study of Superdiversity at Tilburg University (The Netherlands). Her research focuses broadly on digital culture and on identity and meaning-making practices online.

Sam Waldron is a researcher within the reading development team at Coventry University, UK. Her interests include reading development, especially with regards to the impact of modern technology.

Clare Wood is Professor of Psychology in Education at Coventry University, UK. Her research interests encompass all areas of reading development and the impact of technology on learning.

Introduction

Alexandra Georgakopoulou and Tereza Spilioti

Introduction

This Handbook aims to bring together a collection of state-of-the-art chapters that provide an overview of key issues and current advances in language-focused research on digital communication. Since the early 1990s, the study of language, text, discourse, and social interaction in – and through – digital media, often referred to as linguistically focused Computer-Mediated Communication (CMC) research or Computer-Mediated Discourse Analysis (CMDA) as in Herring 2004, has rapidly grown into a thriving area that has earned an important place within the range of socially minded linguistic disciplines (e.g., discourse analysis, pragmatics, sociolinguistics). The area's increasing consolidation is evident in, among other indications, a dedicated peer-reviewed journal (*Language@Internet*), a substantial number of language-focused Special Issues of the *Journal of Computer-Mediated Communication*, and Special Issues in major sociolinguistic and discourse studies journals, e.g. the *Journal of Sociolinguistics* (ed. Androutsopoulos 2006a), *Journal of Politeness Research* (ed. Locher 2010), *Journal of Pragmatics* (Bou-Franch and Blitvich, eds 2014, vol. 73; and Frobenius, Eisenlauer, and Gerhardt, eds 2014, vol. 72); *Pragmatics* (Locher, Bolander, and Hohn, eds 2015). At the same time, a number of state-of-the-art chapters on CMC in linguistically oriented handbooks and the increase of relevant themed panels and colloquia[1] attest to the significance of the area and place it at the forefront of contemporary research in socially minded linguistic disciplines.

Despite this momentum, dedicated publications of collections of state-of-the-art material that both take stock of and register the latest trends remain scarce, particularly if compared to publications on digital communication in the cognate disciplines of sociology, and cultural and media studies. This scarcity of publications that document the area presents the danger of too much diversity and lack of convergence, with scholars and graduate students facing difficulties in building on previous work and identifying agreed upon and well-defined methodologies. To address this gap, we have brought together in this volume work that shows how the study of key issues in the area has benefited from cross-fertilization with a wide range of linguistic fields, including discourse analysis, pragmatics, sociolinguistics, linguistic anthropology, and literacy studies. At the same time, our contributors show how the specificity of focal concerns in the study of language and digital media has necessitated the process of revisiting, extending, fine-tuning, and, where appropriate, moving away from established concepts and methodologies, as we will explain below.

Given the fast-moving nature of digital media and technological advances, we recognize the need for and importance of a broad inclusion of foci of inquiry, some of which inevitably present less consolidation than others: this particularly applies to recent research on social media. The inclusion of an overview of such work has been undertaken in this collection with an awareness of the danger of over-stating the difficulties of taking stock in an area where the sands are forever shifting. But there is arguably no area of human communication shielded from – in many cases overwhelming – socio-cultural changes, including technological developments. To somehow then defer the task of acknowledging and establishing convergence on methods, analyses, and tools that can equip the language and digital media scholar for current and future challenges may be exoticizing the so-called 'new media' as a perennially novel and un-pin-down-able object of enquiry. Our view is that the time is ripe to showcase the critical mass in the area in a confident rather than an apologetic way. This is attested to in the selection and mixing of chapters in each of our Parts to cover both first generation digital media (e.g., email, instant messaging, text-messaging, online forums) and more recent social media (e.g., Facebook, Twitter, YouTube). It is also evident within individual chapters that trace the development of analytical foci, tools, and methodologies across different generations of digital technologies.

Points of convergence

Our decisions on inclusion and coverage have followed broad principles and the topics that we view as having been crystallized in the literature, in that there is both a critical mass to support them and a reflexive dialogue within the field between earlier and later approaches. The first such point of convergence is related to the development of an identity for the field that has gradually found a balance between two competing requirements: on the one hand, the need for some kind of disciplinary autonomy that can ensure the distinctiveness of research priorities and concerns around the study of language and communication on digital media; and on the other hand, the need for interaction and cross-fertilizations with established fields of socially minded linguistic work and related disciplines such as communication, media, and cultural studies. This is a delicate juggling act and is evident in the interdisciplinary perspectives contributors have brought together in their chapters.

In earlier work, it has been argued that not benefiting from sociolinguistic key insights and advances has meant that studies of the so-called 'first wave' of CMC research (Androutsopoulos 2006b) ended up having to deal with the same problems and limitations that had already been addressed in theoretical and methodological developments in related disciplines (Georgakopoulou 2006). This is particularly evident in the case of some of the earlier work on the position of CMC in relation to speech and writing, which could have productively drawn on the advances in contextual linguistic analysis. In contrast to the earlier uneasiness of the CMC field between the centripetal forces of autonomy and the centrifugal forces of intersection, many chapters in this volume show how cross-fertilization with other fields, in particular sociolinguistics, has been fully embraced. Such cross-fertilization is evident in the ease with which studies open up to concepts from media studies and sociolinguistics, such as remediation (e.g., see chapters by Heyd, Puschmann and Hagelmoser, and Squires), translocality (e.g., see chapters by Varis, and Kytölä) and superdiversity (e.g., see chapter by Lee), and, at the same time, borrow and operationalize a range of methods (e.g., network analysis, variationist analysis, and multimodal analysis – see chapters by Paolillo, Hinricks, and Jewitt respectively) for the study of digital communication. This process has facilitated the move away from treating the medium deterministically, restrictively, and uni-dimensionally, as we will see below.

At the same time, research on language and digital media has now developed a distinctive set of concerns and priorities so that relevant studies do not just pay lip service to bigger sociolinguistic or pragmatic concerns but can play a key role in shaping current debates about re-conceptualizations of core concepts within socially minded linguistics, such as context, genre, style, identity, community, and globalization (e.g., see chapters by Angouri, Heyd, Nishimura, Page, and Graham).

Furthermore, there is an increasing development and systematization of concepts that have been gaining impetus in sociolinguistics, such as 'affinity spaces' (see chapter by Knobel and Lankshear) for the study of communities in new learning environments, remixing (see Androutsopoulos and Tereick), personalization (see Kelly-Holmes, and Puschmann and Hagelmoser), publicization (see Squires) and recasting of the private vs the public as for instance in 'social reading' (see Baron). The theorization of the above is intimately linked with the digital environments' affordances of heightened searchability (content can be searched and found), scalability (content can be visible to both known and unknown audiences), replicability (content can be duplicated and shared) and persistence (content is automatically recorded and archived – see boyd 2011).

The second recognized tendency in studies of language and digital media is the definitive move towards contextualized approaches that view language and communication in digital environments as both locally situated and as socio-culturally and historically shaped. The often quoted Special Issue of the *Journal of Sociolinguistics* in 2006 has advocated such approaches as both a desideratum and a prerequisite for the decisive move to the second wave of CMC studies. Almost a decade later, the resonance and prevalence of contextualized approaches to language and digital communication are undisputed. This consolidation has allowed concerns characteristic of the first wave of CMC, such as linguistic creativity, innovation, and genres to be explored away from the technological determinism of earlier approaches and within situated and nuanced perspectives (e.g., see chapters by Heyd, Nishimura, Puschmann and Hagelmoser, Darics, and Waldron, Kemp, and Wood). The advent of ethnography and the influence of New Literacy Studies (Scribner and Cole 1981; Street 1984) on the study of digital literacies have also played a key role in the development of contextualised perspectives in the area (see chapters by Knobel and Lankshear, and Iorio).

This volume does not only attest to the consolidation of a move from medium-related to user-related perspectives, as the second wave of CMC is often described (Androutsopoulos 2006b) but it also reveals a consistent approach to digital environments as multi-layered spaces, mutually constitutive of the language and communication practices that occur in them. Building on the second wave's more nuanced understandings of technological systems in terms of synchronicity and its focus on users' activities and practices, the volume includes latest insights into the ways in which digital environments are designed and engineered; more specifically, it includes insights into how this ecology encourages and engenders specific kinds of communication while constraining others (e.g., see chapters by Graham, Kelly-Holmes, Spilioti, Squires, and Tagg and Seargeant). Contextual approaches are also well placed to explore how people's embodied engagements with digital media and digital environments are interwoven into daily life. This body of work also addresses questions about how such engagements shape physical space (e.g., see chapters by Keating and Herring) and treats the existence and integration of multiple modalities both online and offline as a given and a point of departure for the study of language and communication, placing the concepts of multimodality and multisemioticity as central to current research on language and digital media. As becomes clear in the ongoing methodological reflections of the field, there is still much scope for contextualization to include metrics-based analyses as a way of furthering understanding of digital environments as local contexts where our actions intersect with data exchanges and strings of computer code (algorithms), determining our experience of interacting with texts and with one another and, thus, mediating social interaction and identities (see chapter by Jones).

Another major point of methodological and analytical consolidation and convergence is to be found in the turn to the study of multimodality in digital communication. Jewitt's chapter reminds us that multimodality has always accompanied language use and so it is not exclusively associated with technological changes. In this respect, multimodality is a key area in which to test out insights from a longstanding tradition in research. The current emphasis on multimodality within studies of digital communication is a far cry from the heavy reliance on linguistic means that characterized earlier approaches. Such reliance has been related to the primarily text-based environments typical of first generation digital technologies such as email, text-messaging, etc. That said, visual aspects in terms of typography and pictorial elements (e.g., emoticons) were included in the agenda of first wave CMC. The focus on the visual and its relation to the verbal continues to preoccupy research on digital communication, as is evident in the growing body of work on the use of profile pictures and selfies in social media (e.g., Kapidzic and Herring 2011; Rettberg 2014).

Nonetheless, this volume attests to a further consolidation of this line of inquiry that moves beyond the visual and attends to the interdependence of multiple modes in a more fluid and dynamic way. In this growing approach, multimodality is viewed as encompassing a multitude of semiotic and material resources that not only combine in complex contextually shaped ways within a given site but that can also be transposed and re-semiotized (Iedema 2003) across online and offline sites in different configurations and with different affordances. As Herring's contribution in this volume claims, taking its cue from the increasing use of telepresence robots in many contexts of communication, the task for further studies on the multiplicity of forms, functions, and affordances of different modalities in digital communication is to develop an approach that is capable of 'permitting meaningful comparisons across modes and across platforms'.

The methodological reflection and innovations have been particularly noteworthy in a rapidly changing field. In this respect, too, we see the identity of the field being shaped between drawing on well-established methods in other fields and fine-tuning, creatively adapting or even radically redefining them to suit the needs and complexities of the digital environments. This is the final point of convergence that this Handbook showcases and it is specifically related to the advent of digital ethnographic and multimodal methods, as described above, and to their links with the technological changes that have allowed increasing media convergence. Such methodological perspectives are moving the area away from any neat and clear-cut divisions between the virtual and the real, the online and the offline, and towards nuanced explorations and understandings of their complex interrelationships (see Angouri, and Tagg and Seargeant). The dualities are thus currently being replaced by attention to multiple potential forms of co-presence and relationality that are afforded through multi-dimensional, across- and inter-digital media engagements (e.g., chapters by Abdullah, Baron, Darics, Keating, Newon, and Varis). Such engagements pose new opportunities but also challenges not just for the communicators themselves but also for the analysts: e.g., how can attention to multiple channels be managed and analysed?

In particular, digital ethnography is emerging at the forefront of methodological innovation regarding the blurring of private/interpersonal and public/institutional boundaries and of multiple contextual embeddings, driven by the aforementioned preoccupation with digital environments as multi-layered spaces (e.g., chapters by Iorio, Knobel and Lankshear, Kelly-Holmes, and Newon). Digital ethnography is also closely aligned with the sociolinguistics of globalization, mobility and translocality, feeding into it valuable conceptual and analytical insights (e.g., chapters by Kytölä and Lee).

Overall, as the contributions in this Handbook show, the relationships of methods of researching digital communication with established methods and epistemological perspectives are no longer uni-directional and one-sided. On the contrary, it is not an exaggeration to argue that any further development of well-established methods such as ethnography cannot be undertaken in isolation or oblivious to research on language and digital communication.

The need for creatively combining and integrating qualitative with quantitative methods has long been stressed in the field, not least on the basis of the unrivalled 'easy' access to big data. Many chapters reflect on this need, highlighting the limitations of single method approaches (see Abdullah and Iorio). There is awareness, for instance, that quantitative approaches, such as network analysis, are powerful in terms of examining large bodies of data, but their useful-ness and interpretability are conditioned by the type of questions asked and, in some cases, by the researcher's more nuanced understanding of smaller structural groups and participant roles within the network (see chapter by Paolillo). At the same time, many issues remain ongoing and unresolved. Exactly how qualitative approaches combine with quantitative ones is some-thing to explore further and Page's contribution provides one intriguing way of bringing big data about users to bear on micro-analytically derived insights. In a similar vein, the contribu-tion by Jones stresses the need for methods that can render platform metrics transparent so as to tease out their connections with both communication ideologies and practices. Methodological innovation needs to be extended beyond single platform integration of qualitative with quan-titative insights. The speedy and unprecedented transposition of discourse activities across sites and media platforms makes it imperative to work up methods and tools of analysis suited to this dense intertextual and cross-medial nexus.

Further directions

In the light of the above, we view this collection as firmly placed in the second wave of research in CMC where we can talk about distinct, identifiable, and fairly well developed common con-cerns, methods, and analytical modes. At the same time, at the risk of overdoing the metaphor, the third wave is rapidly upon us: we are offered glimpses of its research priorities in the discus-sion of emerging concerns in several contributions, particularly the concluding ones which look ahead to future challenges. From their discussion, two agendas seem to be shaping further work in language and digital communication, namely the critical and the ethical agendas.

The consolidation of a critical agenda follows on from similar yet peripheral concerns in previous research on language and digital communication. We can somewhat schematically suggest that the first wave of research understandably gave priority to justifying and legitimating the object of inquiry. In the second wave of CMC research, and with the parallel growth of Web 2.0 environments, there has been a tendency towards more celebratory and empower-ing accounts of digital communication, while attesting to its linguistic and cultural diversity (see chapters by Lee, Nishimura, and Waldron, Kemp and Wood). Within the third wave of research, critical approaches to discourses and ideologies of digital communication are rapidly becoming focal concerns. More specifically, relations of power as they are promoted, rein-forced, and constructed in digital environments are put under scrutiny, with particular emphasis on issues of control and surveillance (see chapters by Spilioti, Ess, and Jones). In addition, the growing research on processes of resemiotization and recontextualization in digital media calls for attention not only to the resources employed but also to issues of power and access as those are invoked in the selection of certain resources by certain actors and for certain purposes. Last, but not least, the field is mature enough to adopt a self-reflexive and critical stance towards the digital discourses and ideologies that the analysts themselves implicitly or explicitly subscribe to.

The centrality of ethics in current and future research is prevalent in this volume, with almost every single chapter touching upon this issue. Longstanding concerns about the blurring of boundaries between the public and the private in digital environments are discussed in relation to specific analytical foci and methods (e.g., see chapters by Paolillo, Squires, and Varis). But current research seems to converge on pointing out challenges rather than offering solutions. Taking stock of such challenges is important in order to move forward with an ethical agenda that revisits current procedures and practices for gaining informed consent, addresses the ethics of meta-data in big data research, and is sensitive to data collection processes that can put participants (e.g., political activists) at risk, thus avoiding turning data collection online into another form of surveillance.

A combination of the critical with the ethical agenda should also lead analysts to the scrutiny of how certain social media-afforded communication practices may be ultimately disadvantaging certain socio-cultural groups and individuals as well as promoting non-ethical scenarios of self. We have shown elsewhere (Georgakopoulou 2014) how, in the social media circulation of political stories, certain evaluative perspectives and subjectivities prevail and others are silenced. Those that prevail end up closing down specific interpretative angles for the sake of specific audiences and networks. In this way, in tune with boyd's claim, 'the property of scalability does not necessarily scale what individuals want to have scaled or what they think should be scaled, but what the collective chooses to amplify' (2011: 48). Further research should interrogate the politics and implications of circulation and circulatability of specific communication genres and practices. Similarly, as Ess puts it in his contribution, future work should be mindful of what kinds of scenarios of self and what kinds of literacies are promoted or, equally, undervalued and discouraged in digital communication and what the ethical consequences of any gains and losses are.

Overview

Part I takes stock of the key methods and perspectives that have been used for the study of language and digital communication. The interdisciplinary nature of the field, together with its rapid growth, have resulted in a range of approaches, frameworks, and methods that have been adopted and applied to the study of the specific topics discussed in the following sections of this Handbook. Acknowledging that it is difficult to thoroughly represent the range and multiplicity of these perspectives and methods within a single section, we have aimed for chapters that cluster together and critically discuss methods used for studying: (i) language in terms of linguistic forms, choices, and variation (see Hinrichs); (ii) language as constitutive of webs of relations between individuals and, in turn, of wider social structures and networks (see Paolillo on network analysis); (iii) language as practice embedded in specific activities and cultures of use (see Varis on digital ethnography); and (iv) language as one among many semiotic resources employed for meaning making and communication (see Jewitt on multimodal analysis).

Starting with methods and approaches addressing core linguistic concerns, Hinrichs provides a critical overview of research on language choice and variation in digital environments, by moving through different levels of linguistic description: namely, phonetics/phonology, typography and orthography, morphology and lexis, syntax, and code-choice. In his overview, he sees the development of this area as very much informed by advances in the related fields of linguistics, such as variationist sociolinguistics and corpus linguistics. In addition, the chapter provides guidance for those who wish to design and undertake research in this area by discussing issues of variable selection, sampling and methods for analysis. More specifically, Hinrichs critically discusses a range of quantitative (e.g., descriptive and predictive statistics) and qualitative (e.g., conversation analysis, critical discourse analysis, interactional sociolinguistics) methods used in previous studies of language and digital communication. This discussion concludes with foregrounding the advantages of a mixed methods approach to the study of language variation in digital environments, echoing one of the key points of crystallization in the field, as mentioned above. The issue of 'big data' appears to be amongst the key concerns for future research in the area. Hinrichs points out both the research opportunities from harvesting large amounts of data and the analytic challenges arising from using such data for nuanced and sophisticated under-standings of language variation, human agency, and social context.

The issue of 'big data' is further unpacked and put under scrutiny by Paolillo who introduces the family of approaches known as network analysis. Network analysis draws on the premise that language and communication are mutually constitutive of the basic relations among a set of individuals and, in turn, of the wider social structures that may consist of these basic webs of relations. Applying the 'network' as an abstract mathematical concept to the study of digital communication is deemed appropriate, as digital media include logs and traces that can be easily turned into network data. At the same time, network analysis operates at a level of abstraction that can be useful for processing large bodies of data. In his detailed account of the main types of network analysis, Paolillo reveals not only the strengths of such approaches but also any underlying challenges. For example, research needs to be carefully designed and implemented to avoid any distorting effects caused by poor sampling/analytical methods and being driven by research questions that fail to acknowledge potential differences in the internal structure of social vs technological networks. In terms of future directions, Paolillo sets out the basis for an ethical agenda in the network analysis of 'big data' that includes: the issue of consent in the collection of supposedly public or proprietary data, the increased risk of exposing people or failing to identify vulnerable subjects, and the complications arising from differing perceptions of ethics between the corporate and the academic world.

The following chapter by Varis also introduces a family of approaches that could be clustered under the umbrella term of 'digital ethnography'. Such approaches share an interest in digital culture and practices and they are firmly placed within the second wave of CMC research, moving away from early decontextualized studies of internet log data. Rather than address-ing ethnography as an 'old' method applied to the study of 'new' digital environments, Varis sheds light on how longstanding methodological commitments can now be reflected upon and revisited in light of research on digital communication. The first such commitment concerns ethnography's attention to processes of contextualization which can, at times, appear more visible to the analyst through practices of remixing, copying and pasting, etc. and, at times, become more opaque, when previously separated contexts (e.g., professional, private family, friends, etc.) collapse into one in social media environments ('context collapse', Marwick and boyd 2010). Attention to different layers of contextualization also foregrounds the varying ideological frameworks operating in digital communication: e.g., ideologies embedded in the design of digital media; users' ideologies about the choice and uses of specific media (media ideologies); perceptions of and values assigned to face-to-face communication (see also chapter by Spilioti). Varis's chapter also problematizes a number of methodological issues pertaining to online ethics, degrees of 'immersion' in digital cultures, and the use of 'big data' in digital ethnography. A key point in her chapter is the call for heightened reflexivity and flexibility in designing and undertaking fieldwork online in order to do justice to the complexities and intricacies of digital contexts and practices.

The potential of multi-layered and contextualized approaches to the study of language and digital communication is further foregrounded by Jewitt who discusses relevant approaches for undertaking multimodal analysis in digital environments. A multimodal perspective shifts the attention from language as a single semiotic mode to the interdependence of a range of modes (verbal, visual, aural, etc.) in the production of meaning. After providing definitions for the key terms used in multimodal analysis, Jewitt presents the main ways in which the study of digital communication could benefit from a multimodal perspective. First, inventories of the multiple modes and their interdependencies in digital contexts advance our understanding of different technologies in terms of both their meaning-making potential and their actual take-up by users. As illustrated by Keating as well, multimodal analysis also focuses on embodied engagements with digital tools in specific activities, opening up to the investigation of the interaction between the 'physical' and the 'digital' world. Furthermore, attention to new semiotic resources or new ways of using such resources opens a window on wider social changes (e.g., mobility and globalization) that might be associated with the mobilization of new modal resources. Last, but not least, multimodal analysis paves the way towards a range of methodological innovations in terms of introducing new tools for data collection (e.g., screen-capture and eye tracking software), revisiting processes of transcription and offering new ways to map and analyse visual, embodied and spatial aspects of interaction. Jewitt illustrates the above by taking the reader through necessary steps for designing and undertaking multimodal analysis of digital texts both as multimodal artefacts (e.g., food blogs) and as social interaction (e.g., student interaction over tangible technologies for the learning of science concepts).

What language resources are used and how in different kinds of digital communication has preoccupied analysts since the first wave of research and so the chapters in Part II bring together the early with the latest insights. To begin, there has been a longstanding question of what constitutes a genre and in particular a novel genre in digital communication. In her chapter, Heyd identifies three phases of technological development that have fed into the transition of research from an emphasis on the formal to the functional properties of genres. The difficulties in pinning down genres and relating their formal and communicative features with their wider contexts of occurrence are by no means specific to the genre analysis of digital communication. In this case, however, as Heyd's overview shows, genre analysis that takes into account contextual parameters has been specifically attuned to the sociotechnical aspects of digital communication. In this respect, a concept that has been employed extensively in the identification and analysis of genres and generic features has been that of remediation. Remediation is aimed at capturing the historicity and inter-relationships of new media genres and the ways in which they draw on previous genres as well as departing from them. The latest technological developments regarding the multiplicity of modalities in one particular site as well as the transposition of discourse activities in different media environments have been instrumental in directing analysts' attention to genre overlaps, networks and co-existence – in other words, to their ecology.

The chapter by Nishimura also tackles a longstanding issue, namely (language) creativity and play, the study of which was prompted by first-wave concerns, particularly by how CMC relates to face-to-face interactions that by then had been documented as engendering communicative artistry so as to sustain interpersonal relations. In this respect, early studies of language play and creativity in CMC are reminiscent of foundational sociolinguistic work on the same topic, which set out to demonstrate the verbal artistry of everyday spoken language, which up to then had been viewed as the prerogative of literary language. The widespread view that anonymity and the ephemeral nature of 'virtual' environments automatically resulted in impoverished and largely transactional communication was thrown into doubt by early work in CMC.

As in studies of everyday interactions, reaching a precise definition and identification of devices that count as creative has been a complicated endeavour, not helped by the overlapping reference of the terms creativity, play, and style. Nishimura provides a useful overview of key analyses of such terms in both face-to-face and mediated communication. This shows the shift from text-centred, formal approaches to a view of language creativity as an inter-subjective process, jointly achieved by communicators. She also illustrates how the same linguistic resources can be variously recognized as creative or not, depending on who the 'adjudicators' are. In cases of communication where the audiences are multiple and largely unforeseeable, we can see how there is much scope for multiple evaluations and perceptions of the same language resources.

In the chapters by both Heyd and Nishimura, a shift away from text-based analyses implies a gradual turn to identities, to an exploration of the ways in which communication choices and devices serve as resources for self-presentation and relationality. In the case of digital communication, studies of language creativity and identities have gradually disassociated creative resources from an earlier exclusive association with 'virtual' (i.e. not 'real life') identities, documenting an array of links between online and offline identities through communicative resources. Furthermore, as Nishimura's case study of play and creativity in a Japanese bulletin board site shows, there is multi-semioticity and multimodality involved, including in this case graphemic/script choices, emoticons, etc.

We find the same broad definition of language choices as multi-semiotic and contextually versatile in the chapter by Lee on multilingual resources. Lee shows the gradual transition of the field from the early days of the dominance of work on the uses of English to the redressing of balance with the investigation and documentation of the internet as multilingual. This shift has gone hand in hand with non-Roman scripts becoming available as well as with the increase in audio facilities and multimodal sites. Reflecting on the volume of relevant work (for a comprehensive overview, see Androutsopoulos 2013), Lee's discussion includes emphasis on code-switching as a performative resource for individuals. Lee's chapter subscribes to an increasingly acceptable broad definition of multilingualism as translingualism, i.e. as a more or less rather than an all or nothing knowledge and use of different repertoires of resources from different languages. We see comparable views of multilingualism in the chapters by Androutsopoulos and Tereick, and by Kytölä, which we discuss below. Lee shows how translingual practices connect with digital media-enabled opportunities for employing elements and resources from more than one language, in specific sites and for specific purposes. These opportunities include the sheer prominence, visibility and audibility of minority or non-standard languages (e.g., Cantonese, colloquial Arabic) in many social media platforms (e.g., YouTube). This has implications both for perceptions and practices of language standardization and for vernacular literacies (see chapter by Iorio).

The last chapter in this section by Spilioti turns attention to an issue of increasing importance, namely the ideologies and discourses surrounding the uses of and communication on new media. Any change in communication and literacy practices has historically been accompanied by discourses of fear of the unknown and moral panics and, in this case too, discourses have ranged from the utopian to the dystopian end of the continuum (see Baym 2010), that is, from celebratory views of the internet as a global village to despair about the disruptive effects of the new medium on social relations and communication. To this end, Spilioti discusses four dominant discourses commonly occurring in the old media representations of the new media on the one hand and within the new media themselves, with power-related, monetary and ideological stakes in both of them. These discourses involve the potential of digital media for sociality, equality, and diversity and the representations of young people in relation to digital media engagements and the so-called 'digital language' (see Waldron, Kemp and Wood for evidence that questions such popular assumptions). Spilioti shows how these discourses are densely contextualized and historicized, and closely connected with neo-liberal ideologies. She also discusses how studies of language and digital communication have been instrumental in dismantling certain myths that underpin these discourses. At the same time, as we have argued above, there is much scope and need for interrogating the ideological underpinnings of the academic discourses too vis-à-vis language and digital communication. This will lead to a better understanding of methodological and analytical choices as well as to the uncovering of any more or less conscious biases.

The consolidation of contextualized approaches to the study of language and digital communication has also greatly benefited from developments within the field of literacy studies. The chapters in Part III, especially those by Knobel and Lankshear, and Iorio, firmly root relevant research on digital literacies in socio-culturally oriented perspectives: these understand literacy as a nexus of social practices, identities and meanings embedded and situated in particular activities and contexts of use.

Knobel and Lankshear set the stage by providing a thorough review of research on literacy development and digital media, with a focus on engagements with digital media in primarily out-of-school contexts. Literacy development is examined both in terms of 'personal literacy development' (i.e., improvement of individual literacy proficiencies through engagement with digital technologies) and of 'development in the cultural stock of literacies' (i.e., emergence of new literacy practices, such as blogging, remixing, etc.). The shift of attention to media users, especially children and youths, as producers (as well as consumers) of digital artefacts and the prevalence of 'affinity space' as a useful concept for understanding social learning environments are among the key tenets of current research on the development of literacy practices mediated by digital media. Knobel and Lankshear also reveal a 'new ethos' emerging in digital literacies, 'characterised by deep interactivity, openness to feedback, sharing of resources and expertise, and a will to collaborate and provide support'. Last, but not least, Knobel and Lankshear's chapter aptly demonstrates how the study of digital literacies feeds back into central concerns in the field of literacy studies by foregrounding multiple literacies in action and effectively critiquing the dominant school-centric perceptions of literacy.

The distinction between institutional (e.g., school literacies) and vernacular literacies is taken up by Iorio who probes more into research on vernacular writing in digital contexts. Through the lens of orthography, Iorio shows how traditionally distinct and incompatible literacy practices often co-exist in digital environments, blurring the boundaries between the personal and the professional and between the local and the global. He attests to the vernacularization of institutional literacy practices, evident not only in the expanding use of 'social' digital media in professional contexts but also in the increasingly translocal nature of geographically dispersed working teams. The chapter concludes by pointing out the advantages of a mixed-methods approach to the study of orthography in digital literacies, combining quantitative methods of statistical modelling with qualitative ethnographic research. In doing this, researchers can uncover the multiple and complex contextual embeddings of digital vernacular practices and move beyond medium-restricted understandings of context.

A particular type of orthographic innovation ('textisms') and its relation with language learning are discussed in detail by Waldron, Kemp and Wood. Their chapter reviews primarily research conducted from the perspectives of developmental and social psychology. This line of work provides evidence in support of the idea that there are positive (or, at least, not negative) links between children's use of textisms and literacy abilities, such as spelling, phonological awareness, and word reading. Considering the wide range of data collection methods used in this area (e.g., self-report studies, translation tasks, scenario-based tasks, etc.), the authors critically evaluate each method while discussing the risks of overgeneralizing such results beyond the specific linguistic and cultural context. In their chapter, popular assumptions about the impact of digital media and texting on literacy are called into question by providing ample evidence against moral panic discourses about children and literacy standards. Recommendations for practice are also made regarding the use of mobile technologies as a tool for learning within and outside school environments.

The boundaries between the public and the private, the collective and the personal, have been greatly challenged and debated in recent research on language and digital communication.

Part IV addresses this issue by focusing on different areas of public or professional communication, such as workplace interaction (Darics), advertising (Kelly-Holmes), and corporate blogging (Puschmann and Hagelmoser). Squires's chapter concludes this section by revisiting such debates through the lens of Twitter, the micro-blogging site for (re)broadcasting information to the public.

Darics's chapter shifts attention to the use and integration of digital media in workplace environments, with a focus on text-based interaction via email or instant messaging. Darics advocates the development of an interdisciplinary approach that does not shy away from cross-fertilizations between the fields of business communication research, business discourse studies and computer-mediated (or digital) discourse studies. One of the key challenges in this area of study concerns the communicative complexity of mediated workplace environments, arising from the participants' simultaneous orientation to the highly structured, power-regulated institutional contexts and the more fluid and less conventional digital communicative environments. Darics illustrates how current advances in computer-mediated discourse analysis can contribute to a more nuanced understanding of technological affordances in workplace settings and to a contextualized approach to communicative norms and practices as contextually embedded and emerging in specific situations. As Darics points out, the time is ripe for the study of business digital discourse to expand its analytical agenda, embrace mainstream topics of sociolinguistic research on workplace interaction such as power relations, and contribute to their further theorising.

Moving from workplace interaction to another area of professional communication, Kelly-Holmes focuses on digital marketing communication and examines how digital advertising has been shaped by the recent developments of increased interactivity and participation in web 2.0 environments. Kelly-Holmes reveals the loss of control on the part of the advertiser as communicator, since the public can reinforce or undermine the marketer's message through 'electronic word of mouth' and, effectively, play an active part in co-creating value for brands and products. The increasing potential for consumers to comment on products and generate content relevant to particular brands in social media has played a key role in the rise of the 'working consumer'. At the same time, the discussion unpacks the concept of 'individualised web marketing' whereby individuals (rather than markets or market segments) are tracked and targeted with offering personalized and customized products. The chapter concludes with a critical discussion of methodological approaches (such as ethnography) that can address such complex and multi-layered processes in the area of digital advertising.

The issue of personalization in corporate communication with the public is further discussed by Puschmann and Hagelmoser. In their chapter on corporate blogging and corporate social media, they trace the evolution of blogging from personal blogs to employee blogs that emerged initially for intra-organisational communication and, subsequently, were appropriated for strategic marketing to the wider public. Puschmann and Hagelmoser contextualize this evolution within broader social changes, such as a general loss of trust in public-facing corporate discourse and a shift towards personalization of relationships between institutions and individuals. Research on language use and style in corporate blogging reveals storytelling as a key strategy through which corporate bloggers convey authenticity and affiliate with wider norms and communities appealing to the public. Puschmann and Hagelmoser offer a useful overview of key frameworks for linguistic analysis, such as genre analysis and narrative analysis (for a detailed discussion of narrative analysis in CMC, see Georgakopoulou 2013), which are particularly amenable to this area of research.

Squires concludes Part IV with a compelling chapter on Twitter, its design, any emerging discursive practices and the implications of publicness as promoted and experienced on this specific microblogging site. More specifically, Squires puts under scrutiny the key discursive practices of @mentions, hashtags and retweets, and contextualizes them in relation to the communicative affordances of Twitter that facilitate connectivity and interactivity. In addition to the medium's design, studies of language use on Twitter provide further evidence for the significance of social dimensions (e.g., social identities or goals in using the medium) in understanding language variation in digital environments. Squires also discusses in detail the notion of 'publicization' as a key concept for understanding the communicative dynamics of Twitter vis-à-vis other forms of social media. Publicization is captured in Twitter's potential for 'making text public while de-emphasizing mutuality between users', resulting in mass-scale sharing of information by means of producing new tweets, as well as embedding and appropriating information from previously existing tweets. This dynamic circulates and projects vernacular writing across a multitude of mass media contexts, attesting to the vernacularization of the public sphere, also noted by Iorio. Squires concludes by providing methodological insights about data collection on Twitter and by pointing to avenues for research that include, among others, a shift towards ideological and political aspects in Twitter communication.

Part V moves to what can be seen as focal concerns within the second wave of language and digital communication research, namely the ways in which participants position, manage, present, and perform aspects of themselves in various capacities in (relation to) online environments. All the chapters here present evidence for the porous boundaries between online and offline worlds and lives, which we discussed above. The chapter by Keating illustrates this interdependency vis-à-vis three settings from the author's research: online gaming, sign language in technologically mediated space, and a virtual work environment where engineers located in different continents collaborate on construction plans. In these settings, individuals employ multimodal resources including embodied resources (e.g., gaze, head position, manual signs) so as to co-ordinate their actions in relation to other users, to navigate digital media-related constraints on their body's expressability and to interpret audio, visual and spatial cues when working in teams that are digitally but not physically connected. The chapter brings to the fore certain under-represented yet very significant aspects of multimodality in digital communication that have to do with how people actually renegotiate their habitual embodied communication as well as awareness of space. With new forms of co-presence on the rise, the need for further studies in this line of inquiry is bound to become more apparent.

Abdullah's chapter tackles a similar issue of how individuals construct a sense of place/space and embodiment as part of their online identity and community building within the environment of Second Life. Nonetheless, far from being able to posit a dichotomy between virtual and offline existence, the analysis uncovers the interplay between the online and offline selves of people being (acting and inter-acting) in two places at the same time. This interplay is particularly evident in the choices of person, time and space deictic expressions. At the same time, the discussion shows how identities formed within the online community of Second Life shape language and other semiotic choices: for example, how choices of language play and creativity and the ways in which they are received are intimately linked with the history and participation modes and roles (e.g., novices, experts) of individuals. In the same spirit as other contributors in the volume, Abdullah advocates the synergy of ethnographic, discourse and corpus linguistic analyses for tapping into processes of community (re)formation and their relations with multimodal choices.

In the chapter by Newon, the interplay between online and offline identities is documented in relation to online gaming and how it intersects with people's everyday lives. Newon's overview of different approaches to online gaming shows the transition from functional to more socially oriented approaches where the conceptualization of self becomes increasingly performative: identities can be more or less strategically manipulated and staged. Newon shows how heterogeneous styles of play, practices, and activities of online players interact with multi-semiotic communicative ways of negotiating disputes and disagreement, socializing players into the game and displaying 'distinctiveness' and 'authenticity'. The intriguing suggestion of this contribution is that we need to move beyond the conceptualization of online–offline to more practice-based views of relations, such as, in this case, in-game and out-of-game lives. This refocusing leads us to as yet under-explored topics, for instance, the relations between gamers and designers/developers beyond the game platforms, or the practices of live-streaming of play in different physical spaces. The need to investigate online–offline intersections in (and beyond) gaming environments has also been pointed out by Knobel and Lankshear, who bring to our attention the potential of tapping into such issues through the study of users' engagement with mobile digital technologies (e.g., smartphones, Google glass).

In the chapter by Graham, the ways in which individuals present themselves in different digital environments are studied with a focus on the creation of social relations of friendship, intimacy and alignments. The creation of intimacies and sociality, as Spilioti's chapter reminds us, are interwoven with social media propagated discourses as well as with certain affordances. Graham connects her discussion of the development of social relations with different kinds and types of online community, associated with different generations of digital environments, ranging from communities sustained around a shared interest to communities in which users are primarily interested in one another and their management of self. Social media platforms typically but not exclusively belong to the latter category. As we see in other chapters too, 'new' members in an online community tend to go through processes of socialization and apprenticeship into the accepted communication norms and values of a community. Negotiations around what is acceptable or not by whom, how and why can be discovered empirically with micro-analytic language-focused work, as we see in Graham's analysis of a discussion group of books on My Space.

Individuals' identities cannot be separated from their participation roles and types and degrees of membership in online communities, as the chapters of Part V show. Building on this, Part VI moves to a closer examination of how online communities can be defined and identified. The section begins with a chapter by Angouri, who provides an overview of the definition and conceptual development of online communities. The notion of speech community has been radically redefined in sociolinguistics since the 1970s and studies of language and digital communication have benefited from, as well as shedding more light on, more nuanced understandings. In particular, the initial focus on communities in new media as 'virtual' and therefore separable from 'real life' communication has been replaced by a contextualized focus on 'communities of practice', revolving around shared engagements and interests. Angouri illustrates how users negotiate and construct community through practice with data from a project on an online health forum. The definitional criteria and modes and methods of identification and language-focused analysis of a community are part of an ongoing discussion with many unresolved issues, and, in this respect, Angouri discusses the strengths and limitations of the currently influential Communities of Practice framework.

The chapter by Tagg and Seargeant discusses how making and enhancing social connections is managed on Facebook, a social networking site with unprecedented popularity. Tagg and Seargeant discuss how users perform their identity through individual choices on their profile, their visible network, and their interaction with friends (in status updates and comments). They also show how they employ audience design strategies that include language and style choices, so as to address and in many ways construct and imagine their audience in the semi-public forum of Facebook that comprises 'friends' with a notable heterogeneity in terms of types and degrees of online and offline interaction. This audience design is in turn an important element in constructing or maintaining a community around shared linguistic and cultural practices. As we see in other chapters too, social media environments afford the creation of translocal communities with users co-constructing shared cultures with their interaction from different localities. At the same time, a difference in localities may render the same posting (e.g., an update) open to different interpretations and recontextualizations. Tagg and Seargeant mainly draw on and discuss an ethnographically informed textual analysis of Facebook but they acknowledge the increasing need for metric-based methodologies (e.g., mood analysis) in social networking sites research.

From the well-researched iconic social media environment of Facebook, we move to an equally iconic yet less researched platform, namely YouTube. The chapter by Androutsopoulos and Tereick shows how the few language-focused approaches to YouTube have inevitably recognized and studied the multimodal semiosis of the environment. According to Androutsopoulos and Tereick, this multimodal creativity, often manifesting itself in remixes, is one important level of a complex discourse environment that also comprises the participation framework and the facilities for audience comments and interaction based on the posted videos. The authors advocate multi-layered analyses to capture the interplay of these levels rather than artificial separations of e.g., the comments from the actual video. Related to this, they also recommend a mixed methods research design, based on social semiotics, discourse analysis, and quantitative insights from corpus linguistics, which can be assisted by applications such as the Applications Programming Interface. The chapter illustrates this rich analysis in two case studies: an analysis of YouTube as a site for the performance and negotiation of German dialects, and a corpus-assisted discourse analysis of YouTube as a site of participatory discourse on climate change. The availability of big data on YouTube and the complexity of its environment with the facilities for circulation to and from other social media platforms afford opportunities for mixed methods approaches, but they also pose methodological challenges which Androutsopoulos and Tereick acknowledge.

A similar case for mixed methods and a multi-layered discourse and sociolinguistic analysis that benefits from multidisciplinary perspectives is made in the chapter by Kytölä which brings together insights on translocality, an emerging key concept for the 'investigation of the complex forms of interplay of the local and the global in multi-semiotic digital communication'. Kytölä first contextualizes the conceptual history and development of translocality vis-à-vis other related concepts (e.g., glocalization, hybridity). In cases of proliferating terms with somewhat overlapping reference, it is important to see what kinds of disciplinary traditions each concept has been part of and what explicit as well as implicit associations this has created. An important aspect of translocality in this respect is the fact that it does not marginalize the local but instead views connections between the global and local as mutually feeding and bi-directional. This inter-connectedness is at the heart of social, cultural, and communication activities on digital media, and, as a result, a study that is oblivious to translocality processes is bound to miss out on important aspects of meaning making. Taking this further, Kytölä suggests that future studies should link translocality with the growing importance of multi-semioticity and resemiotization, which are the hallmarks of communication on many social media platforms, e.g. YouTube. The chapter illustrates the benefits of foregrounding translocality concerns in the study of digital communication and the analytical and methodological ways of doing so with contextually diverse case studies, from hip hop to photograph sharing to fandom fiction and comments on YouTube, covering numerous localities (e.g., Tanzania, Finland).

Note

1   Recent themed conferences are as follows: 'Politeness and impoliteness on- and offline' (2010, 5th International Symposium on Politeness, University of Basel, Switzerland); 'Discourse 2.0: language and new media' (GURT 2011, Georgetown University, USA); 'Language and social media: new

challenges for research and teaching linguistics' (2012, University of Leicester, UK); 'Research methods and approaches for analysing social media' (2013, University of Leicester, UK); 'The ethics of online research methods' (2014, Cardiff University, UK); 'ADDA-1 approaches to digital discourse analysis' (2015, University of Valencia, Spain). Relevant themed panels have also appeared in socio- and applied linguistics conferences: e.g. in the bi-annual Sociolinguistics Symposium (e.g., 'Code-switching in electronic writing: the leveling and maintaining of linguistic borders', organized by Laroussi 2008; 'Using multilingual written internet data in language contact studies' by Margreet and Verschik 2012; 'Language and mobility: space, time & social media: communicating (the) here & now' by Georgakopoulou and Angouri 2014) and the bi-annual IPrA conferences (e.g., 'Corpora and methods in computer-mediated discourse analysis', by Androutsopoulos and Beisswenger 2007; '(Im)politeness in computer-mediated communication', by Graham and Locher 2009; 'The pragmatics of quoting in computer-mediated communication', by Bulbitz and Hoffman 2011; 'Digital diaspora: vernaculars and multilingual practices as style resources in mediated communication', by Theresa Heyd and Christian Mair 2013, amongst others).

References

Androutsopoulos, J. (ed.) 2006a 'Special issue: sociolinguistics and computer-mediated communication', *Journal of Sociolinguistics*, vol. 10, no. 4, pp. 419–566.

Androutsopoulos, J. 2006b 'Introduction: sociolinguistics and computer-mediated communication', *Journal of Sociolinguistics*, vol. 10, no. 4, pp. 419–438.

Androutsopoulos, J. 2013 'Code-switching in computer-mediated communication', in S. C. Herring, D. Stein, and T. Virtanen (eds), *Handbook of the pragmatics of computer-mediated communication*, Mouton de Gruyter: Berlin, pp. 659–686.

Baym, N. 2010 *Personal connections in the digital age*, Polity Press: Cambridge.

Bou-Franch, P. and Blitvich, P. (eds) 2014 'Special issue: the pragmatics of textual participation in the social media', *Journal of Pragmatics*, vol. 73, pp. 1–82.

boyd, d. 2011 'Social network sites as networked publics: affordances, dynamics and implications', in Z. Papacharissi (ed.), *Networked self: identity, community, and culture on social network sites*, Routledge: London/New York, pp. 39–58.

Frobenius, M., Eisenlauer, V., and Gerhardt, C. (eds) 2014 'Special issue: participation framework revisited: (new) media and their audiences/users', *Journal of Pragmatics*, vol. 72, pp. 1–90.

Georgakopoulou, A. 2014 'Small stories transposition and social media: a micro-perspective on the "Greek crisis"', *Discourse and Society*, vol. 25, no. 4, pp. 519–539.

Georgakopoulou, A. 2006 'Postscript: computer-mediated communication in sociolinguistics', *Journal of Sociolinguistics*, vol. 10, no. 4, pp. 548–557.

Georgakopoulou, A. 2013 'Narrative analysis and computer-mediated communication', in S. C. Herring, D. Stein, and T. Virtanen (eds), *Handbook of the pragmatics of computer-mediated communication*, Mouton de Gruyter: Berlin, pp. 695–716.

Herring, S. C. 2004 'Computer-mediated discourse analysis: an approach to researching online behaviour', in S. Barab, R. Kling, and J. Gray (eds), *Designing for virtual communities in the service of learning*, Cambridge University Press: New York, pp. 338–376.

Iedema, R. 2003 'Multimodality, resemiotization: extending the analysis of discourse as multi-semiotic practice', *Visual Communication*, vol. 2, no. 1, pp. 29–57.

Kapidzic, S. and Herring, S. C. 2011 'Gender, communication and self-presentation in teen chatrooms revisited: have patterns changed?', *Journal of Computer-Mediated Communication*, vol. 17, no. 1, pp. 39–59.

Locher, M. (ed.) 2010 'Special issue: politeness and impoliteness in computer-mediated communication', *Journal of Politeness Research*, vol. 6, no. 1, pp. 1–150.

Locher, M., Bolander, B., and Hohn, N. (eds) 2015 'Special issue: relational work in Facebook and discussion boards/fora', *Pragmatics*, vol. 25, no. 1, pp. 1–122.

Marwick, A. and boyd, d. 2010 'I tweet honestly, I tweet passionately: Twitter users, context collapse, and the imagined audience', *New Media & Society*, vol. 13, no. 1, pp. 114–133.

Rettberg, J. 2014 *Seeing ourselves through technology: how we use selfies, blogs and wearable devices to see and shape ourselves*, Palgrave Pivot: Basingstoke, UK.

Scribner, S. and Cole, M. 1981 *The psychology of literacy*, Harvard University Press: Cambridge, MA.

Street, B. 1984 *Literacy in theory and in practice*, Cambridge University Press: Cambridge, UK.

Part I

Methods and perspectives

1

Approaches to language variation

Lars Hinrichs

Overview

The study of linguistic variation

In linguistics, the term *variation* refers to the phenomenon of heterogeneity of linguistic form. If the language faculty of the human brain were a simply programmed implementation of rules, one would expect all users of a language to use the same linguistic forms each time they express the same concept or grammatical relation. But they do not: there are many sites in the linguistic repertoires of speakers and writers that force them to choose between alternative ways of expressing something; most of the time, they make these choices automatically, without giving them much thought. For example, in English the possessive relation between two noun phrases can be expressed using either the *of*-genitive or the *'s*-genitive. Speakers and writers are forced to make a choice between those alternatives every time they express the possessive relation between two noun phrases; linguistic study has shown that this choice is conditioned systematically by multiple competing factors (Hinrichs & Szmrecsanyi 2007). Similarly, writers of digital discourse can choose between standard spelling such as <you, aren't> and alternative spellings such as <u, arent>. They can also choose whether or not to insert features specific to Computer-Mediated Discourse (CMD), such as emoticons, into their writings.

The study of variation is one branch of what Susan C. Herring circumscribes in her framework for the study of online language known as computer-mediated discourse analysis (CMDA, Herring 2004). Variation occurs in digital communication at the micro and the macro levels of linguistic analysis, and at all intermediate levels. Likewise, there are different types of cause of variation. In variationist research, the causes of variation are referred to as factors, and they are grouped, at the most fundamental level, into *internal* and *external* types. Internal factors are planes of variation related to the linguistic system. They include grammatical categories, as well as – in multilingual or multidialectal digital communication – the choice of linguistic variety itself. External, or *social*, factors include properties of the interactional context such as age, gender, or ethnicity of the participants, etc.

This chapter first introduces the two subfields of linguistics that most directly inform the study of variation in digital discourse, namely variationist sociolinguistics and corpus linguistics, and then provides an overview of research on variation in online language. The following discussion makes practical suggestions for researchers planning their own studies on issues of variation in digital discourse, and the chapter concludes with some reflections on future developments in the field.

Variationist sociolinguistics

Broadly, *language variation* is an umbrella concept that refers to difference of linguistic form in any of a number of dimensions, for example: differences between one individual's ways of speaking across different situational parameters; differences between multiple individuals' ways of speaking; differences between the language of speech communities located in different areas, i.e. geographical variation; or differences between social groups (e.g., ethnicities, genders, generations).

The fact that language is not always the same everywhere, or that it is fundamentally heterogeneous, is a common observation in daily life. Accents, ways of speaking, and linguistic idiosyncrasies draw attention to themselves in most people's daily experience. In the 1960s, William Labov initiated the field of sociolinguistics when he observed that language variation is in many cases *systematic* rather than random. In the formulation of the foundational article he co-authored with Uriel Weinreich and Marvin Herzog, language displays 'orderly heterogeneity' (Weinreich, Labov, & Herzog 1968: 100). The field of language variation studies is dedicated to discovering and describing the regularity and order of that heterogeneity in language. For example, Labov's well-known study of variation in New York City English (1966a) demonstrated the correlation between the social status of speakers and certain forms of speech, proving the existence of regular, systematic correspondences between higher socioeconomic status and lower frequencies of usage of linguistic features that are socially valued as informal.

The central theoretical construct of language variation studies is the *linguistic variable* (Cheshire 1987; Labov 1966b; Labov 1978; Wolfram 1991). The term refers to any unit of the linguistic system that can be realized in more than one possible shape in linguistic production. To reintroduce an example mentioned above, Standard English has more than one way of expressing the concept of possession linking two noun phrases, i.e. two alternative ways of constructing genitives: the *of-*genitive (*the plan of the administration*) and the *'s*-genitive (*the administration's plan*). In many cases, both genitives are equally possible choices, but it can be shown that variation between the two occurs according to several independent constraints that are statistically significant: if the possessor noun phrase denotes an animate entity, the *'s*-genitive is the more likely choice (e.g. *the man's car*); if the possessor noun phrase ends in a sibilant, the *of-*genitive is the more likely choice (*the angle of the pass*), and so on (Hinrichs & Szmrecsanyi 2007). At the level of phonetics and phonology, linguists may study variation between different pronunciations of the same phonemic speech sound that are all possible according to the rules of the language variety being spoken. For example, in all English-speaking parts of the world, words ending in *–ing* may be pronounced with the final sound realized either as [ŋ] (*reading*) or as [n] (*readin'*). Generally, the variant ending in [ŋ] has been shown to correlate with more formal social features (of the speaker's identity, the situation, the topic, etc.) and the [n]-variant with informal features.

In the early account by Weinreich *et al.* (1968), language variation studies were conceived of as a necessary addition to Chomskyan linguistics, which had by then come to dominate much of linguistic discussion. Transformational grammar presupposes that the human language faculty is a regular system of rules that translates the meanings that speakers wish to express from abstract representations to linguistic forms that are grammatical in the language being spoken. The study of this translational apparatus is the object of Chomskyan linguistics, and for a long time during the initial phase of the field's establishment, its data relied heavily on made-up linguistic examples that were grammatically correct and possible according to the linguist's own judgments.

In other words, Chomskyan (or formal) linguistics emerged as a reflection on language that took an abstract, ideal state of language as its object of study. Spoken language as it was actually used in the speech community was dismissed as unimportant, and variation as noise in the data. But early protagonists of language variation studies pointed to a key fact: over time, language variation leads to permanent changes in the grammar of a language (this is the fundamental claim of Weinreich *et al.* 1968; for elaboration see Labov 1972). Because the responsible study of syntax must therefore incorporate an understanding of language change, as variationists argued, and because language change results from variation, variation and change have come to be viewed as two sides of the same coin.

The quantitative paradigm of language variation studies, whose backbone is sketched above, is also known as the 'Labovian' type of sociolinguistics. In recent years it has been complemented by several influential studies that add ethnographic and qualitative insights to an overall Labovian research design. In an influential review, Eckert (2012) describes three waves in the methodological development of linguistic variation studies. The first wave departs from Labov's work on variation in New York City (Labov 1966a), which inspired similar studies of variation throughout the Anglophone world (e.g., Trudgill 1974; Wolfram 1969), but also in non-English-speaking locales such as Tehran (Modaressi-Tehrani 1978). It marked a fairly radical departure in linguistics because (i) it established beyond doubt that linguistic variation is structured and systematic; and (ii) it 'introduced a new quantitative empiricism into linguistics, with supportive theoretical underpinnings' (Eckert 2012: 88).

Another of Labov's studies initiated what Eckert considers the second wave of variation studies. His work on Martha's Vineyard investigated the link between variation as part of an ongoing sound change and individual identity within the community (Labov 1963). It became an influential model for studies that combined the quantitative angle with ethnographic methods in an effort to gain better insights into the links between local practice, identity, and linguistic variation. Studies in the second wave include Milroy (1980), Cheshire (1982), and Rickford (1986).

The third wave of variation studies takes the ethnographic approach even further, placing ethnography fully at the centre of its methodological paradigm. Unlike the first two waves, which were interested in describing social structure and in correlating dynamics of variation with social categories, the third wave aims to *explain* variation by making the 'social meaning of variation' its overall descriptive goal. In the third wave, the ethnographic method is used to discover linguistic practices and the ways in which they contribute to the construction of locally meaningful social *styles*. Therefore, the social unit of analysis is no longer the speech community, as it was in the first two waves. Rather, third wave ethnographies are located in *communities of practice* (Eckert & Wenger 2005; Holmes & Meyerhoff 1999), i.e. social units which exist and constantly re-construct themselves over time around a common and concrete purpose. For example, Eckert (2000) studied the ways in which high school students participated in social styles that stood in locally meaningful contrast to each other, i.e. the 'jocks' and the 'burnouts'. Variation was shown to systematically contribute to an individual's stylistic identity within, near, or outside of one (or both) of these two macro-identity categories. The community of practice, in this case, was the school where the research was conducted. Other studies in the third wave include Bucholtz (2011), Campbell-Kibler (2007), Mendoza-Denton (2008), and Podesva (2007).

Corpus linguistics and language variation

The sociolinguistic approach is not the only way of looking at language variation. Another tradition that studies variation – and is of particular relevance to written digital language – is corpus linguistics (Biber 2012).

A milestone achievement in the founding days of corpus linguistics was the creation of the Brown corpus and the subsequent publication of Kučera & Francis (1967). Brown is an early example of a digitized collection, consisting of 500 samples of texts written in American English and published in 1961, i.e. representing a specific time slice. The methodological innovation championed by corpus linguistics lay in its strongly empirical approach to language studies, grounded in the study of vast amounts of natural language data, which points to an obvious intellectual kinship with sociolinguistics. Even early corpora were often grammatically annotated in some way, for example through part-of-speech tagging (see Hinrichs, Smith, & Waibel 2010 for a discussion of Brown and three more recent corpora, as well as their levels of annotation).

The major difference between the sociolinguistic and the corpus linguistic approach to variation lies in what each takes as its primary unit of quantitative analysis. Variationist studies focus on individual instances of linguistic forms, while corpus linguistic approaches quantify the number of occurrences for a certain form throughout a text, or across an entire collection of texts (Biber 2012: 12) – usually in order to provide a basis for comparison with other texts, or corpora of texts. A sociolinguistic approach to variation between variant A and variant B of variable X would compile data in long form, which implies keeping a record of each instance of variable X that was encountered in the data, and recording not only its realization as A or B (i.e. the form in which the dependent variable occurred) but also a number of contextual factors (i.e. the independent variables). By contrast, a study in corpus linguistics would typically count all occurrences of A and of B in a given section of their data and then compare these frequencies with those in another subset of data; this way, only one data point would be recorded for the first sub-corpus and another for the second. This form of quantitative data recording is called aggregate-level, or short-form, data collection. For example, one might compare the relative frequencies of two variants of one grammatical form, A and B, in two corpora representing texts from 2000 and 1950, normalizing frequencies in case the sizes of both samples should differ. The differences between the two sets of frequencies would provide a first approximation of language change over time.

The next section discusses how the linguistic interest in variation has been applied to, and developed in, research on digital discourse.

Foci of research on variation in digital discourse

In contrast to the focused research programme of foundational variation studies, which emerged out of an explicit engagement with formal linguistics, research on variation in digital language incorporates a remarkable range of applied research interests and goals. The following thematic overview traces the conventional hierarchy of levels of linguistic analysis. It proceeds from the micro-levels of *typography* and *orthography*, through *morphology* and *lexis* at the word level, to *syntax* at the unit of the sentence/utterance. Further, variation at the level of the linguistic system is considered by discussing *code-switching* in online contexts.

Phonetic/phonological variation in digitally transmitted *speech* has not been widely studied to date, though steady improvements in audio-visual transmission as well as text-to-speech interface technology suggest that such research is imminent (Jenks & Firth 2013).

Typographic variation can be broadly conceived of as the alternation between typographic uses that are accepted in conventional printed language, and those that are not. In contrast to orthography, typography refers to the use of non-alphabetic symbols such as numbers, punctuation, and special symbols. Some of the non-standard, or innovative, uses that occur frequently in CMD have become iconic of online writing in popular perception. A representative list of these features (see Crystal 2006 for an introduction) includes:

- Innovative uses of lower and upper case letters, aS iN tHiS eXaMpLe.
- The use of emoticons, such as :-), ;-), or :-@ to represent emotive expressions – here, a smile, a smirk, and an angry face, respectively. Dresner and Herring (2010) show that the pragmatic force of emoticons is not simply to convey information about emotional states, but also to signal the illocutionary force of utterances.
- The optional use of traditionally required punctuation marks. For example, contracted forms that in standard practice require an apostrophe to mark elisions, such as *can't* or *isn't*, may be written without the apostrophe, as in <cant, isnt>.
- The use of number signs to represent entire syllables or words, as in <4> 'for', <2> 'too'/ 'to', etc. Crystal (2006) refers to such cases as 'rebus-like' symbols. They are often used with the corresponding strategy of using individual letters in the same function, as in <4 u> 'for you'.

A text-linguistic approach to typographic variation quantifies the frequency of a certain feature within a given text or corpus and then compares it with frequencies calculated across other texts. For example, Wolf (2000) quantified the use of emoticons in online newsgroups and compared their relative frequencies in posts written by men to those in posts written by women. Broadly confirming the findings of Witmer and Katzman (1997), Wolf found that emoticons are more frequent in female than in male writing; however, variation was also tied to the topic of interactions (men used particularly few emoticons in threads where mostly men participated, such as the sports-oriented 'Dallas Cowboys' thread, whereas they showed frequencies similar to female writers in mixed-gender threads).

The variationist approach, by contrast, quantifies individual linguistic forms, noting for each instance of a variable which of a given range of possible realizations was selected. For example, Squires (2012) quantified the use of apostrophes in contractions (*isn't*, *we'll*, *let's*) and possessive nouns (*Peter's*) in instant messaging data collected from undergraduate students. She showed that both the gender of the writer and that of their interlocutor were significant factors in the statistical analysis of the frequency of apostrophe deletion (Squires 2012: 306). Male writers were shown to be significantly more likely to delete apostrophes in the two variable contexts than females. The factor of interlocutor's gender was shown to interact with the writer's gender: male writers writing to females deleted apostrophes significantly more often than when writing to males; meanwhile, female writers used more deletions when writing to males than to females. This pattern might be interpreted as a sort of divergence effect, opposite to what is to be expected based on the predictions of the audience design model (Bell 1984, 2001). The effect was neutralized, however, when individual writers' preferences were accounted for in statistical analysis by including a random effect for subject (Squires 2012: 310).

Orthographic variation is an area of particular interest for studies of digital discourse. Since most of the writing system, especially standard language orthography, is so strongly codified, any departure from the rules of convention is highly marked and potentially holds great stylistic weight. In Sebba's (2003) formulation,

[the] study of non-standard spelling derives much of its interest from the fact that spelling generally *is* so highly standardised and rigorously regulated. The symbolic value of deviations thus becomes much greater than it would be if the practice of spelling were not so normative.

(p. 151, emphasis in original)

Linguists have turned to the exploration of non-standard orthography within a framework positing that any departure from standard orthography is potentially richly symbolic, and that this symbolism constitutes 'social action' (Sebba 2012). The emerging subfield has been conceptualized as the 'sociolinguistics of spelling' (Sebba 2007a).

Several studies have considered orthographic *variation* in pursuing the underlying correlational logic of choices between standard and non-standard forms. In Hinrichs (2004) and Deuber and Hinrichs (2007), a quantitative approach modelled on frequency-based corpus linguistics was used to analyse the alternation between standard English spellings and alternative respellings in bilingual digital discourse involving standard English and Jamaican Creole.

In subsequent work (Hinrichs & White-Sustaíta 2011; Hinrichs 2012), this approach was more strictly modelled on the variationist paradigm by regressing over multiple independent variables (including social factors such as the diasporic vs non-diasporic residence of the writer, and the gender of the writer) and thus determining the relative importance and statistical significance of linguistic and social factors.

Iorio (2009, 2010) applied a similar methodological design to a study of monolingual digital discourse among players of the Massively Multi-Player Online Role-Playing Game (MMORPG) *City of Heroes*. Iorio shows that the interactional practices of the virtual world in which players interact create systematic differences among interactions that can help account for selections among standard and non-standard spellings. For example, alternation between the standard spelling <ing> and the non-standard <in> for the verbal suffix *–ing* was shown to be predicted robustly by the interaction between two aspects of the virtual relationships among players' online avatars: their relative proximity within the game world, and their status as role players (not all participants in the game have the status of role player). The highest probability for selection of non-standard <in> was predicted for cases in which both the writer and his/her addressee had role player status, and when both were within close virtual proximity of each other (Iorio 2009: 138). With the non-standard variant being predicted by markers of familiarity, such as closer network ties and higher degree of familiarity among participants, variation between the spellings <ing> and <in> in written digital discourse thus showed remarkable similarities to phonetic variation between the standard form[ɪŋ] and the 'reduced' form [ɪn] that occur in speech, as Iorio notes (2009: 135).

There is little published research on *morphological variation* – alternations in the compositional aspect of words – in online discourse. The few extant studies that target morphology deal with the by now familiar word formation processes underlying 'Netspeak' neologisms (Crystal 2006), such as the prefixes *e–*, *cyber–*, or *hyper–*, acronyms such as *OMG*, *WTF*, and *brb* ('oh my god', 'what the fuck', 'be right back'), or blends (*netizen* from 'network citizen') (examples partly from Herring 2012: 2340). Vandekerckhove and Nobels (2010) consider variation in verbal morphology in Dutch chat conversations among teenagers. Choices among the three possible orthographic representations for the verbal ending *–en* are considered to be constrained by aspects of sociolinguistic identity as well as the economy of writing. The standard Dutch spelling <en> is used in 50.69 per cent of cases. The remaining cases show a clear preference of the young writers for the ending <n> (45.7 per cent) over <e> (3.59 per cent); the authors interpret this distribution as resulting, at least in part, from the conventions of synchronous modes of CMD, which 'urge' writers to choose abbreviated alternate spellings (Vandekerckhove & Nobels 2010: 665). In addition, they attribute the fact that the <e>-variant is dispreferred among the set of reductive spellings to its indexical link with spoken standard Dutch, which deletes the final /n/. The young West Flemish writers who supplied the data for the study, and whose local variety does pronounce final /n/, seem to prefer to project a localized linguistic identity.

Lexical variation – relating to questions of word choice – has been addressed much more frequently. For example, Huffaker and Calvert (2005) studied the online self-presentation of adolescents by quantifying certain keywords occurring in two sub-corpora of blog writing – one written by males and one by females. The keywords were mapped to 33 different thematic dictionaries, among them a dictionary containing self-referential items such as first-person singular pronouns, and a dictionary containing words representing 'resolute and active language'. The authors found a number of differences between the male and female sub-corpora that align with popular stereotypical ideologies of social gender identities, for example higher scores for 'aggression' and 'accomplishment' in the male-authored texts, and higher values for 'communication' in the female corpus. Overall, however, differences were not large, and Huffaker and Calvert concluded that 'perhaps this generation of Internet users is becoming more androgynous in its online communication' (2005: n.p.).

Speelman, Grondelaers, and Geeraerts (2006) examined word choice in two corpora of online writing representing the two main national varieties of Dutch: Dutch from Belgium vs from the Netherlands. Their study, rather than being interested in the linguistic reflections of any of the social phenomena related to online writing, uses digital data as a proxy on pragmatic grounds: it is a conveniently accessible source of written data.

A further body of work has begun to examine *syntactic variation* in digital discourse. The most frequently cited characteristic of digital discourse is its '"telegraphic" and fragmented' nature (Herring 2012: 2342). As a reflection of writers' desire to write more economically, i.e. to save keystrokes, much informal online writing features elisions of grammatical function words such as articles and subject pronouns in positions where they are not strictly needed to guarantee message transparency. Such elisions are often compared to baseline corpora of speech data and of paper-based written texts. Elision rates in CMD usually fall between these two, with synchronous modes showing higher rates of elision and thus greater similarity to speech than asynchronous modes (Ko 1996; Yates 1996).

In addition to facilitating typing efficiency, syntactic elision can be employed as a way of stylising dialects that feature deletions. For example, African-American Vernacular English as well as Creole languages may be stylized through the absence of verbal –s or copular verbs (see Sebba 2007b on the stylized use of Jamaican Creole in Ali G webforums).

Correlations have been reported between usage frequencies of grammatical markers and author gender and sub-genre of blogs (Herring & Paolillo 2006), bloggers' psychological response to the trauma of 9/11 (Cohn, Mehl, & Pennebaker 2004), couples' relationship qualities (Slatcher, Vazire, & Pennebaker 2008), deception in online discourse (Hancock, Curry, Goorha, & Woodworth 2007), and alignment with one of three available varieties of Dutch (Vandekerckhove & Nobels 2010).

In addition to the analytical levels of typography and orthography, morphology, lexis, and syntax, digital discourse varies at the level of the linguistic system: writers may use more than one variety or language in their discourse. If such variation occurs within interactions, and not merely across interactions with different addressees, it is considered *code-switching* (CS). Most research on CS in online language has considered its stylistic motivations and effects, and has generally taken a qualitative approach. However, among the studies cited in this section, several have combined their primarily qualitative perspective with statistical overviews and typologies (e.g., Goldbarg 2009; Hinrichs 2006; Siebenhaar 2006).

Most studies of online CS have considered the use of English in combination with other languages. Early work pursued the proposition that English, given its overall dominance in online discourse, might displace other languages (Warschauer, Said, & Zohry 2002), but such misgivings have been qualified by the observation that the advent of the Internet has also provided avenues of literacy development for previously unwritten (and unstandardized) languages (Eisenlohr 2004; Hinrichs 2006; Rajah-Carrim 2009). Digital CS has also been commented on in work that took a primary interest in other questions, such as the representation of languages traditionally using non-Roman scripts (Sahel 2010 on Moroccan Arabic; Tsiplakou 2009 on

Greek–English CS), or the presence of features of Netspeak in the multi-lingual passages in a corpus of bilingual text messages (Deumert & Masinyana 2008).

Several studies take an interest in how the discourse functions of CS have been affected by the transfer of CS from speech to (online) writing: Montes-Alcalá (2001) proposes a typology of different functions of CS in discourse and compares the frequencies of each functional type in a corpus of Spanish–English CMD and in a corpus of transcribed speech. Siebenhaar (2006) studies the quantitative aspects of vernacular German varieties used in CS with standard German in Swiss chat rooms.

Whenever high numbers of users in an online community are multi-literate, with high proficiency levels in multiple languages, digital discourse can display complex distributions of diverse linguistic resources that perform different functions in interactional identity work (Kytölä 2012; Leppänen, Pitkänen-Huhta, Piirainen-Marsh, Nikula, & Peuronen 2009).

Several recent articles summarize research on CS in multilingual digital communication – see e.g. Androutsopoulos (2013), Dorleijn and Nortier (2009), Leppänen and Peuronen (2012), and Lee (this volume).

Research design in digital language variation

Research projects in digitally mediated language variation are typically undertaken with the goal of answering a question rooted in a broader area of interest – whether in the nature of digital language, the social or psychological dimensions of digital interaction, or other related fields – and these driving interests must take primacy in the process of research design. Herring (2004), for example, warns against a study design that starts from a context-free interest in linguistic phenomena. Valuable findings on variation in digital discourse have grown from primary interests in, for example, the difference between genders in language use, the difference between role-playing and non-role-playing participants in MMORPs, and the difference between diasporic and non-diasporic writers of vernacular language, to name but a few (see summaries in Chapter 4 as well as Table 1.1).

A second step in designing a digital variation study is the selection of a linguistic variable in order to operationalize the study's social interest. The term operationalization refers to the definition of a linguistic phenomenon that (1) is relevant to the research question, in the sense that studying it promises to help answer the research question; and that (2) shows variation, which may mean one of two things: it may be conceptualized as a linguistic variable – a recurring linguistic form which may be realized in two (or more) possible forms according to the grammar and conventions of the variety being studied (for example, both <isn't> and <isnt> are frequently encountered in digital discourse as typographical realizations of the contraction *isn't*; thus, they can be studied as two *variants* of the same *linguistic variable*). Alternatively, there may be *free variation* across sub-samples of the data corpus in the frequency of certain features which may not be describable as having one clear alternative and thus would not fit the definition of a linguistic variable (for example, there is no overt alternative to the use of an emoticon, so it cannot be said to be a variable; a meaningful way of studying emoticons would be to quantify their frequency across sub-corpora of one's data). Further, the phenomenon should be objectively observable (Herring 2004: 355), and the definition should be clear, so as to make the study design reproducible for other researchers.

Different types of data source

Linguistic variation can be studied in any digital genre, synchronous or asynchronous. The most important recommendation for the step of data selection is that the data should fit the research question. There are advantages to both small and large datasets, or *corpora*: small datasets allow the

Table 1.1 Examples of publications studying variation in digital discourse

Publication	Social interest	Type of data	Linguistic variable	Primary method of analysis
Deumert and Masinyana (2008)	Differences in the sociolinguistic norms governing the use of English vs isiXhosa in bilingual text messages	Text messages	(1) Frequency of Netspeak features (abbreviations, paralinguistic restitutions, non-standard spellings) in English vs isiXhosa passages; (2) Code-to-content mapping	Descriptive statistics: (1) Frequency of features in qualitative content analysis combined with a coding scheme and quantification; (2) Analysis of content according to coding scheme, quantification of instances of topics in each code
Herring and Paolillo (2006)	Differences in stereotypically masculine/ feminine language use across author genders and blog genres	Blog posts	Frequency of 'male' vs 'female' function words	Predictive statistics: linear regression modelling
Hinrichs and White-Sustaíta (2011); Hinrichs (2012)	Different language ideologies in diasporic vs non-diasporic Jamaicans	Blogs and emails	Standard-English vs non-standard spellings of four lexical items	Predictive statistics: mixed-effects binary regression modelling[*]
Wolf (2000)	Differences in emoticon usage among male and female CMD writers	Newsgroup posts	Frequency of 14 different emoticons in male-dominated vs female-dominated newsgroups	Descriptive statistics: frequency counts of forms in different sub-corpora
Tsiplakou (2009)	Representation of bicultural identities in emails	.Emails	Code choice (English/ Standard Greek/Cypriot Greek)	Qualitative discourse analysis based on interpretation of observed behaviour by the researcher[**]

Notes
[*] In Hinrichs and White-Sustaíta (2011) the statistical analysis is complemented with a qualitative survey among Jamaican writers of digital discourse.
[**] Tsiplakou (2009) also presents a statistical analysis of the frequency of CS per author using linear regression, which precedes the qualitative analysis of CS discourse functions. The adjusted R^2 amounts to .317 (Tsiplakou 2009: 367).

researcher to know the data more intimately, while larger datasets are more likely to produce generalizable findings and, when quantitative methods of analysis are chosen, statistically significant results.

Samples may be designed in a number of different ways; the guiding principle should again be that the resulting corpus should be suited to answering the questions that will be asked of it. One might, for example, select a random sample, or a sample of writing from a specific type of writer, or only writing on a specific range of topics, etc. (Herring 2004: 351). Depending on the underlying hypothesis, one might seek to balance the sample for certain categories: if the research question concerns gender-based differences in observable behaviour, then the sample ought to be roughly balanced in terms of the numbers of male and female writers included. Similarly, if the question targets a comparison of variation in different digital sub-genres, then the sample should include similar amounts of material from all sub-genres under consideration.

With regard to the ideal size of the data corpus, as a broad tendency one might say that quantitative methods require larger numbers of cases of the variable than qualitative ones; therefore, larger corpora tend to be better suited for quantitative methods. There is no way of generalizing how many words a particular data sample would need to be in order to be suitable for quantitative analysis. Such a prediction would depend on the frequency of the phenomenon. Some orthographic phenomena may be fairly frequent, e.g. the contracted forms studied by Squires (2012); other phenomena may occur less frequently and may require larger corpora in order to obtain a sufficiently large number of cases. A sample is large enough when it allows the researcher to state with confidence which of the observed quantitative tendencies are statistically significant. Ultimately, the ideal size of the corpus needs to be decided on a case-by-case basis, and with a view to the considerations discussed in the next section.

Methods

The range of methods available for the study of linguistic variation in digital discourse includes those that have evolved in the fields of sociolinguistics and corpus linguistics. Which method(s) one selects as most appropriate to the analysis of one's data corpus depends both on the linguistic phenomenon and on the data being studied. Many combinations of research question and data can plausibly be answered by more than one method; in fact, many practitioners encourage the use of 'mixed methods'. While it is impossible within the limits of this chapter to provide actual introductions to the methods mentioned here, it is hoped that the overview and references provided will direct readers toward works designed to perform that function.

Quantitative approaches

In the early days of variationist sociolinguistics and corpus linguistics, both disciplines primarily used *descriptive statistics* (see Johnson 2013 and Gries 2010 for helpful introductions from sociolinguistic and corpus-linguistic viewpoints, respectively). Descriptive statistics, which contrasts with predictive statistics, considers all cases of the variable in the corpus and groups them according to certain criteria. The first analytical step in a variationist study would be to tabulate the frequencies of all variants of the linguistic variable across the corpus; in a corpus-linguistic approach, the first statistical analysis would tabulate the frequencies of the phenomenon under study across the different sub-corpora of the sample. Further analyses might then cross-tabulate the same frequencies against a factor such as gender or age of the writer. On the resulting two-dimensional tables of frequencies, chi-squared tests are customarily performed to obtain a p-value as an expression of statistical significance (the p-value expresses the likelihood that the distribution shown in the table could have been produced by chance alone, so a p of 0.1 states that there is a 10 per cent chance that the results are spurious; when $p < 0.05$, it is accepted that the findings are significant). It is possible to use cross-tabulation with more than one factor at the same time, but the results must then be expressed in increasingly complex tables, or multiple tables.

In order to simultaneously analyse the effects of more than two factors on a linguistic phenomenon, and to determine the extent of each factor's influence while controlling for all other factors in the design, as well as the statistical significance of that statement, one needs to turn to *predictive statistics*. Methods of this type express their results in the form of predictions that a specific outcome will occur, or that a specific linguistic form will be used, given a certain combination of contextual factors. Gorman and Johnson (2013) provide a helpful introduction to predictive statistics.

Methods using predictive statistics are mathematically more complex than those using descriptive statistics. They were widely adopted by sociolinguists once computational equipment was far enough developed for methods using predictive statistics to be automatized and, eventually, packaged in a software programme that made it widely available to the academic community. The methodological innovation of looking at the differential impact of various factors on a statistical outcome within one model was conceptualized under the keyword of 'variable rules' (Cedergren & Sankoff 1974; Sankoff & Labov 1979). A software package implementing a predictive statistics procedure based on the philosophy of variable rules was made widely available to sociolinguists under the name Goldvarb (Sankoff, Tagliamonte, & Smith 2005); it became the de facto methodological standard for quantitative sociolinguistic work published in the 1980s, 1990s, and early 2000s. The statistical modelling procedure that was used in Goldvarb to implement variable rules modelling is called binary logistic regression; it has been superseded in recent years by a procedure known as mixed effects regression modelling, which offers a number of critical improvements (Johnson 2009) over the process used in Goldvarb.

Given the interest of sociolinguistics in the role of social identity, it is not surprising that sociolinguistics adopted predictive statistics, which takes individual instances of linguistic production rather than aggregate measurements in groups of texts as its unit of analysis, before corpus linguistics did. While corpus linguistic methodology for the most part remains centred around descriptive statistics, it has developed descriptive methods to considerable sophistication (Gries 2009), and predictive statistics are being used with growing frequency (Biber, Conrad, & Reppen 1998: 269–274; Gries 2012).

At present, research on variation in digital discourse draws more frequently on descriptive statistics than predictive procedures. However, further proliferation of computational methods among linguists promises to aid in the development of sophisticated CMDA methodology. One development in particular makes a more frequent application of multivariate regression models more likely: the increasing relevance of social network communication in daily life, accompanied by a steady increase in the number of linguistic publications devoted to language use in social network sites. Because participants in social networks (such as Facebook or Twitter) have profiles, much more information is available about them than about participants in some older asynchronous modes of CMD, which informed many of the early studies in the literature (e.g., newsgroups or online forums). In social networks, many users' profiles are publicly accessible, depending on each participant's privacy settings. Bamman, Eisenstein, and Schnoebelen (2012) is an example of a study that utilizes the information in users' profiles in a very large corpus of Twitter posts and combines it with sophisticated methods of statistical analysis.

Qualitative approaches

The range of qualitative methods that can be applied to CMD data is fairly wide. It includes *conversation analysis*, *discourse analysis*, *critical discourse analysis*, *online ethnography* (Kytölä & Androutsopoulos

2012), *interactional sociolinguistics*, and *linguistic anthropology*. The items in that list should be seen less as a group of discrete concepts than as keywords which each refer to a way of data interpretation that highlights different aspects of verbal interaction, but overlaps with the others in certain ways. Conversation analysis focuses rather strictly on the dynamics of conversation and the causes and effects of certain interactional moves, taking the conversational turn as its unit of analysis (Hutchby & Woofitt 2008). Discourse analysis is an intentionally broad and open group of tools (intellectual analytical constructs) that are used to analyse what speakers 'do' in their utterances (Gee 2010; Schiffrin, Tannen, & Hamilton 2003). Critical discourse analysis, while similar to discourse analysis in taking an open-ended qualitative approach to verbal interaction, analyses interactions as expressions of social inequalities (Wodak 2001). Online ethnography requires long-term observation of online communities and analyses that are embedded in the community's broader practices and activities (Kytölä & Androutsopoulos 2012). Interactional sociolinguistics shows aspects of analytical practice from practically all the preceding schools and methods, but uses them to uncover the status of linguistic forms as social symbols (Gumperz 1982). Linguistic anthropology is most similar to interactional sociolinguistics, but its primary interest lies in the observation of communities and ways of interacting, rather than in language per se (Hymes 1974).

The methods sketched above all have in common that they provide moderately formalized frameworks that help researchers organize and focus an otherwise interpretative approach to digital data. Because the analyst's subjective perspective is indispensable to the interpretation and observation of the dynamics of interaction, both within the data and in the context of their production, qualitative methods necessarily provide less objective approaches to online data than quantitative ones. Unlike studies using statistical evaluations of digital data, qualitatively obtained research findings can rarely be verified in follow-up studies reproducing the original study design, because different researchers always bring different subjectivities to their projects. The great advantage of qualitative studies is that their data can be studied in great detail, and even singular observations that would have no quantifiable significance in a statistical analysis can be brought to bear on the research question.

Qualitative studies of variation in digital discourse include, for example, Georgakopoulou's (2011) study of how CS serves as an interactional strategy which writers of personal emails in English and Greek use to 'construct and make sense of the positions, stances, or alignments towards their addressees' (Georgakopoulou 2011: 1). Honkanen (2013) examines the use of non-standard spellings of English elements in Finnish interactions on an online music forum, providing a close analysis and typology of the different motivations for, and interactional functions of, non-standard spellings of English borrowings in dominantly Finnish digital discourse.

Mixing methods

Many researchers have called for greater methodological variety in the analysis of digital language, and it stands to reason that research on variation in digital discourse is among the subfields that would benefit from a diversity of methods. Such variety can be achieved in different ways. First, qualitative studies usually benefit from the addition of quantitative methods. Frontloading a qualitative study with a quantitative survey – or vice versa – can help both to contextualize and to interrogate the findings of the primary analysis. See, for example, Iorio (2010), Hinrichs and White-Sustaíta (2011), and Tsiplakou (2009). And second, even in exclusively quantitative approaches, Gorman and Johnson's (2013) admonition 'against a statistical monoculture' must be taken seriously: the quality of statistical methodology in research on variation in digital discourse benefits from a judicious design of the analytical process in which multiple approaches to the same data are critically applied and compared.

Future directions

By and large, linguists studying variation have hardly tapped the vast resources of the Internet and 'big data'. The frontier for research on variation in digital discourse lies in the further appropriation and development of methodologies that are (1) on a par with the methodological state of the art in sociolinguistics and corpus linguistics; (2) sophisticated enough to help illuminate the complex connections between social context, individual identity, media, and linguistic form; and (3) sufficiently automated to harvest the power of very large amounts of data by letting computers do most of the parsing and pruning.

Along with more ambitious studies of large datasets, case studies based on smaller data samples will continue to be important. The research questions emerging around patterns of digital linguistic variation are becoming increasingly fascinating as linguists' understanding of digital discourse in general continues to evolve. And digital discourse variation research hosts robust discussions of theory, revisiting classic constructs such as the linguistic variety (Seargeant & Tagg 2011) and engaging with emerging theories that posit online language as a hybrid variety in its own right (calling it, for example, a 'supervernacular', Blommaert 2012). Much remains to be understood, too, about the roles of playfulness in online discourse (Ifukor 2011) and about differences in the indexical use of linguistic forms between online and offline language. Research on variation in digital discourse can help improve our understanding of all of these issues.

Related topics

- Chapter 3 Digital ethnography (Varis)
- Chapter 6 Style, creativity and play (Nishimura)
- Chapter 7 Multilingual resources and practices in digital communication (Lee)
- Chapter 10 Vernacular literacy: orthography and literacy practices (Iorio)
- Chapter 11 Texting and language learning (Waldron, Kemp, & Wood)
- Chapter 20 Online communities and communities of practice (Angouri)
- Chapter 23 Translocality (Kytölä)

References

Androutsopoulos, J. 2013, 'Code-switching in computer-mediated communication', in S. C. Herring, D. Stein, & T. Virtanen (eds), *Pragmatics of computer-mediated communication*, Mouton de Gruyter: Berlin, pp. 667–694.

Bamman, D., Eisenstein, J., & Schnoebelen, T. 2012, 'Gender in Twitter: styles, stances, and social networks', *Journal of Sociolinguistics*, vol. 18, no. 2, pp. 135–160.

Bell, A. 2001, 'Back in style: reworking audience design', in P. Eckert & J. R. Rickford (eds), *Style and sociolinguistic variation*, Cambridge University Press: Cambridge, pp. 139–169.

Bell, A. 1984, 'Language style as audience design', *Language in Society*, vol. 13, no. 2, pp. 145–204.

Biber, D. 2012, 'Register as a predictor of linguistic variation', *Corpus Linguistics and Linguistic Theory*, vol. 8, no. 1, pp. 9–37.

Biber, D., Conrad, S., & Reppen, R. 1998, *Corpus linguistics: investigating language structure and use*, Cambridge University Press: Cambridge.

Blommaert, J. 2012, 'Supervernaculars and their dialects', *Dutch Journal of Applied Linguistics*, vol. 1, no. 1, pp. 1–14.

Bucholtz, M. 2011, *White kids: language, race, and styles of youth identity*, Cambridge University Press: Cambridge.

Campbell-Kibler, K. 2007, 'Accent, (ING), and the social logic of listener perceptions', *American Speech*, vol. 82, no. 1, pp. 32–64.

Cedergren, H. J. & Sankoff, D. 1974, 'Variable rules: performance as a statistical reflection of competence', *Language*, vol. 50, no. 2, pp. 333–355.

Cheshire, J. 1987, 'Syntactic variation, the linguistic variable, and sociolinguistic theory', *Linguistics*, vol. 25, no. 2, pp. 257–282.

Cheshire, J. 1982, *Variation in an English dialect: a sociolinguistic study*, Cambridge University Press: Cambridge.

Cohn, M. A., Mehl, M. R., & Pennebaker, J. W. 2004, 'Linguistic markers of psychological change surrounding September 11, 2001', *Psychological Science*, vol. 15, no. 10, pp. 687–693.

Crystal, D. 2006, *Language and the internet*, 2nd edn, Cambridge University Press: Cambridge.

Deuber, D. & Hinrichs, L. 2007, 'Dynamics of orthographic standardization in Jamaican Creole and Nigerian Pidgin', *World Englishes*, vol. 26, no. 1, pp. 22–47.

Deumert, A. & Masinyana, S. O. 2008, 'Mobile language choices: the use of English and isiXhosa in text messages (SMS): evidence from a bilingual South African sample', *English World-Wide*, vol. 29, no. 2, pp. 117–147.

Dorleijn, M. & Nortier, J. 2009, 'Code-switching and the internet', in Barbara E. Bullock & A. J. Toribio (eds), *The Cambridge handbook of linguistic code-switching*, Cambridge University Press: Cambridge, pp. 127–141.

Dresner, E. & Herring, S. C. 2010, 'Functions of the nonverbal in CMC: emoticons and illocutionary force', *Communication Theory*, vol. 20, no. 3, pp. 249–268.

Eckert, P. 2012, 'Three waves of variation study: the emergence of meaning in the study of sociolinguistic variation', *Annual Review of Anthropology*, vol. 41, no. 1, pp. 87–100.

Eckert, P. 2000, *Linguistic variation as social practice: the linguistic construction of identity in Belten High*, Blackwell: Malden, MA.

Eckert, P. & Wenger, E. 2005, 'Communities of practice in sociolinguistics', *Journal of Sociolinguistics*, vol. 9, no. 4, pp. 582–589.

Eisenlohr, P. 2004, 'Language revitalization and new technologies: cultures of electronic mediation and the refiguring of communities', *Annual Review of Anthropology*, vol. 33, pp. 21–45.

Gee, J. P. 2010, *How to do discourse analysis: a toolkit*, Routledge: London.

Georgakopoulou, A. 2011, '"On for drinkies?": e-mail cues of participant alignments', *Language@Internet*, vol. 8, article 4.

Goldbarg, R. N. 2009, 'Spanish–English codeswitching in email communication', *Language@Internet*, vol. 6, article 3.

Gorman, K. & Johnson, D. E. 2013, 'Quantitative analysis', in R. Bayley, R. Cameron, & C. Lucas (eds), *The Oxford handbook of sociolinguistics*, Oxford University Press: Oxford, pp. 214–240.

Gries, S. T. 2012, 'Corpus linguistics, theoretical linguistics, and cognitive/psycholinguistics: towards more and more fruitful exchanges', *Language and Computers*, vol. 75, no. 1, pp. 41–63.

Gries, S. T. 2010, 'Useful statistics for corpus linguistics', in A. Sánchez & M. Almela (eds), *A mosaic of corpus linguistics: selected approaches* (Studien Zur Romanischen Sprachwissenschaft Und Interkulturellen Kommunikation 66), Peter Lang: Frankfurt, pp. 269–291.

Gries, S. T. 2009, 'What is corpus linguistics?' *Language and Linguistics Compass*, vol. 3, no. 5, pp. 1225–1241.

Gumperz, J. J. 1982, *Discourse strategies*, Cambridge University Press: Cambridge.

Hancock, J. T., Curry, L. E., Goorha, S., & Woodworth, M. 2007, 'On lying and being lied to: a linguistic analysis of deception in computer-mediated communication', *Discourse Processes*, vol. 45, no. 1, pp. 1–23.

Herring, S. C. 2012, 'Grammar and electronic communication', *The encyclopedia of applied linguistics*, Wiley-Blackwell: Hoboken, NJ, pp. 2338–2346.

Herring, S. C. 2004, 'Computer-mediated discourse analysis: an approach to researching online behavior', in S. Barab, R. Kling, & J. H. Gray (eds), *Designing for virtual communities in the service of learning*, Cambridge University Press: Cambridge, pp. 338–376.

Herring, S. C. & Paolillo, J. C. 2006, 'Gender and genre variation in weblogs', *Journal of Sociolinguistics*, vol. 10, no. 4, pp. 439–459.

Hinrichs, L. 2012, 'How to spell the vernacular: a multivariate study of Jamaican e-mails and blogs', in A. Jaffe, J. Androutsopoulos, M. Sebba, & S. Johnson (eds), *Orthography as social action: scripts, spelling, identity, and power*, Mouton de Gruyter: Berlin, pp. 325–358.

Hinrichs, L. 2006, *Codeswitching on the web: English and Jamaican Creole in e-mail communication*, John Benjamins: Amsterdam.

Hinrichs, L. 2004, 'Emerging orthographic conventions in written Creole: computer-mediated communication in Jamaica', *Arbeiten aus Anglistik und Amerikanistik*, vol. 29, no. 1, pp. 81–109.

Hinrichs, L., Smith, N., & Waibel, B. 2010, 'Manual of information for the part-of-speech-tagged, post-edited "Brown" corpora', *ICAME Journal*, vol. 34, pp. 189–231.

Hinrichs, L. & Szmrecsanyi, B. 2007, 'Recent changes in the function and frequency of Standard English genitive constructions: a multivariate analysis of tagged corpora', *English Language and Linguistics*, vol. 11, no. 3, pp. 437–474.

Hinrichs, L. & White-Sustaíta, J. 2011, 'Global Englishes and the sociolinguistics of spelling: a study of Jamaican blog and email writing', *English World-Wide*, vol. 32, no. 1, pp. 46–73.

Holmes, J. & Meyerhoff, M. 1999, 'The community of practice: theories and methodologies in language and gender research', *Language in Society*, vol. 28, no. 2, pp. 173–183.

Honkanen, M. 2013, 'Spelling English elements in Finnish CMC: orthography as social practice in a music forum', MS thesis, Albert-Ludwigs Universität, Freiburg.

Huffaker, D. A. & Calvert, S. L. 2005, 'Gender, identity, and language use in teenage blogs', *Journal of Computer-Mediated Communication*, vol. 10, no. 2.

Hutchby, I. & Wooffitt, R. 2008, *Conversation analysis*, Polity Press: Cambridge.

Hymes, D. H. 1974, *Foundations in sociolinguistics: an ethnographic approach*, University of Pennsylvania Press: Philadelphia, PA.

Ifukor, P. 2011, 'Linguistic marketing in " . . . a marketplace of ideas" ', *Pragmatics and Society*, vol. 2, no. 1, pp. 110–147.

Iorio, J. 2010, 'Explaining orthographic variation in a virtual community: linguistic, social, and contextual factors', PhD thesis, University of Texas, Austin, TX.

Iorio, J. 2009, 'Effects of audience on orthographic variation', *Studies in the linguistic Sciences: illinois working papers* 2009, pp. 127–140.

Jenks, C. & Firth, A. 2013, 'Synchronous voice-based computer-mediated communication', in S. C. Herring, D. Stein, & T. Virtanen (eds), *Pragmatics of computer-mediated communication*, Mouton de Gruyter: Berlin pp. 217–244.

Johnson, D. E. 2013, 'Descriptive statistics', in R. Podesva & D. Sharma (eds), *Research methods in linguistics*, Cambridge University Press: Cambridge, pp. 288–315.

Johnson, D. E. 2009, 'Getting off the GoldVarb standard: introducing Rbrul for mixed-effects variable rule analysis', *Language and Linguistics Compass*, vol. 3, no. 1, pp. 359–583.

Ko, K-K. 1996, 'Structural characteristics of computer-mediated language: a comparative analysis of InterChange discourse', *Electronic Journal of Communication*, vol. 6, no. 3, available from: http://www.cios.org/www/ejc/v6n396.htm (accessed 17 June 2015).

Kučera, H. & Francis, W. N. 1967, *Computational analysis of present-day American English*, Brown University Press: Providence, RI.

Kytölä, S. 2012, 'Researching the multilingualism of web discussion forums: theoretical, practical and methodological issues', in M. Sebba, S. Mahootian, & C. Jonsson (eds), *Language mixing and code-switching in writing: approaches to mixed-language written discourse*, Routledge: New York, NY, pp. 106–127.

Kytölä, S. & Androutsopoulos, J. 2012, 'Ethnographic perspectives on multilingual computer-mediated discourse', in S. Gardner & M. Martin-Jones (eds), *Multilingualism, discourse, and ethnography*, Routledge: New York, NY, pp. 179–196.

Labov, W. 1978, 'Where does the linguistic variable stop? A response to Beatriz Lavandera', *Working Papers in Sociolinguistics*, vol. 44, pp. 1–17.

Labov, W. 1972, 'The social motivation of a sound change', in W. Labov, *Sociolinguistic patterns*, University of Pennsylvania Press: Philadelphia, PA, pp. 1–42.

Labov, W. 1966a, *The social stratification of English in New York City*, Center for Applied Linguistics: Washington, DC.

Labov, W. 1966b, 'The linguistic variable as a structural unit', *Washington Linguistics Review*, vol. 3, pp. 4–22, available from: http://eric.ed.gov/?id=ED010871 (accessed 17 June 2015).

Labov, W. 1963, 'The social motivation of a sound change', *Word*, vol. 19, pp. 273–309.

Leppänen, S. & Peuronen, S. 2012, 'Multilingualism on the internet', in M. Martin-Jones, A. Blackledge, & A. Creese (eds), *The Routledge handbook of multilingualism*, Routledge: London, pp. 384–402.

Leppänen, S., Pitkänen-Huhta, A., Piirainen-Marsh, A., Nikula, T., & Peuronen, S. 2009, 'Young people's translocal new media uses: a multiperspective analysis of language choice and heteroglossia', *Journal of Computer-Mediated Communication*, vol. 14, no. 4, pp. 1080–1107.

Mendoza-Denton, N. 2008, *Homegirls: language and cultural practice among Latina youth gangs*, Blackwell: Malden, MA.

Milroy, L. 1980, *Language and social networks*, University Park Press: Baltimore, MD.

Modaressi-Tehrani, Y. 1978, 'A sociolinguistic analysis of modern Persian', PhD dissertation, University of Kansas: Lawrence, KS.

Montes-Alcalá, C. 2001, 'Oral vs written code-switching contexts in English-Spanish bilingual narratives', in I. de la Cruz (ed.), *La lingüística aplicada a fi nales del siglo XX: ensayos y propuestas*, Publicaciones de la Universidad de Alcalá de Henares: Alcalá de Henares (Madrid), pp. 715–720.

Podesva, R. J. 2007, 'Phonation type as a stylistic variable: the use of falsetto in constructing a persona', *Journal of Sociolinguistics*, vol. 11, no. 4, pp. 478–504.

Rajah-Carrim, A. 2009, 'Use and standardisation of Mauritian Creole in electronically mediated communication', *Journal of Computer-Mediated Communication*, vol. 14, no. 3, pp. 484–508.

Rickford, J. R. 1986, 'The need for new approaches to social class analysis in sociolinguistics', *Language & Communication*, vol. 6, no. 3, pp. 215–221.

Sahel, S. 2010, 'Die Rolle der neuen Medien bei der Entstehung neuer Schriftformen: Der Fall einer diglossischen Sprachgemeinschaft', in U. Kleinberger & F. Wagner (eds), *Sprach- und Kulturkontakt in den neuen Medien*, Lang: Bern, Switzerland, pp. 77–96.

Sankoff, D. & Labov, W. 1979, 'On the use of variable rules', *Language in Society*, vol. 8, no. 2, pp. 189–222.

Sankoff, D., Tagliamonte, S., & Smith, E. 2005, *Goldvarb X: a variable rule application for Macintosh and Windows*, Department of Linguistics, University of Toronto: Toronto.

Schiffrin, D., Tannen, D., & Hamilton, H. E. 2003, *The handbook of discourse analysis*, Wiley-Blackwell: Malden, MA.

Seargeant, P. & Tagg, C. 2011, 'English on the internet and a "post-varieties" approach to language', *World Englishes*, vol. 30, no. 4, pp. 496–514.

Sebba, M. 2012, 'Orthography as social action: scripts, spelling, identity and power', in A. Jaffe, J. Androutsopoulos, M. Sebba, & S. Johnson (eds), *Orthography as social action: scripts, spelling, identity, and power*, Mouton de Gruyter: Berlin, pp. 1–20.

Sebba, M. 2007a, *Spelling and society: the culture and politics of orthography around the world*, Cambridge University Press: Cambridge.

Sebba, M. 2007b, 'Identity and language construction in an online community: the case of "Ali G"', in P. Auer (ed.), *Style and social identities: alternative approaches to linguistic heterogeneity*, Mouton de Gruyter: Berlin, pp. 361–392.

Sebba, M. 2003, 'Spelling rebellion', in J. Androutsopoulos & A. Georgakopoulou (eds), *Discourse constructions of youth identities*, John Benjamins: Amsterdam, pp. 151–172.

Siebenhaar, B. 2006, 'Code choice and code-switching in Swiss–German Internet Relay chat rooms', *Journal of Sociolinguistics*, vol. 10, no. 4, pp. 481–506.

Slatcher, R. B., Vazire, S., & Pennebaker, J. W. 2008, 'Am "I" more important than "we"? Couples' word use in instant messages', *Personal Relationships*, vol. 15, no. 4, pp. 407–424.

Speelman, D., Grondelaers, S., & Geeraerts, D. 2006, 'A profile-based calculation of region and register variation: the synchronic and diachronic status of the two main national varieties of Dutch', in A. Wilson, D. Archer, & P. Rayson (eds), *Language and computers: corpus linguistics around the world*, vol. 56, pp. 181–194, available from: http://www.ingentaconnect.com/content/rodopi/lang/2006/00000056/00000001/art00015 (accessed 17 June 2015).

Squires, L. 2012, 'Whos punctuating what? sociolinguistic variation in instant messaging', in A. Jaffe, J. Androutsopoulos, M. Sebba, & S. Johnson (eds), *Orthography as social action: scripts, spelling, identity, and power*, Mouton de Gruyter: Berlin, pp. 289–324.

Trudgill, P. 1974, *The social differentiation of English in Norwich*, Cambridge University Press: Cambridge.

Tsiplakou, S. 2009, 'Doing (bi)lingualism: language alternation as performative construction of online identities', *Pragmatics*, vol. 19, no. 3, pp. 361–391.

Vandekerckhove, R. & Nobels, J. 2010, 'Code eclecticism: linguistic variation and code alternation in the chat language of Flemish teenagers', *Journal of Sociolinguistics*, vol. 14, no. 5, pp. 657–677.

Warschauer, M., Said, G. R. E., & Zohry, A. G. 2002, 'Language choice online: globalization and identity in Egypt', *Journal of Computer-Mediated Communication*, vol. 7, no. 4.

Weinreich, U., Labov, W., & Herzog, M. I. 1968, 'Empirical foundations for a theory of language change', in W. P. Lehmann & Y. Malkiel (eds), *Directions for historical linguistics*, University of Texas Press: Austin, TX, pp. 95–188.

Witmer, D. F. & Katzman, S. L. 1997, 'On-line smiles: does gender make a difference in the use of graphic accents?' *Journal of Computer-Mediated Communication*, vol. 2, no. 4.

Wodak, R. 2001, 'What CDA is about: a summary of its history, important concepts and its developments', in R. Wodak & M. Meyer (eds), *Methods of critical discourse analysis*, SAGE: Thousand Oaks, CA, pp. 1–13.

Wolf, A. 2000, 'Emotional expression online: gender differences in emoticon use', *CyberPsychology & Behavior*, vol. 3, no. 5, pp. 827–833.

Wolfram, W. 1991, 'The linguistic variable: fact and fantasy', *American Speech*, vol. 66, no. 1, pp. 22–32.

Wolfram, W. 1969, *A sociolinguistic description of Detroit Negro speech*, Center for Applied Linguistics: Washington, DC.

Yates, S. J. 1996, 'Oral and written linguistic aspects of computer conferencing', in S. C. Herring (ed.), *Computer-mediated communication: linguistic, social and cross-cultural perspectives*, John Benjamins: Amsterdam, pp. 29–46.

Further reading

Androutsopoulos, J. & Beisswenger, M. 2008, 'Introduction: data and methods in computer-mediated discourse analysis', *Language@Internet* vol. 5, article 2.

In this introduction to a special journal issue, the authors take a synoptic perspective toward research on digital discourse, much of which relates to language variation.

Baayen, R. H. 2008, *Analyzing linguistic data: a practical introduction to statistics using R*, Cambridge University Press: Cambridge.

A reliable and widely used introduction to some frequently employed statistical procedures (including multivariate types of analysis) using the open-source software R. Requires some prior knowledge of R.

Gee, J. P. 2013, *An introduction to discourse analysis: theory and method*, Routledge: London.

A broadly applicable introduction to qualitative research on discourse of any kind, including digital.

Gries, S. T. 2009, *Quantitative corpus linguistics with R: a practical introduction*, Routledge: London.

A basic introduction to elementary statistics which also introduces the beginner to R and demonstrates how R can be used to conduct corpus searches.

2

Network analysis

John C. Paolillo

Introduction

Among the more frequently encountered forms of analysis of digital communication is the family of approaches known as network analysis. These approaches share the notion that important characteristics of communication can be characterized in terms of some basic relations among a set of individuals, and that these relations, though specific to the individuals they relate to, compose a larger-scale structure that bears in some substantive way on the nature of the communication. Researchers from many different fields analyze digital communication using network approaches, and the specific approach to network analysis may vary according to researchers' disciplinary backgrounds and the specific questions they seek to answer.

There are a number of reasons these approaches are so common in digital media. First, the notion of network is a highly abstract mathematical construct and can be applied broadly to anything relational. Communication is naturally viewed as being relational, in that messages are exchanged between individuals and hence relate them to each other. Digital media also provide logs and traces of their use that are easily converted into network data, predisposing it to this kind of analysis. Finally, many of the questions about the use of media—digital or non-digital—involve networks of relations: how does information (or misinformation, or an idea, or a "meme") travel through the Internet to reach the people it ultimately reaches? Where do special Internet language forms originate and how are they dispersed? To what extent is news information controlled by a small group of news organizations, and what routes must alternative stories follow in order to become widely known? These and many other questions are ones that are addressed through a network analysis perspective.

One may wish to know what kinds of structures these relations create, and what they may say about the contexts in which the communication is observed. Network structures inform us about social segmentation into social classes, ethnicities, age cohorts, etc. Network analysis also informs us about processes that create structure and thereby govern social life: social roles, centrality, dominance, systems of exchange, etc. (Degenne & Forsé 1999; Wasserman & Faust 1994). Networks exemplify self-organization, because there is no immediately obvious reason why certain structures are created and not others (Barabási & Albert 1999; Watts & Strogatz 1998). Finally, different network structures may imply different demands on communication and computational resources and so may help us understand how to design and construct digital communication systems that better handle peak and continuing demands. Network perspectives are useful for all of these goals.

Network analysis has a long history, having been developed in different forms at different times. Mathematically it is recognized as an application of graph theory, first formally explored by Leonhard Euler in 1735 but later given a probabilistic treatment by Erdös and Rényi (1959). In sociology, social network analysis is usually traced to Jacob Moreno's work in the 1930s (Freeman 2004; Scott 2012), although it has earlier antecedents as well (Freeman 2004). Network analysis has applications in many other fields, such as computer science, physics, cognitive science, epidemiology, and information retrieval, among others.

A significant challenge for people seeking to understand digital communication in network terms lies in understanding the differences among the different approaches to network analysis and the questions each is intended to answer. For example, a computer scientist whose primary interest may be predicting and planning for peak load demands on a server hosting a social networking site or designing computational architecture required for one is not necessarily deeply interested in understanding the different social roles of specific users on the site. The particular perspective that is most relevant to this question is one that views the network in aggregate, as a single distribution of actors, relationships, and activities, and its specific history is not viewed as deeply relevant. Conversely, a researcher interested in understanding the establishment of norms on a social networking site will favor a network analysis which partitions the participants into structural groups and which foregrounds the roles of specific individuals in bridging more than one group, etc. Because the statistical models for these different types of analysis tend to exclude each other, they also compete as analyses of the structure of the network. Additionally, the models of each type are evaluated according to different criteria. Consequently, it can be difficult to reconcile the different network perspectives with one another.

Network analysis is, by nature, reductive, in that it takes a complex phenomenon like human communication and reduces it, oftentimes to an extreme, so that only a single aspect of the phenomenon is subjected to analysis. While this approach leads to interesting interpretations regarding social structure and process, the fidelity of the analysis to the content and form of e.g., digital communication is low, and this has certain hazards. First and foremost, whether a particular network analysis reveals interesting (or even accurate) interpretations is always open to debate. One can choose from a large number of parameter values to create an analysis (e.g., the definition of a link, thresholds used for interpreting links or recognizing clusters, mathematical transforms for weighting links, etc.); these affect the outcome of the analysis profoundly, but there is little guidance as to how they should be chosen to provide a correct (as opposed to an interesting) analysis. The situation worsens for complex questions from e.g., the sociolinguistics of digital media, where more than one network, or a network plus some other feature, is involved. Such questions include how linguistic variants are distributed in online communities (Paolillo 2001), how digital genres become established (Ferrara, Whittemore, & Brunner 1991; Paolillo, Warren, & Kunz 2011), how Internet or medium-specific forms spread from one medium to another, the role of multilingualism in connecting different online communities (Herring et al. 2007), etc. Network perspectives have much to contribute to these and other questions, but connecting the network and other aspects of the analysis is a problem solved individually for each specific case.

The sociolinguistics of face-to-face speech communities offers some relevant points of reference (Eckert 2000; Milroy & Milroy 1992; see e.g., Paolillo 2001), but many aspects of the methodology do not directly transfer to digital communication, and consequently one cannot always make the same interpretations of the networks that are uncovered. For example, Eckert used face-to-face interviews with specific prompts to generate lists of friends for students at Belten High; interviews like these typically focus on identifying "best friends." Interviews are almost never used with digital media, because the media themselves provide relational information, such as friend lists in user profiles, or "from" and "to" headers in message exchanges; interviews are therefore not necessary for discovering network links. At the same time, social media profiles tend to have many more friends that one can elicit through interviews, and so the connection represented may be more incidental and less socially meaningful—"acquaintance" might be a better term for them. Because none of these definitions can be prescribed, the meaning of any structures discovered may shift depending on the definitions used. Consequently, one must be very careful in conducting and interpreting network analyses.

Foundations

The elements of network analysis are *nodes* and *arcs*. Nodes are the basic unit of analysis; they often represent people but, depending on the context, they may represent more abstract entities as well. Arcs are the relations that hold between two nodes. Again, these often represent a social relationship between individuals, such as friendship or acquaintanceship, but depending on the purpose of the analysis they can be any other type of relationship. Arcs may be *directed* or *undirected*. Directed arcs represent an asymmetrical relationship between two nodes. For example when people name their close friendships, these often turn out to be different depending on who is asked: Bob might name Alice as a friend, but Alice would not necessarily name Bob. "Friendship," construed this way, is a directed relationship. Undirected arcs, also called *edges*, represent a relationship that is necessarily symmetrical. Many social networking sites assume that friendship is undirected, and though a "friend link" typically needs to be initiated by one person and accepted by another (an action that is directed), no distinction is shown between the two people at either end of the link: they are simply shown as "friends," an undirected link.

Nodes and arcs need not always be intuitive, and there are many abstract choices that result in legitimate network analyses. For example, we may wish to examine the structure of relationships among people created by their affiliation with various formal and informal groups, such as would come from a set of subscriptions to different mailing lists. We might adopt the view that two people share a link if they are subscribers to one or more mailing lists in common. This type of data is known as *two-mode data*, as it involves two different kinds of entities—e.g., people and mailing lists—each being a *mode* of the network. Two-mode data has the added benefit of permitting one to draw two networks, in this example a network of people, based on their common subscriptions, and a network of mailing lists, based on their common subscribers. Both can give useful insight. Three-mode and higher networks are also possible but less frequently employed in network analysis because of the complexities of handling the data.

A special case of two-mode data occurs when networks have two fundamentally different types of node, and nodes of each type link only to nodes of the other type. Such a network has a *bipartite* structure. Bipartite networks occur in some natural circumstances, such as in an exclusively heterosexual dating network, where links may occur between a male and a female but not between male and male or female and female. Note that a dating network is not necessarily bipartite, and that a more neutral analytical assumption is that both males and females represent a common mode; the degree to which the network is bipartite can then be investigated. Likewise, two-mode data can always be analyzed as representing a bipartite network, although more commonly we are more interested in the structure within one mode or the other.

Network analyses of face-to-face communication (Eckert 2000; Milroy & Milroy 1992) have tended to favor one-mode data. Two-mode data is common in various social science applications of network analyses, such as court rulings (Doreian, Batagelj, & Ferligoj 2004), congressional committee memberships (Porter, Mucha, Newman, & Warmbrand 2005), and interlocking corporate boards (Borgatti & Foster 2003). In digital media research, both one-mode and two-mode data are commonly used; typically, it is a matter of analytical convenience which is chosen.

One of the chief tenets of network analysis is that a set of nodes is structured based on their connectivity through the arcs; these structures are interesting for their own properties. Networks may have *dense* interconnections, with most nodes linking to many other nodes, or more *sparse* connections, with most nodes linking to few others. There may be a densely connected *core*, along with a less densely connected *periphery*, or there may be multiple *clusters* of densely connected nodes, the clusters being only loosely connected together. Clusters may correspond to interesting groupings such as social classes, ethnic groups, age cohorts, etc.[1] Two or more clusters may be connected by a single node, called a *bridge*,[2] or there may be *chains* of intermediate nodes.

Typical network analyses of social media sites (e.g., LiveJournal, Facebook, YouTube) show that they tend to have densely interconnected cores when "friend," as used by the site, is treated as a link; when actual communicative interactions are used to define links (e.g., posting on someone's wall, or commenting on someone's post), density is typically a lot lower, and sometimes rather extended interchanges encompassing months or years have to be gathered before a core (or any other type of structure) emerges. In a way, "friend" tends to aggregate one's history on a site, whereas the social ties that are currently active, and which may therefore be more interesting for understanding the site's social dynamics from a social perspective, are harder to identify. This is perhaps the greatest challenge for applying network analysis to digital media: finding an appropriate definition of "link" which is operationalizable in terms of the artifacts provided by the digital environment and which leads to a meaningful and insightful analysis from a social perspective.

Other mathematical and algebraic properties of networks interesting to network researchers are *reflexivity* (whether nodes link to themselves), *symmetry* or *reciprocity* (when directed links tend to be reciprocated by both parties in a link), and *transitivity* (when two nodes that link to a common third node tend to be linked to one another). *Density* is the extent to which two nodes that might share a link are actually linked, *homophily* is the extent to which nodes of a similar type are linked (as opposed to links among nodes of different types), and *clustering* is the extent to which nodes in a network form dense clusters. For these and other properties, network analysts have proposed a number of indices (Degenne & Forsé 1999; Wasserman & Faust 1994; Watts & Strogatz 1998). Researchers attempt to use these indices to guide the interpretation of different observed networks, but there are many unsolved statistical problems around the distribution of network properties, along with potentially different interpretations of some of the same empirical cases.

Sampling

Network analysis begins by collecting a sample of nodes and observing the relations among them. This means a decision needs to be made about the nature of the nodes and the type of relationship to be observed. Operational choices among alternatives may appear to yield similar information at first blush but turn out to have consequences whose full import cannot always be determined. For example, one may wish to observe the structure of a community by examining communication among its members, where much of that communication takes place online via a web-based forum. The forum might be configured to allow distinct forum accounts for distinct email accounts; we might therefore choose email account names to identify people. The assumption readily translates to a network analysis of the forum, where nodes are email addresses and forum messages from one email account to another establish a link.

Network analysis of digital communication generally considers a particular kind of operationalization of nodes and arcs where both are located in digital artifacts. One must be aware when doing this that there is an established literature on methodology in Social Network Analysis that emphasizes a different type of observation. These methodological choices have a range of consequences. In the example above, an individual may readily have more than one email and/ or forum account, such that other forum members do not know that the two accounts belong to the same person. Members of the community may also communicate via other channels such as direct email contact and therefore be linked in the sense that is desired, but without evidence of that linkage in the forum messages. Consequently, if the intent is to infer something about relations among people, observing digital artifacts, while convenient, has a potentially distorting effect. This is a common hazard of network analysis, and there is no single remedy for it.

A further issue with network sampling is that random sampling is seldom possible, and, even when it is, its use distorts the structure of what one observes by making the network overall appear less connected than it actually is. Hence, network studies generally use one of two approaches to sampling: they may obtain complete data about some pre-defined context and conduct a network analysis of that; or they may use "snowball sampling" from a number of arbitrary start points. Complete data is typically obtained from archives, such as the Enron email corpus (Klimt & Yang 2004) made public through the legal proceedings against that company, or from gaining access to a company's data or call traffic records, such as the Finland call database used by Onnela *et al.* (2007). Complete data is only complete within the pre-defined context, however, and leaves out any connections outside of that context. In addition, there may be gaps in the data, such as items in the Enron corpus that have been redacted as having personal content.

Snowball sampling proceeds by starting with a seed set of nodes and using the relations to identify new nodes to the set. Seed nodes are selected either at random or by convenience. Relations from these nodes are followed to discover new nodes that are added to the set under study. This procedure is applied iteratively until some limit is reached. This could be a saturation point (no new nodes are found) or a point where the data set is deemed large enough to answer whatever questions are of interest. Search engine indexes of the World Wide Web are gathered in this way, using web pages as nodes and hyperlinks as arcs, as are many other networks, including face-to-face communication networks.

A key point about network samples is that all of them are biased in some way. Complete data only provides information about some specific context; information outside that context yet relevant to it will not be represented. Snowball samples are unlikely to obtain disconnected network components, unless these are in the original starting sample. In contrast, random samples under-represent the connectivity of the network. Hence, inferential statistics based on any of these types of sample will be correspondingly biased. The traditional inference from sample to population—i.e., from characterizing a sample of nodes to characterizing the set of all similar nodes—is not licensed. Network analyses vary in their approach to this problem, from ignoring it entirely to sharply limiting the scope of their conclusions.

Analysis

Analysis of networks is highly abstract and much of it requires tools of advanced mathematics and statistics to perform. Hence, people wishing to do network analysis need a background in the appropriate mathematics and statistics. In this necessarily brief section, it will only be possible to suggest the general outlines of network analysis, emphasizing the most basic concepts; further detail must be found elsewhere. For those with a social science background, Degenne and Forsé (1999) provides a suitable introduction to network analysis rooted in sociological theory, while providing extensive yet accessible discussion of the mathematics; this balance makes it the social network analysis reference of choice for many working with social media. Scott (2012) is similar in approach and accessibility, albeit slightly slimmer, and it lacks reference to interesting work done in the French academic context found in Degenne and Forsé. A more comprehensive treatment of network analysis methods is Wasserman and Faust (1994). All three books predate the current interest in social media, and consequently lack any mention of it. For software-specific introductions to network analysis, Hansen, Shneiderman, and Smith (2011) focus on visualizing social media networks, while de Nooy, Mrvar, and Batagelj (2005) explain a few more statistically sophisticated network models using traditional sociological datasets.

A network analysis begins by building an *incidence matrix* of the network, a basic data arrangement whose exact nature depends on the number of modes in the data. For one-mode data, the incidence matrix is square and the row and column labels are the same; by convention, rows represent the node that an arc originates from and columns indicate the arc's destination. Values are entered into the cells of the matrix indicating the nature of the connection between the respective row and column of each potential pair. Generally, values of zero and one are entered, indicating absence or presence of a relation, respectively. This gives a *binary* incidence matrix. Other values may be used, typically to indicate the relative strength of a connection, resulting in a *valued* incidence matrix. For two-mode data, rows and columns represent the different modes of the network, e.g., subscribers in rows and mailing lists in columns. Again, two-mode data can be binary or valued. Data with more than two modes do not have a single, simple arrangement as an incidence matrix.

The advantage of representing a network as an incidence matrix is that it is convenient for many matrix algebra operations, which in turn have interpretations in network terms. For example, suppose we have a two-mode binary incidence matrix A representing email list subscriptions, where rows are subscribers and columns are mailing lists. If we want to know how many subscriptions any two people share in common, we can use the matrix product AA^T to compute this in one step.[3] Similarly, if we want to know the number of subscribers any two mailing lists have in common, we would compute A^TA instead. These matrix products yield valued incidence matrices for the two different modes of the network. A theorem of matrix algebra, the Singular Value Decomposition (SVD) theorem, relates these two matrix products to each other, expressing a mathematical relationship between the two modes of a network. Similar matrix operations form the basis of Principal Components Analysis and Factor Analysis, two statistical techniques commonly used to analyze network data, further motivating one approach to statistical analysis of network data.

The network–matrix dualism is thus highly productive and permits the direct application of statistical methods to network observations. The incidence matrix representation has one major drawback, however: it is very expensive to compute with. This is because, for a network with n nodes, there are n^2 possible arcs, each of which needs to be a value (e.g., a floating point number) in the matrix. When n is large, such as in the tens of thousands of nodes or more, n^2 can be prohibitively large (hundreds of millions, billions or trillions of arcs), and so programs that require this representation can only be used when vast computing resources are available (supercomputers or supercomputing clusters). This is a non-trivial problem, as many of the digital communication networks which people are interested in characterizing have this kind of size: networks such as the political blogosphere may easily have tens of thousands of active users; typical telephone call graphs involve millions of customers; and Facebook claims hundreds of millions of regular users. For these networks, approaches that do not use the full incidence matrix are generally needed.

Approaches to network analysis generally follow one of three patterns: visualization, structural modeling, and modeling as complex dynamical processes. The first approach is the most common and is used in a wide variety of approaches. Structural modeling is primarily a sociological approach to understanding networks, where the resultant structure of a network is foregrounded. Dynamical process modeling is borrowed from the physics of complex and "self-organizing" systems and uses models that foreground the growth processes of networks. All three approaches make different assumptions about the nature of the network, and their results and interpretations are not necessarily mutually compatible.

Visualization

Visualization is probably the most common and most recognizable form of network analysis. It is also the most intuitive, but visualizations need to be interpreted with caution, because many of their characteristics are arbitrary, and hence what may appear to be interesting visual features could well be artifacts of the analysis.

The usual approach to visualizing a graph is to represent nodes as dots (or polygons) and arcs as lines connecting the nodes. Directed arcs are represented as arrows, while undirected arcs are represented as line segments. The layout of nodes and arcs is arbitrary, and is chosen to make the connections in the network as readable as possible. When a network is simple and has few nodes or arcs, this is generally not too difficult and can be readily done by hand. Visualizations may be further enhanced by adding color, controlling node sizes and shapes, and by composing multiple layout techniques together, as suits the analysis.

For larger networks, choosing an appropriate network layout is more difficult, because, for many possible layouts, arcs and nodes end up superimposed on top of each other, making it harder to tell where arcs originate and terminate. For this reason, different network layout algorithms have been developed, each with its own way of optimizing the arrangement of nodes. Common layouts are the circle, random, Principal Components Analysis (PCA), Multidimensional Scaling (MDS), Fruchterman–Reingold, Kamada–Kawai, and spring embedding layouts. In a circle layout, the nodes are laid out on the perimeter of a circle, making a simple layout that is also difficult to use with large node sets. Random layouts simply assign random positions to nodes in a 2D field; these are seldom used on their own, but often serve as initial configurations for other layout algorithms. Most other layouts make a mathematical or statistical treatment of the incidence matrix: PCA and MDS layouts use some variant of the corresponding statistical procedures, whereas Fruchterman–Reingold, Kamada–Kawai, and spring-embedding are based on physical models where nodes attract or repel each other based on the connections they have.

Nonetheless, all layouts are arbitrary. For most algorithms, different versions exist which employ different assumptions about the data, resulting in different actual layouts that may also vary in their computational efficiency. Even the same layout implementation may produce strikingly different placements of nodes in different runs on the same data, presenting a serious obstacle to interpretation. Figures 2.1–2.4 exemplify this problem. They present four layouts of the same set of network data. The data are the Finnish LiveJournal weblogs from Herring *et al.* (2007), in which a snowball sample was constructed starting with six randomly chosen weblogs and following friends listed in the bloggers' profile pages for two iterations ("two degrees out"). The weblogs are colored by language (a hand-coded content analysis of the weblogs themselves), with Finnish in white, English in dark gray, mixed Finnish–English in light gray, and Russian (one weblog) in black. Layouts were generated using the GUESS system, a Java application for drawing and analyzing networks (Adar 2006).

While the network data are the same in all four plots, the layouts give the appearance of different numbers of clusters: the GEM plots 2.1 and 2.2 appear to show four clusters, while the Kamada–Kawai 2.3 and Fruchterman–Reingold 2.4 plots appear to show three. Moreover, in the GEM plots, the paths between the Russian-language weblog and the large cluster opposite it (upper left in 2.1, lower right in 2.2) appear to go through a common intermediate cluster in 2.1 (middle of figure) but not in 2.2. Hence there are considerable interpretive issues that are not well resolved by these network layouts. For networks that are larger, with hundreds, thousands, and even more nodes, these problems compound further. Hence while network visualizations are often suggestive and interesting, it is unsafe to interpret them on their own without further analysis of the network.

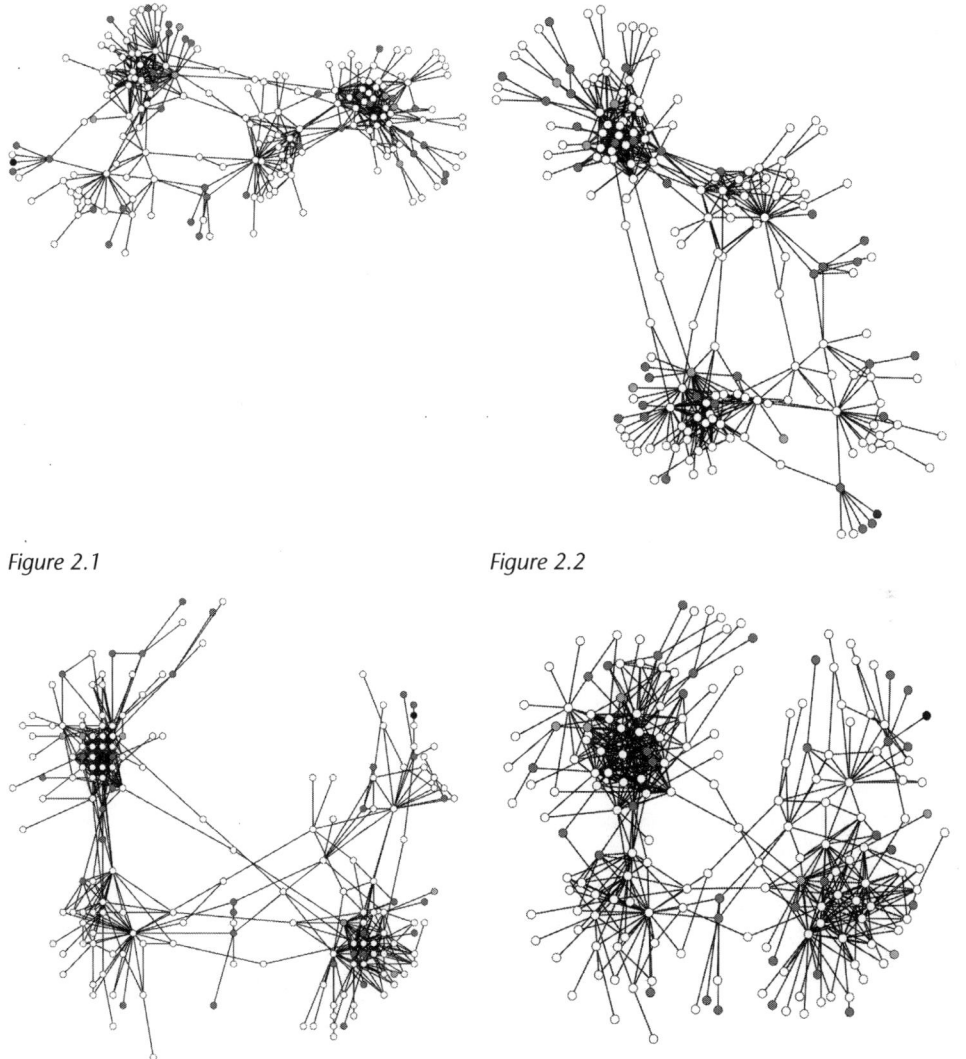

Figure 2.1   *Figure 2.2*

Figure 2.3   *Figure 2.4*

Figures 2.1–2.4 Four different layouts of the same network data: Finnish weblogs on LiveJournal (data from Herring *et al.* 2007). Nodes indicate journals, colored by language: Finnish, white; Finnish–English, light gray; English, dark gray; Russian, black (there is a single Russian weblog, on the left in 2.1, bottom in 2.2, and in the upper right in 2.3 and 2.4).

John C. Paolillo

Structural analysis

In the structural analysis approach, which derives from sociology, statistical models are applied to the network incidence matrix to identify structural properties, which are in turn interpreted in terms of centrality, power, role relationships, and information. The approach features a large number of statistical models whose details are deeply technical and beyond the scope of this chapter; the reader is encouraged to consult the references and the further reading section for specific information about these techniques and their proper application. Broadly, there are two types of model that are most important: block-models and exponential random graph (ERG) models. These two approaches make different assumptions and answer different kinds of questions about network structure.

Block modeling

Block modeling is an approach to network analysis that is focused on social roles and the relationships that define them (Breiger 2000, 2004; Doreian, Batagelj, & Ferligoj 2004, 2005; White, Boorman, & Breiger 1976). It has many applications, including the discovery and analysis of social segmentation, the analysis of political alliances, the economic organization of industries, the patterns of monetary exchange in a society, etc. Its basic assumption is that the network relations constitute a global structure in which equivalent classes of nodes can be characterized as social roles according to their connections to other nodes in the network. Other properties of nodes are potentially distributed according to these role classes. Two kinds of equivalence are recognized: *structural equivalence*, in which nodes that are found in similar structural relationships are grouped into equivalence classes; and the more abstract *regular equivalence*, in which nodes that have similar patterns of relationships are grouped together (Wasserman & Faust 1994).

We present here an example block-model based on the Finnish LiveJournal data. Block-modeling proceeds by conducting a cluster analysis of the incidence matrix; the clusters are used to arrange the matrix into *blocks*, and connections are aggregated block by block. This results in a *reduced incidence matrix* summarizing the connections in an easily interpretable manner. The reduced matrix may be used in additional statistical models, e.g., in regression models for the distribution of different linguistic variants (Paolillo 2001), or it may be visualized and interpreted in place of the full network.

As with network visualization, there is some inescapable arbitrariness in the block-modeling procedure. Clustering requires a *similarity metric*, which expresses how similar two items are, and a *clustering criterion*, which defines how similar items are grouped into clusters, implying different mathematical assumptions about the network and having significant consequences for the results. Common choices of similarity metric are the Pearson correlation coefficient, Manhattan distance, and Euclidean distance; common choices of clustering criterion include nearest neighbor, average distance, and Ward's method.

Cluster analysis may also be performed in different ways. One choice is whether there is a presumed number of clusters (*k*-means clustering) or whether one defines the number of clusters using a hierarchical clustering procedure and a criterion level of similarity at which to perform a *cut*. Hierarchical clustering algorithms may be *agglomerative* or *divisive*, depending on whether they proceed bottom-up by aggregating similar items into successively larger clusters or top-down, partitioning items in the data set into successively smaller clusters. These approaches need not lead to the same solutions. Most hierarchical clustering is agglomerative; in Social Network Analysis, the program CONCOR is used to perform divisive clustering (Breiger 2000; White *et al.* 1976).

Figures 2.5 and 2.6 present the Finnish LiveJournal data, clustered by Euclidean distance and Ward's method, with a cut chosen to yield a total of five clusters. The black and dark gray

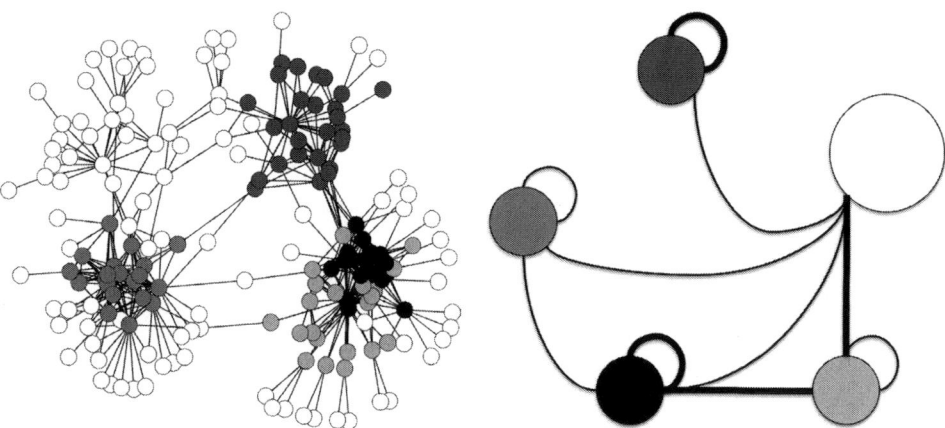

Figure 2.5   Clusters mapped on original
             network

Figure 2.6   Reduced network

Figures 2.5–2.6   Block-models of the Finnish LiveJournal data. Dark gray, medium gray, and
                  black represent the three cores in this network, with medium gray being
                  looser than the other two.

clusters represent densely connected groups around two of the six starting points in the sample. The medium gray cluster represents a third core, more loosely connected than the first two, and the light gray cluster an outer core around the black one. The white cluster contains all other nodes, which are more loosely connected within the network. The two panels present the network in two different forms: in its original form 2.5 using a Kamada–Kawai layout colored by cluster, and in reduced form 2.6 aggregating each cluster into a single node. "Self-ties" are indicated in 2.6, because a connection from one node to another in the same cluster represents a connection from the cluster to itself. Since most of the nodes in the white cluster link only to nodes in another cluster, we represent this group as having no self-tie.

The arrangements in Figures 2.5 and 2.6 allow us to begin interpreting the roles of the different nodes. For example, the black and dark gray nodes represent groups of closely communicating Finnish-speakers on LiveJournal. The black group is the core of a somewhat larger group; its members have slightly less frequent interaction with (and among) members of the light and medium gray groups. The medium gray group is more loosely connected to the black group, being connected by only a small number of bridges, although it also has some (white) intermediaries connecting it to the dark gray group. The light gray group is more connected to the black group than to itself, thus it represents the interactional periphery of the black group. The white group represents a set of more loosely connected (peripheral) individuals that are still accessible to either or both the black and dark gray groups. Two individuals in this group appear to be in a position to broker information between the black and dark gray groups, and two more between the dark and medium gray groups.

Block–model analyses may be used for a range of purposes; they are especially helpful when one wishes to investigate the relationship between network position and social markers such as linguistic elements. For example, Paolillo (2001) used a reduced network to correlate social position on an Internet Relay Chat channel with the variables are/r, your/u, s/z, Hindi and obscenity. Because other demographic information was not available, a traditional sociolinguistic analysis employing class, age, and other demographic variables was not possible in this case.

John C. Paolillo

The social positions (clusters), however, could be treated as social variables in an analysis of the linguistic variables, yielding interpretations in terms of central and peripheral participants, as informed by the reduced network analysis. Similarly, Paolillo, Mercure and Wright (2005) employed a positional analysis of friend links on the LiveJournal blogging site in an attempt to understand how users' interests (as listed in their profiles) worked in the environment. In this case both people's friends and their interests were shown to have robust and stable clusters, but these did not correlate with one another. Yet another example comes from YouTube (Paolillo 2008), in which positional analysis was used to simplify YouTube non-producers (registered users who post no videos) into audiences. In contrast to the previous study, audiences had strong associations with producers of specific types of videos, as indicated by keywords assigned to the videos by the producers. A further example is Rohe, Chatterjee, and Yu (2011), in which the structure of a group of Facebook users is identified using a reduced network analysis over friend links.

ERG models

In contrast to block-models, ERG models do not take the network connections as given but seek to model them as dependent on other factors, potentially including other network connections (Butts 2008). For example, reciprocity and transitivity are two characteristics of a network that show this kind of dependency: if a network exhibits reciprocity, then individuals tend to be linked to other people who link to them; if a network exhibits transitivity, then individuals tend to link to others who are linked to yet others they link to. Such properties need to be modeled together with properties such as group homophily (group members tend to link to their own groups), in order to establish empirically which factor or factors actually influence ties (Shalizi & Thomas 2011). To address this, the ERG approach starts from random graph theory (Erdös & Rényi 1959) and constructs a regression-type model of the ties themselves. In addition to traditional predictors such as (extrinsic) group membership, predictors are introduced into the model to represent various network properties: average connectivity, reciprocity, cycles of different lengths, transitivity, etc. Global network structure is then summarized by the parameter values estimated.

For example, Huang et al. (2009a) investigate the effect of proximity and homophily on structuring network ties among players of the online game EverQuest II using an ERG approach. They are particularly interested in whether players on Everquest II preferentially interact with other players of the same gender, age, and experience with the game, as well as whether physical distance between players results in greater levels of interaction. The types of interaction they measure are partnering in quests, instant messaging (IM), trade exchanges, and mail (all occurring within-game). Their data come from a single server (one of nineteen serving the US/Canada region), for which they had 3,140 players involved in any of these activities between August 25th and 31st, 2006. A table of the results for instant messaging, along with their interpretations, is reproduced as Table 2.1.

As with other regression-type models, the magnitudes of the parameter values are relevant, so that, in the example in Table 2.1, the tendency toward cross-gender interactions in IM is somewhat larger than the decreased tendency for females to interact by IM. Also, as with regression models, one has to be careful in setting up and interpreting the model features so that they represent what is intended. In this example, proximity was measured in geodesic surface distances on the earth's surface, but these distances cover the North American continent, and so cross several time zones; it is possible that the effects attributed to "proximity" have only to do with time zone differences, which were not observed in the study, rather than actual distances.

Table 2.1 ERG model estimates for proximity and homophily in IM. All parameter values are significant at p ≤ 0.01

Type of effect	Parameter	Value	Interpretation
Network	Total edges	−5.251	The network is relatively sparse
	Degree	1.958	Popular differences exist among individuals
	Shared partners	1.073	Interaction is transitive
Homophily	Gender	−0.172	Cross-gender interaction is preferred
	Age difference	−0.025	Same-age interaction is preferred
	Experience difference	−0.050	Same-experience interaction is preferred
Proximity	Log distance	−0.999	Interaction decreases with distance
Control	Gender (female)	−0.086	Females have less interaction
	Age	−0.003	Younger people interact more
	Experience	0.026	More experienced players interact more

Source: Huang, Shen, Williams, & Contractor 2009a.

Investigating this and other competing hypotheses requires the right kinds of observations and careful specification of the ERG model.

Network dependency features can be very difficult to compute; where reciprocity requires computing the n^2 incidence matrix for n nodes, transitivity requires computing a three-dimensional array of n^3 triangles; more complex configurations such as cycles require even greater complexity. As with any form of quantitative network analysis, these problems are exacerbated by the scale of digital media, where n can easily exceed thousands of nodes. In addition, the predictors representing network configurations tend to be highly inter-correlated, and traditional approaches to estimating a regression model cannot be used. Usually, a Bayesian approach is adopted (Robins, Pattison, Kalish, & Lusher 2007), as in the ergm package (Hunter, Handcock, Butts, Goodreau, & Morris 2008) for the R statistical programming environment (R Development Core Team 2012).

Although in development for more than 20 years, ERG models still pose many unsolved problems, including proper model specification (many data sets give degenerate models for what appear to be reasonable model specifications) and the proper handling of changes in the network over time. ERG models are gaining popularity in the analysis of digital communication. Examples of their application to digital media include information-seeking in consulting firms (Su & Contractor 2011), proximity and homophily in virtual worlds (Huang, Shen, & Contractor 2013), the role of information technology in research collaborations (Sayogo, Zhang, & Pardo 2011b; Sayogo, Nam, & Zhang 2011a), organizational crisis (Hamra, Udin, & Hossain 2011) and the structural analysis of Facebook (Traud, Mucha, & Porter 2012) and Twitter (Xu, Huang, & Contractor 2013).

Dynamic process modeling

A third approach to network analysis, and probably the dominant approach to network analysis of digital media in terms of number of published studies, borrows its methods and epistemological framework from physics. It treats the network as an evolving physical process, subject to simple laws that are understood principally in aggregate and probabilistic terms. In some ways, this is a straightforward extension of the network perspective to a dynamic one. Dynamic process modeling uses two types of tools: descriptions of various general properties of an observed network—such as its degree distribution, clustering coefficient, etc.—taken to represent some kind of "final state"; and a dynamic process model that describes how the network evolves over successive time steps. The goal is to develop a dynamic process model that, after a suitable interval of time, reaches a final state that exhibits the same kind of general properties as the observed network.

As with ERG modeling, the starting point is the random graph theory of Erdös and Rényi (1959). However, various aspects of the model are specified differently. First, the descriptions of the observed network's general properties typically take the form of *power laws*, where two quantities of interest are compared on logarithmic scales and described by a straight-line fit, the slope of which characterizes the dynamic process shaping the network. The justification for this treatment comes partly from comparison with physical processes: many phenomena are characterizable by power laws.[4] In addition, power law behavior encapsulates an important hypothesis about real-life social networks, namely that they appear to be *scale free*, i.e., they have the same kinds of properties (degree distribution, clustering, assortativity; etc.) when viewed at several different orders of magnitude (*scales*).

The dynamic process model takes an initial configuration of nodes and links and applies to that a statement of how the network evolves over subsequent time steps. One such starting configuration is a *regular network*, a network in which a simple rule describes the connections among the nodes, for example a rectangular grid, a packing arrangement of spheres, or a circular ring. Another starting configuration is a single node, or no nodes at all. The process model takes a configuration of nodes and arcs and adds or removes nodes and links according to a specific rule. For example, one or more nodes may be introduced at each time step, linking to any of the existing nodes with a probability based on the number of links that that node already has. If the probability of linking to more connected nodes is higher than that of linking to less connected nodes, the rule is a form of *preferential attachment* (Barabási & Albert 1999). Alternatively, rules that remove links between certain nodes and create links between others are called *rewiring* rules.

An important network property that dynamic process models seek to reproduce is the so-called *small world* property. This notion was introduced into the social–psychological literature by Travers and Milgram (1969), in a work which is most cited for the idea that arbitrarily selected people are linked by very short paths through acquaintances.[5] Both preferential attachment and rewiring readily permit this type of network, as do other rules. This property is of keen interest because it not only appears to characterize the human social network but it also characterizes many communications networks, including the Internet (Pastor-Satorras & Vespignani 2004) and has consequences for the spread of information. For example, the small-world characteristic of the Internet permits an endemic spread of computer viruses, such that even when antivirus programs become widespread, a virus can probably never be eradicated. At the same time, model simulations show that virus spread can be limited if the centrally connected "hubs" of the Internet are inoculated (Pastor-Satorras & Vespignani 2004: 180–210). Other applications of dynamic process models to digital media include instant messaging (Leskovec & Horvitz 2008; Smith 2002), mobile phone networks (Onnela *et al.* 2007) and Twitter (Kwak, Park, & Moon 2010; Suh, Hong, Pirolli, & Chi 2010; Weng, Flammini, Vespignani, & Mericzer 2012).

Research ethics

When network data pertain to individual people and their online or real-life social contacts, ethical considerations also deserve special consideration. While network analysis research at universities must observe the usual protocols regarding human subject research, it raises several ethical issues in particularly acute form. Here, I identify six: (1) the scale of network analysis studies, (2) the concerns of non-participant exposure to harm from the conduct of the research, (3) the nature of exposure and/or harm in digital media, (4) feedback into the study population from the research, (5) corporate or government involvement in network analysis, and (6) the network side of digital media studies that do not necessarily concern themselves directly with networks. These issues are the subject of considerable debate across many of the contexts of network analysis.

Regarding the first point, as has been stressed here, network analysis studies favor larger and larger scales of analysis. The Huang *et al.* (2009a, 2009b) study on EverQuest II, with 3,410 players in the study, is on the smaller side of what is being done with network analysis in digital media.[6] Many studies have tens of thousands of participants (e.g., Kramer *et al.* 2014). In such studies, it is not customary to seek permission from any of the participants for the use of their data. Instead, the researchers claim that the data are either public or proprietary, and hence do not require participants' permission. Although the exact circumstances vary considerably from study to study, the question of when the standard of informed consent applies to network studies is currently very hotly debated.

The scale of network studies necessarily raises the second issue, that of non-participant exposure to harm from the research. It is not always reasonable to treat every person one encounters as a research participant: some individuals may have greater vulnerability (e.g., children, prisoners), and for these individuals greater protections are needed. However, it is rare to see such precautions taken in large-scale digital media network research. For example, a study conducted at MIT used an informed consent model in which participants had to download a cellphone application, and were told that this application would forward certain information to a collection site (Eagle & Pentland 2006). However, the application itself collected information on any Bluetooth devices it discovered in the participant's environment: mobile phones, keyboards, computer peripherals, computers, etc. The justification offered for the inclusion of these data is that they are effectively "broadcast" by the devices themselves (and hence are "public data," even though this information is normally only available within a few feet of the participating user's phone). These devices belonged to any of the tens of millions of inhabitants of the greater Boston area, making them unwitting and (non-consenting) participants in the study.

This example raises the third issue: the nature of exposure and harm in network analysis of digital media is distinct from that of other kinds of human subjects research. Specifically, it is possible for sensitive technical information to be exposed; the problem is compounded when the data come from non-consenting participants and/or when the scale of the study is large. For example, the Eagle and Pentland (2006) dataset, which was widely distributed to researchers, contained enough information to permit a number of Boston-area computer networks to be compromised, even when redacted for traditional identifying information such as telephone numbers. Network analysis researchers are therefore potentially responsible for a broader range of possible exposures than other human subjects researchers.

When large numbers of study participants' social network contacts are exposed, feedback into the study population can occur in various ways. For example, when a study on "emotional contagion" on Facebook was published in the Proceedings of the National Academy of Science (Kramer, Guillory, & Hancock 2014), controversy immediately erupted, with a large amount of commentary occurring on Facebook, as well as in the news media. It did not help matters that the authors chose a title phrase that had strong negative connotations in the vernacular (their meaning was closer to "social influence of emotions" and was not restricted to negative emotions); regardless, Facebook users became aware of the research, thereby setting off a chain-reaction of social consequences, including potentially affecting the findings of the original work. When personal inter-connection is relevant to the research context, and especially when it is the object of study, researchers have to be prepared for the fact that their work may have ethical consequences that reach far beyond their original intentions.

A further consideration bearing on the ethical context of network studies of digital media is the provenance of the data. Private companies host most of the servers that generate data on people's digital media use; such companies are not required to observe the same standards of ethical conduct as university researchers. They also sell access to data, and often make "awards" of data to researchers whose projects they approve. The U.S. National Security Administration (NSA), which possesses the largest archives in the world of the digital traces of ordinary citizens, has effectively no ethical oversight on its use of the data for research. Consequently, much network research on digital media is conducted under conditions where the ethical protections for research participants are unclear at best. For example, the Kramer *et al.* study drew sharp criticism for its apparent lack of ethical review; however, Cornell University, the academic home of two of the researchers when the study was conducted, later issued a press release stating that the absence of review was consistent with their policies for "pre-existing data," which in this case had come from Facebook (the institutional affiliation of the first author), allowing the research to be classified as "exempt" from review.

A point generally neglected in the discussion of ethics cases such as this is that the ethical position of corporate entities is quite distinct from that of university researchers, who are generally regarded as being in pursuit of truth. Corporate entities are much more strongly motivated by their stockholders' interests. Notably, in the Kramer *et al.* (2014) case, the researchers were responding to earlier research that had suggested that people's use of social networking sites like Facebook had mostly negative impacts on people's social lives, and were motivated to demonstrate positive impacts as well. It is not difficult to imagine that the financial interests of Facebook played a role in this agenda, just as the U.S. tobacco companies' financial interests informed and guided their research and publications on the health effects of tobacco use.

As a final point on the ethics of network research, one may ask to what extent the concerns raised in this section pertain to digital media, and to what extent they pertain to network analysis. The answer is that they pertain equally to both. While network analysis concerns itself with people's interconnections as the object of study, it also follows that digital media connect people and so, whether or not it is analyzed from a network perspective, all digital media research implicitly involves a network. Recognizing this might or might not suggest a network approach to the research, but it certainly suggests that the ethical context of digital media needs to be considered in terms of the network of connections: the scale of a study may need to be large in order to answer its questions, it may expose non-participants to potential harm, it may cause feedback into the study context through network connections, it may be done with corporate sponsorship or with data acquired through direct contract with a digital media company, and for all these reasons it may have ethical impacts that go beyond those of traditional human subjects research. This is perhaps the place in which network analysis has the greatest significance for digital media research, but it is also the aspect of network analysis that needs the most development, especially as regards its relevance to digital media.

Conclusion

Network analysis is often applied to digital communication because it permits one to ask questions whose answers require the examination of large bodies of data. By reducing individuals and communications to a minimalist abstraction, it is possible to conduct quantitative and statistical analyses of digital media on a very large scale. Often, these analyses exhibit patterns that are readily interpretable. Beyond this, network visualizations often invite interpretation.

Each of the different modes of network analysis has its own hazards. Depending on the size and connectivity of a network, visualizations may or may not be usefully interpretable, simply because of the problems inherent in reducing a high-dimensional geometry to two dimensions.

Block models, while good for identifying role relations, take the ties of the network as given, and do not permit one to investigate relations purely among the ties themselves. ERG models do this, but at the cost of greater model complexity, greater uncertainty in the specification of models for certain types of data, and greater resource needs for computing the models. Dynamic process models permit simpler models with apparently useful resemblances to empirically observed social networks, but lack a means to express social roles, histories, etc., that are important to the social interpretation of network data.

The three different network modeling approaches arise from different intellectual traditions and are directed at different questions about social and technological networks. Consequently, when applied to the same data, they result in disjointed and competing explanations of the observed phenomena. Approaches to network studies are converging to some extent, in that one sometimes finds ERG and dynamic process models in the same study; they have not yet converged to the point of agreeing on a common model, or a research protocol that identifies when it is appropriate to pursue answers to particular types of research questions. In the meantime, interest in networks and their potential for interpretation remains high, and we can expect to see continued development in all three approaches to modeling.

Related topics

- Chapter 1 Approaches to language variation (Hinrichs)
- Chapter 19 Relationality, friendship and identity in digital communication (Graham)
- Chapter 20 Online communities and communities of practice (Angouri)
- Chapter 22 YouTube: language and discourse practices in participatory culture (Androutsopoulos & Tereick)

Notes

1 Clusters are sometimes called "communities" even when the network is not based on social data. Because "community" has other meanings, and clusters in social network data need not be communities in the social sense, I avoid this usage.
2 The term *structural hole* is also used in this sense.
3 The notation A^T indicates the transpose of A, where the rows and columns of A are switched.
4 Among the more well-known examples of power laws is Zipf's law regarding the distribution of word frequencies by their rank-order. Zipf also described a similar law regarding the distribution of bus routes between cities; note that this data implicitly characterizes a (transportation) network and a dynamic process (migration) shaping that network.
5 Popularly, "small world" is also used to mean the common experience that two previously unacquainted people can often discover a common acquaintance who links them. Travers and Milgram (1969) refer to this meaning, but set up an experiment in which randomly chosen people in one part of the US are asked to send a package to a person in another part of the US, forwarding it only through acquaintances. The packages that made it to the destination did so in an average of six steps, giving rise to the idea of *six degrees of separation* but the majority of the packages sent did not actually reach their intended destination.
6 In fact, the larger body of *EverQuest II* studies led by Contractor encompasses a considerably larger scope than this, given that they possess a nearly complete multi-year record of all *EverQuest II* activity. See also Shen (2010).

References

Adar, E. 2006, "GUESS: a language and interface for graph exploration," in R. Grinter, T. Rodden, P. Aoki, E. Cutrell, R. Jeffries, & G. Olson (eds.), *Proceedings of the SIGCHI conference on human factors in computing systems*, ACM: Montreal, pp. 791–800.
Barabási, A. L. & Albert, R. 1999, "Emergence of scaling in random networks," *Science*, vol. 286, no. 5439, pp. 509–512.

John C. Paolillo

Borgatti, S. P. & Foster, P. C. 2003, "The network paradigm in organizational research: a review and typology," *Journal of Management*, vol. 29, no. 6, pp. 991–1013.

Breiger, R. L. 2004, "The analysis of social networks," in M. Hardy & A. Bryman (eds.), *Handbook of data analysis*, SAGE Publications: London, pp. 505–552.

Breiger, R. L. 2000, "A tool kit for practice theory," *Poetics*, vol. 27, no. 2, pp. 91–115.

Butts, C. T. 2008, "Social network analysis: a methodological introduction," *Asian Journal of Social Psychology*, vol. 11, no. 1, pp. 13–41.

de Nooy, W., Mrvar, A., & Batagelj, V. 2005, *Exploratory social network analysis with Pajek*, Cambridge University Press: Cambridge.

Degenne, A. & Forsé, M. 1999, *Introducing social networks*, Sage Publications: London.

Doreian, P., Batagelj, V., & Ferligoj, A. 2005, *Generalized blockmodeling*, Cambridge University Press: New York, NY.

Doreian, P., Batagelj, V., & Ferligoj, A. 2004, "Generalized blockmodeling of two-mode network data," *Social Networks*, vol. 26, no. 1, pp. 29–53.

Eagle, N. & Pentland, A. 2006, "Reality mining: sensing complex social systems," *Personal and Ubiquitous Computing*, vol. 10, no. 4, pp. 255–268.

Eckert, P. 2000, *Linguistic variation as social practice*, Blackwell: Oxford.

Erdös, P. & Rényi, A. 1959, "On random graphs," *Publicationes Mathematicae Debrecen*, vol. 6, pp. 290–297.

Ferrara, K., Brunner, H., & Whittemore, G. 1991, "Interactive written discourse as an emergent register," *Written Communication*, vol. 8, no. 1, pp. 8–34.

Freeman, L. C. 2004, *The development of social network analysis*, Empirical Press: Vancouver.

Hamra, J., Uddin, S., & Hossain, L. 2011, "Exponential random graph modeling of communication networks to understand organizational crisis," *Proceedings of the 49th Sigmis annual conference on computer personnel research*, ACM: Montreal, pp. 71–78.

Hansen, D. L., Shneiderman, B., & Smith, M. A. 2011, *Analyzing social media networks with NodeXL: insights from a connected world*. Morgan Kaufmann: Burlington, VT.

Herring, S. C., Paolillo, J. C., Ramos-Vielba, I., Kouper, I., Wright, E., Stoerger, S., Scheidt, L. A., & Clark, B. 2007, "Language networks on LiveJournal," *HICSS 2007. 40th annual Hawaii international conference on system sciences*, IEEE, pp. 79–79.

Huang, Y., Shen, C., & Contractor, N. S. 2013, "Distance matters: exploring proximity and homophily in virtual world networks," *Decision Support Systems*, vol. 55, no. 4, pp. 969–977.

Huang, Y., Shen, C., Williams, D., & Contractor, N. 2009a, "Virtually there: the role of proximity and homophily in virtual world networks," *Proceedings of the IEEE SocialCom 2009 symposium on social intelligence and networking*, IEEE, pp. 354–359.

Huang, Y., Zhu, M., Wang, J., Pathak, N., Shen, C., Keegan, B., Williams, D., & Contractor, N. 2009b, "The formation of task-oriented groups: exploring combat activities in online games," *International conference on computational science and engineering*, vol. 4, pp. 122–127, IEEE.

Hunter, D. R., Handcock, M. S., Butts, C. T., Goodreau, S. M., & Morris, M. 2008, "ergm: a package to fit, simulate and diagnose exponential-family models for networks," *Journal of Statistical Software*, vol. 24, no. 3.

Klimt, B. & Yang, Y. 2004, "The Enron corpus: a new dataset for email classification research," *Machine learning: ECML 2004*, Springer Verlag: Berlin, pp. 217–226.

Kramer, A. D., Guillory, J. E., & Hancock, J. T. 2014, "Experimental evidence of massive-scale emotional contagion through social networks," *Proceedings of the National Academy of Sciences*, doi: 10.1073/pnas.1320040111.

Kwak, H., Lee, C., Park, H., & Moon, S. 2010, "What is Twitter, a social network or a news media?" *Proceedings of the 19th international conference on World wide web*, ACM: Montreal, pp. 591–600.

Leskovec, J. & Horvitz, E. 2008, "Planetary-scale views on a large instant-messaging network," *Proceedings of the 17th international conference on world wide web*, ACM: Montreal, pp. 915–924.

Milroy, L. & Milroy, J. 1992, "Social network and social class: toward an integrated sociolinguistic model," *Language in Society*, vol. 21, no. 1, pp. 1–26.

Onnela, J. P., Saramäki, J., Hyvönen, J., Szabó, G., Lazer, D., Kaski, K., & Barabási, A. L. 2007, "Structure and tie strengths in mobile communication networks," *Proceedings of the National Academy of Sciences*, vol. 104, no. 18, pp. 7332–7336.

Paolillo, J. C. 2008, "Structure and network in the YouTube core," *Proceedings of the 41st annual Hawaii international conference on system sciences*, IEEE, pp. 156–156.

Paolillo, J. C. 2001, "Language variation on Internet Relay Chat: a social network approach," *Journal of Sociolinguistics*, vol. 5, no. 2, pp. 180–213.

Paolillo, J. C., Mercure, S., & Wright, E. 2005, "The social semantics of LiveJournal FOAF: structure and change from 2004 to 2005," *Proceedings of the ISWC 2005 workshop on semantic network analysis,* vol. 72, no. 7, pp. 69–80.

Paolillo, J. C., Warren, J., & Kunz, B. 2011, "Genre emergence in amateur Flash," in *Genres on the web,* Springer Netherlands: Dordrecht, Netherlands, pp. 277–302.

Pastor-Satorras, R. & Vespignani, A. 2004, *Evolution and structure of the Internet: a statistical physics approach,* Cambridge University Press: Cambridge.

Porter, M. A., Mucha, P. J., Newman, M. E., & Warmbrand, C. M. 2005, "A network analysis of committees in the US House of Representatives," *Proceedings of the National Academy of Sciences,* vol. 102, no. 20, pp. 7057–7062.

R Development Core Team 2012, "R: A language and environment for statistical computing," R Foundation for Statistical Computing: Vienna, Austria. Available at: http://www.R-project.org/.

Robins, G., Pattison, P., Kalish, Y., & Lusher, D. 2007, "An introduction to exponential random graph (p *) models for social networks," *Social Networks,* vol. 29, no. 2, pp. 173–191.

Rohe, K., Chatterjee, S., & Yu, B. 2011, "Spectral clustering and the high-dimensional stochastic blockmodel," *The Annals of Statistics,* vol. 39, no. 4, pp. 1878–1915.

Sayogo, D. S., Nam, T., & Zhang, J. 2011a, "The role of trust and ICT proficiency in structuring the cross-boundary digital government research," *Proceedings of the third international conference on social informatics,* Springer, pp. 67–74.

Sayogo, D. S., Zhang, J., & Pardo, T. A. 2011b, "Evaluating the structure of cross-boundary digital government research collaboration: a social network approach," in *Proceedings of the 12th annual international digital government research conference: digital government innovation in challenging times,* ACM: Montreal, pp. 64–73.

Scott, J. 2012, *Social network analysis,* 3rd edn., Sage Publications: London.

Shalizi, C. R. & Thomas, A. C. 2011, "Homophily and contagion are generically confounded in observational social network studies," *Sociological Methods & Research,* vol. 40, no. 2, pp. 211–239.

Shen, C. 2010, *The patterns, effects and evolution of player social networks in online gaming communities,* Doctoral dissertation, University of Southern California.

Smith, R. D. 2002, "Instant messaging as a scale-free network," arXiv preprint cond-mat/0206378.

Su, C. & Contractor, N. 2011, "A multidimensional network approach to studying team members' information seeking from human and digital knowledge sources in consulting firms," *Journal of the American Society for Information Science and Technology,* vol. 62, no. 7, pp. 1257–1275.

Suh, B., Hong, L., Pirolli, P., & Chi, E. H. 2010, "Want to be retweeted? Large scale analytics on factors impacting retweet in twitter network," in *SocialCom 2010, IEEE second international conference on social computing,* pp. 177–184.

Traud, A. L., Mucha, P. J., & Porter, M. A. 2012, "Social structure of Facebook networks," *Physica A: Statistical Mechanics and its Applications,* vol. 391, no. 16, pp. 4165–4180.

Travers, J. & Milgram, S. 1969, "An experimental study of the small world problem," *Sociometry,* vol. 32, no. 4, pp. 425–443.

Wasserman, S. & Faust, K. 1994, *Social network analysis: methods and applications,* Cambridge University Press: New York, NY.

Watts, D. J. & Strogatz, S. H. 1998, "Collective dynamics of 'small-world' networks," *Nature,* vol. 393, pp. 440–442.

Weng, L., Flammini, A., Vespignani, A., & Menczer, F. 2012, "Competition among memes in a world with limited attention," *Scientific Reports,* vol. 2, article 335.

White, H. C., Boorman, S. A., & Breiger, R. L. 1976, "Social structure from multiple networks: I. Blockmodels of roles and positions," *American Journal of Sociology,* vol. 81, no. 4, pp. 730–780.

Xu, B., Huang, Y., & Contractor, N. 2013, "Exploring Twitter networks in parallel computing environments," *Proceedings of the conference on extreme science and engineering discovery environment: gateway to discovery,* ACM: Montreal, p. 20.

Further reading

Barabási A-L. 2002, *Linked: the new science of networks,* Perseus: Cambridge, MA.

This is an account of the dynamic process perspective on networks, including examples from both the social and physical worlds, from the perspective of one of the chief advocates of this approach in contemporary academic literature.

John C. Paolillo

Degenne, A. & Forsé, M. 1999, *Introducing social networks*, Sage Publications: London.

Scott, J. 2012, *Social network analysis*, 3rd edn., Sage Publications: London.

> These two references provide overlapping but distinct introductions to social network analysis from the sociological perspective. Degenne and Forsé's introduction is a translation from the original French, and includes discussion of work not referenced in most English-language academic publications on social network analysis.

Freeman, L. C. 2004, *The development of social network analysis*, Empirical Press: Vancouver.

> This reference offers an historical account from an insider's perspective on the development of the sociological models and methods in social network analysis, beginning from Auguste Comte in the 1830s to the present day.

3

Digital ethnography

Piia Varis

Introduction

Ethnographic research on online practices and communications has become increasingly popular in the recent years with the growing influence and presence of the Internet in people's everyday lives. This research takes a myriad of forms, appearing within different disciplines and under several different labels such as "digital ethnography" (Murthy 2008), "virtual ethnography" (Hine 2000), "cyberethnography" (Robinson & Schulz 2009), "discourse-centered online ethnography" (Androutsopoulos 2008), "Internet ethnography" (boyd 2008; Sade-Beck 2004), "ethnography on the Internet" (Beaulieu 2004), "ethnography of virtual spaces" (Burrel 2009), "ethnographic research on the Internet" (Garcia *et al.* 2009), "Internet-related ethnography" (Postill & Pink 2012) and "netnography" (Kozinets 2009).

The common denominator for these studies is that they all address different forms of technologically mediated communication and they all employ (a particular version or understanding of) ethnography in the research process. This is basically where the commonalities end; so diverse is the field—if such a field can even clearly be identified—of ethnographic research on digital culture and practices. This is not least because of the various types of data and environments covered in research on digital communication—social network sites, blogs, forums, gaming environments, websites, dating sites, wikis, etc.—but also because of seemingly different understandings of what exactly "ethnography" is, ranging from limiting it to specific techniques or data collection methods (mainly observation and interviews) to seeing it as an approach rather than a set of techniques. This chapter builds on this latter understanding of ethnography; that is, ethnography is not reduced to the employment of certain techniques, but seen as an approach to studying (digital) culture with specific epistemological claims (see e.g., Blommaert & Dong 2010).

Online communications and digitalization—referring not only to the technical aspects of digital media distinguishing them from, for example, print media, but also to cultural forms and experiences emerging thanks to digital media (see Miller 2011)—provide researchers with unprecedented opportunities for accessing and examining people's communicative repertoires. The complexities of the "global," the "local," and the "translocal," and the ways in which people make (globally) circulating semiotic materials part of their own communicative repertoires, can all be traced online (see e.g., Georgakopoulou 2013; Leppänen *et al.* 2014; Rymes 2012; Varis & Wang 2011). Digital ethnography is one approach to capturing the shape and nature of such communicative practices; this chapter discusses its main principles, current applications, and future directions, building on a brief review of "traditional" or "pre-digital" ethnography.

Historical perspectives

Research on technologically mediated communication has come a long way from what Androutsopoulos (2006, 2008: 1) identified as the "first wave," during which "the focus was on features and strategies that are (assumed to be) specific to new media; the effects of communications technologies on language were given priority over other contextual factors." In this early research, as Androutsopoulos points out, "The data were often randomly collected and detached from their discursive and social contexts, and generalizations were organized around media-related distinctions such as language of emails, newsgroups, etc." (2008: 1). The focus was thus on reified end products, texts, and pieces of language, rather than production and uptake of discourse as socially meaningful, context-specific activity.

Broadly, then, the difference between the earlier and later research is a difference between the study of "things" and the study of contextualized "actions"—or the study of texts and cultural practices (see Shifman's 2011 study on YouTube memes for such a conclusion; see also Hine 2000). This largely corresponds with the two phases in social research on technologically mediated communication identified by Hine (2013: 7): the first one was characterized by experimental research, and the second by "growing application of naturalistic approaches to online phenomena and the subsequent claiming of the Internet as a cultural context," with ethnographic research increasingly applied. Indeed, Hine suggests that "our knowledge of the Internet as a cultural context is intrinsically tied up with the application of ethnography" (2013: 8).

Digital ethnography as an approach of course builds on "pre-digital" ethnography. Ethnography, with its roots in anthropology, takes as its object of interest the very lived reality of people, of which it aims to produce detailed and situated accounts—in the words of Geertz (1973), "thick descriptions." As such, ethnography guards against generalization and narrow assumptions regarding the universality of digital experience in general (Coleman 2010), or, in terms of language use, against the kinds of sweeping statements on, for instance, "the language of emails" produced in the first wave of research on technologically mediated communication. Viewed against the background of long-term developments in the study of technologically mediated communication, research under the umbrella "digital ethnography" has deepened our understanding of locally specific digital practices. Using the Internet, and drawing on language and other semiotic means in doing so, are locally situated experiences and entail locally specific practices, platforms, and semiotizations. Ethnography has precisely the tools for capturing this aspect of situatedness, offering a means for understanding informants' life-worlds and their situated practices and lived local realities. To this end, ethnographic fieldwork is essentially a *learning process* where research is guided by experience gathered in the field; it is a mode of discovery and learning (Blommaert & Dong 2010; Velghe 2011). As Dell Hymes put it,

> [Ethnography] is continuous with ordinary life. Much of what we seek to find out in ethnography is knowledge that others already have. Our ability to learn ethnographically is an extension of what every human being must do, that is, learn the meanings, norms, patterns of a way of life.
>
> *(1996: 13)*

While ethnography assumes such a holistic position, the approach, digital and otherwise, is often reduced to specific methodologies and procedures (in many cases, *the* methods consist of fieldwork with participant observation and interviews). As Blommaert and Dong (2010) point out, however, ethnography is not only a complex of fieldwork techniques. It has its origins in anthropology, and "[t]hese anthropological roots provide a specific direction to ethnography, one that situates language deeply and inextricably in social life and offers a particular and distinct ontology and epistemology to ethnography" (p. 7). From an ethnographic perspective, studying language means studying society and larger-scale socio-cultural processes, and any distinction between the linguistic and the non-linguistic is seen as a fundamentally artificial one.

Digitalization has presented scholars of language and communication—also ethnographers—with opportunities to easily collect, store, and sort (e.g., by "tagging" contents in electronic databases) "logs" of interaction, i.e., "characters, words, utterances, messages, exchanges, threads, archives, etc." (Herring 2004: 339; see also Androutsopoulos 2008). While online environments provide opportunities for easy collection of huge amounts of data, from an ethnographic perspective this becomes problematic if the material is taken out of its context—a log of communication only serves as ethnographic data if it is understood in its context. This is where more recent, ethnographically informed research on digital communication dramatically differs from the early studies of technologically mediated communication and their de-contextualized analyses of log data. Ethnographically speaking, context is an interactional achievement, and contexts should be investigated rather than assumed (see, e.g., Blommaert 2007). This is perhaps particularly important in today's complex world of globalization, translocal communication environments, and complex online–offline dynamics, where pre-digital presuppositions regarding contexts and communicators are often invalid.

Critical issues and topics

Context and contextualization are critical issues in digital ethnography, not least due to the fact that, in today's complex world, we are perhaps increasingly encountering polycentric environments—contexts in which multiple normative centres of orientation are simultaneously at work—in which little, if anything, can be taken for granted (see Blommaert 2010: 39–41; Blommaert & Rampton 2011). Today's ethnographers of digital culture and communication need to address new types of contextualization that were unknown or unattested in pre-digital environments.

In an ethnographic study of American teenagers' engagement with social network sites, boyd (2008) documented certain technical properties of online semiotic material that shape interactions in online networks: persistence (semiotic material online is automatically recorded and archived), searchability (semiotic material can be accessed through search), replicability (digital content, made of bits, can be duplicated), and scalability (the potential spread and visibility of semiotic material is great). It is particularly the last two characteristics of digital communication, replicability and scalability, that bear upon the ethnographically important notion of indexicality—links between signs and the macro-level of socio-cultural contexts and meanings (see e.g., Silverstein 2003)—and contextualization in online communication. Thanks to the technical properties of replicability and scalability, semiotic material—linguistic and otherwise—is quickly and easily mobilized, recontextualized, and resemiotized (Georgakopoulou 2013; Leppänen et al. 2014; Rymes 2012), making for complex and often unpredictable uses, reuses, trajectories, and uptakes. Rymes (2012), for instance, shows how widely circulating cultural materials such as elements of YouTube videos become recontextualized and incorporated into a potentially huge range of individual communicative repertoires, in the process gaining new meanings and functions "through repeated viewing, commenting and recirculation" (p. 225). As Rymes points out, the process itself—recontextualization of cultural material and incorporation into individual communicative repertoires—is not something new, exclusively digital, or limited to online forms of communication; what is remarkable, however, is the fact that media such as YouTube make this process and local recontextualizations visible to the analyst.

Contextualization of digital communication is also shaped by other kinds of digital affordances, many of which are platform-specific. Marwick and boyd (2010) discuss the notion of "context collapse" to refer to the idea that in networked online environments such as social media, users' networks potentially include people from different spheres of life (family, friends, co-workers, people one has only met online, people one has not been in offline contact with for years, etc.). In such conditions, the intended uptake for communications may not be clear or transparent at all. Such contextual complexities potentially shape people's communicative practices and need to be ethnographically established (boyd 2008).

We may also mistakenly reduce the context of digital communications to seemingly self-evident abstractions such as "Facebook," when in fact what "Facebook" means for people is by no means a consistent or static thing. It is an ideological construct shaped by the way users view this medium in relation to other media, among other things (see "Current contributions and research" below for a discussion of these notions). Hence, the online environments studied cannot be taken as self-explanatory contexts, but need to be investigated for locally specific meanings and appropriations: Facebook, for example, can be a useful "context" only if we see its features as essentially linked to the commercialization of the Web and the way in which the shape of commercial platforms such as Facebook or YouTube influences semiotic activity. While the shape of any platform does not *determine* the way in which people will use it for their communicative purposes, the design of the site will influence interactions. "Defaults" in digital environments, as van Dijck (2013) points out, "are not just technical but also ideological maneuverings . . . Algorithms, protocols, and defaults profoundly shape the cultural experiences of people active on social media platforms" (p. 32). These coded structures, she maintains, "are profoundly altering the nature of our connections, creations, and interaction. Buttons that impose 'sharing' and 'following' as social values have effects in cultural practices" (2013: 20). This production of social–ideological value is another contextual layer that digital ethnographies of communication need to investigate (Spilioti, this volume).

Online–offline dynamics is another contextually important issue for ethnographers of digital communication. It is becoming increasingly difficult, if not impossible, to make clear-cut distinctions between what is "online" and what is "offline," especially with the recent "de-computerization," i.e., the emergence and increasing popularity of mobile technologies (smartphones, tablets) with Internet access. Understandings of space and place—and indeed, understandings of what constitutes ethnographic "field"—have also been complicated by the fact that mobility is increasingly not confined to physical movement: rather, what we often see is akin to what Raymond Williams (1974) described as "mobile privatisation"—a development where subjects are increasingly mobile, socially speaking, yet they remain "private," as though cocooned. The example of the car, for instance, has been used to describe this seeming paradox: while the car can take its driver anywhere, the driver is self-sealed, isolated in a private space. The same goes for Internet use, and also the smartphone and other mobile devices—these are vehicles of mobility, yet their users do not necessarily have to physically go anywhere in order to be mobile, to be "elsewhere," or to experience a change of context.

Indeed, a lot of the activity that we now see as taking place simply "online" is, thanks to mobile technologies, linked to and influenced by all kinds of offline environments, situations and practices: people do not only sit at home at their desk PC; they also produce what we see as our "online" data in trains, shops, bathrooms, airports, classrooms, restaurants, cars, meeting rooms, concerts and conferences; there are tweets sent from toilet seats and selfies posted from shopping centres. The "finished" communicative products that researchers collect online can thus be shaped not only by the immediately observable *online* context, but also by the *offline* context in which the digital activity has taken place. This may introduce a further normative layer on communicative practices, depending on what kind of digital communication is expected and "acceptable" in a specific physical, offline context. Such normative understandings are visible in normative public and lay discourses regarding digital activities—debates on whether it is, for instance, acceptable to post selfies at funerals, or to be browsing and updating on social media while having an offline, face-to-face conversation. Similarly, broader socio-cultural issues such as Internet censorship can heavily influence communications in certain parts of the world (Varis & Wang 2011). The contexts for online activity are in fact layered and polycentric, and it may be necessary to attend to further layers of context than what is visible on the screen.

The other two technical properties shaping online interactions documented by boyd (2008)—persistence and searchability—are also crucial, from the perspective of those communicating online, as well as ethnographers investigating such communications. To begin with, the fact that online materials can be easily traced and located has implications for how digital ethnographers present their analyses and refer to their informants. Anonymizing data in order to protect people's privacy is of course one familiar step in ethnographic research, and this also goes for usernames and avatars; while it might be argued that these are not people's "real names," such online means of self-representation should rather be seen as very real. The notion that these are not "real names" seems to be based on an ideological understanding of the Internet as "less real" than the offline world, but usernames and avatars are very real to the people who use them to present themselves. They come with often very well-established and well-known online identities; reputations are built on them, and recognising them, if people use the same identifiers for themselves across different contexts and platforms, potentially gives access to intricate worlds of online activity. When necessary, these "not real" names should therefore also be protected.

The searchable nature of digital environments—or the issue of "googleability"—may pose particular problems for ethnographers whose aim is to give justice to people's own voices and present them "in their own words." Even if data is anonymized and people's names are changed, discourse is still searchable: while some platforms and sites are more easily trawled than others, and search engines do not reach every corner of the Internet, there is still the possibility that, simply by entering the online material quoted in a search engine, the data is easily connectable to accounts, usernames and activities. This is of course particularly alarming in cases where extremely sensitive material is being addressed, and people may be put at serious risk. It is the responsibility of ethnographers to see that they do not, for instance, jeopardize political activists in contexts where revealing their actions—or making it easier to establish their offline identities—might put them in danger, or that they are not inadvertently "outing" people with stigmatized sexualities. Difficult compromises may have to be made, such as sacrificing ethnographic detail and accuracy in the reporting, but this should in no way prevent ethnographers from researching sensitive issues and environments.

A closely related issue pertains to the differing understandings of what is "public" and what is "private." These differences persist despite extensive public debate on privacy and surveillance throughout the world: there remains a lack of awareness of what is public and what is private online, and a general underestimation of how persistent online communications can be. These broader concerns and individual understandings of public and private digital communication will influence both the kinds of interactions that are visible for researchers online—what people choose to make public about themselves—and the ethical considerations they must take into account. That is, while semiotic material may be publically available, this does not necessarily automatically mean that it can be used for research purposes, or that people behind the semiotic production accept that what they have entered online will become data unbeknownst to them. The classic example here is the blogger who sees their online writing as a *private* diary, not to be read by anybody else (not to mention to be used for research purposes). This is just one illustration, and a rather extreme one at that, of the differing understandings of "public" and "private" online. In the absence of an official consensus on ethical considerations or strict guidelines for ethnographers in this respect (but see the Ethics Guide by the Association of Internet Researchers at ethics.aoir.org), we can at least be cautioned against seeing the Web as one big, public database readily and voluntarily produced by ordinary Internet users. Case-by-case considerations will have to be made depending on, for instance, the type of platform used, the sensitivity of the issue investigated, and the possible harm caused to those whose communications are being studied.

With ethnography, the kinds of broader macro-contexts discussed here—such as socio-technological developments influencing the shape of online platforms, and socio-cultural issues such as censorship—become part of the investigation. While it is the micro-level that often gains most of the attention from linguistic and discursive interrogations, digital ethnography maintains that the micro-level only makes sense when seen within the macro-level context. Such contexts should be interrogated, and future studies are likely to address ever more complex data sets (both online and offline)—justifiable explorations, considering the online–offline dynamics and the blurred distinctions between "online" and "offline" referred to above.

Current contributions and research

Recent linguistic ethnographic research demonstrates the difficulty—indeed, perhaps the futility—of disentangling "online" and "offline" from one another. In these studies, social media and other online environments are not seen as separate contexts, detached from other spheres of life; and digital communication practices are seen in the wider sociolinguistic context (see e.g., Madsen & Stæhr 2014; Stæhr 2014a, Stæhr 2014b). Such research is multi-sited and employs a number of different methods, adding nuance to our understanding not only of digital communication practices per se, but also of their specific functions in people's communications more generally, as well as of broader online–offline dynamics.

Indeed, current research illustrates that there is no need to "exoticize" online data as particularly difficult to analyze or manage (Georgakopoulou 2013), nor to make the study of digital communication an end in itself—especially if we take it as our goal not simply to take "digital slices" of online interaction, but rather to understand and explain people's life-worlds and communicative practices comprehensively. While early research on technologically mediated communication focused on de-contextualized log data collected online, the research trajectories of much of today's digital ethnographic research may originate online or offline, guided by whatever becomes relevant in the field. Current research is thus more realistic in that it is focused on forming comprehensive pictures of sociolinguistic repertoires and contexts; digital data is an organic part of this rather than an end in itself, and the Internet is no longer seen as a separate sphere of life with no connections to the offline world.

One surprisingly little-explored concept in current research on digital communications is the relatively recently introduced notion of *media ideologies*. Ilana Gershon (2010), drawing on Silverstein's (1979) notion of "language ideology," defines media ideologies as "a set of beliefs about communicative technologies with which users and designers explain perceived media structure and meaning. That is to say, what people think about the media they use will shape the way they use media" (p. 3). Further, Gershon makes use of the notion of "remediation," referring to the fact that people define each technology in relation to the other technologies available to them (p. 5). This means that people make communicative decisions based on what they deem the most appropriate medium for the specific communicative task at hand. This can include all kinds of considerations, ranging from aesthetic ones to the perceived effectiveness or quickness of a medium in offering communications for uptake. Finally, Gershon's highly illuminating study of break-ups in social media introduces the concept of "idiom of practice" to highlight the idea that "people have implicit and explicit intuitions about using different technologies that they have developed with their friends, family members, and coworkers" (p. 6). That is, a group of people with a shared understanding of the use of a specific technology will use it to communicate in a particular way. These notions help explain, for instance, family debates on media use when teenagers may see their parents' phone calls as "embarrassing" and "disruptive," and may prefer text messages or chat software—which they would use with their peers as the default mode of communication—as a preferable means of interaction. Similarly, issues related to "formality" or the "standardness" of language used in communications can partly be explained with these concepts—they have to do with differing understandings of what is appropriate or "good" language in which medium.

Thus far, Gershon's useful concepts remain largely without applications, though they seem to possess plenty of explanatory power for understanding people's digital communication practices. Indeed, in order to explain people's linguistic and discursive choices in digital environments, attending to *both* language ideologies and media ideologies would perhaps provide powerful explanations for what people do and why they do it. Attending to people's media ideologies will also help in making connections to broader socio-cultural issues such as the discussions on privacy referred to above, and hence help explain choice of media for communication and their specific functions.

Digitalization continues to have profound effects on people's everyday lives and communicative practices, and while digital divides persist—with many lacking either Internet or device access, or both—it is not only the lives of the "wired" that are shaped by the recent developments. The lives of people with little or no digital engagement are influenced by the very absence of these tools for communication. Consequently, while appropriations of new communication technologies can provide exciting data on practices and interactions, ethnographic research should also not overlook the new types of "have-nots" appearing as a result of digitalization. Velghe (2011, 2012, and 2014; Blommaert & Velghe 2014), for instance, presents an interesting and informative ethnographic case of resource-scarce digital communication in a South African township. Inquiries into digitally deprived contexts also help shed light on digital communications in a broader sense, and studying local appropriations of technologies adds nuance to how we understand specific digital communication platforms. Studies in this vein help move us away from assumptions of universal digital experience: what "blogging," "YouTubing," or "social networking," for instance, means in each case and particular context is a matter of ethnographic investigation, not assumption.

Main research methods

As mentioned above, this chapter understands ethnography not as a set of field methods, but as an approach, and hence not reducible to specific techniques. Even if ethnography could be reduced to techniques, when it comes to studying "the Internet" or digital environments it would be extremely difficult to outline a simple set of techniques to follow: there is no one-size-fits-all solution, not least due to the myriad of different communicative environments that digital communication encompasses. Ethnography as an approach is always methodologically flexible and adaptive, regardless of its context: it does not confine itself to following specific procedures, but rather remains open to issues arising from the field (Blommaert & Dong 2010). With digitalization and its attendant new communicative environments, debates have emerged over how to study these new forms of interaction, and whether "pre-digital" methodologies and approaches can be successfully applied to digital data. However, rather than discussing which "offline" methodologies could be successfully applied to researching online environments and how, the questions raised by the study of digital environments could be used to reflect more broadly on methodologies and their epistemological nature. As Hine (2013) points out, in line with the ethnographic commitment to reflexivity,

> The question is much more interesting, potentially, than whether old methods can be adapted to fit new technologies. New technologies might, rather, provide an opportunity for interrogating and understanding our methodological commitments. In the moments of innovation and anxiety which surround the research methods there are opportunities for reflexivity.
>
> *(2013: 9)*

Participant observation, traditionally one of the ethnographic staples for understanding local practices and meaning-making, is one example of a technique which has often featured in such "moments of innovation and anxiety." The reasons for this are manifold, yet all have to do with the fact that the study of digital communications always involves the screen in one way or another. One of the issues has to do with the fact that researchers can now lurk—"participate" invisibly and unbeknownst to the people whose activities are being observed—while being entirely immersed in the environment and activities in question; it is as if the ethnographic "fly on the wall" was now wearing an invisibility cloak. Arguments around the invisibility issue range from suggesting that such lurking is not ethnographic observation in the traditional sense (hence "participate" in scare quotes above) and hence not "proper" ethnography, to idealizing the situation by claiming that the invisibility guaranteed by the screen between the researcher and the researched presents a unique opportunity for collecting "natural" data, as the informants are not aware of their informant status and hence do not modify their behavior accordingly (Beaulieu 2004; Garcia *et al.* 2009; Hine 2005; Murthy 2008; Wittel 2000). The latter point of course raises all kinds of ethical questions, a broader discussion of which is beyond the scope of this chapter (but see "Critical issues and topics" above).

As regards the issue of participation, a further point of debate is the fact that online communication is easily collectable, printable, and screenshotable—entire histories of activity can be made into "data" with a couple of clicks without ever having witnessed the interactions while they actually unfolded. This raises the question as to whether the ethnographer should always be "there" to observe interactions as they take place, so as to be "immersed" in the situation and directly experience and witness the interaction as it unfolds—with the lags in communication, the editing and deletion of posts and messages, the floods of commentary in discussion forums and blogs etc.—*in real time*. This would mean in many cases that the poor ethnographer would be able to get very little sleep: with translocal digital communications, one's archive of materials grows potentially non-stop, 24 hours per day. Investigator triangulation is of course an option, with shifts in observation, but this is naturally not always feasible. This means that in many cases the ethnographer will have to deal with *products* rather than *processes* and, modifiable and editable as digital artifacts are, what remains visible is the end result of possibly countless edits, changes and deletions. Some platforms give ethnographers useful research assistance in this respect—for instance, Facebook shows which posts have been edited and which have not (and also gives a separate stamp for mobile posts); time stamps on different kinds of online platforms give indications as to how interactions have unfolded in time, giving possible cues for further inquiries. Such digital traces potentially provide valuable information and leads to follow for the ethnographer, who will also be interested in the processes of semiotization and meaning-making, not just the final product.

However, whatever methods are applied, one thing remains constant in studying digital environments: there is always the unavoidable issue of the screen (Androutsopoulos 2013). Being able to read and watch on the screen can of course be seen as one of the advantages of digital ethnography: field sites are accessible and data available for the ethnographer potentially all the time, even on the go, if smartphones or other mobile devices are used. But the downside of onscreen availability is that we indeed only see what is on the screen. In the case of multi-functional platforms such as Facebook, where multiple channels of communication are available, what is observable on the screen can be misleading or provide only a partial image. For instance, while somebody may seem like an inactive or infrequent Facebook user based on observations of their profile, they may at the same time be actively sending private messages and chatting with their connections; what may seem like status updates without any reaction or commentary from other users may in fact be the subject of heated chatting or private messaging. While a full ethnography of such a multi-channelled site can admittedly be difficult to accomplish, in any case the (semi-)public profile is only *part* of the whole experience of using such a site. What is visible on the screen is thus only part of the story.

Another issue related to the screen is that we do not, for instance, know whether the identities people establish or the facts they disclose about themselves are biographically or demographically "accurate"—that is, that they correspond with what is on the other side of the screen. The authenticity of information is of course a broader issue regarding online materials: it is sometimes difficult, if not impossible, to establish whether information is accurate or not, and the argument could be made that, while there is no way of knowing whether something is "real" or not, such material would not be useful as data. The willingness to deem something as not worthy of research simply because it does not correspond to (assigned) "real" offline identities is in itself an interesting phenomenon, and there often seems to be an ideological understanding of the offline as somehow being primary to the online in terms of "real" selves. An important point here is that identities and self-representation are *contextual*: they appear with a specific function and uptake in mind. This also goes for "false" profiles—these serve a purpose for their creators, and should not be automatically dismissed as uninteresting. However, from the perspective of research which does not go beyond the screen, this of course poses a problem if demographic or biographic accuracy (e.g., of physical location, age, gender) is taken for granted in drawing sociolinguistic conclusions based on demographic correspondence between online and offline. In such cases, an ethnographer would need to go beyond the screen to find out how and for what purposes specific meanings are made. Data mining, or the collection of log data, will not get us beyond the "on the screen" understanding.

However, in going beyond the screen it should also be remembered that people are not "cultural or linguistic catalogues," as Blommaert and Dong (2010) put it: people do not have an opinion on or a straightforward explanation for everything they think or do, nor is every aspect of our behavior easily verbalized (Briggs 1986; see also Blommaert & van de Vijver 2013 for a discussion of "methodological loops"). Interviews are thus not necessarily the magic fix. With digital culture, things have changed—we do have new kinds of socio-cultural activity, and new types of environments, and this may require us to be methodologically creative. At the same time, however, the principles of ethnography remain the same—and ethnography has been through innovations before, incorporating new contexts and new sites and forms of practice. (There was a time, for instance, when ethnography in schools was a new frontier.)

As cultures and societies develop, so does ethnography, using its inherent adaptability and flexibility to try to find out what exactly is going on. And these strengths are of particular use to us now, considering the speed and scope of change that digitalization has brought to social interaction.

Future directions

Broader changes in digital culture and the Internet will continue to shape the nature of ethnography. For instance, the emergence of "nonymous" (Zhao *et al.* 2008) spaces such as Facebook—i.e., private companies providing social network platforms on which people are encouraged to present themselves with their "real" names—has clearly introduced a change in the functions of online environments in everyday life as well as in the study of online environments. It would of course be naïve to assume that simply because nonymity is encouraged, everybody presents themselves with their "real names"—as many of us know from our own contact lists on Facebook, for instance. However, nonymity has clearly been a tendency which has to do not only with the changing face of online sociality, but also with the interests of private companies and other parties (e.g., governments) with a need to access people's "real" identities and their networks. As to the changing face of sociality,

> all kinds of sociality are currently moving from public to corporate space; even as little as ten years ago, the coding of social actions into proprietary algorithms, let alone the branding and patenting of these processes, would have been unthinkable. Today, Facebook, Google, Amazon and Twitter all own algorithms that increasingly determine what we like, want, know, or find.
>
> *(van Dijck 2013: 37)*

Rapid changes in communicative environments continue to introduce changes in the shapes and functions of people's communications. Ethnography will have to follow suit, and it only remains to be seen what kind of transformations lie ahead. Technological innovation thus always forms a context informing our inquiries on digital communications.

A further context that should be invoked here is the ongoing debate on "Big Data," propelled by the perceived ease of collecting huge amounts of ("natural") data from people's online activities. The amount of potential data entered online every day on social network sites alone is astronomical, and a lot of it is easily available to researchers. However, to assume that big data research gives access to *all* the data is misleading—only social media companies themselves have access to "truly big" data; for academics, much of it is beyond reach. This has even prompted some company researchers to suggest that academics should not take the trouble of studying social media, as they themselves are the only ones to have privileged access to all of the data—for instance, all the tweets featuring a specific hashtag (boyd & Crawford 2011).

The availability of data mining techniques has also given rise to innovative approaches such as "ethnomining" (Aipperspach *et al.* 2006), which attempts to bring together ethnographic insight and data mining. Both big data and ethnography have their applications and are suited for different tasks. From an ethnographic perspective, big data research is not necessarily without problems, though. For instance, sampling Twitter accounts to probe into people's communicative practices can be highly problematic if generalizations are made based on the assumption that bigger is better, or that the more representative a sample is, the more accurate it is (see boyd & Crawford 2011 for a broader discussion on the challenges related to big data). Instead of a "the bigger the better" attitude, ethnographers would be more inclined to endorse the idea that "small is beautiful." Thorough ethnographic investigations provide in-depth understandings of the particularities of the cases studied, and provide ecologically valid information. The most recent book by danah boyd (2014), for instance, provides an account of American teens' mediatized lives, and it offers a good example of the kind of rich and detailed account only possible as a result of longitudinal ethnographic engagement in the field. In the future we will hopefully see similar studies focusing specifically on language. Long-term ethnographic engagement is of course time and resource consuming, but such investments are necessary to provide detailed and situated accounts of communicative practices. Indeed, with technological advances, "We've entered an era where data is cheap, but making sense of it is not" (boyd 2010: np).

In some respects, we have come full circle from where we started in the introduction, reviewing the relatively context-poor or decontextualized early research on technologically mediated communication. Data mining is now widely seen as *the* approach to studying online communication: it has the aura of being easy, comprehensive, and objective. Boellstorff *et al.* (2012) recall what could have been an unfortunate example of automated analysis of chat logs from a virtual world gone wrong: in the machine-collected data they discuss, the word "bunnies" appeared as thematically significant, and left the quantitative researcher puzzled as to the apparent heavy interest in rabbits in the data. Had it not been for a colleague with a *contextual understanding* of what exactly had been the object of discussion in the data set, it would have been difficult to establish that the people in the chat were in fact not discussing rabbits at all, but "bunny slippers"—a type of shoe that increases jump height. This is the kind of insight that ethnographers can produce, and the contributions of ethnographers are very much needed in providing realistic, in-depth explanations of digital communications.

In many respects, digitalization has changed and indeed complicated things for ethnographers. However, what could easily be presented as "problems" in digital ethnography should perhaps not be seen as problems at all. The point is not that we should simply keep thinking about these issues in the euphemistic frame of "challenges"; rather, we should see these issues as indicative of the kind of cultural and societal change societies are undergoing thanks to digital technologies. Blommaert and van de Vijver (2013; see also Arnaut 2012; Blommaert 2013) identify complexity, mobility, and dynamics as key features of today's world of rapid social change. The world is increasingly complex, and the changes are in many respects dramatic, and not only for those who have the means and skills—digital and media literacies—required to participate, more or less fully, in these developments. These changes affect all of us: those without the resources and the means to participate digitally are affected by the very fact that they remain excluded from these new means of communication. For charting these socio-cultural developments, digital ethnography is exceptionally well equipped: as Blommaert (2007) puts it,

> One rather uncontroversial feature of ethnography is that it addresses complexity. It does not, unlike many other approaches, try to reduce the complexity of social events by focusing *a priori* on a selected range of relevant features, but it tries to describe and analyze the complexity of social events *comprehensively*.
>
> *(p. 682, emphasis original)*

Related topics

- Chapter 1 Approaches to language variation (Hinrichs)
- Chapter 2 Network analysis (Paolillo)
- Chapter 4 Multimodal analysis (Jewitt)
- Chapter 8 Digital discourses: a critical perspective (Spilioti)

Piia Varis

References

Aipperspach, R., Rattenbuy, T. L., Woodruff A., Anderson K., Canny, J. F., & Aoki, P. 2006, "Ethno-mining: integrating numbers and words from the ground up," Technical Report, Electrical Engineering and Computer Sciences, University of California at Berkeley, available at: http://www.eecs.berkeley.edu/Pubs/TechRpts/2006/EECS-2006-125.pdf [accessed 11 September 2014].

Androutsopoulos, J. 2013, "Online data collection," in C. Mallinson, B. Childs, & G. Van Herk (eds.), *Data collection in sociolinguistics: methods and applications*, Routledge: New York, NY, pp. 236–249.

Androutsopoulos, J. 2008, "Potentials and limitations of discourse-centred online ethnography," *Language@ Internet*, vol. 5, art. 9, available at: http://www.languageatinternet.org/articles/2008/1610/androutso-poulos.pdf [accessed 11 September 2014].

Androutsopoulos, J. 2006, "Multilingualism, diaspora, and the Internet: codes and identities on German-based diaspora websites," *Journal of Sociolinguistics*, vol. 10, no. 4, pp. 520–547.

Arnaut, K. 2012, "Super-diversity: elements of an emerging perspective," *Diversities*, vol. 14, no. 2, pp. 1–16.

Beaulieu, A. 2004, "Mediating ethnography: objectivity and the making of ethnographies of the Internet," *Social Epistemology*, vol. 18, pp. 139–163.

Blommaert, J. 2013, *Ethnography, superdiversity and linguistic landscapes: chronicles of complexity*, Multilingual Matters: Bristol.

Blommaert, J. 2010, *The sociolinguistics of globalization*, Cambridge University Press: Cambridge.

Blommaert, J 2007, "On scope and depth in linguistic ethnography," *Journal of Sociolinguistics*, vol. 11, no. 5, pp. 682–688.

Blommaert, J. & Dong, J. 2010, *Ethnographic fieldwork: a beginner's guide*, Multilingual Matters: Bristol.

Blommaert, J. & Rampton, B. 2011, "Language and superdiversity," *Diversities*, vol. 13, no. 2, pp. 1–21.

Blommaert, J. & van de Vijver, F. 2013, "Good is not good enough: combining surveys and ethnographies in the study of rapid social change," *Tilburg Papers in Culture Studies*, paper 65, available at: https://www.tilburguniversity.edu/upload/61e7be6f-3063-4ec5-bf76-48c9ee221910_TPCS_65_Blomaert-Vijver.pdf [accessed 11 September 2014].

Blommaert, J. & Velghe, F. 2014, "Learning a supervernacular: textspeak in a South African township," in A. Creese & A. Blackledge (eds.), *Heteroglossia as practice and pedagogy*, Springer: New York, NY.

Boellstorff, T., Nardi, B., Pearce, C., & Taylor, T. L. 2012, *Ethnography and virtual worlds: a handbook of method*, Princeton University Press: Princeton, NJ.

boyd, d. 2014, *It's complicated: the social lives of networked teens*, Yale University Press: New Haven, CT.

boyd, d. 2010, "Privacy and publicity in the context of Big Data," WWW 2010, Raleigh, North Carolina, available at http://www.danah.org/papers/talks/2010/WWW2010.html [accessed 11 September 2014].

boyd, d. 2008, "Taken out of context: American teen sociality in networked publics," doctoral dissertation, University of California: Berkeley, CA.

boyd, d. & Crawford, K. 2011, "Six provocations for Big Data," A decade in Internet time: symposium on the dynamics of the Internet and society, Oxford Internet Institute, available at: http://papers.ssrn.com/sol3/papers.cfm?abstract_id=1926431 [accessed 11 September 2014].

Briggs, C. L. 1986, *Learning how to ask: a sociolinguistic appraisal of the role of the interview in social science research*, Cambridge University Press: Cambridge.

Burrel, J. 2009, "The field site as a network: a strategy for locating ethnographic research," *Field Methods*, vol. 21, no. 2, pp. 181–199.

Coleman, G. E. 2010, "Ethnographic approaches to digital media," *Annual Review of Anthropology*, vol. 39, pp. 487–505.

Garcia, A. C., Standlee, A. I., Bechkoff, J., & Cui, Y. 2009, "Ethnographic approaches to the Internet and computer-mediated communication," *Journal of Contemporary Ethnography*, vol. 38, no. 1, pp. 52–84.

Geertz, C. 1973, "Thick description: toward an interpretive theory of culture," in C. Geertz, *The interpretation of cultures: selected essays*, Basic Books: New York, NY, pp. 3–30.

Georgakopoulou, A. 2013, "Small stories research & social media: the role of narrative stance-taking in the circulation of a Greek news story," *Working Papers in Urban Language & Literacies*, paper 100, available at: http://www.kcl.ac.uk/sspp/departments/education/research/ldc/publications/workingpapers/the-papers/WP100.pdf [accessed 11 September 2014].

Gershon, I. 2010, *Breakup 2.0: disconnecting over new media*, Cornell University Press: Ithaca, NY.

Herring, S. C. 2004, "Computer-mediated discourse analysis: an approach to researching online behavior," in S. Barab, R. Kling, & J. H. Gray (eds.), *Designing for virtual communities in the service of learning*, Cambridge University Press: New York, pp. 338–376.

Hine, C. 2013, "Virtual methods and the sociology of cyber-social-scientific knowledge," in Hine, C. (ed.), *Virtual methods: issues in social research on the Internet*, Bloomsbury: London, pp. 1–13.

Hine, C. 2005, "Internet research and the sociology of cyber-social-scientific knowledge," *The Information Society*, vol. 21, no. 4, pp. 239–248.

Hine, C. 2000, *Virtual ethnography*, Sage Publications: London.

Hymes, D. 1996, *Ethnography, linguistics, narrative inequality: towards an understanding of voice*, Routledge: London.

Kozinets, R. V. 2009, *Netnography: doing ethnographic research online*, Sage Publications: London.

Leppänen, S., Kytölä, S., Jousmäki, H., Peuronen, S., & Westinen, E. 2014, "Entextualization and resemiotization as resources for identification in social media," in P. Seargeant & C. Tagg (eds.), *The language of social media: identity and community on the Internet*, Palgrave Macmillan: Basingstoke, pp. 112–136.

Madsen, L. M. & Stæhr, A. 2014, "Standard language in urban rap: social media, linguistic practice and ethnographic context," *Tilburg Papers in Culture Studies*, paper 94, available at: https://www.tilburguniversity.edu/upload/1210cac3-2abf-42d7-84b5-f545916b4d15_TPCS_94_Staehr-Madsen.pdf [accessed 11 September 2014].

Marwick, A. E. & boyd, d. 2010, "I tweet honestly, I tweet passionately: Twitter users, context collapse, and the imagined audience," *New Media & Society*, vol. 13, no. 1, pp. 114–133.

Miller, V. 2011, *Understanding digital culture*, Sage Publications: London.

Murthy, D. 2008, "Digital ethnography: an examination of the use of new technologies for social research," *Sociology*, vol. 42, no. 5, pp. 837–855.

Postill, J. & Pink, S. 2012, "Social media ethnography: the digital researcher in a messy web," *Media International Australia*, available at: http://blogs.bournemouth.ac.uk/research/files/2013/04/Postill-Pink-socialmedia-ethnography.pdf [accessed 11 September 2014].

Robinson, L. & Schulz, J. 2009, "New avenues for sociological inquiry: evolving forms of ethnographic practice," *Sociology*, vol. 43, no. 4, pp. 685–698.

Rymes, B. 2012, "Recontextualizing YouTube: from macro–micro to mass-mediated communicative repertoires," *Anthropology & Education Quarterly*, vol. 43, no. 2, pp. 214–227.

Sade-Beck, L. 2004, "Internet ethnography: online and offline," *International Journal of Qualitative Methods*, vol. 3, no. 2, available at: http://www.ualberta.ca/~iiqm/backissues/3_2/html/sadebeck.html [accessed 11 September 2014].

Shifman, L. 2011, "An anatomy of a YouTube meme," *New Media & Society*, vol. 14, no. 2, pp. 187–203.

Silverstein, M. 2003, "Indexical order and the dialectics of sociolinguistic life," *Language and Communication*, vol. 23, no. 3–4, pp. 193–229.

Silverstein, M. 1979, "Language structure and linguistic ideology," in P. Clyne, W. F. Hanks, W. F. & C. L. Hofbauer (eds.), *The elements: a parasession on linguistic units and levels*, Chicago Linguistic Society: Chicago, IL, pp. 193–247.

Stæhr, A. 2014a, "The appropriation of transcultural flows among Copenhagen youth: the case of Illuminati," in J. Androutsopoulos & K. Juffermans (eds.), *Discourse, Context, and Media*, special issue, Superdiversity and digital language practices, vols 4–5, pp. 101–115.

Stæhr, A. 2014b, "Metapragmatic activities on Facebook: enregisterment across written and spoken language practices," *Working Papers in Urban Language & Literacies*, paper 124, available at: http://www.kcl.ac.uk/sspp/departments/education/research/ldc/publications/workingpapers/the-papers/WP124.pdf [accessed 11 September 2014].

van Dijck, J. 2013, *The culture of connectivity: a critical history of social media*, Oxford University Press: Oxford.

Varis, P. & Wang, X. 2011, "Superdiversity on the Internet: a case from China," *Diversities*, vol. 13, no. 2, pp. 71–83.

Velghe, F. 2014, "'I wanna go in the phone': literacy acquisition, informal learning processes, 'voice' and mobile phone appropriation in a South African township," *Ethnography and Education*, vol. 9, no. 1, pp. 111–126.

Velghe, F. 2012, "Deprivation, distance and connectivity: the adaptation of mobile phone use to a life in Wesbank, a post-Apartheid township in South Africa," *Discourse, Context, and Media*, vol. 1, no. 4, pp. 203–216.

Velghe, F. 2011, "Lessons in textspeak from Sexy Chick: supervernacular literacy in South African instant and text messaging," *Tilburg Papers in Culture Studies*, paper 1, available at: https://www.tilburguniversity.edu/upload/5328eb9d-43bb-47d3-9dbc-f9bc38727c6e_tpcs%20paper1.pdf [accessed 11 September 2014].

Williams, R. 1974, *Television: Technology and cultural form*, Routledge: London.

Wittel, A. 2000, "Ethnography on the move: from field to net to Internet," *Forum: Qualitative Social Research*, vol. 1, no. 1, art. 21, available at: http://www.qualitative-research.net/index.php/fqs/article/view/1131/2517 [accessed 11 September 2014].

Zhao, S., Grasmuck, S. & Martin, J. 2008, "Identity construction on Facebook: digital empowerment in anchored relationships," *Computers in Human Behavior*, vol. 24, no. 5, pp. 1816–1836.

Further reading

Barton, D. & Lee, C. 2013, *Language online: investigating digital texts and practices*, Routledge: London.

This book addresses digital language from a variety of perspectives and includes a useful chapter on researching language online, addressing for instance questions of methodology, ethical issues, and the researcher's stance in online environments.

Blommaert, J. & Dong, J. 2010, *Ethnographic fieldwork: a beginner's guide*, Multilingual Matters: Bristol, UK.

Though it does not address digital environments in particular, this book offers an excellent, accessible introduction to the "basics" of ethnography in general.

Boellstorff, T., Nardi, B., Pearce, C., & Taylor, T. L. 2012, *Ethnography and virtual worlds: a handbook of method*, Princeton University Press: Princeton, NJ.

While specifically focusing on virtual worlds, this book also has wider relevance: it addresses myths and misunderstandings regarding ethnography and provides practical advice and useful suggestions on conducting ethnographic research.

boyd, d. 2008, *Taken out of context: American teen sociality in networked* publics, doctoral dissertation, University of California: Berkeley, CA.

boyd's work in general is highly interesting for anyone engaged in the ethnography of digital culture; this dissertation documents her two-and-a-half-year ethnographic study on American teenagers and their use of social network sites.

Hine, C. (ed.) 2013, *Virtual methods: issues in social research on the Internet*, Bloomsbury: London.

This collection includes several chapters addressing different aspects of ethnographic research and the Internet; the case studies highlight different (methodological, ethical) issues relevant to studying online environments.

4

Multimodal analysis

Carey Jewitt

Chapter overview

There is growing interest in how people communicate through a range of resources such as body posture, gesture, gaze, and speech in interaction; and images, layout, sounds, colour, and writing in texts, particularly in relation to digital texts and interaction in digital environments. A multimodal perspective attends to this full range of communicative forms and the relationships that are created between them. This chapter first introduces multimodality, reviewing its underlying theoretical assumptions and key concepts. The contribution of multimodality to research on digital communication is then briefly discussed. Following this broad introduction and contextualization, a walk-through of the process of multimodal analysis is provided to give a sense of this approach in relation to digital communication. The chapter concludes with a brief discussion of limitations, research challenges, and future directions.

Introducing multimodality

Multimodality is an inter-disciplinary approach that understands communication and representation as more than language and attends systematically to the social interpretation of a range of forms of making meaning. It provides concepts, methods, and a framework for the collection and analysis of visual, aural, embodied, and spatial aspects of texts and interactions (Jewitt 2013; Kress 2010). Multimodality emphasizes situated action, that is, the importance of the social context and the resources available for meaning making, with attention to people's situated choice of resources. It foregrounds the forms of communication or 'modes' that people choose to make meaning with, such as image or writing or gesture, and investigates the social effects of these choices on meaning, asking how choosing to represent something through an image or writing impacts on its meaning.

Multimodality is an approach that provides resources to support a complex, fine-grained analysis of meaning in relation to texts, artefacts, and as face-to-face interaction. From this perspective, meaning is understood as arising in the iterative connection between the meaning potential of a material semiotic text (e.g., a worksheet or website) or artefact (e.g., a tool); the meaning potential of the social and cultural environment where it is encountered (e.g., at home or in a museum); and the resources, intentions, and knowledge that people bring to that encounter. Different intentions and knowledge are in play, for example, when an individual encounters a cup or a website, and when these encounters take place in the home as opposed to a museum. It is this iterative connection between the meaning potential of object, environment, and people that is at the heart of multimodality. That is, it strives to connect the material semiotic resources available to people with what they are used to signify in social contexts. Changes to these resources and how they are configured are therefore understood as significant for communication. Digital technologies are of particular interest to multimodality because they make available a wide range of modes, often in new inter-semiotic relationships with one another. They unsettle and re-make genres, and they often reshape practices and interaction.

Three interconnected theoretical assumptions underpin multimodality. The first is that, while language is widely taken to be the most significant mode of communication, speech or writing are a part of a multimodal ensemble. Multimodality 'steps away from the notion that language always plays the central role in interaction, without denying that it often does' (Norris 2004: 3) and proceeds on the assumption that all modes have the potential to contribute equally to meaning. From a multimodal perspective, language is therefore only ever one mode nestled among a multimodal ensemble of modes. While others have analysed 'non-verbal' modes, multimodality differs in that language is not its starting point, nor does it provide a prototypical model of all modes of communication. The starting point is that all modes that are a part of a multimodal ensemble – a representation and/or an interaction – need to be studied with a view to the underlying choices available to communicators, the meaning potentials of resources, and the purposes for which they are chosen.

The second assumption central to multimodal research is that all modes have, like language, been shaped through their cultural, historical, and social uses to realize social functions as required by different communities. That is, a mode is shaped by the things that it has been used to accomplish socially in everyday instantiations, not by a set of fixed rules and structures. This view of language as a situated resource encompasses the principle that modes of communication offer historically specific and socially/culturally shared potentials (or 'semiotic resources') for communicating. Therefore each mode is understood to have different meaning potentials or semiotic resources and to realize different kinds of communicative work. Multimodality takes all communicative acts to be constituted of and through the social. This also draws attention to the ways in which communication is constrained and produced in relation to social context and points to how modes come into spaces in particular ways. A key question for multimodality, then, is how people make meaning in context to achieve specific aims.

This connects with the third assumption underpinning multimodality: that people orchestrate meaning through their selection and configuration of modes. Thus the interaction between modes is significant for meaning making. Multimodal communication is not only digitally mediated; however, digital media have foregrounded the need to consider the particular characteristics of modes, multimodal configurations, and their semiotic function in contemporary discourse worlds. The meanings in any one mode are always interwoven with meanings in other modes co-operating in the communicative ensemble. The interaction between modes is itself a part of the production of meaning.

A brief history

Multimodality was developed in the early 2000s (see Jewitt 2013, Kress *et al.* 2001, 2005; van Leeuwen 2005). It originated from linguistic ideas of communication, in particular Michael Halliday's work on language as a social semiotic system, which shifted attention from language as a static linguistic system to language as a social system shaped by particular contexts and purposes. In *Language as Social Semiotic* (1978), Halliday offered a theory of language built on a social functional perspective of meaning and a framework for understanding language as a system of options and meaning potentials – in brief, he propounded the idea of meaning as choice. Kress and van Leeuwen (2006) expanded attention from language to other semiotic systems (or modes), laying the groundwork for extending and adapting social semiotics across a range of modes and opening the door for multimodality. As multimodality has developed, it has also looked beyond linguistics for analytical resources to further explore the situated character of meaning making, including sociolinguistics, film theory, art history, iconography, and musicology.

Kress has introduced a strong emphasis on the social character of meaning, foregrounding the agency of the sign maker and the process of sign making. In *Before Writing* (Kress 1997) he offers a detailed account of the materiality and processes of young children's engagement with texts and how they interpret, transform, and redesign the semiotic resources and signs available to them – what has been described as chains of semiosis. From this perspective, multimodal signs are analysed as material residues of a sign maker's interests. Viewing signs as motivated and constantly being re-made draws attention to the interests and intentions that contribute to a person's choice of one semiotic resource over another. This 'interest' connects a person's choice with the social context of sign production, echoing Halliday's emphasis on meaning as choice in his social semiotic theories of communication. The modal resources available to a person are an integral part of that context, which points to the importance of multimodality to understanding the process of meaning making, and to the significance of the changed modal resources of the digital for communication.

Key concepts

This section outlines in detail five concepts that are key for multimodality, some of which have already been mentioned above: mode, semiotic resource, modal affordance, multimodal ensembles, and meaning functions. There is variation among multimodal approaches; here the focus is on a social semiotic approach, thus this section draws primarily on the works of Kress (1997, 2010) and van Leeuwen (1999, 2005) and their joint works (Kress & van Leeuwen 2006).

Mode

This term refers to a set of socially and culturally shaped resources for making meaning: a 'channel' of representation or communication. One definition of a mode is that it has to comprise a set of elements or resources and organizing principles or norms that realize well-acknowledged regularities within any one community. That is, something can only be recognized as a mode when it is a recognized and usable system of communication within a community. The ability for the 'grammar' of the modal system to be broken is seen as a 'test' that it exists. Another 'test' for whether a set of resources can count as a mode is whether it is possible for it to articulate all three of Halliday's (1978) meaning functions: that is, can a set of resources be used to articulate 'content' matter (ideational meaning), construct social relations (interpersonal meaning), and create coherence (textual meaning)? (These meaning functions are more fully outlined in later in the chapter.) Accepted examples of modes include writing, image, moving image, and sound, as well as speech, gesture, gaze, and posture in embodied interaction. Modes are created through social processes; they are not autonomous and fixed but fluid and subject to change. For example, the meanings of words and gestures change over time and context. Modes are also particular to a community or culture where there is a shared understanding of their semiotic, rather than universal, characteristics.

Semiotic resource

This term is used to refer to a means for meaning making that is simultaneously a material, a social, and a cultural resource. In other words, a semiotic resource can be thought of as the connection between representational resources and what people do with them:

> Semiotic resources are the actions, materials and artefacts we use for communicative purposes, whether produced physiologically – for example, with our vocal apparatus, the muscles we use to make facial expressions and gesture – or technologically – for example, with pen and ink, or computer hardware and software – together with the ways in which these resources can be organized. Semiotic resources have a meaning potential, based on their past uses, and a set of affordances based on their possible uses, and these will be actualized in concrete social contexts where their use is subject to some form of semiotic regime.
>
> *(van Leeuwen 2005: 285)*

This definition highlights the historical development of connections between form and meaning, an observation also present in Bakhtin's account of intertextuality (Bakhtin & Voloshinov 1986). Kress (2010) emphasizes that these resources are constantly transformed. This theoretical stance presents people as agentive sign-makers who shape and combine semiotic resources to reflect their interests.

Modal affordance

The term 'modal affordance' is contested and continuously debated within multimodal research. Kress uses the term to refer to the potentialities and constraints of different modes – what is easily expressed, represented, or communicated with the resources of a mode, and what is less straightforward or even impossible – and this is subject to constant social work. From this perspective, the term 'affordance' is a complex concept connected to both the material *and* the cultural, social, and historical use of a mode. The affordance of a mode is shaped by how it has been used, what it has been repeatedly used to mean and do, and the social conventions that inform its use in context. The affordances of the sounds of speech, for instance, usually happen across time, and this sequence in time shapes what can be done with (speech) sounds. The logic of sequence in time is difficult to avoid for speech: one sound is uttered after another, one word after another, one syntactic and textual element after another. This linearity becomes an affordance or meaning potential: it produces possibilities for putting things first or last, or somewhere else in a sequence. The mode of speech is therefore strongly governed by the logic of time. Like all governing principles, affordances do not hold in all contexts and are realized through the complex interaction of the social as material and vice-versa – in this sense, the material and the social are mutually constitutive. These affordances contribute to the different communicational and representational potentials or modal logics of modes (although it is important to note that these are open to change and disruption).

Multimodal ensembles

Representations or interactions that consist of more than one mode can be referred to as a multimodal ensemble. The term draws attention to the agency of the sign-maker, who pulls together the ensemble within the social and material constraints of a specific context of meaning making. When several modes are involved in a communicative event (e.g., a text, a website, a spoken interchange) all of the modes combine to represent a message's meaning. The meaning of any message is distributed across all of these modes and not necessarily evenly. The different aspects of meaning are carried in different ways by each of the modes in the ensemble. Any one mode in that ensemble is carrying a part of the message only: each mode is therefore partial in relation to the whole of the meaning, and speech and writing are no exception. Multimodal research attends to the interplay between modes to look at the specific work of each mode and how each mode interacts with and contributes to the others in the multimodal ensemble. This raises analytical questions, such as which modes have been included or excluded, the function of each mode, how meanings have been distributed across modes, and what the communicative effect of a different choice would be. At times the meaning realized by two modes can be 'aligned', at other times they may be complementary, and they may also produce aspects of meaning that are contradictory or in tension.

Modal affordance in the context of multimodal ensembles raises the question of what modes and modal arrangements are 'best' for in a particular context. The relationships between modes as they are orchestrated in interactions (and texts) may realize meanings through different weightings of modes or 'modal density' in an ensemble (Norris 2013). The structure of hyperlinks in digital texts, for example, realizes connections and disconnections between elements that may contribute to the expansion of meaning relations between elements. An image may be used to link two layers within a text, and the character of what the image links to may elaborate the meaning of the image itself. Further, as meaning makers decide on modal 'best fit' and how to combine modes for a particular purpose, analysis of the moment-by-moment processes of constructing multimodal ensembles can enable the analyst to unpack how meanings are brought together.

Meaning functions

As noted earlier, multimodality is built on a functional theory of meaning, an idea of meaning as social action realized through people's situated modal choices and the way they combine and organize these resources into multimodal ensembles. It distinguishes between three different but interconnected categories of meaning choices (also called meta-functions) that are simultaneously made when people communicate:

- choices related to how people realize content meanings (known as *ideational meaning*) by using resources to represent the world and their experience of it, such as processes, relations, events, participants, and circumstances;
- choices related to how people articulate *interpersonal meanings* by using resources to represent the social relations between themselves and those they are communicating with, either directly via interaction or via a text or artefact – for example, the visual or spatial depiction of elements as near and far, direct or oblique, are resources used to orient viewers or interactants to a text or to one another;
- choices concerned with textual or organisational meaning, for example, the use of resources such as layout, pace, and rhythm for realizing cohesion, composition, or structure in a text or interaction.

Multimodality applies these meaning functions to all modes to better understand their meaning potentials; to discern 'what can be meant' or 'what can be done' with a particular set of semiotic resources; and to explore how these three interconnected kinds of meaning potentials are actualized through the grammar and elements of their different modal systems.

The scope and contribution of multimodality to research on digital communication

This section gives a sense of the scope and potential of multimodality for researching digital communication. The following four potentials of multimodal research are discussed in this section:

- the systematic description of modes and their semiotic resources;
- multimodal investigation of communication and interaction with specific digital environments;
- identification and development of new digital semiotic resources and new uses of existing resources for communicating in digital environments; and
- contribution to research methods for the collection and analysis of digital data and environments within social research.

The systematic description of modes and their semiotic resources

A multimodal approach can be used to create an inventory of the meaning potentials available to people communicating using a technology in a particular context. This may be done through a systematic description of the modes – including their semiotic resources, materiality and modal affordances – and the organizing principles of a device and/or application. Building on the notion of meaning as choice and the concept of meta-functions, some multimodal researchers use a style of diagramming called system networks to map the meaning potentials of a mode. This is a diagrammatic taxonomy of the options that are possible within a semiotic system. It maps the potential of modal resources to articulate content, interpersonal, and textual or organisational meanings (see Kress & van Leeuwen 2006; Jewitt 2013). System networks provide an analytical tool for mapping the range of semiotic resources and options made available by a mode in a given context. In this way, system networks provide a way to push the formal analysis of a mode (or a semiotic resource) to a logical limit.

In the case of digitally mediated interaction and digital texts and environments, multimodal inventories can be of use in both understanding the meaning-making potentials and constraints that different technologies place on representation, communication, and interaction, and apprehending how users of those technologies notice and take up those resources in different ways. This use of multimodality is exemplified in work on how digital technologies re-mediate forms of reading in the English classroom (e.g., Jewitt 2002). This can inform both the re-design of technological artefacts and environments and their introduction into a set of practices, for example for learning or work.

Multimodal investigation of interaction in specific digital environments

Multimodal researchers have also focused on how modal resources are taken up and used in a specific context. They map and compare people's choice of mode, studying the use of semiotic resources in specific contexts; and some examine how these modal choices are jointly shaped by the materiality and affordances of a mode, and the knowledge and experience of research subjects.

Much work has been done on multimodal environments, examining how various modes are taken up and used and attending to how the semiotic resources and affordances of bodily modes and space feature in different digital environments. These inquiries offer insights into the role of the body in digital communication and interaction. When interacting with tangible environments, for example, children's different use of gesture, manipulation of objects, gaze, and body posture is key in how they can develop hypotheses, explanations, and generalisations in the context of learning science (Price & Jewitt 2013; Sakr, Jewitt, & Price 2014). Highly multimodal digital environments also shape how people organize and regulate their talk and writing (Jewitt 2005). Multimodality provides a set of concepts to describe and interrogate these re-mappings, elucidating, for example, the interaction of the 'physical' and the 'virtual' body and what it means for digital communication.

Identification and development of new digital semiotic resources and new uses of existing resources

In addition to creating inventories of modes and semiotic resources and analysing how these are used in a range of specific contexts, multimodality contributes to the discovery and development of new semiotic resources and new ways of using existing ones.

> Studying the semiotic potential of a given semiotic resource is studying how that resource has been, is, and can be used for purposes of communication, it is drawing up an inventory of past and present and maybe also future resources and their uses. By nature such inventories are never complete, because they tend to be made for nature specific purposes.
>
> *(van Leeuwen 2005: 17)*

The discovery and development of new modal resources is linked to social change and society's need for new semiotic resources and new ways of using existing semiotic resources as the communicative landscape changes. Two factors central to this are the potentials of digital technology and the importing of semiotic resources in a global society.

Contribution to research methods

Increasingly, researchers need to look beyond language to better understand how people communicate and interact in digital environments. This places new demands on research methods with respect to digital texts and environments where conventional concepts and analytical tools may need rethinking. Multimodality makes a significant contribution to existing research methods for the collection and analysis of data and environments within social research, including visual digital data such as screen-capture and eye-tracking data (Jewitt 2013); researcher-generated and naturally occurring digital video data; analytical processes of transcription – a focus of much experimentation in multimodal approaches (Bezemer & Mavers 2011); and innovative ways to map and analyse the visual, embodied, and spatial features of interaction with digital technologies (see MODE.ioe.ac.uk).

The next section builds on this introduction to multimodality, offering a 'walk-through' of the process of multimodal analysis of digital communication.

The process of multimodal analysis: a walk-through

As noted earlier in this chapter, a multimodal approach can be applied to investigate the modal meaning potentials of digital texts *and* social interaction. Both of these sites of multimodal application are attended to in this brief walk-through. It draws on two very different multi-modal studies within the large project MODE (multimodal methods for researching digital environments) as illustrative examples. The first study explores the principles of composition of the blog, a significant digital form that involves a range of modes. The study focuses on food blogs – a popular form that is significant for how people create and express social identities – and draws on a corpus of 30 food blogs that display a range of design features. The second study examines how embodied interaction with tangible technologies can be used in the learning of science concepts. The primary data is video recordings of pairs of children (age 10–11 years) completing a series of tasks with a tangible table to explore concepts of light. These studies are used to illustrate the methodological and analytical process. They are distinct in that one attends to a multimodal analysis of digital texts, and the other a multimodal analysis of interaction in a digital environment. The method used here to analyse blogs can be applied to any other digital text or artefact, including websites or online resources, and the example of interaction with a tangible table could equally be applied to interaction within other digital environments and interfaces.

Multimodality pays systematic attention to meaning and the ways in which a range of modes are used to communicate. This process is described in seven steps.

Step 1: collecting multimodal data

The concepts outlined earlier in this chapter are significant for multimodal data collection, as this process has to be fine-grained and holistic enough to ensure that data on each of the relevant modes and semiotic resources in use are captured. This raises challenges – for example, when using video to record interaction in complex digital environments, how can the details of hand movements, facial expression, and body movement be captured? Decisions have to be made regarding how many cameras to use, whether to use a fixed or roving camera, and so on. In the collection of text-based data, a multimodal approach also raises challenges: how can data collection preserve the materiality and dynamic character of complex forms such as animated sequences on a webpage, or depict the texture of a digitally embedded object?

Where a study's focus is on digital texts, such as blogs or websites, the data is often readily available online. Static screen-capture software can be used to capture such digital texts, while dynamic screen capture software can be used to record user interaction with these texts. In the MODE food blog study, for example, where the focus is on the blogs as designed texts, rather than people's interaction with them, a review of popular blogs related to parenting and food was undertaken, and a table constructed to record the different modal features of the blogs. This table was used to select a range of blogs to be collected. The blogs were 'harvested' from the Internet over a six-month period (September 2012–February 2013) using screen-capture tools, and an index of all materials with hyperlinks to their PDF-versions was collated. Screen-capture tools for archiving qualitative data on social media content (e.g. Zotero, LittleSnapper) can be used to collect whole websites as PDFs or images that can then be analysed in an offline setting. In addition, two archives containing snapshots of websites linked to dates ('The Wayback Machine' and 'UK Webarchive') were also used to explore the blog designs from as early as July, making it possible to analyse the changes made to sites over time.

Multimodal studies of interaction, such as the embodied learning with tangibles project, often depend on video recordings as the common primary data, as video can capture fine details of all modes, semiotic resources, materiality, and multimodal ensembles in time-sequential order and in a shareable form that can be manipulated (slowed down, speeded up, etc.). But while video is an excellent observational tool for capturing participants' interaction with the digital environment, it cannot capture the social context of the interaction. For this reason, video recordings are often supplemented by field notes, materials and texts used during the interaction, and interviews. The histories of practices, participants' ideas, the setup of the environment, and the roles of people and their concerns can be collected via fieldwork and interviews, and this provides information to support the analysis of the interaction. (See Jewitt 2012 for a full discussion of the challenges of video data collection).

Step 2: viewing data

Multimodal analysis involves an intensive engagement with data. Viewing the data through the lens of the research questions serves to refine or generate new questions, clarify criteria for sampling, and develop analytical ideas.

When analysing blogs, this intensive engagement involves mapping the modes in play. This may include, for example, covering one mode or part of the page, and focusing on the other and asking 'what sense can I make of this text if I can't see the images?' or 'what sense can I make of the text if I change its layout?' or 'what happens if I view this colour text in black-and-white to get at the "work" of colour in the text?' In the blog study, individual blogs and contrasting examples were viewed together in this way during preliminary analysis to identify the features that were key to the design of a text, for instance.

A similarly intense scrutiny is required for multimodal analysis of video; this involves intensive repeated viewing of the data. In the MODE project on embodied learning with tangibles, for example, the video was viewed repeatedly with both sound and image, honing in on excerpts with vision only, sound only, fast forward, in slow motion – all of which provide different ways of 'seeing' the video, the patterns across it. The focus is on spending significant time with data-discovery and 'noticings' of the detail of the interaction in order to fully appreciate the modes and semiotic resources in use. This helps to recognize customary acts or patterns of gesture, for example, or routines across the time and space of the interaction; and it supports the building of initial hypotheses to be explored. All this observation works towards building a rich holistic sense of the modes, semiotic resources, materiality, and interplay of modes and meaning – in short, doing the work to move from the video as information source to data. This intensive viewing and listening has many similarities with work in ethnomethodology and Conversation Analysis but differs in its commitment to the non-linguistic and the semiotic. That is, the starting point for analysis is not language: the analytical domain is broader and its scale of analysis is larger. The focus in on the semiotic resources of modes and their affordances gives a deeper engagement with these modes and an emphasis on their place in shaping the interaction.

Step 3: sampling data

Multimodal analysis is detailed and labour intensive no matter what kind of data is being used. Given the need to focus on all the modes in use, it may not be feasible or necessary to analyse all of the data collected in fine-grained detail. There are cases where a study focuses on one mode – for example, a recent study of infants' interaction with iPads focused on differences between touch in a paper-based environment and the iPad environment (Crescenzi, Jewitt, & Price 2014); another examined texture in PowerPoint (Djonov & van Leeuwen 2011). In addition, not all modes have the same pace of change and thus some may be less intensive to study – for example, body posture in many contexts may remain relatively static, while in the same context gaze may constantly change. For this reason, the sampling of data for detailed multimodal analysis is a key part of the analytical process in multimodality.

With texts, such as blogs, the question of how to sample is a different one, and is not as laborious as is the case with video data. As blogs are constantly changing, a fine-grained, multimodal analysis of blogs involves decisions about the time frame for harvesting and sampling texts. The fluid, interconnected character of digital texts also raises questions about the level or depth of the data to be sampled and explored: How many levels down should one go? Just the home page? To what extent should links that connect to other sites be followed? What focal texts – e.g. screens from blogs – should be collected? In the MODE blog study, blogs (and blogging platforms) were viewed, compared, and contrasted before zooming in on particular sets of examples.

Using video to collect data produces rich data and often a lot of it. For this reason, once all video data has been viewed, it is usually sampled to select instances (episodes) for detailed multimodal analysis. Sampling may be informed or organized by time, such as sampling every five minutes, or the start and/or ending of an event; or it may be driven by thematic ideas or theoretical concepts that derive from the literature or from preliminary analysis of the video data (Kress *et al.* 2001, 2004). In the study of embodiment and learning in tangible environments (Price & Jewitt 2013), for example, viewing the video data of pairs of students working around a rectangular interactive table enabled us to identify patterns in the students' body-position relative to the table and to one another. It was apparent from the data that different pairs of students chose to position themselves differently around the table, with some pairs choosing to be opposite one another, while others opted to be adjacent to one another along one side of the table. There were also differences in the speed and character of their interaction with objects on the table. In addition, some students were observed to be more verbal than others. Thus, three contrasting pairs were selected for detailed analysis: pair 1 were two boys positioned opposite one another and engaged in a consistent level of verbal articulation; pair 2 were positioned next to one another, and verbal articulation was minimal throughout the activity; and pair 3 were positioned adjacent to one another, with ongoing verbal articulation undertaken primarily by one student throughout the activity. Differences across these dimensions were used to sample the data and to identify three types of multimodal configuration across the pairs, and to sample three pairs typical of these types. During in-depth analysis of these pairs, the data were further sampled for episodes focused on key moments in the interaction related to (1) shifts in the use of modes and semiotic resources, and (2) the work of the manipulation of objects in the interaction. It is important to have a clear rationale for the selection of video excerpts and to ensure they are fully contextualized in the longer stream of interaction.

How best to sample data – whether it is video episodes or focal texts – is a difficult question that is intimately guided by the research question. Multimodal analysis tends to focus on those moments in the interaction or the text where some kind of 'order' is disturbed or where a convention is broken. In the case of the blogs, this might be where the colour of an element is out of place with the overall colour palette of the blog page, or where the connection between image and writing jars or conflicts. It is often on those occasions where power relations and ideologies become manifest (e.g., a student contests the teacher in interaction, or by using an unconventional layout for an assignment). Multimodal analysis focuses on what stands out but it always returns to the whole data corpus to test our analysis of the selected texts against it.

Step 4: transcribing data

There are many ways to transcribe multimodal data, and each shapes the data in significant ways for analysis; the consequences of choosing one method over another therefore need to be considered (this is discussed fully in Bezemer & Mavers 2011).

Multimodal studies of digital texts engage with practices of transcription, through which the 'original' blog pages are transformed for analytical and rhetorical purposes. Blog 'pages' may be captured and frozen, dislocated from time, and made static – even printed out and analysed on paper. Some modes, such as image, writing, layout, and colour, may be available in both media; others, such as moving image and sound, may get lost when moving from a dynamic to static screen or print. Crucially, too, the dynamic character of hyperlinks may not be represented, giving a sense of a 'flat', bounded and contained text rather than an open and fluid one. In the MODE blog study, transcription involved deconstructing and annotating the pages, and noting the use of different modes, semiotic resources, and modal affordances. Similar annotations can be achieved by imagining or even mocking up a re-configuration of the modes, their semiotic resources, and the multimodal ensembles (e.g., transposing image and text, altering the layout or template design, etc.) to get a sense of how the layout is contributing to meaning, for example.

Multimodal transcripts of video interaction set out to capture all the modes and semiotic resources in use in time sequence. For example, transcripts from the MODE embodied learning in tangible environments study make up a parallel record for each student, including time stamps, screen grabs, records of changes in body position and of manipulation of objects, pointing and gesturing, gaze, and speech. The transcripts enabled access to data on the rate at which objects were placed, replaced or repositioned; the number, pattern, and manner of turns taken during the activity; the number of combined modes used at one time and the intensity of modal resources used in the flow; and the quantity and quality (e.g., drawing conclusions or describing behaviour of objects) of their talk. Transcripts can serve an important role in mapping modes along temporal or spatial dimensions of digital communication to illuminate patterns in modal use and configurations. For example, in the tangible table study discussed here, the transcript enabled us to explore the sequencing of modes in the students' interaction, and this enabled us to identify patterns of gesture, gaze, and speech, which gave further analytical insight into the students' reflection and collaboration.

Step 5: analysing individual modes

Multimodal analysis starts with a focus on individual modes in order to build an inventory of the modes and semiotic resources in use, and to gain insights on how these are configured in different contexts of use. This draws on the concepts of mode, semiotic resource, materiality, modal affordance, and the meta-functions outlined earlier in the chapter.

The MODE blog study analysed focal sites and excerpts in detail, attending to each of the different modes in operation (Domingo, Jewitt, & Kress 2014). It builds on and extends the analytical framework of *Reading Images* (Kress & van Leeuwen 2006) and the approach to analysing texts developed by Bezemer and Kress (2008) in their study *Gains and Losses*. The study focuses on each mode and semiotic resource in use, with detailed attention to:

- visuals (e.g., the use of images, drawings, symbols)
- typographic fonts in use (e.g., size, type face, and style – bold, italics, underlining, etc.)
- colour (e.g., palette and effects – saturation, light, transparency, etc.)
- writing
- layout (e.g., framing and orientation – left-to-right arrangements; central elements; horizontally/vertically organized sequence, etc.).

An inventory of the modes and semiotic resources used in each blog is made to build a full modal picture of each. This is then used to compare and contrast the modal realizations across the sample of blogs, to examine how modes and resources are put into action differently in each blog. This analytical phase also focused on understanding the platform template as a semiotic entity in order to distinguish whether the modes being analysed (e.g., the colour template) were customized in any way by the users or if they are technical features that came with the selection of the template from the digital platform. This is where the Wayback Machine and other archival tools assist with the process of analysis to see what changes have been made over time by way of customizing. The concept of meta-functions is used to explore what meaning functions are being realized by these modal resources. That is, what work is being done by each of the modes in a blog? When and why is one mode used over another? What affordances are being exploited, and for what social purpose? These questions focus on how the technological platform of the blog shapes and constrains the modal resources in play. This stage of modal analysis asks how the material semiotic resources convey social meaning – for instance, how are these modes and semiotic resources used to construct the identities of the maker and the imagined reader? It is clear from this analysis that expert bloggers mobilize a range of multimodal resources to create multiple and distinct identities across different social media, including the creation of images of 'frugality' linked to ideas of aesthetics of social class. In addition, the more expert the blogger is, the more embedded and naturalized advertising is within the blog, and the more the visual layout maximizes linkage to a range of the blogger's social media (Domingo *et al.* 2014).

Multimodal analysis of video data proceeds in a similar analytical fashion but usually with a focus on different modes, such as body position, gaze, gesture, and action with objects (e.g., hand manipulation): here the import of time and space for interaction foregrounds the need to attend to the unfolding sequential character of the modes. The materiality of modes and their modal affordances are central to understanding the multimodal interaction that they support. The dimensions that are in focus and the resources in use are often very specific to an environment and the design of the digital technology or platform in use. The embodiment and tangible table study, for instance, examined each mode and semiotic resource in use (in addition to speech) with detailed attention to:

- body position (e.g., opposite one another, adjacent to one another, adjacent and moving around one another during interaction; distance between students – close, mid, far; standing back/near table; crouching down, etc.);
- body posture (e.g., leaning in/over the table, upright, relaxed);
- gesture (e.g., enactment gestures, pointing, etc.);
- gaze ('range' of view, 'shared point' of view, different point of view, reconfigured point of view, etc.);
- action/manipulation of objects (simultaneously picking up objects to use, simultaneous placing them on table, holding, etc.).

Through analysis of how students used the above modes, the study was able to comment on the different ways in which the design and use of the tangible table could contribute to scientific enquiry and collaborative interactions and dialogues (Sakr, Jewitt, & Price 2014; Price & Jewitt 2013).

The modes in focus may differ depending on the technologies being used, the context of use, and the research questions – any of which may require an emphasis on specific modes.

Step 6: analysing across modes

Once a clear picture has been gained of the modes in use and the semiotic resources in play, the next step in multimodal analysis is to investigate the meanings created via the interplay between these modes – that is, to understand the multimodal ensemble. This requires attention to the devices through which relationships are created between modes.

The MODE blog study examined how these modal relations are achieved via the design of layout and cohesive devices, for example. It explored the relationships between image and text and between image and colour in order to identify how a colour palette was used to create coherence across a blog, and how layout was used to design relationships between modes and to indicate a sense of modular elements and the navigation of reading paths. The project explored the design decisions made by bloggers and how these decisions and trends affect which modes are privileged – not only in terms of quantity of use ('is writing used more than image?'), but rather in terms of the functions of modes. That is, is the blog 'image-led' or 'writing-led'? Does it deploy video, still image, or writing with equal frequency and with different functions? In other words, what kinds of modal densities are present in the blog? This study has also examined how aesthetic considerations reflect the social functions of blogs. Genre is a key concept at this level of analysis: in the case of the food blog study, some blogs are collections of recipes, others are narratives/accounts of events, some have advertisements embedded in the writing with hyperlinks to products or services, etc. A range of writing forms materialize in the various pages/levels, and these change over time: a site becomes more commercial as it becomes more popular. For instance, the study indicates a stronger use of embedded hyperlinks within narratives in blogs that become more popular.

One way that a multimodal approach starts to understand the modal features of a blog is to measure the amount of space given to a mode on the screen, as well as the ways in which layout is used to order modal elements. This might involve taking a theme such as 'frugality' or 'commercialism' and exploring where that is articulated on the screen and through which modal features in order to build up a multimodal semiotic map of the site, and then mapping how these meaning elements of a site interact with one another, a part of which would be to explore what discourses are made easily visible and which are more 'hidden'. Semiotically there is also a shift from the linearity of the written text to the modularity of the contemporary written elements of multimodal texts – in this case blogs. Modularity signals the responsibility of the person who engages with the screen, whose reading path and selections 'create' the text. This analysis suggests a shift from the authority of the author to the interest of the reader, from linearity to modularity.

Working with video data, the embodied learning with tangibles project looked across the modes to see the patterns of modes across interactions and to discern how the modes were orchestrated across time. This shed light on the degree of turn-taking and the pace of the interaction across the pairs. By taking this approach, the study was able to comment on the interactional consequences for collaboration of position, gaze, and interaction with objects, the resulting pace and rhythm of interaction, and the potential for reflection and the development of hypotheses. In the interactive table study (Price & Jewitt 2013), for example, a multimodal analysis looking across position, gaze, body posture, gesture, and talk showed that the pace of interaction differed across the pairs. For two pairs (2 and 3), who were positioned adjacent to one another, the pace of interaction was significantly slower and seemed generally more considered and purposeful than for pair (1), in which the students were opposite one another. For pair 1, the ease of simultaneous access to objects meant that they could both pick up and place objects on the table at the same time, contributing to a faster pace of interaction. By this we meant that the number of different objects placed on the table and the changes in configuration were greater throughout the period of the activity (e.g., over 100 for pair 1 versus 30 for pair 2 and 28 for pair 3). While it could be argued that this offers the opportunity for exploring a greater number of 'object' configurations potentially exposing the students to more 'experiences', our analysis suggested that it also reduced the amount of considered 'reflection' time before any one configuration was changed. This contrasts with pair 3, where the degree of verbal articulation and reflection was greater than with pair 1. This 'reflection' time was important both in terms of understanding the science and in enabling them to consider how they structured their activity, i.e. to choose what to do next. Thus, the activity with pairs 2 and 3 seemed more 'purposeful' as opposed to the more 'opportunistic' approach conveyed by pair 1.

While a slower-paced structure to the activity suggests a more methodical and considered approach to exploring the tasks, the students engaging in a faster-paced interaction showed other forms of 'systematic' activity. In particular, they placed each object in the light beam in a planned way to find out which ones displayed a spectrum and which ones did not and they summarized which of the different coloured objects they had used. This systematicity differs from pair 3, the motivation underlying the way they structured their activity being different. Pair 3's methodical approach was driven by exploring the combined physical–digital effects, and what this might mean in terms of light behaviour, while pair 1 were driven by the features of the different objects themselves.

This move from individual mode to understanding the multimodal ensemble is central. As noted earlier, modes have different affordances and materiality, and one aspect of this is the social use of modes. Multimodal studies have shown that it is common for different, often opposing, discourses to be realized in the same text via different modes, and it is this multimodal layering of meaning and the resulting tensions and ambiguities that are revealed via attention to meaning across modes in a text or interaction (Jewitt 2002, 2008). For instance, in a study of sexual health leaflets, image and writing relations were shown to be key in how discourses of masculinity were realized. Notably, analysis of the writing revealed positive and progressive discourses of masculinity and femininity, whilst contradictory and negative discourses of masculinity were 'carried' in the visual elements of the leaflets (Jewitt 1997).

Step 7: combining multimodality with social theories

Multimodality is a powerful approach, providing detailed analysis of the modes and semiotic resources in use as well as the ways that these are integrated in texts and interaction to realize semiotic meaning. It is primarily concerned with the micro-world of interactions and communication and can be used to give a strong semiotic account of a range of social issues, such as how the power dynamics between people are materially realized through their interaction with one another and with objects and devices in digital environments. To move towards stronger sociological or theoretical explanations of the character of these interactions, however, multimodality needs to be combined with social and learning theories – to understand, for example, how issues of power dynamics revealed by a multimodal analysis are infused by gender, class, and race, or, in the case of the tabletop study, by theories of science learning.

The MODE embodiment study turned to theories of scientific inquiry to make sense of the material semiotic analysis afforded by a multimodal approach. Combining the direct observations of manipulation and gesture with theories of science learning, notably the works of Roth (2002) and Mortimer and Scott (2003), the study contextualized this interaction in the processes of scientific description, explanation, and generalization. These theories enabled the analysis to explore how students' descriptions and explanations of scientific phenomena were supported by the manipulation of objects and gestural movements, and the progress from description to explanation. It also showed how manipulation of objects is involved in the construction of scientific explanations, serving – perhaps even facilitating – scientific thought.

Such theoretical understandings may infuse all stages of the multimodal cycle or provide the rationale for an initial research problem space.

Concluding comments

The chapter concludes with a brief comment on the limitations of multimodality and future directions.

Digital environments and devices have changed significantly over the past decade, bringing music, image, and video into many people's everyday communicative repertoire. These changes have expanded the multimodal resources available to people for communication, multiplied the reading paths to be navigated, and introduced practices of re-mixing and redesign of communicative forms. This raises questions about the form and functions of writing and image as well as the body and spatial design in digital environments and it highlights the complexity of communication in digital environments.

A key limitation of multimodality is that it is still at a relatively early stage of development, with much yet to be established, both in terms of theory and in terms of practices of transcription, language of description, and analysis. This raises many methodological challenges. Like any analysis of representation and communication, multimodal analysis is limited in its scope and scale. One challenge is that too much attention to many different modes may take away from understanding the workings of a particular mode; at the same time, too much attention to a single mode runs the risk of 'tying things down' to just one of many ways in which people make meaning. As for potentials and limitations in scale, multimodal analysis is focused on micro-interaction, and therefore questions of how the analysis can speak to 'larger' questions about culture and society are often raised. This can be overcome, at least in part, by linking multimodal analysis with broader social theory and by taking into account historical contexts.

As for the future, no one can really know or predict what will happen with digital technologies and how they will unfold over the next decade or so. New functionalities, new forms of interaction, and new whole-body digital experiences are, however, already emerging on the horizon suggesting an increasing communicative role for touch and other bodily modes. Against that backdrop, the multimodal interaction potentials of digital technologies will continue to increase and expand. New methods will be needed to research these innovations, and multimodality is a good starting point from which these methods might be developed.

Related topics

- Chapter 16 The role of the body and space in digital multimodality (Keating)
- Chapter 22 YouTube: Language and discourse practices in participatory culture (Androutsopoulos & Tereick)
- Chapter 25 New frontiers in interactive multimodal communication (Herring)

References

Bakhtin, M. & Voloshinov, N. V. 1986, *Marxism and the philosophy of language.* Harvard University Press: Boston, MA.

Bezemer, J. & Kress, G. 2008, 'Writing in multimodal texts: a social semiotic account of designs for learning', *Written Communication*, vol. 25, no. 2, pp. 165–195.

Bezemer, J. & Mavers, D. 2011, 'Multimodal transcription as academic practice: a social semiotic perspective', *International Journal of Social Research Methodology*, vol. 14, no. 3, pp. 191–207.

Crescenzi, L., Jewitt, C., & Price, S. 2014, 'The role of touch in preschool children's play and learning using iPad versus paper interaction', *The Australian Journal of Language and Literacy* (Special Issue on Touch), vol. 37, no. 2, pp. 86–95.

Djonov, E. & van Leeuwen, T. 2011, 'The visual semiotics of texture', *Visual Communication*, vol. 10, no. 4, pp. 541–564.

Domingo, M., Jewitt, C., & Kress, G. 2014, 'Multimodal social semiotics: writing in online contexts', in J. Rowsell & K. Pahl (eds.), *The Routledge handbook of literacy studies*, Routledge: London.

Halliday, M. A. K. 1978, *Language as social semiotic: the social interpretation of language and meaning*, Edward Arnold: London.

Jewitt, C. (ed.) 2013, *The Routledge handbook of multimodal analysis*, 2nd edn., Routledge: London.

Jewitt, C. 2012, *An introduction to using video for research*, available at: http://eprints.ncrm.ac.uk/2259/4/NCRM_workingpaper_0312.pdf.

Jewitt, C. 2008, *Technology, literacy and learning: a multimodal perspective*, Routledge: London.

Jewitt, C. 2005, 'Multimodality, reading, and writing for the 21st century', *Discourse: Studies in the cultural politics of education*, vol. 26, no. 3, pp. 315–331.

Jewitt, C. 2002, 'The move from page to screen: the multimodal reshaping of school English', *Visual Communication*, vol. 1, no. 2, pp. 171–195.

Jewitt, C. 1997, 'Images of men', *Sociological Research Online* vol. 2, no. 2, http://www.socresonline.org.uk/2/2/6.html.

Kress, G. 2010, *Multimodality: a social semiotic approach to communication*, RoutledgeFalmer: London.

Kress, G. 1997, *Before writing: rethinking paths to literacy*, Routledge: London.

Kress, G., Jewitt, C., Bourne, J., Franks, A., Hardcastle, J., & Jones, K. 2005, *Urban English classrooms: multimodal perspectives*, Routledge: London.

Kress, G., Jewitt, C., Bourne, J., Franks, A., Hardcastle, J., Jones, K., & Reid, E. 2004, *Urban classrooms, subject English: multimodal perspectives on teaching and learning*, RoutledgeFalmer: London.

Kress, G., Jewitt, C., Ogborn, J., & Tsatsarelis, C. 2001, *Multimodal teaching and learning: the rhetorics of the science classroom*, Continuum: London.

Kress, G. & van Leeuwen, T. 2006, *Reading images: the grammar of visual design*, Routledge: London.

Mortimer, E. F. & Scott, P. H. 2003, *Meaning making in secondary science classroom*, Open University Press: Maidenhead.

Norris, S. 2013, 'Modal density and intensity', in C. Jewitt (ed.), *The Routledge handbook of multimodal analysis*, 2nd edn., Routledge: London.

Norris, S. 2004, *Analyzing multimodal interaction: a methodological framework*, Routledge: London.

Price, S. & Jewitt, C. 2013, 'A multimodal approach to examining "embodiment" in tangible learning environments', in *Proceedings of the seventh international conference on tangible, embedded and embodied interaction,* Barcelona, pp. 43–50, available from http://dl.acm.org/citation.cfm?id=2460632.

Roth, W. M. 2002, 'From action to discourse: the bridging function of gestures', *Cognitive Systems Research*, vol. 3, no. 3, pp. 535–554.

Sakr, M., Jewitt, C., & Price, S. 2014, 'The semiotic work of hands in scientific enquiry', *Classroom Discourse*, vol. 5, no. 1, pp. 51–70.

van Leeuwen, T. 2005, *An introduction to multimodality*, Routledge: London.

van Leeuwen, T. 1999, *Speech, music, sound*, Palgrave Macmillan: London

Further reading

Jewitt, C. (ed.) 2013, *The Routledge handbook of multimodal analysis*, 2nd edn., Routledge: London.

This 32-chapter edited volume on multimodal theory, data analysis, and transcription includes chapters on conversation analysis and early sociolinguistic approaches to 'non-verbal' communication, as well as chapters detailing multimodal research in a range of digital environments including games, film, online environments, and software.

Kress, G. 2009, *Multimodality: a social semiotic approach to contemporary communication*, Routledge: London.

In this book language is theorized in a social semiotic framework of multimodal communication. It refers to a wide range of examples of text and talk, including digital environments.

Part II

Language resources, genres, and discourses

5

Digital genres and processes of remediation

Theresa Heyd

Introduction and definitions

One of the most essential and analytically helpful conceptual tools for theorizing about and working with digital or computer-mediated communication (CMC) is to approach the discourse in terms of digital genres. How does online communication pattern into structured, recognizable, and more or less discrete categories? What properties are central in how we perceive and reproduce digital genres? To what degree are digital genres distinct and genuinely new, or related to older, pre-existing forms that may have fulfilled similar functions in pre-digital communication? And finally, which role does the high level of technical mediation (usage features that are prompted by technical necessities or by intentional design choice) play in the linguistic' and communicative makeup of modern digital genres?

Consider the following example:

Figure 5.1 Example of a tweet.

Theresa Heyd

Depending on our individual familiarity with specific genres, here are a few casual observations that might be made with regard to this snippet of discourse and its relation to the genre continuum:

- The example appears to be a tweet, a discourse turn produced on the platform twitter.com. We might surmise this based on the length of the text, some structural features such as the @-message or the metadiscursive hashtags #YEA and #Jewish, and the characteristic visual–semiotic appearance of the utterance.
- Quite a few of these linguistic features (the restriction to 140 characters; the technical possibility to address other users) are inbuilt design features or programming choices.
- The text is also reminiscent of other, older forms of digital communication. In particular, it seems to share some properties with text messages and Instant Messaging; it displays textual features such as a typical 'Netspeak' abbreviation (lol), informal punctuation, and an overall conversational tone.
- When considering pre-digital genres, it seems more difficult to find spoken or written equivalents of this utterance type. Perhaps telegrams might come to mind, or handwritten notes, or short utterances in spoken conversation.

Genre analysis – that is, a systematic assessment of how textual artefacts group together – provides an essential and useful way to make meaningful abstractions about online discourse, and to uncover and describe its structural features and their communicative purposes and effects. In this sense, genre analysis constitutes an analytical toolbox for doing linguistic and discourse analysis with digital material, in particular where the focus is on comparative work that takes into account neighbouring genres, genre predecessors, and pre-digital antecedents. This chapter will lay out some of the key concepts, ongoing debates, and emerging topics in digital genre research, with a particular focus on remediation – 'the formal logic by which new media refashion prior media forms' (Bolter & Grusin 2000: 273).

The following overview is focused on a discourse–analytical perspective towards digital genres. However, it is worth pointing out that genres of digital documents also play an important role in applied and technical fields of computer-mediated communication, such as data mining, information retrieval, and other forms of empirical research and computational modelling. Automated genre identification and classification, for example, figure prominently in web search interfaces, information retrieval, and automated summarization of information. This highly technical field lies beyond the scope of this chapter, but it may be noted that these applied fields are informed by the same concepts and questions that are being discussed in functional linguistic genre analysis. A good summary of the state of the art is provided in Mehler *et al.* (2010).

This chapter, and many of the approaches outlined here, refers to digital 'genres', but other terms have been used to describe these phenomena – 'text types', 'discourse types', 'styles', 'registers', 'socio-technical modes'. This 'terminological maze' (Moessner 2001) has been noted by many researchers, and it predates the advent of digital communication. Discussions may be found in Giltrow and Stein (2009) or Biber and Finegan (1994). Very simply put, the notion of genre is nowadays often tied to a focus on communicative purpose (Swales 1990) and social action (Miller 1984); Kwasnik and Crowston describe genre as 'the fusion of content, purpose and form of communicative actions' (2005: 76). By contrast, text type refers to 'text categories defined in strictly linguistic terms' (Biber & Finegan 1994: 52). Registers and styles are usually described as situationally determined varieties that are imbued with social meaning. In this sense, the term genre is usually understood as the more functional concept, as opposed to more formal terms such as text type. Importantly, the functional understanding of text categories has been highly influential in genre theory. In particular, Swales's definition of genre as 'a class of communicative events that share some set of communicative purposes' (1990: 58) was widely adopted in many approaches. In this sense, genre is used in this discussion as a functional term that is focused more on communicative purpose and effect than on rigid textual and linguistic features. However, this brief discussion already hints at the formal/functional distinction that is central to genre theory, and this problem is revisited in a later section. A final term that is specific to digital genre theory is 'socio-technical mode' (Herring 2007), which refers to 'technologically defined CMC subtypes' such as blogs, discussion forums, or email – labels which 'are commonly understood to refer not just to CMC systems, but also to the social and cultural practices that have arisen around their use' (Herring 2007). Thus the term refers mainly to established and named types of CMC or communication interfaces and in this way places emphasis on the notion of technological mediation. While Herring (2007) argues for a classification scheme rather than a genre- or modes-based approach to categorizing digital discourse, the notion of socio-technical modes has proven useful to refer to digital genres and their technical component.

The remainder of this chapter on digital genre analysis is structured as follows: in the next section, an historical account traces 1) how the Internet as a genre continuum has emerged in the past three decades, and 2) how digital genre theory has accompanied this development as an emerging field of computer-mediated discourse analysis (CMDA) studies. The discussion then turns to central issues, research topics, and ongoing debates: old vs new; level of granularity; categorization vs classification vs taxonomies; genre ecologies; genre hybridity; technological impact vs technological determinism; and others. Finally, the chapter concludes with a discussion of emerging topics and future directions for research, for example how digital genre theory meshes with the discourse characteristics of social media.

Historical perspectives

A history of digital genres: three eras of development

A history of the Internet (see, e.g., Abbate 2000) can be written in terms of its technical milestones, its global spread, or the evolution of its user numbers. Alternatively, the historical evolution of the Internet can be traced through its genre history, thereby placing the focus on its usability and its communicative means and purposes. The following account identifies three phases: the early days of ARPAnet and the emerging Internet; the subsequent 'golden age' of commercialization and international spread; and the rise of the social web that leads into the present. Importantly, this overview focuses on text-based digital genres rather than other semiotic channels such as primarily audio-visual communication (Internet telephony such as Skype or FaceTime, or video and picture sharing such as YouTube or Instagram). As Herring (2010) notes, 'text-based computer-mediated communication (CMC) enjoys historical precedence . . . typed exchanges have been, and continue to be, the most typical . . . kind of computer-mediated "conversations"'. Some of these quintessential CMC genres – or indeed socio-technical modes – are chronologically outlined here.

1960s to 1980s: the Internet emerges

In its beginnings, the first computer network (ARPAnet) consisted of connections between a few American research institutions and was funded by the U.S. Department of Defense. Initially, data exchange was one of the driving forces behind the project rather than long-distance

communication; allegedly, ARPAnet creator Lawrence Roberts dismissed communicative purposes as 'not an important motivation for a network of scientific computers' (quoted in Abbate
2000: 108). Nevertheless, interactional genres soon emerged and began to thrive. Email was
invented in the early 1970s as a form of personal message exchange. Bulletin Board Systems (BBS),
an early form of public discussion forum, followed soon afterwards. With the gradual spread of
the network in the 1970s and 1980s away from military purposes and toward more generalized
usage in academic settings, email and BBSs became more established and widely available. While
BBSs such as Usenet have nowadays been complemented or overtaken by more recent forms of
discussion-centred platforms, email proved to be 'the acknowledged killer app . . . for most users'
(Herring 2004: 27) and remains one of the quintessential digital genres today.

1990s: launch of the World Wide Web (WWW)

The 1990s brought a radical change to the structure, perception and usage of the Internet.
Through the launch of the World Wide Web and the subsequent commercial rise of Internet
Service Providers, the Internet now became known and available to the general public, and set
out on an ultimately global spread. This influx of new participants led to a more diverse digital
genre ecology. In the words of Herring (2010), '(t)he mid-to-late 1990s was a "golden age" for
CMC, including public, multiparticipant textual interactions, which flourished on electronic
mailing lists, Usenet newsgroups, MUDs and MOOs, and Internet Relay Chat' (Herring 2010).
This list could be extended to include the advent of Instant Messaging in 1997, and, importantly, websites and personal homepages (Dillon & Gushrowski 2000).

2000s: emergence of the social web

The second big paradigm shift in Internet history, the emergence of 'web 2.0', is usually dated
to 2004. The term, and the more general concept of the social web and social media, refers to
a notion of Internet usership that is more active, participatory, and collaborative. It also evokes
applications and genres that are media-rich (incorporating other semiotic modes) and web- or
browser-based. Genres whose emergence falls into this era include wikis and other collaborative knowledge bases (such as Wikipedia, founded in 2001); social networks such as Friendster
(2002), MySpace (2003) or Facebook (2004); blogs (e.g. WordPress, 2003) and microblogs
such as Twitter (2006) or Tumblr (2007); and sharing platforms such as YouTube (2005) and
Pinterest (2010). As noted above, many of these genres display a move away from text-based or
text-centric CMC; nevertheless, many if not most of them still contain communicative interaction that is relevant and lends itself to analysis in terms of genre theory. Indeed, Herring has
put forward the notion of convergent media computer-mediated communication or CMCMC,
'defined as (usually text-based) interactive CMC that occurs on convergent media platforms in
which it is typically secondary, by design, to other activities, such as media viewing or game
playing' (2011: fn 9). Based on this observation, it can be speculated that in future trends
and developments in computer-mediated communication, genres involving (typed) texts and
exchanges will remain relevant regardless of other technical innovations.

Milestones in digital genre research

How did the emerging field of CMC studies frame and analyse the evolution of a digital genre
ecology? The following overview briefly highlights some of the milestone publications that

provide theoretical models and/or case studies of CMC genres. Two phases can be identified: an early phase of more general research about key CMC debates that relate to the notion of genre; and a second phase, in which the notion of digital genres was modelled and empirically explored in a more explicit and principled way.

Online communication began to attract the interest of scholars in different disciplines around the mid-eighties. By the mid-nineties, research focused on the linguistic and discourse features of online communication had somewhat solidified under the umbrella term 'computer-mediated communication'. The inception of the *Journal of Computer-Mediated Communication* in 1995, and the articles on 'Computer-mediated communication: linguistic, social and cross-cultural perspectives' collected in Herring 1996, mark the coming of age of this new discipline. Within this early framework, the notion of digital genre was not a central topic, although some neighbouring disciplines were generating related ideas; for example, Orlikowski and Yates (1994) described email as part of a 'genre repertoire' within organizations, an idea that was taken up by later approaches. However, many early contributions to the study of CMC are relevant to the notion of genre in a more implicit way. Thus many studies were concerned first and foremost with charting the field of emerging discourse modes, the 'parade of passing technologies' (Herring 2004: 36), thereby effectively providing single-genre case studies. Examples are Beißwenger (2001), Collot and Belmore (1996), and Gains (1999), which examine chat, BBSs, and email, respectively. Other approaches were less concerned with particular genres or socio-technical modes but instead addressed some of the key mechanisms and theoretical debates concerning CMC: Is language use on the Internet 'new' or 'old'? Is it more like spoken or more like written discourse? Are its features determined by technological or by social constraints? Many of these debates relate strongly to notions of digital genre, because they were in effect attempts at categorizing the digital discourse universe and uncovering and systematizing structural properties. It is not surprising, then, that many of these debates were carried over into many later works that deal with digital genre overtly.

By the turn of the millennium, the term 'genre' began to feature more prominently in studies of CMC – and increasingly, not just as an incidental descriptive term, but as a purposefully chosen framework of analysis. For example, the discussion in Erickson (2000) of an online communication platform is framed in terms of a 'genre ecology'; Watters and Shepherd (1997) describe digital newspapers as 'an evolving genre'; and Dillon and Gushrowski's (2000) analysis of homepages speculates whether they represent 'the first uniquely digital genre'. Georgakopoulou (2006) frames this changing perspective in the disciplinary evolution of CMC studies as a 'shift from the earlier taxonomic and textualist approaches to CMC genres towards more practice-based views within which genres are orienting frameworks of conventionalized expectations and routine ways of speaking and (inter)acting in specific sites and for specific purposes' (p. 552). For digital genre theory, this tendency culminated in the publication of two collected volumes on genre of digital documents (Kwasnik & Crowston 2005) and genres on the Internet (Giltrow & Stein 2009). Between the more technical, applied orientation of the former, and the broader interest in new rhetoric studies, discourse aspects, and theoretical modelling of the latter, these publications laid the ground for many further single-genre studies that draw on notions such as genre hybridity and genre repertoires or ecologies (e.g., Herring & Paolillo 2006 and Puschmann 2010 on blogs; Heyd 2008 on email hoaxes; Pérez-Sabater *et al.* 2008 on online sports commentary; Nünning *et al.* 2012 on narrative genres).

Today, the notion of genre and the tools of genre analysis have become crucial elements in the analytical repertoire of CMC studies. The following section describes a few of the major concepts, questions, and distinctions that play a role in discussions of digital genre.

Theresa Heyd

Critical issues and topics

As noted above, the study of digital genre was originally inspired by key debates in CMC studies. Nowadays, some of these critical issues and topics are more explicitly linked to the notion of genre itself. Outlining these debates, then, is a good way of approaching the field of digital genre analysis. The following five topics can be identified as central debates, and will briefly be analysed and illustrated with examples:

- level of granularity (micro vs macro, atomistic vs holistic approaches);
- formal vs functional approaches;
- remediation (new vs old, spoken vs written; the notion of bridging or hybrid genres);
- genre repertoires, ecologies, and networks;
- taxonomies, categorization, or classification.

Level of granularity

A first conceptual issue is the question of granularity, or generality, in defining digital genres. Simply put, what counts as a genre? Which level of analysis is adequate, an atomistic or a holistic one? Depending on the chosen level, a genre account of the Internet might consist of only a few broad genre labels that are very central to the digital genre ecology; or it might be very fine-grained and include hundreds or thousands of subgenres – a very detailed, but probably not very operational or meaningful account. In practical terms, this means that in one genre model, the relevant genre terms that form the basis for analysis would be *blog*, *email*, *homepage*, and others. In another, more atomistic approach, the genres under investigation might carry labels such as *corporate blog*, *chain email*, *academic department homepage*, and an open-ended list of other such specific terms.

There is a general consensus in genre theoretical debates that there is no 'right' level of granularity for the analysis of genres; rather, the level of specificity in approaching, labelling and analysing genre candidates depends very much on the theoretical framework that an account operates in. Giltrow and Stein (2009: 4–6) give a helpful overview on this and note that some approaches, such as classical rhetoric or functional linguistics, have gravitated more towards high-generality accounts with a small set of genre labels; other traditions, such as the school of New Rhetoric, have embraced a low level of generality with highly specific and situated genre labels:

> If an 'abstractive' or top-down approach is taken and only a small number of 'basic' genres is distinguished, the number of genres will be small and the issue will be one of establishing hierarchical pedigree . . . In contrast to the traditional 'modes' and to neo-classical rhetorical theory, New-Rhetorical genre theory – with its open set and lower level of generality – would not count 'narration', for example, as a genre. Instead, it would count the workplace-incident report or the medical case-history as genres: habits of speech, techniques of narrating known to some language users at some times and places.
>
> *(Giltrow & Stein 2009: 4–5)*

Regardless of the particular level of granularity that a genre analyst may choose for his or her approach, another helpful way to think about this issue is to see genre as prototypes. While there exists no fully-fledged 'prototype theory' of genre, the connection between genre labels and semantic categorization into prototypes has been made before (see, e.g., Heyd 2008: 192). In fact, Swales (1990) refers to this concept by noting that good representatives of a genre 'will be viewed as *prototypical* by the parent discourse community' (Swales 1990: 58, emphasis added). Building on this notion, it may be a helpful first step in identifying a digital genre candidate to consider whether the specific label – be it general, such as *microblog*, or very specific, such as *community photography blog* – can function as a prototype. That is, can it be categorized more or less precisely, does it refer to a significant number of more or less relevant exemplars, and does it have some recognition in a specific discourse community? Based on such criteria, a genre label may be found to be cognitively and linguistically salient to users, and therefore be identified as a good target for analysis.

Formal vs functional

A second important line of distinction which has attracted major discussion in (digital) genre theory is the form/function debate. While a distinction between formal and functional approaches is a very general epistemological issue, prevalent in virtually all of linguistic theory, its extent in genre research can be summarized along the following lines: what features should be relevant for an accurate description of genres – formal, text-centred ones (such as linguistic and structural features), functional ones (such as communicative purpose, social embedding), or a combination of these? Which features are salient for the genre perception of users? Specifically for digital genres, this discussion also touches on the question of technological determinism and its alternatives: to what degree are digital genres shaped and perceived by technological constraints or other (social) factors?

As noted in the introduction, the formal vs functional debate was at the centre of genre theoretical debates even before the advent of digital genres. A detailed account is given in Heyd (2009). Briefly summarized, many of the earlier linguistic approaches were 'formal' in the sense that their approach hinged on the identification of linguistic or structural features that are essential to particular genres. This is true, for example, in genre studies following the tradition of M. A. K. Halliday and the Sidney School (see Bhatia 1993: chapter 1 for an overview). A formal element is also strongly present in Biber's notion of text types that can be statistically identified and assessed through bivariate analysis; thus they refer to

> text categories defined in strictly linguistic terms. That is, regardless of purpose, topic, inter-activeness, or any other nonlinguistic factors, text types are defined such that the texts within each type are maximally similar with respect to their linguistic characteristics (lexical, morphological, and syntactic).
>
> *(Biber & Finegan 1994: 52)*

With the renaissance of genre theory since the 1990s, a major move toward a more functional framework has taken place. As noted above, this may have been motivated by developments in neighbouring fields such as discourse analysis and pragmatics; Giltrow and Stein (2009: 3–4) point out a 'pragmatic turn' of sorts in more recent genre theory. Influential contributions to this trend include, among others, Swales's (1990) emphasis on communicative purpose in analysing genre, and Miller's (1984) concept of genre as social action: 'a particular type of discourse classification, a classification based in rhetorical practice and consequently open rather than closed and organised around situated actions (that is, pragmatic, rather than syntactic or semantic)' (Miller 1984: 155).

As this debate became extended into the domain of CMDA, the notion of 'formal' properties gained another dimension, namely that of technical constraints and features. Kwasnik and

Crowston (2005: 77–80) acknowledge this when they describe digital genre between 'intrinsic' and 'extrinsic' features:

> Given a definition of document genre as including both socially recognised form and purpose, in studying document genres it is necessary to look at the context of use as well as the formal technical details of the documents. Nevertheless, it is possible to make a logical division between intrinsic genre attributes and the extrinsic function that genre fulfils in human activities.
>
> *(Kwasnik & Crowston 2005: 77)*

What are the implications of this debate for doing digital genre analysis? In the view of Kwasnik and Crowston (2005), this duality of approaches is an asset rather than a problem: researchers can tailor their approach to the communicative practice that they are investigating and focus on intrinsic or extrinsic features according to necessity and circumstances. In reality, many genre studies will often begin with a formal/structural analysis of the genre candidate at hand for purely practical reasons. For example, when charting Twitter as a digital genre, it is quite simply helpful to chart some of its central properties, and how they may be similar to or distinct from other digital genres. The classification scheme suggested in Herring (2007) can be a good starting point for such a formal assessment of digital genres (discussed further below). However, most genre accounts will probably not be limited to a formal description, but will also take into account the 'extrinsic' dimension of a digital genre: what is the communicative purpose, and what are the social practices that go along with this form of communication? What do users try to achieve through it, what are common perceptions or stereotypes associated with it, and what is the societal impact of the genre? The answers to such questions may be more fluid and less easily determined but they certainly contribute to a comprehensive genre analysis. Heyd (2008: chapter 7; 2009) proposes a dual model that attends to both functional super-categories of genres and formally defined subgenres that may be more specific and easily subject to change.

Remediation

Remediation, the notion that '(m)edia are continually commenting on, reproducing, and replacing each other' (Bolter & Grusin 2000: 55), was deeply ingrained in CMC studies from very early on. Just as many scholars, journalists and users have been under the impression of the overall newness of the Internet and its capacity for rapid change, this issue is also highly relevant for assessing digital genres. Indeed, the Internet provides a great testing ground for questions of genre change, genre migration, genre evolution, and other mechanisms. In their opening chapter, Giltrow and Stein (2009) explicitly address these topics with a catalogue of questions, including the following:

> Does a new medium automatically make for a new genre? Is it possible for a traditional genre in the spoken or written media to migrate into the Internet without loss of identity? How much can be lost or changed for a genre to retain its identity? Is it possible to have stability of genre across medium change?
>
> *(2009: 9)*

It can be argued that these issues of remediation are central for any theory of digital genre, and that they inform all the other key topics discussed further below. In this sense, the topic of genre remediation is closely tied to the larger discussions of CMDA, for example the supposed emergence of entirely new digital 'Netspeak' varieties, or the folk linguistic fear of the Internet as a threat to literacy and linguistic standards.

In theoretical models and empirical studies on digital genres, the answers to the questions raised above have in fact been rather moderate and, importantly, attuned to the particularities of each genre and/or sociotechnical setting. Thus genre migration into the digital sphere is possible, but it does not occur for all genres, and those which migrate may do so with adaptations that are specific and unpredictable. For example, academic articles have made a very smooth transition to the web, and even after more than a decade of vigorous online publishing initiatives, only a few structural changes have been established (such as the opportunity to provide additional data or figures online, or embedded links to other publications). In this field, the bigger changes are coming through additional, neighbouring genres that hardly touch on the existent genre, such as academic tweeting or blogging. Another interesting example is that of novels, or more generally 'books' online. Early predictions saw the rise of 'cyberfiction' as a genuinely new genre that would be stripped of most genre conventions such as linearity and be constructed around links. In reality, such experimental literature never transcended the status of a fringe genre. Instead, books have made it to the screen in the most convincing genre mimicry, through digitizing initiatives such as Google Books and through the rise of e-books.

For many digital genres, the process of remediation has indeed been highly relevant, and the resulting genre categories can aptly be described as 'hybrids' that incorporate both old and new aspects. For example, wikis as a knowledge repository certainly have a pre-digital antecedent in printed encyclopaedic references. However, the process of collaborative authoring, and the intricate processes and communicative norms associated with it, are a drastic departure from the old genre norms for the production of such texts. Another high-profile example is that of blogs, whose early popular perception in the media and also by scholars was often that of a 'digital diary' – an impression supported by the names of some of the early blogging interfaces, such as *OpenDiary* or *LiveJournal*. However, subsequent studies (Herring *et al.* 2005; Puschmann 2010) come to different conclusions, as blogging differs not only in its structure (counter-chronological posting) but also in the public communicative setting in which it operates. In this sense, blogging is aptly described as a 'bridging' genre (Herring *et al.* 2005) – a label that is probably fitting for many other digital genre candidates such as discussion forums, online shopping platforms, chat, or news sites.

At the other end of the spectrum, there is the possibility for truly new or 'emergent genres' (Crowston & Williams 2000). As the discussion to this point suggests, it is probably far more difficult to identify genres that are in fact indigenous to the Internet. Most uses of language online are modelled, at least to a degree, after existing human communicative needs; in this sense, it is not surprising that there would be at least a degree of transmedial stability (Zitzen & Stein 2004) between offline and online genre repertoires. However, exceptions to this are possible, particularly in cases where the technological possibilities are fully exploited to create new environments for communication which simply do not have a corollary in face to face communication. In the introductory discussion of a sample tweet, it already became apparent that it is difficult to succinctly trace a pre-digital antecedent for Twitter, either in the spoken or written genre continuum. Similarly, virtual worlds such as Second Life and their communicative repertoires probably have no direct offline counterpart.

A final relevant point in this context is that of genre lifecycles: the communicative relevance or necessity of a genre can change over time, both in online and offline contexts. Because of this, 'new' digital genres may become fossilized or even irrelevant over time, or they may 'recede(. . .) into the shadows' of the Internet (Herring 2004: 30). This has happened to major sociotechnical modes, such as Usenet, virtual reality systems such as MOOs and MUDs, and Internet Relay Chat; it can happen to high-profile instantiations of a sociotechnical mode, such as Friendster or MySpace; and it happens with many smaller and more specific digital genres such as email hoaxes (Heyd 2008). In this sense, it is important to keep in mind that, even on the Internet, 'new' is an unstable and relative category for genres.

Genre networks

The issues discussed so far all relate to individual genres and ways of describing and analysing them in an isolated manner. However, as many scholars have noted, genres do not exist in isolation, and genre analysis will often benefit from taking into account their interrelations. The connections between different genres may be of different types. Genres can be connected temporally, e.g. as predecessors, pre-digital antecedents, hybrid genres, or fossilized forms. They can also form hierarchical structures, e.g. between more general supergenres and more specific subgenres. But typically, genres may be related simply because they share certain features, whether structural or usage-based. For example, a discussion of newsgroups will have to make reference to email for historical reasons; an analysis of Wikipedia may incorporate genres which are structurally distinct but equally relevant, such as Wikipedia Articles, Wikipedia Talk Pages, Wikimedia, Wikiquotes, and others; a genre overview of social network sites might incorporate platforms as disparate as Facebook, last.fm and XING. In all of these cases, it is apparent that a wider perspective that takes into account neighbouring genres may be helpful for a better understanding of the discourse phenomena at hand.

The notion of genre networks, or horizontal genre relations, has been taken up in many genre theoretical and genre modelling approaches (see Heyd 2008: 196–198 for an overview). Thus terms such as 'genre set' or 'genre system' have been used to describe genres that tend to appear in sequential order out of a certain communicative logic. In the digital sphere, a pop-up advertisement, for example, may link to a travel booking website. By completing a booking procedure through several screens, the sending of a confirmation email will be triggered; this may in turn contain a link to a subsequent genre, such as an online check-in website for an air travel company. While such sequential genre patterns certainly have their place on the Internet, it is clear that there are other forms of interrelatedness that are more typical of digital genre. Orlikowski and Yates refer to genre repertoires, which emphasize shared practice within discourse communities:

> Members of a community rarely depend on a single genre for communication. Rather, they tend to use multiple, different, and interacting genres over time. Thus to understand a community's communicative practices, we must examine the set of genres that are routinely enacted by the community. We designate such a set a community's 'genre repertoire'.
>
> *(1994: 542)*

While this approach was initially geared specifically towards discourse communities in white-collar workplaces, it is easy to see how the concept could also be applied to online communities more generally. For example, many bloggers are also users of Twitter (e.g. for reasons of cross-promotion), and this in turn may often prompt the use of embedded genres such as Instagram. It is even conceivable that large-scale social network sites such as Facebook, with their broad array of different communicative functionalities such as liking, following, chatting, messaging and others, could be described as one multi-faceted genre repertoire.

Arguably, the concept that has gained most traction in digital genre theory is that of digital genre ecologies, proposed independently by Erickson (2000) and Spinuzzi and Zachry (2000). In his description of an integrated CMC platform in a specific workplace, Erickson points to

> an ecology of conversational genres, in which the various conversational genres are inter-dependent and act – in a variety of ways – to support the functioning of the system as a whole (. . .) a more relaxed version of a genre system which pays particular attention to how participants are recruited into different genres.
>
> *(Erickson 2000)*

Both Erickson and Spinuzzi and Zachry use visualizations of such genre ecologies to map the interrelatedness and relative closeness or distance of items, as well as the dynamics that exist between them.

The metaphor of a genre ecology to refer to notions of genre co-occurrence, co-existence and overlap has become a part of digital genre theory. This may in part be due to the evocative nature of the metaphor, which equates different genres with organic structures which may have a certain life-cycle and interact with other genres; it is also reminiscent of the use of the word 'ecology' in sociolinguistics (Mufwene 2001; Mühlhäusler 1995). But most of all, this way of modelling simply seems to resonate with the communicative environment of the Internet. Kwasnik and Crowston make this very clear as they adopt the term and generalize it:

> we extend [Erickson's] apt metaphor because it captures succinctly how, like any organism in an ecological community, genres have effects on each other and depend on each other for their effectiveness. They evolve over time, some slowly, some more rapidly. Some genres, under the right conditions, can supplant others. Genres exist in habitats or communities of practice. The notion of genre ecologies becomes all the more salient for digital environments as we observe two phenomena occurring more or less simultaneously: the migration of traditional genres to the web and the emergence of new genres unique to the web. These genres merge or divide, transform and evolve.
>
> *(2005: 81–82)*

This broad sense of genre ecologies has been adopted in a number of case studies, such as Herring *et al.* (2005), Heyd (2008), Puschmann (2010), Freund *et al.* (2011), and others. Such studies demonstrate that the notion of a textual 'ecosystem' meshes well with the nature of genres – particularly digital ones – as it captures the flexible and evolving nature of such systems and pays special attention to the interrelatedness between different genre categories.

Taxonomies, categorization, or classification

Finally, out of the notion of genre interrelatedness arises another issue: where do we look at genre ecologies in context, and how should they and their differences be organized and analysed? This is first and foremost an epistemological question about how we actually perceive discourse continua. However, it also has implications for the actual practice of doing genre analysis. Three ways of structuring genre ecologies are briefly outlined here: taxonomies, categorization, and classification.

Taxonomies do not play a central role in (digital) genre theory. They are usually conceived of as mere lists of genre labels; they evoke notions of closed sets that are considered as final. Miller, in her outline of genre as social action, makes this point:

> Genre study is valuable not because it might permit the creation of some kind of taxonomy, but because it emphasises some social and historical aspects of rhetoric that other perspectives do not (. . .) [Genre] does not lend itself to taxonomy, for genres change, evolve, and decay; the number of genres current in any society is indeterminate and depends upon the complexity and diversity of the society.
>
> *(1984: 151, 163)*

The implication here is very clear: taxonomies are viewed as overly stable and simplistic and do not do justice to the actual richness of genre ecologies. This view is shared by many digital discourse researchers, and the notion of taxonomical lists plays only a marginal role here. (However, see approaches such as Biber and Kurijan (2006), where an attempt is made to chart the field of 'web registers and text types' with the help of multidimensional analysis.)

Categorization is arguably the concept that is most relevant to genre analysis in its most immediate sense. The notion of categories – more or less discrete cognitive and linguistic entities – is closely tied to the notion of prototypes outlined above. In this sense, a genre can be seen as a category; instantiations of the genre would be described as exemplars of the category. This is an epistemological approach that meshes particularly well with digital genres where they are seen in terms of sociotechnical modes – as forms of social action that depend at least to a degree on their technological mediation. Thus it has been observed that some genre labels may suggest a wide diversity of instantiations, where in fact they are typically used to refer to a few select or even a single digital platform. Thus 'microblogging' is almost exclusively used to refer to Twitter usage; and while 'social network' covers a wide variety of applications and genre instantiations, the genre label was used almost synonymously with Facebook for several years. The conceptualization of digital genre as categorization is explored more fully in Giltrow and Stein (2009) (see in particular contributions by Devitt, Heyd, and Puschmann).

Finally, classification is a slightly different way of systematizing genres. In CMDA, it has become an important concept through the influential model suggested in Herring (2007) precisely because it functions in a different way than categorization. Classification, in a way, is a move back to more formal and fine-grained genre descriptions; it is a method of analysis that pays close attention to linguistic and other communicative features and strives to systematize them and make abstractions about them. Herring outlines some of the central issues of digital genres and sociotechnical modes discussed in this overview, such as the unclear level of specificity, or the fact that genres 'are most easily applied to classify discourse that takes place using established, named technologies (cf. Swales 1990), such as those that are popular on the Internet' (Herring 2007). Instead, she proposes a multi-faceted classification scheme that

> cut(s) across the boundaries of socio-technical modes, and combine(s) to allow for the identification of a more nuanced set of computer-mediated discourse types, while avoiding the imprecision associated with the concept of genre. . . . The scheme is intended primarily as a faceted lens through which to view CMD data in order to facilitate linguistic analysis, especially research conducted in the discourse analysis, conversation analysis, pragmatics, and sociolinguistics traditions.
>
> *(Herring 2007, np)*

In this sense, classification as an analytical approach may be of less interest to the researcher who is interested in genre structures per se, and who therefore embraces the holistic view discussed above in terms of genre ecologies. However, classification of texts has its strengths where an in-depth analysis of linguistic and non-linguistic features is needed in order to provide a fine-grained description of specific textual artefacts.

It is beyond the scope of this chapter to fully outline the classification approach. However, it should be noted that categorization and classification are by no means mutually exclusive. Herring emphasizes this point: '[The scheme] is intended to complement genre or mode-based analyses, which can provide a convenient shorthand for categorising CMD types, but are less precise and flexible' (2007). In this sense, both categorization and classification can be seen as valuable tools for CMC scholars who engage with digital discourse and attempt to identify meaningful patterns in their linguistic and communicative makeup.

Current research and future directions in genre analysis

In 2005, Kwasnik and Crowston made the following observation about the state of digital genre research at the time:

> As researchers at this point in history, we have the luxury of observing the transition of forms and traditions of communication from the start of the electronic era to its present tumultuous and lively development and on to an expected future stabilisation. Most of us are not only familiar with life before the web, but have by now experienced some of the transitions in use first-hand and have had an opportunity to reflect on them . . . a viewpoint that may no longer be possible in another ten years. That is, in the near future, we may no longer be able to remember what it was like to participate in organisational life without e-mail, or in a consumer purchase transaction that is not supported at least in part by a web site presence.
>
> *(2005: 77)*

A decade later, we can confirm that much has changed indeed, and that these are far-reaching changes that will have an impact on digital genre theory. For one thing, the first generation of those 'born digital' (Palfrey & Gasser 2008) is coming of age, so that there are an increasing number of users who do not have a concept of life without digital genres. However, the prognosis of an 'expected future stabilisation' of the digital genre continuum has so far not come true. In fact, it seems that the pace of change in the digital world has not slowed down one bit; the 'parade of passing technologies' (Herring 2004: 34) is progressing faster than ever. Two tendencies may be pointed out, both loosely associated with the notion of media convergence (Herring 2011), and both will have to be attended to by digital genre theory, namely browser-based digital communication and mobile computing.

The migration of most digital genres, applications and practices to the web, and specifically to the browser, is almost complete. This development has taken two decades to evolve. It began with services such as Usenet and Internet Relay Chat that were integrated into web environments; next, webmail became a widespread alternative to locally installed email clients. But the trend has not stopped there. Nowadays, browser-based computer use includes practices such as using office applications (e.g. Google Docs), storing data (e.g. Dropbox) and consuming music (e.g. Pandora). Even the distinction between different medium domains such as TV vs Internet is becoming less clear-cut, as many media products do not just migrate to the web, but are in fact being produced exclusively for web-based consumption. Increasingly, these issues fall under the header of 'digital-born materials', and their treatment touches upon many issues that are also relevant to digital genre theory (see Erway 2010 for an overview). In particular, it seems likely that the trend toward indigenously digital material will change our existing notions of how pre-digital and digital genres are related.

Theresa Heyd

This tendency toward convergence is accompanied by the trend for mobile web use. Through smartphones and other handheld devices, the notion of being 'always on' (Baron 2008) has almost come full circle. Many items in daily life now can be connected to the Internet, including TV sets, gaming consoles, (e-)books; this trend toward the 'Internet of things' is currently spreading to cars, garments, and household appliances. The next generation of digital genre studies will have to take into account this turn toward material culture. As the discussion in this chapter has shown, digital genre analysis is firmly anchored in the tradition of CMDA, and as such tends to rely on the methods and parameters that have been established in predigital research on genre. In digital genre studies, this textual tradition has been enriched by a sociotechnical view; the next step might be to embrace a *material* perspective on how we do things with digital discourse: which devices, appliances or other commodities are involved in and needed for the production and reception of digital text? Which are the everyday settings in which these new semiotic codes become relevant?

As a specific first consequence, many digital genres have emerged or migrated to a new instantiation as applications, or apps, for this new generation of digital devices. It is a task for future research on digital genre to illuminate the impact of this large-scale 'appification' on the digital genre continuum: do apps constitute extensions of established genres? Are they sufficiently new formats to be perceived as distinctly new genres? It remains to be seen whether these ongoing changes can also be captured under the notion of remediation, or whether digital genre theory can provide a more tailored description of digital genre change in the twenty-first century.

In a wider sense, it is very likely that entirely new forms of digital communication are emerging. Early case studies such as Honeycutt and Herring (2009) point in the direction for future research on convergent digital genres, but much remains to be done. How will this new digital genre ecology be structured, and how will it be employed and perceived by Internet users? Digital genre theory has yet to chart this evolving discourse continuum and the next phase of digital remediation.

Related topics

- Chapter 1 Approaches to language variation (Hinrichs)
- Chapter 4 Multimodal analysis (Jewitt)
- Chapter 20 Online communities and communities of practice (Angouri)

References

Abbate, J. 2000, *Inventing the Internet*, MIT Press, Cambridge, MA.
Baron, N. 2008, *Always on: language in an online and mobile world*, Oxford University Press, Oxford.
Beißwenger, M. (ed.) 2001, *Chat-Kommunikation. Sprache, Interaktion, Sozialität und Identität in synchroner computervermittelter Kommunikation. Perspektiven auf ein interdisziplinäres Forschungsfeld*, Ibidem Verlag, Stuttgart.
Bhatia, V. K. 1993, *Analysing genre*, Longman, London.
Biber, D. & Finegan, E. (eds.) 1994, *Sociolinguistic perspectives on register*, Oxford University Press, Oxford.
Biber, D. & Kurijan, J. 2006, 'Towards a taxonomy of web registers and text types: a multidimensional analysis', in M. Hundt, N. Nesselhauf & C. Biewer (eds.) *Corpus linguistics and the web*, Rodopi, Amsterdam, pp. 109–131.
Bolter, J. D. & Grusin, R. 2000, *Remediation: understanding new media*, MIT Press, Cambridge, MA.
Collot, M. & Belmore, N. 1996, 'Electric language: a new variety of English', in S. C. Herring (ed.) *Computer-mediated communication: linguistic, social and cross-cultural perspectives*, Benjamins, Amsterdam, pp. 13–28.

Crowston, K. & Williams, M. 2000, 'Reproduced and emergent genres of communication on the World-Wide Web', *Information Society*, vol. 16, no. 3, pp. 201–215.

Dillon, A. & Gushrowksi, B. 2000, 'Genres and the WEB: is the personal home page the first uniquely digital genre?', *Journal of the American Society for Information Science*, vol. 51, no. 2, pp. 202–205.

Erickson, T. 2000, 'Making sense of computer-mediated communication (CMC): conversations as genres, CMC systems as genre ecologies', *Proceedings of the 33rd Hawaii international conference on system sciences (HICSS-33)*, January 4–7, 2000, Big Island, Hawaii, available at: http://ieeexplore.ieee.org/xpl/free-abs_all.jsp?arnumber=926694.

Erway, R. 2010, 'Defining born digital', *Online Computer Library Center*, available at: http://www.oclc.org/research/activities/hiddencollections/bornditgital.pdf.

Freund, L., Berzowska, J., Lee, J., Read, K., & Schiller, H. 2011, 'Digging into Digg: genres of online news', *Proceedings of the 2011 iConference*, New York, NY, ACM, pp. 674–765.

Gains, J. 1999, 'Electronic mail: a new style of communication or just a new medium? An investigation into the text features of e-mail', *English for Specific Purposes*, vol. 18, no. 1, pp. 81–101.

Georgakopoulou, A. 2006, 'Postscript: computer-mediated communication in sociolinguistics', *Journal of Sociolinguistics*, vol. 10, no. 4, pp. 548–557.

Giltrow, J. & Stein, D. (eds.) 2009, *Genres in the Internet: issues in the theory of genre*, Benjamins, Amsterdam.

Herring, S. 2011, 'Computer-mediated conversation, part II: introduction and overview', *language@internet*, vol. 8, no. 2, available at: http://www.languageatinternet.org/articles/2011/Herring.

Herring, S. 2010, 'Computer-mediated conversation, part I: introduction and overview', *language@internet*, vol. 7, no. 2, available at: http://www.languageatinternet.org/articles/2010/2801.

Herring, S. 2007, 'A faceted classification scheme for computer-mediated discourse', *language@internet*, vol. 4, no. 1, available at: http://www.languageatinternet.org/articles/2007/761.

Herring, S. 2004, 'Slouching toward the ordinary: current trends in computer-mediated communication', *New Media & Society*, vol. 6, no. 1, pp. 26–36.

Herring, S. (ed.) 1996, *Computer-mediated communication: linguistic, social and cross-cultural perspectives*, Benjamins, Amsterdam.

Herring, S. & Paolillo, J. 2006, 'Gender and genre variation in weblogs', *Journal of Sociolinguistics*, vol. 10, no. 4, pp. 439–459.

Herring, S., Scheidt, L. A., Wright, E. & Bonus, S. 2005, 'Weblogs as a bridging genre', *Information Technology & People*, vol. 18, no. 2, pp. 142–171.

Heyd, T. 2009, 'A model for describing "new" and "old" properties of CMC genres: the case of digital folklore', in D. Stein & J. Giltrow (eds.) *Genres in the Internet: issues in the theory of genre*, Benjamins, Amsterdam, pp. 239–262.

Heyd, T. 2008, *Email hoaxes: form, function, genre ecology*, Benjamins, Amsterdam.

Honeycutt, C. & Herring, S. 2009, 'Beyond microblogging: conversation and collaboration via Twitter', *Proceedings of the forty-second Hawai'i international conference on system sciences (HICSS-42)*, Los Alamitos, CA, IEEE Press, pp. 1–10.

Kwasnik, B. H. & Crowston, K. (eds.) 2005, *Information Technology and People*, vol. 18, no. 2, Special issue: Genres of digital documents.

Mehler, A., Sharoff, S. & Santini, M. (eds.) 2010, *Genres on the web: computational models and empirical studies*, Springer, Dordrecht, Germany.

Miller, C. R. 1984, 'Genre as social action', *Quarterly Journal of Speech*, vol. 70, no. 2, pp. 151–167.

Moessner, L. 2001, 'Genre, text type, style, register: a terminological maze?', *European Journal of English Studies*, vol. 5, no. 2, pp. 131–138.

Mühlhäusler, P. 1995, *Linguistic ecology: language change and linguistic imperialism in the Pacific Rim*, Routledge, London.

Mufwene, S. 2001, *The ecology of language evolution*, Cambridge University Press, Cambridge.

Nünning, A., Rupp, J., Hagelmoser, R. and Meyer, J. I. (eds.) 2012, *Narrative genres im Internet: theoretische Bezugsrahmen, Mediengattungstypologie und Funktionen*, WVT, Trier.

Orlikowski, W. & Yates, J. 1994, 'Genre repertoire: examining the structuring of communicative practices in organizations', *Administrative Science Quarterly*, vol. 39, pp. 541–574.

Palfrey, J. & Gasser, U. 2008, *Born digital: understanding the first generation of digital natives*, Basic Books, London.

Pérez-Sabater, C., Peña-Martínez, G., Turney, E. & Montero-Fleta, B. 2008, 'A spoken genre gets written: online football commentaries in English, French and Spanish', *Written Communication*, vol. 25, no. 2, pp. 235–261.

Puschmann, C. 2010, *The corporate blog as an emerging genre of computer-mediated communication: features, constraints, discourse situation*, Universitätsverlag, Göttingen.

Spinuzzi, C. & Zachry, M. 2000, 'Genre ecologies: an open-system approach to understanding and constructing documentation', *ACM Journal of Computer Documentation*, vol. 24, no. 3, pp. 169–181.

Swales, J. M. 1990, *Genre analysis*, Cambridge University Press, Cambridge.

Watters, C. R. & Shepherd, M. A. 1997, 'The digital broadsheet: an evolving genre', *Proceedings of the 30th annual Hawaii international conference on systems sciences (HICSS 30)*, January 8–10, 1997, Big Island, Hawaii, available at: http://csdl2.computer.org/comp/proceedings/hicss/1997/7734/06/7734060022.pdf.

Zitzen, M. & Stein, D. 2004, 'Chat and conversation: a case of transmedial stability?', *Linguistics*, vol. 42, no. 5, pp. 983–1021.

Further reading

Bolter, J. D. & Grusin, R. 2000, *Remediation: understanding new media*, MIT Press, Cambridge, MA.

This early classic on digital theory provides key insights on the process of reproduction, recycling and replacement in mediated environments.

Giltrow, J. & Stein, D. (eds.) 2009, *Genres in the Internet: issues in the theory of genre*. Benjamins, Amsterdam.

This collection of essays and case studies provides a broad overview on the theory and practice of digital genre analysis.

Herring, S. 2007, 'A faceted classification scheme for computer-mediated discourse', *language@internet*, vol. 4, no. 1, available at: http://www.languageatinternet.org/articles/2007/761.

This paper provides concise distinctions between terms such as categorization and classification, genre and sociotechnical mode; its classification scheme is widely used in the analysis of digital discourse.

Kwasnik, B. H. & Crowston, K. (eds.) 2005, *Information Technology and People*, vol. 18, no. 2, Special issue: Genres of digital documents.

This special issue is essential reading for anyone interested in digital genre theory as it contains a number of seminal articles for this field of research.

Mehler, A., Sharoff, S. & Santini, M. (eds.) 2010, *Genres on the web: computational models and empirical studies*, Springer, Dordrecht.

This collection provides a state-of-the-art look at more technical aspects of digital genre theory.

6

Style, creativity and play

Yukiko Nishimura

Introduction

This chapter explores how creativity and play can characterize entertainment-oriented, private realms of digital communication such as bulletin board interaction and text messaging. The focus is on style, which is viewed in terms of users' choices in making meaning when interacting with others (Coupland 2007). Style, in its most general sense, refers to a way of doing something; this, however, is a pivotal theoretical construct in sociolinguistic variation studies (Rickford & Eckert 2001) and is employed here as a lens through which to observe manifestations of creativity and play in digital discourse. Creativity is "the ability to come up with ideas or artefacts that are *new, surprising and valuable*" (Boden 2004: 1). Boden (2004: 2) makes a distinction between psychological creativity (P creativity) and historical creativity (H creativity), often referred to as small c creativity and big C Creativity, respectively (Jones 2012: 2). While the latter belongs to distinguished geniuses who have impacted the course of history, the former iss concerned with how ordinary people come up with new things in their everyday experiences, which is the focus of this chapter. Play is used here not only in the sense of text-based language play (e.g., Cook 2000; Crystal 1998), but also refers more widely to various activities including visual and graphic play (Danet 2001), in view of increasing multimodality in digital technologies. Regarding how creativity is related to play, Swann and Maybin (2007) mention that "the use of 'play'/'humor' and 'creativity' by some researchers for similar linguistic and discursive phenomena, sometimes interchangeably, can lead to the potential for conceptual muddiness, if not confusion" (p. 492). They also caution that although playfulness or humor can be a potential characteristic of linguistic creativity, "not all creative episodes are playful" (p. 492). Here, attempts will be made to differentiate the two in communicative behavior, though they characteristically overlap in non-serious online interaction.

The following section surveys how style, creativity and play have been approached in existing literature. This review provides the background for a discussion of current issues and topics concerning creativity and play in digital communication. This body of language-focused research has largely been concerned with textual interactions in English. To address this bias, the chapter extends the investigation of online creativity and play to non-English contexts, specifically Japanese, to reveal common and language-specific features, which broaden our understanding of the nature and variety of ludic digital communication. The discussion then turns to methods for researching these topics, an area where analysts may often face challenges

(King 2009). The chapter concludes with a consideration of future research directions in view of globally expanding digital communication.

Historical perspectives on style, creativity and play

Style

Style is a notion found in a number of disciplines, such as art and architecture. In literary criticism and other language-related fields, "**style** refers to the . . . manners of EXPRESSION in writing or speaking. . . . [style] has EVALUATIVE connotations . . . [and] can be seen as variation in language use, ... **Style variation** occurs . . . according to MEDIUM and degree of FORMALITY" (Wales 2011: 397, original emphases). One classic descriptive study of spoken English identifies intimate, casual, consultative, formal and frozen styles (Joos 1967), which vary according to situations and/or levels of formality.

In sociolinguistics, inspired by Labov's (1966) pioneering study in New York City, the theory of "audience design" posits that "style is essentially speakers' response to their audience" (Bell 1984: 145). A typical example of this is baby talk, or infant/child-directed speech, which demonstrates that a speaker may change his or her way of speaking, or style, according to his or her addressee or audience in order to be accepted in interaction.

In a more contemporary view from socio-cultural/anthropological linguistics, "linguistic style is defined . . . as relentless epiphenomenal process, a context-sensitive interaction between speakers' balance of innovative and conventional elements in their repertoire and hearers' expectations" (Mendoza-Denton 2001: 235). In corpus linguistics, Biber and Conrad (2009) regard style as different from register in the interpretation of the characteristic features observed in text excerpts. From a perspective of register, "features serve communicative functions," while from a perspective of style they are not "directly functional: they are aesthetically valued"; style thus involves "aesthetic preferences" (Biber & Conrad 2009: 18). For this reason, style is more likely to be associated with literary analysis, while register belongs to the terminology of linguistics. The aesthetic or evaluative connotations of style are helpful in the subsequent discussion of creativity and playfulness, as they raise questions about who evaluates or recognizes certain linguistic choices (and hence style) as creative and/or playful.

Another relevant view on style is provided by scholars working on stylistic variation (e.g., Coupland 2007; Eckert 2012; Eckert & Rickford 2001; Schilling-Estes 2004). Style is considered to involve "ways of speaking—how speakers use the resource of language variation to make meaning in social encounters" (Coupland 2007: i). Through stylistic choices, one can achieve the "creation and re-creation of individual and interpersonal identity" (Schilling-Estes 2004: 394), regardless of whether it is in face-to-face or online interaction. While early studies of style classify and label certain linguistic/stylistic features, more contemporary research tells us that stylistic choices are reflections of self-presentation, which involve agency (Eckert 2012). In the context of CMC research, such approaches to style and its evaluative associations are useful in considering creativity and play, in that technologically mediated discourse exhibits elements frequently associated with creativity and play. These "creative styles" are favored and playfully employed by users, as can be readily observed in CMC contexts. As we will see, these conceptualizations of style are relevant for the review of creativity and play that follows.

Creativity

Creativity has also been discussed widely in a number of fields such as psychology (e.g., Runco 2006) and education (e.g., Craft et al. 2001). In linguistics, Chomsky's influential contributions to notions of creativity (e.g., 1965) cannot be overlooked, though his interest in linguistic competence (the speaker–hearer's knowledge of his language) rather than in performance (the actual use of language in concrete situations) places them outside the scope of this chapter.

The distinction between C creativity (of geniuses) and c creativity (of ordinary people) mentioned earlier is articulated by Carter and McCarthy (2004: 83), who claim that creative language use "is not a capacity of special people but a special capacity of all people." More concretely, Carter and McCarthy (1995) observe the creative manipulation of linguistic forms among people in everyday conversation. Vo and Carter (2010: 303) explain such manipulation as "*pattern-reforming*, i.e. creativity by displacement of fixedness, reforming and reshaping patterns of language, and *pattern-forming*, i.e. creativity via conformity to language rules rather than breaking them." Furthermore, the sharp distinction between literary and ordinary language has been recognized to be unhelpful (Carter 2004), because the criteria for literary analyses can also be applied to non-literary, ordinary language. This is due to recent advances in creativity research, especially the availability of electronically stored corpora. Swann and Maybin (2007: 491) state that "creativity may be identified broadly as a property of all language use in that language users do not simply reproduce but recreate, refashion, and recontextualise linguistic and cultural resources in the act of communicating."

Jones (2010, 2012) poses a challenge to these views of language creativity, which have dominated recent sociolinguistics and applied linguistic literature. For Jones, it is problematic to dichotomize big C creativity and small c creativity, or what does and does not count as creativity, because "there is a lot in between" (Jones 2012: 2). Jones further questions whether creativity refers to a text (or artefact), or the process whereby people attempt to produce such an artefact, that is, whether creativity resides in the textual (or other form of) output or in people' activities. Jones thus proposes a "discourse and creativity" approach in which creativity is viewed "as residing not just in language itself but in the actions people take with language" (Jones 2012: 7). Though we can infer creative processes through surface output products when considering creativity, the "discourse and creativity" approach advanced by Jones, as opposed to the "language and creativity" approach of Carter and his colleagues, seems to be more helpful in discussing creative practices. It also allows us to take into consideration how users' choices represent their identities. Just looking at the output product without taking account of its outer contexts makes it difficult to reach a better understanding of this process. A similar approach that incorporates the users and their identities can be adopted in the treatment of "play."

Play and playfulness

Play in online environments covers a wide range of activities such as performing characters/roles, engaging in games, and displaying language play. Indeed, play can be seen as one of the key elements characterising human culture, as Huizinga (1955) notes in his seminal work, *Homo Ludens*. Huizinga (1955: 8) states that the first main characteristic of play is freedom; the second is "that play is not 'ordinary' or 'real life.' It is rather a stepping out of 'real' life into a temporary sphere of activity with a disposition all of its own."

These characterizations are well suited to users' online play, as the Internet affords anonymous environments where participants can be freed from "real" life and can forge, manipulate and experiment with language so as to create online identities (see also Newon, this volume). Participants can thus creatively employ various stylistic resources to enjoy multiple identities, for example, by presenting themselves as the opposite sex in digital environments. Danet (1998) describes such experiments with gender in interactive writing online. Danet (1998: 146–148) concludes her article with a set of research questions for future investigations, which include:

Yukiko Nishimura

"What types of personae do players create? What are the similarities and differences between the games played at RL [real life] carnivals and masked balls and those in MUDs [Multi User Dungeons] and IRC [Internet Relay Chat] channels? What is the wider cultural significance of experimentation with gender on-line?"

Other contributions to researching play online include Danet (1995), Danet et al. (1995), Danet et al. (1997) and Danet (2001), *Cyberpl@y*. The last work explores visual and playful properties in email, chat, IRC and MUDs and the World Wide Web based on nine years of ethnographic observation and research. Danet (2001) discusses textual, theatrical and aesthetic aspects of playful online interactions. Note that these studies by Danet (1998, 2001) and her collaborators appeared at an early stage when the Internet was not as widespread as it is today. In this sense these works, especially Danet's (2001) book-length monograph, are important as the first scholarly efforts to analyze play and playfulness online. No comparable work has appeared since.

Common features characterizing language use online across different genres such as email, chat and text messaging include abbreviation, unconventional spelling, acronyms, emoticons and other features (e.g., Crystal 2001). These are considered to "represent the inherently ludic character of language use on the Internet" (Herring *et al.* 2013: 8). Such language use has been observed widely on the Internet, and much of it can be regarded as playful and/or creative. Here again, a perspective oriented toward users rather than toward text-as-product can be taken to examine play and playfulness in order to understand how each user's linguistic/stylistic choices are related to representing his or her identities.

In the light of the above review of background literature on style, creativity and play, I will move to issues critical to investigating creativity and play in interactions online, including the recognition of certain text styles as creative and/or playful in relation to text-producing agents in broader social and cultural contexts.

Critical issues and topics

Recognition/evaluation of creativity and play

This section will discuss creativity and play from the perspective of those who recognize text excerpts as creative, including participants, addressees, researchers and outsiders such as journalists. A comparison of studies by Werry (1996) and North (2007) is useful here, because these works discuss features generally identified as common to and characteristic of digital communication (Herring *et al.* 2013). The former is representative of an early era of study, when features such as unconventional spelling and abbreviation were felt to be novel, while the latter appeared when knowledge and research on such language use had accumulated.

At the time when CMC was still new, Werry (1996) identified four major properties in Internet Relay Chat (IRC): 1) addressivity, 2) abbreviation, 3) paralinguistic and prosodic cues, 4) actions and gestures. Werry regards orthographic ingenuities as the most interesting and characteristic features of the language used on IRC. Such ingenuities are intended to reproduce "paralinguistic and prosodic" qualities of face-to-face (FTF) conversation such as voice, gesture and tone through unique uses of capitalization, spelling and punctuation. Werry thus finds that participants employ a number of "innovative," "creative" linguistic strategies to compensate for and adapt to the constraints imposed on CMC to reproduce the style of FTF communication. This study was among the first to examine language and interaction online, and Werry shed new light on previously unknown aspects of IRC communication. The recognition of these as "innovative" and "creative"—an assessment presumably made by the analyst—was among the key findings conveyed to his readers.

North's (2007) study gives a different interpretation of "creativity." In her examination of messages posted to an online discussion board, North (2007: 542) states that "the mere fact of using them [emoticons, abbreviations and similar features] cannot be regarded as creative in itself. They have by now become conventional within [the] chat environment." This remark implies that because these features are not new anymore (i.e., they are used by a lot of people), this use is not creative. The recognition or assessment of the use of certain language features as conventionalized, which North's point seems to be based on, can also vary. Indeed, the concept of something being conventional seems irrelevant to the concept of creativity, as everyday creativity is considered to reside in the process of people using language rather than creativity residing in the product (i.e., the text). The assessment of the use of certain features as creative or not cannot be made hastily.

One further comment on the recognition of creativity is how a textual product is received by the public in general, including journalists. It is not surprising that some novel, unfamiliar language use receives unfavorable comments (Tagliamonte & Denis 2008). For instance, a sample of a Scottish schoolgirl's homework, which was widely circulated in British news media, appropriated the style of texting and began with "My smmr hols wr CWOT . . . " (Shortis 2007; Thurlow 2006). These reports generated a number of negative reactions from the public—unfortunately, what may have been recognized as creative by language researchers or by peers did not earn such a favorable assessment from teachers and journalists. Submitting a writing assignment in an educational setting requires adherence to norms of appropriateness that are quite different from those governing texting among friends; the leakage of the schoolgirl's genre-bending style into the public sphere transformed what might have been a minor transgression into a public outcry. Though these innovative communicative practices receive harsh comments from the news media in today's commercialized political world, Thurlow and Bell (2009) and Thurlow (2012) offer outspoken support. Thurlow (2012: 186) suggests that young people's new media practices ought to be properly recognized for their creativity and cultural significance. It is thus necessary for researchers working on creativity to incorporate into their analyses a consideration of who evaluates whose practices and in what way.

Creativity observed in play

Thurlow (2012) analyzes the nature of (small c) creativity in young people's interactions in new media and identifies creativity both in the language use (product-based view) and the process of people using the language. Specifically, Thurlow gives a list of the forms that manifestations of creative practices take in text-based new media, such as "type play" (capitalization), "word play" (punning), "interactional play" (teasing), "identity play" (gender-swapping), "sound play" (accent stylization, and "topical play" (experimenting with norms of appropriateness), many of which are not simply orthographic, but also interactional (p. 179). Such a classification of the kinds of play provides a useful frame of reference for analyzing creativity and play online.

Style in the realization of creativity and play

As Bell (1984) argued in his influential introduction of audience design, style is an interactional phenomenon in which language users take into account the presence of an audience in the production of discourse. Stylistic features associated with texting are widespread in other contexts of digital communication. In a chat interaction or discussion-board environment, where almost everyone employs the creative features of new media language described by Thurlow (2012), a participant employing standard spelling and grammar would stand out and would most likely receive no response. Conversely, where the community interaction normatively takes place in standard language (e.g., a certain community regulator expects its participants to maintain a specific language and follow established guidelines), texting style is not acceptable. Notice also that creativity and play can be achieved in both standard and texting styles. Participants choose the style that is suitable for their presentation of identities, as well as adjusting to their audience's style and complying with community standards. This perspective of style confirms that creative language use is observable in digital communication, as is playful language use. The presumed "creative" (texting) style is not the only kind observed in digital communication.

The research reviewed in this section has mostly been concerned with the English language. In the next section, I will present research findings from non-English contexts, specifically Japanese, to explore common and language-specific phenomena from broader perspectives.

Current contributions and research

Creativity and play in English and non-English digital communication

In this section, current research on interactions in English and non-English languages will be reviewed to broaden our understanding of the nature and variety of creativity and play in digital communication.

A special issue of the online *Journal of Computer-Mediated Communication* on "The Multilingual Internet" (Danet & Herring (eds.) 2003) is among the most prominent works to address the research gap in non-English digital communication. The languages explored include not only other European languages such as Swiss, Greek, Catalan-Spanish and Portuguese, but also non-alphabet-based languages spoken in other parts of the world: Gulf Arabic, Taiwanese Mandarin, Thai and Japanese. The Japanese-focused article (Nishimura 2003b) discusses how young users of a Japanese online discussion board creatively and playfully manipulate language to meet their interactional purposes online, while compensating for and adapting to the digital environment. These collected papers resulted in an edited volume, *The Multilingual Internet: Language, Culture and Communication Online* (Danet & Herring 2007), which incorporates additional articles on languages not included in the online journal, including Hong Kong Cantonese, French, German and Swedish. Another article on Japanese chat rooms discusses emoticons in depth (Katsuno & Yano 2007).

One phenomenon concerning play in CMC is "leet" speak, which is "an alternative alphabet for the English language," according to Wikipedia. The word "leet," an idiosyncratic rendering of "elite," can be expressed as "1337" and "l33t"; "eleet" may be spelled "31337" or "3l33t" (Wikipedia). Wikipedia explains:

> Leet originated within bulletin board systems (BBS) in the 1980s, where having "elite" status on a BBS allowed a user access to file folders, games, and special chat rooms. One theory is that it was developed to defeat text filters created by BBS or Internet Relay Chat system operators for message boards to discourage the discussion of forbidden topics, like cracking and hacking.

For more on hackers' jargons, see Raymond (1998). Leet speak and some hacker terminology is a source of the language play seen online today, such as using the number "2" instead of "to," or replacing words with symbols having similar-sounding names.

Despite huge linguistic differences between English and Japanese in various respects, it is interesting to see that the Japanese language has equivalents to leet speak, which may be due to the shared Internet culture of computer users in both countries. Such orthographic innovations

Table 6.1 Examples of Gal script

Gal script	こ ω L= ちレ£ レ十″ w (キ
Standard (*hiragana*)	こ ん に ち は げ ん き
Roomaji (pronunciation)	ko n ni chi wa ge n ki
English translation	"Hello, are you well?"

can be found throughout Internet (sub)culture, for example in Channel 2 BBS (Nishimura 2003a, 2008). One Japanese equivalent of English leet speak is "gal script," which functions as a secret language among teenage girls to secure solidarity. Table 6.1 above illustrates this.

Notice that all the *hiragana* scripts have corresponding gal scripts. This table shows gal scripts used for the *hiragana*, nん, niに, waは, geげ, and kiき.

As the table indicates, orthography plays an important role in understanding playfulness in Japanese CMC. The Japanese language employs four distinct scripts: two *kana* syllabaries, *hiragana* and *katakana*; the logographic *kanji*; and the *roomaji* or Roman alphabet for transliteration of Western words (Nishimura 2003b). Since one word can be written in several ways, the variety of script choices (Smith & Schmidt 1996) impacts how messages are constructed and interpreted in Japanese CMC. These four Japanese scripts, a number of additional scripts from other languages (e.g. ξ from Greek, д from Cyrillic) and even non-linguistic symbols (e.g., ♂, ♪, ♥, \(ˆoˆ)╱) together form messages that are both textually and visually entertaining and produce the rapport-sharing quality of BBS communication.

One of the four Japanese scripts, *kanji*, can be used as emoticons in Japanese CMC (Nishimura 2003b). Unlike emoticons consisting of punctuation marks and other symbols, meanings conveyed by *kanji* emoticons can be identified instantaneously at a glance, as each *kanji* is an ideograph that carries semantic meanings. Here, the visual shapes and semantic properties of *kanji* are utilized and appreciated more than their linguistic uses as words. These are very powerful visual tools to communicate feelings and actions, even when the pronunciation is unclear. Another factor that may impact on linguistic behavior is the nature and purpose of interaction. BBS interactions are primarily for enjoyment, though BBS websites have purposes other than recreation, such as information seeking.

A number of instances of word play can be identified, such as *kanji* punning and unconventional orthography. Non-standard literacy can be favored by members of online communities (Nishimura 2003a). Users employ unconventional, informal and innovative language and styles that have currency within the community because it is fun to do so. These playful practices, because they can be enjoyed by users, contribute to creating a sense of belonging to the group, and such playfulness seems to be one of the key factors for community bonding and identity. In other words, playfulness and humor, verbal, visual or graphic, can be interpreted as contributing to the formation of online community. Gottlieb (2011) comments that although Japanese CMC may seem to display a new communicative phenomenon enabled by computer technology, it is in fact far from new. Gottlieb (2011: 71) argues that "these practices build on an already existing tradition of orthographic creativity facilitated by the nature of the writing system, the only difference being the practice has now moved into the much wider public arena of cyberspace."

Many of the features identified as common across genres of digital writing (Danet 2001: 17–19) are shared in Japanese CMC (Nishimura 2003b). However, some phenomena are specific to Japanese CMC, based on the word conversion provided by word-processing technology. To write Japanese words or sentences on the computer, it is necessary for writers to use a word-processing programme (mostly preinstalled) to convert *roomaji* input into an appropriate orthographic representation consisting of *kanji* and *kana* to meet the Japanese orthographic system. It so happens that the word-conversion software makes mistakes and totally unexpected, irrelevant output can be produced. These conversion errors occur for two reasons: one is the huge number of homophonous *kanji* (with the same pronunciation but different meanings) in current use; and second, the morpheme boundary is not identified correctly due to the relatively large number of monosyllabic words. Such conversion errors can be the source of humor (or sometimes trouble or irritation, depending on the situation) for writers and recipients.

For example, when someone wants to write on the computer, "We started living abroad" in the Japanese standard orthography, the computer conversion software could produce an output meaning, "Shellfish started living in my stomach." The cause of this conversion error is the interpretation of the morpheme segmentation of *kaigai*, "abroad," which is one word, but the conversion software segments this sequence into *kai* "shellfish"/*ga* subject marker/*i* "stomach."

In English digital writing, what is entered normally appears on the screen without change. An exception is the copyright symbol, ©, which is produced when parentheses enclose the letter "c." A somewhat more systematic conversion takes place when the spell check software detects words that do not belong to its dictionary. For example, an automatic spelling checker corrects "cosplay" into "costly," as depicted on the iPhone display in Figure 6.1.

When Japanese writers write on the computer, what is entered on the computer appears differently on the display. Users sometimes experience conversion errors, and there are various kinds of misconversions. One semi-governmental organization concerned with improving *kanji* literacy among Japanese writers sponsored a "Humorous Misconversion Contest."

Figure 6.1 Example of spell check producing laughter.

Funny misconversions and their intended input were submitted to the contest. This was an opportunity for users to tell stories and jokes about funny misconversions, such as how misconversions created laughter, how careless the user was to send out texts with misconversions, and so on. Japanese digital writing thus offers users such opportunities to enjoy misconversions, and laugh about them. No one but the computer is essentially responsible for these errors, but users can take advantage of this and intentionally and creatively produce texts with misconversions to amuse others.

The automatic spelling correction in English digital writing can sometimes cause a similar phenomenon, but in Japanese such misconversion takes place on a far greater scale than English, as conversion is inevitable in digital writing. There seem to be possibilities for languages other than English and Japanese to have phenomena similar to misconversion, in which writing digitally requires or is assisted by some kind of conversion system. For more details of misconversion phenomena, see Nishimura (2012).

Another area of creativity observed in collaborative online activities of play concerns young Japanese women's practices of crafting novels on mobile phones or *keitai* handsets, which function as handy computers (Nishimura 2011). These young authors create stories and post them on novel-sharing websites. Their readers, who are often writers themselves, offer comments and suggestions to the authors regarding the stories, and the authors incorporate them in their stories. Though the interactive practices of writing and sharing *keitai* novels with peer readers may seem to be observed only in Japan, there are common aspects with English-speaking culture. That is, the novels, particularly the styles employed by young authors, are often the subject of negative comments from adults, including parents, teachers and publishers, just as texting styles are in English. It is of interest to identify the commonality underlying what may seem to be a culture-specific practice, and it is also important to recognize where the cultural specificity and shared social reactions to these phenomena come from.

This section has discussed how play and creativity occur in Japanese CMC by drawing on the unique orthographic resources of the language. Comparative language-focused analysis of play and creativity has suggested that there are language-specific features as well as commonly observed properties between English and Japanese (and probably other languages as well), such as unconventional orthography and abbreviations. The insights from language-specific phenomena could not be obtained if English CMC alone were studied, which reminds us that digital communication is shaped by (and shapes) the technology that enables it. The next section will make a few remarks on research methodology and also explore how evolving technologies affect the study of technologically mediated communication.

Research methodology

This section will present observations on methodological approaches to play and creativity in digital communication, addressing recent trends in research that have bearings on the emerging technologies on which digital communication depend as well as describing methods for data collection and analysis of digital discourse.

In an early study of playfulness in digital communication, Baym (1995) argued against previously held views of digital environments being inhospitable to humor, maintaining instead that humorous interactions abound in online contexts. The methods employed by Baym included not only close textual analysis of Usenet newsgroup messages on soap operas, but also user surveys. Combining textual data and survey data is an excellent way to reach fruitful results, though this type of dual methodology has not always been employed. Androutsopoulos (2008, np) stresses the merit of ethnographic approaches, which not only supply information on the text, but also assist in "reconstructing fields of computer-mediated discourse . . . and participants' literacy practices."

Herring (2013) advances research schemes, foci and approaches within computer-mediated discourse analysis (CMDA) developed in her earlier work (Herring 2004). Some phenomena observed today did not exist in 2004, having arisen alongside the recent development of newer technological platforms such as Facebook and Twitter. In view of today's situation, Herring (2013: 21) foresees that "Discourse 2.0 offers a rich field of investigation for discourse analysts," and stresses the need for incorporating multimodal analysis into qualitative ethnographic approaches and systematic quantitative investigations. Newon's (2011) study on creativity in gaming culture is an example of this multimodal research combining voice and text sources.

One further remark on methodology concerns quantitative corpus-based approaches, which can enable us to find the general nature and patterns of target phenomena. King (2009) outlines how online chat data consisting of mostly gay users are collected and analyzed, while commenting on the challenges attending his corpus compilation and analysis. These include how unconventional spelling, which he calls "cyber-orthography," cannot be properly analyzed using standard corpus tagging tools. Another issue is the difficulty in obtaining participants' permission and accessing their demographic background. Junior researchers will find instructive advice in Nelson's (2010) suggestions for compiling corpora of written data, including discussions of corpus size and text sources.

Recommendations for practice

The field of language-focused research on digital communication has benefited from accumulation of previous research findings in a number of related disciplines. Researchers working on digital discourse are expected to be familiar with fields such as gender and/or age differences, cross-cultural pragmatics, humor and so on. As Internet multimodality continues to increase, analyses must also adapt to incorporate these dimensions of play and creativity. For example, in a case where playful aspects in contemporary multimodal media are to be investigated through an examination of YouTube data, analysts would need to look not only at the videos but also at users' comment-posting functions, which provide a number of entertainment opportunities for users and research opportunities for analysts. One way of capturing interaction would be to collect logs of texts created by participants (viewers of the video) as well as transcripts of the videos in question with contextual notes. Though viewers' backgrounds are difficult to obtain, characters appearing in the video can usefully be incorporated in research. An example of this type of research is Chun and Walters (2011).

Based on each researcher's areas of interest—politics, education, travel, comics and so on—topics for future research are never limited. If, for example, one is interested in overseas travel, websites for hotels in various parts of the world may be the subject of analysis in terms of target audience, translatability and design, including multimodal capabilities (e.g., Vasquez 2014). However, in conducting such research, theories that explain the observed phenomena are always necessary. In this respect, familiarity with other disciplines and an interdisciplinary approach are recommended.

Future directions

This body of empirical work suggests directions for future research in view of the expansion of digital communication globally and among various demographic groups such as seniors. Sociolinguistically motivated CMC research can respond to societal needs such as those of an ageing population. Below are some possible directions that CMC research is expected to take.

Interdisciplinary approaches

In this approach, two or more disciplinary areas are brought together to examine a given phenomenon. One such example already seen is humor research and digital communication. Online interactions are documented and analyzed using theories of humor. Medium specificity needs to be taken into consideration when interpreting the phenomenon in question. Among the research articles that appear in *Humor*, few discuss humor in digital contexts, overlooking perhaps rich cross-fertilizations between this line of research and the discipline of humor studies. As the field of research on digital discourse and communication matures, interdisciplinary research in areas other than humor may be conducted. One such candidate is politeness research, in which "creative" face management in online behavior can be documented and analyzed. Politeness (and impoliteness) in digital communication, in fact, has attracted scholarly interest (Locher 2010), and the author's work (Nishimura 2010) discusses different norms of politeness levels or appropriateness in two discussion forums. Topics include how playfulness and/or creativity in digital communication can relate to politeness, such as whether or not they contribute to the perception of politeness. This area also is promising for future research.

Approaching play and creativity in digital communication

There are at least two directions to take within research on play and creativity in digital communication. One concerns technological innovation in communication platforms, as mentioned in previous sections; and the other concerns stylistic variations in digital discourse. First, new technologies bring about new platforms for digital communication. Because they are new, just as emails or BBS communication were new when they were brought to public attention, there is a lack of descriptive work on their features and usage norms. Description of interactions using newer technologies can advance our knowledge in this area, which can be the basis for more theoretical work in the future.

Second, variations among users can be researched at a time when the use of digital technologies is rapidly expanding among seniors. Responding to "a future priority for sociolinguistics" (Coupland 2004: 83), it is necessary to shift the focus of research to older digital media users, as the area is no longer dominated by young people. A technologically savvy population of seniors is increasingly taking advantage of digital platforms such as blogging, and research is beginning to catch up with these trends. Studies investigating older Japanese women's interactional behavior in face-to-face conversations (Matsumoto 2009, 2011) challenge previously held views of ageing by describing comical and playful aspects of these conversations. Similarly, Nishimura (2013) identifies playful elements in older Japanese bloggers' use of emoticons and other features of style.

Non-English digital communication

Being a non-English speaker myself, I have always felt the need to advance research in languages other than English. The volumes of research conducted on English digital discourse and communication suggest that the research gap between English and non-alphabet-based languages such as Japanese has not diminished, though there have been trends toward improvement in recent years. It is true that tools and theories developed to research English also apply to Japanese digital communication, but the use of these tools and theories may inevitably introduce bias if any target phenomenon is seen through the lens of English. As long as this approach is taken, phenomena specific to particular languages will continue to be overlooked. Research on languages that have received little attention will provide new perspectives on English digital discourse and hence enable us to reach a better, deeper understanding of language and digital communication in general.

Related topics

- Chapter 13 Digital advertising (Kelly-Holmes)
- Chapter 20 Online communities and communities of practice (Angouri)
- Chapter 17 Second Life: language and virtual identity (Abdullah)
- Chapter 18 Online multiplayer games (Newon)

References

Androutsopoulos, J. 2008, "Potentials and limitations of discourse-centred online ethnography," *Language@ Internet*, vol. 5, no. 8, available from: http://www.languageatinternet.org/articles/2008/1610 [accessed March 29, 2013].

Baym, N. K. 1995, "The performance of humor in computer-mediated communication," *Journal of Computer-Mediated Communication*, vol. 1, no. 2, available from: http://onlinelibrary.wiley.com/doi/10.1111/j.1083-6101.1995.tb00327.x/full [accessed December 22, 2012].

Bell, A. 1984, "Language style as audience design," *Language in Society*, vol. 13, no. 2, pp. 145–204.

Biber, D. & Conrad, S. 2009, *Register, genre, and style*, Cambridge University Press, New York.

Boden, M. A. 2004, *The creative mind: myths and mechanisms*, 2nd edn., Routledge, London.

Carter, R. A. 2004, *Language and creativity: the art of common talk*, Routledge, London.

Carter, R. A. & McCarthy, M. J. 2004, "Talking, creating: interactional language, creativity and context," *Applied Linguistics*, vol. 25, no. 1, pp. 62–88.

Carter, R. A. & McCarthy, M. J. 1995, "Discourse and creativity: bridging the gap between language and literature," in G. Cook & B. Seidlhoffer (eds.), *Principle and practice in applied linguistics*, Oxford University Press, Oxford, pp. 303–321.

Chomsky, N. 1965, *Aspects of the theory of syntax*, The MIT Press, Cambridge, MA.

Chun, E. & Walters, K. 2011, "Orienting to Arab Orientalism: language, race and humor in a YouTube video," in C. Thurlow & K. Mroczek (eds.), *Digital discourse: language in the new media*, Oxford University Press, Oxford, pp. 251–273.

Cook, G. 2000, *Language play, language learning*, Oxford University Press, Oxford.

Coupland, N. 2007, *Style: language variation and identity*, Cambridge University Press, Cambridge.

Coupland, N. 2004, "Age in social and sociolinguistic theory," in J. F. Nussbaum and J. Coupland, (eds.), *Handbook of communication and aging research*, 2nd edn., Lawrence Erlbaum Associates, Mahwah, NJ, pp. 69–90.

Craft, A., Jeffrey, B. & Leibling, M. (eds.) 2001, *Creativity in education*, Continuum, New York, NY.

Crystal, D. 2001, *Language and the Internet*, Cambridge University Press, Cambridge.

Crystal, D. 1998, *Language play*, University of Chicago Press, Chicago, IL.

Danet, B. 2001, *Cyberpl@y: communicating online*, Berg, Oxford.

Danet, B. 1998, "Text as mask: gender, play and performance on the Internet," in S. G. Jones (ed.), *Cybersociety 2.0: revisiting computer-mediated communication and community*, Sage, Newbury Park, CA, pp. 129–158.

Danet, B. 1995, "General introduction: playful expressivity and artfulness in computer-mediated communication," *Journal of Computer-Mediated Communication*, vol. 1, no. 2, available from: http://onlinelibrary.wiley.com/doi/10.1111/j.1083-6101.1995.tb00323.x/full [accessed March 29, 2013].

Danet, B., Bechar-Israeli, T., Cividalli, A. & Rosenbaum-Tamari, Y. 1995, "Curtain time 20:00 GMT: experiments with virtual theater on Internet relay chat," *Journal of Computer-Mediated Communication*, vol. 1, no. 2, available from: http://onlinelibrary.wiley.com/journal/10.1111/%28ISSN%291083-6101 [accessed March 29, 2014].

Danet, B. & S. Herring (eds.) 2007, *The multilingual Internet: language, culture, and communication online*, Oxford University Press, Oxford.

Danet, B. & S. Herring 2003, "Introduction: the multilingual Internet," *Journal of Computer-Mediated Communication*, vol. 9, no. 1, doi: 10.1111/j.1083-6101.2003.tb00354.x [accessed March 29, 2013].

Danet, B., Ruedenberg-Wright, L. & Rosenbaum-Tamari, Y. 1997, "'HMMM . . . WHERE'S THAT SMOKE COMING FROM?'" *Journal of Computer-Mediated Communication*, vol. 2, no. 4, doi: 10.1111/j.1083-6101.1997.tb00195.x [accessed March 29, 2014].

Eckert, P. 2012, "Three waves of variation study: the emergence of meaning in the study of sociolinguistic variation," *Annual Review of Anthropology*, vol. 41, pp. 87–100.

Eckert, P. & Rickford, J. R. (eds.) 2001, *Style and sociolinguistic variation*, Cambridge University Press, Cambridge.

Gottlieb, N. 2011, "Playing with language in e-Japan: old wines in new bottles," in N. Gottlieb (ed.), *Language in public spaces in Japan*, Routledge, Abingdon, pp. 71–85.

Herring, S. C. 2013, "Discourse in web 2.0: familiar, reconfigured, and emergent," in D. Tannen & A. M. Trester (eds.), *Discourse 2.0: language and new media*, Georgetown University Press, Washington, DC, pp. 1–25.

Herring, S. C. 2004, "Computer-mediated discourse analysis: an approach to researching online behavior," in S. A. Barab, R. Kling, & J. H. Gray (eds.), *Designing for virtual communities in the service of learning*, Cambridge University Press, New York, NY, pp. 338–376.

Herring, S. C., Stein, D., & Virtanen, T. 2013, "Introduction," in S. C. Herring, D. Stein & T. Virtanen (eds.), *Pragmatics of computer-mediated communication*, Mouton De Gruyter, Berlin, pp. 3–31.

Huizinga, J. 1955, *Homo ludens: a study of the play-element in culture*, Routledge, London.

Jones, R. H. 2012, "Introduction: discourse and creativity," in R. Jones (ed.), *Discourse and creativity*, Pearson, London, pp. 1–14.

Jones, R. H. 2010, "Creativity and discourse," *World Englishes*, vol. 29, no. 4, pp. 467–80.

Joos, M. 1967, *The five clocks*, Harcourt Brace Jovanovich, New York, NY.

Katsuno, H. & Yano, C. 2007, "*Kaomoji* and expressivity in a Japanese housewives' chat room," in B. Danet & S. C. Herring (eds.), *The multilingual Internet: language, culture, and communication online*, Oxford University Press, Oxford, pp. 278–300.

King, B. 2009, "Building and analysing corpora of computer-mediated communication," in P. Baker (ed.), *Contemporary corpus linguistics*, Continuum, London, pp. 301–320.

Labov, W. 1966, *The social stratification of English in New York City*, Center for Applied Linguistics, Washington, DC.

Locher, M. A. 2010, "Introduction: politeness and impoliteness in computer-mediated communication," *Journal of Politeness Research*, Special issue: Language, behaviour, culture. vol. 6, no. 1, pp. 1–5.

Matsumoto, Y. 2011, "Painful to playful: quotidian frames in the conversational discourse of older Japanese women," *Language in Society*, vol. 40, no. 5, pp. 591–616.

Matsumoto, Y. 2009, "Beyond stereotypes of old age: the discourse of elderly Japanese women," *International Journal of the Sociology of Language*, vol. 2009, no. 200, pp. 129–152.

Mendoza-Denton, N. 2001, "Style," in A. Duranti (ed.), *Key terms in language and culture*, Blackwell, Malden, MA, pp. 235–237.

Nelson, M. 2010, "Building a written corpus: what are the basics?" in A. O'Keeffe and M. McCarthy (eds.), *The Routledge handbook of corpus linguistics*, Routledge, London, pp. 53–65.

Newon, L. 2011, "Multimodal creativity and identities of expertise in the digital ecology of a World of Warcraft guild," in C. Thurlow and K. Mroczek (eds.), *Digital discourse: language in the new media*, pp. 131–153.

Nishimura, Y. 2013, "A sociolinguistic study of digital communication among the elderly in Japan: comparison of blog posts by older and younger Japanese," 25th Anniversary Conference of the Nordic Association of Japanese and Korean Studies, The University of Bergen, Bergen, Norway.

Nishimura, Y. 2012, "Puns in Japanese computer-mediated communication: observations from misconversion phenomena," 2012 AAAI Fall Symposium on Artificial Intelligence of Humor, in *Technical Report FS-12-02*, The AAAI Press, Menlo Park, CA, pp. 38–45, available from: http://www.aaai.org/Library/Symposia/Fall/fs12-02.php [accessed March 29, 2013].

Nishimura, Y. 2011, "Japanese *keitai* novels and ideologies of literacy," in C. Thurlow and K. Mroczek (eds.), *Digital discourse: language in the new media*, Oxford University Press, Oxford, pp. 86–109.

Nishimura, Y. 2010, "Impoliteness in Japanese BBS interactions: observations from message exchanges in two online communities," *Journal of Politeness Research*, Special issue: Language, behaviour, culture, vol. 6, no. 1, pp. 35–55.

Nishimura, Y. 2008, "Japanese BBS websites as online communities: (im)politeness perspectives," *Language@Internet*, vol. 5, in J. Androutsopoulos & M. Beißwenger (eds.), Special issue: Data and methods in computer-mediated discourse analysis: new approaches, available from: http://www.languageatinternet.org/articles/2008/1520 [accessed March 29, 2013].

Nishimura, Y. 2003a, "Establishing a community of practice on the Internet: linguistic behavior in online Japanese communication," in P. Nowak & C. Yoquelet (eds.), *Proceedings of the 29th annual meeting of* the *Berkeley Linguistics Society*, University of California Press, Berkeley, CA, pp. 337–348, available from: http://elanguage.net/journals/bls/article/view/3420.

Nishimura, Y. 2003b, "Linguistic innovations and interactional features of casual online communication in Japanese," *Journal of Computer-Mediated Communication*, vol. 9, no. 4, doi: 10.1111/j.1083-6101.2003. tb00356.x.

North, S. 2007, "'The voices, the voices': creativity in online conversation," *Applied Linguistics*, vol. 28, no. 4, pp. 538–555.

Raymond, E. S. 1998, *The new hacker's dictionary*, 3rd edn., The MIT Press, Cambridge, MA.

Rickford, J. R. and Eckert, P. 2001, "Introduction," in P. Eckert & J. R. Rickford (eds.), *Style and socio-linguistic variation*, Cambridge University Press, Cambridge, pp. 1–18.

Runco, M. A. 2006, *Creativity: theories and themes: research, development, and practice*, Academic Press, San Diego, CA.

Schilling-Estes, N. 2004, "Investigating stylistic variation," in J. K. Chambers, P. Trudgill, & N. Schilling-Estes (eds.), *The handbook of language variation and change*, Blackwell, Malden, MA, pp. 375–401.

Shortis, T. 2007, "Gr8 txtpectations: the creativity of text spelling," *English Drama Media*, vol. 8, pp. 21–26.

Smith, J. S. & Schmidt, D. L. 1996, "Variability in written Japanese: towards a sociolinguistics of script choice," *Visible Language*, vol. 30, no. 1, pp. 47–71.

Swann, J. & Maybin, J. 2007, "Introduction: language creativity in everyday contexts," Special Issue, *Applied Linguistics*, vol. 28, no. 4, pp. 491–496.

Tagliamonte, S. & Denis, D. 2008, "Linguistic ruin? LOL! instant messaging and teen language," *American Speech,* vol. 83, no. 1, pp. 3–34.

Thurlow, C. 2012, "Determined creativity: language play in new media discourse," in R. Jones (ed.), *Discourse and creativity*, Pearson, London, pp. 169–190.

Thurlow, C. 2006 "From statistical panic to moral panic: the metadiscursive construction and popular exaggeration of new media language in the print media," *Journal of Computer-Mediated Communication*, vol. 11, pp. 667–701, doi: 10.1111/j.1083-6101.2006.00031.x [accessed March 29, 2014].

Thurlow, C. & Bell, K. 2009, "Against technologization: young people's new media discourse as creative cultural practice," *Journal of Computer-Mediated Communication*, vol. 14, pp. 1038–1049, doi: 10.1111/j.1083-6101.2009.01480.x [accessed March 29, 2014].

Thurlow, C. & Mroczek, K. (eds.) 2011, *Digital discourse: language in the new media*, Oxford University Press, Oxford.

Vasquez, C. 2014, *The discourse of online consumer reviews*, Bloomsbury Academic, London.

Vo, T. A. & Carter, R. 2010, "What can a corpus tell us about creativity?' in A. O'Keeffe & M. McCarthy, (eds.), *The Routledge handbook of corpus linguistics*, Routledge, London, pp. 302–315.

Wales, K. 2011, *A Dictionary of stylistics*, 3rd edn., Routledge, London.

Werry, C. C. 1996, "Linguistic and interactional features of Internet relay chat," in S. C. Herring (ed.), *Computer-mediated communication: linguistic, social and cross-cultural perspectives*, John Benjamins, Amsterdam, pp. 47–63.

Wikipedia 2013, "Leet," available from: http://en.wikipedia.org/wiki/Leet [accessed March 29, 2013].

Further reading

Danet, B. 2001, *Cyberpl@y: communicating online*, Berg, Oxford & New York.

A volume devoted to playful properties in email, chat, IRC and MUDs and the World Wide Web, and exploring textual, visual, theatrical and aesthetic dimensions.

Danet, B. & Herring, S. (eds.) 2007, *The multilingual Internet: language, culture, and communication online*, Oxford University Press, Oxford.

Expands research on digital discourse and communication to non-English contexts and addresses the research gap.

Herring, S. C., Stein, D., & Virtanen, T. (eds.) 2013, *Pragmatics of computer-mediated communication*, Mouton De Gruyter, Berlin.

A comprehensive survey of language-focused CMC research on various topics.

Tannen, D. & Trester, A. M. (eds). 2013, *Discourse 2.0: language and new media*. Georgetown University Press, Washington, DC.

Presents the variety and depth of current discourse-focused CMC research, including works accommodating multimodality.

Thurlow, C. & Mroczek, K. (eds.) 2011, *Digital discourse: language in the new media*, Oxford University Press, Oxford.

Collects sociolinguistically motivated research on digital discourse, including creative and playful activities such as online gaming and collaborative creative writing.

7

Multilingual resources and practices in digital communication

Carmen Lee

The status of English and other languages on the internet

Early studies of computer-mediated communication (CMC), especially those published in the 1990s, tended to focus on *English* on the Internet. There are various reasons for that. First of all, the Internet started and first became popular in the United States where English is the primary language. Second, the dominance of English in the 1990s was reinforced by discourses of the 'hyperglobalisers' (Held and McGrew 2001), who believed that globalization would lead to the homogenization of the world. Linguists also predicted that English, having achieved global status, would remain the dominant language on the Internet (Crystal 1997; Fishman 1998). This discussion also extended to the public sphere, especially in the form of news reports and editorials, as in the following comment in *The New York Times*: '[I]f you want to take full advantage of the Internet there is only one real way to do it: learn English' (Specter 1996: 1).

In view of these beliefs, concerns were expressed as to whether the growth of the Internet in the US would result in linguistic imperialism; Phillipson (1992: 47) noted that 'the dominance of English is asserted and maintained by the establishment and continuous reconstitution of structural and cultural inequalities between English and other languages'. While English may continue to be the lingua franca in many contexts of intercultural communication in the twenty-first century, recent years have seen rapid changes in the distribution of English and other languages online. Between 1998 and 2012, English web content dropped from 80 per cent (Fishman 1998) to 55 per cent (W3techs 2012). In terms of web users' first language, about 71 per cent of Internet users in the world do not speak English as their first language (Internet World Stats 2014). Although no single method developed to date can accurately measure linguistic diversity on the Internet, these surveys show that the presence of languages other than English on the web is on the rise. This also implies that new linguistic data are available for online researchers to investigate digital discourse beyond the English-speaking context.

At the same time, a growing amount of academic research has emerged to confirm the statistical findings mentioned above. The publication of the volume *The Multilingual Internet* (Danet and Herring 2007) marks a significant phase in studies of multilingualism online. Since then, a wide range of platforms, languages, and geographical locations has been researched. Topics range from creative orthography, code choice, and code-switching to language maintenance and identity performance.

The purpose of this chapter is to provide a comprehensive overview of these key topics and recent trends in existing research on multilingual practices in digital communication. Examples from various sociolinguistic contexts will be used to illustrate what web users do with multiple linguistic resources in online interaction, and how interacting or doing things with more than one language becomes an important resource for all web users (including those who are considered 'monolinguals' in the offline world) in a superdiverse world. With the advent of social media and Web 2.0 technologies, the affordance of self-generated contents in social media further encourages and reinforces multilingual encounters online. This chapter also aims to situate multilingual practices within a wide range of platforms, from older media such as email and IRC to newer social media such as Facebook and Flickr.

At this point, it is necessary to define the scope of the chapter and explain how some terms and concepts are used. The notion of 'multilingualism' is used in its broadest sense here. It refers to the co-existence of two or more languages, or 'codes', in any communicative context, including various representations of a language (e.g., Romanized Cantonese and Cantonese represented in characters are treated as two distinct codes, as they may be used for different reasons). The academic area of 'multilingualism online' is also a multifaceted one (see Androutsopoulos 2013a, which identifies five major patterns of multilingualism in digital discourse). Existing studies tend to fall into two major categories: a) statistical surveys of linguistic diversity online; and b) identifying and explaining multilingual practices in a specific form of CMC, as also noted in Leppänen and Peuronen (2012).

At the macro level, public surveys and quantitative research have been conducted to measure linguistic diversity on the Internet. Statistical findings generated from such studies tend to focus on the distribution of English and other languages by recording the dominant language of individual web pages, or by identifying the native language of web users. Some of the most cited public surveys of the Internet population by language include Internet World Stats and W3Techs, both of which are hosted by marketing companies. The methodologies adopted in these marketing surveys are questionable, as Paolillo (2007) pointed out. First, the estimates generated are often based on multiple sources from different countries, which may not share the same set of methods to measure their Internet penetration rates. Second, among the many sources of these surveys are governments and marketing companies, whose interests may shape their findings, leading, perhaps, to biased results or over-estimates. In view of these, Paolillo (2007) proposed a linguistic diversity index that takes into account varieties of languages within a country. With this method, Paolillo was able to reveal that, although North America and China are the least linguistically diverse in offline contexts, these countries, and their associated languages, dominate the Internet. Based on his findings and observations from existing surveys, Paolillo concluded that Internet technologies still favour large languages, especially English. However, one limitation of most quantitative surveys of linguistic diversity is that they seem to assume that an individual web user speaks only one language, and they fail to document an individual's complete linguistic repertoire. Paolillo (2007) also noted that estimates of Internet user populations are far from sufficient in representing multilingualism online, and he called for empirical research on actual instances of language use online. Certainly, a more meaningful and comprehensive investigation of multilingualism online involves understanding what web users actually do with their multiple linguistic resources in authentic contexts and why they do so. People's multilingual practices online are the primary focus of this chapter.

Language choice and code-switching in digital communication

Although quantitative surveys may not accurately represent the actual distribution of English and other languages online, there are reasons to believe that digital communication in languages other than English is on the rise. Technologically, access to the Internet has become relatively easy and cheap in many countries beyond the US and Europe. Processing non-Roman scripts on the computer is now possible, and most foreign language scripts are readable on major computer platforms and web browsers. Still, for a number of technical and social reasons, web users have found creative ways of 'spelling' words in languages that are not typically written in the Roman alphabet. This linguistic characteristic of CMC is one of several features described in studies of multilingual CMC (e.g., Lee 2002, Nishimura 2003, Palfreyman and Al-Khalil 2003, Tseliga 2007). Some of this research takes a largely descriptive approach, comparing participants' use of innovative orthographic or typographic features in CMC with those of English users. For example, Nishimura (2003) shows how Japanese BBS users and their English counterparts adopt a similar set of features of digital writing, such as multiple punctuation, eccentric spelling, capital letters, etc., most of which have been identified in English-based descriptions of 'Netspeak' (Crystal 2006). To date, however, the majority of the multilingual Internet literature tends to be more interested in documenting and explaining language choice and code-switching practices among multilingual web users.

Language choice

Language choice online is concerned with the codes or linguistic resources available to web users and how they negotiate their choice when communicating online with people with or without shared languages. Existing research covers a wide range of platforms and documents users' choices between a number of languages, especially between English and other languages such as Egyptian Arabic (Warschauer *et al.* 2007), Swahili (Mafu 2004), Jamaican Creole (Hinrichs 2006), Cantonese (Lee 2007a, 2007b), Mandarin Chinese (Su 2003), and Thai (Tagg and Seargeant 2012).

To many multilingual web users, English is perceived as the lingua franca in online communication. It is not surprising that language shift to English has been noted among online groups who do not share the same first language. For example, in Durham's (2003) study of a Swiss medical students' mailing list, English – or what Durham refers to as 'Pan Swiss English' – is the dominant language of interaction, although English is no one's first language. According to the participants whose first language is either French or German, switching to English was to ensure mutual intelligibility and because of the commonly accepted lingua franca status of English in Switzerland.

What seems more interesting is when people who do have a shared language communicate in English only online. This trend has been reported on in a number of studies. Warschauer *et al.* (2007), for example, show that a group of Egyptian professionals reported that they use English only, especially in formal email contexts. The participants took pride in their choice of English, interpreting it as demonstrating Egyptian multicultural history, not as a sign of abandoning their local Egyptian culture. Kelly-Holmes (2004) surveyed the linguistic repertoires of over 2000 English-educated bilingual young people in eight different countries. Although no significant shift to English was noted in the group as a whole, the study shows that speakers of languages that have smaller number of speakers, such as Indonesian and Swahili, are more likely to shift to English on the Internet. This confirms Paolillo's (2007) conclusion that the Internet still favours larger languages, including English and Chinese. In some cases, however, English is not the preferred language in online participation. For example, German is the lingua franca among migrant participants in some diasporic discussion forums, as illustrated in Androutsopoulos (2007). In a more recent study, Androutsopoulos (2013c) also looks into the presence of German dialects in YouTube videos. Although YouTube is commonly viewed as a global platform, it also gives rise to local activities, such as discussing local dialects among German speakers. In an initial observation of the situation, Androutsopoulos notes that a great number of videos on YouTube are tagged with German dialect-related key words such as *Bairisch* ('Bavarian'), *Alemannisch* ('Alemannic'), or *Berlinerisch* ('Berlin city dialect'). These dialects are not only present in these videos, but also become the theme of these videos and viewers' comments on them. The increasing presence of smaller languages in multimodal forms in online social networks certainly gives rise to translocal interaction across the globe, which will be discussed later.

It is evident in various studies that the web offers a space for people to write in minority languages or in varieties that do not have any standard writing system in offline contexts. One successful case is the presence of Assyrian, spoken by a small minority group in the Middle East, in English-based CMC (see McClure 2001). Written languages that are no longer used in offline lives have become more visible in digital writing. For example, in Egypt, while English was found to be the common language in formal emails, Warschauer *et al.* (2007) discovered a Romanized form of colloquial Egyptian Arabic used in informal email and online chat. Colloquial Arabic, which used to have very limited use in written contexts offline, is used extensively online alongside English. A similar phenomenon is noted in email and instant messaging (IM) among young people in Hong Kong, where Cantonese, the major spoken language with no standard writing system of its own, is represented in creative forms through alphabetic or character writing systems. Lee (2007b) identified five major codes or linguistic resources available to her Hong Kong participants in their online writing:

- standard English
- standard written Chinese
- Cantonese in characters
- Romanized Cantonese
- morpheme-by-morpheme literal translation.

The first two types, standard English and standard written Chinese, are the written forms commonly used in offline contexts and taught in schools. In addition to these standard codes, the study found that IM users have created innovative ways of representing Cantonese in their IM chat, including borrowing characters from standard written Chinese, spelling out Cantonese words as Romanized words, or even using English transliteration. An interesting example of transliteration is the phrase 'sky and land lessons' found in Lee's IM data. It is a common phrase among university students to mean a long period of spare time between an early lecture in the morning and another one in late afternoon. It is a literal translation of the Cantonese expression 天地堂. What is particularly intriguing in this data is not just the wide-ranging and creative forms of linguistic resources, but how and why these codes are deployed differently for different purposes by different IM users. The study shows that not all of these forms of language were drawn upon in any given chat session. Sometimes the participants would use one code only, while at other times they would mix linguistic codes. And there seems to be no fixed pattern in using or choosing such codes. This is a result of the participants taking up and acting upon the *perceived affordances*, or the action possibilities and constraints, of different languages. In working out what different codes can or cannot do, online participants take into consideration a number of ecological factors: expressiveness of the language, perceived functions of the communication medium, user familiarity with the language, user identification with the language, technical constraints of inputting methods, speed, and perceived practicality of the writing system. These factors are discussed in greater detail elsewhere (Lee 2007a). A similar set of factors is also used to explain code choice between English and other languages in newer social media such as Flickr (Barton and Lee 2013), where the same user may choose to describe a photo in one language and give tags in another.

Carmen Lee

Code-switching

Another theme that is often discussed alongside code choice is code-switching (CS). CS is different from the broader topic of code preference or simply the coexistence of multiple languages on the same webpage (see Lee and Barton 2011 on Flickr). Rather, CS is a more restrictive form of multilingual CMC, in that the co-existence of linguistic codes is required by the discourse structure, and the codes are 'dialogically interrelated by responding to previous, and contextualizing subsequent, contributions' (Androutsopoulos 2013a: 673). Studies of CS in CMC have identified code-switching patterns in a range of platforms and linguistic contexts. These include switching between Assyrian and English in a public mailing list (McClure 2001), between Greek and English in emails (Georgakopoulou 1997), between Finnish and English in blogs (Leppänen 2007), between Wolof/Pulaar and French in SMS (Lexander 2012), and between Swiss German dialects and standard German in IRC (Siebenhaar 2006). While these studies examine CS on one CMC platform, Lee (2007b), in her comparative analysis of Cantonese–English code-mixing practice in email and the instant messaging programme, ICQ, notes that the participants code-mixed significantly more in ICQ than they did in emails. This was explained in terms of synchronicity: ICQ more closely resembles face-to-face context, where participants were already used to the practice of switching between languages. This practice seems to carry over to the writing of Facebook status updates (Lee 2011), in which Cantonese–English bilingual users rarely use mixed code: in that context, status updates are asynchronous and thus the urge to code-switch is lower.

Other studies of CS in CMC have been interested in whether patterns of CS in online interaction conform to or deviate from conversational CS in face-to-face contexts. Theoretical frameworks typically applied to face-to-face CS data, including Myers-Scotton's (1998) markedness model and Auer's (1999) conversational approach, have been applied to CMC contexts. For example, Auer's classification of CS patterns (insertional switching, insertional mixing, alternational switching, and alternational mixing) is applied in Leppänen's (2007) study of the CS practices among Finnish young people, as well as in Siebanhaar's (2006) study of Swiss–German IRC chatrooms. These models may not fully account for CS in digital communication, which is largely written in mode. Sometimes, CS online does not follow conventions of CS in offline interaction, as illustrated in Example (1) below, which is part of an email written by a Hong Kong Cantonese–English bilingual university student:

Example (1)

The ocamp is ok *la*, except that the beach programs and nite journey were cancelled because of the bad weather. And ah sun quarreled with 'ha jong' *lor*, as u know his character *ga la*. But in our ocamp gp ah sun and jessic got along very well with the cores and freshmen *geh*. Ok *la*, keep contact thru email. One yr is not very long.

When Hong Kong Cantonese–English bilinguals code-switch in face-to-face interaction, Cantonese is the matrix code in which lexical items from English are inserted. Example (1), however, shows the opposite: the dominant language is English, while Cantonese discourse particles in Romanized form (italicized) are inserted at the end of the English sentences. This practice is found to be extremely common in digital interaction among Hong Kong users (as discussed in James 2001; Lee 2007b). This needs to be explained within a framework that moves beyond the conventional conversation analysis to take into account situational factors in other modes of communication (but see chapters in Sebba *et al.* 2012). Perhaps what is more important and meaningful is to look at how CS is used strategically in CMC as a particular resource that serves various pragmatic and social functions.

Language choice and code-switching as a resource for self-positioning and identity performance

Though not always discussed explicitly, much of the existing research on CS in online communication points to a common theme: that the negotiation of language choice and alternation between linguistic codes serve as an important resource for self-presentation and identity performance. Lee (2014) examines a case study in which a pre-service teacher in Hong Kong, Tony, addresses his student audience and friends through strategically deploying his linguistic resources on two Facebook accounts. In his primary Facebook site, intended for his friends and family only, Cantonese-based or code-mixed status updates predominate (as in Examples (2) and (3) below) while almost no post was written entirely in English.

Example (2)

收到了Jim Scrivener 2010的新作<<Teaching English Grammar>>,如果我TP之前就買左就好lah . . . . . .

(Translation: Just received Jim Scrivener's new work in 2010 *Teaching English Grammar*. I wish I had bought this before my teaching practice.)

Example (3)

薯片佬,今次我十卜你la!
(Translation: Pringles man, I support you this time!)
[Followed by a link to a piece of local Hong Kong news online.]

Example (2) is a Cantonese-based post with insertion of English expressions such as 'TP' (teaching practice); 'lah' is a Romanized spelling of the Cantonese discourse particle 喇. Example (3) contains a case of phonetic borrowing – the Cantonese pronunciation of '十卜' resembles that of the English word 'support'; 'la' is a variant of 'lah' in the previous example. Tony reported that he had been using Cantonese–English CS in other forms of computer-mediated texts, especially IM, for about ten years. According to Tony's account of his previous language use online, mixed-code chat resembles an everyday conversation with friends. It seems that transferring an existing practice from IM to Facebook enables Tony and his friends to maintain their in-group identity, which is defined by their shared practice of code-switching. As a pre-service English teacher, Tony also keeps in touch with the students in his teaching practice school in his second Facebook account, where he calls himself *Teaching Tony*. His teacher identity is immediately indexed through his language choice. On this site, he writes almost all his posts in English. He said it would have been 'inappropriate' to use Chinese there because, as an English teacher, he had to stick to this medium of instruction in order to encourage students to write to him in English, too. The following two status updates are indicative of his language choice in his teacher Facebook:

Example (4)

Dear 4R students,
I have put copies of three sets of reading practice paper in my cabinet outside staff room. Please come and get it yourself if you need them.

Example (5)

Time to back to school again! Good luck for your homework and the coming tests!

Both messages are primarily directed to his students (and perhaps his colleagues who have access to his Facebook wall). From the content of the other status updates on his teacher Facebook wall, it is clear that Tony was using Facebook not just as a social network site to connect with his students, but also as a teaching and learning tool where he can make class-related announcements and share English learning links and videos and so on with his students. Using different linguistic resources for different kinds of posts also allowed Tony to manage the impression he made on others: Cantonese and code-mixed utterances index his playful, down-to-earth personalities, while English, often used when writing about more serious subject matters on his teacher Facebook page, is used to assert his more 'official' work identity. This echoes Warschauer *et al.*'s (2007) findings that English is reserved for formal email while a Romanized form of Egyptian Arabic is more prominent in informal email and chat. Negotiating language choices for self-positioning and relationship management is also noted in other studies, such as switching between English and Greek in email to enhance solidarity as well as to indicate professional in-group membership (Georgakopoulou 1997). In Senegal, French, rather than African languages, is found to be the dominant language of romantic text messages among lovers (Lexander 2012).

The examples above are related to impression management in private communicative situations, in which the interlocutors are known. When it comes to identity performance on globalized platforms such as the photo-sharing site Flickr, a different scene is observed. Similarly to what happened in previous observations in CMC, Flickr members also negotiate their language choice by taking into account the kind of identity they wish to project to their imagined audience. However, a stronger awareness of *global* and *local* identities is frequently articulated on Flickr, as shown in data from Lee and Barton's (2011) extensive research on multilingual practices on Flickr. For example, a Spanish Flickr user *Carolink* said she had never participated in a global network like Flickr before, and yet she had gradually identified herself as a bilingual global citizen. She explained in the interview that participating in Spanish only is 'too limited for these Internet times. I do not leave Spanish, but I try to use English when I can' (*Carolink*). *Carolink*'s readiness to use English is not surprising because English has been perceived as the lingua franca of online communication, as discussed earlier. However, her remark 'I do not leave Spanish' points to heterogeneity of culture – a salient aspect of the relationship between language and globalization. In other words, instead of seeing the web as a culturally and linguistically unified space, a truly globalized community should be a dynamic and diversified one which allows space for different cultures and languages to develop simultaneously. Users of globalized sites such as Flickr want to be part of the global world without giving up their existing local identities. This can be seen, for example, in that both Chinese and Spanish are lingua francas across a range of countries. Some Spanish users certainly identified the broader Spanish-speaking world as an important audience for them. Similarly, a mainland Chinese informant, *sating*, associated her global Flickr identity with Chinese rather than with English. She explained:

> If Flickr is a global website, as a Chinese, why must I use English, a language that I am not good at? Besides, most of my photos reflect the reality of China. So Chinese has to be the most suitable tool of communication.
>
> (*sating, original interview in Chinese*)

sating's view challenges the globally recognized status of English as the lingua franca on the Internet. Whichever sense of the global is taken, *sating*'s self reflection about her Chineseness and her discourse of resistance to English reveal her strong desire to assert her local identity on Flickr. Such a marker of local identity is useful in that it can attract Chinese-speaking Flickr users within China and beyond, and it helps promote her cultural and linguistic background to the international Flickr community.

This relational tension between the local and global is also expressed by way of the writing systems or scripts associated with different languages. For example, a Singaporean Chinese Flickr user, *Kristie* 遊牧民阿靜, accounts for her bilingual screen-name as follows:

> I want a wider group of people to know me. Not that the Chinese won't know me if I call myself just Kristie but if I attached a more "graphic" Chinese word (that 's how I always see the language), we can connect quicker and better. The name also says a lot about who I am in my whole darn life.
>
> (Kristie 遊牧民阿靜)

This suggests that language choice on globalized sites such as Flickr does not necessarily reflect users' competence in the language, nor does it automatically reveal one's ethnicity. Rather, the choice is closely related to the extent to which participants intend to project themselves as *global* or *local* members. To *Kristie* 遊牧民阿靜, the visual aspect of Chinese and Roman scripts in her screen-name acts as an important symbol of her *glocal* identities, defined as 'a dynamic negotiation between the global and the local, with the local appropriating elements of the global that it finds useful, at the same time employing strategies to retain its identity' (Koutsogiannis and Mitsikopoulou 2007: 143). Similarly, Tagg and Seargeant (2012) note the indexical values of mixing non-Roman scripts with Roman scripts among Thai–English bilinguals on Facebook and IM. Before the age of social media, playing with scripts to assert glocalness was already noted among Greek web users who employed 'Greeklish', or Romanized Greek, in their digital texts (Koutsogiannis and Mitsikopoulou 2007; Tseliga 2007; Spilioti 2009).

The co-deployment of English and local languages in order to project a cosmopolitan identity is also evident in the fan fiction produced by young people around the globe. Black (2009) shows how three Asian fan fiction writers draw on knowledge of their multiple linguistic and cultural resources in their English-based fan fiction texts posted on the site Fanfiction.net. In the texts studied and cited in Black (2009), the three focal participants all start their texts by positioning themselves as incompetent writers of English. For example, one of the writers, Grace, wrote: 'English is not my FIRST LANGUAGE' and admitted to her 'Poor english' in the header. This is actually her way of gaining support from other fan fiction writers. In addition to English, they all drew on other languages in their texts. For example, they inserted Romanized Japanese phrases and lyrics in the header information as well as within the main body of their fan fiction. On the one hand, the addition of Japanese texts and cultural elements allows the writers to enhance the degree of authenticity of the conversations between the characters, whose first language is Japanese in the original manga or anime; on the other hand, their insider knowledge of Asian culture and languages – which is highly valued in fan fiction writing – grants them status in the multicultural fan fiction world. Another participant, Nanako, also incorporated Mandarin Chinese, her first language, into her fan fiction. For example, in a chapter of her text *Crazy Love Letters*, Romanized Chinese with English translation is added in a conversation: 'Meiling turned to Syaoran and grumbled in Chinese. "Dan shi, Xiolang, wo xiang he ta shuo ji ju hua" ("But, Xiaolang, I just wanna talk to her.")' (Nanako 2003, as cited in Black 2009).

This example, as Black argues, immediately indexes Nanako's local identity as Chinese, and at the same time demonstrates her linguistic abilities as a multilingual young person in the fan fiction community. The case of fan fiction clearly demonstrates how the fan fiction site has been transformed into a translocal affinity space (Leppänen and Peuronen 2012), a transborder contact zone in which youth around the world can assert their multicultural and cosmopolitan identities through exchanging mixed-language fan fiction texts.

Carmen Lee

Translingual practices in new social media

While code choice and CS continue to be salient practices in multilingual CMC, particularly for impression and relationship management, 'new' digital media offer new opportunities for multilingual interaction, thus giving rise to new practices. An increasingly common phenomenon in social media is that anyone (including people who see themselves as monolinguals) can experience or do things with multiple languages. The multilingual Internet has gone beyond the question of which language dominates or how users code-switch. It is now a question of how people act differently as they take up new possibilities offered by the different languages on the web. An obvious example is that in a Flickr or YouTube comment thread, it is not uncommon to find people participating in multiple conversations written in different dialects and languages, regardless of the original poster's native language. These multilingual comments may be directed to a specific audience group, while being publicly available to people who may not be directly involved in the conversations. These unaddressed participants may then navigate to a different site to look up these comments on an online translator. This engagement can be seen as a kind of translingual practice (Pennycook 2008; Blackledge and Creese 2009), which emphasizes the *process* of working with different languages rather than the product, and which focuses on communicative practices *across* groups and communities rather than within a specific speech community defined primarily by the geographical locations of speakers. Androutsopoulos (2013b) extends this line of argument to 'networked multilingualism' in social media, where the use of multilingual resources is fluid and unpredictable: 'networked language practices can involve multiple authors, are addressed to different recipients, and draw on network resources' (Androutsopoulos 2013b: 18).

Sometimes, online participants may use only one language in a translingual interaction. Davies (2007) offers a relevant example: On a Flickr photo page, a photo shows an American user, *Saffron*, wearing a 'throw' (as written in the photo description) given to her by her grandmother. A Norwegian Flickr user, *Astrid*, comes across this photo page and asks *Saffron* what the word 'throw' means in her photo description. *Saffron* then explains:

> Hi astrid, yep like a small blanket i guess . . . a pashmina is also used as a wrap and a chunky scarf. this is about a metre and a half long knitted wrap. i guess my grandmother would call this a shawl. I would think a poncho refers to material with a hole in the centre so you slide it on rather than wrap it. aaah such confusion.

The whole exchange between *Astrid* and *Saffron* is delivered in English only. In other words, translingual practices can be understood as the ways in which groups and communities of people experience and do things that involve more than one language, including a mini English lesson like the above example.

Discursive construction of languages online

New media also provide a space for web users with different linguistic and cultural backgrounds to reflect upon their knowledge of languages or the lack of it (see detailed discussion in Lee 2013), as in the following example from a Flickr user's profile page:

Example (8)

My English is Google translator. . . .
Mi español es el traductor de Google. . . .
Mon français est traducteur de Google . . .

(*Angelo*, Italian)

This mixed language text serves multiple purposes: First, it allows *Angelo* to playfully position himself as someone who knows limited English, Spanish, and French, thus seeking support from other Flickr members; on the other hand, this mixed language text nicely illustrates what Jørgensen (2008) calls 'polylingual languaging', playful deployment of linguistic resources regardless of linguistic competence. Similar to the use of foreign languages in fan fiction writing, such playful deployment of languages enables *Angelo* to perform an international identity and widen his Flickr participation. But unlike what was shown in the fan fiction example, *Angelo*'s polylingual resources in this instance are facilitated by the popular online translator Google Translate. Advances in free online translators have presented new translingual experiences and changed the way people engage in translation activities in society. As a result of media convergence, online translators can be incorporated into social network sites. For example, Facebook has added the link 'See Translation' underneath a post that is not written in the user's native language so that the user can click through to see a translation powered by Microsoft Bing. Ordinary web users may also act as translators and eventually 'teach' the web languages of the world. The idea of collaborative or 'cloud' translation is to involve web users in the translation of web contents. The 'translations' application on Facebook is an example of collaborative translation on the web. It is an application that users can add to their Facebook profile page. Once the 'translations' application is added to a profile, the user can then join the 'community of translators' and become a translator of any language of their own choice. Translations of any content on Facebook can be submitted to the community of translators, who then review and approve the translations through a voting system. The original aim of the application is to make Facebook available to everyone regardless of language and ethnicity. These developments raise interesting questions as to whether users really benefit from such multilingual affordances. Lenihan (2011) argues that the Facebook translations application may be just another marketing strategy and suggests it may lead to 'fake multilingualism' (Kelly-Holmes 2005) for a number of reasons. Its translation page interface is available in English only; translations can only be submitted via the U.S. English site; and Facebook administrators can only receive and answer feedback/questions in English. A similar strategy is also adopted by Flickr, which greets its users in a new language every time they log on, from English and Chinese to less common languages such as Mäori, an indigenous language in New Zealand spoken by just a few thousand people. Elsewhere on the site, however, multilingual translations are restricted; official information on the site is available in only a limited number of languages. The multilingual greetings are an instance of what Thurlow (2013) calls 'pseudo-sociality': they are no more than a way of branding the U.S.-based company as one that is committed to reaching out to users around the globe.

Whatever concept is used to describe these emerging practices online, it is evident that web users are faced with unprecedented opportunities to experience multilingual texts, take part in translingual practices, and be reflexive about languages online. At the global level, these practices give rise to new forms of cross-linguistic and cultural exchanges around the world. Locally, minority languages that once were disadvantaged online may now find their place in new social media. For example, Lenihan's (2011) study of Facebook translations looks into how Irish-language translators engage in the translations application on Facebook. The non-expert translators, who can be any users of Facebook, often draw upon a range of ideas about language endangerment, linguistic purism and verbal hygiene when discussing English–Irish translations. A topic that the Irish translators in Lenihan's study often discuss is 'béarlachas', Irish words that are influenced by English, or what are often referred to as Anglicisms. In the following comment, a translator reveals the ideology of linguistic purism while discussing the term 'Anglicism': '"béarlachas" (the modern translation of which is "Anglicism"), while "bastardisation" (the process of corruption or evolution of the meaning of linguistic terms) would be more accurate' (cited in Lenihan 2011:58).

Such talk about translations, as Lenihan argues, illustrates how Facebook and other social media provide the affordances for people to take up new possibilities for translingual practices. In addition, metadiscourses about multiple linguistic resources also reveal web users' attitudes towards their own and others' practices of language choice for digital communication. How smaller languages such as Irish are represented discursively, meta-linguistically and ideologically in new social media such as YouTube and Facebook also becomes an emerging direction for future research (see Spilioti, this volume).

Researching multilingual practices in digital communication

While adopting existing theoretical frameworks for language choice and CS in face-to-face interaction, methods of research on multilingual practices online also tend to follow the discourse analytic or interactional sociolinguistic approach in studies in non-CMC contexts. Previous studies have already provided detailed linguistic analyses of mixed language texts in CMC and have, to some extent, revealed how negotiating code choice allows multilingual users to perform identities. The various translingual and polylingual practices identified in new social media seem to suggest that a) multilingual web users do not simply translate their face-to-face practices to the web context; and b) even people who are considered 'monolinguals' in offline contexts are regularly involved in multilingual interaction. While it is important to describe details of discourse patterns, ethnographic data are useful in revealing the actual social activities and practices surrounding such multilingual writing online, so as to understand better *how* and *what* people write online and *what they do* with their mixed language texts. For example, Eva Lam has carried out a series of case studies of the out-of-school second language literacy practices of young Chinese immigrants to the United States. Similar to much research on CS in CMC, her earlier work (e.g. Lam 2004) also drew upon traditional interactional linguistics and described functions of CS in relation to existing findings in face-to-face contexts. Elsewhere, Lam adopts an ethnographic approach and focuses more on participants' insider perspectives. Lam (2009), for example, draws largely upon interview data to reveal how Chinese students in the US represent and reconstruct their second language learner identities and build transnational networks in online chat. This study and others like it pay more attention to online participants' lives and online activities rather than simply providing detailed discourse analysis of their mixed language texts.

Androutsopoulos (2008) calls for further research that adopts what he calls 'discourse centred online ethnography' (DCOE), an approach that combines observation of discourse online and insights from direct contact with web users. This framework has developed from his work on German-based web environments. For example, one of his projects examines sociolinguistic styles and identity constructions on sites devoted to hip-hop culture (Androutsopoulos 2007). In undertaking DCOE on these sites, Androutsopoulos starts with systematic observation of the discourse of the sites, then interviews Internet actors to elicit insiders' perspectives. The studies of Flickr and Hong Kong-based IM discussed above also share a similar methodological approach in that their objective was to connect texts and practices. In their research on multilingual practices on Flickr, Lee and Barton (2011) started by observing 100 photo-streams to obtain a snapshot of the distribution of English and other languages in different writing spaces on Flickr (e.g. captions, tags, and comments). The next phase of the research involved identifying 30 focal participants, 18 Chinese speakers and 12 Spanish speakers, who were first invited to complete an online survey questionnaire about their general Flickr practices. The survey covered questions about what they used Flickr for, what languages they would use in different areas on the site, and why they made these choices. This was then followed up by a series of online interviews, so as to identify different ways of participating in Flickr and ways in which these users deployed their linguistic resources on their own sites. In the interviews, the questions focused on specific areas of these Flickr sites (e.g. why English was used when describing a particular photo while Chinese was used in the tags) as well as the answers to the initial survey-questionnaire. These interviews allowed the researchers to pay close attention to details about actual situations of Flickr use. As can be seen, a mixed-methods approach is crucial in a DCOE. Lexander (2012) proposes a model for understanding multilingual SMS as literacy practices that also combines text analysis with ethnographic interviews. An important point about this methodological approach is that neither language nor practice should be seen as the sole point of departure in research. Instead, researchers often need to go back and forth between data of language and data of people's practices in understanding the interplay between what is visible on the screen and what people actually do with languages online.

Conclusion and directions for future research

This chapter started with the classic debate of whether the rise of digital communication leads to the dominance of English or a more linguistically diverse Internet. It has shown that there is to date no accurate, reliable, quantitative measurement of online linguistic diversity. At the same time, a number of studies of multilingualism online aim to describe and explain web users' multilingual practices on different CMC platforms. This body of work tends to focus on issues related to language choice and code-switching. While documenting interactional patterns in relation to previous research in face-to-face conversations, researchers have also offered their own interpretation of these phenomena online – that mixed-language texts allow users to manage relationships, perform multicultural identities and build communities.

Much existing research focuses on one type of CMC at one point in time. However, in reality, people are used to multitasking and regularly participate in multiple modes of online communication. The increasing use of smart phones and mobile devices may also bring about changes in patterns of language choice online. Future research needs to take a more holistic view of people's technology-related lives, examining how multilingual practices in one digital medium may or may not carry over to another.

A related question is how language choice and multilingual practices change over time. Many web users have had many years of experience of digital media use, and longitudinal studies are needed to trace changes in linguistic practices at different stages of people's lives (but see Lee (2014) who adopts a techno-biographic approach in her study of Hong Kong young people's Web 2.0 linguistic practices).

Overall, research on multilingual practices in digital communication is certainly on the rise; compared to the volume of English-based studies, however, this body of work is still limited. Some of the topics discussed in this chapter, such as translingual practices in social media, issues of translation and the interplay between language choice and identity performance, still need further development. It is also becoming obvious that existing theories of multilingualism in sociolinguistics cannot capture new forms of multilingual encounters on the web as a result of global flows of people, objects and ideas around the world. Linguists are taking up the notion of *superdiversity* to rethink concepts and terms in sociolinguistics (see, for example, Blommaert and Rampton 2011). For one thing, the traditional notion of 'speech community' does not seem to sufficiently account for the fluidity of languages and the mobility of people online and offline. Research on multilingualism online needs to move beyond comparing CMC with face-to-face conversations in order to illuminate new forms of multilingual participation on the Internet.

In response to these new practices, mixed-methods research combining text analysis with ethnographic data and focusing on details of people's actual writing activities can certainly shed more light on the ever-changing nature of digital communication.

Related topics

- Chapter 3 Digital ethnography (Varis)
- Chapter 8 Digital discourses: a critical perspective (Spilioti)
- Chapter 10 Vernacular literacy: orthography and literacy practices (Iorio)
- Chapter 23 Translocality (Kytölä)

References

Androutsopoulos, J. 2013a, 'Code-switching in computer-mediated communication', in S. C. Herring, D. Stein, and T. Virtanen (eds.), *Handbook of the pragmatics of computer-mediated communication*, Mouton de Gruyter: Berlin, pp. 659–686.

Androutsopoulos, J. 2013b, 'Networked multilingualism: some language practices on Facebook and their implications', *International Journal of Bilingualism*, 1–21, doi:10.1177/1367006913489198.

Androutsopoulos, J. 2013c, 'Participatory culture and metalinguistic discourse: performing and negotiating German dialects on YouTube', in D. Tannen and A. M. Trester (eds.), *Discourse 2.0: language and new media*, Georgetown University Press: Washington, DC, pp. 47–72.

Androutsopoulos, J. 2008, 'Potentials and limitations of discourse-centered online ethnography', *Language@Internet*, 5, article 8, available at: http://www.languageatInternet.de/articles/2008 [accessed 1 May 2012].

Androutsopoulos, J. 2007, 'Language choice and code-switching in German-based diasporic web forums', in B. Danet and S. C. Herring (eds.), *The multilingual Internet: language, culture, and communication online*, Cambridge University Press: New York, NY, pp. 340–361.

Auer, P. 1999, 'From codeswitching via language mixing to fused lects: towards a dynamic typology of bilingual speech', *International Journal of Bilingualism*, vol. 3, no. 4, pp. 309–332.

Barton, D. and Lee, C. 2013, *Language online: investigating digital texts and practices*, Routledge: London.

Black, R. 2009, 'Online fan fiction, global identities, and imagination', *Research in the Teaching of English*, vol. 43, no. 4, pp. 397–425.

Blackledge, A. and Creese, A. 2009, *Multilingualism: a critical perspective*, Continuum: London.

Blommaert, J. and Rampton, B. 2011, 'Language and superdiversity: a position paper', *Working Papers in Urban Languages and Literacies*, paper 70, available at: http://www.kcl.ac.uk/projects/ldc/LDCPublications/workingpapers/70.pdf [accessed 1 May 2012].

Crystal, D. 2006, *Language and the Internet*, 2nd edn., Cambridge University Press: Cambridge.

Crystal, D. 1997, *English as a global language*, Cambridge University Press: Cambridge.

Danet, B. and Herring, S. C. (eds.) 2007, *The multilingual Internet: language, culture, and communication online*, Oxford University Press: Oxford.

Davies, J. 2007, 'Display, identity and the everyday: self-presentation through online image sharing', *Discourse*, vol. 28, no. 4, pp. 549–564.

Durham, M. 2003, 'Language choice on a Swiss mailing list', *Journal of Computer-Mediated Communication*, vol. 9, no. 1, available at: http://jcmc.indiana.edu/vol9/issue1/durham.html#s14 [accessed 17 June 2015].

Fishman, J. 1998, 'The new linguistic order', *Foreign Policy*, vol. 113, pp. 26–40.

Georgakopoulou, A. 1997, 'Self-presentation and interactional alignments in e-mail discourse: the style and code switches of Greek messages', *International Journal of Applied Linguistics*, vol. 7, no. 2, pp. 141–164.

Held, D. and McGrew, A. 2001, 'Globalization', in J. Krieger (ed.), *Oxford companion to the politics of the world*, Oxford University Press: Oxford, pp. 324–370.

Hinrichs, L. 2006, *Codeswitching on the web: English and Jamaican creole in email communication*, John Benjamins: Amsterdam.

Internet World Stats 2014, 'Top ten languages used in the web 2013', *Internet World Stats*, available at: http://www.Internetworldstats.com/stats7.htm [accessed 6 October 2014].

James, G. 2001, 'Cantonese particles in Hong Kong students' English e-mails', *English Today*, vol. 17, no. 3, pp. 9–16.

Jørgensen, N. J. 2008, 'Polylingual languaging around and among children and adolescents', *International Journal of Multilingualism*, vol. 5, no. 3, pp. 161–176.

Kelly-Holmes, H. 2005, *Advertising as multilingual communication*, Palgrave Macmillan: New York, NY.

Kelly-Holmes, H. 2004, 'An analysis of the language repertoires of students in higher education and their language choices on the Internet (Ukraine, Poland, Macedonia, Italy, France, Tanzania, Oman and Indonesia)', *International Journal of Multicultural Societies*, vol. 6, no. 1, pp. 29–52.

Koutsogiannis, D. and Mitsikopoulou, B. 2007, 'Greeklish and greekness: trends and discourses of "glocalness"', in B. Danet and S. C. Herring (eds.), *The multilingual Internet: language, culture, and communication online*, Cambridge University Press: New York, NY, pp. 142–162.

Lam, W. S. E. 2009, 'Multiliteracies on instant messaging in negotiating local, translocal and transnational affiliations: a case of an adolescent immigrant', *Reading Research Quarterly*, vol. 44, no. 4, pp. 377–397.

Lam, W. S. E. 2004, 'Second language socialization in a bilingual chat room: global and local considerations', *Language Learning and Technology*, vol. 8, no. 3, pp. 44–65.

Lee, C. 2014, 'Language choice and self-presentation in social media: the case of university students in Hong Kong', in P. Seargeant and C. Tagg (eds.), *The language of social media: community and identity on the Internet*, Palgrave Macmillan: Basingstoke, pp. 91–111.

Lee, C. 2013, '"My English is so poor . . . so I take photos": meta-linguistic discourse of English online', in D. Tannen and A. M. Tester (eds.), *Discourse 2.0: language and new media*, Georgetown University Press: Washington, DC, pp. 72–84.

Lee, C. 2011, 'Texts and practices of micro-blogging: status updates on Facebook', in C. Thurlow and K. Mroczek (eds.), *Digital discourse: language in the new media*, Oxford University Press: New York, NY, pp. 110–128.

Lee, C. 2007a, 'Affordances and text-making practices in online instant messaging', *Written Communication*, vol. 24, no. 3, pp. 223–49.

Lee, C. 2007b, 'Linguistic features of email and ICQ instant messaging in Hong Kong', in B. Danet and S. C. Herring (eds.), *The multilingual Internet: language, culture, and communication online*, Oxford University Press: New York, NY, pp. 184–208.

Lee, C. 2002, 'Literacy practices of computer-mediated communication in Hong Kong', *Reading Matrix*, vol. 2, no. 2, Special Issue: Literacy and the Web, available at: http://www.readingmatrix.com/articles/lee/article.pdf [accessed 1 May 2012].

Lee, C. and Barton, D. 2011, 'Constructing glocal identities through multilingual writing practices on Flickr.com', *International Multilingual Research Journal*, vol. 5, no. 1, pp. 1–21.

Lenihan, A. 2011, '"Join our community of translators": language ideologies and Facebook', in C. Thurlow and K. Mroczek (eds.), *Digital discourse: language in the new media*, Oxford University Press: New York, NY, pp. 48–66.

Leppänen, S. 2007, 'Youth language in media contexts: insights into the functions of English in Finland', *World Englishes*, vol. 26, no. 2, pp. 149–169.

Leppänen, S. and Peuronen, S. 2012, 'Multilingualism on the Internet', in M. Martin-Jones, A. Blackledge and A. Creese (eds.), *The Routledge handbook of multilingualism*, Routledge, Abingdon, pp. 384–402.

Lexander, K. V. 2012, 'Analyzing multilingual texting in Senegal: an approach for the study of mixed language SMS', in M. Sebba, S. Mahootian and C. Jonsson (eds.) *Language mixing and code-switching in writing*, Routledge: London, pp. 146–169.

Mafu, S. 2004, 'From the oral tradition to the information era: the case of Tanzania', *International Journal on Multicultural Societies*, vol. 6, no. 1, pp. 53–78.

McClure, E. 2001, 'Oral and written Assyrian codeswitching', in R. Jacobson (ed.) *Codeswitching worldwide II*, Mouton de Gruyter: Berlin, pp. 157–191.

Myers-Scotton, C. 1998, 'A theoretical introduction to the markedness model', in C. Myers-Scotton (ed.), *Codes and consequences: choosing linguistic varieties*, Oxford University Press: New York, NY, pp. 18–38.

Nishimura, Y. 2003, 'Linguistic innovations and interactional features of casual online communication in Japanese', *Journal of Computer-mediated Communication*, available at: http://onlinelibrary.wiley.com/doi/10.1111/j.1083-6101.2003.tb00356.x/full [accessed 17 June 2015].

Palfreyman, D. and Al-Khalil, M. 2003, '"A funky language for teenzz to use": representing Gulf Arabic in instant messaging', *Journal of Computer-Mediated Communication*, vol. 9, no. 1, available at: http://onlinelibrary.wiley.com/doi/10.1111/j.1083-6101.2003.tb00355.x/full.

Paolillo, J. C. 2007, 'How much multilingualism? language diversity on the Internet', in B. Danet and S. C. Herring (eds.), *The multilingual Internet: language, culture, and communication online*, Oxford University Press: New York, NY, pp. 408–430.

Pennycook, A. 2008, 'Translingual English', *Australian Review of Applied Linguistics*, vol. 31, no. 3, pp. 30.1–30.9.

Phillipson, R. 1992, *Linguistic imperialism*, Oxford University Press: Oxford.

Sebba, M., Mahootian, S., and Jonsson, C. (eds.) 2012, *Language mixing and code-switching in writing*, Routledge: London.

Siebenhaar, B. 2006, 'Code choice and code-switching in Swiss-German Internet Relay Chat rooms', *Journal of Sociolinguistics*, vol. 10, no. 4, pp. 481–509.

Specter, M. 1996, 'World, wide, web: 3 English words', *The New York Times*, 14 April, pp. 4–5.

Spilioti, T. 2009, 'Graphemic representation of text messaging: alphabet choice and codeswitches in Greek SMS', *Pragmatics*, vol. 19, no. 3, pp. 393–412.

Su, H-Y 2003, 'The multilingual and multi-orthographic Taiwan-based Internet: creative uses of writing systems on college-affiliated BBSs', *Journal of Computer-Mediated Communication*, vol. 9, no. 1, available at: http://jcmc.indiana.edu/vol9/issue1/su.html.

Tagg, C. and Seargeant, P. 2012, 'Writing systems at play in Thai-English online interactions', *Writing Systems Research*, vol. 4, no. 2, pp. 195–213.

Thurlow, C. 2011, 'Fakebook: synthetic media, pseudo-sociality and the rhetorics of Web 2.0', in D. Tannen and A. M. Trester (eds.), *Discourse 2.0: language and new media*, Georgetown University Press: Washington, DC, pp. 225–250.

Tseliga, T. 2007, '"It's all Greeklish to me!": linguistic and sociocultural perspectives on Roman-alphabeted Greek in asynchronous computer-mediated communication', in B. Danet and S. C. Herring (eds.), *The multilingual Internet: language, culture, and communication online*, Oxford University Press: New York, NY, pp. 116–141.

W3techs 2012, 'Usage of content languages for websites', available at: http://w3techs.com/technologies/overview/content_language/all [accessed 6 September 2012].

Warschauer, M., El Said, G. R., and Zohry, A. A. 2007, 'Language choice online: globalization and identity in Egypt', in B. Danet and S. C. Herring (eds.), *The multilingual Internet: language, culture, and communication online*, Oxford University Press, New York, NY, pp. 303–318.

Further reading

Androutsopoulos, J. 2013, 'Code-switching in computer-mediated communication', in S. C. Herring, D. Stein, and T. Virtanen (eds.), *Handbook of the pragmatics of computer-mediated communication*, Mouton de Gruyter: Berlin, pp. 659–686.

This is a comprehensive overview of code-switching research in the context of CMC.

Danet, B. and S. C. Herring 2007, *The multilingual Internet: language, culture, and communication online*, Cambridge University Press: New York, NY.

Chapters in this edited volume report on studies of multilingualism online in a wide range of languages and sociolinguistic contexts.

Leppänen, S. and Peuronen, S. 2012, 'Multilingualism on the Internet', in M. Martin-Jones, A. Blackledge and A. Creese (eds.), *The Routledge handbook of multilingualism*, Routledge, Abingdon, pp. 384–402.

This is a comprehensive review of literature on multilingualism online, with illustrative examples from the author's own research in Finland.

8
Digital discourses
A critical perspective

Tereza Spilioti

Introduction

The study of language use in digital communication cannot shy away from the wider social, cultural and historical discourses about digital media that interplay with the micro-level stylistic, textual and interactional practices of everyday users. Research on discourses about digital media draws on critical approaches to discourse informed by social, media, and cultural theory as well as by sociolinguistics and interactional analysis. Here, the term 'discourse' is not only used to refer to the micro-level practices of language-in-use, or 'little d' discourse (Gee 2010: 34), but it primarily encapsulates the wider communicative and representational practices that naturalize 'socially accepted associations among ways of using language, of thinking, valuing, acting, and interacting', also known as 'Big D' Discourses (Gee 2010: 34). These wider discursive practices are inherently 'ideological' in so far as they articulate particular sets of ideas, perceptions, or received wisdom and, at the same time, they are organized, modulated and reproduced within power-regulating institutional environments, such as the media or the state (Blommaert 2005: 161–164).

The chapter provides a critical overview of the key themes around which contemporary discourses about digital communication often cluster, in an attempt to trace their development over time and understand their popular appeal. The discussion of current research in this area is organized in terms of its focus on the particular power-regulating institutional environments mediating, modulating and reproducing such discourses. More specifically, previous and current research has scrutinized discourses about digital communication that appear primarily in two broad domains: news media environments (with a focus on news items related to digital media that appear in print, broadcast or online), and social media environments, particularly web spaces regulated by social media developers and corporations (e.g., web design interfaces, 'about' pages of social media). Furthermore, this chapter situates the public and popular discourses about digital communication in relation to academic discourses that have been preoccupied with similar themes and have contributed to revealing the ideological underpinnings of public and corporate discourses. In addition to studies that explicitly examine such public discourses from a critical perspective, research on language use and practice from both the so-called first and second waves of Computer-Mediated Communication research (see Androutsopoulos 2006) can also point to potential gaps between symbolic meanings of digital media and actual digital practices.

Tereza Spilioti

Historical perspectives

Investigating the ways in which digital media and language use are talked about, understood and valued is important because it opens up a window into the very ways in which symbolic meanings are assigned to language and digital communication at particular moments in history (Baym 2010: 23; Thurlow & Mroczek 2011: xxiv). As Sturken and Thomas (2004: 1) argue, 'the meanings that are attributed to new technologies are some of the most important evidence we can find of the visions, both optimistic and anxious, through which modern societies cohere'. Such visions of digital communication reflect key concerns about human behaviour, language and technology within a particular social context. At the same time, they are highly 'productive', as they can impact upon the development and integration of digital technologies in people's everyday lives (Sturken & Thomas 2004: 3). For example, the rise of cyberpunk literature in the 1980s (e.g., William Gibson's *Neuromancer*) has fuelled not only collective anxieties but also collective imageries for virtual worlds that we have seen later developed by the 1990s generation of computer programmers and designers (e.g., Second Life; see Abdullah, this volume). In other words, the symbolic meanings assigned to digital media in the 'Big D' Discourses can run ahead or lag behind what seems appropriate at the level of language practice and use at a given historical moment (Coupland 2014: 283).

Popular fascination with 'new media' – together with the ensuing hype and hysteria about its impact on human behaviour, cognition, communication, and/or language – is far from a 'new' or recent phenomenon. Cultural historians' contributions to the critical study of public discourses about communication technologies have been paramount to a better understanding of the historical development of such discourses. As Ong (1982) points out, the then 'new' technology of writing stirred similar debates among Athenian society in the fourth century BC, with Socrates lamenting the demise of memory and 'true knowledge' due to the invention of writing. (Yet of course it is this very invention – and Plato's facility with it – that allowed Socrates' ideas to reverberate through the ages). The rise of more recent technologies for communication, such as the telegraph, the telephone or the television, also engendered a great deal of controversy about their impact on human cognition, behaviour and communication (Fischer 1994; Moran 2013; Standage 1998). Baym (2010: 36) points to Spigel's (1992) work on the ambivalence surrounding television, which was understood both as an opportunity for bringing families together and as a potentially damaging factor in family relationships.

Cultural historians have shown that cultural discourses about technologies – both 'old' and 'new' – present some striking similarities, especially in terms of an underlying tendency to portray 'new media' (whatever this may be at different moments in history) as an evil force or a hopeful blessing. In other words, popular discourses about media appear to form a continuum of primarily utopian and dystopian visions of the world, orienting at times to the technology's empowering and liberating potential, and at times to its 'darker', threatening and destructive side – without excluding cases where both sides are vehemently argued at the same time (Baym 2010: 28). Extreme utopian and dystopian discourses coincide with the early stages of adoption and integration of a given technology in everyday life – for instance, it would be difficult to find many who support Socrates' critique of the invention of writing today. As technologies become 'domesticated' (Silverstone & Haddon 1996) and 'new' media become 'old', the symbolic meanings that popular discourses assign to technologies can become naturalized, dropped or imbued with the personal meanings we (as users) assign to them in our everyday use (Baym 2010: 45). Through this process of domestication (Silverstone & Haddon 1996), media become mundane and relegate their status to other fleetingly 'new' technologies that, in turn, instil 'new' horrors and/or anticipations in the collective public psyche.

In this chapter, key issues in two areas of public discourse – news media contexts and social media corporate or design environments – are traced along the aforementioned continuum between utopian and dystopian visions of digital communication. In doing so, the chapter aims to reveal how particular orientations appear to prevail in certain public domains and to explore the role of institutional ideologies in the articulation and reproduction of such discourses.

Critical issues and topics

Research on discourses about digital communication focuses on four recurrent issues in public debates from the Internet's first boom in the 1990s. The four issues bring together a range of inter-related and sometimes conflicting popular claims and anxieties: (i) discourses about digital sociality, (ii) discourses about digital equality and diversity, (iii) discourses about youth and digital media, and (iv) discourses about digital language.

The rise of public debate about these topics is often associated with and triggered by an extreme and unilateral attention to certain aspects of the digital design that are popularly understood as dictating particular types of social practice, including linguistic and communicative practices (Baym 2010: 22; boyd 2014: 16). In other words, popular representations of digital communication primarily draw on technological deterministic assumptions that see a causal relationship between technology and communication: 'forms of technology actively cause new forms of social relations to come about' (Hutchby 2001: 442). We need, of course, to acknowledge that technological determinism has not only underpinned public (or lay) debates about digital communication, but it has also been influential in shaping academic work on language/society and digital media, especially in the 1990s. For critical reviews of such sociological and (socio)linguistic studies, see Hutchby (2001) and Androutsopoulos (2006), respectively.

In addition to pointing out technological deterministic biases, critical approaches to discourses about digital communication need also to attend to the 'socio-historical circumstances within which such [digital] affordances are created, dropped or promoted' (boyd 2014: 16). This shift of focus within critical studies of such discourses opens up the field to a more profound understanding of the social and cultural forces that shape (and are shaped by) popular views and understandings of digital communication. In order to achieve this, critical perspectives to digital discourses have two inter-related analytic foci: (i) the strategic use of a range of micro-linguistic, stylistic, and narrative resources through which varying discourses about the aforementioned key issues are articulated and modulated; and (ii) the ways in which such discourses interplay and sustain/challenge particular ideological frameworks (e.g., capitalism, neoliberalism, language purism) associated with relevant groups of actors and institutions (e.g., social media corporations). The following discussion attends to both aspects as they become relevant in current studies and research.

Current contributions and research

As mentioned above, research on discourses about digital communication is primarily preoccupied with four key issues that are discussed in detail in the following sections. Each section starts by focusing on mass (particularly news) media and their orientations to utopian and/or dystopian accounts of digital communication. It then describes research on discourses associated with digital media and, particularly, the digital spaces regulated by web developers and social media corporations. At the end of each section, (news) media and corporate discourses are positioned vis-à-vis academic discourses that have been preoccupied with similar themes and engaged with enhancing critical awareness of digital media and communication.

Tereza Spilioti

Discourses about digital sociality

Public discourses about digital communication often revolve around the impact of digital media on human sociality, with a focus on the quality/authenticity of digital communication and the formation of social relationships. Studies of material associated with news media publications – such as news articles, opinion pieces, letters to the editor, cartoons – have demonstrated the rise of public discourses that oscillate between utopian and dystopian visions of communication (e.g., Baym 2010; Thurlow 2006). Discourses orienting towards a dystopian digital reality often portray text-messaging, e-mail, Twitter and other digital media as impoverished forms of social interaction. In such media accounts, digital communication appears to lack the genuine and warm aura of face-to-face interaction and is said to cause the deterioration of existing social relationships. Popular claims about asocial and antisocial behaviour online were particularly prevalent in the early days of text-based digital communication. Although the discourse of 'digital asociality' has been arguably challenged by the rise of the eponymously 'social' media in the early 2000s, public interest in antisocial behaviour online has not subsided, with instances of phenomena like cyberbullying and trolling receiving ample attention and widespread reporting in current news media publications.

At the other end of the utopian–dystopian continuum, we find discourses orienting towards extreme techno-optimistic visions. Such discourses foreground the promise digital technologies offer for enriching our existing social networks and amplifying feelings of intimacy at a distance. With the rise of the so-called 'social' media, these voices become all the more prevalent in news publications, as the boundaries between traditional mass media and digital media become increasingly blurred and their respective vested interests overlap. Regardless of their dystopian and/or utopian slant, discourses in news media environments recurrently draw on a key premise that sees a clear-cut distinction between the 'real', 'unmediated' world and the 'virtual' world of digital communication. It is against the 'standards' of authenticity presumed in face-to-face interaction that virtual worlds, identities and communities are compared and found to be falling short or exceeding expectations.

Popular anxieties and debates about authenticity and the formation of social relationships have been fuelled by heightened attention to certain technological features of digital media, particularly the predominance of text and significant time lags (asynchronicity) in the forms of digital interaction flourishing in the 1990s (e.g., email, text-messaging). The varying scales of interactivity experienced in these forms of mediated communication invited more reflexive accounts of digital uses in newspapers, magazines, and films – but such reflexivity often appears trapped within a technologically deterministic logic, where systemic features are foregrounded as the primary cause for the dystopian and utopian visions described in these popular accounts. The fascination with the technological features and their unidirectional association with the presumed (a-/anti-)sociality in digital communication may be expected from those who do not participate in the development of such technologies, including journalists, politicians, educators and other professionals whose voices are often privileged in news media. Positioning oneself as a 'consumer' with limited engagement in the process of technology production and design is often associated with increased fetishism of technological products and exaggeration of their impact on social relationships. But what about computer designers and developers, for whom the so-called new technologies presumably do not take the form of an untamed beast but appear well integrated in their everyday work and life?

A critical study of the discourse used for the design of digital interfaces foregrounds a similar preoccupation with 'sociality', shaped within a culture that has not escaped from a technologically deterministic thinking. Marwick's (2013) ethnography of the 'tech scene' in San Francisco from 2006 to 2010 demonstrates that their discourses (the 'ideology of Web 2.0') also combine 'technological progressivism (technology always makes things better) and technological determinism (technology determines social effects)' (p. 6). This combination is nicely illustrated in how one of the most popular social media platforms present themselves on their sign up page: 'Facebook helps you connect and share with the people in your life' (Facebook Inc. 2014). In this example, Facebook – both as a technological/systemic interface and as a company – appears as the main agent assisting with the formation of social relationships and, thus, improving people's social lives.

The zeitgeist of 'sociality' not only appears in the corporate discourse of social media that attempts to attract new users/clients but, more importantly, it is often embedded in the 'social' buttons of system interfaces in ways that can be rather opaque to everyday users. As John (2012) points out, keywords such as 'share' or 'like' capitalize on the words' positive connotations and associations with forming and maintaining intimate relations: partners and friends tend to like one another and happily share spaces (e.g., rooms), objects (e.g., clothes, food) and feelings. But a close analysis of how such keywords are used in digital environments reveals that their meaning has gradually been extended to encompass a range of activities that refer to the ways in which users engage primarily with the digital interface rather than with each other. In the case of 'share' in particular, John (2012) argues that it is now used to describe participation on social media platforms in general, invoking and, at the same time, moving beyond its pre-digital meanings of distribution (of goods, products, etc.) or communication (of feelings, thoughts, etc.). Facebook's 'sharing' and 'connecting' imperatives (van Dijk 2013: 45–67) are constitutive of and, at the same time, operative to the modulation and propagation of discourses about digital sociality.

At the same time, the discourse of 'sociality' expands to other domains of practice that are purely commercial: it is by now a truism that exchange of data about users between social media corporations and advertisers is portrayed as 'sharing'. For example, while informing users about privacy controls for tailored ads, Twitter Inc. states:

> We work with ads partners to bring you more useful and interesting advertising content. We may do this based on information that our ads partners *share* with us. [. . .] Here's one way it would work. Let's say a flower shop wants to advertise a Valentine's Day special on Twitter. They'd prefer to show their ad to floral enthusiasts who subscribe to their newsletter. To get the special offer to those people, who are also on Twitter, the shop may *share* with us an unreadable scramble (called a hash) of emails from their mailing list. We can then match that to a hash of emails that our users have associated with their accounts in order to show them a Promoted Tweet for the Valentine's Day deal on Twitter.
>
> *(Twitter Inc. 2014a, emphasis added)*

The story that illustrates the 'sharing' of information between Twitter Inc. and other commercial businesses provides a telling example of how discourses of 'sociality' mystify purely financial and commercial relationships (John 2012: 169). In the quote above, the verb 'to share' with all its positive connotations is used to refer to the commercial exchange of user data (i.e. email lists) that is aimed at increasing sales and overall profit. This financial activity, which appears to target 'floral enthusiasts' rather than 'clients' or 'buyers' is also nicely set against the backdrop of Valentine's Day, evoking other forms of 'sharing' associated with intimacy, like exchanges of gifts and declarations of love between partners and loved ones. Recasting financial and commercial exchanges as 'social' is a key strategy for sustaining and promoting the kind of 'pseudosociality' that enables commercial businesses to hide 'their desire to influence and manage people by

Tereza Spilioti

invoking apparently interpersonal gestures of informality and familiarity' (Thurlow 2013: 244). It is also highly congruent with the neoliberal ideologies of consumer capitalism, where the market logic infiltrates into and (re)appropriates social relations and their associated discourse. As Marwick's (2013: 12) research reveals, neoliberalism – understood in her work as 'a form of governmentality, specifically the theory that the free market has become an organizing principle of society' (see Foucault 2004) – has played a key role in shaping 'Web 2.0 ideology'. Unlike the initial (anti-capitalist) claims of Web 2.0 developers and designers, social media discourses (as manifest in the web design interface of relevant platforms) end up embracing the neoliberal ideals they had set out to challenge or resist.

In sum, a range of utopian and dystopian visions about digital sociality are circulated through news media publications and social media (corporate and design) discourse, with the latter clustering more towards the utopian end of the continuum. Regardless of their orientation, the discourses of digital sociality adhere to technological determinism as a rationale for under-standing social behaviour online and tend to distinguish between the virtual/mediated and real/face-to-face worlds. It is worth noting that similar assumptions underlie early academic work on online sociability, when the influential media richness theory in the 1980s (Daft & Lengel 1984) was modelled on face-to-face communication, and research on online identities and communities echoed 'virtual vs real' dichotomies (see chapters by Angouri and Graham, this volume). Since then, studies from both the first and second wave of CMC research have played a significant role in casting doubt on popular claims about digital media a/anti-sociality by turning attention to the social, playful and creative uses of digital technologies (e.g., Danet 2001) and providing more contextualized and situated approaches to digital (im)politeness (e.g., Herring 1994; Locher 2010). Along with pointing out the gap between popular views in public discourses and users' digital practices, research on language and digital communication has started to explicitly address and critically analyse such public discourses by scrutinising news media texts from a Critical Discourse Analysis (CDA) perspective (e.g., Thurlow 2007) and examining technologists' ideas and discourses through the lens of ethnography (e.g., Marwick 2013).

Discourses about digital equality and diversity

The text-based nature of early digital technologies (e.g., email, echat, text-messaging) offered interactants no visual or audio access to one another's face, voice, gestures, body posture, etc. and has thus been understood to result in the reduction of social cues that readily provide information about one's accent, emotions, race, age, gender and so on. Although such systemic characteristics were held responsible for the demise of trust and authenticity in the formation of social relationships, they have also been celebrated for their potential to liberate digital com-munication from long-established divisions associated with social class, ethnicity, gender, etc.

In news media environments, early utopian visions of the Internet celebrate the reduction of social cues as 'lead[ing] to people valuing one another's contributions for their intrinsic worth rather than the speaker's status' (Baym 2010: 34). In other words, digital communication offered the promise of a more equal, democratic and diverse society. This discourse is still very prevalent in political and media debates, where the concept of 'participatory democracy' draws on the idea of open and transparent communication between high-status government officials and ordinary citizens. The interactivity of social media platforms like Facebook offers ample opportunities for staging this type of communication – for example, when users like, share and comment on President Barack Obama's quotes and statements posted on the official Facebook page of the White House.

On the other hand, discourses orienting toward dystopian visions of digital technologies associate the reduction of social cues with the increasing potential for anonymity and, possibly, deception online. The challenge that online anonymity poses for long-established social divisions can also be understood as a threat to the ways in which a particular society coheres. Although such popular anxieties are less prevalent in current U.S. or U.K. political and media debates, they are nicely illustrated in discourses about the recent controversial ban on Twitter by the Turkish telecommunication authorities. Following the circulation of recordings of corruption allegations targeting the Turkish Prime Minister and his family, telecommunication authorities blocked Twitter in the country in March 2014. One month later, a constitutional court ruling condemned the ban as a breach of freedom of expression, and the government reversed its policy. Nevertheless, the court decision was not well received by the Prime Minister, who argued that it disregarded 'our national and moral values' (*BBC News* 2014), thus portraying social media as incongruent with the core values of Turkish society.

While the perceived anonymity afforded by the web feeds into popular anxieties about loss of control and unwanted challenges to existing structures, it also feeds into dystopian visions of the Internet as a site of extreme control and surveillance. The possibility of deception due to reduced social cues, together with increased 'visibility' and 'spreadability' of online content in social media platforms (boyd 2014: 11), is invoked by technophobic discourses where our online behaviour is portrayed as constantly monitored by third parties. In a recent example of such discourses in news reporting, the *Daily Mail* asks, 'Is the Internet turning into Big Brother?' (Woolaston 2014). The article, whose popularity is demonstrated by '1k shares', draws on the Net Threats report from Pew Research Center and argues that 'by 2025, the web will be governed by a system heavily influenced by governments, large corporations, and security services *all trying to control our behaviours*' (Woolaston 2014, emphasis added). Although the article acknowledges that the report was based on canvassing expert opinions, it omits the original report's disclaimer that 'it is not a representative, randomized survey' (Anderson & Rainie 2014). The article also overlooks the review's more balanced approach, silencing, in other words, any expert opinions that cast doubt on the Big Brother vision of the Internet in 2025. Instead of empowering individuals, the Internet is portrayed here as a tool for empowering established structures and institutions – e.g., governments, large corporations and security services – by means of control and surveillance.

In addition to political and news debates, the 'equality and diversity discourse' also emerges in the corporate domain of digital media. More specifically, we will focus here on issues of language, gender and race representation as manifest in corporate discourse and web design developments in digital media. In terms of linguistic diversity and inclusion, social media like Facebook and Twitter have committed to localizing their sites' interfaces and providing more language options beyond English. For example, Twitter Inc. states that:

> Twitter is a valuable tool for people to exchange timely bits of information, whether it be a momentous news event, a personal story, or a random thought. We want everyone in the world to have the opportunity to engage in this important exchange, so we're calling on the help of real people to translate our site into their own language.
>
> *(2014b)*

As it tunes in to key principles of equality and diversity, Twitter Inc. appears to be primarily concerned with widening participation in 'this important information exchange' and inclusion of people around the world. In order to achieve this, the task of increasing representation in the site's language options is not assigned to professional experts but to a community of translators who are sourced among current users of the social media platform. In other words, the institutionalized discourse of equality and diversity, with its associated themes of widening participation and inclusion, meets the values of information sharing and 'do it yourself' (DIY) ethic of hacker counterculture. The Twitter Translation Center and its forums are portrayed as the realization of techno-optimist visions of open, transparent and democratic communities where status (e.g., the role of 'Twitter Top Translator') is not assumed a priori on the basis of one's expertize, seniority, etc. Instead, this role is achieved through active participation and is legitimated by an algorithm that selects people who are 'submitting quality translations, voting for other quality translations and having translations approved by moderators' (Twitter Inc. 2014b). This presentation of the specific social media service, however, appears oblivious to the additional corporate motivation for localizing the site's interface: namely, the company's need to expand their reach around the globe in order to increase overall profit. Initiatives like the Twitter Translation Center illustrate the interesting combination of the open-source radical counterculture of hackers (evident in the quote above) with the entrepreneurial logic of consumer capitalism that motivates such corporate decisions – indeed, this combination arises as the hallmark of 'web 2.0 ideology' (Marwick 2013: 15).

Regardless of their motives or articulations, such initiatives can be understood as a move toward increased language representation and acceptance of linguistic diversity in digital environments. This is also apparent in the discourse of politico-economic alliances. At the time of writing, the European Union, whose official policy has been to promote linguistic diversity, informs visitors to the European Commission's 'Language Policy' page that 'this information is only available in EN[glish] for the moment. Other language versions will be added shortly' (European Commission 2014). In that respect, having already localized their design interface in a range of languages, social media may appear to be more inclusive, despite their corporate agenda. Nevertheless, research on metalinguistic discourse in social media, like Lenihan's (2013) study of Facebook Translations Application (an app similar to the Twitter Translation Centre mentioned above), reveals that this ideal of inclusivity has its limitations in practice. In an ethnographic study of the Facebook's Irish Language translations application, Lenihan (2011, 2013) nicely demonstrates the gap between Facebook's idealized discourse about linguistic diversity and the ideologies of monolingualism and language standardization, as they emerge in the discourse of the application's interface design and in interaction between the members of the self-appointed translators' community. Similar to Twitter who 'are calling on the help of real people to translate our site into *their own language*' (rather than langua*ges*), Facebook's application architecture 'structures and promotes each language as a separate entity and categorizes users accordingly' (Lenihan 2011: 56). The monolingual ideal of 'one speaker–one language' is also coupled with the availability of the application only in English, resulting in the exclusion of any non-English-speakers from the task purportedly aimed at increasing linguistic diversity and inclusion. Lenihan (2011: 60) also points to the varying agendas of the self-appointed translators, who 'come with their own histories, priorities, and ideologies'. Indeed, the 'new' social media community of self-appointed translators appears to be a site where 'old' debates about language standardization can be played out. In the case of Facebook translators of the Irish language, debates centred around issues of standardness and invoked ideals and beliefs more related to ideologies of language purism than of language diversity.

Although inclusive linguistic diversity has preoccupied Facebook developers' agenda since 2009 (albeit at the level of idealized corporate discourse), gender heteronormativity has been invoked by the interface design of the popular social media platform until very recently. It is only in February 2014 for U.S. users (and in June 2014 for U.K. users) that gender options beyond the two highly contested and heteronormative categories of 'male' and 'female' were made available. Despite the activist and anti-establishment spirit of hacker counterculture that helped set the so-called 'Web 2.0 revolution' in motion, equality and diversity in terms of gender representation in the architecture of web interfaces and in the corporate hierarchies of social media companies remain an issue. Ethnographic studies of tech communities (e.g., Marwick 2013; Neff, Wissinger & Zukin 2005), together with equality and diversity reports published by social media corporations (Williams 2014), provide ample evidence that senior level and technical staff positions (developers, designers, etc.) are occupied by young, white, male graduates of elite schools (or dropouts, as in the case of Facebook CEO Mark Zuckerberg). The utopian vision of the Internet as a gender/race/class-blind environment runs counter to the specific socio-historical circumstances within which digital technologies are designed, developed and used. In terms of design, this becomes especially apparent when racial or social class biases interfere with the product's use, as in voice-recognition software that fails to 'understand' regional accents of English, or image-capture technologies that have difficulty capturing darker-skinned people.

To sum up, news media discourses have capitalized on the concept of 'anonymity' online by orienting toward heightened participatory potentials of digital media and, alternatively, toward their affordances for deception, control and surveillance. In relation to this public debate, social media corporate and technologists' discourses orient primarily toward utopian representations of digital media as sites of equal participation for all. Since the early days of language-focused research on digital communication, the concept of 'anonymity' online has been problematized, and the idea of digital media as gender-blind has been challenged by studies showing that stereotypical associations between gender and language use are often reproduced in digital environments (e.g., Herring 1994; Herring & Paolillo 2006). Digital ethnographies of specific communities (like Lenihan's study of Facebook translators) provide further evidence about the prevalence of pre-established social divisions and language stereotypes in digital environments. For instance, boyd's (2014) research on U.S. teenagers' practices reveals that 'communities where race is fraught maintain the same systems of segregation online and off' (p. 155). Sociolinguistic and media ethnographic research has been paramount in casting a critical eye over popular discourses and shedding light on digital inequalities in the much-celebrated Internet era of global participation. Academic research on control and surveillance is still lagging behind, especially in terms of critically approaching such popular anxieties and reframing the public debate in more informative ways that take into account human agency, social structures and information/algorithmic processing in social media (see Jones, this volume).

Discourses about youth and digital media

Discourses about youth and digital media are particularly prevalent in mass (primarily news) media environments. *Being Five*, an online comic strip created by George Sfarnas, provides a nice illustration of the key ideas that run through such discourses. The main character is 'a kid named Georgie who blogs using voice recognition software (since he can't read or write yet)'. In a 2014 comic strip sequence, little Georgie exclaims in a self-reflective mood:

> i'm a digital native, which means i was born in the age of technology . . . so it comes natural to me! my parents are digital immigrants, which means they can learn technology, but they have to work at it! and my grandparents are digital aliens, which means they barely know how to use a toaster!
>
> *(Sfarnas 2014)*

The above comic strip subsumes ideas about youth and digital media under the prevalent discourse of 'digital nativism'. Digital nativism employs age as a key category for talking about the varying ways in which people engage with and communicate through digital technologies. Based primarily on a widely cited article by Marc Prensky (2001), the discourse of 'digital nativism' appears to recast the generation gap between adults and adolescents in terms of a digital gap between 'digital natives' (younger generations born and raised with access to digital technologies) and 'digital immigrants' (older generations who first started using digital media in their adult life). The 'digital native' metaphor has been rather powerful because it subsumes a number of presuppositions about digital communication and its users. First and foremost, it delineates the digital realm as a separate space or a land with its own 'native' (or immigrant) populations, evoking the online/mediated vs offline/face-to-face divide that also underpins other popular claims (see section on discourses about digital sociality). At the same time, it presupposes that the 'native' populations (i.e. younger generations) naturally inhabit the digital space and thus know how to use the technologies, behave appropriately and communicate effectively in digital environments. As 'digital natives', adolescents and children can also be portrayed as fluent in 'digital language' (see next section).

'Digital nativism' can subsume orientations to both utopian and dystopian visions of young people: at times, digital natives can be heralded as skilful and knowledgeable multi-taskers; at other times, news media discourses focus on adolescents' reduced attention spans, lower literacy standards, Internet addiction and antisocial behaviour like cyberbullying (boyd 2014: 22). Regardless of whether they are presented as 'wired whizzes', 'techno-slaves' (McKay *et al.* 2005; Thurlow & Bell 2009) or as the seemingly less evaluative 'digital natives', the matter of referring to entire generations of users is equally problematic. As Critical Discourse Analysts (e.g., Wodak 2001: 73) have pointed out, labelling and evaluating social actors is achieved through noun phrases stereotypically attributed to entire social groups. The ideological underpinning of such attributions lies in their essentializing logic: for example, the portrayal of younger generations as 'digital natives' erases any intra-generational variation in their digital practices or competencies and treats the cultural construct of 'age' as the main 'causative agent' (Keesing 1981: 72) that explains digital behaviour and communication. More importantly, such attributions conceal – and reproduce – digital inequalities and uneven distribution of Internet access and digital skills among adolescents (like Hargittai's [2010] 'digital na(t)ives'; see also boyd 2014: 179).

The discourse of 'digital nativism' is less prevalent in corporate and web design discourse of popular social media, as from a corporate perspective it is vital to expand rather than limit the target audience. Nevertheless, ethnographic research on tech communities foregrounds the ideal image of the 'young white middle-class male' for would-be designers and developers of social media (Marwick 2013). In addition to such ethnographic research, longitudinal and wide-scale studies of data collected from different regional and socio-economic strata can also attest to inequalities of access to digital technologies, which are often silenced in popular representations of the youth. Examples of this type of research can be found in boyd's (2014) qualitative and ethnographic research on U.S. teenagers from 2003 to 2012 and Koutsogiannis and Adampa's (2012) survey of 4174 students (coupled with qualitative interviews) from a range of geographical regions throughout Greece.

According to boyd (2014: 179), anthropologist Genevieve Bell has also interrogated the implications of the widely cited metaphor of the digital native–immigrant divide. History (especially American history) can provide ample examples where the so-called 'natives' have been displaced or indoctrinated by the 'wiser' immigrants, begging the question whether adults/ immigrants 'intend to recognize native knowledge as valuable or as something that should be restricted and controlled' (boyd 2014: 179). Although it is hard to address issues of 'intent', some of the discourses associated with 'digital nativism' may be associated more with adults' anxieties about youth behaviour and communication and less with the digital technologies per se. This claim is further reinforced by unpacking metalinguistic discourses, as discussed in the following section.

Discourses about digital language

The impact of digital media on language, both in terms of the language produced in digital communication and in relation to language standards, is a recurrent trope in popular discourses about digital technologies. This line of research primarily focuses on corpora of news media texts, where the use of recurrent narrative resources in terms of 'threads' across media publications is put under scrutiny. Thurlow's (2006, 2007) research on popular accounts of digital discourse in English-language press publications from 2001 to 2005 is representative of the type of critical discourse analysis undertaken in this area. As his (2006) study reveals, print media talk about digital discourse is characterized by a preoccupation with the uniqueness and distinctiveness of digital language, which is portrayed as distinct from language use in other non-digital environments. Thurlow identifies a number of verbal strategies through which discourse is articulated and sustained: (i) 'neologistic naming practices' such as 'netspeak', 'netlingo', 'weblish' etc, that uniformly refer to varying genres of digital communication; (ii) the overpowering metaphor of 'digital language' as revolution; (iii) 'relations of equivalence' (Fairclough 2003: 87) whereby 'digital language' is likened to a separate language system, a system not all users/writers are 'competent/fluent' in and texts need to be 'translated' to/from; (iv) the excessive use of numerical citations to describe the spread of the 'new digital language'; and (v) the use of reported speech to give voice primarily to corporate representatives who also exaggerate the distinctiveness of digital communication for marketing purposes (Thurlow 2006: 672–681).

Public debates about digital communication also orient towards utopian and dystopian visions of language practice. While foregrounding its new and revolutionary aspect, 'digital language' is occasionally presented as an expressive, creative, even artful means of communication, akin to the Japanese high literature of haiku. Such positive representations primarily concern language characterizations and descriptions related to digital modes, such as Twitter or text-messaging, where the technological constraints of limited characters are presented as an opportunity for users to improvise and be creative with available resources. Despite the relative scarcity of clearly positive evaluations of so-called 'digital language', they are not altogether absent from metalinguistic discourse in news media, as Spilioti's (2009) study of Greek newspaper articles attests.

Orientations towards dystopian visions of digital language and its overall impact on language standards are particularly prevalent in news media publications. More specifically, in the English-language publications Thurlow (2006) explored, such negative representations tend to portray digital language as 'responsible for a number of wider social and educational ills', such as 'dumbing down the English language' or 'declining standards of literacy' that are subsequently associated with crime, delinquency and amoral behaviour in news media publications (pp. 677–678). Although the focus on digital language per se emerges as a 'new' theme in mainstream news discourse in early 2000, the obsession with 'the deplorable state of the nation's English' is far from a 'new' or 'recent' phenomenon. Cameron's (1995) research on metalinguistic discourse provides numerous examples where national language standards are invoked in public debate about language. The portrayal of a language issue (e.g., language use in digital contexts) as a 'problem', together with value-laden claims in terms of a 'good–bad' or 'right–wrong' ethic, strategically speaks to popular anxieties about language standards. When such anxieties are transformed to widespread fears escalating out of control, they create 'moral panics' (Cohen 2011) that, like newspaper publications on digital language, focus on moral decline.

But as Cameron (1995) points out, 'whatever the specific event or phenomenon that triggers a panic, it will only get going if it mobilizes more general anxieties, and these tend to be about perceived social changes by which important sections of the community feel threatened' (p. 85). Taking into account, therefore, the wider social and historical discourses about language, we realize that moral panic discourse about digital language is related to more general anxieties about language change. Such anxieties often underlie the rise of prescriptive language ideologies that police language practice through correction and prescription of language standards.

Research on media representations of digital communication has also brought to the fore the ways in which discourses about 'digital natives' and 'digital language' often intersect. The focus on distinctiveness is not only typical of digital language discourse, but it also underpins the portrayal of young people as a distinct social group, 'fluent' and competent in the 'new language'. As Thurlow (2007: 216) points out, popular anxieties about technology, youth and language merge into 'a kind of triple-whammy panic' about moral decline and the demise of previously accepted social norms and behaviours. Both CDA (e.g., Thurlow 2007) and ethnographic (e.g., boyd 2014) studies have pointed out the need to look more closely at the people who produce, circulate and clearly voice such value-laden claims. With very few exceptions, they are professional adults – journalists, educators, politicians, etc. – and they primarily voice their own anxieties about a potential loss of control. The loss of control can be two-fold: loss of control over technologies for communication they feel they might not always be 'competent' in, and loss of control over adolescents they are not always able to monitor.

Together with the underlying prescriptive ideologies that regulate and monitor language, the exaggerated discourse about the distinctiveness of digital.language and its users not only constructs adolescents as the 'digital native other', it also both reflects and contributes to the association of 'adulthood' with normativity and standard language. Studies of media representations of adults' language use in digital contexts provide further evidence for the normalization and naturalization of such discourses. More specifically, Squires's (2011: 23) study of recontextualization of adults' texts on TV news broadcasting documented a process of erasing non-standard features that appear in the original texts. This process of erasure has naturalized and reinforced discourses that equate youth with non-standardness and adulthood with standardness. In other words, through policing digital language, adults also invoke wider discourses of 'policing' and disciplining youth.

In sum, discourses about digital language have been primarily examined in news media publications, where language use in digital environments is portrayed as a distinct code. In such public debates, we find an extreme preoccupation with non-standard forms and a general orientation towards dystopian visions of language as under threat by digital technologies. Although the technologists' metalinguistic discourse remains relatively unexplored, it is interesting to note that logos and names for social media platforms capitalize on and echo discourses of non-standardness, as evident in *I Can Has Cheezburger?*, *YAHOO!*, *Flickr*, *Tumblr*, etc. Academic research on digital discourse, and particularly Computer-Mediated Discourse Analysis, has demonstrated that the hype and fetishization of digital language does not do justice to the range of texts, genres and language practices emerging in different digital contexts. In addition to CMDA, studies of digital literacy have provided further evidence and compelling theory for downplaying and contextualising non-standardness in digital environments (see chapters by Iorio and Waldron, Kemp & Wood *et al.*, this volume). As evident in the above discussion, CDA research has scrutinized the ways in which discourses about digital language are articulated and modulated in news media texts; at the same time, it has paved the way for exploring such discourses in relation to longstanding language ideologies and their associated moral panics.

Conclusion and future directions

This chapter has brought together research on discourse about digital communication, as manifest in mass (primarily news) media contexts and in social media environments regulated by web designers and developers. Within the field of Computer-Mediated Discourse Analysis, the critical agenda has been gaining impetus primarily over the last ten years as it has opened to cross-fertilizations from the related disciplines of media and cultural studies. Tracing the development of public discourses about mediated communication over time reveals cultural concerns about human behaviour, language and technology at particular moments in history. In this chapter, I have argued that although the content of such discourses can change over time (e.g., from the 'asocial' to the 'social' and/or 'antisocial' Internet), some aspects have remained relatively stable. Such aspects are primarily related to general anxieties about change and control: be it technological, language or social, change is often accompanied by a sense of loss of control – over once-familiar mediational means, over pre-established language standards and over long-lasting social structures. It is not at all surprising, then, that 'new' debates about digital language capitalize on longstanding language ideologies of standardization (see Lenihan 2011; Squires 2011).

The current overview of research on discourses about digital communication also reveals a relative bias toward discourses and ideologies produced and circulated primarily in what is known as the Western part of the world, particularly in U.S. and U.K. contexts. Marwick's (2013) ethnographic fieldwork on the San Francisco 'tech scene' is particularly enlightening about the discourses shaping the 'Web 2.0 ideology', but similar ethnographic studies of tech communities outside the US (e.g., the Silicon Wadi in Israel, the Silicon Gulf in Philippines, or the 'silicon Allee' in Berlin) are virtually non-existent at the time of writing. Yet, it is only through such detailed and rich ethnographies across different cultures that we can explore and possibly contest the often assumed global currency of such discourses and ideologies. For example, although such communities have acquired the 'silicon' epithet due to their socio-economic growth on the basis of start-up businesses and venture capitalism, it is worth exploring how such discourses interplay with the local socio-economic structures and associated discourses.

The thematic organization of current research has been aimed at revealing how particular discourses cut across different public domains (i.e., news, advertising, corporate, etc.) by focusing on overlapping sets of ideas and topics. Although individual studies usually focus on certain domains of discourse, such thematic overlaps can be discerned and foregrounded. The issue of how such discourses of digital media actually circulate across different domains of practice has been relatively unexplored in the current literature, however. Concepts of 'circulation' or 'en/recontextualization' of discourses are often invoked, but they rarely become the main focus of analysis. (For an important exception, see Squires's (2011) study of the representational practices in a recontextualized thread of text-messages.) There is ample scope for further analytic engagement with such concepts in the study of public debates about digital communication.

Last but not least, media and cultural studies appear to lead the way in offering insights into the socio-historical discourses that shape current ideologies about digital media and communication. 'New' discourses about self-promotion and self-branding (Marwick 2013) as well as perceptions about Big Data and predictive analytics (Andrejevic 2013) have already been scrutinized in research that traces their associations with wider cultural shifts, such as celebrity culture and the decline of symbolic efficiency and expert identity in a post-modern and post-truth world (Zizek 1999). Nevertheless, such accounts would benefit from the detailed attention to the micro-linguistic, stylistic and persuasive devices used to sustain and indeed contest such discourses in different domains of practice, including news media, marketing, social media corporate discourse and, of course, reflexive accounts of the users themselves. This valuable endeavour of looking at discourse across micro and macro scales is well supported by the more language-focused perspectives of critical discourse analysis and critical sociolinguistics.

Related topics

- Chapter 3 Digital ethnography (Varis)
- Chapter 10 Vernacular literacy: orthography and literacy practices (Iorio)
- Chapter 11 Texting and language learning (Waldron, Kemp & Wood)
- Chapter 19 Relationality, friendship and identity in digital communication (Graham)
- Chapter 20 Online communities and communities of practice (Angouri)
- Chapter 17 Second Life: language and virtual identity (Abdullah)
- Chapter 27 Surveillance (Jones)

References

Anderson, J. & Rainie, L. 2014, *Net threats: Pew Research Center's Internet and American life project report,* available at: http://www.pewInternet.org/2014/07/03/net-threats/ [accessed: 15 September 2014].

Andrejevic, A. 2013, *Infoglut: how too much information is changing the way we think and know,* Routledge: London.

Androutsopoulos, J. 2006, 'Introduction: sociolinguistics and computer-mediated communication', *Journal of Sociolinguistics*, vol. 10, no. 4, pp. 419–438.

Baym, N. 2010, *Personal connections in the digital age,* Polity Press: Cambridge.

BBC News 2014, 'Turkish PM Erdogan criticises Twitter court ruling', 4 April 2014, available at: http://www.bbc.co.uk/news/world-europe-26880891 [accessed: 15 September 2014].

Blommaert, J. 2005, *Discourse: a critical introduction,* Cambridge University Press: Cambridge.

boyd, d 2014, *It's complicated: the social lives of networked teens,* Yale University Press: New Haven, CT.

Cameron, D. 1995, *Verbal hygiene,* Routledge: New York, NY.

Cohen, S. 2011, *Folk devils and moral panics: the creation of the mods and rockers,* Routledge: London.

Coupland, N. 2014, 'Language change, social change, sociolinguistic change: a meta-commentary', *Journal of Sociolinguistics*, vol. 18, no. 2, pp. 277–286.

Daft, R. and Lengel, R. 1984 'Information richness: a new approach to managerial behaviour and organizational design', *Research in Organizational Behaviour*, vol. 6, pp. 191–233.

Danet, B. 2001 *Cyberpl@y: communicating online,* Berg: Oxford/New York.

European Commission 2014, *Official languages,* available at: http://ec.europa.eu/languages/policy/language-policy/official_languages_en.htm [accessed: 5 September 2014].

Facebook Inc. 2014, *Welcome to Facebook – Log in, sign up or learn more,* available at: https://www.facebook.com/ [accessed: 15 September 2014].

Fairclough, N. 2003, *Analysing discourse: textual analysis for social research,* Routledge: London.

Fischer, C. 1994, *America calling: a social history of the telephone to 1940,* University of California Press: Berkeley, CA.

Foucault, M. 2004, 'Governmentality', in P. Rabinow & N. Rose (eds.), *The essential Foucault,* The New Press: New York, NY, pp. 229–245.

Gee, J. P. 2010, *An introduction to discourse analysis: theory and method,* Routledge: New York, NY.

Hargittai, E. 2010, 'Digital na(t)ives?: variation in Internet skills and uses among members of the "Net Generation"', *Sociological Inquiry*, vol. 80, no. 1, pp. 92–113.

Herring, S. 1994, 'Politeness in computer culture: why women thank and men flame', in M. Bucholtz, A. Liang, L. Sutton & C. Hines (eds.), *Cultural performances: proceedings of the third Berkeley women and language conference,* Berkeley Women and Language Group: Berkeley, CA, pp. 278–294.

Herring, S. & Paolillo, J. 2006, 'Gender and genre variation in weblogs', *Journal of Sociolinguistics*, vol. 10, no. 4, pp. 439–459.

Hutchby, I. 2001, 'Technologies, texts and affordances', *Sociology*, vol. 35, no. 2, pp. 441–456.

John, N. A. 2012, 'Sharing and web 2.0: the emergence of a keyword', *New Media & Society*, vol. 15, no. 2, pp. 167–182.

Keesing, R. 1981, *Cultural anthropology*, Harcourt Brace: Orlando, FL.

Koutsogiannis, D. & Adampa, V. 2012, 'Girls, identities and agency in adolescents' digital literacy practices', *Journal of Writing Research*, vol. 3, no. 3, pp. 217–247.

Lenihan, A. 2013, 'The interaction of language policy, minority languages and new media: a study of the Facebook translations application', unpublished PhD thesis, University of Limerick.

Lenihan, A. 2011, '"Join our community of translators": language ideologies and/in *Facebook*', in C. Thurlow & K Mroczek (eds.), *Digital discourse: language in the new media*, Oxford University Press: Oxford, pp. 48–64.

Locher, M. 2010, 'Introduction: politeness and impoliteness in computer-mediated communication', *Journal of Politeness Research*, vol. 6, no. 1, pp. 1–5.

Marwick, A. 2013, *Status update: celebrity, publicity & branding in the social media age*, Yale University Press: New Haven, CT.

McKay, S., Thurlow, C. & Zimmerman, H. 2005, 'Wired whizzes or techno slaves? Teens and their emergent communication technologies', in A. Williams & C. Thurlow (eds.), *Talking adolescence: perspectives on communication in the teenage years*, Peter Lang: New York, NY, pp. 185–203.

Moran, J. 2013, *Armchair nation: an intimate history of Britain in front of the TV*, Profile Books: London.

Neff, G. E., Wissinger, E. & Zukin, S. 2005, 'Entrepreneurial labor among cultural producers: "cool" jobs in "hot" industries', *Social Semiotics*, vol. 15, no. 3, pp. 307–334.

Ong, W. 1982, *Orality and literacy: the technologizing of the word*, Routledge: London.

Prensky, M. 2001, 'Digital natives, digital immigrants', *On The Horizon*, vol. 9, no. 5, available at: http://www.marcprensky.com/writing/Prensky%20-%20Digital%20Natives,%20Digital%20Immigrants%20-%20Part1.pdf [accessed: 15 September 2014].

Sfarnas, G. 2014, 'Digital native', *Being Five* [Online] 05 November 2014, available at: http://beingfive.blogspot.gr/2014/11/digital-native.html [accessed 18 December 2014].

Silverstone, R. & Haddon, L. 1996, 'Design and the domestication of information and communication technologies: technical change and everyday life', in R. Silverstone & R. Mansell (eds.), *Communication by design: the politics of information and communication technologies*, Oxford University Press: Oxford, pp. 44–74.

Spigel, L. 1992, *Make room for TV: television and the family ideal in postwar America*, University of Chicago Press: Chicago, IL.

Spilioti, T. 2009, 'Text-messages (SMS): language attitudes and ideological representations in the Greek press', *Communication Issues*, vol. 3, no. 9, pp. 62–74.

Squires, L. 2011, 'Voicing "sexy Text": heteroglossia and erasure in TV news representations of Detroit's text message scandal', in C. Thurlow & K. Mroczek (eds.), *Digital discourse: language in the new media*, Oxford University Press: Oxford, pp. 3–25.

Standage, T. 1998, *The Victorian Internet: the remarkable story of the telegraph and the nineteenth century's online pioneers*, Weidenfeld & Nicolson: London.

Sturken, M. & Thomas, D. 2004, 'Introduction: technological visions and the rhetoric of the new', in M. Sturken, D. Thomas, & S. J. Ball-Rokeach (eds.), *Technological visions: the hopes and fears that shape new technologies*, Temple University Press: Philadelphia, PA, pp. 1–18.

Thurlow, C. 2013, 'Fakebook: synthetic media, pseudo-sociality, and the rhetorics of web 2.0', in D. Tannen & A. M. Trester (eds.), *Discourse 2.0: language and new media*, Georgetown University Press: Washington, DC, pp. 225–249.

Thurlow, C. 2007, 'Fabricating youth: new-media discourse and the technologization of young people', in Johnson, S. & Ensslin, A. (eds.), *Language in the media: representations, identities, ideologies*, Continuum: London, pp. 213–233.

Thurlow, C. 2006, 'From statistical panic to moral panic: the metadiscursive construction and popular exaggeration of new media language in the print media', *Journal of Computer-Mediated Communication*, vol. 11, no. 3, pp. 667–701.

Thurlow, C. & Bell, K. 2009, 'Against technologization: young people's new media discourse as creative cultural practice', *Journal of Computer-Mediated Communication*, vol. 14, no. 4, pp. 1038–1049.

Thurlow, C. & Mroczek, K. 2011, 'Introduction: fresh perspectives on new media sociolinguistics', in C. Thurlow & K. Mroczek (eds.), *Digital discourse: language in the new media*, Oxford University Press: Oxford, pp. xix-xliv.

Twitter Inc. 2014a, *Twitter help center: your privacy controls for tailored ads*, available at: https://support.twitter.com/articles/20170405 [accessed: 15 September 2014].

Twitter Inc. 2014b, *Twitter help center: about the Twitter translation center*, available at: https://support.twitter.com/articles/434816-about-the-twitter-translation-center [accessed: 15 September 2014].

van Dijk, J. 2013, *The Culture of connectivity: a critical history of social media*, Oxford University Press: Oxford.

Williams, M. 2014, *Facebook newsroom: building a more diverse Facebook*, available at: http://newsroom. fb.com/news/2014/06/building-a-more-diverse-facebook/ [accessed: 15 September 2014]

Wodak, R. 2001, 'The discourse-historical approach', in R. Wodak & M. Meyer (eds.), *Methods of critical discourse analysis*, Sage: London, pp. 63–94.

Woolaston, V. 2014, 'Is the Internet turning into BIG BROTHER? Everything we read, watch and buy online will be controlled by government in 2025, claim experts', available at: http://www.dailymail. co.uk/sciencetech/article-2691407/Is-Internet-turning-BIG-BROTHER-Everything-read-watch-buy-online-controlled-government-2025-claim-experts.html [accessed 15 September 2014].

Zizek, S. 1999, *The ticklish subject*, Verso: London.

Further reading

Marwick, A. 2013, *Status update: celebrity, publicity & branding in the social media age*, Yale University Press: New Haven, CT.

This book offers a compelling ethnographic account of San Franscisco's tech community (from 2006 to 2010) and casts a critical eye over the web 2.0 buzz, its culture and ideology.

Thurlow, C. 2013, 'Fakebook: synthetic media, pseudo-sociality, and the rhetorics of web 2.0', in D. Tannen & A. M. Trester (eds.), *Discourse 2.0: language and new media*, Georgetown University Press: Washington, DC, pp. 225–249.

This chapter introduces and examines the concept of 'pseudo-sociality' as played out in different institutional domains (i.e., corporate, political, media, educational and academic discourses) from a critical discourse analysis perspective.

Part III

Digital literacies

9

Digital media and literacy development

Michele Knobel and Colin Lankshear

Introduction

This chapter explores relationships between digital media and literacy development from a sociocultural perspective, looking at how literacies have developed in association with the rise of popular digital media. "Digital media" and "literacy development" are widely researched in tandem, with scholars within education, communication and media studies focusing on important transformations in how people take up, generate and share meanings in everyday life.

For sociocultural theorists, literacy is really *literacies*—social *practices* that involve different configurations of tools, technologies, skills, knowledge and the like, which depend on the socially patterned ways of making and sharing meanings that are recognized as "belonging" to each practice (Street 1984). This orientation towards understanding and researching literacy has become known as the New Literacy Studies. It is characterized by researchers documenting in detail literacy-in-use within people's everyday lives, and its historical development is widely traced to Silvia Scribner and Michael Cole's five-year mixed-methods study of Vai society and its literacy practices in Liberia (1981). Other seminal early studies include Shirley Brice Heath's ten-year ethnographic study of three different communities in the Piedmont Carolinas, USA (1983), and Brian Street's multi-year study of village communities in Iran (1984). All three studies, in their own manner, paid close attention to the ways in which literacy was integral to routinized, socially recognized ways of getting different things done.

Scribner and Cole's conception of social practice is particularly useful to researchers because it grounds social practices in observable and traceable patterned activities and ways of knowing. They define social practices as "socially developed and patterned ways of using technology and knowledge" along with skills—understood as "co-ordinated sets of actions"—to achieve tasks or meet particular purposes (1981: 236). Scribner and Cole argued that a theory of social practice sees technologies, knowledges and skills as dynamically connected to one another, and as mutually evolving in conjunction with people's changing ideas about purposes and tasks (see also Lankshear & Knobel 2011: 36). As social practice, literacy involves "a set of socially organized practices which make use of a symbol system and a technology for producing and disseminating it" (Scribner & Cole 1981: 236). Being literate is not a matter of knowing how to encode and decode a particular kind of script but, rather, of applying "this knowledge for specific purposes in specific contexts of use" (ibid.).

Hence, literacy is really like a family of practices—*literacies*—that include such "socially developed and patterned activities" as letter writing, keeping records and inventories, keeping a diary, writing memos, blogging, participating in an online social news space, and so on. These all vary to some extent from one another in terms of the technologies used (pencil, typewriter, pen, font options, the kind of surface "written" on); the knowledge drawn upon (formatting conventions, tenor choices, information about the topic); and their skill requirements (hand–eye coordination, using a mouse). Literacies may be part of a social practice (such as reading biographies of famous soccer players as part a larger practice of soccer playing or fanship) or may constitute a patterned, socially recognizable communicative practice in their own right (such as reading and writing novels or fan fiction, for example).

Subsequent definitions in the New Literacy Studies tradition include Gee's conception of literacy as "mastery of a secondary Discourse" (Gee 2012) or, in other words, a Discourse acquired within "public sphere" institutions such as schools, religious groups, governments, workplaces and so on (Gee 2012: 155). "Discourses" (with a capital "D") are "distinctive ways of speaking/listening and often, too, writing/reading coupled with particular ways of acting, interacting valuing, feeling, dressing, thinking, believing with other people and with various objects, tools, and technologies, so as to enact specific socially recognizable identities engaged in specific recognizable activities" (Gee 2012: 152). So, a lawyer in a law court will speak and read and write in particular ways as part of being a lawyer. That same person will use quite different ways of speaking and will read, write and view different things altogether, and in different ways, as a basketball player for a local team or a lay reader in their local church. As identities are multiple so, then, are literacies.

Our own work builds on the definitions offered by Street, Scribner and Cole, and Gee to define literacies as "socially recognized ways in which people generate, communicate, and negotiate meanings, as members of Discourses, through the medium of encoded texts" (Lankshear & Knobel 2011: 33). This definition accommodates (as literacies) ways of reading, writing, viewing and listening that extend far beyond conventional texts and traditional analog forms of inscription. We are especially interested in "new literacies" that have emerged with the rise of social practices mediated by digital media (e.g., blogging, social site networking, digital remixing, creating with e-materiales, instant messaging), and that are marked by an ethos characterized by deep interactivity, openness to feedback, sharing of resources and expertize, and a will to collaborate and provide support.

These ideas set the scene for discussing in the remainder of this chapter a particular body of research about digital media and literacy development. This corpus covers research conducted from a sociocultural orientation to literacy and digital media that attends to the social practices, identities and meanings associated with being particular kinds of people engaging in particular kinds of task. It also focuses primarily on out-of-school contexts and includes reference to school practices only to the extent that these are studied and compared to practices engaged outside of school settings or school-sanctioned spaces.

This chapter recognizes two ideas of "literacy development." The first may be called *personal* literacy development. The second is the idea of development in the *cultural stock* of literacies. Scholars interested in the first sense focus on how people change, add to, or improve their literacy proficiencies as they engage with a range of digital media. For example, studies of young people's fan fiction writing often include analyses of how the authors of these texts improve their stories or language proficiencies by means of writing, obtaining feedback from others on their writing and working on their texts in response to this feedback—all facilitated by participating in online fan fiction writing and other related spaces (e.g., Thomas 2007; Black 2008; Curwood 2013; Lammers 2013). "Development" in this sense concerns how people become "better" at and/or become "more" (more capable, more popular, more successful, etc.) in terms of their capacities to create, distribute, share, negotiate, remix (and so on) cultural meanings using digital tools, resources, spaces and networks.

The second sense examines the emergence of *new* and evolving social practices of inscription and meaning-making. From this standpoint, researchers investigate relatively new practices such as blogging, video remixing, digital animation, sound and image editing, among many others in their varying forms, together with how meanings are communicated within such practices. These are often literacy practices that do not rely on an alphabet or syllabary, or on conventional pen and paper, to "work." Research on literacy development in this sense focuses on literacy practices that either did not exist prior to the emergence of digital technologies, or else evolved and gained new prominence as a result of digital media affordances. Examples include studies of digital storytelling (Hull 2003), video remixing (Lankshear & Knobel 2011; Vasudevan 2010), blogging (Davies & Merchant 2007), social networking (Buck 2012; Davies 2012), gaming (Hung 2011; Leander & Mills 2007), and game modding (Durga 2012), to name a few.

For present purposes, digital media is synonymous with new media, referring to content that is digitally created and distributed, as well as to the hardware, tools and networks used in the production and storage process of these media (see also Part II of this Handbook). This runs the gamut from webpages to ebooks to social network pages; from computers to smart phones to the Internet; and so on. Since our focus is primarily on *literacies* and the ways people take up digital media to create meaning within contexts of social practice, the range of digital media addressed in this chapter is circumscribed by the media involved in the literacy studies surveyed.

Bounding this area of study for the purposes of manageable survey and review was a challenge. We have omitted studies of new media, (other) language learning and young children's initial language development, since they are addressed elsewhere (see Waldron, Kemp & Wood, this volume). We have excluded studies conducted entirely within schools and focused on teacher-instigated uses of new media (e.g., teacher-controlled blogs used to improve writing). While interesting in their own right, such studies do not focus sufficiently on the connection between literacy and social practices central to this chapter. Similarly, our sociocultural focus precludes studies that address digital media from the standpoint of psycholinguistic conceptions of reading and writing. Finally, we only survey studies that address literacies and digital media as their central concern, rather than as one focus of interest among others.

Historical perspective

Academic study of digital media and literacies within everyday settings outside classrooms are comparatively recent. Early publications were often commentaries based on observations of and discussions with children and young people concerning their digital technology uses (e.g., video game playing, website building) published in the early 1990s. They focus on palpable changes in how children and young people use digital technologies in their everyday lives to communicate with others, engage with popular culture, and produce their own digital productions around identity, ideas, pleasures and suchlike (e.g., Bigum & Green 1992; Buckingham 1993). The mid- to late-1990s saw a marked increase in academic publications focusing on digital technologies or digital media and literacy. These, again, were mainly theorized commentaries upon and analyses of general trends and observations (e.g., Bruce 1998; Lankshear & Knobel 1995; Luke 1997). There was also a rapid growth of interest in technology and language learning and development (discussed elsewhere in this volume, see Waldron, Kemp & Wood).

The escalating focus on literacies and digital technologies in education and media studies shadowed the growing general academic interest from the early 1990s in new and emerging technologies (see Benedikt 1991; Rheingold 1994), such as email and spam email, jpeg compression for images, PDF capability, the World Wide Web, the rise of the open source movement (Linux), bulletin boards, online discussion forums, the first graphical Internet browsers (Mosaic and Netscape), the launch of Amazon and eBay, CD-ROMs, PDAs (personal digital assistants), MUDs (multi-user dungeons/domains), fifth generation video game consoles and games, notebook computers, bluetooth connectivity, virtual reality modeling language (VRML), zip drives, mobile phones, pagers and the like.

The second half of the 1990s saw a small number of studies that documented what children and young people—often selected purposively—were doing with literacy and digital technologies outside school contexts, and produced findings to inform critiques of classroom practices (e.g., Dudfield 1999; Lankshear & Knobel 1997). Also published during this period were two edited volumes dedicated to documenting and discussing changes in everyday literacy practices in non-school settings when digital technology and media are part of the mix (Hawisher & Selfe 2000; Snyder 1997). Their publication reflected growing academic interest in this area, particularly in Britain, the United States, Canada and Australia. Typical works documented home uses of computers and gaming consoles; personal web page construction; hypertext and reading paths; online MUDs, MOOS and chat spaces; and people's uses of the "World Wide Web."

The first half of the 2000s saw an increase in published studies investigating what children and young people were doing online and/or the digital resources they were using. Gee's major study of games, literacy and learning was published in 2003, doing much to establish video games as a significant focus for academic study within education. Researchers also investigated zines (Duncan & Leander 2000), along with the ways young people used online chat spaces (Merchant 2001; Thomas 2000), constructed fan websites (Lam 2000), wrote and shared fan fiction online (Trainor 2004) and engaged in anime fan practices via discussion lists and online spaces (Chandler-Olcott & Mahar 2003). A small but noticeable subset of studies focused on what young people were doing with digital media and literacy in after-school programs (Hull 2003). Towards the end of this period, studies of very young children and their digital media and literacy development also appeared (Marsh 2004). This body of research emerged at the time when mobile phones, weblogs and instant messaging were burgeoning, along with computer viruses. MySpace was a popular social networking site and shopping online was becoming more common. The iPod was released, along with online music distribution services (and bit torrent sharing became even more popular). Wikipedia was launched in 2001, and the number of Internet users reached 1 billion during 2005.

The period from 2004 onwards brought an escalating surge in published studies of digital media and literacy development within everyday spaces. Many of these addressed fan practices, with fan fiction-writing communities providing a particularly popular research focus (Black 2005, 2008; Curwood 2013; Lammers 2013; Magnifico 2012; Thomas 2007). A strong trend toward researching the phenomenon of writing and producing digital media to share with others became apparent during this period. Studies focused on practices like online zine production and journaling (Guzzetti & Gamboa 2005; Rogers & Winters 2010); digital storytelling (Nelson, Hull & Roche-Smith 2008); media remixing (Leander & Frank 2006; Vasudevan 2010); collaborative writing across time and space (Thomas 2007; Yi 2008); and blogging, microblogging and blog commenting (Davies & Merchant 2007; Gillen & Merchant 2013; Santo 2013).

A second trend in the research during this period involves documenting the ways people across a range of ages make use of social network sites and online social interaction services to build and maintain relationships and/or to perform identity work. This includes analysis of online communities (Thomas 2007); social networking sites (Davies 2012; Knobel & Lankshear 2008; Williams 2010); email (Mavers 2007), virtual worlds (Burke 2013; Marsh 2011); instant messaging and online chat (Lam 2009; Lewis & Fabos 2005); and online discussions (Alvermann 2006).

A smaller discernible trend has been in the growth of studies about how young people "resource" their personal interests. This includes studies of young people using websites as resources for identity construction, sharing interests, and text and media production (Alvermann *et al.* 2012; Guzzetti 2006; Magnifico 2012).

The largest body of research within this period, however, was associated with computer and video game studies, from the standpoints of video games as comprising new literacy practices and as contexts in which gamers develop specialist languages and master related text and media genres. This work covered studies of video games and game playing (e.g., Hung 2011; King 2012; Steinkuehler 2007); video game designing and design communities (Duncan 2012; Leander & Mills 2007; Sanford & Madill 2007), and game modding communities (Durga 2012; Hayes & Lee 2012). Early games research in the area of digital media and literacy had focused mostly on how game structures and mechanics shaped the ways a game is read and played. More recent studies have focused on a wider range of gaming practices, including game creation and modification as forms of writing and production.

Some studies during this period traverse a range of media types and literacy practices as they follow specific research participants online and offline (Buck 2012; Kirkland 2010; McTavish 2009; Smith & Hull 2013; Thomas 2007). A smattering of studies at this time focused on a range of different digital media and literacy practices, including reading conventional books and digital texts such as online encyclopaedias and computer games (Mackey 2007; Davidson 2009), memes (Knobel & Lankshear 2007), and online shopping (Davies 2008).

Research from 2005 onwards saw a marked increase in the study of very young children (e.g., aged seven years and under) and their engagement with digital media and literacies (Davidson 2009; Marsh 2011; Mavers 2007). Explicit studies of adults and their digital media and literacy uses remained rare (Davies 2008; Gillen & Merchant 2013; Mackey 2007). While some social networking and games-related studies likely did involve adults, this was never specified. This period also saw significant growth in media and literacy research conducted in after-school programs, summer programs, alternative programs and the like (Alvermann 2006; Alvermann *et al.* 2012; Steinkuehler & King 2009; Nelson *et al.* 2008; Rogers & Winters 2010; Sanford & Madill 2007; Smith & Hull 2013; Vasudevan 2010).

Major digital technology and media developments during the past decade have included: the emergence of social network sites (e.g., Twitter, Facebook, Bebo), "smart" phones with Internet capability; apps; digital books, journals, magazines; multimedia-sharing social network sites (e.g., Instagram, Pinterest); massively multiplayer online games; DVDs and DVD players; video and music streaming online; Creative Commons copyright licences; Internet archiving for historical purposes; free digital video, image and audio editing software; cloud computing (e.g., Google Docs); online video hosting services (e.g., YouTube); app-driven tablets and so on. These developments have proved fertile ground for researchers interested in the emergence of new kinds of literacy practices as well as in new ways of becoming literate and communicating meanings.

Main research methods

The dominant design in new media and literacy development research is qualitative case study. Case study is best described as an in-depth analysis of a bounded system. The bounded systems in the majority of case studies in this area tend to be people. That is, these studies focus on particular users, remixers, participants, etc., and the ways in which they use particular digital media.

This includes, for example, case studies of fans using and contributing to specific online affinity or shared-interest spaces by means of writing and posting fan fiction, role playing, drawing original anime, game designing, hosting or moderating a fan website, and the like (Black 2008; Chandler-Olcott & Mahar 2003; Curwood 2013; Guzzetti 2006; Lam 2000; Leander & Mills 2007; Magnifico 2012; Thomas 2007; Trainor 2004). Many such studies are conducted entirely or mostly online (some researchers include face-to-face, non-digitally-mediated interviews and some observations of participants using their computers), and often are described as "ethnographic case studies," or as case studies that draw on ethnographic methods. This includes conducting sustained observations, with some studies reporting data collection windows of three years or more (e.g., Black 2008; Burke 2013; Thomas 2007). A number report cases pulled from larger longitudinal ethnographies, too (e.g., Alvermann 2006; Burke 2013; Leander & Frank 2006). Moreover, some ethnographic case study researchers identify themselves as full participants in the practices being studied—such as game modding, fan fiction writing, zining—and have been for some years prior to their formal investigations (Black 2008; Davies 2008; Durga 2012; Magnifico 2012; Rogers & Winters 2010). Such "insiderliness" supports richly descriptive insights into each practice studied.

This body of research also includes case studies of children and young people going about their everyday lives online and offline, and documenting how they make use of digital media for resourcing an interest or pleasure (e.g., sport, lizards, punk music), completing school work, and the like (Davidson 2009; Guzzetti & Gamboa 2005; McTavish 2009). That being said, studies of children and young people and their digital media and literacies at home or outside school seem now to be declining.

Other methodological approaches to studying new media and literacy development include quantitative surveys (Marsh 2004), self-study (Davies & Merchant 2007; Gee 2003; Gillen & Merchant 2013), and observational studies of online communities (Hayes & Lee 2012; Lammers 2013; Thomas 2007). In addition, new kinds of design appear in this corpus of studies that are shaped deliberately around the new media being studied. These include studies of online discussion boards, blog posts and comments, website analysis, video gaming, and social network sites, among others (Davies 2012; Duncan 2012; Gee 2003, 2013; Hung 2011; Knobel & Lankshear 2008; Santo 2013; Williams 2010).

In keeping with the case studies and ethnographic studies that dominate this body of research, reported data collection methods predominantly comprise observation fieldnotes and artefact collection, where artefacts include participant-generated content (e.g., fan fiction narratives, game character builds, game mods, video remixes), as well as resources such as websites and tutorials used by participants. Semi-structured interviews are also common, with formats varying from single participant to group interviews. Interviews are conducted face-to-face or via instant messaging/text chat services, Internet voice services, or email. Data are also mostly used "intact" as they are found, such as discussions in online forums, in email exchanges between observed participants, and in participants' chat logs. Data collection methods for documenting digital media use include videotaping children and young people engaging in online spaces, as well as installing recording software that captures onscreen moves. Less common methods include walk-throughs (whereby the participant "talks" the researcher through a process), time use diaries, user-compiled logs (e.g., of instant messages sent or websites visited), daily saves of work in progress, automated tracking systems that log activity on the network, and keeping a researcher journal.

Data analysis methods tend toward discourse analysis of varying kinds in this set of studies. This is in keeping with researchers' focus on literacy practices and the sociocultural frameworks brought to bear on their studies. Approaches include Gee's D/discourse theory, social semiotics and multimodal analysis, conversation analysis, systemic functional linguistic analysis, critical discourse analysis, and so on. In addition, researchers also make use of basic coding, content analysis, thematic analysis, genre analysis, and nexus analysis.

Key issues and topics

Most sociocultural research on digital technology, literacy and children and young people focuses on their digital media production: for example, writing fan fiction, remixing anime videos, modding and designing video games, running fan sites, creating fan art or generating original digital content to use in virtual worlds and games. This is a valuable corrective to earlier media studies that often emphasized young people as consumers. It also instantiates our two ideas of literacy development, understood as developing our cultural stock of literacy practices and enhancing meaning-making proficiencies.

Many new and emerging literacies have been documented since the 1990s. Studies of zines and electronic zines (e.g., Guzzetti & Gamboa 2005, Rogers & Winters 2010) consider writing as a pastiche or bricolage, using copying and pasting techniques and mixing original textual content with found or original images. Similarly, studies of linguistic innovation within online chat and messaging spaces (e.g., Lam 2009; Lewis & Fabos 2005; Merchant 2001; Thomas 2000) often explore how users weave multiple languages, slang, abbreviations, emoticons and clever—even sophisticated—understandings of how language works in written exchanges. Increasingly, researchers have investigated literacies associated with video game playing and the design of games (e.g., Steinkuehler & King 2009). They study how games can be "read" in multiple layers when learning to play them. Likewise, recent studies of game modding and game creation (e.g., Duncan 2012; Durga 2012; Leander & Mills 2007; Sanford & Madill 2007) focus on "amateurs" learning to modify or generate games and characters, using online-distributed expertise and tutorials together with their own do-it-yourself, trial-and-error approaches to creating something new. Many of these studies show how novice game designers acquire specialist language as they participate in design forums and become more adept at constructing their own games. These studies resonate with a contemporary interest in innovation, active creativity, value-adding practices and social learning approaches. Burgeoning studies of new literacies associated with fanship practices document textual practices involved in coding and hosting fan websites, moderating popular online fansites, and contributing to such sites (e.g., providing original art, fan fiction and writing updates about a popular TV series). Studies of remix practices are common here (e.g., Black 2008; Curwood 2013; Magnifico 2012; Thomas 2007; Trainor 2004). They document how young people combine existing content to create new narratives (e.g., *Harry Potter* or *Hunger Games* fan remixes), or blend existing content with their own content creation (e.g., new characters for stories drawn from movie or television narratives).

Inescapably, all such studies are undertaken within settings and against backgrounds that influence researcher purposes, perspectives and approaches. Some influences are theoretical and conceptual, such as those associated with what can reasonably count as *literacy* and how to reckon with the seamless multimodality of digital inscription. Some are methodological, such as how to conduct research online. Others are more historical or cultural, such as the larger current social and economic significance attached to innovation and active creativity, identity in a "postmodern" age, the ubiquity of social networks, issues concerning intellectual property and copyright or, especially at earlier stages, concerns about slipping "standards," triviality, mistrust of new technologies, and the like, especially in regard to formal education. Such factors inevitably play a role in informing research approaches and decisions about data collection and analysis and often influence the kinds of findings rendered by a study.

For example, Cynthia Lewis and Bettina Fabos's (2003) study of instant messaging (IM), literacies and social identities was centrally concerned with the functions of IM in their seven participants' daily lives, and how their social identities shaped and were shaped by IM. Their study was closely informed by theories of literacies as social and semiotic practices. The sheer dominance of IM as textual practice in young people's lives at the time disposed the researchers to understanding its status and characteristics as a new literacy. This called for "depth" of data that would speak to aspects of identity as well as aspects of IM as literacy. Accordingly, Lewis and Fabos collected data by interviewing and videorecording IM sessions, and used a verbal reporting procedure to track participants' IM strategies. Pursuing richness and depth of understanding, they employed qualitative, open coding techniques to identify substantive recurring patterns. The patterns discerned spoke strongly to diverse and sophisticated aspects of language use: notably, how participants "manipulated the tone, voice, word choice and subject matter of their messages to fit their communications needs" (p. 471). At the level of identity and participation in social networks, the researchers found participants negotiating "multiple narratives" and designing their texting practices to "enhance social relationships and statuses" across multiple contexts" (p. 471).

Studies of identity in relation to literacy practice and digital media use focus largely on identity construction online, with reference to multimodal texts and images created by users that convey information about the kind of person they see themselves as being and would like others to take them as. Other popular foci include maintaining in-person and distributed social relationships via writing and discussion practices, being fans and participants in popular cultural practices, freely sharing expertise, participation in a range of usually popular culture practices, and being a "player" as a mode of engagement with digital media and literacy, as well as for learning and collaborating with peers who share similar interests.

For educationists, a particularly salient issue concerns the relation between young people's "new literacy practices" as organic dimensions of their lives and the literacy practices they encounter within formal education, particularly with respect to a perceived crisis in "engagement in school." While the kind of school versus out-of-school divide that often characterized earlier studies has since been problematized, many researchers nonetheless continue to call for education to pay more and closer attention to the literacies children and young people *already* bring with them to school and to leverage these to help students achieve scholastically. This has especially been a recurring motif among researchers concerned with games and learning, as well as with learning in the context of "participatory culture" (Hayes & Lee 2012; Hung 2011; Lammers 2013; McTavish 2009).

Against a background of games-playing often being blamed as a contributing factor to boys' under-achievement in literacy-related schoolwork, Constance Steinkuehler and Elizabeth King (2009) created an after-school laboratory/incubator space where a group of "at-risk" boys played *World of Warcraft* (*WoW*) in the company of the researchers and graduate student research assistants. Participants engaged in a range of associated literacy practices, such as maintaining a private guild discussion space, in addition to the range of literacy practices that are "an indelible part of progressing through *WoW*" (p. 50), such as seeking out and making sense of online resources (e.g., user-generated manuals, wikis, information data bases) to beat a boss, debating competing models for specializing one's virtual character, and learning how to read the "design grammar" of a game as a semiotic domain (Gee 2003). The researchers were interested, in part, in exploring the extent to which and ways in which such games-related literacies mapped onto formal genres and learning standards recognized in formal school curricula. Their overarching purpose was to try to leverage online games for literacy learning that might have payoffs in school and beyond by creating instructional modules developed around a set of targeted literacy practices in the context of playing the game.

They used ethnographic data collection approaches, in-game and face-to-face, including "participant observation, multimodal field notes . . . videotaped interactions . . . collecting participant artifacts . . . and repeated interviews . . . about their attitudes and general progress in literacy related activities at work, home, and school (e.g. new interests in literacy related issues or topics, improvements in homework)" (Steinkuehler & King 2009: 51). Moreover, individual and group formative and summative assessment data were collected for each instructional module. The data were analyzed in ways designed to map individual and group learning trajectories over time with respect to the targeted literacy practices and their associated language genres and learning standards. Analytic results for a participant named Dumptruck were detailed in the paper. Findings supported the claim that, for Dumptruck, "crucial literacy practices such as researching, assembling, and synthesizing information from online multimodal texts (NCTE Literacy Standards 7, 8, 11, 12; ISTE Technology Standards 3, 4) become tools for solving problems defined by his own goals and with cachet among his own peer group" (p. 57). In short, these are encouraging findings for those who seek closer links between young people's new literacy practices and formal, school-based literacy learning.

Finally, many studies in the body of research we surveyed investigate improvements in young people's literacy proficiencies in their everyday uses of digital media. These are marked by fine-grained studies of young people interacting with more proficient others—whether in a new language or in their first language. Some address young students interacting online among peers and adults, exploring whether their standard written language improves through attending to models of writing expertise, writing about personal interests and the like. This includes studies focused on fan fiction writing and how engaging in the composition-feedback-revision process improves young people's writing over time (e.g., Black 2005; Lam 2000; Magnifico 2012). Yet others document how participants become more and more adept at using social and specialist languages within different interest or affinity spaces (e.g., Chandler-Olcott & Mahar 2003; Lam 2009). A small number of studies focus on website analysis or reading texts in multiple media modes and discuss how these resources support and encourage quite complex reading strategies of the kind valued in schools.

Rebecca Black's (2005, 2008) three-year ethnographic study of online anime fanfic writers focused on English language fan fiction writing by three young women for whom English was not their first language. Black was especially interested in documenting how a particular web service—Fanfiction.net—and its narrative-sharing capabilities, reviewing system, discussion boards and so on, supported and contributed to English literacy development and how this compared to the language-learning support typically offered by schools. Data were collected by means of detailed fieldnotes and organizational charts that mapped social networks among authors within the site and through online semi-structured interviews (Black 2008). Black downloaded and examined participants' public posts to Fanfiction.net, as well as readers' reviews of participants' posted stories. This included tracing the refinement of narratives that were revised by participants in response to reader feedback and tracing the development of particular story structures, the increased clever inclusion of multiple languages within some participants' stories, and characterizations. Artifacts in the form of fan art and community writing forums that discussed "grammar, composition and the etiquette of peer review" (Black 2008: 22), among other items, were also collected and studied. The website itself was closely examined, with Black in the role of full participant–observer, writing and posting her own fanfics, providing feedback on others' writing and interacting with others on Fanfiction.net and related websites, too.

Black found that English language proficiency improved for all participants over time, with the participants themselves attributing this growth largely to their fan fiction writing and the revisions they made in light of reader feedback on plotline, character development, spelling and grammar. Participants also acknowledged the importance of sharing their fan interests with others, sharing story and character ideas among a network of like-minded fans, reading and responding to others' narratives, and being encouraged to write by readers. Black shows that the literacy "work" engaged in by these writers online was sophisticated, well designed, innovative and responsive to audience expectations. Indeed, she recounts how the mother of one of her participants sent an early write-up of her daughter's case (Black engaged regularly in member checking) to the daughter's English teacher as "evidence of the value of her daughter's online, extracurricular writing activities" (2008: 22). Studies like Black's show the value of attending to issues concerning children and young people's literacy development and suggest that many young people may be learning more about literacy outside school than they are in school.

Current contributions to knowledge

Looking at the field of digital media and literacy development studies as a whole, a key contribution made to knowledge is a much-broadened definition and understanding of literacy and what it means to be proficiently literate. Such studies challenge narrow conceptions of literacy as being a process of encoding and decoding alphabetic, character-based or script-based text where the symbol code itself is assumed to have little to do with social contexts or relationships. This is an important contribution because it acknowledges multiple ways of being literate and critiques school-centric conceptions of literacy as a kind of neutral skill—which often exclude a good many students who are actually engaging in quite complex literacy practices as they get things done in the world, but who may not be engaging in school-valued ways of "doing" literacy (e.g., young people who are able to use sophisticated software programs to generate images or games, or who use websites to broker relationships among fans in ways that enhance the website itself through new contributions and shared expertise). A broadened definition of "literacy" and "literacy proficiency" encourages educators to extend the meaning-making affordances they value and make available for students in their own classrooms.

Developments post-2010 reveal the emergence and increasing use of a range of specialist concepts within digital media and literacy development research. These concepts include, for example, participatory culture, chronotopes, premium digital literacy, design and meaning making, affinity spaces, critical literacy and digital media, "new ethos stuff," collaborative production, text fluidity, semiotic choices, identity play, and multimodal meaning making, among others. Space precludes addressing each of these in turn, so only affinity spaces and "new ethos stuff" are examined in more detail below.

Affinity spaces (Gee 2004, 2013) are defined as physical and/or virtual spaces that help to resource and sustain a group's shared interests or affinity with a common endeavour. As such, affinity spaces are not bounded by race, age, gender, ability or class. Newcomers and experts alike make use of the same space, with porous and flexible leadership within the space. Affinity spaces encourage knowledge development—both personal and for the group—and rely on shared and distributed expertize to get things done. Gee outlines additional characteristics of these spaces that emphasize different kinds or degrees of participation and collaboration. What is clear from the research literature is that the concept of "affinity space" is proving to be a useful analytic concept in terms of helping to explain the kinds of learning, social relationships and literacy practices that take place online in relation to identifiable interests and shared passions (see also Hayes & Duncan 2012).

A second conceptual device quite widely employed in recent research is our own account of the different "technical stuff" and "ethos stuff" characteristic of *conventional* and *new/digital* literacies, respectively (Lankshear & Knobel 2011). The technical shift from paper and type to pixels and screen, from material print to digital code, from print and image as distinct pro-duction modes to seamless multimodality, is obvious. Less obvious, however, is the *ethos* shift involved in the transition from conventional to new/digital literacies. The latter are often more participatory, collaborative and distributed, but also less published, less "individuated," and less "author-centric" than conventional literacies. They entail and value new relationships between "authors" and "audiences," a deep valuing of collaboration and participation, quality judged by groups rather than appointed experts, diversity of opinion in decision-making and so on. In this way, new/digital literacies as distinctively contemporary phenomena are distinguishable from conventional literacies reconstituted digitally. This provides a basis for critiquing tenden-cies in formal education to simply digitize longstanding ways of teaching and learning without attending to major cultural shifts associated with new forms of meaning making and social engagement.

Recommendations for research practice

Given the relative "newness" of the field, there is ample room for further research into what people of all ages do with digital media and literacy. Indeed, there is a need for a wider range of literacies to be studied. The field is currently dominated by games studies—including studies of games themselves, game players, game fans, game designers, etc.—to an extent that may impede appreciation of the overall picture of contemporary literacy development in terms of personal proficiency and cultural stock alike.

An important emerging field of inquiry lies in the area of computer programming and a blend of Do-It-Yourself analog and digital media. Work currently underway by Kylie Peppler and colleagues (e.g., Buechley *et al.* 2013) using arduino electronics and programming, mixed with traditional fabric crafts like quilting and cloth accessory-making, marks one leading edge. Digital media pundits outside education are increasingly calling for programming languages to be included in school curricula to help promote key literacies needed for media and content production and valued for employability as well as personal ends.

Another area meriting greater attention involves documenting children and young people's actual composing processes. Studies of young people and their digital media creation work are typically retrospective and enlist participants in talking about works already produced. By con-trast, recent work by Smith and Hull (2013) documents and analyzes *in situ* digital composition processes, and provides a valuable model for subsequent research.

There is likewise a relative paucity of studies of very young children and their digital media and literacy uses, although Jackie Marsh's work (e.g., 2004, 2011) is spearheading a groundswell. Issues concerning class are rarely tackled in this body of studies, and race/ethnicity is often included only by default (e.g., as a result of a particular summer or after-school program). David Kirkland (2010) has begun interesting work with respect to black women writing online, and Black (2008), Lam (2009), Hung (2011), and Yi (2008) have conducted insightful studies of Asian young people and their identities online and offline, but there is certainly room for more. Absence of sustained attention to class and race/ethnicity may be compounded by the difficulty of identifying markers for either when conducting fully online studies. That being said, studies explicitly focusing on either are few and far between.

Perhaps what is needed most, however, are more longitudinal, qualitative studies to evaluate the extent to which what is being claimed about digital media uses and literacy developments and proficiencies at present actually plays out as anticipated in the near and middle future. This would help the field strengthen its reputation for offering informed critiques of formal educa-tion policy grounded in solid understandings of trends and developments in everyday social life.

Michele Knobel and Colin Lankshear

Future directions

Future research directions for the field of digital media and literacy development studies are difficult to predict, since history suggests that technological innovation combines with considerable spontaneity and serendipity and can fly in wildly unanticipated directions. Even so, it is likely that emerging research trends will emphasize mobile media and literacy uses, although studies of literacy and smart phone use are surprisingly under-represented in work to date. Network savviness and practices such as those described by Rheingold (2012), which include technical and social knowhow, are also likely avenues for interesting research. Ideally, studies will emerge that explore literacy development in ways that compare experiences with the "walled garden" Internet (one constrained by access via apps and closed-access interfaces of the kind often developed by schools and companies) and the "creative" Internet (Anderson 2010) that is open to innovation, serendipitous discovery and connection-making. Such studies would afford important insights into the limitations of the former and the opportunities of the latter. Similarly, studies of children and young people engaged in learning and using programming languages to produce a range of diverse digital—and digital–analog—media would be valuable. Ethics is another likely area of research focus, covering users' ethical conduct in relation to digitally mediated literacy practices engaged in and shared with others, as well as government and corporate surveillance of, and restrictions on, digital media and network use.

Work to date in the field of digital media and literacy development has seen theoretical innovation (e.g., in games and learning theory, spatial theory, network theory) and methodological innovation (e.g., traveling ethnography, distributed cases, use of screen capture techniques) emerge on demand and *in situ* to accommodate present research needs and circumstances. We expect this trend to continue in the foreseeable future rather than for any "revolutionary" new approaches to emerge within the sociocultural study of digital media and literacy development. As an adjunct to sociocultural inquiry, the potential for "big data" approaches to researching this theme is huge—but such possibilities fall outside our remit here.

Related topics

- Chapter 4 Multimodal analysis (Jewitt)
- Chapter 10 Vernacular literacy: orthography and literacy practices (Iorio)
- Chapter 11 Texting and language learning (Waldron, Kemp & Wood)
- Chapter 19 Relationality, friendship and identity in digital communication (Graham)

References

Alvermann, D. 2006, "Ned and Kevin: an online discussion that challenges the 'not-yet-adult' cultural model," in K. Pahl & J. Rowsell (eds.), *Travel notes from the new literacy studies*, Multilingual Matters: Clevedon, UK, pp. 39–56.

Alvermann, D., Marshall, J., McLean, C., Huddleston, A., Joaquin, J. & Bishop, J. 2012, "Adolescents' web-based literacies, identity construction, and skill development," *Literacy Research and Instruction*, vol. 51, no. 3, pp. 179–195.

Anderson, C. 2010, "The web is dead? A debate," *Wired*, August 17, available at: http://www.wired.com/magazine/2010/08/ff_webrip_debate/.

Benedikt, M, (ed.) 1991, *Cyberspace: first steps*, MIT Press: Cambridge, MA.

Bigum, C. & Green, B. 1992, "Technologizing literacy: the dark side of the dream," *Discourse*, vol. 12, no. 2, pp. 4–28.

Black, R. 2008, *Adolescents and online fan fiction*, Peter Lang: New York, NY.

Black, R. 2005, "Access and affiliation: the literacy and composition practices of English language learners in an online fanfiction community," *Journal of Adolescent & Adult Literacy*, vol. 49, no. 2, pp. 118–128.

Bruce, B. 1998, "New literacies," *Journal of Adolescent and Adult Literacy*, vol. 42, no. 1, pp. 46–49.

Buck, A. 2012, "Examining digital literacy practices on social network sites," *Research in the Teaching of English*, vol. 47, no. 1, pp. 9–38.

Buckingham, D. 1993, "Towards new literacies: information technology, English and media education," *English and Media Magazine*, Summer, pp. 20–25.

Buechley, L., Peppler, K., Eisenberg, M. & Kafai, Y. 2013, *Textile messages: dispatches from the world of e-textiles and education*, Peter Lang: New York, NY.

Burke, A. 2013, "Stardolls and the virtual playground: how identity construction works in the new digital frontier," in A. Burke & J. Marsh (eds.), *Children's virtual play worlds: culture, learning and participation*, Peter Lang: New York, NY, pp. 38–58.

Chandler-Olcott, K. & Mahar, D. 2003, "Adolescents' anime-inspired 'fanfictions': an exploration of multiliteracies," *Journal of Adolescent & Adult Literacy*, vol. 46, no. 7, pp. 556–566.

Curwood, J. 2013, "Fan fiction, remix culture, and the Potter Games," in V Frankel (ed.), *Teaching with Harry Potter*, McFarland, Jefferson, NC, pp. 81–92.

Davidson, C. 2009, "Young children's engagement with digital texts and literacies in the home," *English Teaching: Practice & Critique*, vol. 8, no. 3, pp. 36–54.

Davies, J. 2012, "Facework on Facebook as a new literacy practice," *Computers & Education*, vol. 59, no. 1, pp. 19–29.

Davies, J. 2008, "Pay and display: the digital literacies of online shoppers," in C. Lankshear & M. Knobel (eds.), *Digital literacies*, Peter Lang: New York, NY, pp. 227–248.

Davies, J. & Merchant, G. 2007, "Looking from the inside out: academic blogging as new literacy," in M. Knobel & C. Lankshear (eds.), *A new literacies sampler*, Peter Lang: New York, NY, pp. 167–198.

Dudfield, A.1999, "Literacy and Cyberculture," *Reading Online*, vol. 7, available at: http://www.readingonline.org/articles/dudfield/main.html.

Duncan, S. 2012, "Kongregating online: developing design literacies in a play-based affinity space," in E. Hayes & S. Duncan (eds.), *Learning in video game affinity spaces*, Peter Lang: New York, NY, 51–83.

Duncan, B. & Leander, K. 2000, "Girls just wanna have fun: literacy, consumerism, and paradoxes of position on gURL.com," *Reading Online*, vol. 4, no. 5, available at: http://www.readingonline.org/electronic/elec_index.asp?HREF=/electronic/duncan/index.html.

Durga, S. 2012, "Learning to mod in an affinity-based modding community," in E. Hayes & S. Duncan (eds.), *Learning in video game affinity spaces*, Peter Lang: New York, NY, pp. 84–102.

Gee, J. 2013, *Good video games + good learning*, 2nd edn, Peter Lang: New York, NY.

Gee, J. 2012, *Social linguistics and literacies: ideology in discourses*, 4th edn, Routledge: New York, NY.

Gee, J. 2004, *Situated language and learning: a critique of traditional schooling*, Routledge: New York, NY.

Gee, J. 2003, *What video games have to teach us about learning and literacy*, Palgrave: New York, NY.

Gillen, J. & Merchant, G. 2013, "Contact calls: Twitter as a dialogic social and linguistic practice," *Language Sciences*, vol. 35, pp. 47–58.

Guzzetti, B. 2006, "Cybergirls: negotiating social identities on cybersites," *E-learning*, vol. 3, no. 2, pp. 158–169.

Guzzetti, B. & Gamboa, M. 2005, "Online journaling: the informal writings of two adolescent girls," *Research in the Teaching of English*, vol. 40, no. 2, pp. 168–206.

Hawisher, G. & Selfe, C. 2000, *Global literacies and the world wide web*, Routledge: London.

Hayes, E. & Duncan, S. (eds.) 2012, *Learning in video game affinity spaces*, Peter Lang: New York, NY.

Hayes, E. & Lee, Y. 2012, "Specialist language acquisition and 3D modding in a Sims fan site," in E. Hayes & S. Duncan (eds.), *Learning in video game affinity spaces*, Peter Lang: New York, NY, pp. 186–211.

Heath, S. 1983, *Ways with words*, Cambridge University Press: Cambridge.

Hull, G. 2003, "At last: youth culture and digital media: new literacies for new times," *Research in the Teaching of English*, vol. 38, no. 2, pp. 229–233.

Hung, A. 2011, *The work of play: meaning making in video games*, Peter Lang: New York, NY.

King, E. (2012), "The productive side of playing in the great indoors," in E. Hayes & S. Duncan (eds.), *Learning in video game affinity spaces*, Peter Lang: New York, NY, pp. 103–128.

Kirkland, D. 2010, "4 colored girls who considered suicide/when social networking was enuf: a Black feminist perspective on literacy online," in D. Alvermann (ed.), *Adolescents' online literacies*, Peter Lang: New York, NY, pp. 71–90.

Knobel, M. & Lankshear, C. 2008, "Digital literacy and participation in online social networking spaces," in C. Lankshear & M. Knobel (eds.), *Digital literacies*, Peter Lang: New York, NY, pp. 249–278.

Knobel, M. & Lankshear, C. 2007, "Online memes, affinities and cultural production," in M. Knobel & C. Lankshear (eds.), *A new literacies sampler*, Peter Lang: New York, NY, pp. 199–228.

Lam, W. S. E. 2009, "Multiliteracies on instant messaging in negotiating local, translocal, and transnational affiliations: a case of an adolescent immigrant," *Reading Research Quarterly*, vol. 44, no. 4, pp. 377–397.

Lam, W. S. E. 2000, "L2 literacy and the design of the self: a case study of a teenager writing on the Internet," *TESOL Quarterly*, vol. 34, no. 3, pp. 457–482.

Lammers, J. 2013, "Fan girls as teachers: examining pedagogic discourse in an online fan site," *Learning, Media & Technology*, vol. 38, no. 4, pp. 368–386, doi:10.1080/17439884.2013.764895.

Lankshear, C. & Knobel, M. 2011, *New literacies: everyday practices and social learning*, 3rd edn, Open University Press: Maidenhead, UK.

Lankshear, C. & Knobel, M. 1997, "Different worlds: technology mediated classroom learning and students' social practices with new technologies in home and community settings," in C. Lankshear, *Changing literacies*, Open University Press: Buckingham, pp. 164–187.

Lankshear, C. & Knobel, M. 1995, "Literacies, texts and difference in the electronic age," *Critical Forum*, vol. 4, no. 2, pp. 3–33.

Leander, K. & Frank, A. 2006, "The aesthetic production and distribution of image/subjects among online youth," *E-Learning*, vol. 3, no. 2, pp. 185–206.

Leander, K. & Mills, S. 2007, "The transnational development of an online role player game by youth: tracing the flows of literacy, an online game imaginary, and digital resources," in M. Blackburn & C. Clark (eds.), *Literacy research for political action*, Peter Lang: New York, NY, pp. 177–198.

Lewis, C. & Fabos, B. 2005, "Instant messaging, literacies, and social identities," *Reading Research Quarterly*, vol. 40, no. 4, pp. 470–501.

Luke, C. 1997, *Technological literacy*, Language Australia Publications: Canberra.

Mackey, M. 2007, *Mapping recreational literacies*, Peter Lang: New York, NY.

McTavish, M. 2009, "'I get my facts from the Internet': a case study of the teaching and learning of information literacy in in-school and out-of-school contexts," *Journal of Early Childhood Literacy*, vol. 9, no. 1, pp. 3–28.

Magnifico, A. 2012, "The game of Neopian writing," in E. Hayes & S. Duncan (eds.), *Learning in video game affinity spaces*, Peter Lang: New York, NY, pp. 212–234.

Marsh, J. 2011, "Young children's literacy practices in a virtual world: establishing an online interaction order," *Reading Research Quarterly*, vol. 42, no. 2, pp. 101–118.

Marsh, J. 2004, "The techno-literacy practices of young children," *Journal of Early Childhood Research*, vol. 2, no. 1, pp. 51–66.

Mavers, D. 2007, "Semiotic resourcefulness: a young child's email exchange as design," *Journal of Early Childhood Literacy*, vol. 7, no. 2, pp. 155–76.

Merchant, G. 2001, "Teenagers in cyberspace: an investigation of language use and language change in Internet chatrooms," *Journal of Research in Reading*, vol. 24, no. 3, pp. 293–306.

Nelson, M., Hull, G. and Roche-Smith, J. 2008, "Challenges of multimedia self-presentation," *Written Communication*, vol. 25, no. 4, pp. 415–440.

Rheingold, H. 2012, *Net smart*, MIT Press: Cambridge, MA.

Rheingold, H. 1994, *The virtual community*, Harper Perennial: New York, NY.

Rogers, T. & Winters, K. 2010, "Textual play, satire, and counter discourses of street youth zining practices," in D. Alvermann (ed.), *Adolescents' online literacies*, Peter Lang: New York, NY, pp. 91–108.

Sanford, K. & Madill, L. 2007, "Understanding the power of new literacies through video game play and design," *Canadian Journal of Education*, vol. 30, no. 2, pp. 432–455.

Santo, R. 2013, "Towards hacker literacies: what Facebook's privacy snafus can teach us about empowered technological practices," *Digital Culture & Education*, vol. 5, no. 1, pp. 18–33.

Scribner, S. & Cole, M. 1981, *The psychology of literacy*, Harvard University Press: Cambridge, MA.

Smith, A. & Hull, G. 2013, "Critical literacies and social media: fostering ethical engagement with global youth," in J. Ávila & J. Pandya (eds.), *Critical digital literacies as social praxis*, Peter Lang: New York, NY, pp. 63–86.

Snyder, I. 1997, Page to screen: taking literacy into the electronic era, Allen and Unwin: Sydney.

Steinkuehler, C. 2007, "Massively multiplayer online gaming as a constellation of literacy practices," *E-Learning*, vol. 4, no. 3, pp. 297–318.

Steinkuehler, C. & King, E. 2009, "Digital literacies for the disengaged: creating after school contexts to support boys' game-based literacy skills," *On the Horizon*, vol. 17, no. 1, pp. 47–59.

Street, B. 1984, *Literacy in theory and in practice*, Cambridge University Press: Cambridge.

Thomas, A. 2007, *Youth online: identity and literacy in the digital age*, Peter Lang: New York, NY.

Thomas, A. 2000, "Textual constructions of children's online identities," *CyberPsychology & Behavior*, vol. 3, no. 4, pp. 665–672.

Trainor, J. 2004, "Critical cyberliteracy: reading and writing *The X-Files*," in J. Mahiri (ed.), *What they don't learn in school: literacy in the lives of urban youth*, Peter Lang: New York, NY, pp. 123–138.

Vasudevan, L. 2010, "Education remix: new media, literacies, and the emerging digital geographies," *Digital Culture and Education*, vol. 2, no. 1, pp. 62–82.

Williams, B. 2010, *Shimmering literacies: popular culture and reading and writing online*, Peter Lang: New York, NY.

Yi, Y. 2008, "Relay writing in an adolescent online community," *Journal of Adolescent & Adult Literacy*, vol. 51, no. 8, pp. 670–680.

Further reading

Alvermann, D. (ed.) 2009, *Adolescents' online literacies: connecting classrooms, digital media and popular culture*, Peter Lang: New York, NY.

This collection documents a range of young people's digital media and literacy practices and examines how these can be leveraged in classroom contexts.

Gee, J. 2013, *Good video games + good learning*, 2nd edn, Peter Lang: New York, NY.

A set of essays that apply discourse analysis to a range of games in order to show how good games encourage deep learning. Gee also addresses how affinity spaces associated with games often entail passion and grit, and can develop premium digital literacies—all of which have important implications for schooling.

Ito, M., Horst, H., Antin, J., Finn M., Law, A., Manion, A., Mitnick, S., Schlossberg, D. & Yardi, S. 2010, *Hanging out, messing around and geeking out: kids living and learning with new media*, MIT Press: Cambridge, MA.

Provides a richly detailed macro-ethnographic perspective on digital media and literacies of contemporary youth within the United States.

Jenkins, H. 2009, *Confronting the challenges of participatory culture: media education for the 21st century*, MIT Press: Cambridge, MA.

Jenkins explains the concept and practice of participatory culture within contexts of digital media production, and shows how such cultures enable people to actively use, contribute to, share, and remix the resources provided by different participatory cultures to create and share meanings.

Lankshear, C. & Knobel, M. 2011, *New literacies: everyday practices and social learning*, 3rd edn, Open University Press: Maidenhead, UK.

This text defines new literacies in terms of social practices, and provides a range of examples of new literacy practices that emphasize collaboration, distributed expertise and social learning.

10

Vernacular literacy

Orthography and literacy practices

Josh Iorio

Introduction

For a growing number of communities, reading and writing are ubiquitous. According to the Pew Internet and American Life Project (2012), 59 percent of adult American Internet users read and write emails as part of their daily routine. Although this research is limited to the United States and its generalizability to other regions may be limited, Internet use is a central contributor to globalization and is thus a driver of social change. Internet World Stats (2013) indicates that the number of Internet users in Africa has increased by 3,606.7 percent and in the Middle East by 2,639.9 percent from 2000 to 2012. When taken together, these data suggest that a large portion of what Internet users do online is grounded in literacy practices and that the number of participants in digital literacy is rapidly growing. Literacy is no longer a practice reserved for the elite or the highly educated. It is becoming a part of everyday life for people from different social, cultural and linguistic backgrounds worldwide. As a result, individuals who engage in digital literacy "are no longer organised solely on the basis of local or national identifications, but are increasingly translocal, consisting in, as well as going beyond local and global identifications" (Leppänen *et al.* 2009: 1080).

Without question, reading and writing are professionally valuable *competencies* (Goody 2000). But literacy is also socially valued because reading and writing have become integrated into daily routines as social *practice* (Street 1988). As a social practice, literacy cannot be properly understood apart from the context in which it is situated (Street 2003). When we think of literacy, we imagine contexts with teachers sitting behind desks piled high with books. We think of grammar lessons and classical literature. We think about writing *correctly* and reading highly edited writing. In fact, you're probably wondering why I'm using so many contractions in this academic handbook chapter. You also may be wondering why I'm making generous use of the first person and why I'm addressing "you" as the reader. I'm breaking all of these prescriptive writing rules to make a point about the nature of literacy: Literacy is complex because it has different meanings for different groups in different contexts. My writing style here may seem out of place because of the formal context in which it is situated. But, in a text message to my sister, use of standard, non-contracted forms may seem standoffish, brusque, or rude. Thus, the way we read meaning in our own writing and in the writing of others changes depending on the context in which the writing is situated. The main goal of this chapter is to provide an overview of current research and future directions for the study of literacy as practices in digital contexts.

Institutional literacy

In the United States, the National Assessment of Adult Literacy defines the literacy rate based on competence in reading prose (e.g., a newspaper), filling out forms (e.g., a train schedule) and processing quantitative documents (e.g., balancing a check book) (National Center for Education Statistics 2012). Reading and writing a text message or updating a status on a social media platform are literacy practices, but also are, unsurprisingly, not included in the assessment. The types of literacy practice that are included can be considered *institutional literacies* because they are promoted, supported and structured by dominant institutions such as education, law and religion (Brandt 1998). In some cases, institutional literacy is dictated by national bodies such as France's L'Académie française that serve to define, for example, the appropriate grammatical, phonological and lexical structures of a given language. Even in countries that do not have these types of language institute, bodies such as the National Center for Education Statistics, which administers the National Assessment of Adult Literacy in the United States, play important roles in defining institutional literacy. Institutions tell people how to write in ways that are acceptable, codified and standardized within particular contexts of social power. Thus, writing can be a means of social empowerment (Goody 2000). The end goal of institutional literacy is not to maximize mutual intelligibility through creating a common and standardized set of reading and writing practices. Rather, the goal is often both to reinforce institutional power structures and to provide a means by which these structures can be challenged (Kaestle 1985).

Conversely, those who lack institutional literacy may be excluded from achieving social or political power. For instance, *legalese* is an institutionally sanctioned literacy practice that affords highly technical language to express the legal rights of individuals. However, to become institutionally literate in legalese, a degree in law or extensive independent study is required. Many individuals whose legal rights are threatened are unable to directly participate in the literacy practices that underlie the legal system. In these cases, institutional literacy suppresses empowerment. From a historical perspective, Martin Luther, a sixteenth-century church reformer, critiqued the power differentials caused by institutional literacy during the Protestant Reformation. The Protestant Reformation sought (among other goals) to shift the language of the Roman Catholic Church from Latin, which was understood only by the elite clergy, to German, the language of the lay people. Because the lay people could not directly understand the ecclesiastical language, the clergy were empowered to shape popular beliefs and the actions that were based on those beliefs. Because of the relationships between power and institutional literacy, it is not surprising that questions of assessment, inequality and access pervade current policy debate (e.g., Street 2011).

Vernacular literacies

In contrast to institutional literacies, individuals also engage in a wide variety of reading and writing practices that are "voluntary and self-generated rather than being framed and valued by the needs of social institutions" (Barton & Lee 2012: 283). This type of *vernacular literacy* has traditionally included personal activities such as creating shopping lists, writing journals or reading letters from family or friends. Vernacular literacy plays an important role in key areas of everyday life where reading and writing play a central role for people, such as in organizing life (e.g., to-do lists, reminder notes), personal communication (e.g., letters to family and friends), leisure activities (e.g., creative writing and journaling), documenting life (e.g., baby books), sense making (e.g., comparing the roster of a sports team across years) and social participation (e.g., wedding speeches and eulogies) (Barton & Hamilton 1998). These types of reading and writing activities are self-generated rather than imposed (Ivanič 1998) and "provide a voice which may otherwise not be heard" (Barton & Lee 2012: 284).

Vernacular literacy practices may differ from institutional literacy practices in terms of: 1) their orthographic form and linguistic structure, 2) their meaning and interpretation, and 3) the contexts in which they are situated. Vernacular writing may not follow standard spelling, punctuation or grammar rules (Sebba 2007) as linguistic and stylistic choices are socially and culturally meaningful (Leppänen *et al.* 2009) in different contexts. Although vernacular literacy differs from institutional literacy in important ways, there is an increasing amount of overlap as the lines between the professional and personal contexts in which literacy is practiced are becoming blurred. Work is increasingly conducted outside of the office. Computer-mediated educational models are becoming more prevalent. Traditionally local contexts are transforming into translocal discursive spaces. These shifts in the traditional delimiters of institutional and vernacular contexts are due in large part to the rise of digital networking technologies and the new opportunities that they provide for vernacular literacy practice.

Historical perspectives

The study of vernacular reading and writing grew out of anthropological and descriptive linguistics as field researchers discovered that communities were developing writing systems based on their local languages rather than reading and writing in the dominant language. The focus of this research is primarily on the form that the languages take and responded to questions such as the following: How can a sound be written in a language without a tradition of literacy if that sound does not exist in the literacy practices of the dominant language? A wide range of research over the past half century has examined vernacular literacy in this way and has highlighted its role as a symbol of opposition to the institutionalized standard and the value system represented by the dominant language (e.g., Crowley 2000).

Vernacular literacy has also been examined from both a variationist and language contact perspective, with a focus on the socioculturally conditioned variability within a language and between languages. For language varieties, there are often no standardized, institutionalized rules for reading and writing. Varieties reflect the ways that individuals speak in the home, the schoolyard and in their local communities. Vernacular varieties of language, e.g., Cockney or African American English, typically exist in opposition to institutional varieties such as Received Pronunciation or Standard American English. The study of vernacular literacy in this tradition often focuses on the orthographic form of the writing and the meaning of these forms to the language users. For instance, Androutsopoulos (2000: 528) describes the relationship between both the intra- and inter-lingual influences on the non-standard orthographic choices of German punk fans and how these choices are, in part, "transgressive with respect to mainstream [institutional] orthographic practices."

Other approaches to the study of vernacular literacy are less concerned with the form that the writing takes and place more emphasis on the uses and meanings of literacy practices in local communities. This line of research focuses more specifically on the contexts in which vernacular literacy practices are situated and on the role that they play in the everyday lives of people. For example, Camitta (1993: 223) describes the practices as "traditional and indigenous to the diverse cultural processes of communities." Her sense of vernacular literacy focuses on the sociocultural context in which the reading and writing occur. In their seminal ethnographic work in a small English community, Barton and Hamilton (1998) explore the events in which literacy occurs, the more general literacy practices which make up the events, and the socio-historical and cultural structures that frame both the practices and the events. Their research very clearly demonstrates that understanding who is writing, to whom, when and why are all questions that are inextricably linked to the contexts in which they are situated.

Taken together, these interrelated but often distinct research traditions form the basis of the emerging study of vernacular literacy in digital spaces. The research on vernacular literacy in non-digital contexts has highlighted the ways that reading and writing are meaningful social practices only when they are analyzed within a particular context. As vernacular literacy has emerged in digital spaces, the challenge for research and theory building has been to account for the role of technological mediation and expanding sociocultural contexts on vernacular literacy practice.

Critical issues and topics

The study of digital vernacular literacy is concerned with: 1) identifying the digital contexts and uses in which literacy is practiced, 2) the orthographic form and linguistic structures that constitute the practices and 3) the relationships between form, structure, context and social meaning. Researchers are re-examining the definition of vernacular literacy within digital contexts, and the resulting new definitions are contributing to an understanding of the implications and meanings of vernacular literacy for local, translocal and global communities. As reading and writing are conducted in a wider range of technologically mediated spaces by members of different language communities, the study of vernacular literacy also has implications for our understanding of literacy more generally. Why do people read and write and what do their literacy practices mean to them? How do literacy practices change when languages (or varieties of languages) come into contact with each other?

Defining digital vernacular literacy: form, context, meaning

As literacy shifted from paper-based media to digital platforms, new frontiers for its study were opened as vernacular literacy practices emerged in digital spaces. As Moje (2009) points out, some literacy practices in digital spaces are entirely new while some are old practices adapted or adopted for a new context. For instance, the practice of writing emails to family members and reading their responses is similar to reading and writing paper letters, but the type of one-to-many reading and writing that occurs on Twitter was only possible in the past through institutional channels and was often not interactive. In many cases, the scope and reach of writing in digital spaces has been dramatically expanded.

In some cases, distinguishing between old and new literacy practices involves examining the vernacular basis of contextually situated orthographic forms and linguistic structures. A social networking site like Facebook can be considered a rich site for vernacular literacy practice given definitions such as Barton and Lee's (2012), because reading and writing are "voluntary and self-generated." But Facebook is also populated by mainstream media companies, which use Facebook as an outlet for their news reporting. The orthographic form and linguistic structure of their news reporting is firmly situated within the journalistic genre and thus typically adheres to institutional literacy prescriptions. However, Facebook users can comment on these news stories through their own vernacular writing practices. This juxtaposition of institutional and vernacular practices is illustrated in Figure 10.1, where the form of the original post, authored by the British Broadcasting Corporation (BBC), is highly standardized and aligned to the institutional literacy practices of traditional mainstream mass media. The institutional form of the framing news story is contrasted with the vernacular form of the comment, which contains non-standard spellings (e.g., <PLZZZzzz>), capitalization (e.g., <kashmiri>) and punctuation

Figure 10.1　BBC Facebook post and comments.

(e.g., <!!!>). This example demonstrates how institutional and vernacular literacy practices are often embedded in a common digital context.

The larger discursive context in which the comment is situated is also important for understanding the meanings associated with the vernacular literacy practices. The comment is advocating for a Kashmiri political movement, while the news article refers to the legal status of migrant workers in Hong Kong. The vernacular orthographic form of the writing is structurally in opposition to the standard form (Sebba 2003) and the vernacular literacy practice here may be oppositional to and subversive of the institutional literacy practices (Maybin 2007) that characterize the framing news article. This example demonstrates how "sound to spelling correspondences [are] exploited in order to produce symbolic value" through which, "by choosing a non-legitimated spelling option, writers can maintain intelligibility but create symbolic distance" (Sebba 2003: 168). In this case, the symbolic value of the comment's vernacular form focuses attention away from both the orthographic norms of the news report and the discursive content of the news story in order to highlight the comment author's oppositional stance.

Note also that, for many readers, the comment may be considered "spam" or "trolling" because it is not related to the content of the original news post. Although spamming is usually considered a practice that has emerged only in online contexts, is it fundamentally different from, e.g., spray-painting political graffiti on top of a corporate logo? It is the presence of these types of questions that require researchers to reassess what we mean by "vernacular literacy" in digital contexts. Because digital literacy practices are often embedded in a shared context, it is not always possible to assert that a particular context entails a singular type of literacy practice. A single post on Facebook can be a site both of vernacular literacy practice and of institutional literacy practice. The same can rarely be said for traditional print-media. Newspapers, even the reader editorial pages, are almost always rooted in institutional literacy practices. The political comment in Figure 10.1 would not likely have been associated with the news article if it had appeared in the Wall Street Journal. Within a single Facebook post, vernacular and institutional literacy practices can (and often do) coexist simultaneously in the same discursive space and thus prove to be common oppositional contexts where literacy practices (and the meanings or ideologies associated with these practices) come into conflict. This coexistence provides exciting opportunities for researchers to explore the role of the vernacular in shaping institutional practices, and in turn the role of the institution in shaping vernacular practices.

The example also highlights the relationship between vernacular orthographic form and meaning. The examples of orthographic non-standardness (i.e., punctuation, phonetic spellings, <z> for /s/ substitutions, and capitalization for emphasis) will probably be familiar to readers from their own experiences with digital literacy. While these forms certainly constitute one aspect of vernacularity that is common in digital contexts, forms such as <Endian>, <Azaadi> and <Aes Che AlllaG> explicitly reflect the cultural meanings of the vernacular forms, where Endian is a Kashmiri spelling of *Indian* and <Azaadi> is a Romanized spelling of the Kashmiri term for *freedom*. The term <Aes Che AlllaG> is less clear. However, the lack of clarity highlights the fact that the intended audience of the comment was not the mainstream audience of BBC Facebook page readers or of an academic writing a handbook chapter. As the commenter notes explicitly, the audience is the "Kashmiri people." By writing <Aes Che AlllaG>, a phrase that is unfamiliar to the audience at large, the commenter is aligning the comment with a particular group of people for whom this vernacular form has a particular meaning. This alignment reflects the discursive theme of the comment, i.e., one of opposition to and subversion of not only the institutional literacy practices represented by the BBC news article, but also Indian politics and the more general practices on Facebook prohibiting spamming. Thus, the vernacular forms that constitute the writing combined with the discursive stance of the comment embedded in the institutional and mainstream context of the BBC's news story demonstrate the complexity of association in which vernacular literacy practices can be situated. Understanding how meanings emerge and are conveyed in this type of embedded discursive context is a critical challenge for digital vernacular literacy research.

Contextual embedding and the vernacularization of institutional literacy practices

Although the BBC is an institutional body, it seeks to establish a social relationship with its readers by cross-posting news articles on Facebook. Davies' (2012) research focuses on the social aspects of Facebook as she demonstrates that Facebook offers new ways of managing friendships. However, the example in Figure 10.1 highlights a different aspect of Facebook—one where friendship is backgrounded and political advocating is foregrounded—and demonstrates that the boundaries between private and public, social and professional, institutional and vernacular are blurred.

Facebook and other digital technologies that tend to be understood as spaces for personal and social interaction are also important in professional interactions. For example, Fluor (NYSE: FLR), a global engineering, construction and project management corporation, uses social networking technology to connect its 43,000 globally distributed employees. Through Fluor's *Connections Tool*, employees are able to interact with each other over a closed intranet through affordances similar to Facebook (IBM News Release 2011). Institutions are not only using digital technologies to connect to their market audience as the BBC does on Facebook, but they are using similar technologies within institutional contexts to encourage social relationship building among their employees. Fluor is not unique in their use of social media in the workplace. In a variety of industries and professions, workers use instant messenger to communicate with co-workers on different floors or in different countries. Technical support personnel in one country respond to service claims by customers in other countries through chat systems or message boards. As many industries are continuing to globalize, geographically distributed workers, clients, customers, managers and executives are interacting with each other through digital writing. Each of these stakeholders brings their local ways of writing to the digital context, and thus development of shared meaning can be challenging.

Within a digital literacy context, opportunity for a wide range of vernacular forms, genres and styles can be embedded in institutional contexts. Consider the following example:

1   Indian_1:   v shal be online for sm 10 mins okie
2   Indian_2:   jus to know comments on our updated model
3   Dutch_1:   This week we did a preliminary cost estimation based on your file
4   Indian_1:   k
5   Indian_1:   u may send mail on that
6   Dutch_2:   Is the use of [construction] phases in [R]evit needed for the planning group? if it is, are you modeller guys able to work with different phases in revit?
7   Indian_2:   phases . . like u need the [building's] foundation. den floor wise?

Example 1   Instant messaging transcript of two Indian and two Dutch speakers of English engaged in engineering work. Brackets indicate insertions by the author for clarity.

Example 1 is an instant messaging transcript of an international team of engineers working on the design of a large freight terminal for Boeing at a major U.S. international airport. Given the scope of the task and the professional context in which it is being conducted, we might expect that the synchronous text communication would follow institutional literacy practices, particularly since the interactions were with workers writing (in some cases) in English as a second language. On the contrary, we observe homophone spellings (Line 5, <u>), phonetic spellings (Line 1, <v>; Line 7, <den>) and so on, juxtaposed with technical engineering jargon (Line 6, *phases*; *Revit*). The examples of non-standard orthography are similar to the types of vernacular literacy practices that Sebba (1998) describes for British Creole. In Sebba's research, he found that British Creole speakers developed innovative orthographic forms to distinguish between the local variety and their English origin, e.g., by spelling *you* as <yu> or <yuh>. The stylistic choices by the Indian engineers are similar because they are based on many of the same underlying non-standard orthographic practices that Sebba describes in his research. Example 1 demonstrates that the vernacular literacy practices of the Indian engineers have transferred into the prototypically institutional context of a work meeting to create a *translocal* interactional space characterized by "the coexistence, mixing and alternation of different languages, registers genres and styles" (Leppänen *et al.* 2009: 1100).

The clearly delimited line that has historically existed between vernacular and institutional literacy practice is becoming increasingly blurred because professional contexts are becoming more translocal. Because of this vernacularization of institutional literacy practice, do institutions have some stake in ensuring, for example, that workers are competent in a range of vernacular literacies? Is it important for the technical support worker in India to understand how vernacular varieties of English are written in the American South, so that they can understand and better connect socially with their customers? Should schools, traditional bastions of institutional literacy, provide students with opportunities to develop their vernacular literacy in addition to or independent of their institutional literacy? Will vernacular literacy become professionally valuable as workers from around the world interact in real-time through digital reading and writing as part of their daily institutional practices? These questions point to the practical implications of a changing dynamic between the vernacular and the institutional and highlight the importance of continued research and theory development on literacy practices in the two merging domains.

Current contributions and research

While research on vernacular literacy in digital contexts is increasing, there is still no unifying theoretical model that integrates the role of the technological affordances, the digital contexts, the orthographic forms, and the meanings that readers share. This type of theorization is challenging because the contexts in which vernacular writing can occur are rapidly expanding. In general, current research has focused on orthographic form and/or its social meanings for readers within a relatively small set of socio-technical contexts. These studies have primarily focused on: 1) describing practices that occur for communities in specific contexts, 2) understanding how traditional literacy practices are extended to new contexts, and 3) understanding how new practices emerge within a given technological context.

Sites of vernacular literacy are emergent and dynamic

The importance of context in terms of understanding vernacular literacy has been examined at the technological level (e.g., Flickr, Facebook, Twitter) and at the community level within a particular "technological context" (e.g., a particular community within an online role-playing game or a friend network within Facebook).

For instance, Barton and Lee (2012) examined the technological context of Flickr with the goal of using Flickr to draw generalizations about uses of literacy in "Web 2.0" or online social networking sites. They show that even on a Web 2.0 platform like Flickr, which is primarily designed to enable sharing of photos, vernacular literacy plays a central role as people read and write image titles, captions and descriptions and interact with others through comments. They argue that vernacular practices on Web 2.0 are a source of creativity, invention and originality. Their findings can be contrasted with Davies and Merchant's (2006: 167) study of academic blogs, which they argue are sites for interactivity through writing that can "reconfigure relationships and can engender new ways of looking at the world." Both Flickr and blogs are Web 2.0 technologies that simultaneously are sites of creativity, as Barton and Lee note, and sites of relationship creation and maintenance. But they are also sites of many other vernacular (and institutional) practices that are enabled through reading and writing. The dynamic nature of digital contexts in which individuals read and write make it challenging for researchers to draw broad generalizations about what individuals do, through their writing, in these spaces. It is thus difficult to state that a one-to-one relationship exists between any particular technological context and the literacy practiced in those contexts.

The contexts in which vernacular literacy practices are situated are constantly emerging and changing as technologies are developed and new uses for old technologies are created. Twitter was originally designed as a personal micro-blogging tool, but has since evolved into a tool for mass marketing, political change and institutional gain. However, Twitter is still used by many on a very personal level, e.g., to keep family and friends updated about the mundane details of day-to-day life. For blogs, Davies and Merchant (2006: 192) argue that "blogging seems to be closely tied up with self-presentation and impression formation." While some (academic) blogs are certainly focused on the individual writer, others are written anonymously or are conduits for the dissemination of information. Still others are collectively authored. The genre of blogs is defined differentially by their literacy practices, not by the properties of the technological context. Whereas blogs had originally started as personal "weblogs" or online journals very much in line with Davies

Josh Iorio

and Merchant's account, like Twitter, they have changed to support a variety of practices. This dynamism and the continued emergence of new technological spaces and uses for existing digital environments are, in part, why development of a unifying theory is challenging. Such a theory must characterize and explain the relationships between socio-technical contexts, orthographic forms, genres, languages, and the meanings of digital vernacular literacy practices.

Vernacular writing is orthographically diverse

In addition to focusing on the contexts in which digital vernacular literacy occurs, research has also focused on developing characterizations of the orthographic form of vernacular writing in digital contexts, with particular emphasis on the meanings associated with the orthographic forms (see, e.g., Hinrichs' (2012) study of Jamaican Creole literacy practices in email and blogs). Sebba (2007: 27–30) describes the multiple ways that orthographic forms can vary from the conventional forms in vernacular literacy practice, including: 1) selection of the script itself (e.g., see Palfreyman and al Khalil's (2003) analysis of choice of the Roman script to represent Gulf Arabic instant messaging), 2) sound-to-character correspondence (e.g., English /z/ represented as either <s> or <z> in words like *legitimise* and *realise*), 3) sound representation in specific positions within a word (e.g., <ck> can only represent /k/ at the end of English words but cannot occur at the beginning of a word), and 4) homophonic representations (e.g., *night* and *knight* are composed of the same sounds but are represented differently and have different meanings). Although this list is not exhaustive, it highlights the linguistic resources that writers draw on to shape the orthographic styles that underlie their vernacular literacy practice.

A growing body of research has examined how these deviations from institutionally sanctioned or conventional orthography are meaningful for digital communities. For instance, Iorio (2010) explored how communities within Massively Multi-player Online Role-Playing Games (MMORPGs) use orthography based on vernacular forms to signal group membership. He demonstrated that the vernacular present progressive suffix <in> in words such as <runnin> were used by the sub-community of role-players to distinguish themselves from other communities within the MMORPG context. The vernacular orthographic form holds special meaning for role-players compared to the conventional form (i.e., *running*). For role-players, the vernacular form is used to signal informality when they are "in character" and thus is interpreted as a textual marker of speech. As in Figure 10.1, where *Endian* is used to signal identification with the Kashmiri community and place this community in opposition to the Indian community, <runnin> is used by role-players to signal differentiation from non-role-players in the MMORPG.

Similarly, Lee (2002) examined the vernacular orthographic character of email and ICQ interactions between people who lived in Hong Kong. She found that there were large differences in writing styles between IM and email interactions in terms of homophone spellings (e.g., <u> for *you*), omission of the first person singular *I*, code-mixed messages (i.e., messages that contained words from different languages), and use of Romanized orthography to represent Cantonese. Her results show that email interactions were orthographically more standard and adhered more closely to institutional writing practice compared to the more vernacular orthography that she observed in ICQ. Thus, Lee's study shows that, for this particular community, the technological medium through which vernacular writing is situated contributes to its systematicity. Her results indicate that "formality and synchronicity are two major factors that determine the frequency of these features in different CMC systems" (Lee 2002: 21). While Lee's results support her claim that "CMC users have less time to type in full forms in a synchronous communicative environment like ICQ," other studies have demonstrated that use of vernacular writing practices are common even in cases where the interactions are less synchronous. For instance, Iorio (2010) demonstrated that there was no statistically significant relationship between an increase in activity level in an MMORPG (implying less time to type) and an increase in shorter, often vernacular orthographic forms. In this study, community members consistently used vernacular orthography when they wanted to signal group membership, regardless of the time demands placed on them by participation in the game. The differences in the findings from Lee (2002) and Iorio (2010) reinforce the role that the interactional context has on the relationship between orthographic form and meaning within different communities. For the role-players, adherence to their character's role through their vernacular writing practices superseded any functional constraints imposed by the speed at which the synchronous interactions were conducted. For the community in Lee's study, while the vernacular forms were meaningful, they were more fully conditioned by the technological context.

Digital vernacular literacy practices are translocal

Through literacy, individuals make meaning of their lives and of the world in which they live. In many digital contexts, individuals from a variety of national, cultural, and linguistic backgrounds interact in a shared space, where new language norms emerge (Blommaert 2005). These emergent norms are often based on a community's negotiation of intersecting local norms that individuals bring to the discursive space. The resulting translocal literacy practices are enabled because of the "transportability [. . .] of styles, aesthetics, knowledges and ideologies that travel across localities and cross-cut modalities" (Alim 2009, pp. 104–105). Leppänen et al.'s (2009: 1098) discussion of Finnish extreme sports fans provides an example of how global cultures are localized through literacy within a digital context. The case study demonstrates how the Finnish fans use the jargon associated with global extreme sports culture and also create different orthographic representations of these terms. For example, one fan discusses how he learned to execute a 360 degree flip on his skateboard by representing *360 flip* as <360flipin>, which reflects an integration of the English jargon into Finnish morphology and word formation patterns. Through their literacy, the Finnish fans localize the orthographic form of the global jargon. By connecting these localized forms to their own experiences, they likewise localize the meanings associated with the forms. Leppänen et al. (2009: 1098) argues that their "language mixing and the appropriation of the terms adopted from English extreme sports jargon seem to be central means for them to negotiate their identities as members of a translocal extreme sports community."

As individuals digitally travel from community to community, they bring with them their sociocultural tools for meaning-making. Thus, the vernacular character of literacy is both conditioned by an individual's local context and their translocal experiences in digital spaces. For example, Leppänen et al. (2009: 1101) describes the ways in which a Finnish teen's digital literacy practices in various environments allow her to "establish and index herself as a particular kind of person, with a particular kind of value system and lifestyle" while simultaneously shaping the broader communities in which she participates. In other words, her vernacular literacy practices both serve as markers of her own identity and contribute to shaping the literacy norms and associated meanings of her online communities. As Leppänen et al.'s research demonstrates, digital vernacular literacy practices are key avenues through which individuals perform identity work in local, translocal and global contexts.

Main research methods

To understand the values, uses and perspectives about vernacular literacy, qualitative methods are appropriate because they are able to capture the dynamic and diverse nature of individual's experiences. Computer-Mediated Discourse Analysis (CMDA) (Herring 2004) focuses primarily on the digital product of writing and how these products are read. This approach allows the researcher to critically examine the forms that writers employ and how readers make sense of these forms. However, unless some of the accessible writing is reflective, it is difficult to determine, using only CMDA, why the orthographic forms have emerged and how people experience digital reading and writing. Combining the analytical focus of CMDA with further ethnographic insights results in Discourse-Centered Online Ethnography (Androutsopoulos 2008), which can include questionnaires, surveys and interviews. By combining ethnography with analysis of discourse, a better understanding of the relationship between form and meaning within a particular context can be established. In some cases, when researchers are part of the communities that they are studying, autoethnography (Davies & Merchant 2006: 167) is appropriate because it "repositions the researcher as both subject and object, and in this way breaks with the more separate stance of traditional cultural ethnographers."

While ethnographic methods are appropriate for communities where the ethnographer has access to a representative subset of community members, for large communities, this type of intimate relationship between researchers and researched is not often possible. For instance, ethnographic methods are appropriate for investigating the literacy practices of a small network of Twitter users, but to be able to discuss literacy practices on Twitter in general, either a large number of ethnographies would need to be synthesized or a single, well-defined quantitative study of Twitter would need to be conducted. To this point, the bulk of research on digital vernacular literacy has focused on its use and meaning in relatively small social contexts, which lack the explanatory power to produce generalizations across communities or contexts. Quantitative analyses (e.g., Hinrichs 2012) allow researchers to determine whether there are in fact systematic variations in the meanings of vernacular literacy practices, e.g., between communities within a given context or across contexts. Quantitative approaches are particularly appropriate for research on digital writing because online texts are often machine readable, which means that they can be processed, searched and analyzed computationally. Computational analysis combined with statistical description can provide detailed descriptions of the orthographic form that writing takes across large populations of community members (e.g., Iorio 2010).

Because of the interface between orthographic form, meaning and the translocal, sociotechnical context in which digital vernacular literacy practices are situated, the most effective way to study digital vernacular literacy blends the quantitative aspects of statistical modelling with the qualitative aspects of ethnography. Thus, statistical descriptions of the distribution of orthographic forms can be combined with the perspectives and experiences of individual community members to produce a more complete account of the meaning and significance of vernacular literacy practice within a community. See *Part I: Methods and perspectives* of this volume for a more detailed description of the methods used to study language and literacy in digital communication.

Recommendations for practice

While much research over the past 50 years has focused on the role of vernacular writing in the classroom, much less has focused on vernacular reading and very little has examined ways to teach individuals how to develop shared meaning in others' vernacular literacy practices. Given the increasing professional value of vernacular literacy, the ability to understand (and appreciate) other literacies will become an increasingly important core learning competency. For instance, in marketing, the ability to connect authentically to a target audience is central to an effective marketing strategy. Marketers must be able to interact with their audience as though they were a member of the community, which requires that they understand the vernacular literacy practices of their audience and adapt their own literacy practices away from the institutional norms to align more closely with the values of their audience. For instance, marketing programs at universities may be well served by allowing students to practice reading and understanding the vernacular writing practices of a range of digital communities to develop competence in adapting their writing to better align with the implied values of their audience based on the meanings associated with their vernacular literacy practices.

Future directions

Elbow (2010) theorizes that vernacular literacy will progress through three stages on a path that ultimately leads to it supplanting institutional literacy. He argues that first, mainstream spoken language will be acceptable for serious writing. Then, mainstream spoken language will be considered acceptable for school writing and academic discourse. Finally, nonmainstream and stigmatized spoken language will be acceptable for all serious writing. While the notion that vernacular writing will eventually replace institutionally sanctioned writing is quite radical, given the incursion of vernacular literacy practices into institutional contexts, Elbow's prediction may hold some merit given a sufficiently long timescale. While institutional literacy practices will likely remain a substantial part of our reading and writing in the foreseeable future, vernacular literacies have nonetheless become ubiquitous. They are on our phones, in our email boxes, on our screens, in our homes and so forth. We are beginning to see them in our schools and in our places of employment. The number of contexts for which institutional literacy is reserved is shrinking.

To a large extent, we are at the very beginning of understanding the types of local/global and professional/personal embedding that surrounds digital vernacular literacy practice. To date, research is beginning to build a qualitative foundation by examining practices on a context-by-context basis, with the bulk of research focused on the social aspects of vernacular literacy. Very little attention has been paid to the juxtaposition of vernacular and institutional practices. Moreover, we lack an understanding of how vernacularization processes operate in institutional contexts, although a few studies have mentioned the institutional aspects of contexts like Facebook and Flickr (see, e.g., Burgess (2007) for analysis of how the business model of Flickr sponsors certain types of vernacular practices). As vernacular literacy continues to become more integrated into institutional contexts, research must strive to better understand these relationships.

In order to develop this understanding, a unified theory of digital vernacular literacy must be developed that can explain the relationship between form and meaning in embedded contexts. Throughout this chapter, I have discussed a number of contexts in which literacy practices emerge. Institutional and vernacular contexts can simultaneously exist within a given technological context. Within either an institutional or vernacular context, individual groups and communities exist, and sub-communities can be embedded within larger communities. Each of these contextual levels can potentially have a range of associated vernacular literacy practices that distinguish its members from communities in other contexts. The differences are not trivial, but fundamentally define the communities. The contextual complexity in which digital vernacular literacy practices are situated is still not very well understood.

As reading and writing continue to play an increasingly meaningful role in everyday lives, the traditional lines drawn between standard and non-standard, correct and incorrect, local and global, vernacular and institutional will continue to become blurred.

Related topics

- Chapter 1 Approaches to language variation (Hinrichs)
- Chapter 3 Digital ethnography (Varis)

Josh Iorio

- Chapter 4 Multimodal analysis (Jewitt)
- Chapter 12 Digital media in workplace interaction (Darics)
- Chapter 9 Digital media and literacy development (Knobel & Lankshear)
- Chapter 11 Texting and language learning (Waldron, Kemp & Wood)
- Chapter 23 Translocality (Kytölä)

References

Alim, H. S. 2009, "Translocal style communities: hip hop youth as cultural theorists of style, language and globalization," *Pragmatics*, vol. 19, no. 1, pp. 103–127.

Androutsopoulos, J. 2008, "Discourse-centered online ethnography," *Language@internet* vol. 5, J. Androutsopoulos & M. Beisswenger (eds.), Special issue, *Data and methods in computer-mediated discourse analysis*.

Androutsopoulos, J. 2000, "Non-standard spelling in media texts," *Journal of Sociolinguistics*, vol. 4, no. 4, pp. 514–533.

Barton, D. & Lee, C. K. M. 2012, "Redefining vernacular literacies in the age of Web 2.0," *Applied Linguistics*, vol. 33, no. 3, pp. 282–298.

Barton, D. & Hamilton, M. 1998, *Local literacies: reading and writing in one community*, Routledge: New York, NY.

Blommaert, J. 2005, *Discourse: a critical introduction*, Cambridge University Press: Cambridge.

Brandt, D. 1998, "Sponsors of literacy," *College Composition and Communication*, vol. 49, no. 2, pp. 165–185.

Burgess, J. 2007, *Vernacular creativity and new media*, available at: http://eprints.qut.edu.au/16378/ [accessed 25 March 2013].

Camitta, M. 1993, "Vernacular writing: varieties of literacy among Philadelphia high school students," in B. Street (ed.), *Cross-cultural approaches to literacy*, Cambridge University Press: New York, NY, pp. 228–246.

Crowley, T. 2000, "The consequences of vernacular (il)literacy in the Pacific," *Current Issues in Language Planning*, vol. 1, no. 3, pp. 368–388.

Davies, J. 2012, "Facework on facebook as a new literacy practice," *Computers and Education*, vol. 59, no. 1, pp. 19–29.

Davies, J. & Merchant, G. 2006, "Looking from the inside out: academic blogging as new literacy," in C. Lankshear & M. Knobel (eds.), *A new literacies sampler*, Peter Lang: New York, NY, pp. 167–197.

Elbow, P. 2010, *A new culture of vernacular literacy on the horizon*, Unpublished manuscript, available at: http://works.bepress.com/peter_elbow/35 [accessed 21 March 2013].

Goody, J. 2000, *The power of the written tradition*, Smithsonian Institution: Washington, DC.

Herring, S. 2004, "Computer-mediated discourse analysis: an approach to researching online behavior," in S. A. Barab, R. Kling & J. H. Grays (eds.), *Designing for virtual communities in the service of learning*, Cambridge University Press: New York, NY, pp. 338–376.

Hinrichs, L. 2012, "How to spell the vernacular: a multivariate study of Jamaican e-mails and blogs," in A. Jaffe, J. Androutsopoulos, M. Sebba & S. Johnson (eds.), *Orthography as social action: scripts, spelling, identity and power*, Mouton De Gruyter: Boston, MA, pp. 325–358.

IBM 2011, "Fluor connects its global workforce and drives innovation with IBM social business software," IBM News Releases, available at: http://www03.ibm.com/press/us/en/pressrelease/40217.wss [accessed 2 April 2013].

Internet World Stats 2012, *World internet users and population stats*, available at: http://www.internetworld stats.com/stats.htm/ [accessed 8 April 2013].

Iorio, J. 2010, *Explaining orthographic variation in a virtual community: linguistic, social and contextual factors*, available at: http://repositories.lib.utexas.edu/handle/2152/ETD-UT-2010-05-727 [accessed 8 April 2013].

Ivanič, R. 1998, *Writing and identity: the discoursal construction of identity in academic writing*, John Benjamins: Amsterdam.

Kaestle, C. F. 1985, "The history of literacy and the history of readers," *Review of Research in Education*, vol. 12, no. 1, pp. 11–53.

Lee, C. K. M. 2002, "Literacy practices in computer-mediated communication in Hong Kong," *The Reading Matrix*, vol. 2, no. 2, pp. 1–25.

Leppänen, S., Pitkänen-Huhta, A., Piirainen-Marsh, A., Nikula, T. & Peuronen, S. 2009, "Young people's translocal new media uses: a multiperspective analysis of language choice and heteroglossia," *Journal of Computer-Mediated Communication*, vol. 14, no.1, pp. 1080–1107.

Maybin, J. 2007, "Literacy under and over the desk," *Language and Education*, vol. 21, no. 6, pp. 515–530.

Moje, E. B. 2009, "Standpoints: a call for new research on new and multi-literacies," *Research in the Teaching of English*, vol. 43, no. 4, pp. 348–362.

National Center for Education Statistics 2012, *National assessment of adult literacy*, available at: http://nces.ed.gov/naal/index.asp [accessed 8 April 2013].

Palfreyman, D. & al Khalil, M. 2003, "'A funky language for teenzz to use': representing Gulf Arabic in instant messaging," *Journal of Computer Mediated Communication*, vol. 9, no. 1.

Pew Internet and American Life Project 2012. *Data trends*, available at: http://www.pewinternet.org/ [accessed 8 April 2013].

Sebba, M. 2007, *Spelling and society*, Cambridge University Press: Cambridge.

Sebba, M. 2003, "Spelling rebellion," in J. Androutsopoulos & A. Georgakopoulou (eds.), *Discourse constructions of youth identities*, John Benjamins: Amsterdam, pp. 151–172.

Sebba, M. 1998, "Phonology meets ideology: the meaning of orthographic practices in British Creole," *Language Problems and Language Planning*, vol. 22, no. 1, pp. 19–47.

Street, B. 1988, "Literacy practice and literacy myths,' in R. Saljo (ed.), *The written world: studies in literate thought and action*, Springer-Verlag: New York, NY, pp. 59–72.

Street, B. 2011, "Literacy inequalities in theory and practice: the power to name and define,' *International Journal of Educational Development*, vol. 31, no. 1, pp. 580–586.

Street, B. 2003, "What's 'new' in new literacy studies? critical approaches to literacy in theory and practice," *Current Issues in Comparative Education*, vol. 5, no. 2, pp. 77–91.

Further reading

Barton, D., Hamilton, M. & Ivanič, R. (eds.) 2000, *Situated literacies: theorising reading and writing in context*, Routledge, London.

This volume is a foundational work that provides a range of perspectives on vernacular literacy practices and their uses and meanings in a variety of non-digital contexts.

Baynham, M. 1995, *Literacy practices: investigating literacy in social contexts*, Longman: New York, NY.

Although not focused on digital contexts, this volume provides a foundational perspective on the sociocultural aspects literacy.

Lankshear, C. & Knobel, M. (eds.) 2006, *A new literacies sampler*, Peter Lang: New York, NY.

This volume is a collection of studies exploring literacy practices in technologically mediated spaces. While it does not focus specifically on vernacular literacy, it provides insight into the interface between literacy and a range of technological contexts.

11

Texting and language learning

Sam Waldron, Nenagh Kemp and Clare Wood

Introduction

The use of text-messaging has increased dramatically across the world in recent years, and with it has come an abbreviated, casual writing style, often called *textese*, characterized by orthographic innovations called *textisms*. The research summarized in this chapter confirms that the use of textese is not associated with poorer literacy skills in general. In children, it is even linked with better reading and spelling ability, although the picture is less clear in adults. The way that textism use is studied is important, as different methodologies can result in different estimates. As the written language of text messaging continues to evolve, investigators should continue to develop ways of collecting and studying the message data in children and adults. Rather than being a distraction in the classroom, mobile technology has the potential to act as a versatile tool for learning, and the research reviewed here could help to inform future studies in this area.

The prevalence of text messaging and its potential effects

Within the last decade there has been considerable media concern over the writing of text-messages on mobile phones and its potential effect on the written language skills of young people. This concern is due to the fact that in these messages words are often spelled in an abbreviated or phonetic form (e.g. *txt*, *nite*) and do not always follow the rules of conventional written language. One of the most extreme examples of negative coverage comes from British journalist John Humphrys (2007) who likened texters to 'vandals' doing to language what Genghis Khan did to his enemies. More recently, Sir Terry Pratchett argued that using text-messaging language demotivates young people to use language correctly and restricts vocabulary (Furness 2012). In contrast, UK Poet Laureate Carol Anne Duffy has stated that 'poems are the original text message' (Hough 2011) – in other words, more recent forms of written language such as texting and tweeting, far from representing the ruination of writing, are simply alternative, modernized types of language whose mechanisms are often seen in poetry. This more positive public view of texting has become increasingly common in recent years, perhaps reflecting the findings of the research that is reviewed later in this chapter. It also fits with the idea that not all of these language changes can be attributed to technology; as Baron (2003) and Crystal (2008) point out, abbreviations and acronyms have been used in English for centuries, and shorthand (which shares some characteristics with text language) was very popular until not long ago.

It is important to study the phenomenon of text-messaging not only because of the ongoing media debate but also because it is so prevalent within modern society. For example, in the UK at the time of writing, 98 per cent of 12–15-year-olds, 47 per cent of 8–11-year-olds and 26 per cent of 8-year-olds own a mobile phone (Ofcom 2011). While 3–4-year-olds do not usually own a mobile phone, 13 per cent of them regularly use one in the home environment to watch TV, play games or use the internet (Ofcom 2012). If using a mobile phone affects children's development, then the potential for such influence must start at an early age and it is important to determine whether these effects are as negative as has been suggested.

The numbers of sent text-messages are also rising year-on-year (Ofcom 2012), especially with the recent (2011–2012) increase in Smartphone ownership for children, as Smartphone owners send more texts than non-Smartphone owners (Ofcom 2012). In theory, sending more texts means the potential for more exposure to non-conventional representations of language. Smartphone ownership and usage is also consistent across all socio-economic groups (Ofcom 2012), and appears to be similar across other Western societies (Lenhart, Ling, Campbell & Purcell 2010). As a result, the concerns about texting and language development are relevant to families from a wide range of backgrounds. Very frequent texting seems to be a life phase effect (Ling 2010), meaning that regardless of cohort, there appears to be an increase in texting during the older teenage years and early twenties, which then declines in later adulthood. We therefore suggest that research needs to focus on participants before and during this period of intense texting, when literacy skills are still developing.

Definitions

An important first step in studying the phenomenon of textese is to code and categorize the spelling transformations that people make in this style of writing. Although some authors have implemented their own coding schemes (e.g., Cingel & Sundar 2012), one which has become widely accepted and used in several studies (e.g., Grace, Kemp, Parrila & Martin 2012; Plester, Wood & Joshi 2009) is that of Thurlow (2003) (see Table 11.1).

Words written in these ways are referred to as 'textisms', and the whole writing system as 'textese' (Crystal 2008) or 'textspeak' (Wood, Kemp & Plester 2014a). This style of writing originally became popular to save on message space, thus saving on cost and time. Many textisms rely on unconventional orthographic representations but have intact phonological

Table 11.1 Textese coding scheme (adapted from Thurlow 2003)

Type of 'textism'	Explanation	Example
Shortenings	Removing word endings	bro, mon
Contractions	Removing letters from the middle of words, usually vowels	ltr, msg
'g' clippings	Removing the 'g' from word endings	borin, tryin
Other clippings	Removing other letters from word endings	hav, wil
Acronyms/Initialisms	Using the first letter from every word in a phrase, to make a short version	lol, BBC
Letter number homophones	Using the sound of a letter or number to spell part or all of a word	l8r, 2morrow
Non-conventional spellings	Spelling phonetically	fone, luv
Misspellings/Typos	Misspelling words non-phonetically	comming, rember
Accent stylization	Writing to reflect spoken language	innit, gonna

representations (*tonite, bak*). Therefore, the creation and understanding of textisms relies heavily on phonological decoding skills, and individuals must already have some letter–sound knowledge in place before they can produce or decipher certain textisms. For example, a child who did not know that *r* and *wr* make the same sound, and that *ite* and *ight* make the same sound, would not be able to create or easily understand the textism *rite*, which could mean either *right* or *write* depending on the context of the message. By providing the opportunity to rehearse such knowledge, texting could also help to develop phonological skills and alphabetic knowledge. Thus, using textese could be encouraging children to play with language and offer a 'safe space' for attempting to spell without the critical eye of an adult, meaning that there is no fear of failure (Crystal 2008). Furthermore, as Baron (2003) has pointed out, there is no master lexicon of abbreviations, either across the world, or within smaller communities. There are multiple ways of spelling various single words; for example, texters might represent the word *tomorrow* with *2moz, 2morrow* or *tmrw* (e.g., De Jonge & Kemp 2012). This lack of a master lexicon means that textisms can and do differ across subcultures, within the same language (especially for *accent stylizations*, such as *init, gonna*, where regional variations on words exist), and across friendship groups, where use of a particular textism can allude to social belonging (Thurlow 2003).

It is also important to look at how messages are written, as large individual differences can be apparent within different samples. For example, differences in the writing style of textisms can also be seen in the fact that some people rely heavily upon creating new words while others simply omit letters, words or punctuation. Such variation was observed by Drouin and Driver (2012), who examined the naturalistic messages composed by American undergraduates. These authors found that textism density was negatively related to reading and spelling ability. However, when the data are considered more closely, it becomes apparent that certain textisms (those that were grammatically incorrect, such as omitted apostrophes) were related negatively to some literacy skills, while others (those that were phonetically based, such as accent stylization) were positively related. This shows the importance of separating textisms into discrete categories, as the relationship with literacy skills in adults seems to differ according to whether the textisms omit conventional features of writing, or creatively re-spell words.

Current research on textese and language skills

Is it possible that excessive exposure to textisms might begin to diminish one's skills in conventional spelling, reading, and/or grammar? The main area of concern raised by the media, parents and teachers has been on the potential damage to conventional spelling ability. However, we argue that such concerns are unfounded in the case of children.

Children and textism use

There is experimental evidence to suggest that, in general, exposure to alternative spellings does not affect everyone's spelling equally. For example, Dixon and Kaminska (2007) found that exposing children to incorrect spellings did not affect their later correct spelling of those words. In contrast, adults *are* affected by exposure to misspellings. Katz and Frost (2001) showed that when adults were exposed to misspellings with the same phonology as the original word but a different orthography (e.g. *fone*), then they were likely to consider these misspellings to be correct. Since most textisms show changed orthography while keeping the same phonology, these results suggest that adults should be affected more negatively than children by text messaging. Furthermore, our own work in this area has shown that not only is spelling and reading ability not compromised by textism use, but spelling development may even be supported by such activity.

Plester, Wood and Bell (2008) conducted one of the first studies to determine whether texting was linked to children's academic ability. They asked 65 11–12-year-olds to translate sentences in standard English into how they would write them in a text message. These authors asked children about their mobile phone usage and considered their responses in relation to their performance on a cognitive ability test. The children who sent the most texts showed the poorest cognitive ability scores, but texting frequency was not related to the density of textisms used. It was found that those who used more textisms also had better verbal reasoning skills and spelling ability. This positive effect could have been due to the increased phonological practice afforded by textism use, but it was equally possible that children who were better at verbal reasoning skills and spelling might be those who understood textisms better, and therefore used them more.

Plester, Wood and Joshi (2009) expanded on this original study to include a measure of reading ability, and a measure of phonological awareness, which they theorized could have mediated the previous study's results. This time, 88 children aged 10 to 12 years wrote hypothetical text messages based upon scenarios. Similar to the previous study, the children who used the most textisms had better word reading, vocabularies and phonological awareness. The authors also found that after controlling for age, short-term memory, phonological awareness, vocabulary and the length of time the children had owned a mobile phone, textism usage could still predict unique variance in word reading ability. This suggested that text messaging was providing some unique positive influence on literacy abilities beyond that attributable to phonological awareness.

Other studies have also found positive links between children's textism use and literacy abilities. Johnson (2012) asked 91 children, aged 8 to 13 years, to translate five text abbreviations into standard English. He found those who defined the most abbreviations correctly had the most superior skills in both reading fluency and sentence comprehension. However, four of the five abbreviations were initialisms, such as *gtg* (*got to go*), and thus their translation relied more on general knowledge of textisms than on phonological awareness. Although this finding suggests that knowledge of phonology cannot be the only factor linked to textism use, the small number of items makes it difficult to draw strong conclusions from this study. In a larger study, Bushnell, Kemp and Martin (2011) asked 227 10–12-year-old Australian children to rewrite a list of 30 spellings as they would if writing a text message. Children who produced more textisms were found to have better general spelling scores.

Most of these studies have been cross-sectional, and therefore do not provide data on the direction of the relationship between fluency with textisms and literacy scores. However, Wood *et al.* (2011b) conducted a longitudinal study to investigate whether text-messaging was helping the development of literacy abilities, or whether literacy ability affected the children's use of textisms. These authors examined the textisms used by 119 children aged 8 to 12 years who owned their own phones, controlling for differences in verbal IQ, phonological awareness and spelling ability at the start of the academic year. Unexpectedly, the relationship was found to be unidirectional; that is, texting ability impacted on spelling development but spelling ability did not impact on the development of textism use. This suggests that exposure to textisms can help children improve their conventional spelling skills.

If it is true that texting has a positive effect upon various language skills, as the studies above suggest, then a texting-based intervention could be used to improve academic success. One such study was carried out to see whether giving mobile phones to children who had never had them before could improve their literacy skills (Wood, Jackson, Hart, Plester & Wilde 2011a).

These authors used a randomized controlled trial with 114 children aged 9 to 10 years, half of whom were given access to mobile phones with credit during the half-term break (one week) and weekends for a period of 10 weeks. Although the improvement in overall literacy skills of children in the phone ownership group did not significantly exceed that of the controls, the spelling development of the children with mobile phones was accounted for by textism use in their messages after IQ was controlled for. This study provided further evidence that texting does not negatively impact upon academic skills, and may even help to improve children's spelling ability.

While these studies have shown a positive link between texting and spelling, there are still several other factors which must be considered. For instance, the way that messages are typed in has changed over time, and varies between phones. Kemp and Bushnell (2011) compared text messages composed by 86 10–12-year-old children who used either predictive texting or multi-press texting (in which number keys are pressed one to four times to get the required letter) to translate messages from standard English. The authors also asked children to read aloud messages written in standard English and in textese. All children took more time and made more errors when reading the textese messages, probably because of the greater demands on phonological coding in this writing style. Predictive texters were faster at both reading and writing messages than multi-press users, but it seems that input method does not affect general literacy skills, as the input method used was not related to reading and spelling scores.

Texting and grammar

In general, then, the links between texting and literacy appear to be positive in children. However, a study by Cingel and Sundar (2012) attracted media attention because of its findings that textism use was negatively related to grammatical knowledge in 'tweens'. A sample of 228 10–14-year-olds was given self-report surveys and completed an in-class grammar assessment. The authors found a significant negative association between participants' scores on the grammatical task and their use of textisms. However, this study has significant limitations. Firstly, the grammar test used was a test for ninth grade students, and even though it was designed to include concepts that should have been covered by sixth grade, the task may still have been relatively difficult for the younger participants. Secondly, the children were asked to analyse their own use of textisms in their last three sent messages, and to count abbreviations only if they were 100 per cent sure that they were textisms. Furthermore, the children were asked to 'only report adaptations that were commonly found in text messaging' (Cingel & Sunder 2012: 8), which may mean that any creative textisms may have been ignored; also individuals may have had different ideas of what constituted 'common' textisms. These self-report measures are prone to error, especially as children with poorer grammatical abilities would be less likely than their peers to be able to identify all the abnormalities in their own writing. Finally, the data from the study were concurrent, and so the implications drawn about the impact of textisms on the development of grammatical understanding have arguably been overstated. Further research is needed to validate the conclusions drawn from this study.

There are three ways in which we would argue that texting could harm grammatical understanding. The first is through the spelling of individual words; within written English, there are many words which sound the same but differ in their orthography because of their grammatical status, often contained in the word ending. For example, the words *mist* and *missed* are pronounced identically, but it is grammatical knowledge that lets us know the *–ed* suffix is required to signal the past tense of the verb *to miss*. Many textisms are written phonetically, and it is possible this could lead to the degradation of knowledge of the grammatical cues for words which are phonetically but not orthographically similar. The second way that exposure to textisms could affect grammatical knowledge is via the popular feature of texting in which word combinations are written as they are often pronounced, as in *hafta* for *have to* or *gonna* for *going to*. This could lead to individuals forgetting or not learning the full versions of these words and in certain situations may reinforce incorrect grammar. For example, children and even adults might find it difficult to learn or remember whether *woulda* is short for *would have* rather than the incorrect but sometimes seen *would of*. The final way that texting might affect grammar is by exposure to the often unconventional use of orthography and punctuation. When texting, individuals often omit punctuation to save on time or space, for example, by leaving out full stops and question marks (e.g., *hi how are you*). Conversely, they may also use excessive punctuation to represent excitement or to reinforce other social cues (e.g., *how are you???!!!*). Excessive use of, or exposure to, examples of unconventional punctuation might make it difficult to remember how to use these spelling rules conventionally in formal writing.

Our recent study (Wood, Kemp, Waldron & Hart 2014b) found little evidence of any relationships between the grammar used in text messages and understanding of grammar or orthography; this was true for both primary and secondary aged school children. However, for adults a relationship emerged between making capitalization and punctuation errors when texting and poorer performance in selecting the grammatically correct orthographic representation of a pseudoword. The cross-sectional nature of the study means that we are not able to determine if making grammatical errors while texting causes adults' poorer performance on orthographic tasks, or vice versa. Another point to consider carefully here is that some alternative forms or omissions of punctuation are deliberate, while others are not. Kemp, Wood and Waldron (2014) examined this point by asking participants to translate a set of text messages into formal English, correcting all spelling and grammatical errors that may be present. The links between the scores on the translation task and incidence of grammatical violations in the participants' naturalistic text messages were not consistent. This suggests that just because participants used poorer grammar in their text messages, it does not mean they do not know how to use correct grammar under other circumstances.

As the use of mobile phones becomes common at very early stages of development, researchers need to include even younger children in their samples. In our own initial research, the youngest participants were ten years old, but now we include children as young as eight, reflecting the changing trends in the uptake of technology. Despite these changes, most research has found no negative impact of texting upon children's literacy skills, and in many cases a positive relationship exists, especially with spelling.

Developmental disorders and textism use

Less research has focused on children with developmental disorders. It is important to remember that this group does not always text in the same way as typically developing children. For instance, unlike their typically developing peers, dyslexic children favour using non-phonetic based textisms (Veater, Plester & Wood 2011), which is perhaps unsurprising as dyslexia is characterized by poor phonological awareness. For dyslexic individuals, there was no evidence of a link between texting and phonological awareness, which is often found in typically developing children (Plester *et al.* 2009). This suggests that, while dyslexic children did not differ from typically developing children in terms of the number of text-messages they sent, dyslexic children's preference to use non-phonetic textisms results in their experiencing no additional benefits for their literacy because of the lack of additional phonological practice afforded by phonetic textism use.

Durkin, Conti-Ramsden and Walker (2011) found that adolescents with Specific Language Impairment (SLI) were less likely to send text messages than their typically developing peers, and that, within the SLI group, those with lower reading abilities were least likely to send texts. These differences could have implications for whether adolescents with SLI are included in texting conversations or in social events organized via text message.

But what about those whose poor reading skills are not poor enough to warrant a clinical diagnosis? Coe and Oakhill (2011) found that good and poor readers aged 10 to 11 years did not differ significantly in the number of text messages sent and received, but that good readers used significantly more textisms than poor readers. This may be because these good readers were better at coming up with phonological alternatives for conventional spellings, or because they had greater metalinguistic skills than their peers, thus finding it easier to switch between multiple registers.

The results reviewed above show that there are differences among children with differential developmental patterns, who may find it difficult to use the technology, but there is no evidence that texting is harming their literacy skills. However, it appears that individuals with language difficulties may not benefit from the technology in the same way as their typically developing peers. For this reason, an intervention for individuals with language difficulties could be useful to allow them to be involved with this social communication tool and also to improve their literacy skills.

Because texting is such a popular activity, it is also exposing many children to more printed words than they would normally see. For example, if a parent doesn't have time to read with a child at home, at least the child may be actively reading and writing text messages, which in turn is increasing his or her exposure to print (Wood et al. 2011b), something which is known to impact positively on literacy development. To date, only one study, by Wood, Jackson, Hart, Plester and Wilde (2011a), has explicitly considered the 'exposure to print' hypothesis with respect to texting. In this intervention study, data on the number of text messages sent and received over the course of the study were tracked. No evidence of a significant association between texting 'traffic' and literacy outcomes was found. However, this outcome may be attributable to the way in which exposure to print via phones was measured: arguably, a more sensitive measure of print exposure would have been to note the number of words in the messages sent and received, rather than the number of messages, as text length can vary a great deal across individuals (Wood, Kemp & Plester 2014a).

Adults and textism use

Compared with research on children, less research into texting and its potential links with literacy has been conducted with adult populations. The results published so far have also been less conclusive. Positive evidence comes from research with U.S. undergraduates, in which self-reported frequency of sending text messages showed no association with spelling skill (Massengill Shaw, Carlson & Waxman 2007). Drouin (2011) found that in a sample of 152 U.S. college students, text-messaging frequency was positively associated with spelling skills and reading skills. However, textese use in online contexts was negatively correlated with reading and spelling skills. These studies both relied on self-reported measures and considered textisms overall, but did not look at relationships with different categories of textism use. In contrast, De Jonge and Kemp (2012) found that in an Australian sample of 52 high school students and 53 undergraduates, textism use in a message translation task was negatively correlated with scores of reading, non-word reading, spelling and morphological awareness. In a study of sent messages, Grace, Kemp, Martin and Parrila (2013) found that greater textism use was associated with poorer general spelling in Canadian undergraduates, but with poorer timed non-word reading (but not spelling) in Australian undergraduates. Clearly the links between texting measures and literacy measures are varied within these age groups, and this could be due to differences in methodology, year of testing or nationality of participants (Grace et al. 2012).

More insight about the varied findings with adult texters might be gained by looking at more experimental research. Powell and Dixon (2011) exposed 94 undergraduates to 30 words, presented either correctly (e.g., *tonight*), as misspellings (e.g., *tonite*), or as textisms (e.g., *2nite*), and compared the effects on subsequent spelling scores. It is important to note that in contrast to Thurlow (2003) and some other researchers, Powell and Dixon (2011) included non-conventional, phonologically plausible spellings under the 'misspelling' category. Powell and Dixon (2011) found that while exposure to these misspellings had a negative effect on spelling, textism exposure actually had a positive effect, which fits with the idea that text messaging can have a positive influence on literacy. Nearly all the textisms in this study were letter/number homophones, which relied heavily on phonological decoding, and the results may not be generalizable to other textism types. Some of the textisms did not seem to be common ones (e.g., *aQr8* for *accurate*, and *LMNt* for *element*), so some participants may not have seen all of the examples before. Powell and Dixon (2011) theorized that these abbreviations were too orthographically different from the real versions of the words to interfere with spelling knowledge. However, as misspellings are usually only slightly different from the real version of the word, they may interfere more with stored orthographic representations. It is not clear how generalizable Powell and Dixon's (2011) findings are to real-world textism exposure, which occurs many more times than the single exposures used in this study. Nevertheless, this study seems to show that certain types of textism (letter/number homophones) do not interfere with, and may even help, adults' spelling. However, it should be borne in mind that other textism types, such as non-conventional spellings, could negatively affect spelling, since they are very similar to the misspelling category. This consideration highlights the need for consideration of the difference in textism types being used.

Much of the research to date has focused on spelling, but writing ability was also examined by Rosen, Chang, Erwin, Carrier and Cheever (2010), who found that, among young U.S. adults with some or no tertiary education (but not among those with a university degree), the (self-reported) more frequent use of textisms was linked to poorer scores on a formal writing task. Future research could consider the potential contribution of general ability and confidence with written language, as these are likely to be intertwined with whether or not participants have a university education. Even among undergraduate students, differences in language skills appear to be associated with differences in the ability to decipher textisms. Kemp (2010) asked 61 Australian students to read and write messages in both conventional English and textese. Overall, the textese messages were faster to write, but they took longer to read and participants made more errors. Participants with better general reading and spelling skills were quicker at typing in dictated messages of both types, and those with better reading skills were better at reading out both types of messages in standard English. However, there were no significant correlations between the proportion of textisms produced when participants translated messages into textese, and their literacy skills. It seems clear that administering different types of tasks can yield different patterns of results in adult texting studies.

It is also interesting to consider if beliefs about texting behaviour align with study results. Drouin and Davis (2009) found that undergraduate students believed that textese use did affect their literacy abilities, even though there was no significant association between texting and literacy in this group. These beliefs may have stemmed from media stories about the perils of textism use. This research highlights the discrepancy between beliefs and measured behaviours, and acts as a reminder of why self-report measures must be taken with caution.

In conclusion, these studies have used a variety of methodologies and most have used experimental rather than naturalistic messages, which make it difficult to draw strong conclusions about the effects of texting in the real world. More research needs to be conducted that takes into account not only textism quantity but also type. These mostly cross-sectional studies also only provide a snapshot of individuals' texting behaviour, meaning that causality is hard to determine, and for this reason more longitudinal data are needed. Overall, it appears that texting has no negative effect on children, but perhaps some negative effect is apparent with adults, although these results are less clear.

Are these findings specific to the English language?

Research on textism use from English-speaking regions may not be generalizable to other areas of the world. This is due not only to differences in available technology but also in language. For example, a single text message can include 160 alphabetic characters, but only 70 Chinese characters (Bodomo 2010), and so people who text in Chinese may seek multiple ways to reduce their expression. However, Grace *et al.* (2012) found significant differences in texting quantity, textism density and uptake of new technology even between two very similar populations: Australian and Canadian English undergraduates. This shows that results may not even be entirely generalizable between English-speaking nations, and for this reason different languages and cultures must be looked at separately.

English spellings are diverse; many sounds can map to the same letter, while spellings in some other languages, such as Italian, are more transparent, meaning that typically only one sound maps to one letter. For this reason it is safe to assume that phonetic textisms in these countries will be more similar to the original word than textisms written by English speakers. For example, the Finnish language has transparent orthography, but, because this language is agglutinative, words can have several endings added to show grammatical meaning, which results in rather long words. Due to this feature, there is a shared understanding between speakers that if intent is clear then the words can be shortened. Plester, Lerkkanen, Linjama, Rasku-Puttonen and Littleton (2011) found that this feature affected children's texting style. Specifically, textese written by Finnish speakers resembled Finnish speech more than Finnish writing, meaning that accent stylization is the preferred textism type used by individuals in this country, unlike in English where homophones are preferred. Finnish speakers generally used the same proportion of textisms in their messages as English speakers, but with a preference for different textism types. In the sample of Finnish children in Plester *et al.*'s (2011) study, there was no significant correlation between proportion of spontaneous textisms and literacy skills, although this should be interpreted with caution because of the small sample size. When a larger sample of children created texts for the study, the authors found that textism use was correlated with reading, phonology and literacy scores, but, unlike most English-language studies, not to spelling. Texting added marginal power to predict the spelling scores of Finnish children, but it was not as powerful a predictor as for English speakers. Thus, texting may have less of a positive influence on Finnish- than English-speaking children because Finnish children gain a better understanding of phonology from their writing system and have fewer sound rules to learn than their English speaking counterparts.

Bieswanger (2006) compared naturally occurring text messages written by German and English adults and found that they had similar message lengths but different writing styles. German speakers tended to use fewer textisms in general than English speakers and did not use letter/number homophones at all, whereas the English users in the study used more contractions, symbols and non-conventional spelling. The lack of phonetic textisms (such as letter/number homophones) in the German messages probably reflects the relatively transparent orthography of this language. It is interesting to note, however, that German messages used fewer symbols, which are often used to reinforce the emotions expressed in a message (Amaghlobeli 2012).

This use of emoticons does not seem to be a reflection of the language but more a social preference which reflects personal choices in writing style.

Texting also occurs in multilingual settings, such as the one Lexander (2011) examined in Dakar, the capital of Senegal, where people use a mixture of French and African languages. Lexander found that texting in this situation promoted 'intellectual code-switching', where individuals used more than one language in a single text message, and changes were often marked typographically by capitals or punctuation. This suggests that texting is improving meta-cognition about language, as individuals have to think about code switching in order to mark it typographically. There are also cultural benefits for using this code-switching, as people can communicate with various friends and family members regardless of the language they speak.

Overall, there are differences between the textisms used by speakers of English compared to speakers of other languages, as English texters tend to rely quite heavily on phonics in the textisms that they produce. There seems to be no evidence so far that texting has a detrimental effect on literacy within other languages, and in some cases it may help metalinguistic awareness.

Methodological issues in texting research

One issue to bear in mind when considering the outcomes of studies on texting is the difference between methods of collecting textism data. Grace *et al.* (2012) compared textism densities across the three most common collection methods. These authors found the highest textism densities in translation tasks, in which individuals are given a traditional English sentence to rewrite as if they were texting it. The next highest textism densities were observed in scenario-based tasks, where individuals are asked to write a message to a friend about a given event. The lowest textism densities were seen within naturally occurring text messages – true sent texts copied directly from the participants' phones. This study shows that participants may experience demand characteristics in the tasks which require them to create new text messages.

Fortunately, the way in which participants are asked to record their messages does not appear to change results in the same way. De Jonge and Kemp (2012) used a translation task and asked individuals to input some messages using a phone with predictive text and to provide others via handwriting. These authors found no significant difference between the two input methods, which suggests that the method of writing texts does not influence textism density, but that task type does. As noted earlier, problems can also arise within methodology when relying heavily on self-report measures.

Constant growth in technology means that there are many individual differences which must be taken into account when examining the results of studies on texting. For instance, the use of predictive text messaging (where individuals type in the first few letters of a word and the phone suggests the rest of the word and inputs it) may have a different effect than typing words out fully. This is especially important to consider now that some predictive text includes words which can be programmed by the user, and thus could input common misspellings of words (e.g., *thier* for *their*). Some predictive text also inputs punctuation and capitalization automatically for the user. Overall, there are a variety of cognitive processes going on. If individuals use predictive text, they do not need to think about punctuation, capitalization and spelling, but they are probably still seeing it used correctly, and so are nevertheless exposed to the conventionally correct versions. If individuals do not use predictive text, but still type in punctuation and full spellings, then they are both thinking about, and being exposed to, the correct versions. However, those who neither use predictive text nor put in punctuation and full spellings are making no conscious effort and receive more limited exposure to conventional writing. This is why the use of predictive text can mediate study results. In addition, such mediation could potentially differ between adults and children, as children may not yet have learned or consolidated these grammatical and spelling rules, whereas adults may be choosing or forgetting to use them.

Another important point to consider when examining text message use is the generational cohort effects. There is a large difference between the early experiences of text messaging for those who are now adults compared to those who are children today. Currently, children are receiving phones at increasingly younger ages, using text messaging more frequently than ever before, and have different technologies available to them, including predictive text and Blackberry Messenger (Ofcom 2012). Children are also still developing both their phonological and orthographical representations of language while using text messaging, whereas adults have a more consolidated understanding of these concepts.

Overall, the evidence presented above suggests that, wherever possible, naturalistic message data should be obtained for a realistic picture of textism use. However, at the analysis stage, it is important to take note of whether individuals have used predictive text or not when composing their messages. When naturalistic message collection is not possible due to issues of access or ethics, or when a highly controlled approach is needed, scenario-based methodology should be used, as it produces a closer approximate of true textism use than straight translation tasks. If an experimental collection method is used, similar densities of textism use are obtained whether participants are asked to type in or handwrite their messages, so researchers should choose the easiest collection method for their sample. Finally, it is important to consider the textism use of adult and child cohorts separately, as different effects can be seen to emerge between different age groups.

Recommendations for practice

Texting is a practice which has begun to permeate every aspect of daily life. This can be very frustrating for teachers if texting leads to disruption during class. Rosen *et al.* (2011) examined this possibility by studying 185 U.S. undergraduates, who agreed to receive texts during lectures and to respond as soon as possible after receiving their text. Participants each received 0–8 texts which related to the lecture material. Those who received more texts remembered less about the lecture, although the effect size was small. It is possible the disruption would have been larger if the texts had not been relevant to the lecture. Nevertheless, this result suggests that strict rules need to be enforced regarding mobile phone use within the classroom.

Mandernach and Hackathorn (2010) argued that, as texting is prevalent within class time anyway, it is better to use this technology to engage students to focus attention, rather than letting the technology distract them. The authors suggest using mobile phones to include students more in lessons through actions such as sending questions, brainstorming ideas, creating summaries, starting discussions, answering quizzes and reviewing exam answers. While it cannot be recommended outright that texting should be used to help within school environments, there have been several studies to show its benefit within this area. For example, Bradley, Weiss, Davies and Holley (2010) showed that students responded positively to using texting within a university class setting. Participants used a program called TxTools (a computer program which can receive texts anonymously) and were encouraged to text questions and feedback during and after lectures. This technology kept data anonymous and encouraged students to ask questions without the embarrassment of having to put their hand up in class. This was especially true of international students with less fluent English skills, as text messages do not have to be spelled correctly. This study provides one example of how texting can be successfully incorporated to enable deeper learning and could offer a model for future work.

Ryker, Viosca, Lawrence and Kleen (2010) proposed a different way of using texting to learn. Many textisms use mnemonics and acronyms, such as *lol* (*laughing out loud*) and *btw* (*by the way*), and thus frequent texters should be more receptive to acronyms to facilitate the learning of helpful phrases. However Ryker *et al.* (2010), in their study of 479 U.S. university students, found that such acronyms were not useful for helping students to remember information if those students self-identified as 'high texters'. The authors suggested that this could be because the students had already reached their full vocabulary limit for acronyms or perhaps had become desensitized to them. This shows that mnemonics and acronyms are not the best way to teach frequent texters new information.

Future directions

From the research discussed here, we can see that texting has a positive effect on children with relation to spelling, phonological awareness and word reading. Research on adults has yielded more mixed results, with much debate over whether or not there is any effect on literacy skills. Future approaches should focus on the educational implications of prior research; there are currently few studies looking at text messaging as a medium to improve literacy, even though any negative effects seem minimal. Texting could prove to be a useful tool for encouraging creativity and playfulness with language, especially in the learning of phonics. Lessons could also be developed to ensure that children learn that certain language rules are only specific to textese, and this could in turn improve metacognition about language and perhaps even reduce some problems with spelling or morphology that can persist into adulthood. Future research could focus on a wider range of language abilities and a wider range of textism types, and could also involve experiments designed to investigate the potential relationship between textism use and the understanding of grammar. Further, investigations could address not only the respelling of words, but the representation of written conventions such as punctuation and capitalization. Most of the research to date has considered the link between textism use and specific language skills such as the reading and writing of single words, but it will also be important to look further at relationships with higher-level writing skills at a more general level.

Related topics

- Chapter 9 Digital media and literacy development (Knobel & Lankshear)
- Chapter 10 Vernacular literacy: orthography and literacy practices (Iorio)
- Chapter 15 Twitter: design, discourse, and the implications of public text (Squires)
- Chapter 21 Facebook and the discursive construction of the social network (Tagg & Seargeant)

References

Amaghlobeli, N. 2012, 'Linguistic features of typographic emoticons in SMS discourse', *Theory and Practice in Language Studies*, vol. 2, no. 2, pp. 348–354.

Baron, N. S. 2003, 'Language of the Internet', in A. Farghali (ed.), *The Stanford handbook for language engineers*, CSLI: Stanford, CA, pp. 59–127.

Bieswanger, M. 2006, '2 abbrevi8 or not 2 abbrevi8: a contrastive analysis of different shortening strategies in English and German text messages', available at: http://studentorgs.utexas.edu/salsa/proceedings/2006/Bieswanger.pdf [accessed 24 March 2013].

Bodomo, A. B. 2010, *Computer-mediated communication for linguistics and literacy: technology and natural language education*, Information Science Reference: Hershey, NY.

Bradley, C., Weiss, M., Davies, C. & Holley, D. 2010, 'A little less conversation a little more texting please: a blended model of using mobiles in the classroom', *Proceedings of the fifth international blended learning conference: developing blended learning communities*, University of Hertfordshire: Hatfield, UK, pp. 1–11.

Bushnell, C., Kemp, N. and Martin, F. H. 2011, 'Text messaging practices and links to general spelling ability: a study of Australian children', *Australian Journal of Educational and Developmental Psychology*, vol. 11, pp. 27–38.

Cingel, D. & Sundar, S. 2012, 'Texting, techspeak, and tweens: the relationship between text messaging and English grammar skills', *New Media and Society*, vol. 14, no. 8, pp. 1304–1320.

Coe, J. E. L. & Oakhill, J. V. 2011, '"txtN is ez f u no h2 rd": the relation between reading ability and text-messaging behaviour', *Journal of Computer Assisted Learning*, vol. 27, no. 1, pp. 4–17.

Crystal, D. 2008, *Txting: the gr8 db8*, Oxford University Press: Oxford.

De Jonge, S. & Kemp, N. 2012, 'Text-message abbreviations and language skills in high school and university students', *Journal of Research in Reading*, vol. 35, no. 1, pp. 49–68.

Dixon, M. & Kaminska, Z. 2007, 'Does exposure to orthography affect children's spelling accuracy?', *Journal of Research in Reading*, vol. 30, no. 2, pp. 184–197.

Drouin, M. 2011, 'College students' text messaging, use of textese and literacy skills', *Journal of Computer Assisted Learning*, vol. 27, no. 3, pp. 67–75.

Drouin, M. & Davis, C. 2009, 'R u txting? Is the use of text speak hurting your literacy?', *Journal of Literacy Research*, vol. 41, no. 1, pp. 46–67.

Drouin, M. & Driver, B. 2012, 'Texting, textese and literacy abilities: a naturalistic study', *Journal of Research in Reading*, vol. 37, no. 3, pp. 250–267.

Durkin, K., Conti-Ramsden, G. & Walker, A. J. 2011, 'Txt lang: texting, textism use and literacy abilities in adolescents with and without specific language impairment', *Journal of Computer Assisted Learning*, vol. 27, no. 1, pp. 49–57.

Furness, H. 2012, 'Sir Terry Pratchett: text and Twitter harming children's development', *The Telegraph*, p.1, available at: http://www.telegraph.co.uk/technology/social-media/9241728/Sir-Terry-Pratchett-Text-and-Twitter-harming-childrens-development.html [accessed 24 March 2013].

Grace, A., Kemp, N., Martin, F. H. & Parrila, R. 2013. 'Undergraduates' text messaging language and literacy skills', *Reading and Writing*, vol. 27, no. 5, pp. 855–873.

Grace, A., Kemp, N., Martin, F. H. & Parrila, R. 2012, 'Undergraduates' use of text messaging language: effects of country and collection method', *Writing Systems Research*, vol. 4, no. 2, pp. 167–184.

Hough, A. 2011, 'Carol Ann Duffy: texting and Twitter "help students perfect poetry"', *The Telegraph*, available at: http://www.telegraph.co.uk/education/educationnews/8743801/Carol-Ann-Duffy-texting-and-Twitter-help-students-perfect-poetry.html [accessed 24 March 2013].

Humphrys, J. 2007, 'I h8 txt msgs: How texting is wrecking our language', *The Daily Mail*, available at: http://www.dailymail.co.uk/news/article-483511/I-h8-txt-msgs-How-texting-wrecking-language.html#ixzz2CCCC4TJH [accessed 24 March 2012].

Johnson, M. 2012, 'Comprehension of standard English text and digital textism during childhood', *The Internet Journal of Language, Culture and Society*, vol. 35, no. 1, pp. 1–6.

Katz, L. & Frost, S. J. 2001, 'Phonology constrains the mental orthographic representation', *Reading and Writing*, vol. 14, pp. 297–332.

Kemp, N. 2010, 'Texting versus txting: reading and writing text messages, and links with other linguistic skills', *Writing Systems Research*, vol. 2, no. 1, pp. 53–71.

Kemp, N. & Bushnell, C. 2011, 'Children's text messaging: abbreviations, input methods and links with literacy', *Journal of Computer Assisted Learning*, vol. 27, no. 1, pp. 18–27.

Kemp, N., Wood, C. & Waldron, S. 2014, 'do i know its wrong: children's and adults' use of unconventional grammar in text messaging', *Reading and Writing*, doi: 10.1007s/11145-014-9508-1.

Lenhart, A., Ling, R., Campbell, S. & Purcell, K. 2010, 'Teens and mobile phones', *Pew Internet and American life project*, available at: http://pewinternet.org/Reports/2010/Teens-and-Mobile-Phones.aspx [accessed 24 March 2013].

Lexander, K. 2011, 'Texting and African language literacy', *New Media and Society*, vol. 13, no. 3, pp. 427–443.

Ling, R. 2010, 'Texting as a life phase medium', *Journal of Computer-Mediated Communication*, vol. 15, no. 2, pp. 277–292.

Mandernach, J. & Hackathorn, J. 2010, 'Embracing texting during class', *The Teaching Professor*, vol. 24, no. 10, pp. 1–6.

Massengill Shaw, D., Carlson, C. & Waxman, M. 2007, 'An exploratory investigation into the relationship between text messaging and spelling', *New England Reading Association Journal*, vol. 43, no. 1, pp. 57–62.

Ofcom 2012, 'UK Children and parents: media use and attitudes report', available at: http://stakeholders.ofcom.org.uk/binaries/research/media-literacy/oct2012/main.pdf [accessed March 24 2013].

Ofcom 2011, 'UK Children's media literacy', available at: http://stakeholders.ofcom.org.uk/market-data-research/media-literacy/medlitpub/medlitpubrss/ukchildrensml11 [accessed 24 March 2013].

Plester, B., Lerkkanen, M., Linjama, L., Rasku-Puttonen, H. & Littleton, K. 2011, 'Finnish and UK pre-teen children's text message language and its relationship with their literacy skills', *Journal of Computer Assisted Learning*, vol. 27, no. 1, pp. 37–48.

Plester, B., Wood, C., & Joshi, P. 2009, 'Exploring the relationship between children's knowledge of text message abbreviations and school literary outcomes', *British Journal of Developmental Psychology*, vol. 27, no. 1, pp. 145–161.

Plester, B., Wood, C., & Bell, V. 2008, 'Txt msg n school literacy: does texting and knowledge of text abbreviations adversely affect children's literacy attainment?', *Literacy*, vol. 42, no. 3, pp. 137–144.

Powell, D. & Dixon, M. 2011, 'Does SMS text messaging help or harm adults' knowledge of standard spelling?' *Journal of Computer Assisted Learning*, vol. 27, no. 1, pp. 58–66.

Rosen, L., Chang, J., Erwin, L., Carrier, M. & Cheever, N. A. 2010, 'The relationship between "textisms" and formal and informal writing among young adults', *Communication Research*, vol. 37, no. 3, pp. 420–440.

Rosen, L., Lim, A., Carrier, M. & Cheever, N. 2011, 'An empirical examination of the educational impact of text message-induced task switching in the class room: educational implications and strategies to enhance learning', *Psicología Educativa*, vol. 17, no. 2, pp. 163–177.

Ryker, R., Viosca, C., Lawrence, S. & Kleen, B. 2010, 'Texting and the efficacy of mnemonics: an exploratory study', *ISECON Proceedings*, vol. 27, no. 1310.

Thurlow, C. 2003, 'Generation txt? The sociolinguistics of young people's text-messaging', *Discourse Analysis Online*, available at: http://extra.shu.ac.uk/daol/articles/v1/n1/a3/thurlow2002003.html [accessed 24 March 2013].

Veater, H. M., Plester, B., & Wood, C. 2011, 'Use of text message abbreviations and literacy skills in children with dyslexia', *Dyslexia: An International Journal of Research and Practice*, vol. 17, no. 1, pp. 65–71.

Wood, C., Jackson, E., Hart, L., Plester, B. & Wilde, L. 2011a, 'The effect of text messaging on 9- and 10-year-old children's reading, spelling and phonological processing skills', *Journal of Computer Assisted Learning*, vol. 27, no. 1, pp. 28–36.

Wood, C., Meachem, S., Bowyer, S., Jackson, E., Tarczynski-Bowles, M. L. & Plester, B. 2011b, 'A longitudinal study of the relationship between children's text messaging and literacy development', *British Journal of Psychology*, vol. 102, no. 3, pp. 431–442.

Wood, C., Kemp, N. & Plester, B. 2014a, *Text messaging and literacy: the evidence*, Routledge: London.

Wood, C., Kemp, N., Waldron, S. & Hart, L. 2014b, 'Grammatical understanding, literacy and text messaging in school children and undergraduate students: a concurrent analysis', *Computers and Education*, vol. 70, pp. 281–290.

Further reading

Crystal, D. 2008, *Txting: The gr8 db8*, Oxford University Press: Oxford.

This paper provides an overview of the media debate surrounding textism usage.

Grace, A., Kemp, N., Martin, F. H., & Parrila, R. 2013, 'Undergraduates' text messaging language and literacy skills', *Reading and Writing*, vol. 27, pp. 855–873, doi: 10.1007/s11145-013-9471-2.

This paper examines textism use and its impact upon literacy skills in both Canadian and Australian undergraduates.

Wood, C., Kemp, N., & Plester, B. 2014, *Text messaging and literacy: the evidence,* Routledge: Abingdon.

This book provides a comprehensive overview of the literature on texting and literacy.

Part IV

Digital communication
in public

12

Digital media in workplace interactions

Erika Darics

Digital communication in today's workplaces

In the last two decades, the need for permanent connectivity and the ever-growing pressure for quick task completion in today's organisations have led to the development and the spread of a wide range of technologically mediated online communications tools. Email is already commonplace in the white-collar workplace, but other tools, including text-based real-time messaging (instant messaging or IM) and online videoconferencing, and convergent media tools, such as knowledge depositories, shared online workplaces and wikis, are also on their way to becoming ubiquitous. Owing to these developing technologies and the resulting range of new communicative modes, as well as the relative ease of accessing them, mediated communication has become commonplace in today's workplaces.

Working virtually

In business communication research, the question of mediated communication and the resulting 'virtualness' of work have long interested researchers. Scholarship on virtual work – in particular from a business managerial point of view – is burgeoning, typically defining virtual work as work that takes place between geographically dispersed, culturally diverse, electronically communicating teams. However, more recent attempts to define virtual work focus on the *extent of virtualness* (for example, Griffith *et al.* 2003) and position workplace interactions along a continuum, where one end represents face-to-face interactions while the other signifies exclusively virtual work arrangements. The validity of such an approach is buttressed by the fact that purely face-to-face work teams that do not use any sort of communication technology are very rare these days. The most important implication of this is the realisation that, in today's organisations, all teams are 'virtual' to some extent (Martins *et al.* 2004: 823). Thus, given the highly important role of mediated communication in the communication ecology of today's workplaces, it is not surprising that social psychologists, communication scholars and representatives of organisational, information and business sciences have undertaken considerable research to discover how these new ways of communication affect workplace life. Leadership and management of dispersed work teams has been extensively researched (e.g., Bell & Kozlowski 2002;

Cascio & Shurygailo 2002; Purvanova & Bono 2009; Skovolt 2009; Solomon 2001) along with issues resulting from the remote nature of collaboration and mediated interactions, such as the creation of trust among colleagues (Crossman & Lee-Kelley 2004; Daim *et al.* 2012; Kraut *et al.* 1990) or the effect of media choice and communication processes on team effectiveness (Ale Ebrahim *et al.* 2009; Berry 2011). At the same time, discourse studies and the academic field of linguistics have also discovered that language use in these highly specialised and mediated environments merits special attention. However – as pointed out by Baron (2010) – the exploration of discursive and linguistic issues of mediated workplace discourse has thus far been sporadic.

It is this gap in particular that this chapter seeks to address: it reviews and assesses the state of research in the academic fields informing studies about mediated workplace communication, establishes the key topics that would further our understanding about digital business discourse, and argues for the need for an interdisciplinary approach. Before further elaboration, however, it is important to note that mediated or digital workplace discourse is in this chapter restricted to text-based forms, that is, when the interaction takes place by sending typed messages to other people's screens. The reason for this focus is twofold: first, in spite of the wide range of available audio-visual channels for work purposes, the most popular communication technologies in the world of work are still text-based (Hoang & Radicati 2011); and second, audio and visual communication channels, such as telephoning or video-conferencing, constitute distinct phenomena from a linguistic/discursive point of view, and deserve to be studied in their own right (see chapters by Jewitt and Keating, this volume).

The development of the study of mediated workplace interactions

Although not intended for interpersonal communication, even the earliest version of the 'Net'– the ARPANET – was soon utilised as a message transmission system, allowing for both real-time interactions and the sending of electronic messages (Hafner & Lyon 1998). Apart from exchanging personal messages, the early users of the Net soon realised its potential as a professional communication tool enabling the dissemination of information between geographically dispersed interlocutors; thus mediated professional communication developed almost alongside the interactive networking itself. Indeed, the earliest strands of research rated computer-mediated communication as appropriate only for work-related communication; owing to its lack of social context cues and non-verbal signalling, researchers claimed it could only moderately allow for the communication of personal–socioemotional information (Ferrara *et al.* 1991; Kiesler *et al.* 1984; Lea & Spears 1992; Sproull & Kiesler 1986). Interestingly, however, in spite of its acceptance as a legitimate means of business communication, language/discourse-focused research seemed to have neglected this field of enquiry in favour of publicly available, mainly recreational and socially-oriented communication modes. This paucity can be accounted for by the difficulty of accessing data from the world of work, as opposed to the readily accessible data from public social domains, but also by the fact that digital business discourse constitutes a highly complex field of enquiry, where the complexities inherent in institutional interactions are combined with the emergent, continuously developing and evolving context of digital discourse. This complexity stems from the fact that, at work, in order to complete tasks and cooperate effectively, people have to be able to communicate their transactional (work-related) messages clearly, preventing any misunderstandings about the content of messages, but also making sure that they maintain good social relations and collegial relationships. This balance is not self-evident, however, and requires significant interactional effort from the people involved, particularly in environments where interactions are often asymmetrical and professional roles are interactionally negotiated (see, e.g., Drew & Heritage 1992). The complex issue of workplace discourse is then further complicated when it is repositioned into the lesser-known, not fully conventionalised digital communicative environment, as will be shown in the following sections.

A language-centred approach to mediated workplace communication

Digital discourse in the workplace is a new field of multidisciplinary scholarship which lies at the intersection of three broad fields – business communication, business or organisational discourse studies, and computer-mediated discourse studies – but which also draws on areas such as (socio) linguistics, organisation studies and sociology.

The field of business discourse studies is a strand of academic enquiry that sets out to bridge the gap between linguistic and organisational disciplines, particularly through the application of linguistic, pragmatic and discourse-analytic approaches and analytical tools, with the aim of providing an insight into the meaning-making processes of organisational interaction (Bargiela-Chiappini 2009b). This field has a strong preference for qualitative research (Bargiela-Chiappini 2009a) – an interest shared with discourse studies in general. Its analytical toolkit often includes close examination of discourse practices, combined with the findings of organisational research discussed above. This approach has successfully been applied in the last decade and has led to a burgeoning literature of business discourse research (see, for instance, Bargiela-Chiappini 2009a; Bargiela-Chiappini et al. 2007; Boczkowski & Orlikowski 2004; Grant et al. 2004). However, as pointed out by Bargiela-Chiappini et al. (2007) and Warren (2013), the field has until now failed to provide adequate answers to questions about the impact of the new communication technologies on corporate communicative practices in general and on interpersonal business discourse in particular.

The scholarly tradition in the field of business communication, although acknowledging the importance of discourse and social interaction, focuses on practical outcomes, such as the creation of trust, managerial issues, or work efficiency. These aspects are particularly important from a business perspective if we consider that in a business environment 'communication is not an end to itself'; there is always also 'an underlying business purpose or objective to be achieved as a result of the communication' (Bargiela-Chiappini et al. 2007: 172). Although the link between organisational studies – specifically organisational communication – and linguistics has increasingly been articulated in recent years (see Alvesson & Karreman 2000; Bargiela-Chiappini 2009a; Grant et al. 2004), research on mediated business communication has thus far neglected this discursive aspect. This apparent lack of communication between the two fields has resulted in two major shortcomings in the academic exploration of digital workplace discourse. First, language and discourse issues within the field of (business) communication studies are approached using long-established frameworks without critique or sufficient overview of the developments in the related fields of linguistics and computer-mediated discourse research. Such popular frameworks include, for example, the 'cues-filtered-out' or social presence theories (Sproull & Kiesler 1986; Kiesler et al. 1984) and the closely related media richness theory (Daft et al. 1987) (see below). In most cases, the application of the theories detailed above is well justified. However, their unconditional application often results in unsupported presuppositions that 'virtual communication is confusing' (Thompson & Coovert 2003), 'impoverished' and 'more laborious and more cognitively taxing' than face-to-face communication (Cornelius & Boos 2003; Purvanova & Bono 2009), failing to provide a complete overview of the complexities of language use and discourse in the virtual work environment.

The second caveat revealed in the literature review – as also pointed out by Skovholt and Svennevig (2006) – is that speculations and observations regarding language use, linguistic competency, strategies and norms often appear in the business and organisational literature, but their claims are based on theoretical considerations, interviews, experience reports and case studies, rather than empirical findings (for instance, see Berry 2011; Cameron & Webster 2005; Churchill & Bly 1999; Handel & Herbsleb 2002; Lam & Mackiewicz 2007; Nardi *et al.* 2000; Reinsch *et al.* 2008; Woerner *et al.* 2007). These academic practices can be criticised for their insufficient empirical underpinning and lack of engagement with scholarship in related linguistic/discourse fields and, consequently, for their inability to accurately reflect how exactly language contributes to the accomplishment of the communicative goals of the players in an organisational setting (Alvesson & Karreman 2000).

The final major academic field informing research in digital business discourse is computer-mediated discourse (CMD) or digital discourse studies. One of the most significant focal concerns of this field is the examination and description of the (new) language variety used in mediated interactions – in particular the identification of the linguistic strategies that distinguish CMD from the language use of other communicative modes, and the exploration of strategies enabling users to achieve their interactional goals via text-based communication modes. Recently, this language-focused direction has also been complemented by studies with broader social concerns, as demonstrated by recent publications such as *The Pragmatics of Computer-Mediated Communication* by Herring *et al.* (2013) and *Cyberpragmatics* by Yus (2011) – both of which have strong discourse analytic/pragmatic approaches – and *Digital Discourse* by Thurlow and Mroczek (2011a), which has an articulated sociolinguistic slant. Language and discourse-centred research has so far produced a wealth of studies ranging from close examinations of micro-level linguistic strategies to studies focusing on the interplay between social phenomena and linguistic manifestations. Interestingly, however, institutional genres and business discourse-related studies have scarcely been represented, and the existing studies draw predominantly on datasets collected in experimental settings – often in educational institutions. Nonetheless, as I will show in the next section, the findings of CMD studies provide an essential foundation for an understanding of how language functions in a virtual work environment, and should therefore be organically incorporated in the field of digital business discourse research.

I have also shown above that, although considerable work is taking place in each of these disciplines, unless these fields open themselves to theoretical and methodological cross-fertilisations, the findings will remain too diverse, hindering the advancement of an interdisciplinary discourse-centred approach to digital workplace communication. This chapter aims to set the grounds for integrating work from the aforementioned areas by adopting an articulated linguistic orientation and shedding light on how people – in a workplace setting, through mediated communicative modes – achieve their communicative goals.

In the next sections, I will therefore examine in greater detail the emergent communicative situations of the virtual work environment. First, I explore the technical affordances that may affect communication, for example the timing and time-related issues of online interactions and the persistent nature of messages; second, I explore in great detail how these new communicative situations affect interactional norms, practices and conventions at the workplace, in particular by looking at the question of style and non-verbal signalling. In the sections below I aim to bring together meaningfully relevant findings from the disciplines discussed above – mainly organisational studies and discourse research – and highlight the under-explored areas of digital business discourse.

Critical issues and topics in digital workplace discourse studies

Communicative complexity of mediated workplace discourse

Since the emergence of computer-mediated communication technologies, there has been a well-articulated distinction between the various degrees of synchronicity of different modes of communication. Email, for instance, has traditionally been considered as an asynchronous mode (Cho 2010; Crystal 2001; Herring 2007; Severinson Eklundh 1994) because the interactional partners do not need to be logged on simultaneously, there is no expectation of immediate feedback, and there can be a considerable time lag between two exchanges. IM, on the other hand, has been viewed as synchronous (Herring 1999, 2001, 2007; Simpson 2005) or quasi-synchronous (Čech & Condon 2004; Markman 2005; Ong 2011) because conversational partners are virtually co-present, and interactions take place almost in real time.

This clear divide between synchronous and asynchronous modes, however, has become blurred in recent years: email is increasingly utilised as a 'synchronous' conversational tool, with almost no gaps between turns; IM, on the other hand, is used in a 'Post-It note' style, for delivering messages that do not need immediate attention. The disappearance of the clear divide between synchronous and asynchronous genres has important implications from a discourse point of view, because synchronicity has traditionally been considered a variable that has a significant effect on language production, synchronous interactions having been described as more speech-like than asynchronous genres (Herring 2007; Ko 1996). This realisation becomes particularly important if we consider that a change in synchronicity can be expected to have a direct effect on language use, and that the discourse previously associated with synchronous and asynchronous modes might display the attributes of both (Crystal 2001: 47). In addition to the grammatical complexity of sentences and any relations to spoken or written linguistic features, however, a more important implication of 'blurring boundaries' is related to the pragmatics of interactions and communicative norms. The emerging communicative practices lead to the re-thinking of previously well-established norms and notions of interpersonal interaction, such as what constitutes a conversation or the norms that govern turn-taking (see, for example, Murray 1990; Darics 2014).

In the workplace context, however, shifts from pre-existing norms or violations of what is perceived as normal may result in frustration and tension between interactants (Reinsch et al. 2008) or wrong impression formation (Cameron & Webster 2005; Churchill & Bly 1999), which then affects communication and consequently work efficiency (Cheshin et al. 2013). An understanding of new or shifting norms in emergent communicative situations in the contemporary workplace is therefore necessary for the exploration of how these affect interaction and conversation (for example Cho 2010; Condon & Čech 2002) or the interpretation of previously existing discursive strategies. Such enquiries could thus provide a basis for organisational sciences to draw upon in discussions of practical issues, such as expectations and impression formation, cooperation, trust and, ultimately, team performance. The following sections provide a brief introduction to the emergent communicative situations and demonstrate the communicative complexity to which they have led, highlighting areas requiring further discourse-focused research.

Timing issues

One of the most prevalent issues resulting from the use of mediated communication technologies at the workplace is the question of time and timing. In the organisational literature, for example, the ability to estimate the probability of success and response time when contacting others has been found to be a key part of the success of people who communicate virtually for work purposes (Handel & Herbsleb 2002; Rennecker & Godwin 2003). In the work environment, time-related expectations as well as the method and context of usage of various communication technologies are often influenced or determined by organisational or team norms and communication policies. Watson-Manheim and Belanger (2002) reported that, in the two firms they observed, one had an expected response time for emails of as long as two days, whereas the other had a time lag of only four hours. Pauleen and Yoong (2001), however, found that the subjects of their study had clear expectations about emails requiring prompt responses, similar to voicemails. The sections below give a short account of how the issues related to timing affect discourse and interactional norms at the workplace, highlighting further areas for academic enquiry.

EMAIL   The timing of messages and response time – chronemic information in general – has been found to be a cue upon which communicators draw, and is particularly important from the point of view of the achievement of communicative goals and the creation and maintenance of an efficient working environment. In their research on the timing of relational emails, Walther and Tidwell (1995), Ledbetter (2008) and Kalman and Rafaeli (2011) found that the reply rate of emails had a direct effect on message perception and impression formation about the interactants. Non-responses and delayed responses have also generated considerable scholarly interest (Kalman *et al.* 2006; Panteli & Fineman 2005; Severinson Eklundh 1994; Skovholt & Svennevig 2013; Tyler & Tang 2003). They have generally been found to be associated with uncertainty and ambiguity and have been identified as a sign of communication breakdown resulting in frustration in the workplace. The lack of conventionality surrounding time-related expectations (Severinson Eklundh 1994; Skovholt & Svennevig 2013), the highly context-dependent nature of response time (Dabbish *et al.* 2005; Tyler & Tang 2003) and the interpretation of chronemic information (Kalman *et al.* 2006) indicate that more empirical work is necessary to gain a clearer picture of the emerging interactional norms of organisational email communication.

IM   With regard to timing in IM, Isaacs *et al.* (2002) identified a link between response time, experience of IM usage, and relationships between participants, and argued that more experienced, 'heavy' users engage in more intense interactions, with short, often intertwining turns. Kalman and Gergle (2010), on the other hand, contend that interactant personality is a key variable affecting timing in IM. In the case of delays in recreational chat, Rintel *et al.* (2003) found that in multi-user synchronous chat environments, users deal with delays or non-responses as if they are problems caused by 'not hearing', a problem often attributed to the system, rather than the users themselves. The study also suggests that users draw on their strategies from spoken interactions in trying the 'easiest solution' for clarifying the reason for the non-response and in pursuing responses, and only after attempts at re-greeting and re-connecting do they move to more 'interpersonally demanding meta-lingual connection checking' (Rintel & Pittam 2003: 12). The participants' orientation to the conventions of spoken interactions in terms of timing is also mentioned in the preliminary study of Markman (2005), who highlights the participants' low tolerance for long pauses – in spite of the fact that in computer-mediated chat, reading, composing and typing should figure in users' interpretation of silences. The above studies suggest that pauses, silences or delays in IM are seen as communication problems, often originating in user expectations based on spoken conversations (Markman 2005), a situation which has serious consequences for task-based co-operation (Kalman & Gergle 2010) and clearly needs to be studied in naturally occurring data.

Persistence of the transcript

Another important feature that is the result of the use of digitally mediated communication technologies at the workplace is the persistent nature of the created texts. Like time-related or chronemic issues, this phenomenon contributes to the creation of new communicative situations and thus results in new or modified interactional norms at the workplace.

The persistence of the transcript and how it affects communication have intrigued CMC researchers from the earliest stages of academic enquiry (see, e.g., the 1999 special issue of the *Journal of Computer-Mediated Communication* on 'Persistent conversation'). This interest is not surprising, since retrievable, readily available and quotable dialogic history made way for communicative practices that had not existed before: in email, such practices include quoting and embedded messages; in IM, intermittent usage allows for messages to be picked up on an as-needed basis. From a practical perspective, as is repeatedly pointed out in the organisational literature, persistent and retrievable texts have become useful resources in the workplace, either as reminders of the actual task in progress, which can be continually re-visited both in IM (Woerner *et al.* 2007) and in email communication (Dabbish *et al.* 2005), or as official documentation of ongoing business issues (Garrett & Danziger 2008; Skovholt & Svennevig 2006).

EMAIL   In email communication, the technology enables previous messages or parts of messages to be included in replies, thus creating novel communicative situations allowing interlocutors to quote or embed dialogic history into ongoing discussion. This new communicative situation has attracted considerable scholarly interest (Crystal 2001; Gimenez 2006, 2014; Ho 2011; Kankaanranta 2006; Severinson Eklundh 2010; Severinson Eklundh & Macdonald 1994; Skovholt & Svennevig 2006; Warren 2013). The practice of 'intertextuality' in emails has been described as a method of creating interactional context both in terms of framing the ongoing work and interaction (Warren 2013) and as a way of contributing to the conversational nature of email interactions (Crystal 2001; Severinson Ekhlund 1994, 2010). However, as with all novel communicative situations discussed in this section, lack of conventionality and context-dependence raises important pragmatic–interactional questions regarding the norms of new interactional behaviour. In line with Crystal's (2001) observations about the lack of agreement regarding the acceptability of altering or adding text to quoted messages, Warren (2013) shows that norms differ considerably, reflecting the nature of the industry and the communicative needs of participants. Ho (2011), through examples of email requests, highlights the need for a deeper understanding of the role such practices play in the achievement of the participants' communicative goals.

IM   In IM, the persistence of the transcript is the feature that enables IM to be utilised as a less 'intrusive' medium in the workplace. If IM is used as an 'asynchronous' medium, it enables the addressed communicative partner not to feel obliged to reply, as they would, for instance, in face-to-face encounters or when answering the phone. IM requests can be left unanswered and can be dealt with at a time that causes less interruption to workflow. From a discourse–pragmatic point of view, this emergent communicative situation means that team members often initiate conversations without ritualistic opening preambles and leave interactions without employing closing sequences (Isaacs *et al.* 2002). In research, however, very little is known about how these interactions are co-ordinated without explicit signalling of the beginning and end of conversations, or about how lack of conventionality contributes to the overall communicative effectiveness of interactional partners.

Communicative norms: practices and conventions

In the section above, the questions of conventionality and the shifting of communicative norms have been raised repeatedly, and I have pointed out that exploration of these new norms and description of the resulting discourse conventions, linguistic patterns and rules have only just begun. However, the definition of what is appropriate and normative in such a changing environment is particularly important for business discourse research for two reasons. First, research has found that work can be considerably affected because violations of what is perceived to be a norm have a negative impact on the success of communication and co-operation (Cheshin *et al.* 2013). Second, the understanding and definition of what is appropriate in the business environment for the achievement of various communicative goals is also essential knowledge for teaching digital business discourse and training effective communicators in the workplace (Gimenez 2000; Kankaanranta 2006). The description of these norms and practices is a complex task, however, because the norms in question can be both externally generated and imposed – for instance in the form of 'netiquettes', guide books or organisational policies – or they can emerge during use as responses to emerging communicative situations, as discussed in the previous section. User awareness of and ability to adapt to these norms in order to 'survive and succeed' (Crystal 2001: 62) in professional encounters over the Internet is therefore essential, particularly when the success of the communication is measurable, financially or otherwise. The 'special skill set' required for effective communication in the virtual workplace can be described as a combination of *electronic communicative competence* (Simpson 2005) and *professional communicative competence*, which includes a tacit awareness and understanding of 'not only what is said, but how, and through what channels' (Turner *et al.* 2006: 242), as well as the ability to appropriately use this knowledge of linguistic features, discourse practices and interactional strategies during the achievement of communicative goals (Gimenez 2000: 248). In the following sections, I briefly introduce two aspects of discourse and language use that constitute the 'how': appropriate style and medium-specific language features.

Appropriate style

Research into the use of appropriate style provides evidence that, because stylistic norms are not fully conventionalised in text-based CMC (Yus 2011), users often draw on their experiences from previously existing spoken and written genres when constructing messages (Baron 2002). Language use, in particular, has been found to be a key aspect of style. For example, it has been found that the use of 'oral features' in IM contributes to the medium being perceived as informal (Nardi *et al.* 2000), whereas email has been positioned somewhere between formal business correspondence and speech, based on the typical linguistic features employed (Cho 2010; Gimenez 2000). Through examination of linguistic practices and grammar, research has already shown the impact of style on the achievement of professional communicative goals – for example, switching to a more formal style might depersonalise correspondence and thus signal greater authority (Skovholt & Svennevig 2006), whereas using a more personal style might result in a higher chance of request compliance (Ho 2011). However, it is important to note that the style attributed to a written message is not solely dependent on the intentions of the writer, but also on the interpretations of the audience (Jansen 2012; Rooksby 2002). In organisational communication literature, the lack of opportunities for the alignment of the usage and meaning of linguistic devices and discourse strategies has been identified as the main cause of miscommunication in the virtual working environment (Berry 2011; Staples & Zhao 2006; Thompson & Coovert 2003); it is clear that more empirical work is needed in this field to address questions regarding the styles attributed to certain linguistic devices or discursive strategies, or questions of conventionality.

Within the broad context of style, linguistic politeness in digital business discourse has also received considerable attention, mainly from a linguistic/discourse perspective. Several researchers have, for instance, examined linguistic politeness in educational institutional settings, and found that the pragmatic competence of writers and their appropriate use of linguistic politeness strategies contribute considerably to the achievement of communicative goals (Biesenbach-Lucas 2006; Chen 2006; Economidou-Kogetsidis 2011). Considerably less work has been done in professional organisational settings; exceptions include studies about how linguistic politeness strategies contribute to the construction of a collegial working environment (Darics 2010a) as well as to the interactional construction of organisational hierarchies (Kong 2006).

Medium-specific features

The 'richness' of text-based CMC channels and user ability to creatively use available resources for the achievement of their communicative goals have also been well researched from the earliest stages of CMC research (see above). In organisational and business communication literature, the fact that people using text-based CMC miss out on interpersonal and situational context cues as well as non-verbal signs that would normally aid interaction and understanding has been found to be a major cause of communication problems (Cornelius & Boos 2003; Thompson & Coovert 2003; Vroman & Kovacich 2002). The exploration of written CMC cues has revealed that users draw on a wide range of resources to convey non-verbal and contextual messages: Lea and Spears (1992) and Byron and Baldridge (2007), for instance, found that usage of even a limited number of written non-verbal cues had a considerable effect on the impressions interactants formed about each other; Berglund (2009), Hancock and Dunham (2001) and Woerner et al. (2007) have given detailed accounts of how textual non-verbal devices contribute to the creation of conversational coherence and to the undisrupted flow of interactions; Panteli (2002) demonstrated how the usage of non-verbal cues in text-based digital communication contributes to the interactional creation of organisational identities; and finally, considerable work has shown that the set of available resources in digital business discourse is effectively used to communicate affect and stance, for example through verbal channels (Hancock et al. 2007), paralinguistic features and backchannel signalling (Darics 2010b), and the use of emoticons (Luor et al. 2010; Walther & D'Addario 2001).

The research strands mentioned above, however, often lack methodological rigour in the description of the range of available cues and fail to account for the highly context-dependent nature of these medium-specific features (see Kalman & Gergle 2010; Thompsen & Foulger 1996). In order to gain a clearer insight into how language functions in the digital business environment, for example in business-critical situations such as customer service encounters, more pronounced emphasis should be put on research examining the role and function of medium-specific linguistic features, such as emoticons, liberated punctuation, spelling, capital letters and the like, in particular so that these usages can be systematically described for training and teaching purposes.

Future directions: theory and practice

Digital business discourse in organisational contexts

Recent manifestos of CMD research have called for approaches that ensure that language is viewed as an organic element of broader socio-cultural practices (Georgakopoulou 2006) and approaches that share a 'commitment to the social function of language, the interactional accomplishment of meaning, the significance of communicator intent and the relevance of social/cultural context' (Thurlow & Mroczek 2011b: xxiii). These agendas have a particular relevance for digital business communication studies, because – as I have shown in the section headed 'A language-centred approach to mediated workplace communication' – professional communication is not simply a means of transmitting information, but also a means of completing work and negotiating goals. At the same time, it is a managerial tool that enables motivation, creation of trust, and resolution of interpersonal conflicts in a work team; and it facilitates the negotiation of professional, personal and team identities, hierarchical status, and relational practices. In order to meaningfully inform both the theory and practice of professional communication, then, it is clear that our observation of the emergent communicative situations created by existing and developing digital media in workplaces and our exploration of the resulting communicative practices must be grounded in overall organisational structure and social practices. It is also true, however, that the various strands of organisational studies need to embrace the 'linguistic turn' and incorporate or draw upon empirical research, mainly through observation of naturally occurring data.

The fusion of these two viewpoints has already begun, as demonstrated by recent publications such as Goodman and Hirsch (2014) and the edited volume *Digital Business Discourse* (Darics 2015a). An increasing number of studies draw on empirical, naturally occurring interactional data to address issues such as the effectiveness of merely text-based communication in group meetings (Markman 2009), the implications of loosened interactional coherence for completing work-related tasks in IM (Woerner *et al.* 2007), specific discursive practices used for the interactional construction of leadership (Skovholt 2009) or interactional strategies used for the construction of organisational hierarchies (Skovholt & Svennevig 2006), email practices used to create accountability (Gimenez 2006, 2014; Ho 2011), or linguistic practices used in IM to accomplish relational work and create a collegial working environment (Darics 2010b). However, in order to gain a full insight into computer-mediated workplace interactions, more work needs to be done to examine how issues previously raised in business discourse research and organisational communication research are affected by mediated communicative genres and emergent communicative situations. Applied research should address, for instance, the relationship between the distribution of power and communication technology, discursive manifestations of power, linguistic construction of gender in professional mediated communication, persuasiveness and negotiations, miscommunication, and other issues related to discourse that could potentially affect the effectiveness of virtual communication and thus virtual work.

Methodological implications

The previous sections have depicted a very dynamic and rapidly changing picture of digital workplace interactions and have shown that lack of conventionality, emergent communicative practices and the disappearance of the synchronous-asynchronous dichotomy have led to new communicative situations, the pragmatic–discursive exploration of which has only just begun. The methodological implications of the complexity inherent in digital workplace discourse coincide with the latest developments of CMD studies, and scholars are recognising the need to re-situate the field's focal concerns in relation to 'issues of physical co-presence and embodiment, sharing (or not) of an immediate context, synchronicity (or not) of interaction, and other contextual dimensions of relevance that have not been fully exploited yet' (Georgakopoulou 2006: 550). Such approaches might require a departure from or re-thinking of traditional analytical perspectives and methodologies (see, for example, problematisations in Cho 2010; Androutsopoulos & Beißwenger 2008). In digital business discourse research, recent attempts have included the application of a conversation–analytic methodology for the analysis of computer-mediated modes previously not treated as interactions (Skovholt & Svennevig 2013) and multimodal approaches where linguistic analysis is combined with observation and description of text production (Marcoccia *et al.* 2008; Markman 2005). Another strand of enquiry employs multidimensional analytical approaches that combine a variety of perspectives, enabling a multi-faceted view of various communicative practices in the workplace (see e.g. Androutsopoulos 2008; Darics 2014, 2015b; Gimenez 2014; Skovholt & Svennevig 2006).

Similar methodological questions are also raised in organisational communication literature: Potter and Balthazard (2002), for instance, urge the research community to 'develop additional theoretical perspectives as well as additional methodologies and research approaches in order to get a deeper insight into computer mediated workplace interactions'. The importance of such new or re-developed methodological approaches, in particular the empirical, data-driven approach for which this chapter argues, is twofold. First, empirical observations could provide a potential starting point for broader generalisations and quantification about business discourse practices (see Bargiela-Chiappini *et al.* 2007), thus providing a theoretical understanding of how communication happens in digitally mediated communicative situations. The second reason is pre-eminently practical. This practical orientation is well articulated in Berry's observation, which argues that

> the effectiveness of virtual teams and resultant outcomes of virtual teamwork is dependent on the resolution of miscommunication and conflict, the development of adequate and competent roles within the team for working together, and facilitating good communication between team members.
>
> *(2011: 202)*

Through the observation of digital workplace discourse, we can gain a clearer insight into how exactly digital media in the workplace affects corporate communication practices. The findings of such enquiries could then provide a useful resource for communication experts and business professionals and inform training materials aimed at professionals communicating via digital media, courses aimed at enhancing online communication, and popular publications on digital discourse in the workplace. The combination of knowledge from organisational studies, business discourse studies, and computer-mediated communication studies could help to avoid problematic workplace communication that could lead to costly negative outcomes, thus enhancing the communication effectiveness of business interactions using digital media.

Related topics

- Chapter 14 Corporate blogging and corporate social media (Puschmann & Hagelmoser)
- Chapter 4 Multimodal analysis (Jewitt)
- Chapter 16 The role of the body and space in digital multimodality (Keating)

References

Ale Ebrahim, N. A., Ahmed, S. & Taha, Z. 2009, 'Virtual teams and management challenges', 1st Executive MBA Conference 2009, Tehran, Iran.

Alvesson, M. & Kärreman, D. 2000, 'Taking the linguistic turn in organizational research: challenges, responses, consequences', *The Journal of Applied Behavioral Science*, vol. 36, no. 2, pp. 136–158.

Androutsopoulos, J. 2008, 'Potentials and limitations of discourse-centred online ethnography', *Language@ Internet,* vol. 5, no. 8, available at: http://www.languageatinternet.org/articles/2008/1610.

Androutsopoulos, J. & Beißwenger, M. 2008, 'Introduction: data and methods in computer-mediated discourse analysis', *Language@Internet*, vol. 5, no. 2, available at: http://www.languageatinternet.org/articles/2008/1609.

Bargiela-Chiappini, F. 2009a, *The handbook of business discourse*, Edinburgh University Press: Edinburgh.

Bargiela-Chiappini, F. 2009b, 'Introduction: business discourse', in F. Bargiela-Chiappini (ed.), *The handbook of business discourse*, Edinburgh University Press: Edinburgh, pp. 1–17.

Baron, N. S. 2010, 'Discourse structures in instant messaging: the case of utterance breaks', *Language@ Internet*, vol. 7, no. 4, available at: http://www.languageatinternet.de/articles/2010/2651/index_html/.

Baron, N. S. 2002, 'Who sets e-mail style? Prescriptivism, coping strategies, and democratizing communication access', *The Information Society*, vol. 18, no. 5, pp. 403–413.

Bell, B. S. & Kozlowski, S. W. J. 2002, 'A typology of virtual teams: implications for effective leadership group and organization management', vol. 27, no. 1, pp. 14–49.

Berglund, T. Ö. 2009, 'Disrupted turn adjacency and coherence maintenance in instant messaging conversations', *Language@Internet* vol. 6, no. 2, available at: http://www.languageatinternet.org/articles/2009/2106.

Berry, G. R. 2011, 'Enhancing effectiveness on virtual teams: understanding why traditional team skills are insufficient', *Journal of Business Communication*, vol. 48, no. 2, pp. 186–206.

Biesenbach-Lucas, S. 2006, 'Making requests in email: do cyber-consultations entail directness? Toward conventions in a new medium', in K. Bardovi-Harlig, J. C. Félix-Brasdefer, & A. S. Omar (eds.), *Pragmatics and language learning*, University of Hawai'i Press: Honolulu, pp. 81–108.

Boczkowski, P. J. & Orlikowski, W. J. 2004, 'Organizational discourse and new media: a practice perspective', in D. Grant, C. Hardy, C. Oswick & L. Putnam (eds.), *The SAGE handbook of organizational discourse*, Sage Publications, London, pp. 359–377.

Byron, K. & Baldridge, D. C. 2007, 'E-mail recipients' impressions of senders' likability the interactive effect of nonverbal cues and recipients' personality', *Journal of Business Communication*, vol. 44, no. 2, pp. 137–160.

Cameron, A. F. & Webster, J. 2005, 'Unintended consequences of emerging communication technologies: instant messaging in the workplace', *Computers in Human Behavior*, vol. 21, no. 1, pp. 85–103.

Cascio W. F. & Shurygailo, S. 2002, 'E-leadership and virtual teams', *Organizational Dynamics*, vol. 31, no. 4, pp. 362–376.

Čech, C. G. & Condon, S. L. 2004, 'Temporal properties of turn-taking and turn-packaging in synchronous computer-mediated communication', in R. H. Sprague (ed.), *Proceedings of the 37th annual Hawaii international conference on system sciences*, Waikoloa, HI.

Chen, C. E. 2006, 'The development of e-mail literacy: from writing to peers to writing to authority figures', *Language Learning & Technology*, vol. 10, no. 2, pp. 35–55.

Cheshin, A., Yongsuk, K., Bos, N. D., Ning, N. & Olson, J. S. 2013, 'Emergence of differing electronic communication norms within partially distributed teams', *Journal of Personnel Psychology*, vol. 12, no. 1, pp. 7–21.

Cho, T. 2010, 'Linguistic features of electronic mail in the workplace: a comparison with memoranda', *Language@Internet*, vol. 7, no. 3, available at: http://www.languageatinternet.org/articles/2010/2728.

Churchill, E. F. & Bly, S. 1999, 'It's all in the words: supporting work activities with lightweight tools', *Proceedings of group '99 conference on supporting group work*, Phoenix, AZ.

Condon, S. L. & Čech, C. 2002, 'Profiling turns in interaction: discourse structure and function', *Proceedings of the 34th annual Hawaii international conference on system sciences 2001*, IEEE, available at: http://ieeexplore.ieee.org/xpl/freeabs_all.jsp?arnumber=926501.

Cornelius, C. & Boos, M. 2003, 'Enhancing mutual understanding in synchronous computer-mediated communication by training', *Communication Research*, vol. 30, no. 2, pp. 147–177.

Crossman, A. & Lee-Kelley, L. 2004, 'Trust, commitment and team working: the paradox of virtual organizations', *Global Networks*, vol. 4, no. 4, pp. 375–390.

Crystal, D. 2001, *Language and the Internet*, Cambridge University Press: Cambridge.

Dabbish, L. A., Kraut, R. E., Fussell, S. & Kiesler, S. 2005, 'Understanding email use: predicting action on a message', *Proceedings of the SIGCHI conference on human factors in computing systems*, ACM, pp. 691–700.

Daft, R. L., Lengel, R. H. & Trevino, L. K. 1987, 'Message equivocality, media selection, and manager performance: implications for information systems', *MIS Quarterly*, vol. 11, no. 3, pp. 355–366.

Daim, T. U., Ha, A., Reutiman, S., Hughes, B., Pathak, U., Bynum, W. & Bathla, A. 2012, 'Exploring the communication breakdown in global virtual teams', *International Journal of Project Management*, vol. 30, no. 2, pp. 199–212.

Darics, E. 2015a, (ed.) *Digital business discourse*. Palgrave: Basingstoke.

Darics, E. 2015b, 'Deconstruction-analysis-explanation: contextualisation in professional digital discourse'. In E. Darics (ed.) *Digital Business Discourse*. Palgrave: Basingstoke. pp. 243–264.

Darics, E. 2014, 'The blurring boundaries between synchronicity and asynchronicity: new communicative situations in work-related instant messaging', *International Journal of Business Communication*, doi: 10.1177/2329488414525440.

Darics, E. 2010a, 'Politeness in computer-mediated discourse of a virtual team', *Journal of Politeness Research*, vol. 6, no. 1, pp. 129–150.

Darics, E. 2010b, 'Relational work in synchronous text-based CMC of virtual Teams', in R. Taiwo (ed.), *Handbook of research on discourse behavior and digital communication: language structures and social interaction*, IGI Global: Hershey, PA, pp. 830–851.

Drew, P. & Heritage, J. 1992, *Talk at work: interaction in institutional settings*, Cambridge University Press: Cambridge.

Economidou-Kogetsidis, M. 2011, '"Please answer me as soon as possible": pragmatic failure in non-native speakers' e-mail requests to faculty', *Journal of Pragmatics*, vol. 43, no. 13, pp. 3193–3215.

Ferrara, K., Brunner, H. & Whittemore, G. 1991, 'Interactive written discourse as an emergent register', *Written Communication*, vol. 8, no. 1, pp. 8–34.

Garrett, R. K. & Danziger, J. N. 2008, 'IM=interruption management? Instant messaging and disruption in the workplace', *Journal of Computer-Mediated Communication*, vol. 13, no. 1, pp. 23–42.

Georgakopoulou, A. 2006, 'Postscript: computer-mediated communication in sociolinguistics', *Journal of Sociolinguistics*, vol. 10, no. 4, pp 548–557.

Gimenez, J., forthcoming, 'Reflections of professional practice: using electronic discourse analysis networks (EDANS) to examine embedded business emails', in F. Sudweeks & H. L. Lim, (eds.), *Innovative methods and technologies for electronic discourse analysis*, IGI Global: Hershey, PA.

Grant, D., Putnam, L. L., Hardy, C. & Oswick, C. (eds.) 2004, *The SAGE handbook of organizational discourse*, Sage Publications: London.

Griffith, T. L., Sawyer, J. E. & Neale, M. A. 2003, 'Virtualness and knowledge in teams: managing the love triangle of organizations, individuals, and information technology', *MIS Quarterly*, vol. 27, no. 2, pp. 265–287.

Hafner, K. & Lyon, M. 1998, *Where wizards stay up late: the origins of the Internet*, Touchstone: New York, NY.

Hancock, J. T. & Dunham, P. J. 2001, 'Language use in computer-mediated communication: the role of coordination devices', *Discourse Processes*, vol. 31, no. 1, pp. 91–110.

Handel, M. & Herbsleb, J. D. 2002, 'IM everywhere: what is chat doing in the workplace', *Computer supported cooperative work '02*, New Orleans, LA.

Hancock, J. T., Landrigan, C. & Silver, C. 2007, 'Expressing emotion in text-based communication', *Proceedings of the SIGCHI conference on human factors in computing* systems, San Jose, CA.

Herring, S. C. 2001, 'Computer-mediated discourse', in D. Schiffrin, D. Tannen & H. Hamilton (eds.), *The handbook of discourse analysis*, Blackwell: Oxford, pp. 612–634.

Herring, S. C. 1999, 'Interactional coherence in CMC', *Journal of Computer-Mediated Communication*, vol. 4, no. 4, available at: http://onlinelibrary.wiley.com/doi/10.1111/j.1083-6101.1999.tb00106.x/full.

Ho, V. 2011, 'What functions do intertextuality and interdiscursivity serve in request e-mail discourse?', *Journal of Pragmatics*, vol. 43, no. 10, pp. 2534–2547.

Hoang, Q. & Radicati, S. 2011 'Survey: instant messaging, social networking, unified communications, 2011–2012', The Radicati Group: Palo Alto, CA.

Isaacs, E., Walendowski, A., Whittaker, S., Schiano, D. J. & Kamm, C. 2002, 'The character, functions, and styles of instant messaging in the workplace', *Proceedings of the 2002 ACM conference on computer supported cooperative work*, ACM, New York, NY.

Jansen, F. 2012, 'The putative email style and its explanations: evidence from two effect studies of Dutch direct mail letters and direct marketing emails', *Language@Internet*, vol. 9, no. 1, available at: http://www.languageatinternet.org/articles/2012.

Kalman, Y. M. & Gergle, D. 2010, 'CMC cues enrich lean online communication: the case of letter and punctuation mark repetitions', available at: http://129.105.146.12/pubs/MCIS2010-KalmanAndGergle-CMCCues.pdf.

Kalman, Y. M. & Rafaeli, S. 2011, 'Online pauses and silence: chronemic expectancy violations in written computer-mediated communication', *Communication Research*, vol. 38, no. 1, pp. 54–69.

Kalman, Y. M., Ravid, G., Raban, D. R. & Rafaeli, S. 2006, 'Pauses and response latencies: a chronemic analysis of asynchronous CMC', *Journal of Computer-Mediated Communication*, vol. 12, no. 1, available at: http://onlinelibrary.wiley.com/doi/10.1111/j.1083-6101.2006.00312.x/full.

Kankaanranta, A. 2006, '"Hej Seppo! Could you pls comment on this!": internal email communication in lingua franca English in a multinational company', *Business Communication Quarterly*, vol. 69, no. 2, pp. 216–225.

Kiesler, S., Siegel, J. & McGuire, T. W. 1984, 'Social psychological aspects of computer-mediated communication', *American Psychologist*, vol. 39, no. 10, pp. 1123–1134.

Ko, K. 1996, 'Structural characteristics of computer-mediated language: a comparative analysis of InterChange discourse', *Electronic Journal of Communication/La Revue Électronique De Communication*, vol. 6, no. 3, available at: http://www.cios.org/www/ejc/v6n396.htm.

Kong, K. C. C. 2006, 'Accounts as a politeness strategy in the internal directive documents of a business firm in Hong Kong', *Journal of Asian Pacific Communication*, vol. 16, no. 1, pp. 77–101.

Kraut, R. E., Fish R. S., Root, R.W. & Chalfonte, B. L. 1990, 'Informal communication in organizations: form, function, and technology', *Human reactions to technology: Claremont symposium on applied social psychology*, Sage, Beverly Hills, CA, pp. 145–199.

Lea, M. & Spears, R. 1992, 'Paralanguage and social perception in computer-mediated communication', *Journal of Organizational Computing and Electronic Commerce*, vol. 2, no. 3–4, pp. 321–341.

Ledbetter, A. M. 2008, 'Chronemic cues and sex differences in relational e-mail', *Social Science Computer Review*, vol. 26, no. 4, pp. 466–482.

Luor, T., Wu, L., Lu, H. & Tao, Y. 2010, 'The effect of emoticons in simplex and complex task-oriented communication: an empirical study of instant messaging', *Computers in Human Behavior*, vol. 26, no. 5, pp. 889–895.

Marcoccia, M., Atifi, H. & Gauducheau, N. 2008, 'Text-centered versus multimodal analysis of instant messaging conversation', *Language@Internet*, vol. 5, no. 7, available at: http://www.languageatinternet.org/articles/2008/1621.

Markman, K. M. 2009, '"So what shall we talk about": Openings and closings in chat-based virtual meetings'. *Journal of Business Communication*, vol. 46, no. 1, pp. 150–170.

Markman, K. M. 2005, 'To send or not to send: turn construction in computer-mediated chat', in C. Sunakawa, T. Ikeda, S. Finch, & M. Shetty (eds.), *Proceedings of the twelfth annual Symposium About Language and Society (48)*, Texas Linguistic Forum, Austin, TX, pp. 115–124.

Martins, L. L., Gilson, L. L. & Maynard, M. T. 2004, 'Virtual teams: what do we know and where do we go from here?', *Journal of Management*, vol. 30, no. 6, pp. 805–835.

Murray, D. E. 1990, 'CMC', *English Today*, vol. 6, no. 3, pp. 42–46.

Nardi, B. A., Whittaker, S. & Bradner, E. 2000, 'Interaction and outeraction: instant messaging in action', *Proceedings of the 2000 ACM conference on computer supported cooperative work*, ACM, New York, NY, pp. 79–88.

Ong, K. K. W. 2011, 'Disagreement, confusion, disapproval, turn elicitation and floor holding: actions as accomplished ellipsis marks-only turns and blank turns in quasisynchronous chats', *Discourse Studies*, vol. 13, no. 2, pp. 211–234.

Panteli, N. 2002, 'Richness, power cues and email text', *Information & Management*, vol. 40, no. 2, pp. 75–86.

Panteli, N. & Fineman, S. 2005, 'The sound of silence: the case of virtual team organising', *Behaviour and Information Technology*, vol. 24, no. 5, pp. 347–352.

Pauleen, D. J. & Yoong, P. 2001, 'Facilitating virtual team relationships via internet and conventional communication channels', *Internet Research*, vol. 11, no. 3, pp. 190–202.

Potter, R. E. & Balthazard, P. A. 2002, 'Virtual team interaction styles: assessment and effects', *International Journal of Human Computer Studies*, vol. 56, no. 4, pp. 423–443.

Purvanova, R. K. & Bono, J. E. 2009, 'Transformational leadership in context: face-to-face and virtual teams', *The Leadership Quarterly*, vol. 20, no. 3, pp. 343–357.

Reinsch, N. L., Turner, J. W. & Tinsley, C. H. 2008, 'Multicommunicating: a practice whose time has come?', *The Academy of Management Review*, vol. 33, no. 2, pp. 391–403.

Rennecker, J. & Godwin, L. 2003, 'Theorizing the unintended consequences of instant messaging for worker productivity', *Sprouts: Working Papers on Information Environments, Systems and Organizations*, vol. 3, no. 3, pp. 137–168.

Rintel, E. S. & Pittam, J. 1997, 'Strangers in a strange land: interaction management in Internet Relay Chat', *Human Communication Research*, vol. 23, no. 4, pp. 507–543.

Rintel, E. S., Pittam, J. & Mulholland, J. 2003, 'Time will tell: ambiguous non-responses on Internet Relay Chat', *The Electronic Journal of Communication*, vol. 13, no. 1, available at: http://www.cios.org/Ejcpublic/013/1/01312.HTML.

Rooksby, E. 2002, *E-mail and ethics: style and ethical relations in computer-mediated communications*, Routledge: London.

Severinson Eklundh, K. 2010, 'To quote or not to quote: setting the context for computer-mediated dialogues', *Language@Internet*, vol. 7, no. 5, available at: http://www.languageatinternet.org/articles/2010/2665.

Severinson Eklundh, K .1994, 'Electronic mail as a medium for dialogue', in L. van Waes, E. Woudstra & P. van den Hoven, (eds.), *Functional communication quality*, Rodopi, Amsterdam, pp. 162–173.

Severinson Eklundh, K. & Macdonald, C. 1994, 'The use of quoting to preserve context in electronic mail dialogues', *IEEE Transactions on Professional Communication*, vol. 37, no. 4, pp. 197–202.

Simpson, J. 2005, 'Conversational floors in synchronous text-based CMC discourse', *Discourse Studies*, vol. 7, no. 3, pp. 337–361.

Skovholt, K. & Svennevig, J. 2013, 'Responses and non-responses in e-mail interaction', in S. Herring, D. Stein & T. Virtanen, (eds.), *The pragmatics of computer-mediated communication*, Mouton De Gruyter: Berlin, pp. 589–612.

Skovolt, K. 2009, Leadership communication in a virtual team. *42nd Hawaii International Conference on System Sciences*, 2009. HICSS'09. 1–12.

Skovholt, K., & Svennevig, J. 2006, 'Email copies in workplace interaction'. *Journal of Computer-Mediated Communication*, vol. 12, no.1, pp. 42–65. doi: 10.1111/j.1083-6101.2006.00314.x.

Solomon, C. M. 2001, 'Managing virtual teams', *Workforce*, vol. 80, no. 6, pp. 60–65.

Sproull, L. S. & Kiesler, S. 1986, 'Reducing social context cues: electronic mail in organizational communication', *Management Science*, vol. 32, no. 11, pp. 1492–1512.

Staples, D. S. & Zhao, L. 2006, 'The effects of cultural diversity in virtual teams versus face-to-face teams', *Group Decision and Negotiation*, vol. 15, no. 4, pp. 389–406.

Thompsen, P. A. & Foulger, D. A. 1996, 'Effects of pictographs and quoting on flaming in electronic mail', *Computers in Human Behavior*, vol. 12, no. 2, pp. 225–243.

Thompson, L. F. & Coovert, M. D. 2003, 'Teamwork online: the effects of computer conferencing on perceived confusion, satisfaction and postdiscussion accuracy', *Group Dynamics: Theory, Research, and Practice*, vol. 7, no. 2, pp. 135–151.

Thurlow, C. & Mroczek, K. 2011a, *Digital discourse*, Oxford University Press: Oxford.

Thurlow, C. & Mroczek, K. 2011b, 'Introduction: fresh perspectives on new media sociolinguistics', in C. Thurlow & K. Mroczek, (eds.), *Digital discourse*, Oxford University Press: Oxford, pp. xix–xliv.

Turner, J. W., Grube, J. A., Tinsley, C. H., Lee, C. & O'pell, C. 2006, 'Exploring the dominant media: how does media use reflect organizational norms and affect performance?', *Journal of Business Communication*, vol. 43, no. 3, pp. 220–250.

Tyler, J. R. & Tang, J. C. 2003, 'When can I expect an email response? A study of rhythms in email usage', in K. Kuutii, E. H. Karsten, G. Fitzpatrick, P. Dourish & K. Schmidt (eds.), *Proceedings of the eighth European conference on computer supported cooperative work*, Springer: Netherlands, pp. 239–258.

Vroman, K. & Kovacich, J. 2002, 'Computer-mediated interdisciplinary teams: theory and reality', *Journal of Interprofessional Care*, vol. 16, no. 2, pp. 159–170.

Walther, J. B. & D'Addario, K. P. 2001, 'The impacts of emoticons on message interpretation in computer-mediated communication', *Social Science Computer Review*, vol. 19, no. 3, pp. 324–347.

Walther, J. B. & Tidwell, L. C. 1995, 'Nonverbal cues in computer-mediated communication and the effect of chronemics on relational communication', *Journal of Organizational Computing and Electronic Commerce*, vol. 5, no. 4, pp. 355–378.

Warren, M. 2013, '"Just spoke to . . . ": the types and directionality of intertextuality in professional discourse', *English for Specific Purposes*, vol. 32, no. 1, pp. 12–24.

Watson-Manheim, M. B. & Belanger, F. 2002, 'Exploring communication-based work processes in virtual work environments', *35th annual Hawaii international conference on system sciences*, available at: http://ieeexplore.ieee.org/stamp/stamp.jsp?tp=&arnumber=994459&isnumber=21442.

Woerner, S. L., Yates, J. A. & Orlikowski, W. J. 2007, 'Conversational coherence in Instant Messaging and getting work done', *40th annual Hawaii international conference on system sciences*, available at: http://ieeexplore.ieee.org/stamp/stamp.jsp?tp=&arnumber=4076526&isnumber=4076362.

Yus, F. 2011, *Cyberpragmatics: Internet-mediated communication in context*, John Benjamins: Amsterdam.

Further reading

bargiela-Chiappini, F. 2009. *The handbook of business discourse*, Edinburgh University Press: Edinburgh.

The Foreword is a particularly useful summary of the aims and scope of business discourse studies. Chapter 10 specifically addresses mediated workplace communication.

Herring, S. C., Stein, D. & Virtanen, T. 2013, *Pragmatics of computer-mediated communication*, Mouton De Gruyter: Berlin.

Chapters 2–9 provide an overview of the various mediated communication modes and contain up-to-date reviews about the field, particularly from a pragmatic point of view. Chapters 24–25 address workplace-specific issues.

13

Digital advertising

Helen Kelly-Holmes

Introduction

Advertising was originally conceived as a one-to-many, primarily verbal/textual mode of communication. As web-based advertising evolved, it tended to retain these features; however, a number of developments have created parallel and powerful trends in digital marketing communication. The first is the evolution of Web 2.0, characterised by user-generated content, peer-to-peer communication and interactivity, which has, on the one hand, forced advertisers to consider the interactive dimensions of their communication, and, on the other, enabled consumers to create texts about products, which are outside of the control of the advertiser. Consumers are thus in a powerful position to recommend products through electronic word of mouth ('eWOM'), which can either reinforce or undermine the marketer's message. The second development is the evolution of the concept of the 'working consumer' who co-creates value for brands and products; this, too, involves a loss of control on the part of the advertiser as communicator, since the consumer can also devalue a product or brand or subvert message content through remediation and comment. The final dimension is the increasing role of 'personalisation' in web-based advertising and marketing, which allows for customised and localised offerings to be made to consumers on an individual or one-to-one basis. Following an introduction to digital advertising and a brief history of its evolution, these key factors and trends will be discussed in terms of current research and illustrative examples, and methodological approaches for exploring and investigating advertising and digital communication will also be addressed.

Historical overview

While it may not be as apparent as in traditional media such as print, radio, and television, the web and other digital media are primarily funded by advertising. From the marketing point of view, media (traditional and digital) are where promotion – in the form of advertising – takes place. Promotion is one of the 'four Ps' in the standard marketing mix, along with price, product and place; this mix has traditionally been the focus of marketers, with each dimension requiring equal but distinct attention and strategy. In contrast to earlier media, however, which were mainly focused on promotion, the web and other digital media are able not only to promote products, but also to act as distribution and transaction channels as well. Consequently, the web and digital technology have forced a reconsideration of the very fundamentals on which marketing and advertising were built. Constantinides (2002) argues that the marketing mix, which has been the basis of marketing since the 1960s, has been rendered obsolete by technological changes. He identifies a move from a mass market to a virtual marketplace, which is 'increasingly segmented, niche dominated or even mass-customised, highly interactive and global' (p. 59). The key components of this virtual market are the growth of personalisation in terms of 'satisfying individual rather than collective needs', and a ceding of control to a new generation of consumer who is 'better informed, wired and wealthier' (Constantinides 2002: 59).

Until recently, a web presence for many companies involved just that – being present. When the Internet opened to companies in the early 1990s, commercial uses grew rapidly, despite objections by the 'original users' (Hammill 1997: 303) in the education and research domains, who wanted the Internet to remain a space where information could be freely exchanged and kept apart from commercial applications. From the point of view of companies, web and digital marketing has many advantages and tends to reduce many of the previous disadvantages experienced by small and medium-sized companies in particular. For example, it reduces economies of scale and allows for markets made up of tiny niches or even individual consumers to be profitable. It also allows for internationalisation at a much more rapid pace and with much reduced costs, since companies can reach overseas markets without the need to set up a subsidiary company or appoint an agent or distributor, which previously would have been the case. Additionally, issues of temporal and spatial distance from customers are far less important. There is no longer a need to have an impressive headquarters, and large and successful businesses can be run from a very small physical space with minimal numbers of employees (see Hammill 1997 for an overview of these issues) as the web allows for the development of 'non-personal' interaction with customers (Bitner *et al.* 2000: 141).

Consumers have different motivations for using websites and applications, and research suggests that the design of digital marketing needs to take these differences into account and allow for differentiated design that will accommodate such diverse categories as 'goal directed immediate purchasers', 'goal directed future purchasers', 'hedonic immediate purchasers', as well as those 'who just land on the website and then directly leave' (Ström, Vendal, & Bredicam 2014). Unsurprisingly, the conversion rate for website visits to purchases varies greatly between these different types of consumer (Ström *et al.* 2014).

The first phase of web marketing began in the mid-1990s and was mainly concerned with providing information to the customer. With the emergence of social media in the early 2000s, a second phase began to focus on interacting with customers and on allowing for many of the marketing functions to take place in one space (price, promotion, product and place). The current phase, which probably began with Google's introduction of personalisation in 2005, is dominated by the notion of 'intelligence': the idea that information can be constantly gathered about individuals as they use the web, which can be used to differentiate them from other users to allow for personalised and individualised targeting.

In the initial phase of web-based marketing, as stated above, marketers simply saw the web as another medium through which to promote their products. Commercial web presence thus had two important functions: first, to enhance credibility and support offline promotion in other media and distribution channels, and, second, to provide information to consumers. Offline methods and messages tended simply to be transferred to the web page of the particular company or product. Such an approach involved primarily one-way communication, in line with traditional approaches in mass-marketing and advertising in print, radio, television, etc. Interestingly, while web marketing has since widely embraced the intelligence-gathering and interactive features afforded by Web 2.0 in particular, the one-to-many corporate web persists, as we shall see below – sometimes on its own and sometimes in conjunction with more interactive approaches. Interactivity between individuals and groups is at the heart of the new marketing imperative, with the intensity of the interactivity being measured by the extent of two-way communication, the magnitude of synchronism, and the degree of control the participants have over the communication (Ström *et al.* 2014). Other key concepts are intermediality, which involves the dependence of different media on each other, and integration, which describes the incorporation of all media platforms and channels into one campaign with a coherent, repeated message.

Mobility (in terms of technology usage and access through tablets, smart phones, etc.) is also taken for granted in current marketing campaigns. Mobile marketing combines all of the phenomena outlined above with the introduction of mobility and the intensification of the omnipresence of marketing in people's everyday lives. This mobility brings both restrictions, such as smaller screen sizes and limited functions in comparison to laptop or desktop computers, and opportunities – for example, mobility offers the possibility of targeted marketing during the shopping experience, since people will have their device with them when they are in the physical retail landscape and/or actually using the product. (See Ström *et al.* 2014 for an overview.)

These technical changes have both responded and contributed to a philosophical change in the marketing concept of the consumer. A major shift in the perception of the consumer has taken place: once seen as a passive recipient of marketing messages, the consumer has now become not just an active participant in the marketing communication process, but an equal co-creator of value in terms of products, services and the whole marketing process. Co-creation refers to the processes by which both consumers and producers collaborate, or otherwise participate, in creating value. Thus, we now talk of 'working consumers, co-production, prosumption, consumer empowerment, consumer resistance, consumer agency, and consumer tribes' (Pongsakornrungsilp & Schroeder 2011: 304). Alongside this there has been a deconstruction of the very concept of value, and a subsequent repositioning of value as something 'complex and multidimensional' (p. 305), in opposition to its previous narrow meaning as something understood in functional or economic terms. These philosophical shifts in marketing, along with the technological changes in digital media, have resulted in a very different marketing and advertising landscape.

Critical issues and current research

We have seen how advances in digital technologies and changing communicative practices in digital environments have contributed to the evolution of marketing. We will now address two issues that are particularly relevant to the inter-relationship between marketing and digital communication: first, the loss of control on the part of the marketer, a result of the move from predominantly information-giving to interactive and peer-to-peer-based communication; and second, the rise of individualised web marketing in the forms of mass personalisation and mass customisation, which now track and target individuals instead of markets or market segments. We will now examine and illustrate each of these in detail, and attempt to assess their implications for digital communication.

The active consumer

Web 2.0 has at its core the concept of user participation and user-generated content (Constantinides & Fountain 2008). This means that user input is not just welcomed; it is now a key dimension of marketing strategy. As Constantinides and Fountain note, 'Web 2.0 applications support the creation of informal users' networks facilitating the flow of ideas and knowledge by allowing the efficient generation, dissemination, sharing and editing/refining of informational content' (2008: 232–233). So, for example, while previous communication eras encouraged marketers to achieve brand or product loyalty by 'locking in' customers with restrictive contracts and terms or using price to compete with alternative brands and products, in the current era, technological affordances and cultures of use (Jones & Hafner 2012), including peer influences, are likely to have just as much if not more impact on customer loyalty.

The way in which Web 2.0 is structured and the principles on which it operates mean that not only have individual and group behaviours been transformed, but there has also been a very significant shift in the 'power structures in the marketplace, causing a substantial migration of market power from producers or vendors towards customers' (Constantinides & Fountain 2008: 232). Consumer choice has grown exponentially: the web has made available vastly more products and boundless quantities of information about alternative products; and, as a result of the interactive nature of Web 2.0, consumers now have much more choice about how and when (and when not) to interact with the marketer (Constantinides & Fountain 2008: 232). Consequently, the active role played by the 'free consumer' (Zwick, Bonsu, & Darmody 2008) is increasingly understood as a threat to marketers, who may be seen to be losing power in the market (Cova & Dalli 2009). Furthermore, this active consumer role can be credited with transforming basic market dynamics and the marketing relationship by shifting power from producers to consumers and blurring the boundaries between firms and customers (see Pongsakornrungsilp & Schroeder 2011).

The development of digital marketing can be seen to have advantages and disadvantages for both consumers and marketers. From the marketer's point of view, consumers are engaged in web-based communities, where they discuss and evaluate products, test products, and add value to products (see Pongsakornrungsilp & Schroeder 2011 for a case study). Such communities provide companies with a naturalistic environment in which to gather valuable naturalistic data; they no longer have to rely exclusively on artificial settings such as focus groups or on reported data gathered through surveys. These new kinds of feedback allow marketers to carry out 'real-time' improvements to web applications, products sold online, and processes of sale, delivery, and information-giving. As a result, web marketing sites and applications are in a 'perpetual beta' state, never completely finished, always changing and evolving in response to consumers' feedback and suggestions (Constantinides & Fountain 2008: 236).

It is interesting to note that, alongside technology, the key influence today is seen to be peers. In fact, the technological changes heralded by the Web 2.0 environment have meant a greater connection with fellow consumers and increased possibilities for discussion with and influence by peers. As Drury (2007) points out, 'when discussing social media, pundits often emphasize "media" as being most important, when in reality the "social" element is key . . . social media enables "content" to become more democratised than ever before' (p. 274). Thus, for the marketer, marketing is no longer about delivering a message to a consumer but 'building a relationship and conversation with your audience' (Drury 2007: 275) and between members of the audience, who are cast as equals in the communication process.

This move towards democratisation or perceived democratisation means that the information monopoly is no longer in the hands of the marketer: 'Marketing with social media is not just about telling and giving a message, rather it is about receiving and exchanging perceptions and ideas' (Drury 2007: 275). Not surprisingly, then, the emphasis in this new communication context is no longer on directing a message from the company to the potential consumer but rather on attempting to manage interactions with users in social networks (Pantano & Carvello 2013: 214), and this represents a particular challenge in an always-on environment where consumers expect 24/7 interaction.

The main job of the marketer in the Web 2.0 context is now to attempt to influence consumers by directing their social media interactions. Electronic word-of-mouth (eWOM) sites allow and encourage consumers and friends to share information and give product tips. Through their work and contribution to value by liking, sharing, linking, inviting, etc., consumers play a major role in determining whether or not an advertising message goes viral – the marketer alone cannot achieve this. Good viral marketing involves 'effortless transfer to others', 'exploits common motivations and behaviours', 'utilizes existing communications network'; and 'takes advantages of others' resources' (Wilson 2000: 1). We can see how much of this success relies on having not just positive but also active consumers. The possibility of a viral campaign also has a negative side, and those features that make it possible for a positive marketing message to go viral can just as easily have the opposite effect – 'one unsatisfied customer can become thousands in a nano second' (MacLaren & Cattarell 2002: 320). Furthermore, Web 2.0 has also seen the evolution of 'anti-brand communities' (MacLaren & Cattarell 2002: 320) directed at large global brands such as McDonald's, Walmart, and Starbucks (see Hollenbeck & Zinkhan 2006).

It is not just in designated spaces such as eWOM sites or even anti-brand communities (e.g., the anti-McDonald's community McSpotlight) that word of mouth plays a role. Mainstream social media and peer-to-peer communication technologies such as Youtube and Facebook are increasingly important sites of influence for consumers, and it is almost impossible for marketers to control or even monitor the content of such sites. The following example illustrates the advantages and disadvantages of the advertiser's loss of control in Web 2.0. Laurensboutique is a YouTube channel featuring an American teenager who posts regular videos of herself. In the videos, which are categorised as 'howto' on YouTube, she gives advice about make-up and fashion and also talks about herself. 'Everyday neutral makeup for teenagers' is a typical presentation. It is shot as a 'selfie' video, with the presenter, Lauren, sitting on the floor of her bedroom in front of the camera. The following extract gives a good example of the informal style of presentation:

L1:   To start out I'm going to be using my Garnier fruitease under eye roller and apply this
L2:   underneath my eyes just to brighten them up a little bit. Next, I'm going in with my MAC
L3:   NW20 concealer and applying this to any blemishes that I have with a little Sigma
L4:   concealer brush and this is going to give a nice flawless finish. I'm taking some Clean and
L5:   Clear oil blotting sheets and going over and just soaking up all that oil that's just sitting on
L6:   our faces and don't worry it doesn't take off your make up. Then I'm going off with m-
L7:   going in with my Sephora mineral powder and just mattifying everything on my face to get
L8:   my nice light finish and skipping foundation because this neutral look is very simple and
L9:   easy. Then I'm going in with this elf contouring and blush palette and I'm taking my big
L10: powder brush and just applying my blush to my cheeks. And this is just going to give a
L11: nice look. Then I'm going in with a concealer and I'm going to be applying this as our base
L12: and blending it in. I didn't end up using the Naked 2 at all so I don't know why I'm
L13: showing it. But I'm going with virgin and applying this all over my eyelids to brighten
L14: them up a little and also applying this into the inner corner of my eyes as well. Then I'm
L15: going to be going in with naked and I'm going to be applying them to my crease with a
L16: nice matte colour to warm up our crease a little bit and then I'm going to go in with the
L17: buck which is a darker matte colour and applying this to the outer corner of my eye with
L18: that same brush. Then I'm taking virgin again and applying this as a highlight to my
L19: {unclear} {laughter}. Okay. And then I'm curling my eyelashes with my Revlon
      eyelash
L20: curler and then I'm taking my favourite mascara, I LOVE this mascara, it's a L'Oreal
L21: telescopic or L'Oreal clean, no, L'Oreal's shocking extensions mascara and I'm applying

L22:   this to the bottom and top lashes and I love this mascara so much guys, it's like my
L23:   favourite mascara.

('Everyday neutral makeup for teenagers', laurensboutique, http://www.youtube.com/
watch?v=nwVRSQr7ZhQ)

As we can see from the transcript, she mentions numerous different brands and products in the course of her video (underlined above). She is doing many of the functions of advertising (giving information, naming the products and showing them, praising the positive features of products, promoting them), but this is happening in a very different way to a professionally created, produced, and delivered advertisement. The communication style is very repetitive with overused constructions ('I'm going in with' in L2, L7, L9, L11, etc.), which would not feature in scripted advertising or promotion. This type of eWOM is also very different to testimonials, which are part of standard advertising communication and tend to feature top models and celebrities praising the product and claiming to use it. The video itself is only one part of the communication (see Burgess & Green (2009) and Lange (2007) for an overview of YouTube as a site of complex communication and multiple modes). This video has had 141,139 views, 3,140 likes and 54 dislikes, as well as 161 comments (March 2014). The comments are also an important part of the eWOM process, with posters generally agreeing with her tutorial and praising her looks and use of make-up, for example:

you are so adorableee ! <3 lol I love this video c; thumbs up babygirl c:
U attuly have perfect skin!
Love this video , and how u do ur makeup . . . Thumbs up all the wayy !

However, the nature of YouTube, as a peer-to-peer medium, means that negative or critical comments are also posted and appear along with the video, as the following examples show, which is very different to the traditional type of controlled environment of advertising:

Why did you have mascara on before you put mascara on
Love this look but in your introduction you were eyelinerr , and your not applying that in the look , do you want to do a eyeliner tutorial?
You should have used the oil absorbing sheets BEFORE putting the concealer on because, 1, there is oil on your blemishes, and the concealer covers them up, so the oil stays, and 2, some of your concealer could come off

Individual products are also discussed and commented on by posters, and again this would not happen in a traditional advertising format, which would focus exclusively on one particular product or brand in an attempt to create a strong message. In fact, as we can see from the extract below, posters also offer Lauren advice on her makeup:

If you like lenghtening mascaras you should definitely try the megalenghts mascara by wet in wild its cheap and amazing :)

The posts also feature direct requests to laurensboutique for future content, and in fact, some of them comment on that fact that this video seems to be in response to a previous request.

omg i requested this on your last video and you actually di it (: you're amazing lauren!
Can you do a video like this but with drugstore only products?

YouTube statistics for laurensboutique's channel show that she has uploaded 154 videos with 5,875,315 views, and has 131,491 subscribers to her channel. Even allowing for multiple views by the same person, the number of views shows the reach of these 'howto' videos and their potential to influence the audience, especially given the obvious impact the videos have on the posters, who respond to them as the products of a peer rather than an advertiser. We can see this in the informal style of communication in the posts.

As the extracts above illustrate, there is also a large amount of redundancy in these posts – this, too, is not a feature of traditional advertising, where redundant content is kept to a minimum as advertising space and time are generally at a premium. However, in this digital culture of peer production, these posts and contributions can also be seen to add value:

> You are purf!
> you have beautiful freckles <3
> i love this look Lauren! This is such a great look, and i am in love with your shirt (like can i marry it?)

On the one hand, this seems like free advertising for all those brands lucky enough to feature in laurensboutique's videos. But, as outlined above, eWOM can also be negative – not just for those brands that do not feature, but also where products are evaluated negatively, either by laurensboutique or by the various posters (Pantano & Carvello 2013: 214), and/or where she gets information wrong or makes mistakes (e.g., L20–21 in relation to the L'Oreal mascara). This type of recast would never happen in a traditional advertising message.

The death of distance and the 'many-to-many communications environment' (MacLaren & Cattarell 2002: 320) is also a stressful one for marketers. Positive or negative feedback is as public as the advertising message itself – information about whether a product or advertisement has been viewed and liked, including the comments about the product or advertisement, is available to all. However, we can also see the power of the peer-to-peer communications environment in influencing purchaser. Consider this post by a laurensboutique fan:

> Thanks to you I have purchased the loreal telescopic shocking extensions mascara in water-proof and I absolutely LOVE it!!! :) It makes my eyelashes look super long and really holds the curl, thank you so much <3 Also really cute look on this video :)

What also emerges from examining these transcripts is that many of the posters are regular viewers of laurensboutique's videos and make up the subscriber base. For them, this is not perceived as an advertising communication, it is simply part of their everyday interactions on the web. This points to the challenge the current context poses for marketers, namely to make advertising messages mainstream and normal and place them 'into existing communications between people' (Wilson 2000: 2) rather than making them explicit advertising messages. Although consumers are exposed to exponentially more advertising than previously, they are also in a much stronger position to block these messages. In addition, media usage today is much more tied up in personal relationships, free time, hobbies and interests, entertainment, and leisure. The barriers between traditional media and 'everyday life' were much stronger and less blurred. Therefore, it could be argued that experiencing advertising in traditional media was just part of the medium, which was demarcated from everyday life. However, digital and especially social media are hugely integrated into everyday life: the distinctions between online and offline are much more blurred, and people are more likely to be engaging in personal communication with friends using digital media. Therefore intrusions into this private and/or social space in the form of advertising can be considered much more negatively than, for example, advertising in traditional media (e.g., television, newspapers), which are not an intimate part of people's lives and which they see as clearly detached from themselves. For this reason, 'pull technologies', which give the consumer more control over deciding whether or not to access information (as opposed to 'push technologies' like email, which push messages out to the consumer) are seen to be more appealing and successful in the longer term in winning over consumers. (See Watson, McCarthy, & Rowley 2013 for a study of these issues in relation to smart phones.)

It is worth contrasting this dynamic environment with the rather static, one-to-many-oriented websites of many of the brands mentioned by laurensboutique. For example, the Garnier.com site gives plenty of information, but in a controlled one-to-many context of high production values, conceptualised, proofed and edited text, and slick design. The consumer can access 'expert advice' – not peer advice – on the site. The only question and answer content on the site is in the form of frequently answered questions:

Do self-tanning products prevent 'real' tanning from the sun?

No, not at all, because self-tanning products are not sun-protection products. If you are going in the sun, remember to use a sun-protection product, which can be applied over your self tan without problem.

(www.garnier.com)

This type of polished, edited communication contrasts sharply with the peer production on the laurensboutique channel, which very much mirrors everyday communication on the web and reads like unscripted, spontaneous communication between young people, including mistakes, false starts, repetition, redundancy, etc.

The only interaction encouraged on the Garnier site is for customers to submit a question by email to the site or sign up for a newsletter. It is hard for this kind of mass, impersonalised communication to compete with the bottom-up, 'authentic' communication created on peer-to-peer sites. As Constantinides and Fountain (2008) point out, 'there is evidence that customer reviews posted in different forms on online commentaries, web blogs and podcasts are much more powerful as marketing tools than expert product reviews' (p. 240). However, in the current era marketers need to attend to both: on the one hand, traditional, one-to-many communication is needed in order to get the brand 'out there' and give it credibility, so it is important to have one-to-many corporate sites, if for no other reason than to show that the brand is real and credible; on the other hand, new, interactive, many-to-many communication needs to be attempted and harnessed in order to take advantage of the ways in which people now communicate and to attempt to become an ordinary part of everyday interaction.

Finally, it is important to point out that the consumer also loses an important aspect of control when engaging in online and digital marketing – namely, a loss of control over private data. Using social networks, companies can 'gain knowledge of consumers' past experiences with . . . products as well as their needs and preferences' (Pantano & Corvello 2013: 214). This brings us to our next main topic, the issue of individualisation.

From segmentation to individualisation

As highlighted above, digital marketing in the Web 2.0 and mobile media environment 'permits the promise of relationship marketing, one-to-one marketing and mass customization to be fulfilled . . . [and] allows one-to-one dialogue between marketer and customer' (MacLaren & Cattarell

2002: 319). In fact, Friedman (2005) describes the current era of globalisation (globalisation 3.0, as he terms it) as characterised by the increasing role of the individual, mainly as a result of changes wrought by digital technology. Similarly, 'projects of the self' are widely acknowledged as a key dimension to contemporary life (see Coupland 2010). Not surprisingly, then, the aspiration of the current era in marketing is the 'market of one' (Kumar 2007), where the focus is on individualisation.

Individualisation can be seen as an extreme form of segmentation, which was one of the defining features of – and key reasons for – the development of modern marketing and the evolution of mass consumer markets. Based on economies of scale, the role of marketing was to come up with ideas for products that had widespread appeal and that could be manufactured and sold on a mass scale. With increasing supply, marketing moved towards the creation of niche and specialist markets, using crude segmentation strategies based on location, gender, age, lifestyle, education, etc. Given the relatively high cost of advertising in traditional media such as television and print, the aim was to create a message that would target a composite or ideal individual, representing a much larger group of consumers, a segment of the mass market. The development of digital media, with the technological possibilities it affords, has in many ways reversed this model of marketing.

Two types of individualisation may be identified. In the first of these, personalisation, the marketer personalises the offering to the consumer based on information known about them. The best known and most frequently cited example of personalisation is that of online book and media retailer Amazon. Personalisation works by using 'input about a customer's interests to generate a list of recommended items. Many applications use only the items that customers purchase and explicitly rate to represent their interests, but they can also use other attributes, including items viewed, demographic data, subject interests, and favourite artists' (Linden, Smith, & York 2003: 76). The Amazon.com model uses 'recommendation algorithms to personalize the online store for each customer. The store radically changes based on customer interests, showing programming titles to a software engineer and baby toys to a new mother' (Linden *et al.* 2003: 76). Such techniques are now the basis of many eCommerce websites. Google ads also use this type of tagging to identify likely targets for advertising based on searches carried out using its search engine. The basis of personalisation is the recognition that the web is being constantly fed by users, and that this dynamic allows companies to learn something new about those users every time they go online (Pariser 2012).

The other type of individualisation in marketing is customisation, which is bottom–up and driven or controlled by the consumer. In customisation, the marketer enables the user to customise their product within certain limits and adapt it to their own needs – iGoogle, myyahoo, MyO2, Facebook and YouTube profiles are examples of this type of customisation. Many of these are also used for personalisation, since, for example, Facebook uses algorithms to suggest possible new friends, groups and sites to users. A number of sites combine customisation and personalisation. For example, Flipboard allows individuals to select particular news media and combine them into a personalised 'magazine', as well as using intelligence to select stories that will be of interest to particular individuals. The possibility of customisation means that every web page is slightly different for every individual. Both of these individualisation approaches represent a major departure from the mass marketing and segmentation of previous eras: 'Mass marketing focuses on articulated needs as stated by customers, or the marketer's perception of consumers' articulated needs. Customization focuses on both the articulated and unarticulated needs by guiding the customer through a design and discovery process' (Wind & Rangaswamy 2001: 21). Technology now allows marketers to guide the consumer through a discovery process for satisfying needs which they may not even be conscious aware of: 'They [consumers] cannot say exactly what they want, but know it when they see it. Technology offers ways to give customers product use experiences before the company produces the product' (Wind & Rangaswamy 2001: 21). Thus, marketing and advertising messages have been transformed from 'seller-centric' to 'buyer-centric' (Wind & Rangaswamy 2001: 14).

It is also no coincidence, given the shift toward targeting the individual and away from mass targeting outlined above, that *you* has become the most prominent pronoun in contemporary marketing. In fact, *you* was chosen as *Time* magazine's Person of the Year in 2006 (Grossman 2006). The international site Cafepress is a good example of the potential of individualisation in terms of customisation and personalisation. The site describes itself as follows:

> CafePress is where the world's creative minds join forces to provide an unparalleled marketplace. We give you the power to create custom products and personalised gifts on a variety of high-quality items such as t-shirts, hoodies, posters, bumper stickers and mugs. CafePress also allows you to set up online shops where you can design and sell your own unique merchandise. Our design tools make it easy to add photos, text, images, and even create cool designs or logos from scratch. As if it couldn't get any better, you can even find content from major entertainment partners such as The Hunger Games, Big Bang Theory and Star Trek as well as products dedicated to hobbies, birthdays, the military and more. At CafePress we print each item as it's ordered and many products ship within 24 hours.
>
> *(www.cafepress.com)*

In the description of the business above, we can see a number of the tropes of the digital marketing era: the 24/7 interactivity and availability ('we print each item as it's ordered and many products ship within 24 hours'); the empowering of consumers ('we give you the power to create custom products'); the focus on personalisation; and the treatment of the consumer as an equal ('Cafepress also allows you to set up online shops where you can design and sell your own unique merchandise'). The language and informal style also indicate the blurring of barriers between consumer and marketer ('As if it couldn't get any better'; 'cool designs and logos from scratch'). The extract below shows even more extensive use of this informal lexis for communicating with the consumer ('get sketch-y', 'super-unique', 'take it up a notch', and 'only could've come from you'). The site relies on learned genres of eCommerce and offers all the usual and predictable options and routines of such a site (in terms of the shopping basket, checkout, payment methods etc.). However, its core message is, ironically, an anti-mass marketing one. In addition to all of the standard tabs like 'shop', 'gifts', etc. there is a tab for 'create'. When users click this tab they enter a site with the heading 'Design your own . . . anything'. The text below contains an anti-mass marketing message with a strong focus on empowering the consumer and taking for granted their work and contribution to creating the product:

> Give the gift that really counts. Think personalized gifts and personal style, shirts that celebrate team spirit, family reunion items, or just a way to promote your favorite cause.
>
> *(www.cafepress.com)*

The following extract from the promotional text illustrates many of the assumptions of the current era of globalisation and digital communication, for example, the primacy of projects of the self and the declining value of professional input:

> Ready for super-unique, 'only could've come from you' gift ideas? Give a thought that counts exponentially when you give gifts you create yourself. Time to get sketch-y and design your own T-shirts, pajamas, flip flops, tanks & hats, or maybe phone cases, tote bags, drink ware, stationery and other great gear. You can have designs on (just about) anything you can think of! Add your sense of flair to everyday items like bags and water bottles, or take it up a notch and custom-create jewelry, keepsake boxes and home accessories.

> Make gifts for him, gifts for her, and even 'gifts' for yourself. Just start with your own image, photo or quote, and add it to any product you choose. This is one great way to put your personal stamp on a gift for someone special (or tailor it specifically to that someone special's style). Ready? Personalize!
>
> *(www.cafepress.com)*

Users are encouraged to 'celebrate the designer in you', and this imperative can be seen as a symptom of the current declining value of the role of the professional (Coupland 2010), which has seen a number of previously professional roles becoming devalued and mainstreamed as something ordinary people can do. It is worth reflecting on the extensive use of *you* throughout the site – in the above extract alone, there are five instances of *you*, four of *your*, and two of *yourself*.

A site like Cafepress.com is premised entirely on the working consumer. After all, if consumers are not interested in interacting with brands and with each other in relation to brands, there is no real point in digital marketing based on interaction and exchange. The success of the loss of control model of Web 2.0 marketing is premised on an interested and engaged consumer. Ironically, consumers are demanding increasing levels of customisation and personalisation while at the same time also raising more and more concerns about privacy and the nature and quantity of personalised data that are being gathered about them via the web (Ho 2006).

Personalisation and customisation are also relevant to issues of language choice. Many social networking sites and search engines are practising a type of hyper-differentiation in relation to language, whereby more and more languages are achieving their own bounded spaces and places of use on the web. For example, Facebook is available in Irish, Northern Sámi, and Pirate English, while Google offers its search engine in Klingon, the fictional language of the *Star Trek* science fiction television series and movie franchise. Furthermore, search engines use information about users' geographically based Internet protocol (IP) addresses to tailor user content and trajectories to their assumed linguistic profile. And online translation tools automatically 'warn' users of content in languages other than the one associated with that geographic location, offering to localise the 'foreign' content for them (see Kelly-Holmes 2013 for an overview of issues here).

Research methods and future directions

Researching marketing communication online requires a multi-methods and adaptive approach which virtual ethnography offers (see Domínguez *et al.* 2007; Fay 2007; Greenhow 2011; see also Varis, this volume, for a discussion of digital ethnography). Ethnographic studies are very useful for investigating such mundane and taken-for-granted issues as offerings, options and practices on websites, since an ethnographic sensitivity 'makes explicit the taken-for-granted and often tacit ways in which people make sense of their lives' (Hine 2000: 5). Virtual ethnography allows for a number of possible types of engagement with a range of marketing spaces on the web, from corporate sites to brand communities and eWOM sites: surfing the web while searching for a particular product or brand and logging that surfing experience; observing a particular corporate or eWOM or eCommerce site; lurking (systematic and long-term engagement with a site without open participation, see Paccagnella (1997)) on an eCommerce site or within a brand community. Not every ethnographic study will involve or require all these stages of engagement; the level of engagement should be determined by the research questions and purpose of the study. For some purposes, lurking/observing and downloading/archiving may be sufficient in order to document multilingualism on the web, although interviews with site originators and participants can enhance the data gathered.

A number of studies by marketing theorists have enhanced our understanding of communication in digital environments. For example, Pongsakornrungsilp and Schroeder (2011) carried out a long-term ethnographic study of the ThisIsAnfield (TIA) online community of Liverpool FC football fans in order to examine peer co-production of brand value. This involved observing 'consumer-to-consumer interactions on the TIA community, acting both as a participant and a non-participant with the permission of the site moderators and other members' (p. 308). They formed 'direct relationships with group members', becoming a 'recognized culture member' (Kozinets 2002). One of the authors was a football fan who engaged in the community, while the other author did not – a division of roles which allowed them to maintain both insider and outsider perspectives on their data. The authors downloaded relevant online conversations between members and adopted an iterative approach to analysing the data, categorising the conversations and communications recorded and observed. The study concludes that 'consumers may act as providers and beneficiaries within the value co-creation process, and that the co-consuming group is . . . a source of value or a platform on which consumers may co-create value' (Pongsakornrungsilp & Schroeder 2011: 309). An obvious future direction is for these kinds of studies to converge with studies by communication and sociolinguistic theorists, as marketing studies would benefit from the fine-grained attention to discourse that figures in computer-mediated discourse analysis (e.g., Herring 2004) and in discourse-centred online ethnography (e.g., Androutsopoulos 2008). This is particularly important given the omnipresence of marketing communication in individuals' lives as a consequence of digital marketing. The impact of this normalisation of marketing messages and its implications for communication would be a fruitful area to study.

In addition, the results of various algorithmic processes utilised by marketers will clearly have effects on digital communication, and this is only beginning to be understood. Pariser (2012) outlines how individuals are increasingly guided through the web in 'filter bubbles' – in other words, they only come into contact with sites, information, cultures and even other individuals who are likely to appeal to their digital profile. This is one area in which communication theorists and marketers could profitably collaborate in order to understand how this will impact on our communication in both online and offline contexts.

Related topics

- Chapter 3 Digital ethnography (Varis)
- Chapter 14 Corporate blogging and corporate social media (Puschmann & Hagelmoser)
- Chapter 21 Facebook and the discursive construction of the social network (Tagg & Seargeant)
- Chapter 22 YouTube: language and discourse practices in participatory culture (Androutsopoulos & Tereick)

References

Androutsopoulos, J. 2008, 'Potentials and limitations of discourse-centred online ethnography', *Language@ Internet*, vol. 5, no. 9, available at: http://www.languageatInternet.org/articles/2008/1610.

Bitner, M-J., Brown, S., & Meuter, M. 2000, 'Technology infusion in service encounters', *Journal of the Academy of Marketing Science*, vol. 28, no. 1, pp. 138–149.

Burgess, J. & Green, J. 2009, *YouTube: online video and participatory culture*, Polity: Cambridge, MA.

Constantinides, E. 2002, 'The 4S web-marketing mix model', *Electronic Commerce Research and Applications*, vol. 1, no. 1, pp. 57–76.

Constantinides, E. & Fountain, S. 2008, 'Web 2.0: Conceptual foundations and marketing issues', *Journal of Direct, Data and Digital Marketing Practice*, vol. 9, pp. 231–244.

Coupland, N. 2010, 'Introduction: sociolinguistics in the global era' in Coupland, N. (ed.), *The handbook of language and globalization*, Wiley-Blackwell: Oxford, pp. 1–27.

Cova, B. & Dalli, D. 2009, 'Working consumers: the next step in marketing theory?', *Marketing Theory*, vol. 9, no. 3, pp. 315–339.

Domínguez, D., Beaulieu, A., Estalella, A., Gómez, E., Schnettler, B., & Read, R. 2007, 'Virtual ethnography', *Forum: Qualitative Social Research*, vol. 8, no. 3, pp. 3–7.

Drury, G. 2007, 'Opinion piece: social media: should marketers engage and how can it be done effectively?', *Journal of Direct, Data and Digital Marketing Practice*, vol. 9, no. 3, pp. 274–277.

Fay, M. 2007, 'Mobile subjects, mobile methods: doing virtual ethnography in a feminist online network', *Forum: Qualitative Social Research*, vol. 8, no. 3, article 14.

Friedman, T. 2005, *The world is flat: the globalised world in the twenty-first century*, Penguin: London.

Greenhow, C. M. 2011, 'Research methods unique to digital contexts: an introduction to virtual ethnography', in N. K. Duke & M. H. Mallette (eds.), *Literacy Research Methodologies,* 2nd edn., The Guilford Press: New York, NY, pp.70–86.

Grossman, L. 2006, 'You – yes, you – are TIME's Person of the Year', *Time*, 25 December 2006, available at: http://content.time.com/time/specials/packages/0,28757,2019341,00.html.

Hammill, J. 1997, 'The Internet and international marketing', *International Marketing Review*, vol. 14, no. 5, pp. 300–323.

Herring, S. C. 2004, 'Computer-mediated discourse analysis: an approach to researching online behavior', in S. A. Barab, R. Kling & J. H. Gray (eds.), *Designing for virtual communities in the service of learning*, Cambridge University Press: New York, NY, pp. 338–376.

Hine, C. 2000, *Virtual ethnography*, Sage: London.

Ho, S. Y. 2006, 'The attraction of Internet personalization to web users', *Electronic Markets*, vol. 16, no. 1, pp. 41–50.

Hollenbeck, C. R. & Zinkhan, G. M. 2006, 'Consumer activism on the Internet: the role of anti-brand communities', *Advances in Consumer Research*, vol. 33, pp. 479–485.

Jones, R. H. & Hafner, C. A. 2012, *Understanding digital literacies*, Routledge: London.

Kelly-Holmes, H. 2013, '"Choose your language!" categorisation and control in cyberspace', *Sociolinguistica*, vol. 27, pp. 132–145.

Kozinets, R. V. (2002) 'The field behind the screen: using netnography for marketing research in online communities', *Journal of Marketing Research,* vol. 39, no. 1, pp. 61–72.

Kumar, A. 2007, 'From mass customization to mass personalization: a strategic transformation', *International Journal of Flexible Manufacturing Systems*, vol. 19, no. 4, pp. 533–547.

Lange, P. A. 2007, 'Publicly private and privately public: social networking on YouTube', *Journal of Computer-Mediated Communication*, vol. 13, no. 1, pp. 361–380.

Linden, G., Smith, B., & York, J. 2003, 'Amazon.com recommendations: item-to-item collaborative filtering', *IEEE Internet Computing*, January-February 2003, pp. 76–80.

MacLaren, P. & Cattarell, M. 2002, 'Researching the social web: marketing information from virtual communities', *Marketing Intelligence and Planning*, vol. 20, no. 6, pp. 319–326.

Paccagnella, L. 1997, 'Getting the seat of your pants dirty: strategies for ethnographic research on virtual communities', *Journal of Computer Mediated Communication*, vol. 3, no. 1.

Pantano, E. & Corvello, V. 2013, 'The impact of experience on companies' reactions to negative comments on social networks', *Journal of Direct, Data and Digital Marketing Practice*, vol. 14, pp. 214–223.

Pariser, E. 2012, *The filter bubble: how the new personalized web is changing what we read and how we think*, Penguin: New York, NY.

Pongsakornrungsilp, S. & Schroeder, J. E. 2011, 'Understanding value co-creation in a co-consuming brand community', *Marketing Theory*, vol. 11, no. 3, pp. 303–324.

Ström, R., Vendel, M., & Bredican, J. 2014, 'Mobile marketing: a literature review on its value for consumers and retailers', *Journal of Retailing and Consumer Services*, available at: http://dx.doi.org/10.1016/j.jretconser.2013.12.003i.

Watson, C., McCarthy, J., & Rowley, J. 2013, 'Consumer attitudes towards mobile marketing in the smart phone', *International Journal of Information Management*, vol. 33, no. 5, pp. 840–849.

Wilson, R. F. 2000, 'The six simple principles of viral marketing', *Web Marketing Today*, 2000, available at: http://webmarketingtoday.com/articles/viral-principles/ [accessed 10 October 2014].

Wind, J. & Rangaswamy, A. 2001, 'Customerization: the next revolution in mass customization', *Journal of Interactive Marketing*, vol. 15, no. 1, pp. 13–32.

Zwick, D., Bonsu, S. K., & Darmody, A. 2008, 'Putting consumers to work: "co-creation" and new marketing govern-mentality', *Journal of Consumer Culture*, vol. 8, no. 2, pp. 163–196.

Further reading

Constantinides, E. & Fountain, S. 2008, 'Web 2.0: conceptual foundations and marketing issues', *Journal of Direct, Data and Digital Marketing Practice*, vol. 9, pp. 231–244.

This article gives an overview of the development of digital marketing and the impact of technological change on marketing thinking and theory.

Hine, C. 2008, 'Virtual ethnography: modes, varieties, affordances', in N. G. Fielding, R. M. Lee, & G. Blank (eds.), *The SAGE handbook of online research methods*, Sage: London, pp. 257–270.

This provides an updated and abbreviated introduction to Hine's (2000) study, explaining the methods of virtual ethnography.

Pariser, E. 2012, *The filter bubble: how the new personalized web is changing what we read and how we think*, Penguin: New York, NY.

This book explains how personalisation happens on the web and how our online behaviour feeds marketing intelligence.

Pongsakornrungsilp, S. & Schroeder, J. E. 2011, 'Understanding value co-creation in a co-consuming brand community', *Marketing Theory*, vol. 11, pp. 303–324.

This provides a methodological and theoretical review of marketing studies of online consumer communities and a detailed reporting of one case.

14

Corporate blogging and corporate social media

Cornelius Puschmann and Rebecca Hagelmoser

Introduction

Social media increasingly plays a significant role not only in interpersonal communication, but also in the electronic discourse between corporations, public institutions, NGOs, and private individuals. In the course of the last decade, blogging, microblogs and social networking sites (SNS) have become increasingly mainstream instruments of corporate communication (Kaplan & Haenlein 2010). Social media have proven to be versatile tools in a variety of functions (marketing, PR, lobbying, recruiting, knowledge management), yet they also challenge the stakeholders involved in their use and force them to develop new communicative approaches. Companies are under pressure to reconcile new ways of sharing and socialising with their established communications strategies. They must appear as competent sociocommunicative actors and minimise a potential loss of face, while also showing that they 'get' social media.

In this chapter we will discuss corporate blogs and corporate social media and examine how both have adjusted to the institutional needs of their users. We discuss the setting of organisational communication as the backdrop against which corporate social media is used and outline the historical development that corporate blogs have taken. We then turn to some of the critical issues related to corporate social media that have been raised in current research from discourse analysis, communication studies and media studies, as well as in business and organisational studies. Finally, we discuss genre analysis and narrative analysis as important methodological instruments for the study of corporate social media and discuss the case of the Whole Foods Blog as an example of how strategic communication is conducted in a blog. We close by providing a brief outlook on future developments in corporate social media.

Definitions

Weil (2006) defines corporate blogging as 'the use of blogs [by business professionals] to further organizational goals' (p. 1). Weil's book was one of the earliest publications on corporate blogging aimed at business practitioners and offering a hands-on approach to social media. Blogs had yet to become widespread at the time, and the observation that they could be productively adopted for institutional communication, rather than for personal aims, was less obvious than it may seem today. Online presence in social media such as Facebook and Twitter is increasingly seen as a requirement for global businesses, especially with regards to branding and public relations (Kaplan & Haenlein 2010). The speed and ease of disseminating information and responding to criticism makes social media essential to any business, and especially to consumer companies with significant brand exposure. Blogs and other social media channels are socio-technical entities which are adopted by different actors to reach out to different audiences and serve a range of purposes.

Corporate social media is strategically deployed by companies, rather than taken up out of curiosity or for entertainment, as is most frequently the case with private users. Institutional communication is characterised by a strong emphasis on strategic aims, which are pursued by professionals (marketers, public relations experts) and are generally stable and consistent over a long period of time (Horton 1995). While individuals are equally goal-oriented when they communicate, their aims are more likely to be immediate or short-term, and less clearly articulated and reflected. Private interpersonal communication often revolves around the negotiation of social relationships, and identity management through the expression of thoughts or emotions plays an equally central role (Walther 2007). By contrast, in institutional contexts the goals of individuals are superseded by those of the organisation (winning customers, increasing profits, cutting costs), all of which are long-term and require concerted action. From this vantage point, a series of assumptions can be made about organisational communication:

- Organisational communication is distinctively goal-oriented.
- There is a tendency towards explicitness and structure that coincides with more explicit goal-orientation.
- Meta-language is often used to talk about the communicative process itself.
- Specialised lexis (jargon) is often used, especially in internal communication.

According to Horton (1995), corporate communication can be divided at the most basic level into intra-organisational and extra-organisational discourse, then further separated into internal communication between colleagues, departments, and employees of different influence; and external communication with customers (existing and potential), partners, and the general public. This model also reflects the basic dichotomy of corporate-internal and corporate-external communication, which is significant in the context of blogging. Other salient factors include:

- Who communicates (e.g., CEO, sales manager, software engineer)?
- Who is the intended audience (e.g., customers, investors, government regulators)?
- In what mode (e.g., spoken, written, technologically mediated)?
- What is the genre (e.g., advertisement, mission statement)?

These factors shape and constrain organisational communication in specific ways and provide the backdrop against which corporate blogs should be evaluated and understood. The emergence of corporate social media can be regarded both as the appropriation of a personal mode of expression for organisational purposes, and as a conscious reaction on the part of companies to the novel communicative setting of the Internet. Traditional corporate-to-public communication is generally highly vetted, planned and shaped by organisational goals. The realisation of such goals is not simply a side effect, but constitutes the core motivation behind communicating with external stakeholders (customers, competitors, regulators) in all circumstances. Following Horton (1995), discourse surrounding business transactions (marketing) is the most archetypal form of external corporate communication and has the simultaneous goals of providing customers with information about a product and persuading them to purchase it. In traditional mass media, such discourse lacks the interactional element of interpersonal communication, but in social media, these elements are consciously mixed and intertwined. In what follows, we describe some of the stylistic properties and rhetorical functions of corporate blogs in organisational settings.

Historical perspectives

Corporate blogging and corporate social media are offshoots of personal blogging (Puschmann 2013). Estimates of the total number of corporate blogs vary, but it can be assumed that they do not exceed 10 per cent of the global population of well over 100 million blogs (Halzack 2008; Sobel 2010). Puschmann (2010) based his research on a corpus of 137 English-language company blogs operated by large multinational companies – a limited picture of the global population of corporate blogs, especially in relation to the strong growth of online content in languages other than English.

Historically, corporate blogging evolved from employee blogging. In their study of employee blogging at Microsoft, Efimova and Grudin noted that corporate blogging is a term 'which suggests action that is authorized, acknowledged, or in a formal way associated with an organization' (2007: 2), a characteristic not universally applicable to employee blogging. The authors describe the genesis of blogs at Microsoft that began in 2000 and 2001 with the externally hosted blogs of interns and newly hired employees. An internal blog platform was launched as a grass-roots effort, as was a curated list of employee blogs in 2002, which finally led to the establishment of a company-wide blog network. Today, blogs are tightly integrated into MSDN (Microsoft Developer Network), the company's developer knowledge management platform. The changes occurred gradually and incrementally and were initially relatively independent from any central planning mechanism.

While there is no historically precise account of who started the first employee blog in the sense described by Efimova and Grudin (2007), it is plausible to assume that a similar evolutionary process – from scattered private blogs of junior staff to blogs jointly hosted on corporate servers – took place in a similar fashion at other software companies such as IBM, Sun, Adobe and Oracle, all of which today maintain large employee blog hubs (portal sites where employee blogs are hosted) that bundle the content from several thousand individual blogs. The style and content of early employee blogs approximated those of private blogs, specifically the filter variety (blogs that filter news and other informative content based on the interests of the author). In Efimova and Grudin's description, corporate blogging that had been adjusted to management guidelines followed quietly on the heels of these early practices: 'By mid-2003, a server hosting externally visible weblogs was operating. Because some managers perceived a benefit in using weblogs to communicate with customers, this server had formal budget support' (2007: 3). A recurring theme in usage-based research on employee blogging is the persistent tension between organisational goals and personal preferences, both in relation to the corporate hierarchy and among employees (Agerdal-Hjermind 2014). Interpretations of what goals a set of company blogs should achieve vary strongly, posing significant challenges to management.

Blogging proved to seamlessly complement software development as knowledge-intensive and highly specialised work: writing software and writing *about* writing software fit together extremely well. At the same time, as blogging expanded into other sectors beyond coding, senior management keenly felt the difficulties of merging an organic blog movement that had evolved from the bottom up with a top-down structured communications hierarchy. Efimova and Grudin (2007) describe the conflicting perspectives on corporate blogging between two corporate vice presidents at a technology company (p. 4). While one supported blogging as a way of presenting the company as open and transparent, the other was initially sceptical, feeling that blogs upset the corporate organisational structure by creating a stage for self-appointed spokespeople.

These issues became magnified as blog audiences grew from small and reasonably intimate circles to mass audiences. There have been incidents of employee bloggers being fired for disclosing confidential company information in their blogs. This phenomenon is part of the larger new theme of 'doocing' – to lose one's job because of one's website – associated with various forms of user-generated content on the Net (Lorenz 2005; Wallack 2005). However, the enthusiasm for novel technology and the need to optimise both internal knowledge flow and customer service led managers to support rather than hinder the proliferation of blogs. Corporate leadership recognised that employees' blogs had better business potential when presented to the public; blogs kept exclusively private offered less potential for control and none of the corporate benefits. This realisation led the software industry to adopt a strategy of 'extend and embrace', providing a technical infrastructure and a basic behavioural code (called blogging guidelines or blogging policies) for employees to follow, together with continuous measurement and reviews of the perceived risks and benefits of employee blogging.

Two other processes increased the popularity of blogs in a business context: a crisis in the perception of public-facing corporate discourse, and a general trend towards personalisation and 'democratisation' in the relationship between institutions and individuals. One impetus for the latter trend may have been *The Cluetrain Manifesto*, a dual book and open-access Internet publication by Rick Levine, Christopher Locke, Doc Searls and David Weinberger (2000). The book consisted of 95 theses challenging widely held practices and assumptions about mass marketing and the relationship between corporations and consumers in a tone reminiscent of political activism. While this kind of enthusiasm is likely to have since died down, the practical utility of corporate blogs and social media, not only for marketing and PR, but also for internal knowledge management, is widely recognised, not only because these corporate media support the claim that marketing has reinvented itself in a more egalitarian communicative environment, but also because social media is increasingly superior to broadcast media for targeting younger target groups.

Another issue that gave rise to corporate adoption of social media is trust. In a study conducted by a U.S. public relations company, 68 per cent of the American respondents named 'a person like me' as the person they would trust most as a source of information on a company, outranking corporate and political leaders, public institutions, and academia as trusted sources (Edelman 2008). This marked a significant shift from 2003, when only 20 per cent nominated 'a person like me' (Edelman 2006). In the 2008 poll, peers outranked experts and institutions in Brazil, Canada, Germany, the Netherlands, Spain, Sweden and the United States, while financial experts ranked at the top in France, India, Ireland, Mexico, Poland, South Korea and the United Kingdom, and academics were most trusted in Italy, Japan, Russia and Spain (Edelman 2008: 6). The study highlights the importance of direct recommendations and 'word of mouth' marketing in social networks rather than traditional approaches. The boom in digital interpersonal communication via the Internet – both within existing networks of friends and family and among strangers – arguably goes hand in hand with at least a partial erosion of trust in institutional sources of information. Based on the study, the authors formulate the following advice for corporate communicators:

> Share your content with your employees, passionate consumers, and bloggers, allowing them to co-create, repurpose, and improve their knowledge through dialogue. Change your tone from one that pronounces to one that invites participation, ceding some control in return for credibility.
>
> *(Edelman 2008: 5)*

The advice to 'change your tone from one that pronounces to one that invites participation' and to 'cede some control' is based on the impression that only a communicative style that emphasises parity and equality can succeed. While Edelman's focus is on public relations and not marketing, the message is similar: corporate actors should emulate the socio-communicative behaviour of their customers to gain trust and be perceived as competent partners and not manipulators. The issue is not seen primarily as ethical but rather as behavioural: communicate differently and you will be perceived differently.

As the examples in the following sections show, company blogs are consciously used for the purpose of reinventing and redressing the interactions between corporations and their external stakeholders. Blogs, both from a purely technical perspective and because of the social practices they foster, represent a suitable platform for achieving this goal. The inherent assumption in public-facing corporate blogging is that the crisis postulated by *Cluetrain* and reflected in the loss of trust in established corporate communicators and genres can be overcome by adapting to a new environment and its practices. Using an external blog to address a wide variety of stakeholders (potential and existing customers, potential employees, public officials, interest groups) means being on par with the perceived democratic nature of the blogosphere; it also opens the door to a number of new challenges.

Critical issues and topics

What are the precise incentives for corporations to blog? While the goal of connecting more effectively with outside stakeholders is apparent, the exact motivations are varied and depend crucially on the target audience, on communicative goals and on how the individual company conceptualises blogging.

One reason to blog – at least initially – may be to simply follow a trend, with no clear knowledge of how blogging contributes to the achievement of specific organisational goals. In a study conducted by agencies Porter-Novelli and Cymfony, nearly two-thirds of respondents stated that their company began its first blog not to satisfy a specific need, but because of 'pressure to participate in the medium' (Hirsch & Nail 2006: 7). The advice given by consultants, which is often vague and based on stereotyped claims about the changing discourse environment, reflects this hype to join in without clear objectives. Weil claims that as blogging has emerged as a new way of interacting with a company's stakeholders, the way to lead a conversation has turned from 'packaged, filtered, controlled' to 'open, two-way, less than perfect' (2006: xvi). This observation points toward the notion of a changed environment that demands adaptation from corporate actors and justifies the targeted use of blogs for companies. However, it is clear that blogging and the move towards social media in general are broader phenomena that institutions need to pay attention to, if they do not wish to lose touch with their external stakeholders.

To meet the demands of interpersonal communication between corporation and consumer, corporate blogs often opt to let individuals communicate on behalf of the organisation. Yet this poses its own risks for companies, as the individual blogger may become too powerful in his role as spokesperson, or his personal goals may run counter to the strategic objectives of the company. Corporate blogging guidelines and other codes of conduct are implemented to prevent such issues, and many company blogs are written by teams, not single authors, to prevent any conflicts arising. The need to personalise communication in an environment that demands uniformity is challenging because of the increasing complexity of objectives that form the *raison d'être* of external corporate communications. Companies need to constantly balance the need for authenticity and appropriate marketing strategies against the conflicts arising from this gap for the blogging employee.

Corporate blogs written in an accessible or informal style borrow from the personal and subjective character of personal blogs, which makes them available to a readership that does not necessarily consist of experts. A subjective perspective transforms corporate blog posts from a collection of formal, distant press releases to a set of informal and more emotional experiences.

Corporate blogs are generally created with the objective of furthering organisational goals. However, since a variety of goals exist and many individuals from different departments and branches can potentially be involved, the corporate blog is far from being a single, clearly delineated genre. Instead, it branches out into different subtypes that address different communicative needs, are aimed at different reader communities, and are written by different departments inside an organisation. Zerfaß (2005) points this out in an early study and proposes a typology of corporate blogs, first differentiating topic-oriented and personal blogs. The types he presents are related closely to a set of organisational goals: internal communication, market communication, and public relations. Since Zerfaß's (2005) study, companies have gained more experience with new forms of embedding, streaming, sharing and socialising. They have developed strategies to react to criticism and quickly disseminate information. As the University of Massachusetts's 2012 Inc. 500 Social Media Report shows, the numbers of fast-growing companies running a corporate blog rose to 44 per cent from 37 per cent a year before (Barnes & Lescault 2012). The report also shows an increase in the use of social media: in 2012, LinkedIn has taken the lead as platform most used by these companies (81 per cent), whereas the use of Facebook has decreased. Twitter is the third most commonly used platform (67 per cent) among the 500 fastest growing private companies in the United States.

Current contributions and research

Researchers from a variety of fields have approached corporate social media and corporate blogging with different questions and using different methods. Early research examined aspects such as the role of workplace email for internal communication (Sproul & Kiesler 1986) or the disclosure of financial information online (Craven & Marston 1999). Kaplan and Haenlein (2010) note the potential of social media for redefining organisational communication and provide a set of guidelines for companies seeking to integrate social media strategically.

In a comprehensive approach to corporate blogging, Zerfaß (2005) outlines more specific features. Like Weil, Zerfaß emphasises that a clear strategic objective is required for a company blog. Thus, while personal blogs can be characterised by lack of a fixed external purpose, corporate blogs are not viable without explicit communicative goals. Blogging cuts across the organised and structured processes of internal communication, market communication, network communication and public relations that form the framework within which corporate communication takes place. This makes blogging difficult to plan and control, which runs counter to the assumed prerequisite of concerted organisational action. In corporate blogging, it can be difficult to determine the author, the addressee, and the overall tone of communication. It must be clear who is communicating, who is addressed and how the communication is conducted, but the stability of these factors is undermined in blogging, since anyone can create or consume a blog; and the content and style of corporate blogs are largely in the hands of individual employees who may feel unprepared to achieve strategic objectives through blogging. The degree of organisational purposefulness intrinsically required for corporate blogs is therefore extremely hard to combine with the prototypical characteristics of private personal blogs. This situation thus calls for a reconceptualisation of corporate blogs along the lines of topic blogging and publishing, where topic and the addressee are two distinct (albeit overlapping) considerations. It is possible to subsume a range of activities and goals ranging from knowledge management to product promotion and crisis de-escalation.

Before a blog can be launched, five steps should be taken by practitioners, according to Zerfaß:

- Practitioners should make themselves familiar with blogs and post/message feeds to gain an understanding of the format.
- A form of blog monitoring should be implemented to control the blog and measure its success.
- Opinion leaders and critics should be identified.
- Companies should gain experience by launching a non-public blog on the company intranet.
- If prior experiences are positive, a public-facing blog on the Internet can be launched.

Such a measured and careful approach reflects organisational considerations for coherence and sustainability. Since they have much more to lose by unsuccessful ventures into the blogosphere than individuals, corporations must plan step by step how they want to implement blogs. Similar suggestions for the successful integration of planned corporate blogging into a company's corporate communications strategy are given by countless marketing and public relations experts, new media consultants and researchers with backgrounds in communication studies and economics. However, two core recommendations offered by Zerfaß – adopting a form of blog monitoring and identifying (and addressing) opinion leaders and critics – are more problematic than they initially appear. Despite attempts to measure the impact of blogs, questions remain regarding how well any metric, list of stakeholders, or feedback sample can capture the actual quality of response given by the readership.

Puschmann (2010) proposes a typology of different blog types based on communicative function. The typology is based on authorship, assumed function, and suggested audience. It identifies shared communicative purposes that we infer from the description given in the blogs themselves, as well as the aims that are associated with them. Table 14.1 summarises different types based on these parameters. Neither Zerfaß's nor Puschmann's taxonomy is by any means the only way to categorise corporate blogs. However, authorship appears to be a good predictor of a blog's aims insofar as specific corporate units have the task of conducting certain kinds of strategic communication such as marketing and public relations. This in turn has implications both for the envisaged target audience and the goals associated with blogging.

Main research methods

In the studies discussed above, an important role is assigned to genre analysis as a methodological framework for the study of corporate social media. *Genre theory* is a popular approach in disciplines studying recurring patterns in language use and communication, because it offers an explanation for the typified nature of discourse and for the specific norms that evolve as genres become culturally entrenched (Bhatia 2002; Freadman 2012; Swales 1990). Genres are recurring textual patterns used by specific communities for a set of communicative goals. Swales (1990) argues that a shared concept of genre 'helps to clarify relationships between texts and media, as well as between texts and society' (p. 948). Organisational discourse in particular is strongly shaped by genre, as a result of its transactional nature (Yates & Orlikowski 1992). A complex organisation can only function if there are rules of form and style imposed on various formats of communication, both inside a company and in interaction with consumers, competitors and

Table 14.1 Different functional types of corporate blogs

Corporate blog type	Department	Target audience	Functions
Product blog	Marketing, customer service	Consumers	a) to promote a product directly b) to generate a discussion centred on the product c) to address issues closely related to the company's products d) to provide customer support
Image/lobbying blog	Public relations/ communications	Consumers / focal group	a) to create a positive public perception of a company b) to actively shape the public discussion of a company and its products c) to advance company interests in regards to policy (lobbying) d) to preempt or react to criticism (crisis management)
Recruitment blog	Human resources	Potential employees	a) to capture the interest of potential employees b) to communicate directly with potential employees and respond to their questions
Executive blog	Management	Consumers, investors, partners	a) to discuss the position of the corporation and its products in the market b) to evaluate competitors and their products c) legitimate management decisions such as layoffs, restructuring, expansion, etc. d) to outline future strategic goals
Knowledge blog	Subject-matter expert	Other small/ medium enterprises	a) to share specialised knowledge in a subject matter (e.g. engineering/software development/hardware r and d) with stakeholders inside or outside of the company b) to seek information and advice from other experts about such issues c) as as a mnemonic instrument for the author

other stakeholders (Berkenkotter & Huckin 1995). More recent approaches to genre theory include social actors, their communicative goals and the texts they produce in a model of underlying communicative principles that govern specific types of interaction. The mutual recognition of the forms that genres take is essential to discourse participants who need to anticipate the aims and expectations of communicative partners, especially online (Lüders, Prøitz & Rasmussen 2010). Weil's definition emphasises the goal-oriented nature of corporate blogs and hints at the fact that the corporate blog forms a sub-genre which, like other forms of corporate communication, is subject to its own communicative situations and conditions.

Narrative analysis provides a second analytical lens for the study of corporate social media (Bamberg & Georgakopoulou 2008; Georgakopoulou 2006). Digital narrativity and corporate blogging not only present a challenge for website owners who have to adapt to new developments, but also for the recipients who need to adapt their narrative competence in order to read stories that are largely composed of multimodal content and characterised by a high degree of interactivity. In a similar vein, Ryan (2006: 11) stresses the multimodal character of digital narratives when she argues that 'the property of being a narrative can be predicated of any semiotic object produced with the Internet to evoke a story to the mind of the audience', noting the interplay between storytellers and readers in digital environments. According to Ryan, the narrative potential of a text is perceived individually and the recipient takes an active role in turning the offered information into a meaningful narrative.

Storytelling offers the opportunity to enrich corporate strategy with emotional and adaptive impressions through interaction, as the technical affordances of Internet communication allow narratives to spread across different social media platforms that may be only loosely linked. This migration of stories can establish, preserve and strengthen corporate identity on the Internet. A narrative following a canonical structure may not succeed in holding its audience's attention, as users find their way through webpages according to their individual interests, with links diverting them toward various competing narratives. Nevertheless, transmedial strategies try to align the different self-representational channels and tools on relevant websites and social media, so they can be associated with the company or its brands.

Quite often, a transmedia approach is taken when placing products in various channels in order to reach the target audience wherever they are mostly likely to engage. In addition to increasing reach, this adds a medial subtext specific to the respective contribution; as Jenkins (2006) notes, 'stories . . . unfold across multiple media platforms, with each medium making distinctive contributions to our understanding of the world' (p. 334).

A case study: the Whole Foods Market blog

As we argued in the previous sections, it is the combination of personal and organisational goals that we encounter in organisational blogs that makes them stand apart as a distinct (sub)genre. Particularly in cases where 'tellable' incidents are told from a personal point of view, storytelling must be seen as an essential element of the blogging strategy. Bruner (1991) highlighted the importance of storytelling for the shaping of identity, and since then there has been extensive research on how companies actually tell stories in digital environments (Boje 2009; Gabriel 2008). Today, storytelling has established itself as a marketing technique intended to associate the company with specific values. The corporate blog is a tool that can be easily used for storytelling strategies, as this genre adapts to narrative purposes as well as to informational purposes; further, its use of combined media can reach multiple target groups efficiently and effectively.

In this section, we discuss the Whole Foods Market blog as an example of how a corporate blog can be strategically deployed. The chain of Whole Foods grocery stores runs three corporate blogs: the 'Whole Story', 'John Mackey's Blog', and 'Walter Robb's Blog'. The 'Whole Story' is a topic blog focussing on the presentation of different stores and discussing topics like whole food nutrition, sustainable ways of living, environmentally responsible products, recipes, etc. A team of bloggers updates this blog almost daily, and though the blog offers no information on whether there is a permanent team of bloggers, it does provide links to short profiles of each contributor. Another topic blog, named after CEO John Mackey ('John Mackey's Blog'), focuses on conscious capitalism and other topics related to the conjunction between corporate responsibility and business. Despite the blog's title, it is evident from the headings of each post that employee Kate Lowery has authored most of the posts. However, the CEO appears in this blog as an interviewee and/or as a figure of authority writing or lecturing on the topic of conscious capitalism.

Co-CEO Walter Robb and COO A. C. Gallo run a third blog entitled 'Walter Robb's Blog' which primarily posts announcements concerning the brand Whole Foods Market, reports about formal speeches and keynotes, etc. According to Table 14.1, the three blogs are representatives of the executive ('John Mackey's Blog', 'Walter Robb's Blog') and image

('Whole Story') blog types. According to Zerfaß's typology, their organisational goals range from 'persuasion and the coverage of important topics' to 'market communication'. By raising issues pertaining to 'a sustainable way of life', 'corporate responsibility' or the Whole Foods company in general, the company covers a wide range of topics related to what is considered to be a sustainable, responsible and healthy lifestyle. Covering these topics works to align the brand with these specific concepts, thereby constructing a corporate identity that brands these topics as the values of the company. Similarly, these values shape the company's storytelling strategy, which is also carried out through corporate blogging. By linking the stories told on a corporate blog with central goals and values, storytelling becomes an important aspect of the corporate communications strategy. Blogs by employees and CEOs on topics largely aligned with the company's core values contribute to the construction of an image where everybody works towards a shared higher value that can be identified with the brand.

The following example from the Whole Foods Market blog shows how this impression can be achieved through the stories a company shares with its followers and readers.

> One of my greatest passions, other than food, is riding motorcycles. I love it even though it is not exactly the most carbon-neutral activity. Sure, the gas mileage is better than a car, but there is always room for improvement. That's where the Brammo Enteria electric motorcycle comes in.
>
> *(posted by Chad Lott, March 26, 2013)*

The example above appears under the blog category 'environmental stewardship' and narrates the experience of a blogger with an electric motorcycle. Although the issue of electric motorcycling is not explicitly linked with nutrition, it falls within the range of topics related to a sustainable and responsible lifestyle, making such a story 'tellable' in the specific context. But the commercial purpose of the post has not been forgotten, as a link to the motorcycle manufacturing company is embedded within the first third of the post, in the form of the blogger's meta-comment: 'Note: I received no compensation from Brammo other than the use of their motorcycle'. The rest of the blog post focuses on the advantages and the disadvantages of the motorcycle from the blogger's first-person perspective. As suggested before, the presence of a human protagonist and the narration of their experiences transform a product-focused press-release or commercial into a more personal and emotional description of a real-life experience. It is thus the first-person perspective that contributes significantly to the emotional effect of a blog post. As Uri Margolin points out,

> Every 'I' sayer has by definition immediate epistemic access to his or her own sensations, mental states and episodes. On the other hand, any 'we' sayer who makes assertions such as 'we felt that . . . ' or 'our current state of mind is . . . ' combines in fact immediate inside knowledge as regards his/her own internal states with beliefs (second or third person attributions), based upon inference from external data, concerning the internal states of the other individuals in the 'we' reference class.
>
> *(1996: 117)*

It is this distinction between first-person 'I-narratives' and 'we-narratives' that makes a corporate blog post written in first-person singular appear more authentic than a blog post written in a 'we-narrative' mode. While the 'I-narrative' appears to be rooted to the experiences of the speaker, the 'we-narrative' is more open to interpretation as to who exactly feels, sees or describes.

Although an individual, first-person perspective contributes to the credibility and perceived authenticity of a blog, the reporting of commonly valued actions through a 'we-narrative' mode can contribute to feelings of affiliation with wider norms and communities. The following post is categorised as 'Company Info' and is part of the series 'Our Hidden Gems.' This series of interview posts introduces local branches by interviewing the leader of the marketing team. The team leader answers questions about the store, the best team member, the tastiest dish offered, and any common activities team members share. The questions invite a 'we narration' and contribute to the creation of a shared corporate identity.

At the same time, such interviews enable the global website to show how the globally predefined goals and values are transferred into the local branches and how these goals and values (positively) affect the everyday life of the team members.

> We've just opened HWY, our licensed bar, and the bar menu features a fantastic pulled pork sandwich and has a great selection of local beers and wines. We also have a green roof made of sedum [. . .] and reclaimed wood panelling that covers the front walls of the store [. . .]
>
> *(posted by Elizabeth Beal, March 26, 2013)*

The interview on Whole Foods Blog shows that various strategies – storytelling, commercially oriented interviews, personal reports – are used to establish and reinforce a corporate identity. With key topics framing the company's overall narrative, individual storytelling about experiences connected to these topics shapes and projects the company's identity. While individual perspectives contribute to a more authentic picture of the company, global actions like the county-wide lead interview series show that global values and goals are individually played out in local branches.

Future directions

Blogging has established itself as a tried and tested instrument of corporate communication. At the same time, companies are expanding their strategic communication to Social Networking Sites (SNS) such as Facebook and LinkedIn, and microblogging services such as Twitter. These platforms make use of basic structural elements that are quite similar to blogs, while offering the advantage of a large-scale centralised infrastructure and interface. The pre-set design of SNS offers few possibilities to personalise sites, as the major part of available service is strictly defined, but this also has advantages for users and for companies, as it presents pre-set combinations of multiple modes (texts, images, video clips) across different platforms.

The continuing diversification in corporate social media is a reaction to growing numbers of Internet users globally and to a diversification of devices and platforms. Apps are increasingly integrated within a company's multimedia portfolio, and the new standard for corporate websites is responding to demand for content that can be easily read and navigated on smart phones. Companies increasingly realise the impact of tweeted news, publicised 'likes', and shared and uploaded content, and they encourage their followers and fans to share their opinions, pictures and videos related to the brand. With followers and fans engaging with the brand, companies are constantly interacting with consumers in a variety of digital contexts. Beyond medial diversification, aspects such as cultural differences in the usage of social media must be accounted for, as the Internet increasingly establishes itself in emerging markets (Jeon, Yoon & Kim 2008).

Whether directly embedded and integrated via newsfeeds on the corporate website or connected via hyperlink, different social media platforms have become seamlessly integrated into company websites. As a result, web strategies have become more complex, coordinating many platforms at once, and this development has opened up new possibilities and genres that a company can use for self-representation. Genres on the Internet quickly adapt to new trends; new media formats emerge as well as new ways of narrating stories. Like no other medium, the Internet assimilates new media formats and furthers the process of remediation, in which 'hypermedia applications (. . .) import earlier media into a digital space in order to critique or fashion them' (Bolter & Grusin 2000: 53). Corporate blogs have already taken this step and have merged typical business narratives, like reports, with the Internet-specific phenomenon of blogging – which is itself a re-mediated genre, if you consider its often-stated diary-like quality. Like no other medium, the Internet draws on various semiotic modes in a fragmented, sequenced and simultaneous way.

Related topics

- Chapter 1 Approaches to language variation (Hinrichs)
- Chapter 12 Digital media in workplace interaction (Darics)
- Chapter 13 Digital advertising (Kelly-Holmes)
- Chapter 20 Online communities and communities of practice (Angouri)
- Chapter 21 Facebook and the discursive construction of the social network (Tagg & Seargeant)

References

Agerdal-Hjermind, A. 2014, 'Organizational blogging: a case study of a corporate weblog from an employee perspective', *Corporate Communications: An International Journal*, vol. 19, no. 1, pp. 34–51, doi:10.1108/CCIJ-09-2012-0066.

Bamberg, M. & Georgakopoulou, A. 2008, 'Small stories as a new perspective in narrative and identity analysis', *Text & Talk*, vol. 28, no. 3, pp. 377–396, doi:10.1515/TEXT.2008.018.

Barnes, N. G. & Lescault, A. M. 2012, 'Social media settles in among the 2012 Inc. 500', Center for Marketing Research, University of Massachusetts Dartmouth, available at: https://www.umassd.edu/cmr/socialmediaresearch/2012inc500/.

Berkenkotter, C. & Huckin, T. N. 1995, *Genre knowledge in disciplinary communication: cognition, culture, power*, Lawrence Erlbaum Associates: Hillsdale, NJ.

Bhatia, V. K. 2002, 'Applied genre analysis: a multi-perspective model', *Ibérica*, vol. 4, no. 1, pp. 3–19.

Boje, D. M. 2009, *Storytelling organizations*, Sage: London.

Bolter, J. D. & Grusin, R. 2000, *Remediation: understanding new media*, MIT Press: Cambridge, MA.

Bruner, J. 1991, 'The narrative construction of reality', *Critical Inquiry*, vol. 18, no. 1, pp. 1–21, doi:10.1086/448619.

Craven, B. M. & Marston, C. L. 1999, 'Financial reporting on the Internet by leading UK companies', *European Accounting Review*, vol. 8, no. 2, pp. 321–333, doi:10.1080/096381899336069.

Edelman 2008, '2008 annual Edelman trust barometer', available at: http://www.edelman.com/assets/uploads/2014/01/2008-Trust-Barometer-Executive-Summary.pdf [accessed June 17, 2015].

Edelman 2006, '2006 annual Edelman trust barometer', available at: http://www.edelman.pl/en/trust/siodma_edycja/FullSupplement_final.pdf [accessed June 17, 2015].

Efimova, L. & Grudin, J. 2007, 'Crossing boundaries: a case study of employee blogging', in *Proceedings of the fortieth Hawaii international conference on system sciences (HICSS-40)* IEEE Press: Los Alamitos, pp. 86–96.

Freadman, A. 2012, 'The traps and trappings of genre theory', *Applied Linguistics*, vol. 33, no. 5, pp. 544–563, doi:10.1093/applin/ams050.

Gabriel, Y. 2008, 'Seduced by the text: the desire to be deceived in story, memoir and drama', *TAMARA: Journal of Critical Postmodern Organization Science*, vol. 7, no. 2, pp. 154–167.

Georgakopoulou, A. 2006, 'Thinking big with small stories in narrative and identity analysis', *Narrative Inquiry*, vol. 16, no. 1, pp. 122–130, doi:10.1075/ni.16.1.16geo.

Halzack, S. 2008, 'Marketing moves to the blogosphere', *The Washington Post*, August 25, p. D01, Washington, DC, available at: http://www.washingtonpost.com/wp-dyn/content/article/2008/08/24/AR2008082401517.html

Hirsch, P. & Nail, J. 2006, 'Corporate blog learnings: the discovery age', available at: http://www.actulligence.com/images/0609/corporate_blog_learnings.pdf.

Horton, J. L. 1995, *Integrating corporate communications: the cost-effective use of message and medium*, Quorum Books: Westport, CT.

Jenkins, H. 2006, *Convergence culture: where old and new media collide*, New York University Press: New York, NY.

Jeon, S., Yoon, S. N. & Kim, J. 2008, 'A cross cultural study of corporate blogs in the USA and Korea', *International Journal of Information Technology and Management*, vol. 7, no. 2, pp. 149, doi:10.1504/IJITM.2008.016602.

Kaplan, A. M. & Haenlein, M. 2010, 'Users of the world, unite! the challenges and opportunities of social media', *Business Horizons*, vol. 53, pp. 59–68, doi:10.1016/j.bushor.2009.09.003.

Levine, R., Locke, C., Searles, D. & Weinberger, D. 2000, *The cluetrain manifesto: the end of business as usual*, Perseus: New York, NY.

Lorenz, K. 2005, April, 'Avoid getting fired for blogging', available at: http://edition.cnn.com/2005/US/Careers/04/05/blogging/ [accessed April 8, 2014].

Lüders, M., Prøitz, L. & Rasmussen, T. 2010, 'Emerging personal media genres', *New Media & Society*, vol. 12, no. 6, pp. 947–963, doi:10.1177/1461444809352203.

Margolin, U. 1996, 'Telling our story: on "we" literary narratives', *Language and Literature*, vol. 5, no. 2, pp. 115–133, doi:10.1177/096394709600500203.

Puschmann, C. 2013, 'Blogging', in S. C. Herring, D. Stein, & T. Virtanen (eds.), *Pragmatics of computer-mediated communication*, Mouton De Gruyter: Berlin, pp. 83–108.

Puschmann, C. 2010, *The corporate blog as an emerging genre of computer-mediated communication: features, constraints, discourse situation*, Universitätsverlag: Göttingen.

Ryan, M-L. 2006, *Avatars of story*, University of Minnesota Press: Minneapolis, MI.

Sobel, L. 2010, 'Technorati state of the blogosphere 2008', available at: http://technorati.com/state-of-the-blogosphere-2010/ [accessed June 17, 2015].

Sproull, L. & Kiesler, S. 1986, 'Reducing social context cues: electronic mail in organizational communication', *Management Science*, vol. 32, no. 11, pp. 1492–1512, doi:10.1287/mnsc.32.11.1492

Swales, J. M. 1990, *Genre analysis: English in academic and research settings*, Cambridge University Press: Cambridge.

Wallack, T. 2005, 'Beware if your blog is related to work', *San Francisco Chronicle*, January 24, p. C1, available at: http://www.sfgate.com/business/article/BLOGS-Beware-if-your-blog-is-related-to-work-2703354.php [accessed June 17, 2015].

Walther, J. B. 2007, 'Selective self-presentation in computer-mediated communication: hyperpersonal dimensions of technology, language, and cognition', *Computers in Human Behavior*, vol. 23, no. 5, pp. 2538–2557, doi:10.1016/j.chb.2006.05.002.

Weil, D. 2006, *The corporate blogging book: absolutely everything you need to know to get it right*, Portfolio: London.

Whole Foods Blog, available at: http://www.wholefoodsmarket.com/blog/whole-story [accessed June 17, 2015].

Yates, J. & Orlikowski, W. J. 1992, 'Genres of organizational communication: a structurational approach to studying communication and media', *The Academy of Management Review*, vol. 17, no. 2, pp. 299–326, doi:10.2307/258774.

Zerfaß, A. 2005, 'Corporate blogs: Einsatzmöglichkeiten und Herausforderungen', BIG BlogInitiative Germany, available at: http://www.zerfass.de/CorporateBlogs-AZ-270105.pdf [accessed April 8, 2014].

Further reading

Kaplan, A. M. & Haenlein, M. 2010, 'Users of the world, unite! The challenges and opportunities of social media', *Business Horizons*, vol. 53, no. 1, pp. 59–68, doi:10.1016/j.bushor.2009.09.003.

> Compares the characteristics of different forms of social media with regards to their respective potential for social presence and self-presentation and evaluates their usefulness for corporate communincations.

van den Hooff, B. & de Ridder, J. A. 2004, 'Knowledge sharing in context: the influence of organizational commitment, communication climate and CMC use on knowledge sharing', *Journal of Knowledge Management*, vol. 8, no. 6, pp. 117–130. doi:10.1108/13673270410567675.

> The authors explore the relation of knowledge sharing via CMC and organizational climate to evaluate the role of CMC for knowledge management.

Yates, J. & Orlikowski, W. J. 1992, 'Genres of organizational communication: a structurational approach to studying communication and media', *The Academy of Management Review*, vol. 17, no. 2, pp. 299–326, doi:10.2307/258774.

> A foundational paper on the relevance of the concept of genre to organizational communication.

15

Twitter

Design, discourse, and the implications of public text

Lauren Squires

Introduction

Launched in 2006, Twitter is a service for *microblogging*—the practice of publishing short bursts of content. Through Twitter's website (http://www.twitter.com), mobile device interfaces, or third-party applications, users broadcast and read short messages called *tweets*. At the time of writing, Twitter was the tenth-most-visited website globally (http://www.alexa.com/topsites; 13 March, 2013). The goal of this chapter is to provide an overview of language-related questions that arise regarding Twitter, considering especially the unique position of Twitter within contemporary media ecologies. The first half of the chapter discusses the communicative affordances of Twitter, the distinctive practices that have emerged as part of discourse on the site, and the linguistic character of tweets. The second half of the chapter focuses on the consequences of the high degree of publicization given to text on Twitter, which I suggest sets it apart from other (older) forms of social media.

Design features and discourse practices

Though social practice on Twitter is often characterized as microblogging, the functions of discourse on Twitter are variable and dynamic. In an early study of Twitter posts, Mischaud (2007) reports that, while Twitter's textual prompt at the time was "What are you doing?," the majority of tweets analyzed did not directly answer this prompt. Rather, people included content related to family/friends, personal information, information sharing, technology, "small talk," work, and reporting on past activity. Similarly, in an analysis of Twitter activity from their own perspectives as users, Gillen and Merchant (2013) describe multiple functions of tweets, including citizen journalism, political activism, maintaining a fan base, corporate advertising, crowd-sourcing, and social networking. Additionally, note that Twitter is in use among a wide variety of people—the service has a vast global reach, and users tweet in many languages. Though my discussion here focuses on English, multilingualism in Twitter is an important area of research (e.g., Bastos *et al.* 2013; Borau *et al.* 2009; Volkova *et al.* 2013).

At least to some extent, Twitter's multifunctionality and popularity result from its specific communicative affordances (Hutchby 2001). Twitter's network creates connections and

collective content that are felt to exist but are not necessarily individually articulable: it constitutes a form of distributed knowledge and sociality. A term often used to describe this is *ambient*,
as in "ambient sociability" (Gillen & Merchant 2013), "ambient affiliation" (Zappavigna 2011,
2012), and "ambient journalism" (Hermida 2010). As I discuss below, Twitter's design features,
and the discourse practices that they afford, contribute to its ambient quality.

As with many new media platforms, the material experience of using Twitter is device-
dependent, differing based on how one accesses the content: via the Twitter website on a web
browser or mobile device, via Twitter's official standalone applications, via a third-party application specifically made for Twitter, or via some other means (Gouws *et al.* 2011; Zappavigna
2011). Additionally, features of Twitter undergo regular change, which cannot be anticipated.
I limit my description here to the major design features of the Twitter website as they appeared
in mid-2013, discussing how many of these represent evolutions from earlier phases of Twitter's
existence; some features will undoubtedly have changed by the time this chapter is published.

Once signed in to the Twitter website, a user is taken to her Home page, the bulk of which
consists of a "stream" or "feed" of Twitter posts. This stream of tweets is reverse-chronologically
ordered (Figure 15.1); newer tweets automatically load periodically, and scrolling down to the end
of the page loads older tweets. Once a user posts a tweet, it is broadcast instantly to the user's stream.

Twitter's most iconic feature has remained stable since its inception: the 140-character limit
on tweet content (Figure 15.2; for technical discussion of what the system counts as a character,
see https://dev.twitter.com/docs/counting-characters). This feature was the focus of much early

Figure 15.1   A Twitter home page.

Figure 15.2 140-character limit in entering text.

news coverage of the service (Arceneaux & Schmitz Weiss 2010) and continues to mark the site as distinctive. When entering text, the system displays to users their current character count (spaces included), affording in-the-moment editing for length. This may in turn produce qualitative changes in the text people use, if the short length requires adaptation. However, Eisenstein (2013) and Schnoebelen (2012) have found that length of tweet is not always a predictor of expected lexical shortenings, questioning the direct influence of the character limit on practice. Though users are undoubtedly aware of the constraints the tweet format places on their text, and adapt to it, the medium is not determinate in terms of the orthographic or lexical resources used—rather, as discussed below, speakers construct individual and group styles out of textual features.

While the system began as a bare-text means of posting these short "status messages" via SMS (http://blog.twitter.com/2006/09/whats-your-status.html; 13 March 2013), Twitter now offers robust options for linkable and interactive tweets. In addition to user-entered URLs, several bits of text within a tweet may be hyperlinked. Twitter usernames, prefixed with <@> (as in *@ SquiresLauren*), create an automatic link to user profiles—known as *@mentions* ("at-mentions"). *Hashtags*, prefixed with <#> (as in *#Twitter*), create an automatic search for other tweets containing the same tag. Users also have several options to interact with a tweet they see in another user's stream. Figure 15.3 shows an "expanded" view of a tweet, which reveals a timestamp, number of retweets and favorites, and a reply box. "Reply" creates a pop-out reply box. "Retweet" allows a user to directly re-broadcast another user's tweet to her own followers. "Favorite" lets one express approval or appraisal of a tweet (similar to the "Like" button on Facebook), and to mark it for future reference. "More" presents the option to embed the tweet (code to display the tweet graphically on a webpage) or to email it (a box to enter an email address and message along with the tweet).

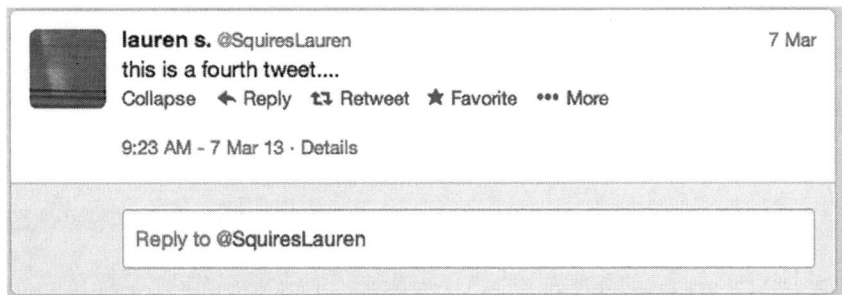

Figure 15.3 Options for interacting with a tweet.

Figure 15.4   A conversation.

These features have been gradually added to the site design, and many of them are institutional-ized responses to user innovation, making what was once emergent user practice part of "offi-cial" Twitter design. I will discuss this dynamic with regards to three central discourse practices in Twitter: @mentions, hashtags, and retweets.

The use of an *@mention* accomplishes several things at once: it establishes addressivity for a tweet, it triggers a notification to the @mentioned user that they have been addressed, it cre-ates a link to that user's profile, and it establishes the conditions for threading multiple tweets together as a "conversation." Figure 15.4 above gives an example. Here, I address my tweet to @prof_squires, and, within the tweet itself, any viewer can now click on "@prof_squires" to be taken to that user's profile. Users are notified when they have been addressed in this way (users can set preferences for the method of notification).

@mentions may occur anywhere within a tweet, and as such may occur in different syntac-tic slots to accomplish different goals. In the hypothetical tweet in (1a), @prof_squires is being addressed; in (1b), @prof_squires is being referred to; in (1c), @prof_squires is "tagged" as a way to suggest that the tweet is relevant to her, though she is neither directly addressed nor referred to.

(1a)   @prof_squires will I see you at the conference?

(1b)   I saw @prof_squires at the conference!

(1c)   Headed to the conference this weekend! @prof_squires

Early Twitter users imported the <@> prefix from Internet Relay Chat (boyd *et al.* 2010), where it had been used to address users by their nicknames (see Werry 1996).

Honeycutt and Herring (2009) provide an extensive analysis of <@> on Twitter; they note that the large volume of tweets in a user's stream creates a "noisy" environment, and the <@> symbol helps to capture the attention of an addressee. This addressivity facilitates interactivity and enables coherence among tweets as components of a larger conversation, which would be difficult to do in the environment in the absence of address cues. Zappavigna (2012) further argues that <@> mentions offer a way to introduce other voices into tweets, constructing heteroglossic texts (Androutsopoulos 2011a). As the system evolved, Twitter increased its support for the interactional threading of tweets, as shown above in Figure 15.4. When at least one other user has replied directly to a user's tweet, the two (or more) tweets are packaged by the system as a "Conversation," and the entire thread can be viewed. This feature was responsive to users' treatment of Twitter as a conversational medium despite the poor fit of its earlier affordances for maintaining threaded conversations (Honeycutt & Herring 2009).

Like @mentions, *hashtags* serve as a means of organizing material within Twitter, but they are based on topics or ideas, rather than users. Hashtagging—the use of <#> before a string of text—also has a precursor in IRC practice, which prefaces channel names with <#> (boyd *et al.* 2010; Werry 1996). A hashtag consists of the <#> symbol before a word or phrase, which instantly creates a searchable phrase for other tweets tagged in the same way. Hashtags specify a metadiscursive topic for or commentary on a tweet, and may be officially suggested by some entity (such as a university encouraging all students to use the same hashtag) or emergent from Twitter users (which may come to constitute memes (Zappavigna 2012) or "Trends" on Twitter). As with @mentions, hashtags may occur anywhere within a tweet and in any syntactic position the user wishes; this diversity is exemplified in the hypothetical examples in (2a–d).

(2a) I wish #springbreak lasted longer
(2b) I am so ready to be on vacation next week #springbreak
(2c) #Iwish spring break lasted longer
(2d) #thingsiwishfor a longer spring break

In one of the most extensive linguistic discussions of Twitter to date, Zappavigna (2011) characterizes the use of hashtags as discourse "where the primary function appears to be affiliation via 'findability'" (p. 789; see also Zappavigna 2012). This creates what Zappavigna calls "searchable talk." Hashtags function to internally organize the information on Twitter, and offer a means of "ambient affiliation" through dynamic and shifting moments of communal evaluation by those who do not know each other and may not ever connect again. The searchability of talk created by hashtagging may have social rewards if one's tagged tweets lead to more readers or followers, or if they are picked up for circulation by another entity, such as a blog or entertainment media. Of course, tweets are not always re-circulated with positive framings: there are also blogs dedicated to "shaming" Twitter users whose tweets reveal bigotry (see, e.g., http://publicshaming.tumblr.com/).

Hashtags may be used to construct communities with either short- or long-term persistence. For instance, users have harnessed hashtags to create interactive information streams that function like topic-specific chat channels. One example of this is #lingchat, a hashtag used during pre-planned meeting sessions in which interested Twitter users discuss specific linguistic issues (or interact with specific linguists). This hashtag permits subsequent access to the tweets generated during the session, and to the participants of the chat—connections that are professionally or personally useful. Bastos *et al.* (2013) show that similar communities emerge surrounding issues of political activism, which may be more or less global and multilingual.

A final major design feature important within Twitter is the *Retweet* button. Retweeting is the re-broadcasting of another user's tweet through one's own stream, fostering a sense of ambient connection among users. According to boyd *et al.* (2010: 1), retweeting "contributes to a conversational ecology in which conversations are composed of a public interplay of voices that give

Figure 15.5 Retweeting, emergent and standardized.

rise to an emotional sense of shared conversational context." boyd *et al.* (2010) found multiple motivations for retweeting, including spreading information more widely, entertaining a specific audience, demonstrating public agreement, demonstrating friendship, and self-promoting.

Before retweeting was built in to Twitter's design, users would copy and paste tweet content and include some indicator that the text was not their own, the most frequent being the message prefix <RT> (boyd *et al.* 2010). Figure 15.5 illustrates both the earlier, emergent practice of retweeting (top tweet) and the standardized manifestation of retweeting (bottom tweet).

Interestingly, the integration of retweeting as a system feature made some of the practices discussed by boyd *et al.* (2010) unnecessary. Since shortening or modifying original tweets is not necessary for space purposes alone, the official retweet button has standardized the practice to provide the verbatim text of the original user's tweet. However, users still do retweet manually using the <RT> prefix, and some use <MT> for "modified tweet"; other users simply quote a tweet through copy-and-paste and the use of quotation marks. These methods continue to permit modifying original tweets or adding commentary to them. As they are incorporated into texts outside of Twitter, tweets may also be modified, for instance for editorial purposes (Georgakopoulou 2013; Squires & Iorio 2014).

Retweeting highlights the fact that tweets are, by design, especially *portable* bits of text—in the terms of Bauman and Briggs (1990), they come with a *detachability* that makes them particularly amenable to de- and re-contextualization (see Georgakapoulou 2013; Spitulnik 1997; Squires & Iorio 2014). While standardized retweeting facilitates rebroadcasting *within* Twitter, Twitter's features have also evolved to embellish the form in which tweets may be transported to discourse *outside* of Twitter. The relatively new *embedding* feature gives a one-click option for people to embed a tweet with its full graphical context on another website. Such a feature facilitates the effortless verbatim quoting (and faithful visual representation) of tweets outside of Twitter, including on blogs and newspaper websites.

The features discussed above—@mentions, hashtags, and retweets—are emblematic of discourse on Twitter, and they have all undergone change as Twitter's design has responded to users' practice within the site. Importantly, all three of the features are multifunctional. Yet they all share in common that they make using Twitter more interactive than simply broadcasting one's own short messages. These practices also increase the visibility of one's own tweets—and visibility is major social currency on the site, as users aim for more readers and ultimately more followers (boyd *et al.* 2010: 9; Marwick & boyd 2010; Page 2012a).

Yet many Twitter users have widespread public recognition that predates their time on Twitter: Twitter is full of celebrity accounts, for which Twitter offers a "verified" service to sort imposter accounts from celebrities' real presences. Page (2012b) shows how celebrities leverage Twitter accounts to post "small stories" that promote a desired public identity (see also Ivanova 2012), offering fans access to personal details about celebrity lives that have typically not been available, or have not been offered by celebrities themselves. Twitter's prevalence in public discourse has partially been prompted by this perceived audience–celebrity collapse (see Marwick & boyd 2010). As Page (2012b: 104) writes, "Mainstream media has sensationalized celebrity use of Twitter as a means of accessing the intimate details of their private life." The status of celebrities within Twitter's discursive space has prompted Page (2012a) to challenge other characterizations of Twitter as extremely "conversational" in nature: the asymmetrical relationships that accrue to public entities' Twitter accounts may not be conducive to what is traditionally understood as interactive conversation.

Twitter provides the same discursive resources to celebrities as it does to non-celebrities, but those resources are marshaled differently. Page (2012a) found that hashtag usage differed across three types of Twitter accounts: celebrities, corporate entities, and "ordinary" people. Hashtags were most frequent among corporate users, less frequent among "ordinary" users, and least frequent among celebrity users. Thus, hashtagging—while frequently characterized as a conversational practice—is the most used (and perhaps the most useful) for corporate promotion and branding. Page also found syntactic differences across the three user groups. For instance, celebrity users had more imperative updates than either corporate or ordinary users. By contrast, questions occurred most often by ordinary users. This reflects the differing goals that different users have on Twitter; Page found that celebrities urge followers to action, while "ordinary" people elicit conversation. There is a wealth of future research that could be done to identify how different users' purposes for being on Twitter—and their status among Twitter users and elsewhere—affect their use of the features afforded by the medium.

Language variation

Beyond distinctive discourse practices that respond directly to Twitter's communicative affordances, what is the general nature of language on Twitter? Zappavigna (2012: 20) claims that "Microposts [such as tweets] typically contain non-standard orthography," and she mentions that her 100-million-word corpus includes frequent use of emoticons, the repetition of letters or punctuation marks, vowel omission, and what she calls "Internet slang" such as *LOL* and phonetic spellings. However, she notes that the use of these features even within single tweets is highly variable, and that tweets contain both standard and nonstandard text. For instance, <u> and <you> and <2> and <to> co-occur within single tweets, which Zappavigna interprets as indicating a lack of stabilization for formal norms within the medium. The use of typographic and syntactic features in Twitter, its variation across speaker groups (including language groups), its comparison to other forms of CMC, and its change over time are important areas for continued research; here, I give examples of recent studies that speak to these issues.

A few studies have examined the co-occurrence of multiple features in Twitter. Schnoebelen (2012) studied emoticon usage in Twitter posts, finding that the most frequent emoticons were the smiley, wink, and frown, all with no noses. Moreover, the "nose" variants of emoticons (e.g., < :-) > rather than < :) >) tended to pattern differently with regards to the words they occurred with. In spite of the pressure put on users by Twitter's character limit, Schnoebelen found that nose-includers tended to have longer tweets than those who did not. That is, while one might predict that people omit noses in order to accommodate length limits, this was not the case. Rather, by comparing multiple features and @mentions among tweets, Schnoebelen inferred that the variation in nose usage was partly a function of age: nose-omitters were younger than nose-includers. Nose-omitters used more emoticons, more expressive lengthenings, more common misspellings, more contractions without apostrophes, and more taboo words; nose-includers used longer tweets and more correctly spelled words.

Stylistic correlations between text features were also studied by Callier (2011), who investigated the use of <d> for word-initial <th> in Twitter posts, an orthographic analogue to "DH-stopping" (for instance, in *dis* and *dem* for *this* and *them*). Callier identified two stylistic clusters for <d> users: those who also tend to use r-lessness, and those who also tend to use *LOL* (in other words, *LOL* and r-lessness were themselves not associated). These seem to be different groups of Twitter users constructing different linguistic styles in their tweets. Styles may also relate to social goals on Twitter, as I have shown (Squires 2014). I investigated two sets of features—nonstandard spellings and informality markers—in the tweets of speakers who used a novel lexical item associated with a media celebrity. I found that tweets directed at the celebrity via @mention were overall more "standard" than tweets that were not. That is, people using Twitter to attempt communication with a celebrity had fewer nonstandard spellings and fewer informality markers than those using Twitter for more "ordinary" interpersonal communication. These styles seem to mark different types of speakers, who also have different social goals in the moment of tweeting.

Just as spoken language patterns often align with social similarities or differences between speakers, research has shown that social affiliation between Twitter users predicts linguistic patterns. Bamman *et al.* (2014) found that female-associated words included pronouns, emotion terms, "CMC words" (e.g., *LOL* and *omg*), emoticons, prepositions, and hesitation markers; male-associated words included numbers, technology words, and swear words. Using cluster analysis, they identified more fine-grained clusters of users who tend to use similar word sets, grouping them into "gendered clusters" (male-dominated and female-dominated), showing how groupings of features are associated with either gender (and how not all users conform to these patterns). Further, Bamman *et al.* found that females with more female-dominant networks used more female-dominant features, and the same was true for male-dominant networks. Similar to this "homophily" effect, Danescu-Niculescu-Mizil *et al.* (2011) found that Twitter conversants stylistically accommodate to each other.

Thus, research to date has demonstrated that variation in the use of both medium features and textual features on Twitter relates to social dimensions. These studies show that individual linguistic style in Twitter may be associated with social identities, goals in using the medium, or both; importantly, use of resources in the medium is facilitated by, though not determined by, the design features of the medium. Because Twitter users represent such a diverse span of types of people—both in traditional socio-demographic terms and in less stable categories, such as "celebrities" versus "ordinary users"—language variation on Twitter should continue to be of great interest to researchers who want to know the linguistic correlates of social meaning (Eckert 2012) in digital communication. In being variable in this way, language on Twitter is no different from language in face-to-face communication or language on other popular digital media platforms. However, Twitter is set apart from its social media precursors due to its intensive design focus on public information. This creates a new set of sociolinguistic dynamics for language in the public sphere, which I discuss in the next section.

Publicization

In addition to the more detailed features described above, the design of Twitter has one overarching feature that influences its use: it emphasizes making text public while de-emphasizing mutuality between users. That is, the average Twitter user does not know how many people—or which people—may read her tweets. Twitter otherwise meets the definition of social network sites (SNSs) as provided, for instance, by boyd and Ellison (2007: 211): "web-based services that allow individuals to (1) construct a public or semi-public profile within a bounded system, (2) articulate a list of other users with whom they share a connection, and (3) view and traverse their list of connections and those made by others within the system." However, among SNSs, Twitter distinctively permits (and even fosters) asymmetrical connections. A Twitter user has a list of *followers*, who subscribe to receive the user's tweets in their streams; she also has a list of other users she is *following*, whose tweets she subscribes to in her stream (see Figure 15.1).

Followers and those-following are not necessarily reciprocal. In fact, much site activity revolves around asymmetrical relationships, where those following outnumber those followed, as in the case of the millions of followers of celebrities or brands (Marwick & boyd 2010; Page 2012a, 2012b: 98–99; Zappavigna 2012: 27–28). Asymmetrical relationships are furthermore supported by the normative expectation of Twitter as a site of *public* information broadcast. The default setting for tweets is public, which makes them searchable within Twitter, searchable via search engines, and publicly retrievable via the site's application programming interface (API). A user may elect to restrict tweets to those following her, whom she must approve as followers. However, if a user restricts her tweets in this way, then tweets she sends to any user who does not already follow her will not be seen: messages to celebrities or companies will go unnoticed, and hashtags will not attain search currency. Further, a large part of Twitter's popularity stems from the perception that it lessens barriers between "ordinary" people and celebrities (Page 2012b) and networks unknown users around common interests (Zappavigna 2011). For a user to fully take advantage of these functions requires maintaining a public account.

Twitter's stated central function also sets it apart from many SNSs, including Facebook. As I wrote the initial draft of this chapter, Twitter's "About" page defined itself as "an information network" (http://twitter.com/about), and the message on its main page was, "Find out what's happening, right now, with the people and organizations you care about" (http://twitter.com). Facebook's front page, by comparison, entreated visitors to "Connect with friends and the world around you on Facebook" (http://facebook.com). This distinction—between *finding out what's happening* and *connecting with friends*—sums up many of the differences between the two sites. Twitter centers on text, information, and publicity, while de-centering reciprocity, privacy, and multimodality.

Twitter's asymmetrical network structure, norm of public accessibility, and predominance of text (rather than other semiotic modes) have potentially dramatic implications for language in the public sphere. Twitter represents an unprecedented convergence of mass-scale information sharing and casual writing. As discussed above, the discursive space of Twitter is shared by celebrities, journalists, politicians, "ordinary" people, and representatives of non-human entities such as brands, corporations, products, and other types of organizations. Though most linguistic research on Twitter has focused on users' *production* of tweets, many of these users also *consume* tweets in specific ways—by re-using others' tweets for their own ends. Within a mass media-saturated culture such as the US or UK, even a person who doesn't use Twitter may encounter tweets in news stories, on television, or on other websites.

Any tweet is potentially *doubly publicized*: first by a user on Twitter, then by another agent who embeds it in another website, quotes it in a news story, or displays it on a television show (for instance). Agents of mass media use Twitter not only to broadcast information about their own entities, but also to find other users' tweets that may suit their needs. I consider the former a *productive* use of Twitter, and the latter an *appropriative* use of Twitter. For scholars interested in mass and new media as sites of language–ideological reproduction, circulation, and contestation

(Squires 2010), this represents a ripe area for investigation, as language produced in a specific media context is detached and recontextualized within others. To illustrate the relevant dynamics between Twitter users and uses, I will discuss two different sites of mass media: entertainment media such as television shows on the one hand, and journalistic media such as newspapers on the other.

For entertainment media, consider *Dancing with the Stars*, an American television show that pairs celebrities with professional dancers to compete for best celebrity dancer. The show airs live twice a week, and viewers are partly responsible for choosing the winner by voting (via text message, phone call, or website). The show itself has a Twitter account, as do the various professional dancers and celebrity contestants. On the bottom of the show's website (http://beta. abc.go.com/shows/dancing-with-the-stars), a "Tweeting with the Stars" banner displays real-time updated tweets from the show's cast. The show's official Twitter account, @DancingABC (Official DWTS), posts behind-the-scenes pictures and videos from rehearsals, retweets from cast members, exhorts followers to follow them on other social media, and makes promotional announcements, as in (3a–c).

(3a)   Get an exclusive look at this season of #DWTS TONIGHT at 9|8c on ABC!

(3b)   Get to know the Season 16 professional dancers! http://abc.tv/16mBzz7 Which seasoned dancer is your favorite? pic.twitter.com/II36xG651m

(3c)   Cheryl Burke @CherylBurke
       Just had a great rehearsal today with @RealDLHughley! Salsa is comin along. #DWTS16

[Retweeted by Official DWTS]

This official account works as a clearinghouse for information about the show, as well as setting discursive norms for viewers' use of hashtags, which highlights that while hashtags are often created by users in a "bottom-up" fashion and gain popularity by diffusion across users, they are also often prescribed by media entities in a "top-down" fashion. These practices exemplify entertainment media's *productive* use of Twitter.

The show's *appropriative* use of Twitter includes displaying viewers' tweets on screen during the television broadcast. In screen graphics and live host announcements, viewers are encouraged to tweet with the hashtag #DWTS, and to use @mentions for the stars and @DancingABC. The show's producers presumably use these indexes to locate relevant viewer tweets and select some to broadcast onscreen during the broadcast (the selection processes involved in these re-broadcasts would make for a useful ethnographic investigation). The deployment of the appropriate hashtags or @mentions is presumably taken as consent for the tweet to be used by the show. I have seen similar displays of tweets on cable news broadcasts, sports broadcasts, weather reports, other reality competition shows, industry awards shows, and syndicated narrative television shows.

Journalism has also been transformed by the presence of Twitter. News stories may now take shape collaboratively through both professional and non-professional contributors to local, national, and international conversations (Hermida 2010; Arceneaux & Schmitz Weiss 2010). More significantly from a linguistic standpoint, utterances on Twitter may be treated as on-the-record comments about events, even though they are not elicited with respect to specific stories. I will illustrate the news media's productive and appropriative uses of Twitter by examining *The Guardian*, one of the UK's most popular newspapers in print and online. *The Guardian* maintains several verified Twitter accounts, its main one being @guardian (The Guardian), which posts links to stories, including @mentions of other *Guardian* accounts, as in (4a–b).

(4a) Guy Bourdin's fashion photography from 1978—in pictures http://gu.com/p/3ecqa/tw via @GuardianCulture

(4b) Shakespeare scholars unite to see off threat of the "Bard deniers" http://gu.com/p/3ez8a/tf

This account serves the promotional purpose of notifying followers of stories they may be interested in, as well as directing them to other Twitter accounts that they may wish to follow. This is a standard productive use for a journalism entity.

The Guardian's appropriative use comes in at least two forms: it uses readers' tweets to create story content, and it uses public figures' tweets as sources for quotes. I searched the paper's website (http://www.guardian.co.uk/) for the term "*tweeted*," which returned over 38,000 results. These include article tags such as "Tweet ur Trip (Travel)" for stories explicitly centered on aggregating tweets from readers. Tweets also occur within more traditional stories, in the form of quoted content. For instance, articles about the recent banking crisis in Cyprus, the football player Rio Ferdinand, and the death of a transgender teacher all contain at least one quote from a tweet posted by relevant parties. Twitter has become a *source of news*, as when talk on Twitter constitutes a story (or when notable figures tweet, such as the Pope), but also a *source for news producers*, as when quotes are gathered from public figures' Twitter accounts and re-embedded within news stories.

One might expect appropriative uses of tweets to be more prevalent in some genres of mass media or news than others. For instance, Georgakapoulou (2013) writes about the quoting of tweets within celebrity gossip columns, where tweets provide sources of "breaking news." Squires and Iorio (2014) likewise examine reported tweets within entertainment and sports news. These are personality-focused genres, and tweets become another symbolic resource in the culture of celebrity. However, tweets also occur in more formal sub-genres of political and global news, as noted above, and future research should continue examining which mass media genres appropriate tweets, for what reason, and with what linguistic consequences, including how different genres of news might deal differently with tweets.

The mass media's appropriation of Twitter content is especially interesting in terms of language. It brings audience voices directly into entertainment media content, and it brings the unsolicited voices of story participants into news media content (see Cotter 2010 and Van Hout *et al.* 2011 for discussions of traditional news sourcing practices). If, as researchers suggest (Eisenstein 2013; Zappavigna 2012), tweets on the whole are characteristically not wholly "standard" in their orientation, then this dynamic potentially amounts to an extraordinary increase in the amount of *vernacular writing* that is *publicized* for mass audiences. CMC has in general amplified the public spaces in which casual writing is seen (Androutsopoulos 2011b). Twitter's unique position within media culture could *vernacularize* elements of the public sphere in new ways, where even traditional figureheads of linguistic propriety, such as broadcasters, politicians, writers, and professors, are producing nonstandard language, making it public, and having it made doubly public via appropriation (see Iorio this volume; Squires & Iorio 2014).

The re-circulation of tweets by mass media may engender contrasts between the expected "standard" language of public discourse and the language of tweets. In particular, tension may arise between the non-standard linguistic form of a quoted tweet and the standard linguistic form of the journalistic writing within which it is (re-)embedded. Indeed, Squires and Iorio (2014) found that although the number of "reported tweets" in news sources increased dramatically from 2009 to 2011, the overall profile of the tweets as they were quoted remained largely standard. Thus, journalists may select tweets that conform to their entrenched expectations of standard language (Cotter 2010), or use tweets with "vernacular" features only in order to portray tweets as exotic (Cotter 2011). Nonstandard features have also been found to decrease the perception of a tweet's credibility (Morris *et al.* 2012), so it is possible that reporters are sensitive to this perception and select more standard tweets when credibility matters more. One wonders, further, what the effect is on social impression formation, and language ideologies, when public figures who are assumed to be credible (such as well-known public broadcasters) do tweet using "nonstandard" features. This discussion has only scratched the surface of potential issues regarding the publicization of tweets—an important area to track as Twitter's role in public discourse continues to evolve.

Data collection

This section discusses some of the research findings of projects that have taken advantage of *data collection* (or *data mining*) from Twitter. The public accessibility of large quantities of tweets fostered by Twitter has created an unprecedented focus on CMC that is not for the sake of understanding language in CMC specifically, but rather for understanding the modeling of human language more generally. Twitter's application programming interface (API) permits streaming of tweets outside of the Twitter website. While most programmers use programming interfaces to access the stream, there are ways to capture tweets via the API that require less technical sophistication. For instance, there is a package for collecting tweets using the environment R, which is familiar to many linguists (http://cran.r-project.org/web/packages/twitteR/); and there are online services that collect tweets for export so that no programming is required (including ContextMiner, which is designed for academic use, and 140kit, TweetArchivist, and HootSuite, all designed for marketers). Using these methods, even a technically unsavvy researcher can easily gather thousands of tweets, targeting specific keywords, users, or hashtags, in a single day. Data mining can also be considered an appropriative use of Twitter, though of course the aims are quite different from those of the mass media discussed above.

Unsurprisingly, the most sophisticated uses of such Twitter corpora come from the realm of computational linguistics, where Twitter data has been used to formulate models of natural language processing, and to apply computational modeling techniques to sociolinguistic issues such as large-scale patterns of language variation and change. Out of this work have come many findings of interest to sociolinguistic researchers; importantly, these studies make claims about language generally speaking, not "language in digital media" specifically.

Geographical variation is a central area of sociolinguistics, and several studies have exploited the availability of Twitter data to explore large-scale patterns of synchronous variation in the US. Eisenstein *et al.* (2010) and Russ (2012) investigated geographic lexical variation, taking advantage of the fact that many Twitter posts are "geotagged" with GPS metadata acquired from mobile devices. Eisenstein *et al.* (2010) found that lexical features associated with a certain topic (e.g., "sports"), including nonstandard orthographic forms and "slang" terms, patterned differently across regions. Examining more canonical geographical variation, Russ (2012) tracked three dialect variables for U.S. English. The geographical patterns in the Twitter data replicated those found in speech, but also provided intriguing new data about the possible spread of patterns beyond those previously reported in the dialectology literature (see also Brown 2012 on Spanish features). Further investigating diachronic diffusion, Eisenstein *et al.* (2012) tracked the spread of words across U.S. Twitter users over a span of almost two years. They found that demographic similarities in racial/ethnic and socioeconomic characteristics of metropolitan areas made it more likely for them to influence each other linguistically.

Moving beyond geography, O'Connor *et al.* (2011) used cluster analysis to reveal associations between groups of demographic properties and groups of lexical items. For instance, in their model, phonetic spellings were associated with clusters with more lower-income and fewer white users. Emoticons were associated with a cluster having a high percentage of Hispanic users. Such analyses show the complexity of lexical and orthographic patterns across macro-level demographic characteristics, highlighting the notion of intersecting identities and linguistic style as they are constructed from clusters of features, rather than singular features or monolithic demographic categories (Eckert 2012). As with Bamman *et al.*'s (2014) multi-layered analysis of gendered tweets, this work offers enormous potential for sociolinguistic insight, offering a testing ground for theories of wide-scale variation and change (see Maybaum 2012).

Within these and other studies, natural language processing (NLP) researchers have consistently noted the difficulties that appear to be inherent to modeling Twitter data—especially the prevalence of non-standard orthography. Eisenstein (2013) provides an insightful discussion of this problem, which he characterizes as one of "bad language on the Internet," where language at all levels—including vocabulary, spelling, and syntax—differs from the standard corpora (often news texts) on which NLP applications are trained. Eisenstein surveys the approaches that NLP researchers have used to accommodate the unexpected forms found in social media texts, which often includes glossing nonstandard forms into standard forms (erasing the very variability that many other linguistic researchers are likely to care about). He ultimately argues for NLP researchers to create programs that are sensitive both to linguistic variation and to social factors that may condition that variation. This position highlights the importance of real collaboration between researchers with different methodological and theoretical approaches to language in Twitter (and in digital communication more generally).

Beyond the details of automating data processing, a potential problem for researchers using Twitter data is a tradeoff in quality for quantity. While computational methods have yielded valid inferences regarding some demographic categories of the users whose tweets they are analyzing (such as gender and region), data collected from Twitter is "demographically lean" (Iorio 2009). That is, while one can easily retrieve information such as username and geographical location, there is no automatic metadata specifying gender, race or ethnicity, class, etc. This makes knowing with certainty the demographic features of users unlikely, and inferences based on usernames, geographical locations, or other combinations of metadata may yield false categorizations. The true population from which any sample of tweets is taken is arguably unknowable at anything but the largest level of abstraction (e.g., "English speakers," "people in London"), though hashtags may offer some opportunity for narrowing the population based on interest (e.g., "Guardian readers," "Dancing with the Stars viewers"). While the quantity of language available via Twitter is unprecedented and undoubtedly useful, researchers must think critically about the research questions to which the data are validly suited (Herring 2004).

Finally, ethical questions have always arisen with Internet data, particularly surrounding user privacy (for recent discussions, see D'Arcy & Young 2012; Bolander & Locher 2014). Researchers should be aware of more general cross-disciplinary debates regarding the dynamics of Twitter's API (and similar systems) and the rights of end users. For instance, Burgess and Puschmann (2013) discuss how Twitter's "ecosystem" has transitioned over time to being advertising-heavy (one now sees "promoted" posts from brands regularly in one's stream). From a business standpoint, the API facilitates advertisers' analysis of patterns that let them target consumers; just as academic researchers see access to the API as an easy way to retrieve data on a population, so do advertisers. Though users with accounts set to private are never accessible through the API, the system incentivizes remaining public, and so, as Burgess and Puschmann (2013) say, for most users, "Privacy concerns . . . are effectively traded for free access to the platform." Researchers collecting data from Twitter should be aware of these dynamics. (For a broader discussion of the use of "big social data," see Burgess and Bruns 2012).

Conclusion

In this chapter, I have tried to outline what makes Twitter distinctive from other digital communication platforms, focusing on its emblematic features and the rather large impact it has had on language in the public sphere. Twitter provides a massively popular space for text-focused interaction, and it has simultaneously made those interactions readily available for re-use by those within and outside of its immediate domain. Assuming that Twitter maintains or expands its reach, each set of issues discussed above will remain relevant to understanding language and digital communication; here, I consider four specific areas for future research.

First, Twitter should continue to be of great interest for scholars researching how humans accommodate social and linguistic practice to new or changing technological systems and their attendant affordances and constraints. It is a site in which it is clear how technical design features motivate particular discursive practices, but it also shows that users' practices are not wholly determined by the design features of a system. Indeed, while many observers initially mocked Twitter's 140-character limit (Arceneaux & Schmitz Weiss 2010), users clearly find pleasure in this generic format of a tweet, and it is a linguistic and sociological question as to why. Importantly, Twitter offers observable examples of language users' "bottom-up" practices becoming codified by "top-down" design decisions, giving a glimpse of how language use and interface affordances evolve independently or in tandem. Studying this more closely can reveal important dynamics of institutional power that potentially have widespread sociolinguistic implications. The more we turn to mediating technologies to communicate, the more the form of our communication is influenced by the agents who design the technologies. This is no more true of Twitter than of any other mediating technology, but Twitter seems to offer an unprecedented opportunity to observe changes in progress.

Second is Twitter's rapidly changing role in consumer and media culture, the relatively short history of which can illuminate societal relations between mass and interpersonal media (Arceneaux & Schmitz Weiss 2010) and the role of language therein (Squires & Iorio 2014). Within Twitter lies a discursive environment with sociolinguistic dynamics that heretofore could have seemed peculiar. For just a few examples, consider that on Twitter, corporations "speak" directly to consumers, ordinary people's statements are quoted by other people who they didn't even know existed, and fans of television shows create textual content in the hopes that it will cross media from Twitter to the television. As language in the public sphere continues to change via technologies like Twitter, researchers can track how language is interwoven with other forms of interpersonal and mass communication and with the dynamics of power that manifest in these connections. Of particular interest for sociolinguists is whether the increasing publicization of casual, vernacular texts like tweets leads to a longer-term shift in ideologies about what kind of language is suited to the public sphere.

Third, Twitter is an important site of study for those interested in studying the discursive construction of contemporary attitudes and ideologies about a range of social issues. Twitter is a public platform through which users can organize social action and discuss social causes, and indeed some of the most talked-about "events" on Twitter have involved political issues. People have effectively leveraged Twitter to draw public attention to both large-scale and small-scale social causes (from the Arab Spring to local issues on university campuses). Many users of Twitter see tweeting itself as a potential form of activism, giving voice to those unrepresented by mainstream dialogue elsewhere in mass media. Thus, Twitter provides fertile ground for critically analyzing discourse.

Fourth and finally, as with other digital communication technologies, there is still work to be done to better understand the diversity of language use on Twitter. Here are just some of the potential research areas: the use of different codes among multilingual users, including code-switching; cross-cultural communication between users in different parts of the world; the use of lexical items or orthographic features among different social groups; the representation of spoken dialect features in this casual sphere of text; the relationship of syntactic patterns to tweets as a genre; and the ways that medium features, like hashtags and @mentions, are used differently across groups (e.g., Page 2012a). Twitter's public data makes it an especially exciting site through which these questions can be explored with large quantities of language at once. To best investigate these issues will require collaboration between those with expertise in studying language through highly technical computer-assisted methods and those with expertise in studying language variation and society. I believe that researchers in both areas will benefit from such collaboration—as will the study of language and digital communication.

Related topics

- Chapter 1 Approaches to language variation (Hinrichs)
- Chapter 2 Network analysis (Paolillo)
- Chapter 6 Style, creativity and play (Nishimura)
- Chapter 10 Vernacular literacy: orthography and literacy practices (Iorio)
- Chapter 19 Relationality, friendship and identity in digital communication (Graham)
- Chapter 21 Facebook and the discursive construction of the social network (Tagg & Seargeant)

References

Androutsopoulos, J. 2011a, "From variation to heteroglossia in the study of computer-mediated discourse," in C. Thurlow & K. Mroczek (eds.), *Digital discourse: language in the new media*, Oxford University Press: Oxford, pp. 277–298.

Androutsopoulos, J. 2011b, "Language change and digital media: a review of conceptions and evidence," in T. Kristiansen & N. Coupland (eds.), *Standard language and language standards in a changing Europe*, Novus: Oslo, pp. 145–161.

Arceneaux, N. & Schmitz Weiss, A. 2010, "Seems stupid until you try it: press coverage of Twitter, 2006–09," *New Media & Society*, vol. 12, no. 8, pp. 1262–1279.

Bamman, D., Eisenstein, J., & Schnoebelen, T. 2014, "Gender identity and lexical variation in social media," *Journal of Sociolinguistics*, vol. 18, no. 2, pp. 135–160.

Bastos, M. T., Puschmann, C., & Travitzki, R. 2013, "Tweeting across hashtags: overlapping users and the importance of language, topics, and politics," in *Proceedings of the 24th ACM conference on hypertext and social media*, ACM, New York, NY, pp. 164–168.

Bauman, R. & Briggs, C. L. 1990, "Poetics and performance as critical perspectives on language and social life," *Annual Review of Anthropology*, vol. 19, pp. 59–88.

Bolander, B. & Locher, M. 2014, "Doing sociolinguistic research on computer-mediated data: a review of four methodological issues," *Discourse, Context & Media*, vol. 3, pp. 14–26.

Borau, K., Ullrich, C., Feng, J., & Shen, R. 2009, "Microblogging for language learning: using Twitter to train communicative and cultural competence," in *Proceedings of the 8th international conference on advances in web based learning*, pp. 78–87, available from: ACM Digital Library [accessed 29 March 2013].

boyd, dm & Ellison, N. B. 2007, "Social network sites: definition, history, and scholarship," *Journal of Computer-Mediated Communication*, vol. 13, no. 1, pp. 210–230.

boyd, d, Golder, S. & Lotan, G. 2010, "Tweet, tweet, retweet: conversational aspects of retweeting on twitter," in *Proceedings of the 2010 43rd Hawaii international conference on system sciences*, pp. 1–10, available from: ACM Digital Library [accessed 29 March 2013].

Brown, E. 2012, "'Cuando gustes, me envías un DM': experiential *gustar* in tweets in the capital cities of Spanish-speaking countries in Latin America and in Spain," presented at *New Ways of Analyzing Variation 41*, Bloomington, IN.

Burgess, J. & Bruns, A. 2012, "Twitter archives and the challenges of 'big social data' for media and communication research," *M/C Journal,* vol. 15, no. 5, available from: http://journal.media-culture.org.au/index.php/mcjournal/article/viewArticle/561 [accessed 29 March 2013].

Burgess, J. & Puschmann, C. 2013, "The politics of Twitter data," in K. Weller, A. Bruns, J. Burgess, M. Mahrt, & C. Puschmann (eds.), *Twitter and society,* Peter Lang: New York, NY, pp. 43–54.

Callier, P. 2011, "Stylistic co-variates of DH-stopping on Twitter," presented at *New Ways of Analyzing Variation 40,* Washington, DC.

Cotter, C. 2011, "Diversity awareness and the role of language in cultural representations in news stories," *Journal of Pragmatics,* vol. 43, pp. 1890–1899.

Cotter, C. 2010, *News talk: investigating the language of journalism,* Cambridge University Press: Cambridge.

D'Arcy, A. & Young, T. M. 2012, "Ethics and social media: implications for sociolinguistics in the networked public," *Journal of Sociolinguistics,* vol. 16, no. 4, pp. 532–546.

Danescu-Niculescu-Mizil, C., Gamon, M., & Dumais, S. 2011, "Mark my words! linguistic style accommodation in social media," in *Proceedings of the 20th international conference on World Wide Web,* pp. 745–754, available from: ACM Digital Library [accessed 29 March 2013].

Eckert, P. 2012, "Three waves of variation study: the emergence of meaning in the study of sociolinguistic variation," *Annual Review of Anthropology,* vol. 41, pp. 87–100.

Eisenstein, J. 2013, "What to do about bad language on the Internet," *Proceedings of NAACL 2013,* available from: http://www.cc.gatech.edu/~jeisenst/papers/naacl2013-badlanguage.pdf [accessed 13 April 2014].

Eisenstein, J., O'Connor, B., Smith, N. A., & Xing, E. P. 2012, "Mapping the geographical diffusion of new words," in *NIPS 2012 workshop on social network and social media analysis,* available from: http://arxiv.org/abs/1210.5268 [accessed 29 March 2013].

Eisenstein, J., O'Connor, B., Smith, N. A., & Xing, E. P. 2010, "A latent variable model for geographic lexical variation," in *Proceedings of the 2010 conference on empirical methods in natural language processing,* pp. 1277–1287, available from: ACM Digital Library [accessed 29 March 2013].

Georgakopoulou, A. 2013 "Storytelling on the go: breaking news stories as a travelling narrative genre," in M. Hatavara, L-C. Hydén, & M. Hyvärinen (eds.), *The travelling concepts of narrative,* John Benjamins: Amsterdam, pp. 201–224.

Gillen, J. & Merchant, G. 2013, "Contact calls: Twitter as a dialogic social and linguistic practice," *Language Sciences,* vol. 35, pp. 47–58.

Gouws, S., Metzler, D., Cai, C., & Hovy, E. 2011, "Contextual bearing on linguistic variation in social media," in *Proceedings of the workshop on language in social media (LSM 2011),* pp. 20–29, available from: http://aclweb.org/anthology/W/W11/W11-0704.pdf [accessed 29 March 2013].

Hermida, A. 2010, "Twittering the news: the emergence of ambient journalism," *Journalism Practice,* vol. 4, no. 3, pp. 297–308.

Herring, S. C. 2004, "Computer-mediated discourse analysis: an approach to researching online behavior," in S. A. Barab, R. Kling, & J. H. Gray (eds.), *Designing for virtual communities in the service of learning,* Cambridge University Press: New York, NY, pp. 338–376.

Honeycutt, C. & Herring, S. C. 2009, "Beyond microblogging: conversation and collaboration via Twitter," in *Proceedings of the 42nd Hawaii international conference on system sciences,* pp. 1–10, available from: IEEE Xplore Digital Library [accessed 29 March 2013].

Hutchby, I. 2001, *Conversation and technology: from the telephone to the Internet,* Polity Press: Cambridge.

Iorio, J. 2009, "Effects of audience on orthographic variation," *Studies in the Linguistic Sciences: Illinois Working Papers,* vol. 2009, pp. 127–140.

Ivanova, A. 2012, "Presidential talk online: Barack Obama's use of Twitter," in Elorza, I., Carbonell i Cortés, O., Albarrán, R., García Riaza, B., & Pérez-Veneros, M. (eds.), *Empiricism and analytical tools for 21 century applied linguistics: selected papers from the xxix international conference of the Spanish Association of Applied Linguistics (AESLA),* Universidad de Salamanca, pp. 189–198.

Marwick, A. E. & boyd, d 2010, "I tweet honestly, I tweet passionately: Twitter users, context collapse, and the imagined audience," *New Media & Society,* vol. 13, no. 2, pp. 114–133.

Maybaum, R. 2012, "Evolving innovations: a real time study of changing slang in Twitter," presented at *New Ways of Analyzing Variation 41,* Bloomington, IN.

Mischaud, E. 2007, "Twitter: expressions of the whole self: an investigation into user appropriation of a web-based communications platform," MSc Thesis, London School of Economics and Political Science, London, UK.

Morris, M. R., Counts, S., Roseway, A., Hoff, A., & Schwartz, J. 2012, "Tweeting is believing? Understanding microblog credibility perceptions," in *Proceedings of the ACM 2012 conference on computer supported cooperative work,* ACM, New York, NY, pp. 451–450.

O'Connor, B., Eisenstein, J., Xing, E. P., & Smith, N. A. 2011, "A mixture model of demographic lexical variation," in *Proceedings of NIPS workshop on machine learning in computational social science*, vol. 14, available from: http://www.cc.gatech.edu/~jeisenst/papers/nipsws2010.pdf [accessed 24 June 2015].

Page, R. 2012a, "The linguistics of self-branding and micro-celebrity in Twitter: the role of hashtags," *Discourse & Communication*, vol. 6, no. 2, pp. 181–201.

Page, R. E. 2012b *Stories and social media: identities and interaction*, Routledge: New York, NY.

Russ, B. 2012, "Examining large-scale regional variation through online geotagged corpora," presented at the *American Dialect Society Annual Meeting*, Portland, OR.

Schnoebelen, T. J. 2012, "Emotions are relational: positioning and the use of affective linguistic resources," PhD Dissertation, Stanford University, Palo Alto, CA.

Spitulnik, D. 1997, "The social circulation of media discourse and the mediation of communities," *Journal of Linguistic Anthropology*, vol. 6, no. 2, pp. 161–187.

Squires, L. 2014, "From TV personality to fans and beyond: indexical bleaching and the diffusion of a media innovation," *Journal of Linguistic Anthropology*, vol. 24, no. 1, pp. 42–62.

Squires, L. 2010, "Enregistering Internet language," *Language in Society*, vol. 39, no. 4, pp. 457–492.

Squires, L. & Iorio, J. 2014, "Tweets in the news: legitimizing medium, standardizing form," in J. Androutsopoulos (ed.), *Mediatisation and sociolinguistic change*, Mouton de Gruyter: Berlin, pp. 331–360.

Van Hout, T., Maat, H. P., & De Preter, W. 2011, "Writing from news sources: the case of Apple TV," *Journal of Pragmatics*, vol. 43, pp. 1876–1889.

Volkova, S., Wilson, T., & Yarowsky, D. 2013, "Exploring demographic language variations to improve multilingual sentiment analysis in social media," *Proceedings of the 2013 conference on empirical methods on natural language processing*, pp. 1815–1827.

Werry, C. C. 1996, "Linguistic and interactional features of Internet Relay Chat," in S. C. Herring (ed.), *Computer-mediated communication: linguistic, social and cross-cultural perspectives*, John Benjamins: Amsterdam, pp. 47–64.

Zappavigna, M. 2012, *Discourse of Twitter and social media*, Continuum: London.

Zappavigna, M. 2011, "Ambient affiliation: a linguistic perspective on Twitter," *New Media & Society*, vol. 13, no. 5, pp. 788–806.

Further reading

Bamman, D., Eisenstein, J., & Schnoebelen, T. 2014, "Gender identity and lexical variation in social media," *Journal of Sociolinguistics*, vol. 18, pp. 135–160.

Provides a complex analysis of language use in Twitter according to gender, including lexical variation, co-variation, and the relation between social network structure and variation. Offers discussion of the benefits of large-scale computational data analysis techniques for sociolinguistic theory.

Page, R. 2012, "The linguistics of self-branding and micro-celebrity in Twitter: the role of hashtags," *Discourse & Communication*, vol. 6, pp. 181–201.

Distinguishes between user groups on Twitter to show that celebrities, corporate entities, and "ordinary" users put the discursive affordances of Twitter (specifically hashtags) to different functions; gives in-depth discussion of Twitter practice as self-presentational rather than conversational.

Zappavigna, M. 2012, *Discourse of Twitter and social media*, Continuum: London.

Analyzes a massive Twitter corpus from a Systemic Functional Linguistics perspective, with especially rich coverage of the notion of "searchable talk." Investigates Twitter-specific features (such as <@> mentions and hashtags) and features found in other domains (such as emoticons and respellings) to establish a quantitatively robust profile of Twitter use.

Part V

Digital selves and online–offline lives

16

The role of the body and space in digital multimodality

Elizabeth Keating

Introduction[1]

Language is a tool of unparalleled power for creating and sharing information, perspectives and plans, and has been a focus of countless fascinating research studies. Other non-verbal modalities for communication have been far less studied for what they contribute to culture and social transmission (see Jewitt, this volume). This is in part because of prior difficulties in studying and recording human interaction, and in part due to the historical privileging of written texts in scholarly work. The recent development of low-cost digital image recording technologies, however, has enabled the close analysis of multimodality in human communication, and studies are proliferating on the topic of multimodality. This includes both discrete aspects of visual semiotic modalities, such as gesture (e.g., Kendon 2004; Kita 2003; Streeck 2009), gaze (e.g., Goodwin & Goodwin 1987; Kendon 1990), the body, and space, as well as the inter-relatedness of modalities (e.g., Deppermann 2013; Goodwin & Goodwin 1996; Jewitt, Kress, & Mavers 2009; Mondada 2011; Streeck, Goodwin, & LeBaron 2011). Video recordings have enabled researchers to better understand the coordination of modalities in terms of simultaneity and sequentiality. The world's many sign languages, now being extensively documented, are also a resource for multimodality study. In sign language, signs made with the hands work in complex coordination with signs made with the face, head movements, torso shifts, gaze, gestures, and mimetic moves.

The plasticity of human facial expression, the properties of eye movement, the mobility of the hands, the seemingly "natural" attitudinal displays of the limbs, and the body's relation to space and to others' bodies are all conventionalized to some degree within cultures and are an essential resource for those communicating something and those trying to understand what is going on. Digital communication tools, such as web cameras and mobile phones, and digital interaction spaces, such as gaming, alter habits and possibilities for multimodal expression and provide new challenges for the integration of modalities (see e.g., Jewitt, this volume; Keating 2005; Wasson 2006). In this chapter, several aspects of the role of the body and space in digital multimodal communication are considered: semiotic resources such as gesture, gaze, manual signs, head position, facial expressions, body attitude, and the use of the environment. Also considered are the integration of multiple communication modalities in digital environments and the influence of digital environments on the body and space. Three particular settings are used to illustrate multimodal practices: online gaming, sign language in technologically mediated space, and a virtual work environment where engineers located in different continents collaborate on construction plans. The chapter's focus is on multimodality in interaction, and the settings are chosen from the author's research.

The topic of multimodality has relevance for better understanding precisely how culture and sociality are maintained and how collaboration in meaning-making is accomplished, including status negotiations, alignment or conflict, displays of physiological responses (or feigned responses) of emotion, maintenance of norms and identities, learning new tasks, innovation, and much more. Bodies interacting in space are expected to be giving off information (Goffman 1961), which is then used to infer such important aspects of social relationships as rights of participation, hierarchy, and role, both as these relate to particular individuals and actions, and as they are projected to future actions. By reading embodied behaviors, people infer how another might be likely to interact within a range of contexts, sometimes based on a single multimodal interchange. A variety of multimodal expressions and interpretations are key in these inferences. The openings and closings of interactions with others, for example, although quite routinized and conventionalized, are rich sites for reading and displaying social attributes as each uses his or her body in concert with others and the environment, by gaze, gesture and use of space in combination with language (Duranti 1992). In some societies, such as Pohnpei, Micronesia, where status differentiation is highly valued and elaborated, hierarchy is displayed and inferred through multiple simultaneous modalities at public events: by the sequence of serving food or drink, by where a person sits horizontally in space in relation to others, by a person's vertical height in seating arrangements compared to others, by language used, by gaze direction, and by body attitude (Keating 2000). An absence of any one of these expressive signals is cause for criticism about appropriate behavior.

Historical perspectives on multimodality

A separation between the study of linguistic forms and other semiotic modes of expression (often called paralinguistic forms) and the neglect of the latter have been unfortunate historical products of the valorization of written texts and literacy practices, and the results of an early research focus on literary works when formally examining properties of meaning (Volosinov 1973). Linguists' reliance on introspection as a tool for analyzing and describing linguistic structures has also contributed to overlooking the importance of so-called paralinguistic, non-verbal elements of communication. A legacy of the status division between text or verbal language and other modalities of communication remains in the lack of good terms for categorizing or describing aspects of multimodal communication, and an unhappy distinction between verbal and non-verbal, or text and context. One remedy suggested for transcending the problematic verbal vs non-verbal distinction is to use descriptive categories for modalities, such as "vocal/aural" vs "visuospatial" (Enfield 2005). Another is to stress the inseparability of modalities (Kendon 1977; Streeck et al. 2011), citing the importance of interstitial meaning-making practices (or the way meaning can emerge from elements distributed across or between people—see, e.g., Hutchins 1995). The human attunement to emergent, situational, relational and co-occurring aspects of meaningful activity resists the categorization of multimodal elements into independent distinct phenomena. Multimodality researchers recognize meanings that lie not entirely in talk or sign, but "somewhere in between" talk and other signals (Levinson 1992). All face-to-face interaction is by definition multimodal (Stivers

& Sidnell 2005). Readers will encounter below both the advantages and the limitations of discussing modalities separately.

A corollary problem to the historical privileging of text and verbal structures (reflected in the way other modalities are defined by what they are not, especially in terms of text, as in "non-verbal" or "context") is that non-verbal actions and contextually dependent signals have been rather crudely dumped into a single oppositional category. The primitiveness of the category is evident, for example, in the wry term "the bucket theory of context" (Heritage & Clayman 2010). The bucket has been discovered, however, to be a source of riches, something already noted in the long tradition of analyzing visual aspects of communication, including the body and the visual field, in art history, film studies, and media education. The "multisemiotic nature" of contemporary media exploits not only multiple discrete sign systems, but how meaning is extracted from new ways that sign systems interact with each other (Fairclough 2000: 162). When language, the body, space, and material objects are taken together to create worlds and to respond to others, this involves indirectly invoking key knowledge not explicitly mentioned in ways that are not yet well understood.

Moving beyond a focus on text and a privileging of verbal forms, scholars have been emphasizing that even when not actively trying to communicate something, people "secrete semiotic material" (Goodwin 1995), giving off signals through their posture, facial expressions, dress and other signs that others are constantly interpreting. These semiotic discharges are treated by interactants as having meaning, whether these interpretations are attested or not. An example is a yawn, taken to mean the hearer is losing interest, but probably actually a sign of too little sleep. Yawns and other signs, such as eye gaze, are considered as being specific indications of what about a person's ongoing talk is being considered relevant and meaningful (Schutz 1964).

Although there are cautions about analyzing multimodal resources discretely as mentioned above, there is an active field of scholars focusing on gesture. Others take a more holistic approach, for example, building on Gumperz's (1982) notion of "contextualization cues" in order to better understand how listeners are able to infer so much from the sometimes sparse, minimal units of speakers' talk, given the rich amount of information listeners gather from them. Some aspects of contextualization cues have been more systematically researched than others (e.g., prosody and codeswitching), but some (e.g., the role of the body) remain underspecified in the literature on the topic, and there remains much to be researched about multimodal aspects of communication.

Critical issues and topics

A key principle in studying multimodal interaction is that people generate interdependent patterns using resources from different semiotic systems (see, e.g., Streeck & Jordan 2009), so it is important to focus not only on the discrete elements of these signs as people produce and understand them, but also on a larger unit than one individual's sign production. People, for example, design their communication for specific others and in collaboration with them. Together, they constantly negotiate topics, reciprocal perspectives, assessments, and shared perception. Each body behaves interdependently, acting in response to other bodies, and joint activities have an intercorporeal character (Streeck et al. 2011). The achievement of what Goffman (1961) referred to as a focused gathering—a first step toward engaging together—is dependent on cues from the body, as focused attention is typically shown in non-verbal ways (such as withholding yawns). In Japan, for example, focused attention includes overt displays in the form of head nods (aizuchi) of different types, such as "singular nods" and "stretched nods" (Aoki 2011).

Developing attunement to the gaze, gestures, and embodied behaviors of others likely constitutes a preverbal set of engagements with the world (Lerner *et al.* 2011; Tomasello 2008). Coordinating with others in multimodal interactions with objects is key to passing on belief systems and mastery of skills. Multimodal resources influence the communication of findings and concepts that scientists innovate in collaboration with others, including communication with images, programming languages and experiments (Suchman 1992).

The advent of digital technologies has not only made interactional multimodal research possible, but the image recording potentials of digital technologies have spawned sweeping innovations and adaptations of communication for long-distance multimodal interaction. Digital communication technologies provide enhancements and constraints to the body's expressability, and people have to renegotiate their habitual embodied communication. Technologically mediated spaces challenge multimodal integration and awareness of the other, as discussed below. Interpreting audio/vocal and visuo/spatial cues or interpreting contextualization cues can be a problem, for example, for those engaged in global teamwork from different localities, such as designers, engineers, and others working together in digital spaces. Digital social media have been widely discussed for their potential to reorganize culturally mediated social barriers of communication, such as those erected between genders to control mobility of women (Ling & Donner 2009; Maroon 2006; Steenson & Donner 2008). With digital communication, members of societies in some parts of the world are experiencing a kind of emancipation from the social rules inscribed for certain members of society on physical space. Children's access to different types of settings, for example, is changing. With the introduction of personal computers into the home space, parents have found they must judge the implications of placing computers in either shared, common family spaces (e.g., the living room) or more private, unshared spaces (e.g., children's rooms). Decisions have an impact on how much interaction adults and children have with others via computer and the general supervision of technological spaces by adults (Aarsand & Aronsson 2009).

In the next sections, the role of the body and space in multimodal communication are discussed in more detail.

The body

The body is considered by sociologists and anthropologists as a nexus of culture. As such, the body is a highly managed sign system, beginning at a very young age. Body comportment is considered to be a key symbol for conveying normativity, for example, displaying "literacy" in culturally approved choices of body adornment. To be able to read the displays of others is one of the foremost ways to show cultural competence. Training in techniques of the body varies with each culture. The body has been described as "man's first and most natural technical object, and . . . technical means" (Mauss 1973: 75). The body is such an important expressive medium that when polled, people regularly report that someone's "body language" is more convincing than their talk if the two modalities are displaying contradictory messages.

Clothing and which parts of the body must be adorned is linked during early childhood socialization to feeling structures including shame and disgust or approbation. Identity, authority, status, and role can be deduced from properties of attire and attitude, and people use attire and body comportment to make predictions about role behavior. The semiotics of dress and appearance (Entwistle & Wilson 2001) can in turn influence decisions about talk, gesture, gaze, and body attitude. In Pohnpei and other Pacific islands, people used to elaborately tattoo the body as a record of clan history, making the body quite literally a text to be read (the word for writing is also the word for tattoo).

Research on one aspect of embodied behavior—gesture—has shown that gesturing is far from a mere expression of dramatic emphasis or exuberance; rather, it is a complex semiotic resource that has relevance for multiple meaning-making projects and for shared cognition. Gestures establish reference points and perspectives for discussion, including adoption or rejection of proposals, and are important signals in the achievement of joint understanding. They can also foreground resistance and opposition to another's stance or position. Gestures portray aspects of thought (see, e.g., McNeill 2006)—for example, speakers' mental maps are made visible to others when using gestures in wayfinding (Haviland 2000) and in other types of explanations. Gestures treat the human mind as something that extends beyond the skin to include social and material worlds (Meyer *et al.* forthcoming). A gesture can fill in for a lexical item. Gestures structure space itself through pointing (Kita 2003), one of the most powerful forms of gesturing. Gestures link past experiences of tactile contact with the physical world by replicating them in an abstracted form. In both signed and spoken languages, gestures display a range of important cues. In the case of multimodal interactions with technologies, new tactile aspects of the body's "interaction with the world" are experienced, and resources are available for extending properties of the body beyond its gestural boundaries.

One of gesture's most powerful properties is that it can make visible particular relationships and actions and enable conceptual understandings. For example, a gesture can represent an imagined idea in a collaboration about design that later results in a built form (LeBaron & Streeck 2000). Gestures help people to imagine jointly (Enfield 2009). Gestures structure interactions, too, in the case of organizing mechanisms such as turn-taking (Mondada 2011). Gestures are used in combination with other multimodal resources for a complex coordination of people and action, such as when online gamers organize complex forays into game world territories. Gamers who organize activity in technologically mediated worlds utilize multimodal forms in their planning of future moves—for example, by sketching in the air a sequence of actions planned to take place online (Keating & Sunakawa 2011). The hands' manipulation of real and imagined objects and space in gesture is a resource for coordinating people and activities (Keane 2003; Lave & Wenger 1991; Luff *et al.* 2003).

The body and its presentation and comportment, including its gesture and gaze behaviors, are culturally made into a conventionalized field of communication, not only through early childhood socialization, but through life stage rituals involving activities performed by or on individual bodies and witnessed by others as part of a building of collective experience—an experience emphasizing individual requirements and benefits of group membership (Durkheim 1995). Digital media applications such as advertizing utilize imagery of bodies with sound and language in a similar way to create and share collective ideas. Types of body presentation and styles of consumption are linked to social identities and beliefs. Gaze plays an important part in this meaning-making and circulation. When people are gazing together at a common event or object, this is taken as a signal of a certain type of participation, one with direct and often exclusive access. A single hearer's gaze behavior can influence the course of an interaction—for example, the organization and content of a speaker's ongoing utterance (Goodwin & Goodwin 1987).

Interactive digital environments significantly alter experiences of gaze and other aspects of communicative systems of the body. Shifts in body orientation, which usually have consequences for organizing participation face to face, do not influence structures of participation in digitally mediated environments such as Skype or video conferencing in the same way. In face-to-face interaction, displaying a focused formation or orientation and attention to others' bodies depends particularly on the attitude of the lower part of the body (Kendon 1990), but the lower part of the body is often not even visible in many digitally mediated conversations.

Elizabeth Keating

Video-mediated gaze is also experienced differently from face-to-face interaction. People find they cannot gain others' attention through simply gazing at them in digitally-mediated interaction, meaning that gaze is not as effective in gaining attention and does not function the same for monitoring the behavior of others (Heath & Luff 1993).

Space

Space is more than a backdrop in which human activity takes place; it is an instrument of meaning, "a tool of thought and of action" (Lefebvre 1991: 26). Space is an important piece of the multimodal repertoire—in fact it may be impossible to abstract space from human activity in general (Auer & Schmidt 2010). The spatial arrangement of letters on this page and the spatial organization of this book influence readers' understanding, for example. Built space structures the natural landscape and creates a culture's representation of key social relationships and views of the world. Cultures or groups then order themselves "in accordance with this representation" (Bourdieu 1977: 163). An American house and a Berber house contain certain assumptions about family roles and practices. The analogy of a text has been used to show how the meaning properties of houses, like those of bodies, are places for "writing" and "reading" status differentiation (Bourdieu 1973)—thus, for example, the body conforms to certain manners of entrance to a house according to a person's status and role (Frake 1964). The legacy of buildings shapes the behavior of present and future generations and can visibly incorporate the past. Physical space is an effective way to make tangible the sacred or invisible. Structures become important reference points and concretize relationships between space and other multimodal behaviors. Space influences identities and subjectivities. And once localized in meaning, these can be dispersed and amalgamated across a wide range of regions both human and mechanical (Deleuze & Guattari 2004).

Digital worlds offer new terrain for cultural inscription of space. They have given rise to discourses about how to appropriately organize digital spaces and how to interpret behaviors within them. With digital spaces, some scholars argue that the once-familiar relationship of dialect or regional language variety to a particular local space is increasingly fragmented and ad hoc (Auer & Schmidt 2010). At the same time, online communities sustain participation of multiple diverse members in new ways and over significant time periods. One is not now limited to being influenced or socialized through localized positions in time and space, or restricted to local meanings; one can occupy multiple positions and locations in space, as in digitized texts and images, for example, which are easily replicated to other locations (Poster 1990). Moral boundaries which formerly depended on space as an enforcing tool (such as the concept of maintaining moral purity through the spatial segregation of genders) are being undermined by a "mobile sociability" (Maroon 2006) of space. Disparate groups are brought together, and with them different senses of space and how to behave within it. Studies of virtual shared office spaces linked by video and audio over periods of years show adjustments in the body's orientation to mediated space emerging (Dourish et al. 1996). In the past, the probability of people communicating within an organization was related to the distance separating them (i.e., rapidly decreasing past the first 30 meters of physical desk separation; see Allen 1984). However, the complex combination of spaces made possible by digital tools differently impacts the role of space in communication today. If workers sitting in an open-style office with their desks next to each other collaborate with (for example, in another culture across the world) a group where members sit in separate, walled cubicles, working more independently, the groups will generate different assumptions about what information each group or individual has access to, and presumptions made on the basis of shared information can be faulty (Jarvenpaa & Keating 2011).

Digital applications can be used by people with a wide variety of sensory and modality impairments or capabilities. Blind people, for example, can use digital tools to transform relationships to physical space, as when GPS devices transform location coordinates into the spoken modality to provide an audible description of spatial features. Blind people using a mobile phone camera can capture visual aspects of space—surroundings and landmarks, street signs or storefront signs—and the images can be sent to sighted friends. In this way, blind people can utilize digital communication as a prosthetic pair of eyes to recruit navigational help outside of the immediate spatial environment. What blind people refer to as modality-induced perceptive barriers to participation can be reduced (Keating & Hadder 2010). For deaf people, digitally mediated space enables communication with hearing people using sign language interpreters, who now transcend physical space limitations to appear virtually and instantly in many locations. Deaf signers find that digitally mediated communication space affords them the ability to gaze at representations of themselves to see the effectiveness of their own sign production, crucial information for building and maintaining reciprocal perspectives (Keating & Mirus 2003). In these ways, digitally mediated space can introduce new forms of copresence, including a mobile one (Haddington et al. 2012; Hutchby 2001; Luff et al. 2003; McIlvenny et al. 2009), and new forms of intimacy within distance (Arminen & Weilenmann 2009), with different challenges for maintaining joint attention.

Camera phones and Skype make it possible to merge near space and far space, and these capabilities are used to manage the participation of distant others, such as in the practice of sending photos and updates, but also impact collaboration on how the audience may interpret the behaviors now within the parameters of their gaze. Webcams expand gaze parameters across geographical space, but also restrict gaze parameters in other ways through reduced visual area of the screen and camera lens. In digitally mediated Skype interactions, elderly parents who are located far away can materialize in the room, but can't physically touch or hold their grandchildren. They engage in highly valued observations of behavior to see for themselves that the children and grandchildren are doing well (Sunakawa 2012). In some digital spaces, one can manipulate visibility of one's body to maintain an "ambiguous ethnic identity" despite being known by others, for example, to be a certain ethnicity (Sebba 2007). Space is a semiotic tool of great potential, providing new meaningful elements of choice, contrast, sequence, and simultaneity.

In the next sections, three specific contexts are discussed in more detail as examples of digital influences on multimodal expression and perception: technologically mediated sign language, online gaming, and engineers working in global collaborations through digital media.

Signed communication and digital contexts

Actions made with the hand are a distinguishing aspect of sign languages. Hand shapes are combined with gaze, facial expression, head and body orientation, motion, and touch. Signers produce a variety of visual signs simultaneously. Eye gaze is a critical resource for grammatical marking, but also for understanding and for addressee specification, among other functions. Combinations of signals such as squinting and head position are similarly meaningful; for example, a squint can signal to the addressees that they should retrieve information not readily accessible, roughly translatable as: "I think you know this item, so, please, search your memory and bring the item into your consciousness, because this item is what I am talking about" (Engberg-Pedersen 1990: 123).

Digitally mediated sign language environments pose problems for some of these properties of signing in several ways. There is often diminished clarity of visual signs due to screen resolution, speed of transmission, and the flattening of dimensions. This limits the effectiveness of signals such as gaze, squinting, and brow movement. The reduced size and dimensionality of technologically mediated space for communication affects coherence for manual signs, too. Aspects of both person and place reference that depend on spatial pointing become complicated when qualities of space change. For example, signers have to reanalyze the effects of finger pointing in space to negotiate whether they mean "here" in "my" space or "there" in "your" space (which is on "my" screen). The communication of the concept "behind," for example, made by pointing behind the speaker (where something is located in three-dimensional space), is difficult to effectively produce for viewers who have only a screen view of the sign (with only two onscreen dimensions). Signers have learned to adapt their signs, e.g., changing the visibility of the finger or thumb direction from behind them (not visible) to rather point in space "beside" them, which has visibility in two dimensional space, and can actually explicitly reference something or someone actually located behind them (Keating & Mirus 2003). This transformation of physical space to align with a digitally mediated representation of space is a good example of the way that digitally mediated space influences both language and the use of space as a flexible signifier of meaning.

Another way signers have adapted sign language to digital communication environments is that they have redistributed the production of meaning across modalities, including eyebrows, mouth, hands, and head position, to maximize clarity of communication. For example, to overcome problems in understanding the target of eye gaze (in terms of addressee specification), finger pointing is substituted for gaze to identity an addressee. Gaze direction is problematic in digitally mediated communication partly because the camera lens is situated differently than the actual co-participant's eyes, and the view is thus mediated through the position of the lens rather than the position of the person being gazed at (Keating, Edwards, & Mirus 2008). Signers have shown that they are very flexible in using the range of modalities available to them. They exploit the gaze properties of the technology, for example, positioning a hand closer to the camera lens to enlarge the hand in the addressee's field of vision, creating a new way to indicate emphasis. Multimodal sign systems function interdependently but differ in their adaptive capabilities for particular environments.

In gaming space, to be discussed below, properties of space and bodies are even more radically innovated, and ways of achieving shared perspective involves both resource flexibility and recognizing and capitalizing on new potentials.

Online gaming and multimodality

The gaming environment has been a thrilling space for novel interaction in unusual spaces with unfamiliar attributes. Players can change attributes of themselves as well as of the space they are participating in in dramatic ways. Online worlds include magical properties that reconfigure boundaries of the individual body and its abilities, and space and its attributes. In games, players are able to manipulate space in new ways—they might re-make a game space into an ice-covered landscape or engage in some form of "illusion control." They might alter gravity, and find that space supports them as they fly through it. Bodies can be made impermeable to the expected effects of actions of others. It is not unusual for players to remark about their bodies' new experiences in space, for example saying "I fell down. Oh. I fell up" (Keating & Sunakawa 2011). Part of the enjoyment of the virtual world is new forms of participation, including the manipulation of properties available to enhance the body and change its relationship to space and others. The digitally mediated game space allows perspective shifts not possible with "real" bodies. The game space can be viewed from multiple angles controlled by the player and the software, and players transition continually from textual representations of space to iconic representations of landscapes. They may switch between a first-person perspective on space and another person's perspective, using language to inform others of what they see; or they may control virtual eyes and body through tactile mode. Avatars, however, are more limited than people in their abilities to talk, use facial expressions, and gesture, although skilled players can manage to cause an avatar to point while running. Language plays an important role in coordinating and sharing new forms of multimodal actions together. Through language, players plan how to behave in digitally mediated game space, and they can coordinate the actions of a team of players. They also critique each other's actions and build new conventions and attitudes about what constitutes appropriate ways to use a digital body and what the game is. Although communicative visual behavior includes "anything an individual does that is visible to another" (Kendon 1973: 31), gamers expand communicative visual behavior by making audible verbal descriptions of what individual avatars are doing that is not visible to all, such as when playing together in LAN party gaming activities. In these complex technical environments of coordination, language makes activity hearable in a way that affects individual coordinating moves. The gamers constantly update reciprocal perspectives, describing their own and others' moves in space, spatial positions, and features of the site; through language, they supply multiple views of the space of collaborative activity. In the multisemiotic game world, successful participation depends on displaying and interpreting a range of cues distributed across different modalities. For example, in one interaction (Keating & Sunakawa 2011), players tell each other about their sensory perceptions. One says, "I see it, I see it, I see it" and another player responds by saying, "I hear it, I hear it, I hear it" (they are looking for a particular signal). Moments later, a third player says "Keep him OFF me," using language to direct one of the other players to take an action in the game world to defend him. In another example, as one player moves his mouse to move his cursor from left to right, shifting the virtual space to enable looking around another player's temporarily inactivated avatar body, searching for potential threats, he informs the others while he looks: "Okay. Let me make sure that it's safe," in order to coordinate the actions of all. After several seconds he says, "I think it's safe now" (Keating & Sunakawa 2011). These examples show the importance of language in organizing and interpreting multimodal action. The effects of actions in space are also mediated through culture and through the skills of gamers, and the imaginations of programmers, developers, and designers.

This goal-directed activity of team gaming is similar to some professional environments which require intricate coordination, such as the collaborations of design engineers discussed below, with some notable differences.

Globalized work teams and multimodality

A third case of digital adaptation of multimodal communication returns us to our earlier discussion of the verbal vs non-verbal divide and how it understates the role that embodied behaviors play in interaction and culture, and our discussion of the body as the nexus of culture. In the case of those whose everyday work has recently come to include global workspaces, the situation they must adapt to is similar to gaming, where not all "players" have access to the same information or the same view of the world, and the world in play is constantly changing. However, it is dissimilar in that in the case of the global office there is very little visual or background information provided between distant locations. In one case of engineers collaborating from geographically distant cities and cultures (Keating & Jarvenpaa 2011), the engineers experienced missed cues about behavior and made wrong assumptions about the intentions of others. With limited access to the embodied cues that colleagues rely on for understanding others and checking understandings, and because of geographical and time differences which limited hours of mediated co-presence, resources were missing for communicating key aspects of work style and preferences, and for coordinating knowledge with other engineers. For example, as mentioned earlier, gestures can enable the visualization of abstract concepts and can establish reference points and orient perspectives on information. Gestures are interpreted as portrayals of aspects of others' thought patterns. Focused interactions are facilitated not only by gesture but by multiple cues from the body, and listeners' attention is typically shown in non-verbal ways.

Virtual global teams experience infrequent interactions with counterpart team members across the world and must make others' actions and words coherent with reduced visual cues about the behaviors and habits of others. Given what has been discussed about what can be shown through gesture, gaze, the body's attitude, and the semiotics of attire, appearance, and space, this means the virtual interactants experienced an impoverished range of communicative clues and a more limited range of opportunities for negotiating meaning. This impacted their skill acquisition, especially concerning adapting to others' cultural practices and negotiating points of understandings among varying cultural habits. Engineers collaborating virtually between Romania and the US and India and the US, for example, were not able to observe the others' work habits, leading to anxieties about cooperation, integrating work styles, and meeting deadlines. The engineers in the study described their frustrations with trying to understand structures and sequences not only of other styles of engineering work, but of interactional routines for showing respectful consideration of others, and appropriate ways to convey nonalignment or criticism (Keating & Jarvenpaa 2011), such as the familiar "why do they say 'yes' when they mean 'no'!" Without access to a wide range of multimodal expressions and coordinating mechanisms and context, communications were vulnerable to being misunderstood or considered rude or "too" direct (see also Murphy & Levy 2006). The sometimes subtle non-verbal expressions which signify and produce power relations and alignment or disalignment differ markedly from those communicated with linguistic forms. The engineers in interviews constantly expressed a nostalgia for face-to-face working conditions, which they were convinced gave them tools to better understand how to work well with other engineers. Goffman noted of gesture, "we have to introduce the human and material setting in which the gesture is made" (1964: 164); the same applies to other semiotic forms as well. The setting or the "surround," including gaze and the body, is integral to the making of meaning and to developing strategies to predict and make sense of the behavior of others. With home, work and in-between becoming increasingly multidimensional (Castells 2001), there is much to be learned about digitally mediated multimodality in interaction. Meaning is an aggregate of many coordinated signals with differing potentials. The importance of understanding meanings that are produced by gaze, gesture, and other signals made by the body (see Jewitt, this volume) is being recognized not only by engineers.

Conclusion and future directions

The development of digital media has enabled the close analysis of multimodality in human communication, both discrete aspects of different semiotic modalities, and the inter-relatedness of modalities in terms of simultaneity and sequentiality. Digitally mediated space has introduced interesting challenges to working and communicating, and has resulted in interesting adaptations in human multimodal communication that are still underway.

In this chapter, the body (including gesture and gaze) and space have been discussed in terms of the communicative potential of modalities as well as the integration of multiple modalities. The influences of digital environments on multimodality have been explored, and three particular settings were used for illustrative purposes: online gaming, sign language in technologically mediated space, and engineers located across continents working together through digitally mediated communication settings. Each of these settings shows aspects of digitally influenced multimodal behavior and co-presence that engage participants in creative ways. The topic of multimodality has relevance for better understanding precisely how culture and social life are maintained and how work and play are achieved, as well as the flexibility of humans in new interactive settings.

Related topics

- Chapter 4 Multimodal analysis (Jewitt)
- Chapter 12 Digital media in workplace interactions (Darics)
- Chapter 18 Online multiplayer games (Newon)
- Chapter 25 New frontiers in interactive multimodal communication (Herring)

Note

1 I would like to express my sincere appreciation to the Freiburg Institute for Advanced Studies for the time and support to work on this chapter.

References

Aarsand, P. & Aronsson, K. 2009, "Gaming and territorial negotiations in family life," *Childhood*, vol. 16, no. 4, pp. 497–517.

Allen, T. J. 1984, *Managing the flow of technology: technology transfer and the dissemination of technological information within the R & D organization*, MIT Press: Cambridge, MA.

Aoki, H. 2011, "Some functions of speaker head nods," in J. Streeck, C. Goodwin, & C. LeBaron (eds.), *Embodied interaction: language and body in the material world*, Cambridge University Press: Cambridge, pp. 93–105.

Arminen, I. & Weilenmann, A. 2009, "Mobile presence and intimacy: reshaping social actions in mobile contextual configuration," *Journal of Pragmatics*, vol. 41, no. 10, pp. 1905–1923.

Auer, P. & Schmidt, J. E. 2010, "Introduction: language and space," in P. Auer & J. E. Schmidt, *Language and space: an international handbook of linguistic variation*, Walter de Gruyter: Berlin, pp. 7–16.

Bourdieu, P. 1977, *Outline of a theory of practice*, Cambridge University Press: Cambridge.

Bourdieu, P. 1973, "The Berber house," in M. Douglass (ed.), *Rules and meanings*, Penguin: Harmondsworth, pp. 98–110.

Castells, M. 2001, *The Internet galaxy*, Oxford University Press: Oxford.

Deleuze, G. & Guattari, F. 2004, *Anti-Oedipus*, trans. R. Hurley, M. Seem, & H. R. Lane, Continuum: London.

Deppermann, A. (2013) "Turn-design at turn-beginnings: multimodal resources to deal with tasks of turn-construction in German," *Journal of Pragmatics*, vol. 46, no. 1, pp. 91–121.

Dourish, P., Adler, A., Bellotti, V., & Henderson, A. 1996, "Your place or mine? Learning from long-term use of audio-video communication," *Computer-Supported Cooperative Work*, vol. 5, no. 1, pp. 33–62.

Duranti, A. 1992, "Language and bodies in social space: Samoan ceremonial greetings," *American Anthropologist*, vol. 94, no. 3, pp. 657–691.

Durkheim, E. 1995, *The elementary forms of religious life*, trans. K. E. Fields, Free Press: New York, NY.

Enfield, N. J. 2009, *The anatomy of meaning: speech, gesture, and composite utterance*, Cambridge University Press: Cambridge.

Enfield, N. J. 2005, "The body as a cognitive artifact in kinship representations," *Current Anthropology*, vol. 46, no. 1, pp. 51–81.

Engberg-Pedersen, E. 1990, "Pragmatics of non-manual behaviour in Danish Sign Language," in W. Edmondson & F Karlsson (eds.), *SLR '87: Papers from the fourth international symposium on sign language research*, Signum: Hamburg, pp. 121–128.

Entwistle, J. & Wilson, E. 2001, *Body dressing*, Berg Publishers: Oxford.

Fairclough, N. 2000, "Mutiliteracies and language: orders of discourse and intertextuality," in B. Cope & M. Kalantzis (eds.), *Multiliteracies: literacy learning and the design of social futures*, Routledge: London, pp. 162–181.

Frake, C. O. 1964, "How to ask for a drink in Subanun," *American Anthropologist*, vol. 66, no. 6, pp. 127–132.

Goodwin, C. 1995, "Seeing in depth," *Social Studies of Science*, vol. 25, no. 2, pp. 237–274.

Goodwin, C. & Goodwin, M. H. 1996, "Seeing as situated activity: formulating planes," in Y. Engeström & D. Middleton (eds.), *Cognition and communication at work*, Cambridge University Press: Cambridge, pp. 61–95.

Goodwin, C. & Goodwin, M. H. 1987, "Concurrent operations on talk: notes on the interactive organization of assessments," *IPrA Papers in Pragmatics*, vol. 1, no. 1, pp. 1–55.

Goffman, E. 1964, "The neglected situation," *American Anthropologist*, vol. 66, no. 6, part 2, pp. 133–136.

Goffman, E. 1961, *Encounters: two studies in the sociology of interaction*, Bobbs-Merrill Company: Indianapolis, IN.

Gumperz, J. J. 1982, *Discourse strategies*, Cambridge University Press: Cambridge.

Haddington, P., Nevile, M., & Keisanen, T. 2012, "Meaning in motion: sharing the car, sharing the drive," *Semiotica*, vol. 2012, no. 191, pp. 101–116.

Haviland, J. 2000, "Early pointing gestures in Zinacantán," *Journal of Linguistic Anthropology*, vol. 8, no. 2, pp. 162–196.

Heath, C. & Luff, P. 1993, "Disembodied conduct: interactional asymmetries in video-mediated communication," in G. Button (ed.), *Technology in working order*, Routledge: London, pp. 35–54.

Heritage, J. & Clayman, S. 2010, *Talk in action*, Blackwell: Malden, MA.

Hutchby, I. 2001, *Conversation and technology: from the telephone to the Internet*, Polity Press: Cambridge.

Hutchins, E. 1995, *Cognition in the wild,* MIT Press: Cambridge, MA.

Jarvenpaa, S. & Keating, E. 2011, "Hallowed grounds: the role of cultural values, practices, and institutions in TMS in an offshored complex engineering services project," *IEEE Transactions on Engineering Management*, vol. 99, pp. 1–13.

Jewitt, C., Kress, G. & Mavers, D. E. 2009, *The Routledge handbook of multimodal analysis*, Routledge: London.

Keane, W. 2003, "Semiotics and the social analysis of material things," *Language and Communication*, vol. 23, no. 3, pp. 409–425.

Keating, E. 2005, "Homo prostheticus: problematizing the notions of activity and computer-mediated interaction," in A. Duranti (ed.), *Models of language, interaction, and culture*, Special issue of *Discourse Studies*, vol. 7, no. 4–5, pp. 527–545.

Keating, E. 2000, "Moments of hierarchy: constructing social stratification by means of language, food, space, and the body in Pohnpei, Micronesia," *American Anthropologist*, vol. 102, no. 2, pp. 303–320.

Keating, E., Edwards, T., & Mirus, G. 2008, "Cybersign and new proximities: impacts of new communication technologies on space and language," *Journal of Pragmatics*, vol. 40, no. 6, pp. 1067–1081.

Keating, E. & Hadder, R. N. 2010, "Sensory impairment," *Annual Review of Anthropology*, vol. 39, no. 1, pp. 115–129.

Keating, E. & Jarvenpaa S. 2011, "Interspatial subjectivities: engineering in virtual environments," *Social Semiotics*, vol. 21, no. 2, pp. 219–237.

Keating, E. & Mirus, G. 2003, "American Sign Language in virtual space: interactions between deaf users of computer-mediated video communication and the impact of technology on language practices," *Language in Society*, vol. 32, no. 5, pp. 693–714.

Keating, E. & Sunakawa, C. 2011, "Participation cues: coordinating activity and collaboration in complex online gaming worlds," *Language in Society*, vol. 39, no. 3, pp. 331–356.

Kendon, A. 2004, "Some contrasts in gesticulation in Neapolitan speakers and speakers in Northamptonshire," in R. Posner & C. Mueller, (eds.), *The semantics and pragmatics of everyday gesture*, Weidler Buchverlag: Berlin, pp. 173–193.

Kendon, A. 1990, *Conducting interaction: patterns of behavior in focused encounters*, Cambridge University Press: Cambridge.

Kendon, A. 1977, *Studies in the behavior of face-to-face interaction*, Peter De Ridder Press: Lisse, The Netherlands.

Kendon, A. 1973, "The role of visible behavior in the organization of social interaction," in M. Von Cranach & I. Vine (eds.), *Social communication and movement: studies of interaction and expression in man and chimpanzee*, Academic Press Inc: London, pp. 29–74.

Kita, S. (ed.) 2003, *Pointing: where language, culture, and cognition meet*, Lawrence Erlbaum: Mahwah, NJ.

Lave, J. & Wenger, E. 1991, *Situated learning: legitimate peripheral participation*, Cambridge University Press: Cambridge.

LeBaron, C. & Streeck, J. 2000, "Gestures, knowledge and the world," in D. McNeill (ed.), *Language and gesture*, Cambridge University Press: Cambridge, pp. 118–138.

Lefebvre, H. 1991, *The production of space*, trans. D. Nicholson-Smith, Blackwell: Oxford.

Lerner, G., Zimmerman, D. & Kidwell, M. 2011, "Formal structures of practical tasks: a resource for action in the social life of very young children," in J. Streeck, C. Goodwin, & C. LeBaron (eds.), *Embodied interaction*, Cambridge University Press: Cambridge, pp. 44–58.

Levinson, S. C. 1992, "Activity types and language." In P. Drew & J. Heritage (eds.), *Talk at work: interaction in institutional settings*, Cambridge University Press: Cambridge, pp. 66–100.

Ling, R. & Donner, J. 2009, *Mobile communication*, Polity Press: Cambridge, UK.

Luff, P., Heath, C., Kuzuoka, H., Hindmarsh, J., Yamazaki, K., & Oyama, S. 2003, "Fractured ecologies: creating environments for collaboration," *Human-Computer Interaction*, vol. 18, no. 1, pp. 51–84.

Maroon, B. 2006, "Mobile sociality in urban Morocco," in A. Kavoori & N. Arceneaux (eds.), *The cell phone reader*, Peter Lang: New York, NY, pp. 189–204.

Mauss, M. 1973, "The techniques of the body," *Economy and Society*, vol. 2, no. 1, pp. 70–88.

McIlvenny, P., Broth, M. & Haddington, P. (eds.) 2009, "Communicating place, space and mobility," Special issue, *Journal of Pragmatics*, vol. 41, no. 10, pp. 1879–1886.

McNeill, D. 2006, "Gesture, gaze, and ground," in S. Renals, & S. Bengio (eds.), *Machine learning for multimodal interaction: second international workshop* (MLMI 2005), revised elected papers, Springer: Edinburgh, UK, pp. 1–14.

Meyer, C., Streeck, J. & Jordan, J. S. Forthcoming, *Intercorporeality: beyond the body*, Oxford University Press: Oxford.

Mondada, L. 2011, "The interactional production of multiple spatialities within a participatory democracy meeting," *Social Semiotics*, vol. 21, no. 2, pp. 283–308.

Murphy, M. & Levy, M. 2006, "Politeness in intercultural email communication," *Journal of Intercultural Communication*, vol. 12, pp. 1–11.

Poster, M. 1990, *The mode of information: poststructuralism and social context*, University of Chicago Press: Chicago, IL.

Schutz, A. 1964, "The dimensions of the social world," in A. Schutz, *Collected Papers, Vol. 2*, Martinus Nijhoff: The Hague, pp. 20–63.

Sebba, M. 2007, *Spelling and society: the culture and politics of orthography around the world*, Cambridge University Press: Cambridge.

Steenson, M. & Donner, J. 2008, "Beyond the personal and private: modes of mobile phone sharing in India," in *The reconstruction of space and time: mobile communication practices*, Transaction: Piscataway, NJ, pp. 231–250.

Stivers, T. & Sidnell, J. 2005, "Introduction: multimodal interaction," *Semiotica*, vol. 156, pp. 1–20.

Streeck, J. 2009, *Gesturecraft*, John Benjamins: Amsterdam.

Streeck, J., Goodwin, C., & LeBaron, C. 2011, *Embodied interaction: language and body in the material world*, Cambridge University Press: Cambridge.

Streeck, J. & Jordan, J. S. (eds.) 2009, *Projection and anticipation in embodied interaction*, Special double issue of *Discourse Processes*, vol. 46, no. 2-3, pp. 93–102.

Suchman, L. 1992, "Technologies of accountability: of lizards and aeroplanes," in G. Button (ed.), *Technology in working order: studies of work, interaction and technology*, Routledge: London, pp. 113–126.

Sunakawa, C. 2012, "Virtual 'ie' household: transnational family interactions in Japan and the United States," Unpublished dissertation, University of Texas at Austin.

Tomasello, M. 2008, *The cultural origins of human cognition*, MIT Press: Cambridge, MA.

Volosinov, V. N. 1973, *Marxism and the philosophy of language*, trans. L. Matejka and I. R. Titunik, Harvard University Press: Cambridge, MA.

Wasson, C. 2006, "Being in two spaces at once: virtual meetings and their representation," *Journal of Linguistic Anthropology*, vol. 16, no. 1, pp. 103–130.

Elizabeth Keating

Further reading

Goodwin, C. 1994, "Professional vision," *American Anthropologist*, vol. 96, no. 3, pp. 606–633.

> This article discusses how the body, language, and environment can be used to produce different versions of "reality."

Mondada, L. 2014, "The local constitution of multimodal resources for social interaction," *Journal of Pragmatics*, vol. 65, pp. 137–156.

> This article introduces a set of articles that discuss embodied behavior and multimodality as well as multimodal research issues.

Streeck, J. 2009, *Gesturecraft: the manu-facture of meaning*, John Benjamins: Amsterdam.

> This book explores gesture and the communicative ecologies in which it occurs.

17

Second Life

Language and virtual identity

Ashraf R. Abdullah

Introduction

When users visit secondlife.com, they arrive on the threshold of a virtual world – in fact, Second Life (SL) is 'the largest-ever 3D virtual world created entirely by its users' (www.secondlife. com 2014). Established in 2003, the online virtual social world (OVSW, Sherman 2011) now has millions of registered users worldwide and hosts tens of thousands online at any one time – users whose interactions and activities necessarily take place through digitally mediated communication. Second Life is ideologically based on freedom and creativity, offering an escape from the constraints of reality and the liberty to do and be whatever one pleases. As its name implies, it presents not just an alternate reality, but indeed an *anti*-reality, fuelled by anonymity and unconstrained freedoms. Language is only one of these freedoms. In the course of several years of research on SL, I have seen at first hand how *SLers* say 'in SL I feel comfortable, I can be myself' and Boellstorff (2008) quotes users of SL also saying things like 'In Second Life I feel I can truly be myself, my inner self' and 'we wear our souls in here'.

In this chapter, I explore how the residents of SL use language in their construction of a virtual identity. The approach to identity adopted here builds on Omoniyi and White's (2006) concept of *(co)construction*. Identity has always been a 'problematic and complex concept', at once both 'non-fixed and non-rigid and always being (co)constructed by individuals of themselves (or ascribed by others)' (Omoniyi & White 2006: 1). Not only can we ourselves actively be multiple and play with our identities, as Bell (2000) puts it, but the virtual environment and the people around us can also have their effects on our virtual identity.

The discussion begins with an introduction to the attributes and history of SL, then describes related research on SL from a variety of disciplinary perspectives. The focus then shifts to work in linguistics in particular, including corpus-based research methods, data collection techniques, and sociolinguistic analysis, which has offered investigations of linguistic features used by SL residents as part of their acquisition of a virtual SL identity, such as lexis and SL-specific code, word formation and structure, deixis and indexicality, and pragmatic acts (Mey 2001). This chapter concludes with a consideration of gaps in research and recommendations for future work.

Ashraf R. Abdullah

Second Life

The cultural sphere of cyberspace is generally viewed as radically new, post-modern, even revolutionary. This signifies a break in traditional cultural patterns, not only in terms of communication, but also in notions of community and identity. Virtual worlds are often described in futuristic terms; they are 'harbingers of a coming utopia of unforeseen possibilities' (Boellstorff 2008: 32). But virtual worlds like SL have been around for over a decade, and the fact that millions of people continue to inhabit them means that something is staying the same. Today's virtual worlds are described as 'imagined places', a concept that originated with inventions like the camera obscura and the printing press and flourished in the everyday correspondence of pen-pals and in the extended narratives of the novel. But it was with the rise of mass media – particularly communication technology such as the telephone and television – that the notions of 'other places' and 'other visual spaces' really came to the fore. The introductions of Cinerama and Cinema-scope in the 1950s were attempts to develop experiences of a more immersive 'virtual reality', and, in 1956, Morton Heilig came up with an attraction that would offer the virtual experience of a motorcycle ride: one would sit on a structure resembling a motorcycle and feel the force of 'wind' blowing at a speed that corresponded to the movement in a scene (Krueger 1991). Throughout the twentieth century, fantasy literature and science fiction imagined richly detailed virtual worlds. The Internet created new virtual spaces for social life, and with the emergence of Web 2.0 and the development of digital communication, virtual environments like SL became possible.

Indeed, today's virtual identity has many characteristics of the Utopian.

> In Cyberspace, space, time and identity it would seem are no impediment to doing whatever we want to do, or being whomever we wish to be. Identity on the Internet is playful, creative, impressive and limitless, and (so popular discourse would have it) an entirely different proposition from identity in the 'real world'.
>
> *(Benwell & Stokoe 2006: 243)*

Only in a perfect world would we be able to do and be whatever we want – only in a world, that is, like the online virtual world Second Life.

Second Life is a three-dimensional virtual world that has the special feature of being imagined, designed and created by its residents. It was established by Linden Laboratories (LL) in 2003, and, for millions of users, it lives up to the promises of its name. LL provides virtual resources of land and sea, which form the bases of all virtual construction, in addition to software that allows the creation of anything and everything by *residents* (users or players of SL). It is indeed a 'second life', and anyone with Internet access can have it. SL has millions of residents worldwide, and tens of thousands are logged in and immersed *inworld* (i.e., taking part in the SL virtual environment) at any one time. SL's universe includes thousands of cyber-geographic regions, from London, Paris, New York, and Chinatown to Bora Bora, Blarney Stone Irish Bar, Habiby's Club, Arab Avatar, and many more. Just as in 'real life', each region hosts different communities of residents. Each user is embodied by an avatar, which can be customized to any shape and size, and the list of possible virtual activities is endless in everyday SL:

> A man spends his days as a tiny chipmunk, elf, or voluptuous woman. Another lives as a child and two other persons agree to be his virtual parents. Two 'real'-life sisters living hundreds of miles apart meet every day to play games together or shop for new shoes for their avatars. The person making the shoes has quit his 'real'-life job because he is making over

five thousand dollars from the sale of virtual clothing. A group of Christians pray together at a church . . . Not far away a newsstand provides copies of a virtual newspaper with ten reporters on staff; it includes advertisements for a 'real'-world car company, a virtual university offering classes, a fishing tournament, and a spaceflight museum with replicas of rockets and satellites.

(Boellstorff 2008: 8)

These are but a few of the activities and ways people interact in SL with each other and with the virtual world. The array of unfettered possibilities and capabilities SL offers, in addition to its affordances and reach, is its primary attraction. In SL there are *arguably* no social constraints due to the 'anonymising conditions of the Internet, its spatial and temporal indeterminacy, and the escapist, transient and above all postmodern complexion of cyberspace' (Benwell & Stokoe 2006: 245). A person can literally be, do, and say whatever he pleases. As in the case of the man as a chipmunk or elf (Boellstorff 2008: 8), or a woman as a man, cat, or dinosaur, anonymity is a key factor allowing and even fuelling this kind of identity play. Part of the logic of the game (I refer to 'logic' as there are no rules, and 'game' in the sense of role-playing, although many residents do not regard SL as a game) is to successfully construct a virtual identity, which is the basis of being accepted into SL communities. Acceptance into the community is the outstanding social constraint (Abdullah 2014), hence my emphatic use of 'arguably' above; sometimes *noobs* or 'novices' are avoided, rejected, or mocked by the more established *residents* or 'experts'.

The term 'virtual identity' suggests that it is opposed to 'real' identity in that it is existent online, whereas the real identity is the one in our offline lives. But there are materialistic issues involved with having an SL identity (or *SLidentity*), such as having a virtual residence, a virtual job, a relationship, a family, a network of friends, and a social life. There is also a linguistic element to SL identity, as one has to possess the necessary linguistic knowledge for different social situations in SL (Llamas & Watt 2010), such as familiarity with the use and meaning of SL lexis, showing an awareness of the virtual surroundings by using appropriate indexical and deictic expressions, and recognising and acting upon pragmatic acts (Mey 2001).

Second Life is a 'non-ludic' virtual world, and it means different things to different people. A non-ludic game is aimless – that is, unlike in many video games, where the goal is to pass levels or 'save the world', there is no clear objective. Rather, the protagonists in SL are free to make their own objectives and aims. The SL community is full of 'creative designers, educators, students, researchers, business people, event organizers, tourists, shoppers, or simply vagrants' (Ensslin & Muse 2011: 1); earnings in SL currency are even transferrable to U.S. dollars. There is much overlap between these categories, too, as many users who fall under one of the above categories may also pursue another. An individual can have more than one SL account – for example, a user may keep one *main* account and one or more alternative accounts (*alts*), each playing a different role in different communities.

In order to have a second life through SL, one must set up an account on the SL website and download the software. Setting up an account involves, as any account would, choosing a name and login password. SL has changed this process as it has aged. When I created my account in 2008, I chose a first name and then was asked to choose a last name from a list provided by the site. I was then provided with a basic or what is known as a *noob* (beginner, one unfamiliar with the ways of the virtual world) avatar. Nowadays, the choice of username is more flexible and one's *inworld* display name can be changed once a fortnight. There is a wider range of choice of beginner avatars that are much more sophisticated than the *noobish* one of 2008. Once the SL viewer software has been downloaded and the login process completed, a new user appears

in *Help Island*, where a first-time user becomes acquainted with the mechanics of avatar movement, interaction with objects, communication, and transportation between *sims* ('simulations' –
the different regions in SL). When these skills are acquired, the journey of SL begins.

It is not unusual to start out by visiting the heavily populated *sims* and interacting with
other *SLers*. SL has a search option through which one can look for places, events, people, and
even objects. When searching for places and events, the resulting menu mentions the *traffic*
of that particular place – that is, how many people are there at that particular time. Usually
the most densely populated places and events are clubs and parties where people would go to
enjoy good music, good conversation and dance (singles' and couples' dance routines are made
possible through *pose balls*, objects used to enable animation of the avatar). Communication is
practised either through the public chat stream, or through private instant messaging between
avatars.

Figure 17.1 shows a typical screen shot of the SL viewer. There are multiple viewers in addition to the viewer provided by secondlife.com, namely *Phoenix* (Figure 17.1), *Singularity*, and
Catznip, among others. The general features are the same in that they all show the tabs along
the top of the screen, as well as the location bar and search bar. The public chat stream appears
on the bottom left, and the interactive chat window at the right in Figure 17.1 can be moved
anywhere. My avatar (*Ashy Viper* or AV) is dancing with a friend while also engaged in conversation that cannot be seen by the other attendees at the club.

One soon discovers that the aim of having a second life is not merely dancing at clubs and
chatting, although many vagrants do spend most of their time in such activities. *SLers* occupy
a social hierarchy ranging from *noobs*, or novice newcomers, to *Residents*, who are 'experts'
in Zimmerman's (1998) sense. To move up the social ladder is to acquire a virtual identity or
SLidentity (my neologism). This involves presentational skills, such as knowing how to walk and
dress, as well as social capital, such as having a virtual home and displaying wealth. In addition,
the acquisition of a successful virtual identity depends on the acquisition of linguistic competence. Knowledge and frequent use of SL-specific vocabulary, appropriate deictic expressions,
and acknowledging and fulfilling pragmatic acts are all valuable signs of in-group identity.

Figure 17.1   SL viewer screenshot showing avatars dancing at a club.

SL's design was focused on 'fostering creativity and self-expression in order to create a vibrant and dynamic world full of interesting content' (Ondrejka 2004: 1). Creativity in SL can take different forms, from the architecture of the game, to the various virtual activities possible, to the language of SL Residents. It is this latter type of creativity that I focus on in this chapter. It is a crucial part of (co)constructing a virtual identity on SL, and *inworld* digital communication offers an opportunity to observe it at work. Linguistic communication in SL may be text-mediated, voice-mediated, or a mixture of both. Audible language is more revealing of a resident's real-life (RL) regional dialect than text, whereas text shares more attributes with e-English or *Netspeak* (Crystal 2001), such as the recurrence of abbreviations, acronyms, brevity, and nonstandard grammatical forms. A voice option is available for those users who have activated microphones and have no objection to their voices being heard online, though this is restricted in some areas. In my experience, Arabic speakers particularly prefer voice communication due to the fact that Arabic – a right-to-left discursive language – appears left-to-right and non-discursive when in text form unless specific software is bought and installed. Although there are many places dedicated to voice communication such as *voice geek community, voice island* and *voice vixens*, the preference among English speakers (who dominate the population of SL) is text chat through the public and private chat streams.

Current research

Previous research has been concerned with giving introductory, instructional and descriptive accounts of SL (Rymaszewski *et al.* 2007; Robins & Bell 2008) as well as anthropological exploration (Boellstorff 2008), ethnomethodology (Boellstorff , Nardi, Pearce, & Taylor 2012), personal narrative (Guest 2007; Winder 2008), sociology (Mennecke, Triplett, Hassall, Conde, & Heer 2011), intercultural communication (Diehl & Prins 2008), multi-disciplinary construction of virtual identity (Ensslin & Muse 2011), virtual literacy (Gillen 2009), medical and health education (Boulos, Hetherington, & Wheeler 2007), business and economy (Laumer, Eckhardt, & Weitzel 2008) and virtual learning and teaching innovation (Murga-Menoyo 2011), to name but a few. Boellstorff (2008) arguably provides 'the most academic and empirically rigorous exploration' (Ensslin & Muse, 2011: 2) of SL in a book-length publication. As an anthropologist, Tom Boellstorff conducted over two years of ethnographic fieldwork in Second Life. He dwelled among the residents and observed them, learning about their cultures and social groups. 'Tom Bukowski' (Boellstorff's SL name) roamed the virtual world applying anthropological methods to study many facets of SL, including issues of identity, race, gender, sex, economy, violence, and role-play, in addition to the interplay of self and group and the social construction of place and time. Boellstorff *et al.*'s (2012) *Ethnography and Virtual Worlds* is one of a kind – a concise, comprehensive, and practical guide for students, teachers, designers, and scholars interested in using ethnographic methods to study online virtual worlds, including both game and non-game environments. Focusing on the key method of participant observation, the book provides invaluable advice, guidelines, and principles to aid researchers through every stage of a project, from choosing an online fieldsite to writing and publishing the results. Ensslin and Muse (2011) provide insights into how 'second lives' – in the sense of virtual identities and communities – are constructed textually, semiotically, and discursively, specifically in the online environment of SL and in massively multiplayer online games such as World of Warcraft. The book's approach is multi-disciplinary, and its goal is to explore the question of how we as gamers and residents of virtual worlds construct alternative online realities in a variety of ways, particularly through text. Guest (2007) and Winder (2008) provide journalistic accounts of their virtual experiences, giving valuable information about the mechanics, social structure, and culture of the virtual world and complementing the instructional and descriptive accounts provided by Rymaszewski *et al.* (2007) and Robins and Bell (2008).

There is, however, a gap in the current literature regarding more specific linguistic investigation of the language of *SLers*, and few studies have adopted the tools and approaches of corpus linguistics to study communication in SL. Abdullah (2014) addresses this gap, exploring the linguistic construction of virtual identity in a collected SL corpus (see data collection and methodology). The study observes identity projection through language and elucidates its relationship to the real-life identities of a selection of English-speaking and Arabic-speaking residents from SL. The corpus-driven study investigates how users' language in SL reflects their customs, habits, cultural behaviour, and points of difference. This is accomplished by analysing their use of vocabulary, deictic and indexical expressions and pragmatic acts.

SLexipedia

As Benwell and Stokoe (2006: 263) note, 'lexis is one dimension of language which has been profoundly affected by CMC'. This impact is apparent in Second Life. In Abdullah (2014), I have used the term *Slexipedia*, a neologism combining SL with Crystal's (2004) term, *lexipedia*, to describe the particular forms of SL vocabulary (Table 17.1), which display characteristic word formation processes, creativity and playfulness. The study's SL-specific lexical analysis contributes to a discussion about lexical implications for virtual identity.

As a form of synchronous digital communication, text in Second Life is influenced by *Netspeak* (Crystal 2001) and *Textspeak* (Crystal 2004), particularly their features of brevity, grammatical tolerance, and typography (manipulating the appearance of text for decorative purposes or to convey a particular meaning; see Danet 2001). For instance, in Example 1, CP graphically enhances her comment with colons, a graphic heart and capitalization, following it up with a representation of a vocalization that is extended and elaborated with alternating upper and lower case characters.

1   < PCbbMAY11.CC>
     [16:13] CP :::::: I ❤ ❤ THIS T U N E ! ! ! :::::: HOoOoOUlalalala :)

The graphic norms of chat language originating with older digital communication modes are common practices in SL, but a number of additions are site-specific to SL. It is these that are of special interest here. New vocabulary items have emerged, some in the form of neologisms (*TP*, *SLex*), others semantic extensions of existing terminology such as *lag* (slow connection speed affecting movement in SL) and *rezz* (or *rez*, short for 'resurrect', which refers to making an item or oneself appear in the virtual world; see Table 17.1).

Some forms of language play that are familiarly associated with digital communication are evident in the vocabulary items in Table 17.1, for example initialisms (*SL*, *LM*, *TP*), clipping (*sim*, *rez*) and compounding (*SLex*). However, there are interesting forms that seem to be quite specific to SL.

2   < AVSWhomeOCT10.SC>
     [17:20] AV: cant you see snow?
     [17:20] SW: no i am not fully **rezd**

SW in 2 refers to the process of her avatar and the surrounding environment loading or gradually appearing on her screen. *Rez* is a frequently used word by *SLers*, and it would seem strange and *noobish* behaviour to refer to this process with any other word – *appear*, for instance.

Table 17.1 Second Life terminology

AO	'Animation overrider' – an object that can be attached to an avatar and provide realistic movement animation when walking, sitting and standing
av/avie	'avatar'
HUD	'Heads up display' – control panel that controls various animations such as AOs, hugging and kissing
Lag	Sluggishness in movement, connection, and loading
LM	'landmark' – location card
Lindens/L$	Linden Dollars
Noob	A newcomer, unfamiliar with the ways of SL
Prim	'Primitive' – structural unit that all SL objects are made from
Log/relog	Logging out of the world and back in to fix bugs
Resident	Established user, knowledgeable about the ways of SL
Rez	'resurrect' – make appear
RL	'real life'
Sim	'simulator' – one location (or island) in SL
SL	'Second Life'
SLex	'Second Life sex'
SLT	'Second Life Time' (-7 GMT)
SLURL	'Second Life web address'
TP	'Teleport' – transportation between *sims*

In addition to the forms of language play mentioned in previous works (Danet 2001), some reconfigured (structural reshaping of some discourse phenomena that takes place in Web 2.0 environments) forms (Herring 2013) can be found in the data, especially in *SLArabic*.

3   <PCaaAPR2011.IE>
SS: /welkəmu::::::::/
Welcome him!
Welcome hiiiiiiiiiiiiiiiiiiiim!

In Example 3, we see the prolongation of the final vowel in /welkəmu::::::::/ and hence its equivalent in the three tier transcription and translation method. What also can be seen in this example is the fact that this is the English word *welcome* with the Arabic morphemes [/u:/ you pl.] and [/hu/ him] affixed to it, though the full Arabic form is /welkəmu:hu/ in which the [him] morpheme is fully formed, rather than elided as in the SL form. Mixed-code and cross-language agglutination is a common feature of *SLArabic* – the particular type of Arabic used in Second Life – with English being the lingua franca. The corpus contains many cases of English words with Arabic morphemes attached to them, including:

- plurality /lānd-āt/ (lands), incorporating the Arabic noun plural morpheme -āt(final),
- determination /ʼal-mayk/ (the-mic(rophone)), incorporating the Arabic determiner ʻal-(initial),
- preposition /fil-rīl/ (in real(life)), incorporating the Arabic preposition fil-,
- possessive /stāyl-ak/, (your style), incorporating the Arabic second-person plural possessive morpheme -ak (final).

Holes (1995: 81) states that 'The principle of Arabic derivational morphology is that of root and pattern'. Here, English words are treated in the same way as Arabic root words (or base morphemes), and the addition of Arabic inflectional and derivational morphemes results in these quasi-Arabic words.

Cross-language morpheme agglutination, typography, capitalization, and acronymy are all instances of language play that is characteristic of Second Life. This playfulness has led to the unique formation of new words. Some of these words are formed by well-documented word-formation processes, while others are quite innovative in their word formation technique, either being SL-specific or bringing together two languages in one word as in the case of *SLArabic*.

A virtual place

> Second Life is a 3D world where everyone you see is a real person and every place you visit is built by people just like you.
>
> *(www.secondlife.com, 2014)*

Second Life's (2014) own definition of their virtual place is one that emphasizes the 'real': a 'place' 'built' by 'real' people. It also refers deictically to the potential user, 'you'. Without the people who build Second Life, the grid would be empty. The word *build* here takes on a wider meaning than its dictionary entry. Every physical, graphical aspect of a virtual location is built out of *prims*, from buildings and structures to trees, plants, and furniture. Only the land, water, and sky are essentially and primarily provided by Linden Laboratories. The virtual world is also made real by the company: 'everyone you see is a real person'. As people roam through SL embodied by an avatar, they can see other avatars – 'real' people who are also online and roaming the virtual world, each with their own aims and objectives. The laws of physics will inform us that we cannot be in two places at once, but when online and engaged in Second Life, a resident is physically sitting at a computer in the 'real world' and present on the SL grid in the 'virtual world', or *in SL*. Recognising that we are in a virtual world and appropriately engaging with our virtual surroundings is part of the process of acquiring a virtual identity. Knowledge of how to move in SL and *teleport* around the SL grid is a necessity, but this is not a complex skill to master. However, the cognitive process of knowing we are in two places at one time poses a linguistic challenge, and one worthy of investigation.

Our perceptions of the world are expressed through linguistic means in our communication with others, and the language we use reflects our perceptions of the virtual setting, including place, time, and persons (whether participants involved in interaction or not). The study of deictics can contribute to the general discussion of 'real' versus 'virtual' identities (showing that a real dichotomy is hard to sustain even in SL, as my participants move between those spaces/times/personhoods). *Indexicality* refers to the ability of language to pick out particular referents (Grundy 2000) – or, as Mey (2001) puts it, indexical expressions are referential in that 'in the semantics of their "naming", their *sense*', they include a 'reference to the particular context in which that sense is put to work' (Mey 2001: 54). A knowledge of context is required for the understanding, interpretation, and use of these lexical items or *deictics*.

I now turn to indexical issues of person, place, and time in SL, focusing on personal pronouns and adverbials of place and time. The SL virtual environment enables a new sense of space, time, and personhood. The use of deictic expressions in the social context of SL reflects a user's perceptions of the virtual context, which in turn has implications for virtual identity. If a user perceives himself to be immersed in the virtual world and linguistically shows himself to be deeply embedded in his virtual surroundings, then we can say that he has displayed an important aspect of virtual identity, notwithstanding the fact that users can also slip in and out of their virtual identities as they situate themselves in the real and the virtual worlds simultaneously.

The first-person singular *I* and the second-person *you* are by far the most frequently used personal pronouns among residents of SL. *I* is more frequent than *you*, which suggests that *SLers* talk most frequently about themselves, which is expected in a first-person player perspective. The pronoun *I* is necessarily deictic: its referent can only be identified in relation to the context. Halliday's (1994) notions of transitivity and relational processes serve us well in identifying the functions of pronominal deictic expressions. He notes that relational processes are those that classify and identify one experience with other experiences and that relational processes can be of three types: intensive (*x is a*), circumstantial (*x is at a*), and possessive (*x has a*) (Halliday 1994). An observation of a data example from the SL corpus would serve well here:

4   <AVHcreamy12AUG2011.IE>

  1   [10:04] H: But this av is an alt
  2   [10:04] H: And although **I** am not hiding who **my** main is
  3   [10:04] H: The reason **I've** been logging on as **her** is because **I**
  4   associate **my** main with having certain relationships with people who
  5   hang at this club
  6   [10:04] H: Whereas even though it's still **me**. And all **my** friends
  7   know it. **I** don't feel like **I** have the same um . . . expectations with this av

To put this example into context, so as to gain a better picture of 'the deictic field' (Hanks 2005), a model which can be adopted to capture the multimodal dimensions of the data, we can use an image that is associated with this data context.

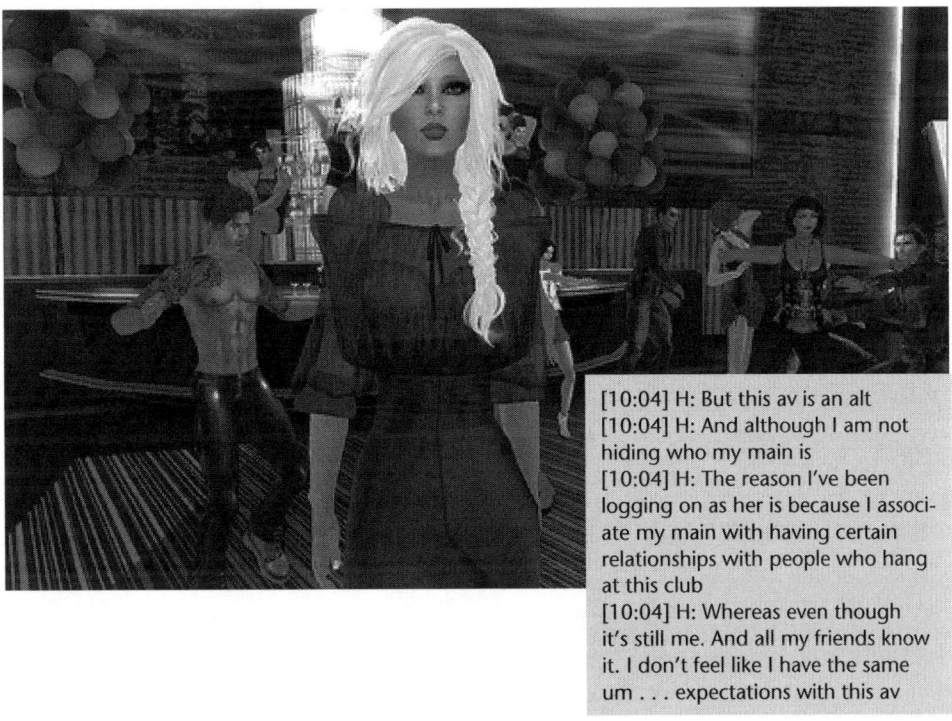

[10:04] H: But this av is an alt
[10:04] H: And although I am not hiding who my main is
[10:04] H: The reason I've been logging on as her is because I associate my main with having certain relationships with people who hang at this club
[10:04] H: Whereas even though it's still me. And all my friends know it. I don't feel like I have the same um . . . expectations with this av

Figure 17.2   Snapshot of H at Club Creamy Kittens.

In this example, H is talking to AV (my avatar) about herself, mentioning that she has more than one account (*this av is an alt*) and justifying why she does so. H and AV are in close proximity to each other in a nightclub setting in the evening. Because she is revealing facts about herself that she does not want other persons to know, she chooses to use the private chat option, even though AV is standing right in front of her. The *who* aspect of this conversation is interesting: the speaker refers to three persons that are associated with her alone: her real world self, her *main* (account/avatar) and her *alt*(ernative account). The referent of the deictic expression *I*, though, seems to be the real-world self of H; when she refers to the other (virtual) self, she uses the third person pronoun *her* (*The reason I've been logging on as her*). The relational process in Hallidayan terms is intensive and of an identifying nature, so the pronoun must have an antecedent; *her* refers to only one of H's three possible identities, namely the alt. So even though the use of *I* by H refers to her real self, the use of the third-person object pronoun *her* refers to her other self. This shows that there is a relationship between the 'real' person behind the screen, and their virtual self or selves. When a person is represented in the virtual world by a *main* and an *alt*, this relationship changes. Identity play is clearly involved with the use of different avatars and ways of deictically referring to them. SL has been described as being an escape from reality, and it seems that the *main* provides the means for that escape. But according to the above example, it also seems that an *alt* can be an escape from the escape. The main account turns into the main second life, which is also susceptible to danger, discomfort and disappointment; in these contexts, an *alt* provides an easy escape route to a new identity within SL. In order to identify the referent of *her* in the example above, one must resort to the context of the situation, which not only includes time, place, and gesture, but crucial background information on the language of Second Life in general, and on the specific clipped terms *av* and *alt* that are used.

Deictic terms of place such as *here*, *there*, and *behind* reflect a *Resident's* conception and awareness of their virtual surroundings. A person is in two places at once when engaged in the virtual world, the real world and the virtual, and *Residents* can distinguish between these in various ways. When a user converses about the real world as if it was *the other* or an outside concept, this choice has implications for *SLidentity*. Linguistically, this can be investigated by examining the use of the deictic place expression *here* and the collocation *in SL* across the corpus.

There is an important distinction between *here* and *in SL*. The former occurs more frequently in the SL corpus but can be rather ambiguous. Quite often one does not know which *here* the speaker is referring to – the immediate surroundings *in Second Life* or in the real world – and clarification is often needed. Hanks (2005) states that the meaning of *here* 'depends upon its contrasts with other related terms including *there*, *this* and so on' (p. 192), and in the context of Second Life, *in SL* can be added to those related terms. *Here* can refer to the immediate virtual context and surroundings, or *in the real world*. In the former case, it is almost synonymous with *in SL*.

Time is also an issue in Second Life. *Residents* originate and are physically located all over the globe in very diverse real-world locations across different time zones. SL provides one unified time zone, namely Second Life Time (SLT), and that is the time zone which most residents refer to and use in the announcement of events and in their SL activities. But, like space, time in SL is not always straightforward. When referring to future time, *Residents* can get rather confused if their interlocutors live in different time zones in RL.

    5   \<AVAJhomeJUL09.FM\>

        1   [5:21] AJB: so, what time is 2:30 pm SLT in Iraq?
        2   [5:22] AV: I dont know . . . my SL clock says PDT★
        3   [5:22] AJB: that is the same thing
        4   [5:22] AJB: pdt and slt are the same

5   [5:22] AV: ok . . . so its 5:22 am SLT **now**
6   [5:22] AJB: some people use SLT to mean Second Life Time
7   [5:23] AV: which is 3:22 pm in Iraq
8   [5:23] AJB: so +10 hours
9   [5:24] AJB: so 2:30 pm SLT is 12:30 am Iraq time
10   [5:24] AV: thats right
★ PDT: Pacific Daylight Time

Now usually refers to the same (immediate) time for all interlocutors in a conversation. But as in long-distance telephone calls, pinpointing the meaning of *now* is more complicated in digital communication, where the speakers may be in different time zones, and RL time has effects on the conversation. The time deictic *now* in line 5 relates to the other temporal lexical collocations preceding and following it in the conversation in the process of understanding the 'when' of a future time. The lexical combinations *my SL clock*, *SL time*, *Iraq time*, *my time* and quantities of time: *3:22 pm SLT*, *5:22 am*, *+10 hours* help to determine the temporal context of the conversation, which in turn can be used to calculate future time (2:30 pm SLT is 12:30 am in Iraq). The unspecific grammatical word *now* is given new meaning through all of these specific lexical items to refer to different times and different time zones in the SL context.

When SL *Residents* are dispersed around the globe, they must use all types of deictics at their disposal in order to deliver their messages unambiguously and to display their understanding and awareness of time and place. These examples have shown how person, place, and time deictics work together to contextualize and disambiguate conversation in SL.

Doing virtual

The title of the section is derived from Winder's (2008) *Being virtual: Who you really are online*. The verb *doing* implies a connection to Austin's *How to do things with words* (Austin 1962), in which he introduced his notion of speech acts. No investigation of language use in a virtual environment would be complete without a section on pragmatics. Linguistic practices (Page, Barton, Unger, & Zappavigna 2014) are what people do with language and the ways in which language is used to perform particular identities. In my data, I investigate *pragmatic acts* (Mey 2001) and their significance in identity (co)construction. It is assumed that the pragmatic acts gathered from corpus – for instance, instructing *noobs* to wear virtual clothing and avoid wearing a box on their avatar's head (which is common) to save them embarrassment – have implications for the (co)construction of a virtual identity in Second Life, where experts instruct novices and in turn help them shape their identities.

Conversations that take place in SL clubs, for instance, differ from those that take place in SL homes, academic surroundings, and business settings. *Residents* employ language in different ways with different intentions – in other words, they perform different speech acts or pragmatic acts. Example 6 from the data provides a good example of how context and intentionality are important in understanding virtual communication in SL.

6   <AVSWs'shomeJUL09.SD>

1   [9:58]   SW: STAND UP BEFORE YOU TP OUT
2   [9:58]   AV: ok . . . good u told me

SW and AV were dancing at a club, when AV revealed that he was 'hungry' and wanted to go to a restaurant. As he took his leave and offered to send a teleport request to his interlocutor, she stated the above (line 1), which at first glance is a simple command. Without prior knowledge of the social context, it would be unclear to an outsider why SW would order AV to stand up, as he was not 'sitting down' in the first place. The utterance's meaning and intention cannot be understood through semantic or syntactic means. Clearly there is a pragmatic act in play here. In SL, when an avatar is being animated by a particular pose or action, that pose or action will continue into the destination teleported to. To 'stand up' in this case actually means to stop the animation and not the verb's literal meaning 'to stand'. Once *rezzed* at the new destination, AV's avatar will appear dancing in a place or new social context where dancing may be inappropriate (though it is possible that one would not want to suddenly appear in dance mode, no matter where the destination is). The act is not a simple speech act of ordering, as the semantic meaning implies. It *is* an order in literal terms, as SW is a more established *Resident* than AV, higher up the SL social hierarchy. There are no clear conditions of authority in SL, and a *noob* is not obliged to obey a *Resident's* command, but will usually do so willingly – indeed, appreciatively. This is because commands from *Residents* are also valuable warnings. This one is intended to save AV potential embarrassment and prevent him from being viewed as a *noob* upon arrival in a new setting.

It has been established that pragmatic acts are complex. They combine a speech act, situated in and affected by a particular context, with a certain communicative intention and function – in the above example, the act is at once face-threatening and face-saving. It would be safe to claim that further complexity is possible and further, perhaps long-term, aims can be achieved through the utterance of a series of pragmatic acts. Speakers and the addressees are not likely to have one simple goal in mind for each pragmatic act. There are different goals, some short-term and others long-term. A short-term goal of a warning could be to help an addressee avoid humiliation and save face, but the long-term goal maybe to aid the novice in learning what is appropriate in such circumstances, acquiring the required skills for future action and interaction, and helping the addressee construct an identity one step at a time.

Data collection and methodology

The data in this study were collected according to ethnographic methods through *participant observation* (see chapters by Varis and Newon, this volume). Second Life is a virtual world, and virtual worlds are 'places of imagination that encompass practices of play, performance, creativity, and ritual' (Boellstorff *et al.* 2012: 1). Levon (2013) defines ethnography as 'the study of how members of a community behave and why they behave in that way' (p. 69) and Boellstorff *et al.* (2012) call it 'an approach for studying everyday life as lived by groups of people' (p. 1). A central method in ethnography is participant observation, as Johnstone (2000) states: 'participant observation is the primary research technique of ethnography or the description of cultures' (p. 82). Ethnography as a method involves understanding local identity through participating in the culture and practices – a key element of understanding SL. The method presents challenges for data collection, including identifying a fieldsite, constraining the boundaries of this fieldsite to make it manageable (Page *et al.* 2014: 107), and ensuring systematicity, in addition to designing a research sample that is representative of the communities under observation. One danger of this method is that it can lead to the production of a researcher-centred data set. Page *et al.* claim that

> ethnographic approaches accept that the researcher is central, and that all views are partial and therefore the researcher is always positioned in some way in relation to the research. The researcher is not an outsider to the research site but a crucial part of it.
>
> *(2014: 110)*

Corpus building

My intention in SL research has been to formulate a corpus that is truly representative of the English and Arabic used in SL for the purposes of identity portrayal. The corpus comprises data in two formats, text and video (with incorporated text). The text data were simply gathered by a copy/paste process of text-based conversations from the public and the private chat channels available in SL, stored in *.doc* format initially and then transferred to *.txt* format to enable compatibility with corpus analysis software such as *Wordsmith Tools* (Scott 2012), which allows for quantitative analysis. The video data were gathered using an electronic video-recording program called Camtasia Studio (TechSmith Corporation 2009). This program records the screen, including any audio going in through the microphone, and also output audio, in addition to having an edit option, which allows the video captions to be manipulated to suit the researcher's needs.

Combining ethnography and corpus linguistics in this sense has many advantages. Instead of conducting structured or semi-structured interviews, as is sometimes the norm in ethnography, gathering a corpus of data allows for more profound linguistic investigation of language as it is actually being used in context. Linguistic patterns, frequencies of particular lexical items, concordances, and collocations can all be observed and commented upon. By keeping field notes and an ethnographer's daily journal, parts of the data can be linked with journal entries and notes to provide a more accurate sense of context and setting. All of these tools for data management and manipulation require a level of familiarity with recording and corpus analysis software.

My SL multimodal corpus comprises approximately 200,000 words in text format and 24 hours of video recording with incorporated text. It is a small and very specialized corpus. Figure 17.3 shows the distribution of the text corpus according to conversational genres. As my avatar AV was engaged in more than one type of virtual community, it is only logical for the conversations to be of different natures and focuses. The English text data were collected from different

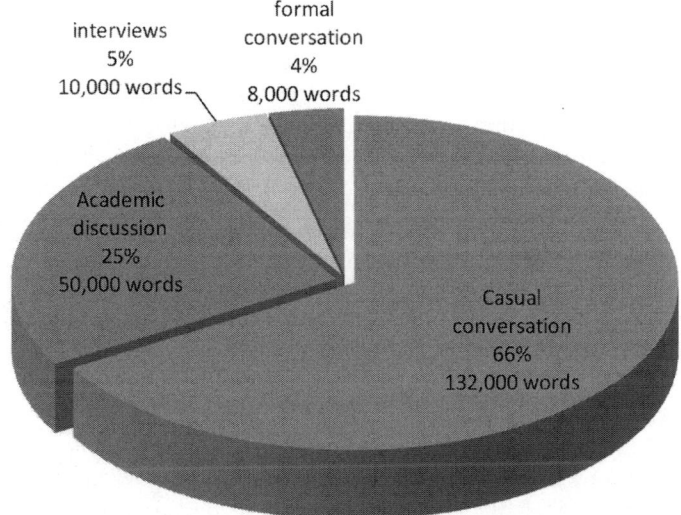

Different types of conversation in the SL Corpus (English)

- interviews 5% 10,000 words
- formal conversation 4% 8,000 words
- Academic discussion 25% 50,000 words
- Casual conversation 66% 132,000 words

Figure 17.3 Conversational genres in SL corpus.

perspectives in the participant observation process and from different chat streams: public chat (taken from clubs, business environments, and academic surroundings); private chat (conversations with close friends and family, some work-related conversations, initial encounters at clubs); and interviews (sociolinguistic interviews conducted by the researcher and during virtual job interviews at the stage of job-hunting).

The video data is mostly in Arabic and comprises excerpts ranging from 5 minutes to 2.5 hours long. The population represented in the video excerpts were predominantly Arabs, including Saudi Arabians, Egyptians, Syrians, Palestinians, and Arab Americans. Some of them were or eventually became virtual friends of AV, while others are total strangers. There are quite a few naturally occurring conversations that involve more than two interlocutors, often four or more, in which my avatar was not a participant.

Methodological suggestions

This discussion of the methodological aspects of data collection in SL brings to mind two specific recommendations for practice in corpus-based research on language in virtual worlds. The first of these is the adoption of a comprehensive file naming procedure. The second is the importance of a consistent transcription technique for any data. I address them each briefly here.

We have seen throughout this chapter that the examples all have titles. These titles signal the file that each example is located in:

    7   \<PCclub4AUG2011.PARTY>
    8   \<AVGThawaiiAUG09.CC>

My method for naming individual files includes several components. At the beginning of each file name, in capital letters, are the initials of the names of the interlocutors in the conversation. In the case of 7, the interlocutors are 'PC', or public chat, which denotes multiple (unnamed) participants in the conversation; in 8 it is AV and GT. Each of these participant codes is followed by the cyber-location in which the conversation takes place – a random club and Hawaii, respectively. The approximate date of recording comes next, followed by (dot), and finally a code describing the nature of the conversation – an encounter at a party in 7 and casual conversation ('CC') in 8. This naming system enables the organization of the corpus according to who participates in the conversation, where it takes place, and the date and nature of the conversation. These tags ensure that if a reader or a future researcher was interested in, for instance, initial encounters, these could easily be segregated in a subcategory of the corpus. Other conversational subcategories are academic discussion (AD), business meetings (BM), and interviews (INT).

A standardized transcription method is essential for comparison within a corpus and could further enable comparison across different corpora. I suggest the adoption of a system like the three-tiered transcription method demonstrated in example 3 above, which follows Gail Jefferson's notation script (Atkinson & Heritage 1999).

Conclusion

Second Life, like life itself, is continuously evolving. Avatars and *sims* have developed, as well as the SL viewers and the software itself. From one look at SL very recently, I have noticed its new compatibility with the Oculus Rift headset developed by *Oculus VR*. This virtual reality headset technology provides a fully immersive virtual reality experience in Second Life and instantly changes notions of place, and even personhood. Communication via text becomes arduous. Perhaps the future of SL communication is voice-dominant, and the luxuries of anonymity will become constrained. I look forward to the future of research on the new and developing facets of place, language, and identity in Second Life.

Related topics

- Chapter 3 Digital ethnography (Varis)
- Chapter 6 Style, creativity and play (Nishimura)
- Chapter 18 Online multiplayer games (Newon)
- Chapter 19 Relationality, friendship and identity in digital communication (Graham)

References

Abdullah, A. R. 2014, 'An ethnographic sociolinguistic study of virtual identity in Second Life', PhD thesis, University of Leeds.

Atkinson, J. M. & Heritage, J. 1984, 'Transcript notation', in J. M. Atkinson & J. Heritage (eds.), *Structures of social action*, Cambridge University Press: Cambridge, pp. ix–xvi.

Austin, J. L. 1962, *How to do things with words*, Oxford University Press: Oxford.

Bell, D. 2000, 'Cybercultures reader: a user's guide', in D. Bell & B. Kennedy (eds.), *The cybercultures reader*, Routledge: London, pp. 1–12.

Benwell, B. & Stokoe, E. 2006, *Discourse and identity*, Edinburgh University Press: Edinburgh.

Boellstorff, T. 2008, *Coming of age in Second Life: An anthropologist explores the virtually human*, Princeton University Press: Princeton, NJ.

Boellstorff, T., Nardi, B., Pearce, C., & Taylor, T. L. 2012, *Ethnography and virtual worlds: a handbook of method*, Princeton University Press: Princeton, NJ.

Boulos, M. N. K., Hetherington, L., & Wheeler, S. 2007, 'Second Life: an overview of the potential of 3-D virtual worlds in medical and health education', *Health Information & Libraries Journal*, vol. 24, no. 4, pp. 233–245.

Crystal, D. 2004, *A glossary of Netspeak and Textspeak*, Edinburgh University Press: Edinburgh.

Crystal, D. 2001, *Language and the Internet*, Cambridge University Press: Cambridge.

Danet, B. 2001, *Cyberpl@y: communicating online*, Berg: New York, NY.

Diehl, W. C. & Prins, E. 2008, 'Unintended outcomes in Second Life: intercultural literacy and cultural identity in a virtual world', *Language and Intercultural Communication*, vol. 8, no. 2, pp. 101–118.

Ensslin, A. & Muse, E. (eds.) 2011, *Creating second lives: community, identity and spatiality as constructions of the virtual*, Routledge: New York, NY.

Gillen, J. 2009, 'Literacy practices in Schome Park: a virtual literacy ethnography', *Journal of Research in Reading*, vol. 32, no. 1, pp. 57–74.

Grundy, P. 2000, *Doing pragmatics*, Edward Arnold: London.

Guest, T. 2007, *Second lives: a journey through virtual worlds*, Hutchinson: London.

Halliday, M. A. K. 1994, *An introduction to functional grammar*, Edward Arnold: London.

Hanks, W. F. 2005, 'Explorations in the deictic field', *Current Anthropology*, vol. 46, no. 2, pp. 191–220.

Herring, S. C. 2013, 'Discourse in Web 2.0: familiar, reconfigured and emergent', in D. Tannen & A. M. Trester (eds.), *Discourse 2.0: language and new media*, Georgetown University Press: Washington, DC, pp. 1–26.

Holes, C. 1995, *Modern Arabic: structures, functions and varieties*, Longman: London.

Johnstone, B. 2000, *Qualitative methods in sociolinguistics*, Oxford University Press: Oxford.

Krueger, M. W. 1991, *Artificial reality II*, Addison-Wesley: Reading, MA.

Laumer, S., Eckhardt, A., & Weitzel, T. 2008, 'Recruiting IT professionals in a virtual world', in W. Huang & H. H. Teo (eds.), *12th Pacific Asia conference on information systems*, pp. 862–871.

Levon, E. 2013, 'Ethnographic fieldwork', in C. Mallinson, B. Childs, & G. Van Herk (eds.), *Data collection in sociolinguistics: methods and applications*, Routledge: New York, NY, pp. 69–79.

Llamas, C. & Watt, D. 2010, *Language and identities*, Edinburgh University Press: Edinburgh.

Mennecke, B. E., Triplett, J. L., Hassall, L. M., Conde, Z. J., & Heer, R. 2011, 'An examination of a theory of embodied social presence in virtual worlds', *Decision Sciences*, vol. 42, no. 2, pp. 413–450.

Mey, J. 2001, *Pragmatics: an introduction*, Blackwell: Oxford.

Murga-Menoyo, M. A. 2011,'Information technology and innovation in teaching: concept map editors: possibilities and limitations', *Revista Espanola de Padagogia*, vol. 69, no. 249, pp. 273–288.

Omoniyi, T. & White, G. 2006, 'Introduction', in T. Omoniyi & G. White (Eds.) *The sociolinguistics of identity*, Continuum: London, pp. 1–10.

Ondrejka, C. 2004,'Escaping the gilded cage: user created content and building in the metaverse', *New York Law School Law Review*, vol. 49, no. 1, pp. 81–101.

Page, R., Barton, D., Unger, J. W., & Zappavigna, M. 2014, *Researching language and social media: a student guide*, Routledge: New York, NY.

Robins, S. & Bell, M. 2008, *Second Life for dummies*, Wiley Publishing: Indianapolis, IN.

Rymaszewski, M., Wagner, J. A., Wallace, M., Winters, C., Ondrejka, C., Batstone-Cunningham, B., & Second Life Residents from all around the world 2007, *Second Life: the official guide*, Wiley Publishing: Indianapolis, IN.

Scott, M. 2012, *WordSmith Tools* version 6, Lexical Analysis Software: Liverpool.

Second Life Homepage 2008, 2010, 2014: www.secondlife.com.

Sherman, K. M. 2011, 'An imagined community of avatars? A theoretical interrogation of Second Life™ as nation through the lens of Benedict Anderson's imagined communities', in A. Ensslin & E. Muse (eds.), *Creating second lives: community, identity and spatiality as constructions of the virtual*, Routledge: New York, NY, pp. 32–53.

TechSmith Corporation 2009, *Camtasia studio* (Version 7) [Computer Program], available at: http://www.techsmith.com/camtasia.html [accessed 12 July 2009].

Winder, D. 2008, *Being virtual: who you really are online*, John Wiley and Sons: West Sussex.

Zimmerman, D. 1998, 'Identity, context and interaction', in C. Antaki & S. Widdicombe (eds.), *Identities in talk*, Sage: London, pp. 87–106.

Further reading

Boellstorff, T. 2008, *Coming of age in Second Life: an anthropologist explores the virtually human*, Princeton University Press: Princeton, NJ.

Provides perhaps 'the most academic and empirically rigorous exploration of Second Life to date' (Ensslin & Muse 2011: 2). Boellstorff provides an expansive account of SL, including its history, culture and technological features.

Boellstorff, T., Nardi, B., Pearce, C., & Taylor, T. L. 2012, *Ethnography and virtual worlds: a handbook of method*, Princeton University Press, Princeton, NJ.

A guide for all those interested in using ethnographic methods to study online virtual worlds.

Ensslin, A. & Muse, E. (eds.) 2011, *Creating second lives: community, identity and spaciality as constructions of the virtual*, Routledge: New York, NY.

A multi-disciplinary look at gamers and residents in virtual worlds and the ways they construct alternate realities.

18

Online multiplayer games

Lisa Newon

Introduction

In a relatively short period of time, online multiplayer games have become a significant cultural and social phenomenon. Today, there are more than half a billion people worldwide who play online games for at least an hour a day, making the digital gaming industry one of the fastest-growing sectors in the world (McGonigal 2011). Multiplayer online games, by definition, are computer games that are played over an Internet connection, and are thus designed to be played socially, with other players. These games typically require players to engage with other networked individuals in the context of the game itself, in the form of partnership, competition, or rivalry. As gaming requires players to coordinate and collaborate with other players, gamers often construct social networks and communities composed of people who engage in regular play together. Through engagement, these groups co-construct subcultures centred on shared social practices, experiences, ideologies, and interests. These constructed groups may be thought of as *communities of practice* (Lave & Wenger 1991) in that they are composed of players who join together in common endeavour and mutual engagement.

As technologies continue to develop and improve, players have access to a range of semiotic resources which they can use in communication with other players. Language and communication in multiplayer games are defined as the ways in which players use digital semiotic tools, like voice-chat, text-chat, sounds, emotes, and other types of in-game signalling, to coordinate, strategize, and socialize with other players in the midst of game-play. This dialogue occurs in all settings and contexts, ranging from situated joint activities where players collaborate to accomplish game tasks, to less calculated situations, where players use the setting of the game for casual conversation. As multiplayer online games span numerous genres, players adopt and innovate styles of language and communication that allow them to coordinate and collaborate with other players according to specific game contexts.

Studying language and communication in online multiplayer games is important for multiple reasons. According to the *Sales, Demographic, and Usage Data* of the Entertainment Software Association (2014), 59 per cent of Americans play video games, of whom 52 per cent are male and 48 per cent are women. These gamers represent a wide range of age groups, including under 18 years (29 per cent), 18–25 years (32 per cent), and 36+ years (39 per cent). As gaming may no longer be considered a niche interest held by a small minority, but rather a popular and pervasive activity undertaken by people of all ages, genders, and geographies, it is important to understand how gaming and digital media intersect with people's everyday lives. More

Lisa Newon

specifically, it is important to understand how interacting and engaging in games influences the ways in which people learn, socialize, participate, and build relationships. Further, studying language and communication in online multiplayer games, as well as in digital communication more broadly, allows us to rethink and expand the concept of community to account for more than just geography and language code, but also media and multimodality, spaces and temporalities, notions of local and global, online and offline.

Historical perspectives

Research on language and digital communication in online multiplayer games is a relatively recent enterprise. Although research based on ethnography and digital communication has become more popular over the past five years, these types of studies are still very few in number. Since multiplayer online games developed as a genre approximately fifteen years ago, much of the literature that has been produced examines the general function of language in games as opposed to players' in-game discourses and interactions. Drachen and Smith (2008) outline three perspectives on types of player communication in online multiplayer games that are not mutually exclusive and therefore used together in game-play. As games are ultimately competitive and goal-driven, they discuss language in gaming as being functional and strategic. Further, they discuss the social nature of online multiplayer games and thus the social nature of language in these contexts.

Language as functional

In this perspective, communication between players serves as a resource for coordination, information sharing, and negotiation of appropriate behaviour. For example, using this type of functional language, players might ask, 'Where should I place this ward?' or 'Does anyone know what spell the opponent will use first?' or 'Is it okay if I tank this fight?' Players use language to negotiate next moves and behaviours and to collaboratively achieve game-goals and tasks. Multiplayer online games are often designed to require teams of people, ranging from an additional teammate to forty or more, to coordinate complicated actions in joint, goal-driven activities. Wright, Boria, and Breidenbach (2002) also refer to this type of talk in games as *performance talk*. This kind of engagement between players is highly focused on the game itself, as opposed to external topics, and includes tactical questioning, explanations of game features, teaching talk, supportive praise, ability evaluation and assessment, and apologies for failure talk.

Language as strategic

VanDeventer and White (2002) examine how young people use language functionally in video games to strategize, teach novice players and observers, problem-solve, anticipate events and future actions, classify similarities and differences in game play, and to display game expertise. For example, players on an allied team might say, 'Don't hit the tank, focus fire on the ranged DPS opponent first', or 'We can beat them if we first use Player A's stun, Player B's grab, and then Player C's ultimate'.

In this perspective, which has ties to game theory, communication is viewed as a rational, goal-driven activity that calculates wins and losses. Players use communication in contexts that further their own game success (Drachen 2011). For instance, in competitive gaming, players may engage in cooperative, functional communication with their own teammates or short-term

290

alliances, as discussed above. Players are less likely to communicate or share information with players on opposing teams, as they do not individually benefit from helping players they compete against. In some cases, threatening or teasing language may be used to distract or derail opposing players for personal benefit. According to Wright *et al.* (2002), this type of language refers to *insult/distancing talk*, which includes speech such as taunting, trash talk, and ritual insults. Strategic language, which is often tightly focused on the game itself, is ultimately discussed as a tool for furthering the goal-oriented interests of the individual player.

Language as social

In this perspective, players engage in communication that may not focus on game activities or contexts, including greetings, word play, debating, popular culture referencing, joking, and story-telling. For example, players using an in-game chat box might write, 'GLHF (good luck, have fun)', 'Victory is *Garenteed* (League of Legends)', 'Chuck Norris can slam a revolving door', or 'Sorry, I'm really drunk right now . . . '.

Gaming is perceived as an activity context in which social communication may take place. Sociability, defined here as playful conversation (Simmel 1949), is facilitated through the structure of online games themselves. The term 'third places' (Oldenburg 1989) describes the physical places outside the home and workplace that people use for social interaction. To many scholars, online spaces, such as those found in online multiplayer games, are third places that allow for real-time conversations with other players through text-chat, voice-chat, and other modes of social communication (Brown 2005; Ducheneaut, Moore, & Nickell 2007; Rheingold 1993; Steinkuehler 2005; Steinkuehler & Williams 2006). Similarly, within these third places, players bring together discourses used in their homes, communities, and informal social interactions, along with more secondary discourses endorsed by formal institutions, to form a sort of 'third space' online, used for these and other types of communication as well (Bhabha 2004; Gutiérrez, Baquedano-Lopez, & Tejeda 1999; Vygotsky 1962). In this perspective, language and communication in online multiplayer games may not necessarily have anything to do with the present activity or game play itself, but may instead be used to construct a sort of *sense of community* or connectedness.

Critical issues and topics

Although work in the field of language and digital communication is broad and evolving as game technologies change, scholars have identified and discussed certain key topics and themes that have made a lasting impact in the understanding of how people construct their social worlds online through digital play. These topics, as discussed below, include language and identity, language and community, language and strategic work, language and heteroglossia, and language and learning. Together, these themes build on historical perspectives of language in games and inspire future discussions and research trajectories.

Language and identity

In multiplayer games, a player's game identity, or public self-image (Goffman 1963) is what he or she projects when interacting socially. The relationship between language and identity is a complex mix of individual, social, and political factors, which function to construct people as belonging to or excluded from a social group (Bucholtz & Hall 2003). Scholars who study language and identity in online games work from several core understandings (e.g., Boellstorff 2008; Nardi 2010; Newon 2011). First, identity is discussed as an accomplishment rather than a predetermined state or object. Identity work occurs through discourse, talk, and various practice-based styles of communication (Eckert & Rickford 2001). For instance, what a player says in-game and the manner in which he/she says it may linguistically and symbolically index a range of different identities, attitudes, and subgroups of players, tied to understandings of gender, age, nationality, social class, style, subculture, and so forth. Identity may also be constructed through other semiotic markers, such as the customized representations of players' avatars in game space. Second, language-focused scholars discuss identity as being fragmentary and constantly in flux. In online games, players may engage in one style of communication only part of the time, or in certain contexts of game play. For example, players may engage in practices like role-playing where they shift linguistic styles according to specific characters they are playing in game and particular activity frameworks (Yee 2014). Third, identity is discussed as varying according to contexts, audiences, and situations. In online games, players use different speech styles according to what game they are playing, what they are doing in game, and who they are playing with. This research is similar to sociolinguistic research on identity involving interactional, face-to-face data, but instead focuses on the method of digital rather than face-to-face ethnography. Like offline language and identity researchers, digital game scholars focus on how players use innovative linguistic and material styles to construct their personas in game and how these styles relate to community and social memberships.

Language and community

As discussed previously, online multiplayer game environments are conceptualized as third places and spaces where spatially distant networked players engage together through social interaction with other players. In studying sociability, researchers often focus on groups of players who engage regularly, share common interests and understandings, and have similar discourses and ways of speaking. While ethnographers have long made use of the analytic concept of community in linguistic and social analysis, the concept's definition has been multiple and contrasting, influenced by scholars' methodological preferences, different schools, and paradigms. Related terms include *speech community* (Hymes 1972; Gumperz 1962; Labov 1972; Morgan 2004); *imagined community* (Anderson 1983); *community of practice* (Bourdieu 1977; Lave & Wenger 1991); *community of interest* (Brown & Duguid 2000); *discourse community* (Bazerman 1978; Porter 1992); and *online community* (Jones 1998; Rhinegold 1993; Wallace & St-Onge 2003; Wellman & Haythornthwaite 2003). Older approaches to the term community, and in particular speech community, focussed on groups of people who share the same linguistic features (see Saussure 1916; Bloomfield 1926), while other approaches focus on groups of people who share the same set of norms, attitudes, and ways of speaking (see Gumperz 1962; Holmes & Meyerhoff 1999; Hymes 1972; Labov 1972). Nevertheless, Duranti writes that speech community is:

> the widest context of verbal interaction . . . any notion of speech community . . . depends[s] on two sets of phenomena: (1) patterns of variation in a group of speakers also definable on grounds other than linguistic homogeneity and (2) emergent and cooperatively achieved aspects of human behavior as strategies for establishing co-membership in the conduct of social life . . . the ability to explain (1) ultimately relies on our success in understanding (2).
> *(1988: 217–218)*

Digital media scholars often focus on how groups of players, such as 'guilds', fit into traditional definitions of community and simultaneously call for a re-thinking or expanding of established understandings. These scholars also focus on how players co-construct community. For instance, they might study how players establish behavioural norms, determine group roles and statuses, resolve conflicts, organize events, and participate in ritual practices (Nardi 2010; Newon 2011, 2014; Pearce 2011; Taylor 2006). In addition to exploring how players construct local cultures in cyberspace through interaction (Guimarães 2005), language-focused scholars are interested in how players align themselves with other players through stance, assessment, and other linguistic forms of negotiating moral participation and the boundaries of community membership. For some scholars, it is important to study how group organization online may be both similar to and different from interaction in offline contexts, while, for others, it is more revealing to discuss how people interact in community groups using a wide-range of semiotic resources that are uniquely suited to online multiplayer gaming environments. These researchers may also focus on how game developers' software and designs shape interaction in online groups. For example, Banks (2013) and Newon (2014) found that online gaming communities are co-constructed through developer and player interaction, centred on design and the game, as well as company and player ideology and culture. As a result of this contact and interaction, digital gaming communities are co-constructed mutually, top-down and bottom-up, institutionally and endogenously.

Language and strategic work

While some scholars research communities as a core unit of study, others focus on activity frameworks that occur in game in order to study how players use language and other semiotic resources strategically to organize and successfully complete group activities in online multiplayer games, such as *raiding*, *questing*, and *player-vs-player battlegrounds* (Chen 2011; Nardi 2010; Newon 2011). For example, dungeon raiding is a competitive activity in *World of Warcraft* that typically requires five to forty players in order to fight a series of powerful game-generated monsters. With the possibility of lasting several hours, dungeon raids are composed of fast-paced individual fights that must be completed in a limited amount of time. That is, each fight is a test of the coordination and skill of the group, and, as such, raids require participants to cooperate and coordinate, using functional language, in order to respond and perform quickly under duress. Functional, cooperative language in games is very much a negotiation of language, community, and identity, requiring players of varying expertise, status, and authority to accommodate to one another.

Language and heteroglossia

Heteroglossia is the notion that the speech of any one person is filled with many different and competing voices, authors, and sources (Bakhtin 1981; Bauman 2004; Duranti 1997). Even in everyday language and dialogue, which is full of quotations and references, people selectively assimilate the discourse of others and make it their own. Words have histories, and, as such, individuals inherit words that have rich indexical histories, some of which they have direct understanding of and some they have limited control over. In online multiplayer games, as with other digital media, language and interaction is full of quotations and references to popular memes, current events, prominent media forms, and other types of information. These types of references are meaningful to others in conversation as many players share similar kinds of knowledge and exposure. One explicit example of this type of voicing can be found regularly in *World of Warcraft*'s general text-chat, where people continuously relay popular jokes about the action-series actor, Chuck Norris. While some of these jokes are improvisational, many of these sayings are found on popular websites and blogs and thus referenced in the game to contribute to the fun, off-topic nature of the communicative space.

Although there has not been systematic research on language and heteroglossia in the context of online multiplayer games, these ideas have not been absent from other studies of communication and digital media (Androutsopoulos 2011). The semiotic environments of online games are not closed systems, but in fact open ecologies where rich, complex layering and voicing occur. Androutsopoulos (2011) suggests that language-focused scholars should move beyond cataloguing linguistic differences in digital discourses and instead engage more holistically with relevant issues of multi-authorship, translocality, and multimodality in digital communication.

Language and learning

Many scholars are interested in the ways in which multiplayer online games are mechanisms for learning and cognition (De Freitas & Maharg 2011; Gee 2013; Jenkins 2006; Prensky 2001; Squire 2002). This body of research is focused on how players develop competencies, literacies, and skills through participation and language use in games and online gaming communities. Examples of these competencies include strategic thinking, planning, teamwork, negotiating, and decision-making. Much of this work takes an applied perspective and explores the possibilities of using computer games to support young people's learning, and thus aims to inform educational policy-makers, researchers, and game designers. While much of this work is not ethnographic and does not explicitly discuss language and communication between players in games, it touches on the importance of language and communication in peripheral, participatory communities and engaged learning. McGonigal (2011), for instance, suggests that online games help players build collaborative and networking skills that can be applied to 'real world' problem-solving. By bringing diverse people together from around the globe to develop these skills through interaction and teamwork, she suggests that online games have the potential to significantly impact the future of higher education. (See also Knobel & Lankshear, this volume.)

Current contributions and research

Over the past ten years, and especially the last five, there has been an effort to discuss digital games empirically using ethnographic methods. As a set of research methods, digital ethnography requires scholars to fully immerse themselves in the online games and communities of play on which they focus their work. Through long-term participation, researchers gain a more complete understanding of how players co-construct notions of subculture, community, and identity. They also gain a more complete understanding of how players use language in these types of environments and groups. Players in games use language and communication in social and cultural contexts and settings, and ethnographic research is key to understanding the nuances of situated, complex player interaction in online multiplayer games.

This section reviews several key ethnographic studies of various online multiplayer games and communities. Taylor's (2006) book, *Play Between Worlds: Exploring Online Game Culture* describes the practices of gamers in and around the massively multiplayer online game *Everquest*. Like many games in this genre, Everquest requires players to create game character avatars in order to band together with other players to complete quests and kill monsters. Drawing from her own experiences as an Everquest player, Taylor also uses ethnographic research, semi-structured interviews, and documentary analysis (e.g., game manuals, supporting websites) to explore how meaning and culture are socially co-constructed. She investigates how different types of players, particularly women and what she refers to as 'power gamers' (players who play in ways that closely resemble work) engage in different types of practices, strategies, and interactions that often blur the line between in-game life and out-of-game life. In doing so, she problematizes the stereotyped categories of gamers and argues that, through studying what gamers actually do, rather than what they are perceived to do, scholars can better understand the heterogeneity of players' interactions and the practices through which they co-construct culture in games. For example, Taylor discusses how a growing body of studies on massively multiplayer online games typically focus on a generic, or imagined player, when in fact, there is a variety of types of activities that different people prefer and participate in, and many different ways of engaging with others in multiuser game worlds. The terms 'casual gamer' and 'power gamer' evoke particular stereotyped figures, yet do not critically analyse real styles of play, everyday experience, and what motivates players.

In her book, Nardi (2010) uses ethnography to investigate the history, structure, and culture of *World of Warcraft*, a massively multiplayer online game, much like Everquest and other games of the genre. Based on three years of participatory research, Nardi discusses the game as an aesthetic experience in which players both work and play. She explores the cultural logics involved in online games, looking particularly at player addiction, gender, and the ways in which players engage in 'theorycraft'. Theorycraft is the term given to the ways in which players strategically analyse game mechanics in order to gain a better understanding of the inner workings of the game. Players take part in these types of practices in order to make more favourable decisions, predictions, behaviours, and outcomes in course of gameplay. In her participatory work both in the United States and in China, Nardi describes how these types of practices co-construct game culture.

Mark Chen (2011) discusses similar methods in his work, drawing on his experiences leading a raiding guild in *World of Warcraft* over the course of ten months. Chen suggests that players in the guild assume specific roles, forming a network of responsibility and interdependence. In raiding, players learn through failure, as unsuccessful team tasks lead to negative interaction (e.g. blaming, evaluation, teasing) that requires players to continuously negotiate group boundaries, statuses, and roles. Through analysis of players' conversations, Chen suggests that social capital and expertise are meaningful markers of players' identities in and out of game.

My own work (Newon 2011) explores how distant, multicultural players of the digital game *World of Warcraft* use voice and text-based chat concurrently – a phenomenon referred to as multi-layered, platform-based code-switching (Boellstorff 2008) – to organize collaborative group activities online. Based on transcribed data derived from sixty hours of recorded video and audio-recordings, this project demonstrates how players use linguistic structures in the midst of game-play to construct community membership, confer responsibility, and negotiate authority and social roles in the group. The linguistic structures players use for these purposes include directives (Becker 1982), assessments (Pomerantz 1984), and stance and alignment through turn-taking (DuBois 2007; Goodwin 2006); the data show that expert players socialize novice players engaged in group game-play through a specific style and register that both demonstrates authority and mitigates social difference.

Another empirical study of how participation, connectivity, and sense-making unfold in the everyday interactions of a global network of players and developers is Newon 2014. Through the lens of a global gaming community built around the game *League of Legends*, the study investigates how translocality (Greiner & Sakdapolrak 2013) and transidiomatic practices (Jacquemet 2005) inform how people understand, construct, and experience a voluntary and avocational community and identity in their everyday lives. Distributed players and developers co-construct a sense of community, belonging, and connectivity through language and interaction, both online and offline. I argue that as technology and globalization continue to impact, transform, and recreate communities, there is a great need to expand our understanding of speech communities to account for the changing forms of meaningful participation in a society or culture. Players and developers co-construct community and identity through language, distinctiveness, and authenticity – they co-construct a *sense of community* through linguistic and communicative styles, signalling community membership through lexical resources and wordplay. Players use specific technical registers in order to distinguish themselves as authentic *League of Legends* players who share common references and experiences.

Developers and players promote feelings of inclusion and connectivity by negotiating what constitutes appropriate community membership and behaviour. For example, various codes of conduct and software are created and implemented by the company institutionally as a means of managing disputes and inappropriate community behaviour. At the same time, community members manage endogenous disputes and disagreements outside of formal institutional structures. Through interaction, players and developers form evaluative stances of what appropriate player community behaviour should entail, but these stances are fluid, overlapping, and at times competing.

Further, players and developers co-create community through understandings and narrative experiences of translocality and temporality. Drawing from interview data collected over the course of fieldwork, I examine what developers and players mean when they use words like 'global' and 'local' to describe different and overlapping communities in the greater *League of Legends* community. Discussions among players are often about co-constructing a sense of community and belonging in spite of regional, cultural, and linguistic differences in the global network. When players and developers work together to make sense of both global and local experiences, as well as a range of much more complex, translocal experiences, they co-create a sense of community and belonging. These findings suggest that the process of community in the digital and information age is very complex and nuanced, and an expanded or reimagined analytic model for understanding community is critically needed in order to account for the fluid ways in which people come to experience and organize their everyday social worlds.

Main research methods

The following ethnographic methods are key in the study of language and digital communication in online multiplayer games.

Participant observation

Participant observation involves taking part in the daily activities, rituals, interactions, and events of a group of people as the primary means for observing and learning the implicit and unspoken aspects of their life routines and culture as they unfold (Bernard 1998; Dewalt & Dewalt 2002). In the contexts of online multiplayer games, where the researcher must engage in both play and research simultaneously, this non-elicited data might include naturally occurring conversations, activities, embodiments, movements through space, and built environments (Boellstorff, Nardi, Pearce, & Taylor 2012: 55). Through this type of holistic, long-term engagement in the cultural community, and through detailed field notes (Emerson, Fretz, & Shaw 1995), the researcher is better able to identify the practices and beliefs of a social group of which they may have been unaware (see also Varis, this volume).

Ethnographic interviews

While interviewing on its own provides inadequate ethnographic context in online research, open-ended, semi-structured interviewing (Briggs 1986; Mertz 1993) alongside participant observation is a key method in studying language and digital communication in online multiplayer games. Semi-structured interviewing involves presenting participants with a list of questions and prompts in order to increase the likelihood that all topics will be covered in each interview in more or less the same way. In open-ended, semi-structured interviewing, participants are also permitted to introduce new topics, dismiss presented topics, and expand on prompts of their preference to fit the flow of the conversation. Group interviewing (Kratz 2010), or focus group interviewing, is also a useful method, as it allows for conversations that might not emerge in one-on-one contexts. This method may be used online using video-conferencing or audio-recording software or offline in face-to-face contexts. Interviewing is an important supplement to ethnographic participation as it 'provides opportunities to learn about people's elicited narratives and representations of their social worlds, including beliefs, ideologies, justifications, motivations, and aspirations' (Boellstorff 2012: 92).

Computer-mediated discourse analysis

Computer-mediated discourse can be defined as the communication that occurs when people interact on the Internet with one another, e.g. by email, instant messaging, chat channels, video blogs, web discussion boards (Herring 2001, 2004). This type of analysis uses similar methods and key concepts found in disciplines such as conversation analysis and ethnography of communication to study how people use language and draw upon unique digital resources and environments when communicating on the Internet. Computer-mediated discourse analysis enables the researcher to see interconnections between all levels of interaction and may shed light on participant frameworks, online identity performance, and online communities (Androutsopoulos & Beißwenger 2008).

Capturing digital data and transcription

Digital records such as screenshots, chatlogs, video, and audio can be captured in games using available software to document how people are actually behaving rather than how people believe they behave or would like others to believe they behave. Alongside participant observation and interviewing, video and audio recording in online contexts, when transcribed according to conversation and discourse analysis conventions (Atkinson & Heritage 1984), provide the researcher with rich ethnographic and interactional data that illuminates the ways in which people construct and perform relational identities and social roles in their everyday interactions (Duranti 1997; Kulick & Schieffelin 2004). Digital records can also be captured off-game in social media websites, wikis, blogs, and other types of websites. Because of the possible sensitivity of recorded digital data, it is crucial that data collection abides by e-research, disciplinary, and institutional ethical guidelines (see also Jewitt, this volume).

Recommendations for practice

The following recommendations may prove helpful for researchers interested in studying language and digital communication in online multiplayer games.

Lisa Newon

Play the game you are studying

In order to understand how players use language and communication in a particular game or gaming community, it is important that the researcher plays the actual game (Aarseth 2003). As an active participant, the researcher will better understand game objectives, narratives, and cooperative strategies, as well as the mechanics designed by developers to shape player communication. Additionally, the researcher may gain nuanced understandings of how, in what contexts, and for what means players use the semiotic tools available in game-play.

Follow related social media and websites

It is also important for the researcher to read and become familiar with the discourse present on websites and other digital content associated with the game. These websites may be different depending on the specific game and network of players, but in general include websites and message-boards sponsored and developed by the game company, fan websites and strategy guides, popular news forums like *reddit*, and social media sites like Facebook, Twitter, and YouTube that feature gaming pages and channels. By engaging with these websites, the researcher not only gains a broader understanding of how players interact out-of-game, but might also use these sites to 'enter the community', making contact and building rapport with potential informants and gaming groups.

Read what has already been written and determine the unique contribution of your work

As with any topic of study, the researcher must begin by thoroughly reading and reflecting on the existing literature in the field. The researcher may find it useful to begin with the work listed in the 'References' and 'Further reading' sections of this chapter. Because the field is continuously growing and changing as technologies develop, it may also be useful to join an active game/media-research listserv that maintains regular, ongoing conversation (for example, see *Association of Internet Researchers*). By becoming familiar with the existing literature, the researcher may be more successful in developing their particular research objectives and determining their unique contribution to the field.

Become familiar with e-research ethics

Through all steps of the research process, ethical issues may arise and need to be addressed. In Internet-based research specifically, these issues may involve discussions of what constitutes human subjects, concepts of public and private, and identifiable personhood in datasets. The researcher should become familiar and abide by existing e-research, disciplinary, and institutional ethics guidelines.

Determine your methods and software

The researcher should determine which methods are best suited to his or her particular research questions and objectives. Based on this research plan, the researcher should become familiar with different types of software for data collection. Examples include applications for audio-recording, video-capture, transcription, video-conferencing, and social media monitoring. Since software changes regularly as technologies develop, it is in the researcher's best interest to keep up with the wide market of research tools available.

Create a searchable archived database

In doing digital ethnography and computer-mediated discourse analysis, the researcher will inevitably collect a multitude of text, video, images, audio, websites, and other online data. It is recommended that the researcher organize this data according to date, media genre, and/or keyword in a searchable database that sorts and stores this information in a single collection. This attention to organization and meta-tagging will greatly aid the researcher during data analysis. It is also crucial that files be saved and backed up regularly.

Attend gaming conventions and events

Gaming conventions, consumer shows, and other sponsored events offer opportunities to network and engage with both game developers and game fans. These local events are often easily accessible, and they are key sites for additional observation and ethnography in offline contexts. Some examples of these events include *Penny Arcade Expo (PAX Prime)* in Washington, *GamesCom* in Germany, *DreamHack* in Sweden, *China Joy* in China, *G-Star* in South Korea, *BlizzCon* in California, and *League of Legends Champion Series and World Finals* in California.

Get in touch with developers

Many game developers have personal public social media accounts (e.g., Facebook, Twitter) in which they encourage fans to follow and engage through tweets and postings. Game developers are typically passionate about the games they create and often welcome conversation and feedback from players. The researcher may wish to get in touch with developers through social media if relevant to their research objectives.

Future directions

Research on language and digital communication in online multiplayer games is a new field, and this chapter offers a preliminary review of what has been written to date. As digital technologies and online games continue to evolve and engage more people, there is much more work to be done. Examples of research topics that could be addressed in future work include the following:

Community construction and identity work in games

Much of the language and digital communication research that has been done so far explores how players engage in community co-construction and identity work in online multiplayer games. Nevertheless, as games, technologies, ideologies, and communities are ever-evolving, this area of research has not been exhausted. Due to pervasive computing technologies and the proliferation and popularity of social networking websites, texting and messaging, video conferencing, blogging and online gaming, rethinking, redefining, and reconceptualizing 'community' is essential. It is important to understand how players participate in online games and construct corresponding groups and communities, how they engage with different community audiences to negotiate norms and moral behaviour, how they cooperate to strategize and achieve game goals, and how they use new semiotic resources, registers, and styles to perform in-game identities.

Lisa Newon

Community management, gamers and game developers

A useful next step would be not only to explore the affordances of digital media in gaming – i.e., the social identities, communities, and worlds that media facilitates – but also to study how these phenomena relate to the teams of media developers who structure and shape the games and their corresponding online communities. This type of work may include analysing the discourse and media on external websites and platforms produced by community managers for the community. This work might also examine the language, practices, and programs utilized by developers to monitor both positive and negative player behaviour. Further, this type of future work might look at how the interaction between players and developers on various forms of social media (e.g., game message boards, Twitter, Facebook, YouTube, reddit) may influence future game developments and features.

Games, temporalities, and space

There is a lack of work addressing how people play and interact across various temporalities and spaces. More ethnographic research is needed to explore the popularity of live-streaming as it becomes a way to broadcast players' game-playing abilities, commentaries on games, and, more broadly, players' thoughts and opinions. Further work should also examine live streams of competitive gaming tournaments from all parts of the world and their instant availability in multiple languages. Language-oriented researchers should engage in research on the physical and social spaces of gaming, such as PC cafes, PC bangs, organized LAN parties, and gaming houses. The language and interaction that occurs in these spaces may be especially helpful for providing insights into theories of localness, distance, and community. Further, much work is needed in studying the processes and practices of localization and translation that occur in development studios for different language and geographic regions world-wide. Alongside this work, researchers should examine how players engage in cross-cultural or cross-code communication in games and out of games on corresponding community websites.

Language, competition, and strategy

Another topic for future work involves looking at how people use language to cooperate and strategize at different skill levels, including the highest level of competitive play. E-sports and competitive gaming events are organized at various conventions and locations for players and fans, as well as live-streamed on the Internet. At these events, players compete in teams using headphones with attached microphones to communicate with each other. By analysing how players communicate and strategize in-game using not only speech, but other semiotic resources like clicking, text-chat, avatar movement, and sounds, researchers may better understand how players use communication to coordinate, cooperate, and achieve successful game outcomes. Shoutcasting – improvisational, broadcasted narrating and commenting on competitive games – is another under-studied area to which scholars should attend.

Gaming economies, work, and language

'Gold farming' is a new form of digital industry that employs hundreds of thousands of people in mostly developing countries. These employees produce digital goods, currency, and services to sell to other players, often from developed countries, for tangible currency. Alongside other employed players, these 'farmers' work long hours and sell their digital goods, often illegally, through extensive social networks. As these economies continue to grow, despite laws, regulations, and taxation, more work is needed to explore how these companies are organized and how employees interact with each other and their customers; how players use language and digital communication to sell their products and sustain their work; and how developers position themselves with respect to these economies through discourses and practices.

Language, socialization, and learning in games

In the future, scholars will continue to study how online games facilitate learning and how new games might be designed with education and socialization in mind. In education, digital games are gaining recognition as learning tools that provide personalized and engaged experiences for students. Games teach students to be digitally fluent by acquiring new types of technical and interpersonal skills, particularly those related to play, multitasking, simulation, performance, judgment, and networking (Jenkins 2006: 4). Research is also needed to address how developers discuss and design games for learning, and how these structures shape game narratives and other in-game experience. Additional digital ethnographies of gaming and gaming communities will also help us to better understand how people learn, socialize, and play in their everyday lives.

Related topics

- Chapter 3 Digital ethnography (Varis)
- Chapter 6 Style, creativity and play (Nishimura)
- Chapter 9 Digital media and literacy development (Knobel & Lankshear)
- Chapter 19 Relationality, friendship and identity in digital communication (Graham)
- Chapter 20 Online communities and communities of practice (Angouri)
- Chapter 23 Translocality (Kytölä)

References

Aarseth, E. 2003, 'Playing research: Methodological approaches to game analysis', Paper presented at the Melbourne, Australia DAC conference, May 2003.

Anderson, B. 1983, *Imagined communities: reflections on the origin and spread of nationalism*, Verso: New York, NY.

Androutsopoulos, J. 2011, 'From variation to heteroglossia in the study of computer-mediated discourse', in C. Thurlow & K. Mroczek (eds.), *Digital discourse: language in the new media*, Oxford University Press: Oxford, pp. 277–298.

Androutsopoulos, J. & Beißwenger, M. 2008, 'Introduction: data and methods in computer-mediated discourse analysis', *Language@internet*, vol. 5, available from: http://www.languageatinternet.org [accessed 20 March 2013].

Atkinson, J. and Heritage, J. 1984, *Structures of social action: studies in conversation analysis*, Cambridge University Press: Cambridge.

Bakhtin, M. 1981, 'Discourse in the novel', in M. Holquist (ed.), *The dialogic imagination: four essays*, trans. by C. Emerson & M. Holquist, University of Texas Press: Austin, TX.

Banks, J. 2013, *Co-creating video games,* Bloomsbury Academic: New York, NY.

Bauman, R. 2004, *A world of others' words: cross-cultural perspectives on intertextuality*, Blackwell: Malden, MA.

Bazerman, C. 1978, 'Written language communities', Paper presented at the *Convention of college composition and communication*, Minneapolis, MN.

Becker, J. 1982, 'Children's strategic use of requests to mark and manipulate social status', in S. Kuczaj (ed.), *Language development: language, thought, and culture*, Erlbaum: Hillsdale, NJ, pp. 1–35.

Bernard, R. 1998, *Research methods in cultural anthropology*, Sage: Newbury Park, CA.

Bhabha, H. K. 2004, *The location of culture*, Routledge: Abingdon, UK.

Bloomfield, L. 1926, 'A set of postulates for the science of language', *Language*, vol. 2, no. 3, pp. 153–154.

Boellstorff, T. 2012, 'Rethinking digital anthropology', in H. Horst & D. Miller (ed.), *Digital Anthropology*, Berg: New York, NY, pp. 39–60.

Boellstorff, T. 2008, *Coming of age in Second Life: an anthropologist explores the virtually human*, Princeton University Press: Princeton, NJ.

Boellstorff, T., Nardi, B., Pearce, C., & Taylor, T. 2012, *Ethnography and virtual worlds: a handbook of method*, Princeton University Press: Princeton, NJ.

Bourdieu, P. 1977, *Outline of a theory of practice*, Cambridge University Press: New York, NY.

Briggs, C. 1986, *Learning how to ask: a sociolinguistic appraisal of the role of the interview in social science research*, Cambridge University Press: Cambridge.

Brown, B. 2005, 'Play and sociability in There', in R. Schroeder & A. Axelsson (eds.), *Work and play in shared virtual environments*, Springer: New York, NY.

Brown, J. & Duguid, P. 2000, *The social life of information*, Harvard Business School Press: Boston, MA.

Bucholtz, M. & Hall, K. 2003, 'Language and identity', in A. Duranti (ed.), *A companion to linguistic anthropology*, Blackwell: Oxford, pp. 369–394.

Chen, M. 2011, *Leet noobs: new literacies and digital epistemologies*, Peter Lang: New York, NY.

De Freitas, S. & Maharg, P. 2011, *Digital games and learning*, Continuum Press: London.

Dewalt, K. & Dewalt, B. 2002, *Participant observation: a guide for fieldworkers*, AltaMira Press: Walnut Creek, CA.

Drachen, A. 2011, 'Analyzing player communication in multi-player games', in G. Crawford, V. Gossling & B. Light (eds.) *Online gaming in context: the social and cultural significance of online games*, Routledge: New York, NY, pp. 201–223.

Drachen, A. & Smith, J. 2008, 'Player talk: the functions of communication in multiplayer role-playing games', *ACM Computers in Entertainment*, vol. 6, no. 4, pp. 1–36

Du Bois, J. 2007, 'The stance triangle', in R. Englebretson (ed.), *Stance in discourse: subjectivity in interaction*, Benjamins: Amsterdam, pp. 139–182.

Ducheneaut, N., Moore, R., & Nickell, E. 2007, 'Virtual "third places": a case study of sociability in massively multiplayer games', *Computer Supported Cooperative Work*, vol. 16, no. 1–2, pp. 129–166.

Duranti, A. 1997, *Linguistic anthropology*, Cambridge University Press: Cambridge.

Duranti, A. 1988, 'Ethnography of speaking: towards a linguistics of the praxis', in F. J. Newmeyer (ed.), *Linguistics: the Cambridge survey, vol. IV, Language: the socio-cultural context*, Cambridge University Press: Cambridge, pp. 210–228.

Eckert, P. & Rickford, J. 2001, *Style and sociolinguistic variation*, Cambridge University Press: Cambridge.

Emerson, R., Fretz, R., & Shaw, L. 1995, *Writing ethnographic fieldnotes*, University of Chicago Press: Chicago.

Entertainment Software Association 2014, *2014 Sales demographic and usage data: essential facts about the computer and video game industry*, available from: http://www.theesa.com/facts/pdfs/esa_ef_2014.pdf [accessed 14 June 2014].

Gee, J. 2013, *The anti-education era: creating smarter students through digital learning*, Palgrave/Macmillan: New York, NY.

Goffman, E. 1963, *On face-work: an analysis of ritual elements of social interaction*, Anchor: New York, NY.

Goodwin, M. 2006, *The hidden life of girls: games of stance, status, and exclusion*, Blackwell: Oxford.

Greiner, C. & Sakdapolrak, P. 2013, 'Translocality: concepts, applications and emerging research perspectives', *Geography Compass*, vol. 7, no. 5, pp. 373–384.

Guimarães, M. 2005, 'Doing anthropology in cyberspace: fieldwork boundaries and social environments', in C. Hine (ed.), *Virtual methods: issues in social research on the Internet*, Berg: New York, NY, pp. 141–156.

Gumperz, J. 1962, 'Types of linguistic communities', *Anthropological Linguistics*, vol. 4, no. 1, pp. 28–40.

Gutiérrez, K., Baquedano-Lopez, P., & Tejeda, C. 1999, 'Rethinking diversity: hybridity and hybrid language practices in the third space', *Mind, Culture, & Activity*, vol. 6, no. 4, pp. 286–303.

Herring, S. 2004, 'Computer-mediated discourse analysis: an approach to researching online behavior', in S. A. Barab, R. Kling, & J. H. Gray (eds.), *Designing for virtual communities in the service of learning*, Cambridge University Press: Cambridge, pp. 338–376.

Herring, S. 2001, 'Computer-mediated discourse', in D. Schiffrin, D. Tannen, & H. Hamilton (eds.), *Handbook of discourse analysis*, Blackwell: Oxford, pp. 612–634.

Holmes, J. & Meyerhoff, M. 1999, 'Communities of practice: theories and methodologies in language and gender research', *Language in Society*, vol. 28, no. 2, pp. 173–183.

Hymes, D. 1972, 'Models of the interaction of language and social life', in J. Gumperz & D. Hymes (eds.), *Directions in sociolinguistics: the ethnography of communication*, Blackwell: Oxford, pp. 35–71.

Jacquemet, M. 2005, 'Transidiomatic practices: language and power in the age of globalization', *Language and Communication*, vol. 25, no. 3, pp. 257–277.

Jenkins, H. 2006, *Fans, bloggers, and gamers: exploring participatory culture*, New York University Press: New York, NY.

Jones, S. 1998, *CyberSociety 2.0: revisiting computer-mediated communication and community*, Sage: Thousand Oaks, CA.

Kratz, C. 2010, 'In and out of focus', *American Ethnologist*, vol. 37, no. 4, pp. 805–826.

Kulick, D. & Schieffelin, B. 2004, 'Language socialization', in A. Duranti (ed.), *A companion to linguistic anthropology*, Blackwell: Oxford, pp. 349–368.

Labov, W. 1972, *Sociolinguistic patterns*, University of Pennsylvania Press: Philadelphia, PA.

Lave, J. & Wenger, E. 1991, *Situated learning: legitimate peripheral participation*, Cambridge University Press: Cambridge.

McGonigal, J. 2011, *Reality is broken: why games make us better and how they can change the world*, Penguin: New York, NY.

Mertz, E. 1993, 'Learning what to ask: metapragmatic factors and methodological reification', in J. Lucy (ed.), *Reflexive language: reported speech and metapragmatics*, Cambridge University Press: Cambridge, pp. 159–174.

Morgan, M. 2004, 'Speech community', in A. Duranti (ed.), *A companion to linguistic anthropology*, Blackwell: Oxford, pp. 186–219.

Nardi, B. 2010, *My life as a night elf priest: an anthropological account of World of Warcraft*, University of Michigan Press: Ann Arbor, MI.

Newon, L. 2014, 'Discourses of connectedness: globalisation, digital media, and the language of community', PhD Dissertation, University of California, Los Angeles.

Newon, L. 2011, 'Multimodal creativity and identities of expertise in the digital ecology of a *World of Warcraft* guild', in C. Thurlow & K. Mroczek (eds.), *Digital discourse: language in the new media*, Oxford University Press: Oxford, pp. 203–231.

Oldenburg, R. 1989, *The great good place*, Marlowe & Company: New York, NY.

Pearce, C. 2011, *Communities of play: emergent cultures in multiplayer games and virtual worlds*, MIT Press: Cambridge, MA.

Pomerantz, A. 1984, 'Agreeing and disagreeing with assessments: some features of preferred/dispreferred turn shapes', in J. Atkinson & J. Heritage (ed.) *Structures of social action: studies in conversation analysis*, Cambridge University Press: Cambridge, pp. 57–101.

Porter, J. 1992, *Audience and rhetoric: an archaeological composition of the discourse community*, Prentice Hall: Englewood Cliffs, NJ.

Prensky, M. 2001, *Digital game-based learning*, McGraw-Hill: New York, NY.

Rheingold, H. 1993, *The virtual community: homesteading on the electronic frontier*, MIT Press: Cambridge, MA.

Saussure, F. 1916, *Cours de linguistique générale*, Payot: Paris.

Simmel, G. 1949, 'The sociology of sociability', *American Journal of Sociology*, vol. 55, no. 3, pp. 254–261.

Squire, K. 2002, 'Rethinking the role of games in education', *Game Studies*, vol. 2, no. 1, available from: http://gamestudies.org/0201/Squire/ [accessed 25 March 2013].

Steinkuehler, C. 2005, 'The new third place: massively multiplayer online gaming in American youth culture', *Tidskrift Journal of Research in Teacher Education*, vol. 3, no. 3, pp. 17–32.

Steinkuehler, C. & Williams, D. 2006, 'Where everybody knows your (screen) name: online games as "Third Places"', *Journal of Computer-Mediated Communication*, vol.11, no. 4, pp. 884–909.

Taylor, T. 2006, *Play between worlds: exploring online game culture*, MIT Press: Cambridge, MA.

VanDeventer, S. & White, J. 2002, 'Expert behavior in children's video game play', *Simulation Gaming*, vol. 33, no. 1, pp. 28–48.

Vygotsky, L. 1962, 'Thinking and speaking', in E. Hanfmann & G. Vakar (eds.), *Lev Vygotsky archive transcribed by Andy Blunden*, MIT Press: Cambridge, MA.

Wallace, D. & St-Onge, H. 2003, 'Leveraging communities of practice', *Intranets: Enterprise Strategies and Solutions*, May–June, pp. 1–5.

Wellman, B. & Haythornthwaite, C. 2003, *The Internet in everyday life*, Blackwell: Oxford.

Wright, T., Boria, E. & Breidenbach, P. 2002, 'Creative player actions in FPS online video games', *The International Journal of Computer Game Research*, vol. 2, no. 2.

Yee, N. 2014, *The Proteus paradox: how online games and virtual worlds change us – and how they don't*, Yale University Press: New Haven, CT.

Further reading

Chen, M. 2011, *Leet noobs: new literacies and digital epistemologies*, Peter Lang: New York, NY.

> This book explores how a group of *World of Warcraft* players establish styles of communication and material practices in order to organize and engage in a 40-person joint activity known as raiding.

Nardi, B. 2010, *My life as a night elf priest: an anthropological account of World of Warcraft*, University of Michigan Press: Ann Arbor, MI.

> Based on three years of ethnographic, participatory research, Nardi explores how players of World of Warcraft interact, adopt, and use technology, and construct social practices in both the United States and China.

Newon, L. 2011 'Multimodal creativity and identities of expertise in the digital ecology of a *World of Warcraft* guild', in C. Thurlow & K. Mroczek (eds.), *Digital discourse: language in the new media*, Oxford University Press, doi:10.1093/acprof:oso/9780199795437.003.0007.

> Based on transcribed data derived from 60 hours of recorded video and audio-recordings, this chapter explores how expert and novice members of a *World of Warcraft* guild use linguistic structures in the midst of game play to construct community membership, confer responsibility, and negotiate authority and social roles in the group.

Paul, C. 2012, *Wordplay and the discourse of video games: analyzing words, design, and play*, Routledge: New York, NY.

> This book explores the ways in which designers, players, and society negotiate the discourse of games through words, design, and play.

Taylor, T. 2006, *Play between worlds: exploring online game culture*, MIT Press: Cambridge, MA.

> This book explores how multiplayer online games, in particular *Everquest*, are social spaces where people co-construct emergent player cultures.

Relationality, friendship, and identity in digital communication

Sage Lambert Graham

Introduction

According to the Pew Internet and American Life Project (sponsored by the Pew Research Center), as of December 2012, 67 percent of online adults use social networking sites. A November 2010 study by the same group also found that:

- Social networking sites are increasingly used to keep up with close social ties.
- The average user of a social networking site has more close ties and is half as likely to be socially isolated as the average American.
- Facebook users are more trusting than others.
- Facebook users have more close relationships.
- Internet users get more support from their social ties and Facebook users get the most support.

Facebook revives "dormant" relationships.[1] It is common in much of Western society for people to have a Facebook or some other social media account that they use to keep in touch with others. Social networking sites, moreover, are not the only ways that we interact online—we also use email, Twitter, IM, and discussion boards to discuss topics of interest, form relationships, and otherwise interact with others. Identities—how we choose and project our personae in these environments—play a key role in the types of relationships we form and the friendships (or animosities) we develop when interacting in these settings. In examining the ways we form relationships online, we must first consider how we define relationality, friendship, and identity—all key concepts. At its core, relationality is the navigation of closeness or distance between individuals or groups. The foundation of relationality is our degree of alignment with others, and constructing that alignment requires an ongoing dance which may change from context to context and moment to moment.

Alignments are critical to our ability to form friendships online. What is "friendship"? A clear definition is a tricky thing, but ultimately I would argue that friendship results when there is alignment with another. There are degrees of alignment, of course, and being aligned with someone does not necessarily mean that a friendship exists, but some amount of alignment/shared value/common experience must be present in order to label someone as a friend. We can argue, then, that in any interaction, we negotiate alignment to establish our level of relationality with others, and at one end of that "relationality spectrum" are those we would label as friends.

A critical component of both relationality and friendship is identity. Identity is dynamic and constantly re-negotiated. It depends on the participants in any interaction, the degree of alignment they share, and the contexts in which they are interacting. And, ultimately, our relationships with one another are based on our conception of the others' identities. Identity, moreover, is not just an individual construct. In addition to the individual identities we construct for ourselves (and project onto others), we also form group identities that are based on common denominators—shared alignments that bind us to others in a group. Individual versus group identities will be discussed more thoroughly below.

In the past 40 years, the advent and growth of digital communication has radically redefined our notions of alignment, friendship, relationships, and identity. Where friends and communities were once determined by physical proximity, and we took for granted that gathering together in the same space was a marker of our closeness with one another, digital communication has now allowed us to connect with one another without the constraints of time and space. We can form friendships, romantic relationships, and communities without ever seeing the others with whom we have formed these ties. As interactions via digital media have become more and more frequent, and as technology advances and new media enter the scene, we have had to adjust our ideas about what friendships and relationships are, and this makes the ways that we form identities and relationships online a worthy (and fascinating) area of study.

Historical perspectives

Foundations in linguistic identity research

The desire to understand human interaction is nothing new, and it makes sense that the rise of digital communication in many parts of the world would have a profound influence on that interaction. Linguists have examined the construction of identity through language in *non*-digital contexts for some time, using a variety of theoretical and disciplinary approaches and perspectives. Considerations of space do not allow a complete discussion of all of these approaches here, but a brief discussion of a few particularly influential ones is warranted (for a more comprehensive overview, see e.g., Benwell & Stokoe 2006; De Fina *et al.* 2006).

In sociolinguistics, much of the exploration of identity builds on the work of Erving Goffman (1959, 1974, 1981). Goffman argues that we construct our identities within the frame of any interaction by displaying a *footing*. Footing, according to Goffman, is "the alignment that speaker and hearers take toward each other and toward the content of their talk. Interlocutors jointly construct frames by signaling their own ever-shifting footings while recognizing and ratifying those of co-participants" (1981: 128). The Social Constructivist model of identity construction has grown from this notion of footing. Proponents of social constructivism argue that we create our identities within the context of every interaction we have, that identity construction is ongoing within interaction, and that our identities evolve as the interaction proceeds rather than being static (see De Fina *et al.* 2006).

A related framework in analyzing identity is Positioning Theory, first developed by van Langenhove and Harré (1999) and Davies and Harré (1999). Positioning theory proposes that when we interact, we *position* ourselves (and others) in relation to the individuals and groups involved, creating either alignment or distance. According to this approach, identities are co-constructed, with speakers positioning both themselves and others with regard to their alignments.

Yet another trend in research on identity construction is seen in frameworks that draw on broad categories as a way to understand individuals' identity construction. Membership Categorization (Antaki & Widdecombe 1998; Sacks 1972), for example, is built on the idea that identity is constructed using categories that individuals draw upon when making language choices (for more in-depth discussion of these approaches, see Benwell & Stokoe 2006 and De Fina *et al.* 2006). As De Fina *et al.* note,

> scholars in the Membership Categorization Analysis movement . . . have drawn attention to the fact that identity construction is often related to . . . identification with typical activities and routines. This, in turn, has prompted a reflection on the nature of identification categories and on the relationships between individual identity and group membership.
>
> *(2006: 2–3)*

Identity categories can be useful tools in understanding people's identities. While a rigid use of this framework could certainly be problematic, the theoretical underpinnings (that all people organize the world into categories that help them make sense of the world) are reasonable. The danger lies in the difficulty of identifying categories that are too rigid or that do not allow us to account for the fluid nature of interaction and identity; I will return to this idea of identity categories later in the chapter. I would argue, however, that these approaches are not incompatible—individuals can (and do) use categories to organize and structure their language choices and create an identity, and that identity (and the categories that contributed to forming it) can also change as the discourse develops. Take, for example, a circumstance where a mother was called to a school principal's office because her child hit another child. In such a circumstance, the parent might initially present herself using an idealized identity as a "responsible parent" and highlight how she encourages good behavior in her child. As the interaction continues, though, the parent might shift toward a "warrior" identity if she feels that her child is being criticized too harshly and needs an advocate. In such a case, the identity the parent projects shifts from one who gives the child instruction about social responsibility to one who will fight for the rights of her child if warranted.

The idea that people draw on idealized concepts to create their identities is reasonable—categories help us make sense of the world around us, and it is therefore logical that we would draw on our conceptions of those categories in our daily interactions. This does not mean, however, that a "categorization" strategy is incompatible with emergent identity—we may switch our references to and alignments with multiple categories within a single interaction. I would argue, in fact, that all of these approaches co-exist in any interaction: we index different identity *categories* as one strategy to *position* ourselves in relation to others, and as our interactions with others unfold, our identities shift and *emerge* according to our conversational and interactional needs and desires.

Identity in digital environments

While the Social Constructivist, Positioning Theory, and Categorization Membership models were originally developed to examine identity construction in *non*-digital contexts, researchers were beginning to explore how computers were affecting our interactions and relationships as early as the 1990s. And while identity exploration had been a focus of linguistic exploration for some time, researchers who began to focus on digital/online identities argued that the computer medium brought new factors that influenced the ways we formed our identities in virtual settings.

Rheingold's (1993) *The Virtual Community* is regarded by many as the first ethnographic examination of the ways that a group of geographically separate individuals formed a close-knit, functioning, interactive community (with its own identity) via the Internet. The papers in Herring's (1996) edited volume also had great influence as some of the first linguistic analyses of online communication.

As of the mid-1990s, researchers from wide-ranging disciplines began exploring how people form relationships and communities online. As with Rheingold, some explored how people form ties online in establishing virtual communities (see Baym 1995, 1998; Jones 1995, 1998; Smith & Kollock 1999). Others explored whether computer-mediated communication (CMC) would give people the ability to overcome aspects of themselves that, in real-world contexts, could lead to discrimination—things like gender, physical disability, race, etc. Herring (1993, 1996) and Poster (1998) were among the first to argue that people assign identities to others online, so prejudices that would exist in face-to-face (f-t-f) environments are no less present in computer-mediated contexts. Still others examined how CMC affected our expectations for others' behavior—the rules of "Netspeak" and how people form identities for themselves and judge others for their ability to keep up with and appropriately use the language that is unique to CMC (Crystal 2001; Shea 1994).

Norms of CMC interaction from these early days of research may, in some cases, seem dated now; media modalities have evolved to the point where many of the issues early researchers identified are no longer even at play. For example, at one time, computer users used dial-up modems, and the rates they paid were determined by the amount of information they down-loaded. The result was a "netiquette" rule that people sending emails would edit email responses so that their messages did not include long chunks of previous conversation—this way the recipients would not have to pay to download long strings of unnecessary data. While many of the concerns of this early research are now outmoded, however, they have nevertheless informed the questions we now raise with regard to how we use mediated communication to form relationships, what types of relationship we form online, and how the various computer modalities we have available influence the strategies we use in forming our identities and our relationships. As communication via electronic media becomes more prevalent and modalities continue to emerge and change, investigation of the ways we relate to one another in digital contexts will continue to merit careful reflection.

Critical issues and topics

As more of our daily interactions occur in mediated environments, examining how we relate to one another in these contexts is both a challenging and a fascinating endeavor. When we begin to examine digital identities in a systematic way, two questions that we might ask are:

1 What interactional patterns and constraints exist in different digital media (Facebook vs email vs Twitter, etc.) and how do they impact the relationships and identities we form online?[2]
2 What current trends exist in CMC identity research and are the topics they raise actually different from f-t-f? If so, how?

Factors in creating relationships in different modalities

Just as in f-t-f environments, some interactions lend themselves more readily to forming online relationships than others. And my attempt to construct a particular identity, while pivotal to forming a relationship, will not necessarily result in one. For example, I might put a sign in my yard declaring support for a political candidate, but that act is not necessarily intended to spark an interpersonal relationship with a viewer. I am making a declaration about my identity, but not one that is negotiable and emergent in a way that would foster a relationship. (Such a contingency might arise if there were a subsequent discussion about my views in a f-t-f conversation in my yard, but that possibility is not related to my putting the sign up). Similarly, some online platforms are more conducive toward establishing relationships than others. We sometimes have a tendency to lump all digital communication together and focus on the fact that it has the potential to link people of all different nationalities and backgrounds. We see CMC as a relational nirvana that opens all kinds of possibilities for connecting with others from around the world. This does not mean, however, that every computer medium is a good context for examining relationality, and we must keep in mind that all relationships and identities are not the same.

In examining relationality and identity online, three factors emerge as having an influence on the strategies we use:

- perceptions/expectations of audience;
- limitations/capabilities of different media;
- goals of interaction.

I will discuss each of these and their link to relationality in digital communication in turn.

Perceptions and expectations of audience: who's out there?

One element in constructing our relationships online involves our intended audience and their level of anonymity. As stated earlier, relationality is dependent upon alignments, and the potential for anonymity (which might make it more difficult to verify alignments) and/or our perceptions of privacy in some digital formats complicates our ability to establish ties to others. When we communicate online, in many cases we cannot be sure exactly who our audience is, and we therefore cannot assess our level of alignment with them. Are there lurkers? Does a hierarchical power relationship exist? Is my audience comprised of many people or just a few (or only one)? Are they close friends or workplace superiors or something in between? In writing a private email to my boss, for example, I am aware that I am writing to one person, I understand the power dynamic between us, and I know that s/he will be able to identify me as the sender (and since I am not anonymous I will be held accountable for anything I say). In posting a message to a discussion forum, however, I cannot be sure exactly who will read my post and may have difficulty in identifying and then possibly modifying any relationship that exists—and this will change the strategies I employ in establishing my identity and alignment with my interlocutors.

In the 1990s, there was speculation that the anonymity of CMC environments would lead to chaos and harassment by people who could not be held accountable for their behavior. While that belief proved to be overblown, relationality and anonymity (and privacy), are linked nevertheless. As my relationship with someone else increases and I grow more comfortable in my assessment of his/her motives, I may reduce my anonymity by disclosing more details about myself, but my emergent identity and the relationship(s) it indexes will still be influenced by my perceptions regarding the level of anonymity that exists. Similarly, my expectations of privacy will shape my projection of my identity, since my ability to control exactly who my audience is directly determines how I choose to present myself (see boyd & Hargittai 2010 and Marwick & boyd 2014 for further discussion of privacy and context in social media). Unquestionably, our ideas about who our audience is and what kinds of information about us they should (or already do) have access to has a direct impact on the strategies we employ when attempting to establish relationships in digital environments.

Limitations and capabilities of different media

A second influential factor in constructing online identities and relationships relates to the technical constraints of the various media platforms we use. Can you use video/pictures or is the communication solely written? Is the communication linear (i.e. top-to-bottom) or can you navigate freely? Is the platform geared toward synchronous or asynchronous communication? Is it designed to be interactive or "read-only"? The signature line in an email message, for example, allows the sender to construct his/her identity in one way; it is most often comprised of only text, and is read in a linear, top-to-bottom way (for a discussion of email closings, see Spilioti 2011). In contrast, a Facebook profile's format allows the inclusion of visual elements like pictures, and the layout does not require that information be read top-to-bottom.

It is worth noting here that, while everything we do contributes to our construction of an identity (see Walther *et al.* 2008 for discussion of this phenomenon on Facebook), some digital environments lend themselves more readily to the interactive co-construction of identity and relationality than others. Pinterest, for example, allows individuals to "pin" photos they find noteworthy to a board and let others (who can "follow" them) see what they have pinned. In turn, one person's followers can comment on or re-pin those photos to their own boards. In this case, users are clearly constructing an identity by choosing which images to pin, but the platform does not lend itself to in-depth discussion and the negotiation of relationships. Rather than sparking conversations that would lead to alignment (or distance), it is more accurate to say that, just as in my earlier example about political yard signs, the focus of these platforms (e.g., Pinterest, Blogs, Twitter) is to "put an identity out there" and try to make it entertaining enough for others to acknowledge it in some way. This keeps the focus on the individual rather than the formation of group identities.[3]

Other types of online interaction, such as discussion boards, lend themselves quite well to establishing relationships between groups of people because the interaction is largely egalitarian. Messages are posted to discussion boards with the expectation that the subsequent interaction will link people by allowing them to share their thoughts and feelings in their own constructed identities. The distinction between this type of setting and individual-oriented ones like Facebook and Pinterest is akin to the difference between attending a cocktail party at which you mingle and chat with others about common interests (discussion boards and email groups) and a stage performance where one individual performs and the other attendees are expected to give feedback (Facebook).

Goals of interaction

Finally, in addition to the structural constraints in different media platforms, the goals of online interaction also influence how both individual and group identities are formed. Schwämmlein and Wodzicki (2012) identify two different types of group identities: 1) common-bond communities, and 2) common-identity communities. Individuals in common-bond communities exist only because the members are interested in one another, while in common-identity communities individuals focus on interests that are shared by the community members. In common-identity communities, "social identity builds on shared characteristics (such as interests, attitudes, or values), on shared social categories (such as gender, nationality, or organizational affiliations), or on a common task or purpose (such as sports teams or work groups)" (Schwämmlein & Wodzicki 2012: 388).

These two types of online communities are often correlated with different computer media. According to Schwämmlein and Wodzicki, common-bond communities like blogs and Facebook tend to focus on member posts and friends' responses to an individual's projected identity. In this case, the focus is on forming bonds between the people while the topic is less prominent and may even be altogether unimportant. Consider, for example, how often people update their Facebook status with pictures of their meals. In the majority of these cases, the point is probably not to talk about the food itself. Instead, the goal is to form a bond with the audience who can relate to your enjoyment or disappointment. Common-bond communities are often profile-based (i.e., the focus is primarily on the individual constructing him/herself and allowing others to respond). Alternatively, in common-identity formation there is greater focus on the topic, which results in a more cohesive and unified group identity. Discussion boards and email discussion lists lend themselves to common-identity communities since they are created with a purpose in mind (e.g., discussing books, debating theology, talking about sports).

If we take this framework as valid, there are striking implications for how we understand online relationships. We think of Facebook as revolutionary in bringing people together, but Facebook does not create a commonly shared group identity. Instead, individuals on Facebook form relationships with one another that are individually-based.

Schwämmlein and Wodzicki's division is useful because it gives us a window into how identity (particularly group identity) is accomplished differently in different electronic media. I would argue, however, that the distinction between the two types of communities is by no means straightforward and is not solely determined by the medium. A group that begins as a common-identity community devoted to discussing literature, for example, might very well evolve and the members might also take on characteristics of a common-bond community. Indeed, this is quite common—groups who meet online, though they might begin by talking about books or some other specific topic, often develop friendships that bridge multiple media formats (Georgakopoulou 2011).

If we are to explore identities and relationships online, it would be useful to have a more complete understanding of the mediation process—the ways different computer media facilitate different types of identities and relationships. While Schwämmlein and Wodzicki's work is a step in that direction, it does not provide a very complete picture of how the formation of group and individual identities work in different modalities. Baron's (2008) book *Always On* addresses communication in multiple formats, but if we are to understand how forming relationships and identities online truly works, more comparative examinations of identity across various media platforms is warranted.

Prominent themes in identity and relationships in CMC (but are they really different from f-t-f)?

Since identities and relationships are so multifaceted, there are seemingly an infinite number of ways we might explore identities and relationships online. Following Herring's (1996) work, the frenzied research conducted in the 1990s and 2000s on computer-mediated communication tended to operate on the assumption that CMC was inherently different from f-t-f interaction. Scores of studies in multiple disciplines and representing multiple theoretical approaches examined CMC in terms of its a/synchronicity, its blend of oral and written strategies, and its potential for anonymity—all characteristics that seemed to dramatically distinguish CMC from f-t-f interaction. A large number of these studies, however, simply applied research on f-t-f communities to CMC contexts, using variationist methodologies to examine factors such as gender, age and ethnicity.

Early research on CMC was also decisively English-centric, and this was problematic for obvious reasons—the Internet was touted as providing a means for people around the globe to connect and communicate, but research that only examines English-speakers misses a large part of the global picture of relationships and identity online. Danet and Herring's (2007) collection of papers in *The Multilingual Internet* was a step toward rectifying this discrepancy, and recent years have seen a rise in research that explores the impact of multi-ethnic and multilingual inter-action in establishing and negotiating identities and relationships online (see Angouri & Tseliga 2010; Georgakopoulou 2011; Lee, this volume; Paolillo 2011).

Gender is another dimension of sociolinguistic variation that has been used extensively as a lens through which to examine computer-mediated behaviors and identities. Beginning in the early 1990s, researchers began to explore gendered power dynamics in both synchronous and asyn-chronous communication (Danet 1998; Herring 1992; Rodino 1997). More recent research has revisited the role of anonymity (discussed above) as a potential factor in how gendered identities are constructed and performed online, particularly in light of the changing levels of anonymity that "Web 2.0" formats such as Facebook have brought. While the research on gendered language online is far too vast for a comprehensive overview here, Herring and Stoerger (2014) provide a rich overview of the history and most current developments in the field.

Finally, another prominent trend in examining online identities and relationships focuses on politeness and impoliteness online as researchers have attempted to assess the role of (im)polite behaviors in negotiating alignment (and therefore relationships). Despite their (often extreme) dif-ferences, seminal works in Politeness Theory (e.g., Brown & Levinson 1978; Fraser 1990; Leech 1983; Spencer-Oatey 2000) all identify politeness as a factor in negotiating interpersonal relation-ships and alignments. Locher and Watts' (2005) framework of Relational Work is particularly use-ful when examining the ways that we form relationships online, since it allows us to focus on the results of (im)polite acts in negotiating alignments (and therefore relationships) with others. While researchers have examined the impact of politeness on identity construction for some time, older explorations often focused on Brown and Levinson's (1978) notions of positive and negative face, which, it has since been argued, are not fully adequate to understand the complexities of interac-tion and participant alignments (Watts 2003). More recent studies have attempted to address the interconnectedness of *im*politeness and identity construction in computer-mediated contexts (e.g., Graham 2007a, 2007b; Locher 2010; Spilioti 2011), and this is an area that is rapidly growing.

While multilingualism, gender, and (im)politeness are all very commendable areas of explo-ration (as evidenced by the amount and breadth of research conducted), these areas are not unique to CMC and are no less present or worthy of examination in f-t-f interactions. This might lead us to ask how or even whether CMC is different from other interactional contexts. Benwell and Stokoe (2006), approaching the question from a social constructivist perspective, discuss this idea and note that if we take identity as discursively constructed, then *all* identities are performances of an imagined identity (e.g., gender identity, cultural identity, etc.) and so the differentiation between "virtual" and "real-life" identities becomes a red herring: "With these arguments in mind, we may decide that 'virtual identity' is simply a prosaic term for the identity work that just *happens* to occur online" (2006: 245).

In a similar vein, some scholars have pointed out that *all* communication is mediated in some way, and therefore the "mediated" label in CMC is a misnomer (Scollon 2001; Thurlow & Mroczek 2011). If we take this view, then the fact that CMC operates in new and developing modalities is not, of itself, noteworthy. That does not mean, however, that online communica-tion is not worth studying.

The answer to the question of whether CMC and f-t-f identities are different, then, is that they are not *as* different as was once assumed. This does not mean that computer-mediated discourse is not a worthwhile area of exploration. It simply means that the *mediated* element does not set it apart as much as was initially assumed and should not be our only focus of exploration.

Gaining membership in the "in-group" of a digital community

Thus far, we have examined: 1) the ways that identity, alignment, and relationality are connected; 2) some historical perspectives; and 3) some of the critical questions we might ask when we explore these concepts in online environments. At this point, we will shift our attention to the negotiation of identity in a specific online community, with a brief investigation of how one individual gains entry into a discussion forum "in-group," thereby achieving greater power through an enhanced relationship with the e-community.

Roles in computer-mediated communities

Most people who have participated in any online group are familiar with certain terms that index status within the group: "Lurkers" are silent observers, "Newbies" are inexperienced newcomers who are expected to make mistakes, and "Moderators/Operators" are those who have administrative authority over the group and can control posted content, layout, and even access to the community itself. There are also less clearly delineated categories like "Participant" (someone who has contributed frequently enough not to be classified as a Newbie, but who has not yet acquired the social capital to be considered a member of the "Core/Ratified/Elite" group), and "Core Member" (part of the "in-group"). Core Members tend to post the most frequently and are privy to the group's history and humor (Benwell & Stokoe 2006; Graham 2008). In e-communities, it is the Core Group Members who have the social authority to define and enact all of these elements.

It is reasonable to assume, given the power of the Core Group Members, that at least some people would want to gain greater status within the group by shifting their role from Newbie to Core Group Member. This might not be an easy transition, however. Benwell and Stokoe (2006) note that there is a "social order in which 'newbies' lack status and must 'earn' it from regulars on the board, who may be hostile" (p. 274). Honeycutt, in her (2005) examination of hazing online, found that elite group members may employ threats and even violence in an effort to maintain the group's boundaries and protect the Core Group from outsiders. It is no surprise that a Newbie might find exposing him/herself to this type of negative response daunting.

For a Newbie, one difficulty is that there are few resources to guide him/her in the quest for acceptance. While many groups publish FAQs (Frequently Asked Questions) that they say will instruct newcomers in the ways of the group, in Graham (2008), I found that FAQs, while they claim to serve as a guide, are actually ineffective because 1) by the time they are published the group norms have frequently already evolved beyond them, and 2) more importantly, FAQs are not really reflective of communicative practice within the group anyway; Core Group Members break FAQ rules frequently without negative effects because they hold the power to ratify the behavioral expectations in the group. They might say that typos are unforgivable, for example, but then suffer no ill effects when there are typos in their own messages. How can newcomers overcome the fact that they do not have a guide (FAQ) that will allow them to be successful, and they do not have the power to ignore the rules the way the Core Group Members do? Why does one Newbie fail while another does not?

In exploring how one Newbie makes the transition from Newbie to Core Group Member, I will use examples taken from a corpus of MySpace discussion group postings. The group was devoted to the discussion of books, and membership included approximately 650–700 subscribers at any given time (although membership in any such group is fluid). Schwämmlein and Wodzicki (2012) would classify this as a common-identity group, since they came together with the purpose of discussing literature. Core Members of the group place high value on being knowledgeable about the literary canon, understanding and being adept at both interpreting and manipulating language, and attending to careful use of language by avoiding grammatical and spelling errors. These characteristics all index the "real-world" purpose of the group (which often manifests as being a member of the literary elite), but there are also group-centric characteristics that index the community identity. These include a passionate dislike for spammers and "pimpers" (individuals who post messages that "shamelessly promote" their own writing), a desire to engage in "intellectual" discussion, and a dislike for anyone who does not respect the history of the group.

Gaining membership into the "in-group"

In this particular group, the most passionately declared rules are: "no spamming and no pimping" (in this group of readers/writers, "pimping" involves promoting your own writing to the group). Brandon[4] is a Newbie who posts the following, fairly standard, introductory post:

Example 1

guess it's time to formally introduce myself . . . i'm brandon and i'm a fictionphile. started one summer back in high school by going through most of steinbeck's work. went through some dickens and hemingway then drifted into anything with a neat cover. i then realized that neat covers didn't always translate into neat books. i read the stranger during my senior year in high school and 30 years later i still can't shake meursault loose . . . bastard! i attribute my first two years of university debauchery to him . . . and my 0.4 gpa (yes the point is in the right place). also learned that punching a teacher doesn't earn as good a mark as giving them apples.

dropped out of school. toured the south by bicycle. worked in the oilfield, on shrimp boats, and painted houses. went back to school when my friends started drinking and driving into trees or taking more chemicals than their bodies were capable of handling. ended up with a degree in landscape architecture and changed my gpa by shifting that damned point over to the right one notch.

live and learn and never regret. thanks for having me . . . oh yeah, i get lazy with the shift key.[5]

Here, Brandon introduces himself with the information commonly associated with introductions—he gives biographical background information (e.g., his failure at school, former jobs) and he explains his motivation for coming to the group. He also identifies himself as a topic enthusiast/competent reader by including references to authors like Steinbeck, Dickens and Hemingway. Overall, however, this introduction does nothing to make Brandon stand out—it is essentially the same as the other 207 introductions posted there.

Brandon's next posting to the group comes when he initiates a thread about the book he is reading.

Example 2

. . . i was looking for a quick read, a quick fix, and picked up Joyce Carol Oates' **Rape: A Love Story**. Anyone read this? Found the title interesting. Found the short description even more intriguing.

While this post mirrors the ones that Core Group Members use to spark discussion on the list by asking for feedback from other readers, Brandon, a Newbie, is ignored. Shortly after his failed attempt to initiate conversation, however, an author posts a message "pimping" her new book *A Prescription for Love*. In addition to the problem of pimping, moreover, the book is a formulaic romance novel—the kind that often receives criticism in the group for not being "true literature." The author is immediately attacked by several Core Group Members (some more venomously than others); one says "I wish I could be there [at your book signing] to beat the shit out of you in person."

Within this series of attacks, Brandon's next move is to post the following 2 messages:

Example 3

Here's the opening paragraph from Leeanne Marie Stephenson's whirlwind romance novel.

> *The decks were strung with lights that soared high above the calm sea, framing the deepening darkness of the night. As Nicole Danley gazed upon the water far below the deck, the reflection of the full moon scattered into a thousand reflective crystals.*

Now it appears that when I eventually make this transition from 19th century Russian literature to a gripping tale of romance from the 21st century I'll be going from a scene of poverty and hopelessness to a world of wealth and prestige . . . and steamy affairs, *"Take me now Travis, now and forever"*.

I'm not sure how I'll be able to make this transition. I'm not sure what to expect. I'm not even sure why I'm doing this. Last year marked the first time I ever read a Russian author. This year I lose my literary virginity to romance novels.

Example 4

After numerous brews of the Mexican variety I went home to spend some time with Nicole and her violet eyes and heart-shaped face, the face framed with curly brown hair. Of course all she could think about was Travis with his piercing blue eyes and powerful arms. I kept having to prop her up on her rubbery legs . . . cheap horny bitch that she is.

SPOILER ALERT (Ha . . . really . . . it's so predictable there's not much to spoil)

So what's this story about so far? Nicole is a nurse with a large trust fund. She's loaded but keeps it a secret from everyone but her best friend and boyfriend. Her boyfriend is Ron, a stupid bitch man with jealous rages and a large debt. He's an incompetent doctor and lies a lot. Travis is a surgeon that makes Nicole's knees rubbery. Ron appears to Nicole to be stable, a go to man. She doesn't really know him. Travis appears to be a man-whore, but he really isn't. She's afraid of Travis because her father was a man-whore and left her mom and she . . . yada, yada, yada. She's torn between the two. A lady has a heart attack and they fix it. A lady has an ulcer and they fix it. A prisoner has a gun shot wound and they fix it. The prisoner tries to rape Nicole. Travis fixes it. Ron leaves sponges in his surgery patients . . . yawn . . .

No one has had sex. No one has died. This just sucks. *END SPOILER ALERT*

In Example 3, Brandon directly indexes the object of the Core Group's venom, and, although he says he does not know why, he says that he will read this book that the Core Members are attacking. While on the surface this might seem to position him as someone who reads romance

315

novels (who are viewed as not being capable of reading and appreciating "true" literature), he mitigates this by mentioning that he's never read a romance novel before and he has read Russian authors (who do not tend to fall into the romance novel category). The same day, he posts a follow-up message that includes a parody of the formulaic nature of *Prescription for Love* (also referred to within the group as PFL).

By the time he gets to his fourth message, Brandon has also added language choices that illustrate his ability to understand and manipulate language. He mimics the simplistic syntax and word repetition of PFL. He openly criticizes the book by inserting "yawn" throughout his parody and ends the message by saying "This just sucks." Brandon's next two messages come after he has finished the book.

Example 5

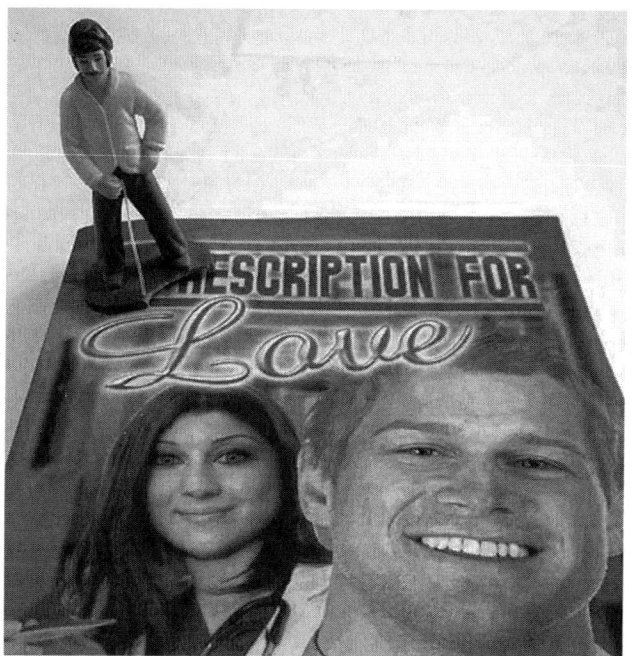

Example 6

Brandon reads this review of the book "Devil in the White City" and thinks about his copy sitting on his bookshelf, a bookshelf cluttered like the stickers on a fast moving racing car. Then he reads the line that implies Olmsted's Japanese garden design should be boring stuff. With nostrils flaring and hands clenching he storms up to Sam[6] and says, "I read that you think Olmsted's garden design should be boring! I'll have you know that anything concerning Olmsted is riveting stuff! His landscape ideas shine like the moon over the sea creating little sparkling jewels! That . . . " He looks into Sam's sparkling eyes as he passes his hands through his short cropped hair and wonders why he feels intensely about this subject, an intensity that intensifies as he confronts Sam. The tension is extensive. The tension can be cut with a knife, a cut no sutures could hold. Then he thinks about hr and Olmsted and storms off back to his desk thinking maybe I should read this book, or better still, a short review about it. Then she'll know how deeply I feel about this landscape stuff.

By the time Brandon had completed this sequence of postings, he had become a fully ratified member of the Core Group. Unlike his posts in Examples 1 and 2, Brandon's subsequent posts garnered multiple very positive responses from other Core Group Members, which marked his full initiation as a Core Group Member.

The obvious question we must ask is "How did he do it?" A previous attempt to transition into the Core Group had different results. In that instance, the individual posted criticism about Harry Potter and the Death of Literature. Although that poster (Don) adopted the stance of a literary elitist the same way Brandon did when he attacked a romance novel, Don was criticized for rehashing the same tired topics that the group had discussed before (i.e., he did not respect the history of the group). Don was also criticized for not proofreading his message for typos. As noted above, part of the group identity is that the Core Members respect those who take care with their language, and while members will be forgiven for typos and grammatical errors after they have achieved Core Group Member status, those who are still trying to gain entry into the in-group will not. As Don's result shows, being a literary elitist is not enough. In addition, participants must show an awareness and respect for the group history by not recycling topics that the Core Group has already debated and showing the commitment to be meticulous in their language use.

The key element of Brandon's success, however, was likely his willingness to defend the group against a "common enemy" who violated the published rules while *also* framing his defense in a way that demonstrated his talent at manipulating language through his parody. In Don's case, his attack was not prompted by an external violation of the rules, it was based solely on literary elitism. Brandon's success indicates that the literary elitism that links the group to their common-identity purpose must be combined with a willingness to attack a "common enemy" who violates the rules of the group.

Conclusions and future directions

Identities and the relationships we create through our negotiation of them are ever-present in our daily interactions, and as different media evolve and our "toolbox" of ways to construct our identities expands, there is no reason to believe that we will run out of questions to ask.

One area that would benefit from further research is a closer examination of the interplay between group and individual identities. While individual identity is somewhat easier to grasp, group identities are more nebulous, perhaps because group membership is constantly shifting. They are not simply the straight sum of all of the individual identities of the participants. Rather, they are a conglomeration of those individual identities that merge and form a set of "common denominators" that reflect the features of the group as a whole. And, like individual identities, group identities are also emergent—in essence, as the group grows and interacts with others, the identity of that group will evolve and it will have its own set of norms and expectations regarding "who we are" and what kind of behavior/talk is appropriate. While much of the current research on digital communication and identity discusses the ways that individuals display their identities and alignments, there is much less research on what the parameters of a given digital community are—how they are defined/identified by community members, and how they are renegotiated on an ongoing basis. As the different modes of digital communication affect our relationality, it is worth exploring how the parameters of each modality affect our relationships and interactions with one another and how we use/manipulate these factors in forming both group and individual identities.

Another fruitful area of further research would involve impoliteness as a means of creating distance (rather than intimacy). While politeness in digital environments has been a long-standing focus of research, there is significantly less about *im*politeness in mediated environments—the papers in Locher's (2010) special issue of the *Journal of Politeness Research* are exceptions, but this is certainly an underexplored area that deserves further attention.

Related topics

- Chapter 3 Digital ethnography (Varis)
- Chapter 7 Multilingual resources and practices in digital communication (Lee)
- Chapter 20 Online communities and communities of practice (Angouri)

Notes

1 http://pewInternetInternet.org/Commentary/2012/March/Pew-Internet-Social-Networking-full-detail.aspx.
2 Here, I will primarily use Facebook and discussion forums/email lists as illustrative examples. While many different media platforms have their own norms for identities and relationships, the rate of change is frequent, and space precludes a comprehensive discussion here. Facebook and discussion forums, on the other hand, appear to have a certain longevity and are adequate to illustrate the underlying concepts with regard to relationship parameters.
3 This is not to say that people *can't* form relationships with one another based on comments/responses to a Pinterest post or blog—only that these types of media do not facilitate relationality and community in the same way as some others like discussion boards and email lists.
4 While the data listed here comes from a publicly available Myspace discussion group, all names are psuedonyms.
5 Unless otherwise noted, all examples are printed as they appeared on the discussion board, including typos, grammatical discrepancies and formatting.
6 While the other names included are part of the fictional canvas B is painting, S is actually a member of the discussion group.

References

Angouri, J. & Tesliga, T. 2010, "'you HAVE NO IDEA WHAT YOU ARE TALKING ABOUT!': from e-disagreement to e-impoliteness in two online fora," *Journal of Politeness Research*, vol. 6, no. 1, pp. 57–82.
Antaki, C. & Widdicombe, S. (eds.) 1998, *Identities in talk*, Sage: London.
Baron, N. S. 2008, *Always on: language in an online and mobile world*, Oxford University Press: New York, NY.
Baym, N. K. 1998, "The emergence of on-line community," in S. Jones (ed.), *Cybersociety 2.0: Revisiting computer-mediated communication and community*, Sage: London, pp. 35–68.
Baym, N. K. 1995, "The emergence of community in computer-mediated communication," in S. Jones (ed.), *CyberSociety: computer-mediated communication and community*, Sage: Thousand Oaks, CA, pp. 138–163.
Benwell, B. & Stokoe, E. 2006, *Discourse and identity*, Edinburgh University Press: Edinburgh.
boyd, d & Hargittai, E. 2010, "Facebook privacy settings: who cares?" *First Monday*, vol. 15, no. 8, doi:10.5210/fm.v15i8.3086.
Brown, P. & Levinson, S. 1978, *Politeness: some universals in language usage*, Cambridge University Press: Cambridge.
Crystal, D. 2001, *Language and the Internet*, Cambridge University Press: Cambridge.
Danet, B. 1998, "Text as mask: gender, play and performance on the Internet," in S. Jones (ed.), *Cybersociety 2.0: Revisiting computer-mediated communication and community*, Sage: London, pp. 129–158.
Danet, B. & Herring, S. C. (eds.) 2007, *The multilingual Internet: language, culture, and communication online*, Oxford University Press: New York, NY.
Davies, B. & Harré, R. 1999, "Positioning and personhood," in Harré, R. and van Langenhove, L. (eds.), *Positioning theory: moral contexts of institutional action*, Blackwell: Oxford, pp. 32–52.
De Fina, A., Schiffrin, D., & Bamberg, M. (eds.) 2006, *Discourse and identity*, Cambridge University Press: Cambridge.
Fraser, B. 1990, "Perspectives on politeness," *Journal of Pragmatics*, vol. 14, no. 2, pp. 219–236.

Georgakopoulou, A. 2011, "'On for drinkies?': email cues of participant alignments," *Language@Internet*, vol. 8, article 4.

Graham, S. 2008, "A manual for (im)politeness?: the impact of the FAQ in e-community formation and socialization," in D. Bousfield & M. Locher (eds.), *Impoliteness in language*, Mouton de Gruyter: Berlin, pp. 281–230.

Graham, S. 2007a, "'Do unto others': gender and the construction of a 'good Christian' identity in an e-community," in A. Jule (ed.), *Language and religious identity: women in discourse*, Palgrave MacMillan: Basingstoke, UK, pp. 73–103.

Graham, S. 2007b, "Disagreeing to agree: conflict (im)politeness and identity in a computer-mediated community," in H. Spencer-Oatey & S. Ruhi (eds.), *Journal of Pragmatics*, vol. 39, no. 4, pp. 742–759, Special issue: Identity perspectives on face and (im)politeness.

Goffman, E. 1981, "Footing," in *Forms of talk*, University of Pennsylvania Press: Philadelphia, PA, pp. 124–159.

Goffman, E. 1974, *Frame analysis: an essay on the organization of experience*, Northeastern University Press: Boston.

Goffman, E. 1959, *The presentation of self in everyday life*, Doubleday: New York, NY.

Herring, S. (ed.) 1996, *Computer-mediated communication: linguistic, social, and cross-cultural perspectives*, John Benjamins: Philadelphia, PA.

Herring, S. C. 1993, "Gender and democracy in computer-mediated communication," *Electronic Journal of Communication*, vol. 3, no. 2, pp. 1–17.

Herring, S. C. 1992, *Gender and participation in computer-mediated linguistic discourse*, ERIC Clearinghouse on Languages and Linguistics: Washington, DC.

Herring, S. C. & Stoerger, S. 2014, "Gender and (a)nonymity in computer-mediated communication," in S. Ehrlich, M. Meyerhoff & J. Holmes (eds.), *Handbook of language, gender, and sexuality*, John Wiley & Sons: Hoboken, NJ, doi: 10.1002/9781118584248,ch29.

Honeycutt, C. 2005, "Hazing as a process of boundary maintenance in an online community," *Journal of Computer-Mediated Communication*, vol. 10, doi: 10.1111/j.1083-6101,2005,tb00240,x.

Jones, S. (ed.) 1998, *Cybersociety 2.0: revisiting computer-mediated communication and community*, Sage: Thousand Oaks, CA.

Jones, S. (ed.) 1995, *Cybersociety: computer-mediated communication and community*, Sage: Thousand Oaks, CA.

van Langenhove, L. and Harré, R. 1999, "Introducing positioning theory," in R. Harré & L. van Langenhove, *Positioning theory: moral contexts of intentional action*, Blackwell: Malden, MA, pp. 32–52.

Leech, G. N. 1983, *Principles of pragmatics*, Longman: New York, NY.

Locher, M. 2010 (ed.), "Special issue: Face, identity and im/politeness," *Journal of Politeness Research*, vol. 6.

Locher, M. & Watts, R. 2005, "Politeness theory and relational work," *Journal of Politeness Research*, vol. 1, pp. 9–33.

Marwick, A. & boyd, d 2014, "Networked privacy: how teenagers negotiate context in social media," *New Media and Society*, doi: 10.1177/1461444814543995.

Paolillo, J. C. 2011, "'Conversational' codeswitching on Usenet and Internet Relay Chat," *Language@Internet*, vol. 8, article 3.

Poster, M. 1998, "Virtual ethnicity: tribal identity in an age of global communications," in S. Jones (ed.), *Cybersociety 2.0: Revisiting computer-mediated communication and community*, Sage: Thousand Oaks, pp. 184–211.

Rheingold, H. 1993, *Virtual communities: homesteading on the electronic frontier*, Addison Wesley: Reading, MA.

Rodino, M. 1997, "Breaking out of binaries: reconceptualizing gender and its relationship to language in computer-mediated communication," *Journal of Computer-Mediated Communication*, vol. 3, no. 3, doi: 10.1111/j.1083-6101.1997.tb00074.x.

Sacks, H. 1972, "An initial investigation of the usability of conversational data for doing sociology," in D. N. Sudnow (ed.), *Studies in social interaction*, Free Press: New York, NY, pp. 31–74.

Schwämmlein, E. & Wodzicki, K. 2012, "'What to tell about me?' Self-presentation in online communities," *Journal of Computer-Mediated Communication*, vol. 17, no. 4, pp. 387–407.

Scollon, R. 2001, *Mediated discourse: the nexus of practice*, Routledge: London.

Shea, V. 1994, *Netiquette*, Albion Books: San Francisco.

Smith, M. & Kollock, P. (eds.) 1999, *Communities in cyberspace*, Routledge: London.

Spencer-Oatey, H. 2000 "Rapport management: a framework for analysis," in H. Spencer-Oatey (ed.), *Culturally speaking: managing rapport through talk across cultures*, Continuum: London, pp. 11–46.

Spilioti, T. 2011, "Beyond genre: closings and relational work in text messaging," in C. Thurlow & K. Mroczek (eds.), *Digital discourse: language in the new media*, Oxford University Press, Kindle edition.

Thurlow, C. & Mroczek, K. 2011, "Introduction: fresh perspectives on new media sociolinguistics," in C. Thurlow & K. Mroczek (eds.), *Digital discourse: language in the new media*, Oxford University Press, Kindle edition.

Walther, J., Van Der Heide, B., Kim, S., Westerman, D., & Tong, S. 2008, "The role of friends' appearance and behavior on evaluations of individuals on Facebook: are we known by the company we keep?" *Human Communication Research*, vol. 34, no. 1, pp. 28–49.

Watts, R. 2003, *Politeness*, Cambridge University Press: Cambridge.

Further reading

Benwell, B. & Stokoe, E. 2006, *Discourse and identity*, Edinburgh University Press: Edinburgh.

This book provides a foundational overview of approaches to discourse and identity in general, with Chapter 7 focusing specifically on virtual identities.

Schwämmlein, E. & Wodzicki, K. 2012, " 'What to tell about me?' Self-presentation in online communities," *Journal of Computer-Mediated Communication*, vol. 17, pp. 387–407.

This article provides a solid introduction to Membership Categorization as a way to examine online identities.

Thurlow, C. & Mroczek, K. (eds.) 2011, *Digital discourse: language in the new Media*, Oxford University Press: Oxford.

The papers in this volume provide an overview of the latest themes in online communication, with a comprehensive introduction by the editors and an impressive array of chapters based on empirical data.

Part VI

Communities, networks, relationships

20

Online communities and communities of practice

Jo Angouri

Introduction

An ever-increasing number of users access the World Wide Web on a daily basis. This has brought changes to the ways people look for information, share personal experiences, and pursue personal or professional interests – to name but a few of the activities being transformed in the online era. Computer supported interaction in particular has become part of the daily routine for a large percentage of those living in technologically advanced societies (Seyber 2012) following the popularization of the Internet in the 1990s. 'Netizens' interact across borders, meet others who may or may not have met before in on- or off-line contexts, and online formations multiply (Barton & Lee 2013). In this context, research on Computer Mediated Communication (CMC) has grown from its early stages as the pariah of the 1980s to become a priority for scholars across many disciplines and schools of thought. Online assemblages, which constitute the focus here, operate at the interface of geographical, regional, temporal, linguistic and other boundaries and create the context within which users interact with multiple audiences. The now widely used term of collapsed contexts (Marwick & boyd 2011) succinctly foregrounds this reality.

In the 1960s, Licklider and Taylor foresaw the ways in which users would reorganize life around the infrastructure that was becoming accessible and the growing significance of interacting online with other users. They suggested that online formations 'consist of geographically separated members, sometimes grouped in small clusters and sometimes working individually. They will be communities not of common location, but of common interest' (1968: 30). Groups of people interacting *across boundaries* of the past is also in line with Lévy's (2005) idea of a *cosmopedia*, a knowledge space where users or 'global citizens' form groups and share knowledge across geographical and national boundaries. The widely cited remark that 'no one knows everything, everyone knows something, all knowledge resides in humanity' (Lévy 1999, cited in Jenkins 2006: 139) succinctly illustrates Lévy's conceptualization of a universally distributed intelligence with the transformational potential to change societal power structures. Although Lévy's work presents an *attainable utopia* (see Jenkins 2002, 2006), what is particularly relevant for the discussion here is the tremendous socio-political and economic implications deriving from the fact that users in different geographical locations routinely and effortlessly come together around some common interest. These online formations are commonly referred to as 'online communities'.

In early research following Rheingold's influential work in 1993, the term of favour was 'virtual communities'. Rheingold suggested that 'virtual communities are social aggregations that emerge from the Net when enough people carry on those public discussions long enough, with sufficient human feeling, to form webs of personal relationships in cyberspace' (1993).

As the term 'virtual communities' suggests, work of that period framed the online space as a different 'mode', almost diametrically opposed to that of face-to-face interaction, and often as a distinct channel or medium (see Herring 2001). In contrast, more recent work has shown the nuanced relationship between online and offline and the need to go beyond binaries (e.g., Preece & Maloney-Krichmar 2005). Technology has afforded new possibilities for interaction: social media have become part of the fabric of life, and the boundaries between the face-to-face and the online have thus become blurred. This does not mean, however, that technology affordances can simply pre-determine human behaviour and communication. In fact, research has criticized a deterministic link between the two (e.g., Georgakopoulou 2011b; Jones 1997). The conceptualization of what constitutes an online community and how it operates is constantly evolving for lay users and scholars alike, in line with changes in the broader socioeconomic and technological environment. This includes but is not limited to the development of communication technologies.

The notion of the 'community', both on- and off-line, occupies a central position in socio-linguistic literature. It sits at the interface of theoretical and analytical decisions that researchers need to make in order to study social phenomena in context – but the term affords multiple meanings and readings depending on the researchers/readers' stance. Traditionally, it has been adopted as a unit of analysis in research addressing key issues in sociolinguistic variation, which seeks to describe how the language used by individuals varies in systematic ways and indexes membership in different social groups – e.g., linguistic variation associated with social class or age groups has been prominent in sociolinguistic research. The definition of the 'online community' is also a focal point for CMC researchers, for whom it is a 'legacy term that is engrained in Internet culture', as Preece and Maloney-Krichmar (2005) observe.

Against this backdrop, this chapter discusses the notion of the online community, paying special attention to the community of practice (CofP) framework. It is organized in four parts and addresses different research approaches and ethical issues surrounding the study of online groups. I draw on examples from my current and recently completed research, as well as representative studies from the sociolinguistic field. I close the chapter with a discussion of the issues future research might usefully address.

Unpacking the notion of on-/off-line communities

Scholars in a range of disciplines, such as sociology, linguistics and psychology, to name but a few, have debated what constitutes a community and the criteria that can be used to delimit it. The term is typically used to refer to a set of people grouped together around shared characteristics. The concept therefore carries connotations of cohesion – members have something in common – and belonging. This can also be seen in dictionary definitions of the term. In socio-linguistic literature, 'speech community' has traditionally been related to the language variety that a social group is understood to have in common and that distinguishes it from other groups (for an overview of the sociolinguistic notion of the speech community, see Patrick 2002). The boundaries of the community in relation to other broad or narrow assemblages depend on the researchers' standpoints, particularly concerning how language relates to social and cultural contexts. As a result, the term has been used to denote large demographically based categories (e.g., women) as well as much narrower ones (e.g., the users of one forum) and researchers' understandings of the *scale* or *homogeneity* of the assemblages under study vary. Gumperz (1982) questioned the distinct boundaries of the community unit as follows: 'The assumption that speech communities, defined as functionally integrated social systems with shared norms of evaluation, can actually be isolated . . . becomes subject to serious question' (p. 26). More recently, Gumperz and Levinson (1996: 11) referred to 'networks of interacting individuals' in an attempt to capture the dynamic relationship between the individual and group membership.

The use of the term says at least as much about the researchers' theoretical and methodological stance as it does about the assemblage under study. Simply put, research taking a positivist view – according to which there is an objective reality that can be known and measured – clusters individuals according to macro categories such as age, gender or ethnicity (among others), determined and defined by the researcher. Constructionist approaches, on the other hand, understand reality as emergent and negotiated in interaction, existing within the social order. Hence, categories cannot be defined on the basis of abstract criteria but are context dependent, complex and dynamic (see Angouri, forthcoming, for an overview). According to the latter perspective, a community is a construct emerging and negotiated between members who claim/reject membership. This approach avoids creating a rigid frame for the study of communities (both on- and off-line) and is attuned to current, ethnographically informed studies of the web. Given that the 'online community' was seen from the beginning as a social formation transcending traditional, geographically defined boundaries, a positivist approach is both limited and limiting, and more flexible designs have been proposed by researchers. I return to this point later.

A number of typologies have been introduced over the years in an attempt to delineate the 'online community' in particular. Some researchers (e.g., Weinreich 1997) have argued that online 'communities' cannot exist, as the membership traits and rapport management between the users are substantially different from the face-to-face experience. Many, however, have attempted to distinguish between formations that will become 'communities' and those that will not develop further (see Jones 1997; Preece & Maloney-Krichmar 2003). Although there is no agreed-upon approach (or definition), typical criteria include the demographics of the members, the frequency/purpose of interaction, evidence of group norms, and the technological characteristics of the environment within which online users operate (see also Androutsopoulos 2006).

Given the multiplicity of factors that have been identified as relevant, definitions are varied and broad; de Souza and Preece (2004: 580), for instance, understand an online community as 'a group of people, who come together for a purpose online, and who are governed by norms and policies', while Lazar, Hanst, Buchwalter, and Preece (2001) note that the online community is often conceptualized as 'a group of people who share a similar interest, share networked resources, and communicate using a computer-mediated communication tool' (p. 2). These definitions reflect the development of thinking in the field and the need for a dynamic approach to the study of the online community – one that cannot rely on prescriptive top-down criteria.

To take this further, turning from what an online community *is* to what the community *does* provides the theoretical tools for capturing members' understanding of their various contexts and practices. The criteria that can be used to delimit a community not only constitute the subject of academic debate, but are also negotiated in everyday discourses when members claim/reject membership to a community. Research shows how speakers mobilize a range of resources in constructing connections between 'self' and the 'group' (e.g., Wodak, de Cillia, Reisigl, & Liebhart 2009 on national identity; Wodak & Angouri 2014). *Perceptions* of similarity/difference and cohesion are particularly relevant from this point of view, as they form part of the social imaginary (see Castoriadis 1987 for a discussion on imagination). As such, they are useful in unpacking how the members construct community in interaction (see examples 1 and 2 below). Following this line of enquiry, boyd (e.g., 2008) has usefully expanded the notion of *imagined communities*, introduced by Anderson (1991) in relation to national identity. boyd refers to imagined audiences and highlights how communities are defined through their membership instead of a priori categorizations by the researcher. Given the porous boundaries of the various (either on- or off-line) communities and the complexity of negotiating belonging, taking a bottom-up approach to analyse how membership is negotiated by the *users* provides a more nuanced understanding of the characteristics of any assemblage, one that goes beyond the researcher's own view.

This is in line with current research, which argues against rigid definitions and criteria for top-down framing of the online formations. In a useful summary of relevant literature, Herring (2004) has identified six sets of relevant criteria for operationalizing the online community:

> 1) active, self-sustained participation; a core of regular participants; 2) shared history, purpose, culture, norms, and values; 3) solidarity, support, reciprocity; 4) criticism, conflict, means of conflict resolution; 5) self-awareness of group as an entity distinct from other groups; 6) emergence of roles, hierarchy, governance, rituals.
>
> *(2004: 355)*

This useful classification is compatible with work by Wellman (1999, 2001) who identified a tripartite characterization of the community as providing sociability, support, and identity to members (see also Herring 2007).

Despite the diversity of researchers' perspectives, there is consensus that not all online assemblages constitute communities. A focus on how the members themselves define the community and how they position themselves in relation to others provides, in my view, powerful insights that go beyond top-down descriptions and can feed back into the theoretical development of current models and frameworks. Sociolinguistic research is well placed to provide and further develop the methodological and analytical tools for the analysis of online community as emergent in discourse. One particular theoretical concept is of special relevance here, namely the notion of communities of practice (CofP).

Communities of practice and beyond

CofPs have become particularly popular in sociolinguistic research (Meyerhoff & Strycharz 2013) and the framework is increasingly adopted as a unit of analysis instead of the more traditional speech community or social network[1] (Holmes & Meyerhoff 1999). The CofP construct and framework originates in research by Lave and Wenger (1991) on the social theory of learning and was originally adopted by sociolinguists in the context of research on language and gender (Eckert & McConnell-Ginet 1999).

Wenger (1998) identifies three dimensions of a CofP:

> a) What it is about – its joint enterprise as understood and continually renegotiated by its members. b) How it functions – mutual engagement that bind[s] members together into a social entity. c) What capability it has produced – the shared repertoire of communal resources (routines, sensibilities, artifacts, vocabulary, styles, etc.) that members have developed over time.
>
> *(1998: 73)*

It is particularly the discourse practices that CofPs develop over time that have become the focus of sociolinguistic work. The axiomatic position of discourse as socially constitutive, socially conditioned and socially consequential (for a detailed discussion on these notions see Wodak and Meyer 2009) is well aligned with practice theories in general and the CofP framework in particular – which explains, at least partly, why the field embraced it. The framework provides a way to study language use locally and to link the micro context to the broader socio-cultural environment. It provides the tools to capture and explain members' practices and is well tuned with ethnographic studies. For instance, recent studies (see, e.g., Thurlow & Mroczek 2011) take a CofP approach to show how users construct the community through *doing* – engaging with the joint activity (e.g., support newly diagnosed users in online health groups, as we will see in Example 1) – and to illustrate how both language use and what is (or not) appropriate for a community are negotiated by members (as we will see in Example 2; see also Graham 2007 on conflict in an online community). In this context, the CofP framework offers a detailed view on communities' norms as well as the work of 'core' and peripheral users, and it enables researchers to analyse and, to an extent, interpret the situated nature of interaction. These strengths largely account for the popularity of CofP in sociolinguistic studies of online groups.

More than a decade ago, Johnson (2001) carried out a survey of research on online communities of practice and attempted to delimit the boundaries between the online community and the CofP. He defined the two as follows: 'Virtual communities are groups that use networked technologies to communicate and collaborate. Communities of practice are cultural entities that emerge from the establishment of a virtual or nonvirtual organization' (2001: 56).

Others have also suggested typologies which attempt to capture the characteristics of the online CofP, focusing on the profile of the members, the technical characteristics of the environment and the context of the community (see, e.g., Hara *et al.* 2009). The strengths and weaknesses of these approaches resonate with the attempts to define the online community as discussed earlier. At the same time, as Corder and Meyerhoff have suggested, 'the term [CofP] has spread faster than familiarity with the analytic presuppositions and methods that are fundamental to a CofPs analysis' (2007: 441). Indeed, the term is often used without further discussion of the notions of practice and community which are central to it.

This is also reflected in literature that has problematized the CofP framework mainly from two perspectives. The first critique notes that although the two terms, *community* and *practice*, are 'bound' together in Lave and Wenger's (1991) work, the actual relationship between them is not straightforward. As Nicolini (2012) argues, 'Communities of practice are, in fact, communities of practitioners constantly busy positioning themselves within the ongoing practice' and further 'it is practice which performs community and not the other way around' (2012: 94).

The relationship between practice and membership is particularly relevant to the online communities where members take different roles and negotiate the group's identity with other core users (as in Example 1 below). The different roles members take and the implications for the group's norms and life cycle have been discussed since early ethnographic research on online communities. For instance, Baym's (1995) work on online soap opera fandom has shown that a small number of members do the posting while most are lurking (see also Radin 2006); and those who are most prolific tend to be powerful in influencing the group's norms (see also Graham, this volume).

These issues bear directly on how community is operationalized in research. Wenger (1998) clearly warns against seeing the 'community' as a single whole, but given the connotations of the notion (see Gee 2005 and earlier discussion) and the fact that the framework has become fashionable, the terms CofP and its components are at times used loosely and without further probing. Useful to note here is that in more recent work by Wenger, McDermott and Snyder (Wenger *et al.* 2002: 4) CofPs are defined as 'groups of people who share a concern, a set of problems, or a passion about a topic, and who deepen their knowledge and expertise in this area by interacting on an ongoing basis'. This broader definition creates more space for diversity in the formations that scholars label as CofPs and is something research can probe in more detail in relation to the affordances of the framework.

The second common criticism of the CofP framework is related to the operationalization of 'legitimate participation' and issues of power. In a useful dialogue in the *Journal of Sociolinguistics* (2005, vol. 9, no. 4) the notions of power and hierarchy were scrutinized and the extent to which the CofP allows for a study of relations between individuals was brought to debate (e.g., Davies 2005). The most relevant issue here is that community participation involves negotiating gatekeeping mechanisms. In other words, CofPs develop 'fencing' strategies, and access to the discourse resources for doing 'core' membership is not always equally shared across all members. As nicely put by McElhinny (2003: 30), 'different (perhaps hierarchical) positionalities within communities of practice' can be identified. The legitimate peripheral participation process as discussed in original work (e.g., by Lave & Wenger 1991) captures, in my view, the complexities of negotiating power in the context of the community. The operationalization of the concept, however, has not always been consistent. I would argue that there is agreement in that 'novices' negotiate participation, and this is visible to members of communities – both face-to-face and online. In the online context, norms of participation are learnt before active contribution, and the terms 'lurking' or 'de-lurking' (Radin 2006) succinctly reflect this.

Overall, CofP has been a significant development for the study of language use in general and can be usefully applied to the study of online formations in particular and the analysis of the members' experience. Conceptual clarity is necessary however. The increase in studies taking a 'beyond CofPs' approach (e.g., Amin & Roberts 2008) indicates that the time is ripe for revisiting the framework and re-opening the debate on its affordances. The recent notion of affinity space (Gee 2005), for example, has been introduced in an attempt to go beyond issues related to community and membership. Hayes and Gee (2010) refer to semiotic spaces and sees affinity spaces as 'places – real world or virtual on Internet sites or in virtual worlds like *Second Life* – where people interact around a common passion' (p. 187). They identify 11 features of membership, participation and the context within which users interact. These features constitute the complete definition and an analytical frame for analysing new 'learning sites'. The notion has been usefully adopted in research on online gaming fan sites; more generally, however, it also indicates the need for theory-grounded research that goes beyond single cases studies and adds to the conceptual tools that have so far been adopted for theorising social affiliations on the web.

In order to illustrate in further detail how users negotiate and construct community through practice, I now turn to one example taken from an online arthritis forum (Angouri & Sanderson in prep). The excerpt is from an ongoing collaborative project with a patient association that aims to explore how members of the forum understand and define their online space and how they participate in the group. The excerpts below are part of a thread initiated by a newly diagnosed user, named here Marjanna (postings not included here), who claims a post-diagnosis member identity and receives a number of responses from more experienced users.

Example 1: part of a thread from an arthritis forum

Anamaria

You poor woman, what an awful time you are having. I have been crying all week about my own troubles which fade into nothing compared to what you are dealing with. [drug name] is a great drug if you don't get any of the side effects. If it doesn't work for you there are many other drugs on the market, so don't give up.

[. . .]

Keep on this site, there is loads of wisdom and a huge amount of experience that is there for the asking. We all know exactly what you are going through and we are all here to help in any way we can, so keep in touch and let us know how you are doing. X

Marjanna

Thanks Anamaria, Am already feeling better from all this support xx

Milly

Hiya,

Oh my gosh, this was me exactly 2 years ago, diagnosed 6 weeks after giving birth, my [diagnosis] and thought my life was over; consultant told me mine was aggressive also; husband had to dress me ect, I could barely walk and changing nappies when you can't bend your fingers!!! I can fully empathise.

You've had some amazing replies, but I just wanted to let know how similar we are

[. . .]

Good news is that my RA [rheumatoid arthritis] was under control within [details] and I have been in medically induced remission ever since. I work part time, manage the gym and would say 90% better.

I wrote a blog about my experience if you fancy reading it

[. . .]

Although I feel very lucky, I often think back to where you are now, it was the hardest time in my life as it is for you right now. I also felt my Husband should just leave and that he shouldn't have to look after me. I never dreamt that I would get back to normal again. This is just a blip, a big fat stupid blip thats a pain in the arse but you'll get there just as soon you find the right meds for you. I feel very sad to have missed out on all the things a new Mum should be doing at that time. I make up for it now ☺

Take care and feel free to PM me if I can help at all xx

Members of the forum categorize self and other on the basis of the experience of living with the condition. As is common on health sites, a 'diagnosis' constitutes legitimation of membership and a way into the group. Newcomers address the forum as one homogenous group and position self as a novice seeking advice or support. Individual members, in their response, take up the group identity by aligning with the interactional and behavioural norms of the group (see also Stommel & Koole 2010); they construct the forum as a community where advice and information is available. This is visible in this short excerpt where Anamaria projects a set of roles and functions to the group and is acknowledged by Marjanna in her response. At the same time, individual users also put forward their own individual cases, converging or diverging from the newcomer's experience. Milly's posting shows some of the common moves for creating common ground and easing the newcomer's entry into the group. Narratives of sameness play an important role in health communities, particularly those related to chronic illnesses where empathy, solidarity and managing the emotional side of living with the condition are constructed by the members as both a reason for and an outcome of participation in the community (Barak *et al.* 2008). This is also the case in our data (Angouri & Sanderson in prep; Sanderson & Angouri 2014) and is visible in this short excerpt, where the users collaborate to provide

Marjanna with encouragement and hope for living with the condition. A number of resources are used here: Anamaria's posting on the effectiveness of drugs and Milly's description of the trajectory of the condition both create a frame for a positive outlook of living with the condition. This is also reflected in the linguistic choices the users make (e.g., the enactment of solidarity in the address term *poor woman* used to open the posting). In the context of this health-related forum, the members seem to take different roles depending on their perceived audience (e.g., in interaction with newcomers, the senior users claim an advisor's role and enact authority by drawing on their own experience of living with the condition).

Although space does not allow for a detailed analysis here, I consider practice theories particularly useful for the analysis of online health care communities and the ways they are constructed through members' practices. The members in this community carry out social activities and get together for online social events such as tea and cakes as much as they exchange information on new drugs and treatment. A detailed analysis of these practices can contribute to the development of theoretical frameworks that address the perceived function of online formations and provide a nuanced understanding of how membership is negotiated by the users. As far as the subject matter is concerned, this can also contribute to a better understanding of the significant role of online health discussion forums, which are understood by their members as communities.

To conclude this discussion, I would align here with those who argue for resisting the temptation to explain away the online community on the basis of predefined criteria. In keeping with current research, I argue for a dynamic and multilayered approach to the analysis and interpretation of online practices. I discuss this further below.

CMDA, online ethnography and other issues in sociolinguistic studies of the web

While sociological, psychological and media studies research in CMC has focused on the profile and identity of online communities as well as the behaviour of online users, the discussion of these phenomena in mainstream sociolinguistic research is more recent (e.g., Androutsopoulos 2006; Herring 2004). The expansion of the Internet and the text-based tools of CMC (e.g., email, instant messages, discussion forums and so on) triggered a series of influential studies on the graphological, lexical, syntactical and grammatical features of 'netspeak' (e.g., Cherny 1999; Crystal 2001) and the relationship between the format of the text and the speed, immediacy and interactivity typical of electronic communication (for a critique of first-wave CMC studies, see Androutsopoulos 2006). The early language-focused CMC research has contributed to a shift to CMD (Computer-mediated discourse), where the emphasis is online language *use* (Herring 2001) and discourse is taken as the starting point of inquiry. CMD research has challenged the purportedly deterministic character of technology and, as Herring (2001) suggests, 'not all properties of CMD follow necessarily and directly from the properties of computer technology'; rather, 'social and cultural factors . . . contribute importantly to the constellation of properties that characterizes computer-mediated discourse' (p. 625). Like any other type of language interaction, then, CMD shapes and is shaped by the situational context and the interactants' choices (Georgakopoulou 2011a and 2011b).

Herring (2007) has proposed an analytical (though not exhaustive) classification scheme incorporating some of the most important medium and social factors ('facets') that are relevant to the use of language in online environments. Herring (2007) identifies ten major medium factors that previous studies have found to exert influence on the language variation noted in electronic environments, including: *synchronicity, persistence of transcript, channels of communication, anonymous messaging, quoting and message format*, along with eight situation factors (including *topic, purpose, participant characteristics* and *norms*). Herring's framework constitutes a major contribution to the development of the CMDA agenda, paving the way for new theoretical discussions in CMD research (see, e.g., Androutsopoulos & Beißwenger 2008).

Although a detailed discussion exceeds the scope of this chapter, CMDA constitutes a pioneering approach for the study of online communities. It describes research at four levels as defined by Herring – a) structure, b) meaning, c) interaction, and d) social behaviour – moving from the more detailed linguistic analysis to the broader discussion of social phenomena (see Herring 2004 for detailed definitions and discussion) and bringing together the micro context of the interaction and the wider social order. Firmly placed within the discourse analytic tradition, CMDA provides the theoretical tools for the analysis of the discursive construction of a community and can be used to address the following questions:

a) 'What are the discourse characteristics of a virtual community?' (b) 'What causes an online group to become a community?' c) 'What causes a virtual community to die?' d) 'How do virtual communities differ from face-to-face communities?' e) 'What happens to face-to-face communities when they go online?' and f) 'In what ways do communities constituted exclusively online differ from online communities that also meet face-to-face?'

(Herring 2004: 348)

Not all CMDA research addresses all these questions; conversely, asking these questions does not necessarily index a CMDA approach. A lot depends on the researchers' specific interests, levels of access to the group, pragmatic constraints, theoretical allegiances and methodological decisions. However, Herring's CMDA framework provides an agenda for systematic and detailed online ethnographies and invites a debate on how current tools and traditions in sociolinguistic enquiry can (or cannot) be used for the study of online communities' discourses in general (e.g., Androutsopoulos & Beißwenger 2008), and the analysis of the community as emergent in interaction in particular. This is also particularly relevant for the study of identity in online contexts.

Given the variety of practices and the multiple and fast-paced changes in online contexts, ethnographically informed research designs have been common in CMD and are still considered most suitable and necessary for the study of users' practices and the management of interpersonal relationships on the web. Looking into this in more detail, Baym's (1995) pioneering research of a group of soap opera fans shows how a group identity is constructed through the members' participation in the sharing and exchanging of information with other users. Baym's work also shows the role humour plays in constructing self/group identity and how a detailed linguistic analysis can contribute to our understanding of the ways in which group belonging is enacted through a range of discourse strategies. This work constitutes a widely cited example of a classic 'online ethnography': Baym took a participant role in the forum and worked toward an emic understanding of the group's life as a community (see also Georgakopoulou 1997; Varis, this volume). In the same vein, Cherny's (1999) work shows how members of a group develop specific ways of interacting and introduce new members to the group norms.

From a methodological point of view, a range of terms such as 'online ethnography' or 'virtual ethnography' (e.g., Hine 2000) are widely used to denote fieldwork designs that focus solely on online communities; to describe the adaptation of traditional instruments for capturing data (in, for example, observation logs or interviews) to the affordances of digital medium; or to acknowledge the growing significance of the 'online' in all domains of life. At the same time, new terms are being introduced – for instance, 'netnography', a term deriving from marketing research (e.g., Kozinets 2010) that refers to a set of steps for carrying out research in online contexts. Kozinets (2010) makes a case for a new set of methodological procedures that sets this approach apart from 'mainstream' ethnography – assuming that one common understanding exists. I find these new terms useful in continuing the dialogue on the appropriateness of our current tools and practices for carrying out online research and in probing the meaning we, as researchers, attribute to terms we currently use.

Further, Androutsopoulos (2008) introduced the term 'discourse centred online ethnography' (DCOE) to go beyond participant observation and heavy reliance on single datasets, most commonly text/data logs. As he argues, carrying out ethnography online requires exploring the nexus of relationships between members and the activity that is being produced. As with all ethnographic studies, developing an emic understanding (even when long-term longitudinal designs are not feasible) requires more than 'gazing at' (Androutsopoulos 2008: 5) people – or at the screen, for that matter. He unpacks the notions of systematic observation and contact with informants and argues against 'narrow' investigations. By moving from the core to the periphery in a systematic way and by using a range of both qualitative and quantitative data (including, e.g., descriptive statistics and linguistic analyses), a case is made for a well-rounded approach to online ethnography. Androutsopoulos provides a detailed account of methodological choices through two examples, opening a dialogue that should be continued. Given that research in the field has now come of age, I argue that sharing the lived experience of doing online research has the potential to further the development of our methodological tools and provide a more nuanced understanding of the phenomena under investigation.

Combining data from various sources and going beyond an on-/off-line binary conception of research (Georgakopoulou 2011a) is a view I also take, and as an illustration I turn to an example from a completed project on discourse practices and online communities of practice (see Angouri & Tseliga 2010). The project aimed to explore how regular members of online forums construct and reflect on group norms, and we specifically addressed perceptions of impoliteness and disagreement practices. I am going to draw on excerpts from one particular professional academic forum here, run by a scholar who self-categorizes as a Greek based in the US. The members are also scholars from Greece and elsewhere. It is an open-access forum which features high activity on various academic topics (such as the role of the Senates of Greek Universities, scholarship schemes, the restructuring of Greek higher education, and so on). Four datasets were collected and analysed for the needs of the project, consisting of observations of the group's activities, micro-analysis of postings, and survey and interview data with core participants. As our interest was on perceptions of members' practices, we found the ongoing collaboration a *sine qua non* for addressing our questions.

Although this design is undoubtedly time-consuming and resource-intensive, it allowed us to approach a topic holistically. After completing the first stage of our work, which was concerned with observing, understanding and analysing popular threads, we approached core informants and collected interview data, which fed back into the analysis of the linguistic data. We were thus able to go beyond binaries (such as off-/online or real/virtual) which were not conceptualized in our project as clear-cut categories, but rather blurred and coexistent realities for the members. As with the study of other abstract notions (e.g., identity – see Angouri in press), a critical issue is whose voice is heard in research: that of the researcher, or that of the participants. From this point of view, the first- and second-order levels of analysis common in politeness theory, addressing participants' and researchers' perspectives, respectively (see Watts, Ide, & Ehlich 1992), can be usefully applied to the understanding of complex phenomena, such as the understanding of the role and modus operandi of online communities. In order to capture first-order perceptions, though, research designs need to allow for the voice of the participant to be heard. A holistic approach like the one briefly described here is conducive to this (see also Androutsopoulos 2008).

Example 2: two postings from two users (one core) debating acceptable norms of interaction

MK

Κ αν πραγματικα περιμενεις να σου απαντησω, το πρωτο που θα
πρεπει να κανεις ειναι να απολογηθεις για τους υβρισμους σου,
ή τουλαχιστον να τους σταματησεις. Ειλικρινα πιστευεις οτι πρεπει να
ανεχομαι το απαραδεκτο υφος σου?

'If you really expect me to respond, the first thing you should do is to apologize for your swearing or at least stop. Do you honestly think I should put up with your tone?'

NickShultz [replies]

@MK, Δεν σε βρίζω αγαπητέ, οποιαδήποτε ένσταση για το ύφος είναι
δεκτή αλλά δες το με χιούμορ, άλλωστε απευθύνομαι προς ένα
nickname, όχι σε κάποιον που γνωρίζω προσωπικά.
Μας χωρίζει ένα interface! :)

'I didn't intend to offend you sir, I accept you objecting to the tone but show some wit, besides I am addressing a username not someone I personally know, we are kept apart by the interface ! :)'

MK and *NickShultz* both identify as members of the group, but *MK* is one of the core members. In this excerpt, *MK* challenges the tone of an earlier posting and explicitly refers to the breach of 'politic' – perceived as unmarked and acceptable (Watts 2003) – behaviour. *MK* refers to the group's netiquette in a range of threads we analysed and repeatedly sanctions what seems to be perceived as inappropriate behaviour. The analysis of the ethnographic interview data, where core users talked the researchers through the data (see Angouri & Tseliga 2010 for a discussion of the research design), showed that this is seen as an 'educational duty' where peripheral members need to be 'taught the rules' – a position taken by *MK* and other core members of the group who tend to adopt a formal style and explicitly react to postings perceived as offensive. This relates to the perceived role of the forum, which is defined by the members as a space for the exchange of academic ideas and which aims to foster specific suggestions for policy reform. Thus the core members, who have known each other for years, according to the data, expect peripheral users to be 'mature', not to abuse 'anonymity' (as the members put it), and to use an 'appropriate' tone. The norms of interaction are subject to scrutiny by the members, however, and *NickShultz*'s response is a good example of how the members of a community might challenge what is considered politic.

Developing a relationship initially with the forum moderator and later with a group of core users was particularly significant for collecting rich data, and this process led to the construction of a 'thick description' of the group. We were able to access 'first-order' views on the forum and perceptions of appropriateness, which informed our accounts on situated impoliteness. Although a detailed discussion goes beyond the scope of this chapter, it is important to note that, for core users, the group is constructed as a community with a clear purpose and identity, while peripheral members keep a distance. This, too, is visible in this short excerpt by *NickShultz*'s distinction between a 'username' and a 'real' person. A core member describes the group as follows: 'Our blog is not an airtight vessel but there is solidarity between old and new members. We know each other for years [referring to the core members] if someone attacks [refers to other core member] I will intervene' (Angouri & Tseliga 2010: 76).

The different levels of membership in a group are particularly relevant for self- and other-positioning and related to engagement (or not) with the group's core activities. Members' claimed and projected roles of participation in a dynamic reality changes over time (core members may become peripheral and vice-versa). Accordingly, research on online formations needs to allow for the necessary flexibility to capture this dynamic reality. Practice theories – either under the Community of Practice framework or some other approach (e.g., Nicolini 2012) – can provide the theoretical underpinning for unpacking how users construct their online context and negotiate norms of interaction.

In closing this discussion, I briefly raise the issue of ethics in carrying out research on online communities. Ethical issues are not typically discussed in detail in online research (but see Androutsopoulos 2008). Although projects that have been or are currently being carried out are approved by universities' ethics committees, the guidelines for online research are still a grey zone. Almost twenty years ago, King (1996) wrote on the potential for harm arising from the analysis of postings in the public domain and made a case for clear guidelines to ensure that research respects the participants' space. The 'public' domain constitutes a significant factor in determining whether consent is necessary or indeed appropriate. More recently, researchers have debated the strengths and limitations of different guidelines, suggesting that sets of criteria be determined on a case-by-case basis (e.g., Berry 2004; Hudson & Bruckman 2004). Although this work is invaluable, what is in my view still rare is an open discussion of the dilemmas our students and we face in carrying out research, as well as what we consider 'good practice'. Given the pace of change of technology, the porous boundaries between public and private, the diversity of online groups, and the variety of research questions posed, one set of criteria for online research is inherently impossible. An open dialogue, however, can contribute to clarifying some of the questions that need to be addressed by future research and advance our field's understanding of good practice in relation to the study of online communities.

Conclusion and future directions

Many complexities must yet be addressed by future research, including the theoretical frameworks and methodological tools that best capture the complex relationship between the individual and the group, as well as how researchers can best engage with practice in online contexts. In this chapter, I have attempted to provide a brief overview of some key theoretical issues related to the study of the online community, such the very notion of the 'community' in sociolinguistic inquiry; the benefits and limitations of CofP and CMDA frameworks; the challenges for carrying out ethnographic research online; and the implications for research ethics. I have also discussed influential studies that have contributed to the development of the field, and provided two analytical examples to illustrate the themes of membership and practice addressed here.

The 'online community' has been used to denote a range of formations and has been defined in relation to multiple criteria. Going beyond definitions that are based on rigid criteria and set categories defined by the researcher (such as gender, age, ethnicity), the current focus on the *discursive construction* of online communities allows space for members' perceptions to feed into the development of theoretical frameworks for multilayered research into online groups and the practices of their members. This is still an open issue that further research must continue to probe.

I also discussed in some detail the CofP framework, which has been fruitful for the analysis of language use in on- and off-line communities. Despite the significant contribution CofP research has made to our understanding of variation, the CofP framework and terminology are often used without clarifying how the notions of *community* and *practice* are conceptualized and operationalized in a given research context. Given the strong connotations of belonging and sameness that accompany the term *community*, and given the complexity of the relationship between the 'community' and the notion of 'practice', terminological clarity is in my view pertinent, for it will contribute to a better understanding of the research rationale of projects taking a CofP approach. From this point of view, it can be useful for the field to revisit the framework and continue the debate on its constitutive elements. Future research can take stock of how the term is currently being used and what this signifies for the affordances of the framework. This can usefully pave the way for a new range of theoretical and empirical questions to be addressed in the CofP context.

Finally, the time is right for CMD research to begin to pay more attention to professional and institutional interactional contexts. The analysis of online communities in the corporate and health care world has attracted attention in business studies and medical literature, but there is still *comparatively* little work from a sociolinguistic perspective. Given the significance of online communities for their members – health discussions being an important case in point – this is an area that future research can fruitfully address.

Related topics

- Chapter 1 Approaches to language variation (Hinrichs)
- Chapter 2 Network analysis (Paolillo)
- Chapter 3 Digital ethnography (Varis)
- Chapter 19 Relationality, friendship and identity in digital communication (Graham)

Note

1   The notion of a network is widely used to refer to online formations, too (typically to capture the relationship between users within or across communities). Network analysis (Milroy & Milroy 1992) has been traditionally related to the diffusion of typically nonstandard linguistic variables. This, however, does not map onto the online context. As an example, Paolillo's (1999) well known study on IRC (Internet Relay Chat) has shown that network ties do not correspond to vernacularisation of variables as they do in off-line communities. See Paolillo 1999 for a discussion.

References

Anderson, B. 1991, *Imagined communities: reflections on the origin and spread of nationalism*, Verso: London.

Androutsopoulos, J. 2008, 'Potentials and limitations of discourse-centred online ethnography', *Language@ Internet*, vol. 5, article 8, available at: http://www.languageatinternet.org/articles/2008/1610 [accessed 24/10/2014].

Androutsopoulos, J. 2006, 'Introduction: sociolinguistics and computer-mediated communication', *Journal of Sociolinguistics*, vol. 10, no. 4, pp. 419–438.

Androutsopoulos, J. & Beißwenger, M. 2008, 'Introduction: data and methods in computer-mediated discourse analysis', *Language@Internet*, vol. 5, article 2, available at: http://www.languageatinternet.org/articles/2008/1609 [accessed 24/10/2014].

Angouri, J. Forthcoming, 'Identity', in Zhu Hua (ed.), *Research methods in intercultural communication: a practical guide*.

Angouri, J. & Sanderson, T. in prep. '"You'll find lots of help here": unpacking the function of an online rheumatoid arthritis (RA) forum', unpublished manuscript.

Angouri, J. & Tseliga, T. 2010, '"You have no idea what you are talking about!": from e-disagreement to e-impoliteness in two online fora', *Journal of Politeness Research*, vol. 6, no. 1, pp. 57–82.

Amin, A. & Roberts, J. 2008, 'Knowing in action: beyond communities of practice', *Research Policy*, vol. 37, no. 2, pp. 353–369.

Barak, A., Boniel-Nissim, M. & Suler, J. 2008, 'Fostering empowerment in online support groups', *Computers in Human Behavior*, vol. 24, no. 5, pp. 1867–1883.

Jo Angouri

Barton, D. & Lee, C. 2013, *Language online: investigating digital texts and practices*, Routledge: Abingdon, Oxon.

Baym, N. K. 1995, 'The performance of humor in computer-mediated communication', *Journal of Computer-Mediated Communication*, vol. 1, no. 2, doi: 10.1111/j.1083-6101.1995.tb00327.x.

Berry, D. M. 2004, 'Internet research: privacy, ethics and alienation: an open source approach', *Internet Research*, vol. 14, no. 4, pp. 323–332.

boyd, d 2008, 'Why youth (heart) social network sites: the role of networked publics in teenage social life', in Buckingham, D. (ed.), *Youth, identity, and digital media*, MIT Press: Cambridge, MA, pp. 119–142.

Castoriadis, C. 1987, *The imaginary institution of society*, Polity Press: London.

Cherny, L. 1999, *Conversation and community: chat in a virtual world*, CSLI Publications: Stanford, CA.

Corder, S. & Meyerhoff, M. 2007, 'Communities of practice in the analysis of intercultural communication', in H. Kotthoff & H. Spencer-Oatey (eds.), *Handbook of intercultural communication*, Mouton de Gruyter: Berlin, pp. 441–465.

Crystal, D. 2001, *Language and the Internet*, Cambridge University Press: Cambridge.

Davies, B. 2005, 'Communities of practice: legitimacy not choice', *Journal of Sociolinguistics*, vol. 9, no. 4, pp. 557–581.

De Souza, C. S. & Preece, J. 2004, 'A framework for analyzing and understanding online communities', *Interacting with Computers*, vol. 16, no. 3, pp. 579–610.

Eckert, P. & McConnell-Ginet, S. 1999, 'New generalizations and explanations in language and gender research', *Language in Society*, vol. 28, no. 2, pp. 185–201.

Gee, J. P. 2005, 'Semiotic social spaces and affinity spaces', in D. Barton & K. Tusting (eds.), *Beyond communities of practice: language power and social context*, Cambridge University Press: Cambridge, pp. 214–232.

Georgakopoulou, A. 2011a, 'Computer-mediated communication', in J-O. Östman & J. Verschueren (eds.), *Pragmatics in practice*, John Benjamins: Amsterdam, pp. 93–106.

Georgakopoulou, A. 2011b, '"On for drinkies?": email cues of participant alignments', *Language@Internet* 8, article 4, available at: http://www.languageatinternet.org/articles/2011/Georgakopoulou [accessed 24/10/2014].

Georgakopoulou, A. 1997, 'Self-presentation and interactional alliances in e-mail discourse: the style- and code-switches of Greek messages', *International Journal of Applied Linguistics*, vol. 7, no. 2, pp. 141–164.

Graham, S. L. 2007, 'Disagreeing to agree: conflict, (im)politeness and identity in a computer-mediated community', *Journal of Pragmatics*, vol. 39, no. 4, pp. 742–759.

Gumperz, J. J. 1982, *Discourse strategies*, Cambridge University Press: Cambridge.

Gumperz, J. J. & Levinson, S. C. (eds.) 1996, *Rethinking linguistic relativity*, Cambridge University Press: Cambridge.

Hara, N., Shachaf, P. & Stoerger, S. 2009, 'Online communities of practice typology revisited', *Journal of Information Science*, vol. 35, no. 6, pp. 740–757.

Hayes, E. & Gee, J. P. 2010, 'Design, resources, and affinity spaces', in J. A. Sandlin, B. D. Schultz & J. Burdick (eds.), *Handbook of public pedagogy: education and learning beyond schooling*, Routledge: Oxon, pp. 185–194.

Herring, S. C. 2007, 'A faceted classification scheme for computer-mediated discourse', *Language@ Internet*, vol. 4, article 1, available at: http://www.languageatinternet.org/articles/2007/761 [accessed 24/10/2014].

Herring, S. 2004, 'Computer-mediated discourse analysis: an approach to researching online behaviour', in S. A. Barab, R. Kling & J. H. Gray (eds.), *Designing for virtual communities in the service of learning*, Cambridge University Press: New York, NY, pp. 338–376.

Herring, S. 2001, 'Computer-mediated discourse', in D. Schiffrin, D. Tannen & H. E. Hamilton (eds.), *The handbook of discourse analysis*, Blackwell: Malden, MA, pp. 612–635.

Hine, C. 2000, *Virtual ethnography*, Sage: London.

Holmes, J. & Meyerhoff, M. 1999, 'The community of practice: theories and methodologies in language and gender research', *Language in Society*, vol. 28, no. 2, pp. 173–183.

Hudson, J. M. & Bruckman, A. 2004, '"Go away": participant objections to being studied and the ethics of chatroom research', *Information Society*, vol. 20, no. 2, pp. 127–139.

Jenkins, H. 2006, *Fans, bloggers, and gamers: exploring participatory culture*, New York University Press: New York, NY.

Jenkins, H. 2002, 'Interactive audiences? The collective intelligence of media fans', in D. Harries (ed.), *The new media book*, British Film Institute: London, pp. 157–170.

Johnson, C. M. 2001, 'A survey of current research on online communities of practice', *The Internet and Higher Education*, vol. 4, no. 1, pp. 45–60.

Jones, Q. 1997, 'Virtual-communities, virtual settlements & cyber-archaeology: a theoretical outline', *Journal of Computer-Mediated Communication*, vol. 3, no. 3, doi: 10.1111/j.1083-6101.1997.tb00075.x.

King, S. A. 1996, 'Researching Internet communities: proposed ethical guidelines for the reporting of results', *The Information Society*, vol. 12, no. 2, pp. 119–128.

Kozinets, R. V. 2010, *Netnography: doing ethnographic research online*, Sage: London.

Lave, J. and Wenger, E. 1991, *Situated learning. Legitimate peripheral participation*, Cambridge University Press: Cambridge.

Lazar, J., Hanst, E., Buchwalter, J. & Preece, J. 2001, 'Collecting user requirements in a virtual population: a case study', *WebNet Journal: Internet Technologies, Applications & Issues*, vol. 2, no. 4, pp. 20–27.

Lévy, P. 2005, 'Collective intelligence, a civilisation: towards a method of positive interpretation', *International Journal of Politics, Culture, and Society*, vol. 18, no. 3, pp. 189–198.

Licklider, J. C. R. & Taylor, W. 1968, 'The computer as a communication device', *Science and Technology*, vol. 76, no. 2, pp. 21–40.

Marwick, A. E. & boyd, d 2011, 'I tweet honestly, I tweet passionately: Twitter users, context collapse, and the imagined audience', *New Media & Society*, vol. 13, no. 1, pp. 114–133.

McElhinny, B. 2003, 'Theorizing gender in sociolinguistics and linguistic anthropology', in J. Holmes & M. Meyerhoff, M (eds.), *The handbook of language and gender*, Blackwell: Malden, MA, pp. 21–42.

Meyerhoff, M. & Strycharz, A. 2013, 'Communities of practice', in J. K. Chambers & N. Schilling-Estes (eds.), *The handbook of language variation and change*, Wiley-Blackwell: Malden, MA, pp. 428–448.

Milroy, L. & Milroy, J. 1992, 'Social network and social class: toward an integrated sociolinguistic model', *Language in Society*, vol. 21, no. 1, pp. 1–26.

Nicolini, D. 2012, *Practice theory, work, and organization: an introduction*, Oxford University Press: Oxford.

Paolillo, J. 1999, 'The virtual speech community: social network and language variation on IRC', *Journal of Computer-Mediated Communication*, vol. 4, no. 4, doi: 10.1111/j.1083-6101.1999.tb00109.x.

Patrick, P. L. 2002, 'The speech community', in J. K. Chambers & N. Schilling-Estes (eds.), *The handbook of language variation and change*, Blackwell: Malden, MA, pp. 573–597.

Preece, J. & Maloney-Krichmar, D. 2005, 'Online communities: design, theory, and practice', *Journal of Computer-Mediated Communication*, vol. 10, no. 4, doi: 10.1111/j.1083-6101.2005.tb00264.xo. 4.

Preece, J. & Maloney-Krichmar, D. 2003, 'Online communities', in J. Jacko & A. Sears (eds.), *Handbook of human-computer interaction*, Lawrence Erlbaum Associates: Mahwah, NJ, pp. 596–620.

Radin, P. 2006, ' "To me, it's my life": medical communication, trust, and activism in cyberspace', *Social Science & Medicine*, vol. 62, no. 3, pp. 591–601.

Rheingold, H. 1993, *The virtual community: homesteading on the electronic frontier*, Addison-Wesley: Reading, MA.

Sanderson, T. & Angouri, J. 2014, ' "I'm an expert in me and I know what I can cope with": Patient expertise in rheumatoid arthritis', *Communication & Medicine*, vol. 10, no. 3, pp. 249–261.

Seyber, H. 2012, 'Internet use in households and by individuals in 2012', Eurostat, available at: http://epp.eurostat.ec.europa.eu/cache/ITY_OFFPUB/KS-SF-12-050/EN/KS-SF-12-050-EN.PDF [accessed 24/10/2014].

Stommel, W. & Koole, T. 2010, 'The online support group as a community: a micro-analysis of the interaction with a new member', *Discourse Studies*, vol. 12, no. 3, pp. 357–378.

Thurlow, C. & Mroczek, K. (eds.) 2011, *Digital discourse: language in the new media*, Oxford University Press: Oxford.

Watts, R. 2003, *Politeness*, Cambridge University Press: Cambridge.

Watts, R. J., Ide, S. & Ehlich, K. (eds.) 1992, *Politeness in language: studies in its history, theory and practice*, Mouton de Gruyter: Berlin.

Weinreich, F. 1997, 'Establishing a point of view toward virtual communities', *Computer-Mediated Communication*, vol. 3, no. 2, available at: http://www.december.com/cmc/mag/1997/feb/wein.html [accessed 24/10/2014].

Wellman, B. 2001, 'Physical place and cyberplace: the rise of personalized networking', *International Journal of Urban and Regional Research*, vol. 25, no. 2, pp. 227–252.

Wellman, B. 1999, 'The network community', in B. Wellman, *Networks in the global village*, Westview: Boulder, CO.

Wenger, E. 1998, *Communities of practice: learning, meaning, and identity*, Cambridge University Press: Cambridge.

Wenger, E., McDermott, R. A. & Snyder, W. 2002, *Cultivating communities of practice: a guide to managing knowledge*, Harvard Business Press: Cambridge, MA.

Wodak, R. & Angouri, J. 2014, 'From Grexit to Grecovery: Euro/crisis discourses', *Discourse & Society*, vol. 25, no. 4, pp. 417–423.

Wodak, R., de Cillia, R., Reisigl, M. & Liebhart, K. 2009, *The discursive construction of national identity*, Edinburgh University Press: Edinburgh.

Wodak, R. & Meyer, M. (eds.) 2009, *Methods for critical discourse analysis*, Sage: London.

Further reading

Gee, J. P. 2005, 'Semiotic social spaces and affinity spaces', in D. Barton & K. Tusting (eds.), *Beyond communities of practice: language power and social context*, Cambridge University Press: Cambridge, pp. 214–232.

A good look at new trends in the study of online communities. The paper introduces a new approach and aims to move beyond the CofP framework. Also a useful treatment of the conceptualization of online spaces.

Herring, S. 2004, 'Computer-mediated discourse analysis: an approach to researching online behaviour', in S. A. Barab, R. Kling & J. H. Gray (eds.), *Designing for virtual communities in the service of learning*, Cambridge University Press: New York, NY, pp. 338–376.

An influential work on the characteristics of online communities. The article provides good coverage of research in the area and a holistic framework for operationalising the 'online community'.

Hudson, J. M. & Bruckman, A. 2004, '"Go away": participant objections to being studied and the ethics of chatroom research', *Information Society*, vol. 20, no. 2, pp. 127–139.

A good discussion of the ethical dilemmas in research on Internet communities, clarifying the issues that need to be taken into consideration in the design and execution of research on online communities.

21

Facebook and the discursive construction of the social network

Caroline Tagg and Philip Seargeant

Introduction: society and the social graph

In his letter to accompany Facebook's stock market launch, the company's founder Mark Zuckerberg wrote:

> Personal relationships are the fundamental unit of our society. Relationships are how we discover new ideas, understand our world and ultimately derive long-term happiness. At Facebook, we build tools to help people connect with the people they want and share what they want, and by doing this we are extending people's capacity to build and maintain relationships. People sharing more – even if just with their close friends or families – creates a more open culture and leads to a better understanding of the lives and perspectives of others.
>
> *(2012)*

In the relatively short period of time since its conception, Facebook has become the most successful social network site (SNS) in the world. The idea for the site was conceived in a college dorm in 2004 by twenty-year-old Mark Zuckerberg as a means by which fellow students at Harvard University could connect with each other. It has since grown from a college start-up to a worldwide platform which, in 2012, reached one billion users and which continues to expand, develop and diversify. It has evolved from a place where users go in order to check the social networks of friends to something that allows a huge range of different means of communication and social action, from sharing photos and interacting with friends to organising street protests and house parties. But Facebook is more than just a communication tool that helps people to do online the sorts of things they had previously been doing offline. As Zuckerberg's quote indicates, Facebook as a company has ambitions to alter the ways in which people relate to each other and to transform the nature of human society. The ambition is to map the social connections that constitute the network of relationships that individuals have with one another – what in Facebook terms is known as the 'social graph' – and in so doing create a society where the ability to connect and interact is as frictionless as possible.

At the base of this ambition is the way the site allows individuals to, in Zuckerberg's words, 'connect with the people they want and share what they want', and central to these processes is a particular form of phatic communication which is blurring the boundaries between the interpersonal and the informational. People today can increasingly solicit and access information from others via social networks formed on Facebook, thus using interpersonal connections as a way to stream, filter and evaluate information which can then be acted upon or forwarded in a similar way to others (Vitak & Ellison 2013). It is this ready sharing of opinion and phatic expression on Facebook – of information as a means of interpersonal connection – that is having an impact on how we build and manage relationships, and on how, as a society, we access and evaluate knowledge.

In this chapter, we highlight the importance of socially oriented language study as a way of understanding how connections are made and exploited on Facebook, and the implications the site has for social relationships and, by extension, society as a whole. We start by describing the nature of the site, the kinds of interactions and practices it affords, and the wider social media landscape it inhabits. We go on to pinpoint three issues that are central both to the site and to socially oriented linguistics: *identity* (the way users present themselves on Facebook), *audience design* (the way they imagine and address the audience that exists in the semi-public forum of Facebook), and *community* (the multiplex connections that form through Facebook interactions). These observations are then illustrated through an extended example of Facebook-mediated communication, before we step back to consider research methods and recommendations for practice. As noted above, as Facebook grows and expands, it enables an ever-wider range of communication modes, including synchronous and asynchronous private messaging as well as public posts such as status updates, wall posts, and comments. In this chapter, however, we focus predominantly on the use of the status update and subsequent comments, as these arguably have the greatest implications for social life.

Facebook and the rise of the social network site

Facebook and social media

The history of Facebook – as documented in books such as *The Facebook Effect* (Kirkpatrick 2010) and *The Boy Kings* (Losse 2012), and dramatized by Hollywood in *The Social Network* (2010) – is now enshrined in popular culture. The site was named after the printed directories of student information distributed on American college campuses. The idea was partly inspired by Mark Zuckerberg's first online venture, Facemash, which enabled Harvard students to compare and rank student photos. From the start, then, and in contrast to many online forums of the time, the site was grounded in offline practices and focused on connecting people to those they already knew. The rapid uptake by Harvard students led Zuckerberg to open it up, first to other universities and then, in 2006, to anyone who wanted to join. By this stage, many of the affordances we still associate with the Facebook platform were already in place. Users connected to people they usually knew from offline contexts via a system of mutual contracts (that is, users had to offer and accept invitations to become 'Friends'), and they constructed member profiles (the section on the site where users provide a photo and personal information). They were encouraged to 'update their status' in postings resembling short written broadcasts which were then displayed to Friends in their 'News Feeds' (constantly updated streams of Friends' Facebook activity). They also had the option of interacting on a one-to-one basis by posting on others' 'walls' (a page within each user's profile where their recent activity is listed) or via a private messaging function.

The subsequent rise and continuing development of the platform since 2006 must be understood within the context of a rapidly changing social media landscape, increasingly characterized by integration and convergence, mobility and multimodality. The site was conceived at a time when the web was altering from a place that was understood in terms of a metaphorical library or information highway – i.e., somewhere people went to get information – to what is commonly described as 'Web 2.0', characterized by user-generated content, a participatory culture, and increasingly *social* media. Captured by the term 'social media' is the fact that the production of Internet content has moved from being predominantly the reserve of traditional media and publishing institutions and emerges instead from the participation of, and interaction between, its users. This blurs the dividing line between publishing or broadcasting and private or personal communication. The platforms on which this happens range from social networking services (SNSs) – for which social connection and user interaction are key – to those sites and services which have a different primary purpose (e.g., broadcasting news, selling books, giving travel information) but which now also include affordances which allow users to comment, network or share. Meanwhile, there is a growing tendency towards integrating distinct services – so that, for example, sharing options via Facebook or Twitter are incorporated directly into operating systems – and this links a user's social networks with activities performed in external applications.

As an SNS, Facebook can be seen as being at the forefront of the move towards the web becoming powered by the actions and engagement of all those who use it. At the same time, the wider social landscape leaks into and shapes the very architecture of Facebook and the practices available to people engaging with the technology. For example, Facebook users operate within a space which is also exploited by social media-savvy commercial companies and political groups seeking to shape users' communicative practices for their own ends. Products, celebrities and political campaigns have Facebook pages which users can endorse through the affordance of 'Liking' – a user clicks 'Like' on a particular page, the click is added to the number of Likes a page has, and the user's endorsement is then displayed to his or her Friends. This process has, of course, been facilitated not only by companies' attempts to tap into people's very visible social networks for advertising purposes (and by many users' readiness to align themselves with what is being promoted), but by the Facebook company itself as it seeks to increase its revenue. The affordances that Facebook provides, therefore, and the ways in which these are promoted, perceived, regulated and used, now exist at the intersection of technology, social practice, political debate and commercial imperatives.

Mobility and multimodality

Since the inception of Facebook in 2004, the Internet has also become more mobile with the rise in popularity of smart phones and tablets. In 2012, for example, more than half of Facebook's users were accessing the site through a mobile device (Sengupta 2012). While this shift toward mobility has clear corporate implications – for example, mobile devices permit fewer advertisements than computers – its most significant impact is on the extent to which users can integrate social media into the everyday routines of their lives. Being able to access the Internet while on the move and/or engaged in other activities (that is, while being mobile) allows for constant connectivity, and it alters the relationship between people's online communication practices and the locale in which these happen, with implications for both what is communicated (on the spot reports, geolocation tags, etc.) and the form that communication takes (for example, different patterns of deixis and other context referents). Increasingly, then, Facebook is becoming deeply entrenched in the offline activities of an individual's life in much the same way that text messaging was when it first became popular. Another important factor is that multimodality – the integration of images, videos and photos as a part of people's interactions (see also Jewitt, this volume) – is increasingly central to users' experiences of Facebook, and allows users to create further links between offline and online activity. Although text persists as a very prominent mode, the use of other modes, especially images and videos, is also a fundamental part of the communicative ecosystem.

Constant incremental change

Partly in response to what it sees as changing user practices and expectations (both commercial and individual), Facebook has continually developed its site. Since 2006, status updates have been a central feature of the site, but the varied and creative ways in which users exploit this affordance have led to a series of changes to the prompt given to them: the original prompt '*[Username] is . . .* ' was replaced by the question 'What are you doing right now?' and later 'What's on your mind?'. Other developments include the way that, since 2011, users have been able to target status updates at particular audiences by creating groups within their list of 'Friends', in a move prompted by ongoing user concerns about privacy. Tagging is another practice that has developed over the years. Originally this was a means by which users could tag other users when they appeared in photos, but now a similar practice can also be applied to draw Friends' attention to status updates.

Other changes, such as the replacement of users' walls with the Timeline – which organizes posts chronologically into a kind of online, multimodal diary – seem more closely aligned with the central tenets of sharing and openness espoused by the company than with a particular response to user behaviour. Indeed, not all changes are immediately popular. When the News Feed was introduced to the home page in 2006, users complained both about violations of their own privacy and the unwelcome clutter it caused.

Against this backdrop of constant incremental change, any study or overview of Facebook must be seen as a snapshot of the particular time at which it was conducted. As noted above, however, we have grounded the discussion in this chapter in those affordances which have been fundamental elements of Facebook since the early stages of its incarnation, and which define many of the changing patterns of communication for which the site is responsible.

Critical issues and topics

The sociolinguistics of Facebook

As suggested in the introduction to this chapter, Facebook (and other SNSs) do not simply allow users to engage online in the same forms of communicative interaction that are available offline, but instead introduce a range of new or extended interaction patterns. Certain features and combinations of affordances are unique to Facebook, but the site shares three key elements with other sites, which combine to produce the communicative dynamics which underlie all SNSs. These are the capacity for:

1   constructing and presenting a member profile;
2   establishing (a network of) links with other members; and
3   viewing and searching the networked links of members in your network.

(boyd & Ellison 2008)

These three elements allow users to maintain and make visible their social networks, and this visibility operates as an important part of users' projected image and the way they are perceived by others. In other words, the fundamental social dynamics at the heart of Facebook use are self-presentation (issues that pivot around notions of *identity*), and the building and maintenance of networked relationships (issues relating to concepts of *community*). Linking these two concepts is the notion of *audience design* – the way that speakers' perceptions of the people they are addressing shape what they say (Bell 1984) – which has particular relevance for an individual's attempts to form communities in the noisy, semi-public environment of Facebook. In the rest of this section we show how these three sociolinguistic concepts are shaped by – and shape – communicative practices on Facebook.

Identity

Performances of identity on Facebook are sociolinguistically interesting for two main reasons: first, because the resources which people have at their disposal differ markedly from those typically associated with identity construction in face-to-face spoken contexts; and second, because the online context of Facebook allows for a high degree of selectivity in how people present themselves. These factors resonate with, and extend, contemporary ideas about the way that identity operates as a set of resources which people draw upon in presenting and expressing themselves via interaction with others, rather than being a stable, predetermined property of an individual. This constructivist view of identity views people as actively and repeatedly co-constructing and negotiating their identity (within the constraints afforded by various social and individual factors), and thus presenting themselves in different ways depending on the particular contextual circumstances (see also Graham, this volume). Seen in this light, there are a number of places and practices on Facebook where identity (or acts of self-presentation) can be performed. It happens by means of an individual's member profile (which offers a limited and formulaic method for listing demographic attributes and alignments), but also in the visibility of a user's Friend network, and dialogically through the updates and comments they exchange with this network.

Facebook users must portray themselves not through social cues available in settings of physical co-presence but through the use of a set of largely text-based visual resources. As in other online contexts, these resources include discourse, typography, arthography and the creative combining of different scripts (Tagg & Seargeant 2012), while attributes available to speakers – tone of voice, facial expression, gesture, gender, age and accent – are much less salient, if accessible at all. To paraphrase boyd (2001: 119), social media participants therefore engage in *writing* themselves into being.

The practice of posting and sharing photos and other media is, of course, also a significant aspect of identity construction on Facebook – according to McLaughlin and Vitak (2011: 306), in their study of Facebook norms among American college students, it was photos that participants went to first to get 'a feel' for an individual. However, although photos may appear to ground otherwise disembodied interactions in the offline world, again Facebook allows for the careful management and co-construction of identity through these resources. Users are free to select their profile picture in order to present a particular view of themselves, and may choose images not of themselves but of objects, people or places that foreground actual or desired attributes and alignments. In addition, photos posted by other people can be carefully monitored, either by the person posting them or post-hoc by those appearing in the photos (Marwick & boyd 2011; McLaughlin & Vitak 2011).

Given that Facebook is grounded in offline social networks, the site tends not to afford users the anonymity and complete freedom to 'reinvent' themselves that was associated with online forums in the 1990s. Users can, however, foreground certain aspects of their identity and present themselves in ways appropriate to the new online situations in which they find themselves. For example, McLaughlin and Vitak (2011) identified implicit rules among their participants against posting confrontational, sensitive, or 'overly emotional' status updates. The college students they surveyed also appeared to be aware that the identities they constructed on Facebook did not fully resonate with their overall image about themselves. One participant, Lindsay, said:

> I think there's probably a disproportionate amount of me, of pictures of me at parties [on Facebook] . . . if someone was only to look at my Facebook profile to get an impression of me, they would think that I go out way more than I do.
>
> *(McLaughlin & Vitak 2011: 306)*

Despite this partial nature of online self-presentation, a central concept for identity management on Facebook is the idea of authenticity – the extent to which an online persona is seen to relate to the person behind it – as well as the social value placed on this perceived authenticity. The perception that there should be a direct connection between the online persona and the offline self becomes very evident in the case of scams or online impersonations when people's sense of authenticity is violated (Page 2014). Authenticity is an important issue because of the investment interlocutors make in terms of personal disclosure which, according to the Gricean notion of the co-operative nature of conversation, they do on the basis of a contractual agreement that the interlocutor will respond in kind.

The construction of identity on Facebook is further constrained by users' perceptions of the online audience – of who they are addressing, and who may or may not read their posts. The notion of 'context collapse' describes the way that, on Facebook and other SNSs, a user's potential audience may comprise a combination of people from various domains of their lives – family, current friends, former lovers, colleagues – and, thus, what in everyday offline encounters would tend to constitute several different contexts are brought together in one conflated audience (Marwick & boyd 2011). The attendant implications for identity construction and acts of self-presentation are that people cannot vary how they come across to different people with the same amount of control as they do in offline or one-to-one contexts, so they need to negotiate the presentation of an identity which a variety of different groups will simultaneously judge to be authentic (Ellison, Steinfield, & Lampe 2011). As we discuss later in relation to audience design, Facebook users thus develop linguistic strategies for distinguishing between different segments of the audience and for targeting certain individuals and groups while excluding others.

Community

Identities online and offline are performed to some extent through the alignments people make with different groups, opinions and cultural issues, and thus an individual's identity must also be understood in relation to the communities with which they align themselves (see, for example, boyd's 2006 notion of 'imagined egocentric communities'). These alignments are very prominent on an SNS like Facebook, which is predicated on the notion of connectedness. As noted above, affordances built into the infrastructure for establishing social networks include the visible display of one's network of followers or Friends, the capacity to comment on status updates, and the ability to 'like' posts, and for this information then to be shared across one's network. Research into online communication has explored the extent to which structural affordances allow users to form 'virtual communities' and whether or not these meet the criteria required of offline communities, such as a shared set of cultural references, a regular pattern of interaction, and some sense of belonging (Herring 2008). The observations that emerge from such work – that online communities as the product of networked connections are flexible, shifting and interactively constructed – resonate with contemporary conceptions of offline communities in an increasingly mobile, intricately interconnected and globalized world (Blommaert 2010).

On Facebook, however, social networks operate in a context where the dynamics of space and time are distinct from most offline contexts. In the age of social media, geographical distance is far less important than it used to be, even compared to earlier technologies such as the telephone or radio, as communication can be instantaneous to almost any destination without difficulty, expense or much inconvenience. Wherever people have access to a computer or a mobile device with an Internet connection – which of course remains a major proviso for large parts of the global population – access to social media is practically ubiquitous. Meanwhile, the convergence of different media and modes allows people to integrate and move between different platforms and types of communication in complex, fluid ways (Jones, Schieffelin, & Smith 2011). Sites such as Facebook also allow for time delays not possible in spoken interactions, so that people may not respond immediately if at all, particularly as status updates seemingly operate by a 'pull' rather than 'push' dynamic (Marwick & boyd 2011: 11) in the sense that users are not obliged to read others' posts, but instead pick and choose what they engage with and when.

The various factors outlined above shape the types of communities that people form on Facebook. One consequence is that several communities on Facebook, as with other forms of social media, are bounded not by geographical proximity and shared background but by people's affiliation to shared interests, in what Gee (2004) calls 'affinity spaces'. That is, social alignments on Facebook can involve the development of new, often transient and weak social relations with strangers around particular topics, causes or experiences. This can take place not only through Facebook pages for celebrities, products, political parties and so on, which can then be Friended and 'Liked', but also through Facebook groups, which range from those set up to support a one-off event such as a party, outing or political petition, to more lasting efforts based, for example, around a cause, mutual hobby, or shared social characteristic such as age or sexuality.

Like other social media sites, Facebook allows individuals to find each other and rally around a shared affiliation regardless of their national background or current geographical location, and this can often have the effect of extending and transforming a local concern or a locally situated group's practices and turning it into a global issue. Monaghan (2014), for example, describes how the Liverpool Football Club's supporters' union *Spirit of Shankly* adopted the use of social media, including Facebook, as part of their campaign against the club's new owners. In one aspect of their campaign they asked geographically dispersed fans to hold up protest posters in front of world landmarks, which were then photographed and uploaded online. *Spirit of Shankly* was tapping into an existing global fanbase that identified to some extent with the club, but in offering people the opportunity to become actively involved with practices such as this, social media had the effect of creating a sense of deeper attachment and allegiance to the club's concerns, which in turn strengthened its local bargaining power. This example also highlights the porous boundaries between the online and offline activities of many modern-day interest groups or social activist networks, where what happens on social media complements, reflects or extends practices happening outside the digital world.

Alongside the development of interest-based communities, Facebook is perhaps more closely associated with a different kind of alignment, one which emerges from personal connections with other people. Facebook is grounded in offline spaces in the sense that Friends tend to comprise people with whom users have existing, offline relationships, rather than those they meet online (boyd & Ellison 2007: 211). Facebook can then be used to maintain these pre-existing offline social relationships across time and space in a way that would be impossible, or very difficult, without the Internet. However, while geographical location is of little importance for the maintenance and performance of community relations, a sense of 'local' shared knowledge can persist in these online communities, despite the participants' current real-world contexts and affiliations. In other words, despite communicating in a virtual space with a potentially global reach, people's discourse is often very context-specific and replete with in-group reference points (Seargeant, Tagg, & Ngampramuan 2012). These 'translocal' interactions – which bring various locally defined meanings and values together into one space (Blommaert 2010; see also Kytölä, this volume) – also generate their own shared culture: they produce new reference points for the community to orient to (such as the development and spread of Internet memes). These online communities are not, therefore, simply replications of offline ones, but result in the development or expansion of shared community practices and affiliations.

One of the key features of Facebook, then, is how particular affordances of the site – that is, the way in which people are able to manage their communication across time and space – facilitate patterns of group interaction which often differ from or extend the types of social organization available offline. The effort and engagement needed to sustain communities on Facebook is often low, but in many cases can be seen as usefully strengthening weak ties – with implications for an individual's ability to widen their access to information and support through their social network – while not precluding an individual's maintenance of stronger, local ties (see also chapters by Graham and Angouri, this volume).

Audience design

Audience design is founded on the insight that people construct an *idea* of their audience for the purpose of giving context to their utterances and that this is then reflected in the ways they shape their communication (Bell 1984). It has particular salience for a non-face-to-face context like Facebook, in which a largely unseen audience must be imagined into being. Although there are options for conducting one-to-one conversations on Facebook, the audience for most Facebook posts can be described as 'semi-public' in that, although a user decides who to friend, they cannot be entirely sure which of their Friends will read a post and respond. In this sense, as with broadcast audiences, the audience is largely unknown or invisible (Marwick & boyd 2011). This is further complicated by the conflated nature of the audience, potentially comprising people from different parts of a user's life. The different segments of this audience, and their likely effects on a user's posts, can be explored by adapting Bell's (1984) audience design model for spoken interactions into the following five categories (Tagg & Seargeant 2014).

- *Poster* of the status update or comment (the 'speaker' in Bell's model);
- *Addressee/s* (as in Bell's model, those to whom an update or comment is explicitly addressed);
- *Active Friends* (the people who someone typically interacts with on Facebook and who in some cases pertain to Bell's 'auditors,' those not directly addressed but whose participation is ratified by the speaker);
- *Wider Friends* (the wider circle of social acquaintances, family, and professional contacts, who might in Bell's analysis be termed 'overhearers', those whose presence is known but for whom a post is not intended);
- *The Internet as a whole* (pertaining to Bell's 'eavesdroppers', those whose presence can in some circumstances become suddenly known to the speaker with implications for their language style and choice of utterance – seen in numerous cases on social media where ostensibly private messages are picked up on by the authorities or news media).

The implication of this adapted model for Facebook interaction is twofold. First, a user's awareness of their peripheral Friends (the overhearers) is likely to have some influence on what they say, even when they have closer friends in mind (addressees and auditors); second, in posting a status update, a user must draw on a number of audience design strategies to target and exclude particular parts of their potential audience.

The audience design strategies that Facebook users adopt in order to negotiate collapsed contexts and largely unknowable audiences are likely to vary. One possible response is to avoid communicative topics or language practices that potentially exclude or may be considered inappropriate by some groups. Another is to develop highly nuanced self-presentation strategies in an attempt to target and address particular audiences within the semi-public site (Marwick & boyd 2011). Although there are several structural options for audience design embedded into the site itself – such as the development of an 'audience selector' function so that each status update can be restricted to a particular 'group' or 'list' of Friends – research suggests that certain groups, for example American teens (Marwick & boyd 2014: 1059), distrust these in-built affordances and see status updating as 'performing for others to see'. The teens in boyd and Marwick's study choose instead to use social and linguistic practices to signal boundaries, to target some users, and to exclude others. For multilingual groups, language choice can operate as another audience design strategy (Seargeant *et al.* 2012; Tagg & Seargeant 2014).

One of the implications of the semi-public nature of Facebook and the invisibility of audiences is that Facebook users are not so much targeting or responding to an audience as actually constructing it. Audience design entails drawing on what are perceived to be shared practices, and at the same time enacting and elaborating upon these practices (such as code-switching, or style-shifting). As such, audience design is an important element in constructing or maintaining a community on Facebook: it is a means of constructing the links between a user and those in their network, and of building these links around shared cultural and linguistic practices. In this sense, communities on Facebook (and elsewhere) can be seen as emerging from a user's perception of shared communicative practices, as reflected in their audience design strategies – the decisions they make and enact about style, language choice, topic of conversation, and so on.

Current contributions and research

Language choice as audience design on Facebook

In a number of recent research studies focusing on multilingual users of Facebook from various countries, we have explored the role of language choice (largely between English as a lingua franca and various other 'local' languages) as one salient aspect of an audience design strategy in the interactive construction and maintenance of communities on Facebook (Seargeant *et al.* 2012; Tagg & Seargeant 2014). In this section, we draw on an extended example to illustrate the particular ways in which identity, community and audience design are configured on Facebook. The data collected comprise status updates posted over a three-month period by our informant and the comments made in response to the updates, which we collected from the informant's wall. We then analysed the form and function of code-switches in the data, informed by data drawn from interviews and questionnaires with our informant. Informed consent was given by the informant and by participants in the data, and all names were anonymized. Issues related to the data and the methods used are discussed further later in this chapter.

Kickboxing in Athens

The exchange below begins with a status update by Mariza, a Greek woman based in Athens who has a history of migration and residence abroad and who uses Facebook multilingually to connect with users from across Europe. Specifically, Mariza was 28 at the time of data collection and had previously worked and studied in the UK, Belgium and Luxembourg. She speaks Dutch, French and Italian as well as Greek and English, and used them all on Facebook (although English and Greek were her main languages of communication on the site). At the time, she was using Facebook on a daily basis. The time stamp grounds this exchange in a particular period in the development of practices on Facebook, before the introduction of affordances enabling users to target status updates at particular audiences or to tag them in their posts. At the time of the study, Mariza had 654 Friends, 50 of whom (mainly Greeks and other Europeans) she considered to make up her active circle of Friends. Turns in the interaction are numbered, and translations of the non-English utterances, provided by Mariza, are given in square brackets after the relevant posts where necessary.

Example 1

1	Mariza	is kickboxing again after a looong time . . . ♥
		(Time stamp: December 13 2010, at 9:27)
2	Elena	I love to kick!
3	Adriano	ζηλεύω . . . θέλω κι εγώ!!!
		[I envy you . . . I want too!!!]
4	Mariza	Haha!I love to box!;) Adriano Ela k sy!oi eggrafes tha arxisoun tin paraskeyi!:)
		[Adriano come on! Registrations will start on Friday!]
5	Adriano	που? *[Where?]*
6	Mariza	Stelnw minima!
		[I am texting you!]
7	Sofia	Steile k se mena!
		[Text me too!]
8	Carmen	Cool!!!!! come to brussels and we do it together!!! BTW happy Xmas!!!
9	Mariza	Guapa! Donde estas?feliz navidad tambien!besitos!:)
		[Pretty! Where are you? Merry Christmas to you too! Kisses!]
10	Carmen	still still in brussels, flying back on the 24th, are you ok?
		how is the work hunting going? I whish you all the best. miss you!

Mariza's status update strikes a lighthearted tone, which is signalled by language play such as repeated letters ('looong'), the heart symbol, and the teasing tailing off of the ellipsis (. . .) and which can be compared with others across our data sets:

- Dream is packing up for Paris!! :D *(Thai user)*
- Pauline is back. or is she? *(French user)*
- Eva has found her mojo again! *(Dutch user)*

As with these other status updates, Mariza's post can be seen as playfully eliciting responses from across her active Friends. The use of English suggests that the update is not targeted specifically at Greek Friends, but instead that people are included or excluded depending on such things as their relationship with Mariza, their interest in her hobby (kickboxing), and the varying ways in which they can interpret the update. As Mariza put it to us, 'Sometimes whoever interested they will react to the post'. At the same time, the reference to her kickboxing is vague enough to exclude acquaintances at the periphery of her Friends list who will not have the contextual background about her to know exactly what it refers to (that is, 'is kickboxing again' does not include information as to where or when she is 'kickboxing', why she has taken it up again and after how long – or indeed whether she means the term literally or figuratively). What she does present them with is a particular (carefree, light-hearted) display of identity – in other words, she is to some extent performing in front of these wider Friends even though the status update is not primarily intended for them. Her post, then, is shaped by her perception of the different relationships she has with the varied groups that make up her potential Facebook audience.

What then emerges in the comments can be seen as the discursive co-construction of an online group identity as mutual Friends of Mariza's respond to her status update. This group identity is signalled by the shared communicative practices – that is, largely phatic responses delivered in the same jocular tone as the status update, as suggested by the repeated exclamation marks (turns 2, 3 and 8). A sense of community is particularly evident when a number of participants begin to arrange to attend the boxing class (turns 4–7). In these turns, the participants can be seen as using Facebook as one of a set of communicative tools available to them in achieving a shared communicative purpose (boyd & Ellison 2007).

However, despite this suggestion of affiliation between participants, the 'commenters' largely do not remark on each other's comments, but instead direct their posts back to Mariza, the initial status-updater and central node in the 'community' emerging as a result of her status update. This 'node-oriented' interaction pattern has the effect of creating a series of distinct duologues rather than anything that can be seen as a coherent 'conversation' (Tagg & Seargeant 2014). Both Elena and Adriano (turns 2 and 3), for example, address Mariza directly with little evidence that they have read the other's comments, while Carmen uses her turn as an opportunity to instigate a more personal conversation, wishing Mariza 'happy Xmas!!!' (turn 8). Interestingly, this distinct communicative pattern of parallel duologues is built upon by Mariza, who responds separately in turn 4 to both of the previous participants, signalling the shift in addressee through accommodation to their different language choices and the use of a vocative ('Adriano'). This communicative dynamic reflects a pattern we noted across our data sets. For example, in one exchange initiated by a Dutch user, Eva, two commenters berate themselves for using her status update to chat among themselves (what they call 'spamming her profile'):

Example 2

| 1 | Josja | let's not put spam on Eva's profile too. |
| 2 | Julia | yeah . . . I was thinking that too :P Sorry Eva :P ♥ |

The expectation for these users appears to be that comments should orientate around the node user (the status updater) and that interaction between commenters which does not directly include the node user should be avoided. Thus we might see in this pattern a shared communicative norm emerging according to which a lack of interaction between 'commenters' is tolerated or even expected.

In the various language choices and switches in the comments following Mariza's update, it is difficult to identify a clearly interpretable set of norms dictating which language should be used when, nor is there any consistent attempt to accommodate to others' choices. While Elena echoes Mariza's use of English (turn 2), Adriano writes in Greek (turn 3), Mariza switches to romanized Greek (turn 4), and Carmen (a Spanish speaker) continues in English despite Mariza's use of Spanish to address her (turns 8–10). While further analysis may reveal patterns across a broader set of data, factors beyond audience design are clearly playing a part in motivating language and script choices here: personal identity and choice, concurrent activity or technology constraints (which may shape, for example, Mariza's initial choice of romanized Greek), as well as the attempt to create and follow different conversational threads. Topic was also stated by our participants as a motivating factor in determining language choice; Eva, for example, noted, 'The only times I post in Dutch is when I really don't think it will be of any use to any foreigners'. Within exchanges across our data sets, there is generally a shared tolerance for an individual's language choice. The communicative expectations appear not to be that commenters adhere to the language initially used in the status update, nor to one particular language, but that they draw on any language resources shared between themselves and the node – in this case, Mariza.

The use of English between Greek users in our example (e.g., turns 1 and 2), and between speakers of other languages in other exchanges we analysed, appears at least in part to be motivated by the semi-public nature of the site – that is, by users' awareness of their wider, multilingual audience. Another participant in our study, the Thai user Dream, explained that she and her Thai Friends adopted very mixed language practices of the kind illustrated below, although she claimed that they would not do so in spoken conversations. Dream and many of her Friends were in the UK, and their use of English on Facebook constituted an attempt to create a sense of 'Thainess' on what they saw as an international (i.e., English-speaking) site (Seargeant *et al.* 2012).

Example 3

Panita: dreamdream jaaa . . . miz u wa and c u today na
babyyy. yeahhh rice with duck sounds great mak. I have been soooo sick with food here laaa
[Dream Dream . . . (I) miss you, and will see you today baby. Yeah, rice with duck sounds absolutely great. I have really been so sick with the food here.]

As alluded to above, what is also interesting about Mariza's update is the extent to which it is embedded in – and yet operates separately from – a local context. Mariza's status update is grounded in a temporal and spatial offline context, but it opens up a space on Facebook where this offline situation is not necessarily always relevant (see Elena's decontextualized 'I love to kick!') or where it can be challenged ('come to Brussels and we do it together!!!' [turn 8]). For participants also based in Athens, however, the context is made immediately relevant as they arrange to attend the class (turns 4–7). Interestingly, the localized nature of this part of the exchange, together with the switch from a largely interpersonal to a specific instrumental function, appears not only to motivate the continuation of the conversation in Greek but to initiate a move to another mode, text messaging. This highlights the converged nature of digital media and the motivated way in which participants select and move between them. The public comment function is embedded in this local activity but clearly not seen here as appropriate or optimal for making private plans.

This exchange thus illustrates the dynamic between a local offline context and the translocal space opened up on Facebook. That is, the status update plays a role in the ongoing relationships between Mariza and some Athens-based Friends who use Facebook, via texting, to organize a face-to-face activity; but while Mariza's update is grounded in her offline activities, it is simultaneously open to interpretation and recontextualization by participants based in other localities, who construe and respond to the update in relation to their own interpersonal relationship with Mariza. Despite the varied motivations of the participants, however, there are signs of shared community practices here: the use of repeated punctuation to signal light-hearted exclamations, the interactional pattern created by participants rallying around the node, and the shared tolerance for individual language choices.

Summary

Facebook's current popularity can in great part be put down to network effects: nothing attracts someone to an SNS like the realization that all their friends are using it. Many users thus have hundreds of Friends who are, by default, gathered together in a crowded semi-public environment as potential audiences for the written broadcasts for which Facebook is typically used. In this novel and emerging context, users must find new ways (using a reconfigured set of resources) to present themselves as individuals, and to form and maintain connections with other people. We have shown in this section how the sociolinguistic concept of audience design can, if adapted to fit the semi-public, written context, be a useful tool in explicating the links between identity and community and in revealing how communities on Facebook can emerge not simply through structural features of the site, such as those which allow users to group Friends together or to select audiences, but also in the way in which an invisible audience is perceived, discursively co-constructed and thus imagined into being through semiotic practice.

Research methods and recommendations for practice

The research discussed above draws largely on textual analysis of the forms and functions of code switches to and from English, supplemented by participant interviews which seek to obtain post-hoc accounts of the motivations underlying the language choices in order to explore their possible functions and indexical values. While this aspect of our approach does not have the same range and depth as discourse-centred online ethnography (Androutsopoulos 2008), it can supplement inductive inferences based on textual analysis with emic insights based on participants' own perceptions of their use of various linguistic resources. It must be noted, however, that these interviews consist of the participants' post-hoc reflections on the interactions and cannot of course be considered straightforward or objective records of the motivations behind the interactions; they are constrained by factors such as the scope of their metalinguistic terminology, the perspectival nature of their interpretation, and so on. The method of interpretation is framed by this caveat.

Much of the social research being conducted around social media draws upon metric-based methodologies – mapping user networks, measuring user traffic, exploring language distribution, charting the rise and fall of discussion topics, and so on (see, for example, 'mood-analysis' studies that examine the frequency of certain indexical terms used in relation to a particular event or issue, such as Mislove, Lehmann, Ahn, Onnela, & Rosenquist 2010) – but such large scale studies of the *what* and *how* of user behaviour cannot adequately answer questions as to *why* people are using a particular site, how their practices online emerge from and complement their offline lives, and in what ways people themselves justify, explain and indeed understand their communicative practices. We have shown in this chapter how sociolinguistic concepts can help explain social processes of identification and connection. In particular, language-related studies which draw to varying extents on an ethnographic epistemology are crucial in understanding the impact which Facebook, and social media in general, is having on people's lives (Lee 2011, 2014; Page 2014).

Future directions

Socially oriented studies that seek to understand interactions on Facebook and other SNSs (see for example the studies in Seargeant & Tagg 2014) face a number of challenges which sociolinguists are only now beginning to come to terms with. Chief among these are issues related to the online/offline divide, the increasingly multimodal and multilingual nature of the site, and the transfer of speech-like practices to the written mode.

The online/offline divide can be seen as part of the wider issue of delimiting what constitutes the object of enquiry and its context. It raises questions about the nature of the relationship

Caroline Tagg and Philip Seargeant

between people's offline lives and their online practices (and how the two are interwoven), about the many ways in which people can access and navigate Facebook (through mobile devices, through being directed to particular interactions by email alerts, by scrolling down News Feeds, and so on), and about which elements on the multi-channel, multimodal Facebook platform are relevant as frames for research (is it everything that Facebook chooses to include in a News Feed – or in a Timeline? Should it include hyperlinked external texts or site-generated peripheral elements such as targeted ads?). Ongoing and future work will need to address these questions, bearing in mind the ever-changing affordances and architecture of Facebook and the shifting practices of its users, as well as the wider social media landscape.

Given the prominently multimodal nature of the Facebook platform, data collection for any holistic exploration of people's practices becomes a multi-layered, complex operation, calling into question the utility of very large-scale studies or text-only investigations and suggesting the potential limitations of a corpus-based approach. In addition, the highly multilingual and mixed-language nature of the site (given its global reach and the translocal communicative practices employed within it) poses challenges for existing frameworks of code-switching. Models of code-switching in spoken interaction cannot necessarily be assumed to apply to written contexts such as Facebook, where participants are separated in time and space and where the written mode offers additional resources such as use of script, image and hyperlinks, all of which create a different conversational dynamic. It is in these areas that future work is likely to be focused, in order to build a sound empirical understanding of the sociolinguistics of social network sites, and to establish a theoretical basis for the analysis of language and style choice in written, multimodal communication contexts such as Facebook.

Related topics

- Chapter 4 Multimodal analysis (Jewitt)
- Chapter 7 Multilingual resources and practices in digital communication (Lee)
- Chapter 15 Twitter: design, discourse, and the implications of public text (Squires)
- Chapter 19 Relationality, friendship and identity in digital communication (Graham)
- Chapter 20 Online communities and communities of practice (Angouri)
- Chapter 22 YouTube: language and discourse practices in participatory culture (Androutsopoulos & Tereick)
- Chapter 23 Translocality (Kytölä)

References

Androutsopoulos, J. 2008, 'Potentials and limitations of discourse-centred online ethnography', *Language@ Internet*, vol. 5, article 8.
Bell, A. 1984, 'Language style as audience design', *Language in Society*, vol. 13, pp. 145–204.
Blommaert, J. 2010, *The sociolinguistics of globalization*, Cambridge University Press: Cambridge.
boyd, dm 2006, 'Friends, friendsters, and top 8: writing communities into being on social network sites', *First Monday*, vol. 11, no. 12.
boyd, dm 2001, 'Taken out of context: American teen sociality in networked publics', PhD thesis, University of California, Berkeley, CA.
boyd, d.m. & Ellison, N. B. 2008, 'Social network sites: definition, history, and scholarship', *Journal of Computer-Mediated Communication*, vol. 13, no. 1, pp. 210–230.
Ellison, N. B., Steinfield, C. & Lampe, C. 2011, 'Connection strategies: social capital implications of Facebook-enabled communication practices', *New Media & Society*, vol. 13, no. 6, pp. 873–892.
Gee, J. P. 2004, *Situated language and learning: a critique of traditional schooling*, Routledge: New York, NY.
Herring, S. C. 2008, 'Virtual community' in L. M. Given (ed.), *Encyclopedia of qualitative research methods*, Sage: New York, NY, pp. 920–921.

Jones, G. M., Schieffelin, B. B. & Smith, R. E. 2011, 'When Friends who talk together stalk together: online gossip as metacommunication', in C. Thurlow & K. Mroczek (eds.), *Digital discourse: language in the new media*, Oxford University Press: Oxford, pp. 26–47.

Kirkpatrick, D. 2010, *The Facebook effect*, Simon and Schuster: New York, NY.

Lee, C. 2014, 'Language choice and self-presentation in social media: the case of university students in Hong Kong', in P. Seargeant & C. Tagg (eds.), *The language of social media: identity and community on the Internet*, Palgrave Macmillan: Basingstoke, UK pp. 91–111.

Lee, C. 2011, 'Micro-blogging and status updates on Facebook', in C. Thurlow & K. Mroczek (eds.), *Digital discourse: language in the new media*, Oxford University Press: Oxford, pp. 110–128.

Losse, K. 2012, *The boy kings: a journey into the heart of the social network*, Free Press: New York, NY.

Marwick, A. E. & boyd, d.m. 2014, 'Networked privacy: how teenagers negotiate context in social media', *New Media and Society*, vol. 16, no. 7, pp. 1051–1067.

Marwick, A. E. & boyd, d.m. 2011, 'I tweet honestly, I tweet passionately: Twitter users, context collapse, and the imagined audience', *New Media & Society*, vol. 13, no. 1, pp. 114–133.

McLaughlin, C. & Vitak, J. 2011, 'Norm evolution and violation on Facebook', *New Media & Society*, vol. 14, no. 2, pp. 299–315.

Mislove, A., Lehmann, S., Ahn, Y-Y., Onnela, J-P. & Rosenquist, J-N. 2010, 'Pulse of the nation: US mood throughout the day inferred from Twitter', available at www.ccs.neu.edu/home/amislove/twittermood.

Monaghan, F. 2014, 'Seeing red: social media and football fan activism', in P. Seargeant & C. Tagg (eds.), *The language of social media: identity and community on the Internet*, Palgrave Macmillan: Basingstoke, pp. 228–254.

Page, R. 2014, 'Hoaxes, hacking and humour: analysing impersonated identity on social network sites', in P. Seargeant & C. Tagg (eds.), *The language of social media: identity and community on the Internet*, Palgrave Macmillan: Basingstoke, pp. 46–64.

Seargeant, P. & C. Tagg (eds.) 2014, *The language of social media: identity and community on the Internet*, Palgrave Macmillan, Basingstoke.

Seargeant, P., Tagg, C. & Ngampramuan, W. 2012, 'Language choice and addressivity strategies in Thai-English social network interactions', *Journal of Sociolinguistics*, vol. 16, no. 4, pp. 510–531.

Sengupta, S. 2012, 'Facebook's prospects may rest on trove of data', *The New York Times*, 14 May 2012.

Tagg, C. & Seargeant, P. 2014, 'Audience design and language choice in the construction and maintenance of translocal communities on social network sites', in P. Seargeant & C. Tagg (eds.), *The language of social media: identity and community on the Internet*, Palgrave Macmillan: Basingstoke, pp. 161–185.

Tagg, C. & Seargeant, P. 2012, 'Writing systems at play in Thai–English online interactions', *Writing Systems Research*, vol. 4, no. 2, pp. 195–213.

Vitak, J. & Ellison, N. 2013, ' "There's a network out there you might as well tap": exploring the benefits of and barriers to exchanging informational and support-based resources on Facebook', *New Media & Society*, vol. 15, no. 2, pp. 243–259.

Zuckerberg, M. 2012, Facebook registration statement, as filed with the Securities and Exchange Commission on February 1, 2012, available at www.sec.gov/Archives/edgar/data/1326801/00011 9312512034517/d287954ds1.htm#toc287954_10).

Further reading

Papacharissi, Z. (ed.) 2011, *A networked self: identity, community, and culture on social network sites*, Routledge: Abingdon, UK.

This book brings together new work on identity and social connection on social media sites from a range of different disciplines.

Seargeant, P. & Tagg, C. (eds.) 2014, *The language of social media: identity and community on the Internet*, Palgrave Macmillan: Basingstoke.

This book brings together studies from researchers at the leading edge of language and social media research, exploring issues of identity and community on a range of online sites. Several of the studies deal with communication via Facebook, while others look at different forms of social media, from Twitter and TripAdvisor to YouTube.

22

YouTube

Language and discourse practices in participatory culture

Jannis Androutsopoulos and Jana Tereick

Introduction

YouTube, the globally leading video-sharing website and one of the iconic environments of the social media era, has received less attention from language scholars than other social media platforms such as Facebook or Twitter, let alone older communication modes such as discussion forums. One reason for this could be the impression that YouTube is mainly about the moving image, with language playing a peripheral role. In this chapter, we argue that language is a key resource in the semiotic landscape of YouTube. We discuss a number of approaches to its analysis and suggest that researchers have conceptualized the role of language in YouTube in different ways, such as a resource for multimodal semiotic creativity, for digital multi-party interaction, or for participatory discourse on social and political issues. Our discussion is based on a survey of literature as well as on our own research. In the following section, we outline the development and growth of YouTube in the ten years of its existence to date. We then examine YouTube as a complex discourse environment at three levels: the 'big picture' of discourse structure and participation framework; the range of multimodal digital recontextualization practices that are often termed 'remix'; and the realm of audience comments and interaction. We then present two research approaches to language and discourse practices on YouTube, which originate in our own research. The first outlines a social-semiotic and sociolinguistic approach to YouTube as a site for the performance and negotiation of dialect, and the second outlines a corpus-assisted discourse analysis of YouTube as a site of participatory discourse on climate change. We conclude with recommendations for practice and suggestions for future research.

Historical perspectives

Founded in 2005 and bought by Google in 2006, YouTube is currently the third most popular website globally.[1] Its exponential growth in the ten years of its existence to date has played out at various levels. In terms of technological facilities, YouTube constantly increases the size of uploaded videos, and has refined available viewer statistics, introduced features to increase coherence among comments, and extended its range of localized versions, which now amount to 73 countries and 51 different languages.[2] At the same time, certain features have ceased to be available, including the option of video response, which was removed in August 2013. In terms of social penetration, YouTube claims that 'More than 1 billion unique users visit YouTube each month' and 'YouTube reaches more U.S. adults aged 18–34 than any cable network'.[3] While the latter information is limited to U.S. audiences, there is little doubt that YouTube is among the core features of the contemporary global digital media landscape. The viewing figures of certain YouTube videos probably exceed the reach of any single broadcast show in most of the world's countries. For example, the (apparently) original 'Harlem Shake' video has reached 52,386,603 views and 47,354 comments, and a YouTube compilation of popular videos of the year 2012 reached 146,497,785 views and 249,160 comments.[4]

These ten years have also seen a massive diversification of the individuals and/or organizations that upload and make available content on YouTube. Soon after its launch, YouTube became a key site for practices of civic engagement, grassroots activism, and vernacular semiotic creativity at the interface of mainstream media and participatory culture (Burgess & Green 2009; Jenkins 2006; Lovink & Niederer 2008). As early as 2006, media scholars celebrated YouTube as a prototype of participatory culture because it offered alternative publics a much broader reach than earlier niche media (Jenkins 2006, 2009). At the same time, its rapid mainstreaming meant that YouTube now hosts video channels by all kinds of political, religious or commercial actors, including the Vatican (channel name: *vatican*); the German federal government (*bundesregierung*); the International Olympics Committee (*olympic*); Coca Cola (*cocacola*); luxury vehicle brands (e.g., *Porsche*); NGOs (e.g., *GreenpeaceVideo*); educational institutions (e.g., *Harvard*); media organizations (e.g., *BBC*); manufacturers of consumer goods (such as *durex*, the globally leading producer of condoms); and so on. Providing a platform for the distribution of video content by almost any author and/or producer imaginable, YouTube has gained massive importance in contemporary media culture from a global to a very local scale. Besides consuming a large amount of web traffic and filling people's time with pastimes such as watching funny cat videos, it has gained considerable political power as a publishing space for videos which document, among other things, police violence, war crimes and natural catastrophes. YouTube's development into a resource for civic activism has increased the potential impact of contributions 'by the people' on the unfolding of a particular event, but this has also led to its perception as a threat by certain governments, which have blocked or censored YouTube in a number of countries (see the Wikipedia entry on 'Censorship of YouTube').

YouTube's rise in popularity and present-day de facto market dominance can be described as a network effect (Sundararajan 2008). Simply put, the more users are already using YouTube, the more likely it is that new users are going to use it too, and once a critical mass is reached, user numbers grow exponentially. In this respect, YouTube's success story is similar to that of Facebook or other social media. However, YouTube is not a social networking site like Facebook (despite efforts to integrate it into *Google+*). Though users have the option of setting their videos as 'private', uploaded videos and comments are by default publicly accessible to an infinite audience. While YouTube users clearly do not constitute a homogenous community, YouTube is accessible to members of online communities (in the sense of Herring 2004) and enables user interaction centred on, and sometimes sparked through, video content, in ways which we discuss below.

Critical issues and topics

Research on YouTube tends to follow different strategies for reducing its sheer volume of content to analytically meaningful and manageable samples. In this process, the research priorities of each discipline determine to a large extent how YouTube is studied. Researchers in socio-cultural linguistics have focused either on videos or comments or – perhaps more typically – on videos together with their comments. In this section, we first take an integrative view on YouTube from the perspective of the discourse structures and user activities it hosts. We then focus on YouTube videos in terms of multimodality and remix practices, and finally consider comments in terms of interaction structure and audience engagement.

Discourse structure and participation framework

What we see on any YouTube page is neither just audio-visual content nor just a thread of comments, neither just image nor just language, but rather a complex configuration of semiotic components. YouTube was the first digital environment that introduced a tripartite order of content that may seem rather common today, but revolutionized the structure of multimodal web platforms in its early days. Its centre part is a (usually short) video clip that is publicly available for users to watch, save, share and discuss. This central piece of content is complemented by audience responses, which are likewise publicly available and open to counter-responses by other users. Finally there is the hosting space, i.e. the individual webpage on which each video is framed by additional information, such as viewing statistics, recommendations of similar content, navigation bars and other elements. Defined by this tripartite configuration, YouTube pages share in our view four characteristics that shape their discourse structure: they are *multi-authored*, *multi-semiotic*, *dialogic* and *dynamic* units of discourse (Androutsopoulos 2010, 2013; Tereick 2011). We briefly discuss each one in turn.

YouTube pages are *multi-authored* in that their three dimensions of content (i.e., videos, comments and framing elements) are contributed by different sources. Videos are produced and/or uploaded by different kinds of people (a point to which we return below), and even the components of a single video sometimes have different origins, this being the case with compilations, remixes and so-called 'buffalaxed' videos – i.e. short movie clips with added subtitles that provide a phonetic pseudo-translation (see Leppänen & Häkkinen 2012). Comments are obviously contributed by multiple authors. Many post one-off comments to a video, but some contribute multiple comments as they get engaged in a debate with other YouTube users (see Bou-Franch & Garcés-Conejos Blitvich 2014). Surrounding elements are based on the site's algorithms, in part related to user tags, and are therefore beyond the agency of video uploaders and commenters.

YouTube pages are *multi-semiotic* in that they combine multimedia and multimodal characteristics. By multimedia, we mean the combination of audio and visual media that is generally typical for YouTube videos, whereas the notion of multimodality focuses on the distinct semiotic resources that make up a video, e.g., spoken and written language, music and other sounds, moving and still images. From a language studies perspective, YouTube has been pivotal in extending the modalities of language in computer-mediated communication. Whereas spoken language was marginal in earlier CMC, being limited to video conferencing and online phone calls, it has gained a much wider presence through video-sharing sites. This development is of particular interest to sociolinguists, since YouTube videos raise questions about the public online representation of linguistic diversity (e.g., dialects, multilingualism) and of the hybrid combinations of linguistic resources (see Androutsopoulos 2010; Leppänen & Häkkinen 2012).

YouTube pages are *dialogic* in a number of ways. In the most obvious sense, dialogues can be carried out in the uploaded videos, either among the characters or in terms of a character addressing the viewer. There is, further, dialogue in comments responding to the videos (see discussion of video turns below), video responses addressing the main video, and dialogue carried out among commenters. To this we can add the special cases of collaborative video annotation (Herring 2013: 18) and 'bufallaxed' videos (Leppänen & Häkkinen 2012), which extend the dialogic qualities of YouTube videos in media-specific ways.

YouTube pages are *dynamic* in that even though the posted video remains unaltered, new comments can be added at any time. Readers might be anecdotally familiar with the phenomenon of 'tribute comments' after the death of an artist or other personality whose YouTube videos suddenly receive new viewers. The surrounding textual elements, too, are ever-changing depending on the website's algorithms. To paraphrase the famous statement by Heraclitus of Ephesus, no man ever visits the same YouTube video page twice, as each new visit alters its overall configuration. This raises methodology issues with regard to 'freezing' a corpus, as we discuss further below.

Androutsopoulos (2010, 2013) proposed to conceptualize the discourse structure of YouTube as a 'vernacular spectacle', thereby drawing on a pair of metaphors from Goffman's frame analysis (Goffman 1986). Goffman distinguishes between 'game' and 'spectacle', i.e. 'between a dramatic play or contest or wedding or trial and the social occasion or affair in which these proceedings are encased' (p. 261). In this analogy, a YouTube video can be likened to a 'game', while the webpage that encases this video alongside its comments and surrounding elements can be likened to a 'spectacle'. From the viewpoint of user practices, an entire YouTube video page could be likened to a game, with each individual instance of reception constituting a spectacle. Either way, the notions of game and spectacle foreground the performance qualities of YouTube discourse. Exceptions of private settings notwithstanding, videos are uploaded to be displayed to an audience and to prompt responses by members of that audience.

The participation framework proposed by Dynel (2014) draws on research on media talk and mediated interaction to distinguish three levels of YouTube interaction: a) speakers and hearers in the factual or fictional dialogues of the videos; b) speakers and hearers of comments; and c) senders (uploaders) and recipients (viewers) of YouTube videos. Part of this last level is a tripartite classification of YouTube videos in terms of authorship: 'authorial videos' by private YouTube users, which Dynel calls 'vlogging' (from 'video blogging'); videos that 'do not differ from televized programmes'; and those based on 'programmes and films released earlier but purposely modified by YouTube users' (Dynel 2014: 7). These three categories are common in the research literature, albeit with different terms, including amateur videos, corporate content and pirated material, respectively. With regard to reception roles, Dynel suggests that YouTube viewers 'resemble traditional media viewers in many ways' – apart, that is, from their capacity to comment on the videos and interact with other commenters. As a result, Dynel claims, the participation framework of YouTube is much more complex than traditional broadcasting.

Another important dimension of YouTube content is its detachability and potential for intermedia circulation. By default, YouTube videos can be embedded on other websites and are thus commonly found in social media timelines, online journalism, or personal blogs, where they are combined with new textual elements and recontextualized. Detachability and recontextualization afford YouTube videos a high potential for circulation and 'virality' (Georgakopoulou 2013; Shifman 2012), a process by which even low-budget, amateur videos can become very popular in one particular country or even world-wide, sometimes sparking off a series of imitations or remixes. Shifman (2012) examines such a remix series of one scene from the movie *Downfall*. Leppänen and Häkkinen (2012) analyse how the practice of Buffalaxed videos is adopted in Finland by a local YouTube user who subtitles clips from a Bollywood movie and a Kurdish wedding band with mock translations that acoustically resemble the original lyrics. The authors point out the tension between the sexist and racist content of the mock translations, on the one hand, and the unexpected popularity that the parody offered to the Kurdish wedding singer among Finnish audiences. The boundaries between online and offline practices are particularly permeable on YouTube, and one avenue for future research could be to complement the analysis of online discourse with ethnographic explorations of how people 'read', view and interact with YouTube spectacles, including practices such as visiting a page, playing and replaying a video, commenting, browsing through and rating others' comments, forwarding and sharing, downloading and remixing, and so on.

Remixing and embedding: multimodal recontextualization practices

In a discourse environment that is characterized by diversity and collaborative authorship, one important question is how participants engage with material that is produced by others and does not legally belong to them. On YouTube, this concerns video material produced 'outside YouTube', in particular by mass media and multinational corporations, as well as material from 'within YouTube', i.e. produced and/or provided by other users. Engagement with others' video material is one of the most common and characteristic, even defining, practices of YouTube's participatory culture (see Shifman 2012: 188).

Such an engagement materializes in remixing and embedding as practices of recontextualization (Bauman & Briggs 1990). We understand embedding and remixing to refer to a range of semiotic modification procedures which are closely linked to conceptual transformations in the frame of a particular discourse. More specifically, remix 'means to take cultural artifacts and combine and manipulate them into new kinds of creative blends' (Knobel & Lankshear 2008: 22); embedding means using an existing artefact without changing it – as in quoting, for example. In the YouTube context, a common form of embedding is to upload an existing video, which has been produced by others, and to recontextualize it by assigning it a new title, short description and set of tags.

Unlike the notions of parody or piracy, the concepts of remixing and embedding do not entail semantic or evaluating aspects; however, the digital literacy practices of embedding and remixing are closely linked to modifications of meaning. We illustrate this with examples taken from Tereick's research on representations of climate change on YouTube (Tereick 2012; see below). For example, think of a YouTube user who takes an extract from a television programme on climate change produced by a public service broadcaster, then adds the new caption, 'The climate change hoax', and a fitting video description. This is an instance of embedding that is likely to influence the interpretation of the resulting artefact. To bring in an example of remixing, think of a user who collates snapshots of mass media coverage on climate change into a collage and adds a voice-over that characterizes this coverage as 'media hysteria' (Tereick 2012). The original bits of mass media content have now become part of a new proposition. Such remixing of mass media material can take the form of a (pseudo-) dialogue between the original material and the producer – for example, by adding subtitles or captions which pose questions that are apparently 'answered' by excerpts from the broadcast content (Tereick 2012: 242).

Remixing can involve the modification of a single video or collaging and montaging excerpts from several pre-existing videos into a new artefact. An example from Tereick's ongoing research is the remix of a promotional video clip produced by RWE, a large German electric utilities company. The original clip, called 'Der Energieriese' ('The Energy Giant'[5]) features an animated benevolent giant who plants windmills and fermentation plants. The giant here stands for the company; through this metaphor, the clip aims to enhance the perceived value of RWE's activities in the renewable energy sector. However, a number of NGOs and individual users deployed various remix techniques in order to subvert the clip's promotional message. An analysis of such remixes uploaded to YouTube in July and August 2009 identified procedures of commenting, blending and transformation.

Figure 22.1   Remixed YouTube video frame.

More specifically, *commenting* refers to the practice of using the original material and adding a second layer to it, such as overlay captions which challenge the discourse of the original video with counterfactual propositions. The resulting remix is reminiscent of the practices of marginal comments and overwriting in medieval manuscript culture; it is, so to speak, a *palimpsest* of competing meanings. In the video 'Energieriesen-Lüge' (which can be translated as 'energy giant lie' or 'giant energy lie'),[6] counter-facts are inserted at the clip's relevant points, such as the statement 'Windmill plants make up only 0.1 % of RWE's power plants' (0:16, see Figure 22.1). The producers also point at aspects that are missing from the promotional clip, for example by asking 'Where are RWE's five nuclear power plants in this video?' (1:35), thereby exposing RWE's implicature that the power sources represented in their clip are the only ones they use.

Transformation refers to remix practices that modify, instead of just overlaying, the original video. An example from Tereick's study is the remix video 'Atom-Energieriese' ('nuclear energy giant') in which several parts of the original clip are reversed in order to represent the giant as actually removing windmills instead of planting them; here, the reversal of the semiotic material corresponds to a reversal of meaning. This technique is also used in the remix 'RWE Energieriese – Director's Cut', which in addition repeats a short sequence with the giant extracting coal. Here, the reiteration of the sequence metaphorically indexes RWE's prolific use of coal.

Blending refers to a set of elaborate and technically challenging techniques by which new material is added to the original video. For example, a remix video by the NGO Greenpeace begins with the unmodified RWE clip, and the camera then zooms out to reveal that the clip is shown on a TV set standing on the site of a nuclear power plant after a nuclear hazard (0:28, see Figure 22.2). A set of decapitated windmills completes this post-apocalyptic scenario. This video demonstrates a complex blend of embedding, 'quoting' the original material and literally adding a new frame to change its meaning. The resulting blend follows the composition structure termed 'ideal/real' by Kress and van Leeuwen (2006: 186–192), in that it first shows RWE's 'ideal' untouched and then slowly reveals the 'real' scenario, which adds to the dramatic effect. However, blending does not necessarily have to follow this structure. For example, the remix video 'Atom-Energieriese' ('nuclear energy giant') just adds a nuclear power plant to the original clip's idyllic panorama.

Figure 22.2   Frame from remix video by Greenpeace.

As these examples suggest, remixing can be used to re-key (Goffman 1986) a video, i.e. to change its original tone and message by modifying its formal structure. It is also noteworthy that all these remix techniques entail orientational metaphors in the sense of Lakoff and Johnson (2003). The formal structure of remix – overlay, reversal, counterpart – is reproduced at the content level, while the propositional structure of the original video is modified in analogy to the images. While in these examples remix techniques are used for the purpose of adbusting or culture jamming (Firat & Kuryel 2011), they can also serve other purposes of subversion in other contexts.

Audience comments: on-line polylogues and YouTube discussion culture

Research on YouTube comments is of two kinds, broadly speaking. The first approaches YouTube comments as a site of computer-mediated interaction and aims to describe their sequential structure and coherence-building devices. The second views YouTube comments as a resource for discourse participation and examines the attitudes they express towards the reference video and/or their contribution to an on-going discourse. Both lines of inquiry will be discussed in this section. Apart from these, hardly anything is known about how YouTube users actually read comments. Jones and Schieffelin (2009) suggest that most users only read the most recent comments, but this needs to be further researched (see Bou-Franch, Lorenzo-Dus, & Garcés-Conejos Blitvich 2012). It is worth noting that in non-linguistic scholarship, the number of comments a video receives has been viewed as an index of audience attention.

An analysis of YouTube comments as computer-mediated interaction begins with their sequential structure and coherence. As in other public modes of CMC, interaction is prompted by an initiating contribution, in this case the uploaded video. It is constrained by the technological conditions of the platform, which include the limitation to verbal signs, the linear mode of a single thread of comments, and the recently introduced format in which direct replies to a comment are subordinated to it. Finally, interaction varies according to factors such as the discourse framing of the respective video and the socio-demographic characteristics of its viewership. In this largely unregulated space of discourse, and in view of the massive amounts of comments that popular videos receive, one might expect comments to be haphazard and incoherent. However, this is not validated by research, which attests to thematically coherent threads of comments and sustained interpersonal interaction among commenters (e.g., Androutsopoulos 2013; Bou-Franch *et al.* 2012; Jones & Schieffelin 2009; Pihlaja 2014; Sharma 2014).

Bou-Franch *et al.* (2012) propose a framework for the analysis of YouTube comment threads in terms of discourse reference, turn-taking management and cohesion establishment. Their empirical data are two discussion threads on two thematically different YouTube videos. The analysis is limited to the first 150 comments from each thread, so that the question of whether coherence can ever be maintained over long threads of comments remains unanswered. In terms of participation structure, they calculate the number of participants, the mean number of turns per participant, the number of one-turn contributors and of multiple contributors, these figures providing an index of interactional engagement. This study includes two coding schemes. The first is concerned with discourse reference; each individual comment (or, in conversation–analytic terminology, each author's 'turn') is coded in terms of the contribution it refers to. Five turn types are distinguished (Bou-Franch *et al.* 2012):

1   Adjacent Turn: Turn referring to immediately prior turn.
2   Non-adjacent Turn: Turn that refers to a turn other than the immediately adjacent turn.
3   Video Turn: Turn referring to triggering video clip.
4   Multiple Turn: Turn referring to multiple prior turns.
5   Mixed Turn: Turn combining two or more of the above turn-types.

Their findings show that adjacent turns have the largest share (more than 60 per cent of both sample threads), followed by video turns (19 per cent) and those referring to a non-adjacent turn (12 per cent). These figures suggest a considerable degree of adjacency in these two threads. The pattern of adjacent turns indexes on-going interaction among commenters, while that of video turns indexes audience responsiveness to the 'game', i.e. the uploaded video. The study distinguishes between two patterns of video turns, serial and 'sprinkled' ones. The first is a series of references to the video, a pattern typical for the early phase of a thread; the second consists of references that appear in-between turns and have no coherent connection to their adjacent turns.

The authors propose a second coding scheme concerned with turn-management devices. It identifies eight categories in terms of how a contribution ties into the on-going discussion, the most frequent in the sample being the following:

1   Turn-entry devices, which link the contribution to a prior turn (e.g., *by the way, you see*).
2   Turn-exit devices, which close the turn and link it to a next turn (e.g., *That's all, full-stop*, question tags and aphorisms like *sad but true*).
3   Cross-turn addressivity, when a turn selects an addressee by their screen name.
4   Indirect addressivity, when a contribution addresses another user only indirectly.

A sequential analysis of this kind mainly focuses on relations among comments in a thread. By contrast, other approaches pay more attention to discourse relations between comments and reference video – focusing, in other words, on relations of intertextuality within a specific YouTube spectacle. Comments are viewed as sites of audience engagement and discourse participation, and they represent a multi-authored 'negotiation' (Androutsopoulos 2013; Chun & Walters 2011) of the reference video and its discourse context. In this vein, Jones and Schieffelin (2009) examine audience responses to commercial clips posted on YouTube in terms of how commenters recontextualize advertising slogans. Both this study and Androutsopoulos (2013) show how comments (or, more precisely, video turns) echo scenes and voices from the reference video in a manner reminiscent of audience practices during television reception. Pihlaja (2011) compares video responses and comments as two modalities of responsivity and finds that video responses are longer, more elaborate and more interactively oriented than text comments to the same reference video.

Research has also established that YouTube offers a site for language–ideological discourse. Sharma (2014) examines how transnational speakers of Nepalese respond to a speech in English by a Nepalese politician at an international meeting. His analysis of the comments shows how the minister is mocked and ridiculed for her heavily accented English. Sharma argues that digital spaces such as YouTube offer channels for (oppositional) political involvement and engagement with the nation of origin for diasporic populations. Androutsopoulos (2013) examines the negotiation of German dialects on YouTube (see also next section) and finds that comments on (and often in) dialect are prompted by the video's reflexive orientation to dialect. This study also found that comments have different ways of engaging in the negotiation of dialect. Some users focus on dialect performance (often in terms of authenticity) in the reference video, whereas others employ the video as a mere occasion to discuss a dialect. Comments may also use certain linguistic features of the dialect staged in the video. In the analysis of two videos referring to the Berlin city dialect, Berlin dialect features occur in 40 per cent and 63 per cent of the comments, respectively (Androutsopoulos 2013). Commenters may use dialect features in their own voice or in quotations from the video, and dialect often serves as a resource for identity work in the process of discussing the performance of dialect in the reference video.

Doing YouTube research: two case studies

The two studies presented in this section illustrate two research approaches to YouTube as a site of language and discourse practices. The first study focuses on dialect performance and metalinguistic discourse, the second on the negotiation of knowledge and participation norms. Different as they may be in their empirical objects and disciplinary points of reference, they both converge on advocating a mixed-methods research design based on social semiotics, (critical) discourse analysis, and corpus linguistics. Both case studies tackle a number of methodological challenges that arise in YouTube research and show how such issues can be dealt with in empirical practice.

Performing and negotiating dialect: a social semiotic and sociolinguistic perspective

The first case study examines the representation of German dialects on YouTube (Androutsopoulos 2010, 2013). Data collection started by doing YouTube searches for around 20 German dialect labels, including *Schwäbisch* (Swabian, 6,870 results in June 2011); *Kölsch* (Cologne dialect, 6,600); *Bayerisch* (Bavarian, 5,390) and *Sächsisch* (Saxonian, 1,330). Southern German dialects are featured more frequently on YouTube than northern and eastern ones, a distribution that presumably reflects their higher vitality and stronger presence in popular culture. Some of these dialect-tagged videos had reached more than two million views and a few thousand comments at the time of research. These figures clearly suggest a keen interest in the representation of German dialects on YouTube. The analysis proceeded in two parts. The first was an analysis of metalinguistic discourse based on a sample of 310 dialect-tagged videos which were coded for type of authorship, genre, dialect use, metalinguistic discourse on dialect, and orientation to the region where the dialect in question is spoken. The second part was a micro-analysis of selected videos that feature *Berlinerisch*, the Berlin city dialect. It examined the use of six dialect features in video characters' performances of the Berlin dialect. All comments on these videos were coded for their use of dialect features, overt metalinguistic attitudes to dialect, and reference to their authors' own dialect usage. Qualitative analysis then identified common themes of dialect discourse.

The framework developed for this study centres on the notions of dialect performance, stylization and negotiation. Dialect-tagged videos share characteristics of performance, defined as a mode of speaking that is characterized by orientation to an audience, attention to the form and materiality of speaking, and heightened metalinguistic reflexivity (Bauman 1992; Bell & Gibson 2011). Many dialect videos on YouTube explicitly orient to a dialect and put it on display for an imagined or assumed audience. Even when the subject matter of a video is not explicitly reflexive (as in the case of, say, a stretch of everyday social interaction that is video-recorded and then uploaded), its display on YouTube frames it as a moment of performance. In addition, the study took into account the visual dimension of YouTube videos and the ways in which remix practices create new conditions for dialect performance. In engaging with a dialect, YouTube users appropriate semiotic resources and assemble them anew by means of techniques such as separating and recombining video and audio tracks, layering footage with a new audio track, and so on. They remix different materials, creating patterns of contrast or incongruence, which can for example generate humour or challenge dialect stereotypes. In order to account for the multimodal and multimedia aspects of this material, the analysis drew on the four levels of the social semiotics framework proposed by van Leeuwen (2005), i.e. discourse, genre, style, and mode. We briefly outline these here.

At the level of *discourse*, the analysis focused on the metalinguistic knowledge that producers and audiences of YouTube dialect videos engage with. Questions for analysis include: What are the topics of these videos in word and image? What stances towards a dialect and its typical speakers do they communicate? The analysis identified comments that discuss the geographical reach of a dialect, its distinctive features, its history and status, and issues of dialect decline and maintenance. Many of these comments reproduce social, cultural and political differences, which historically shape dialect discourse in the German-speaking area. For example, comments that debate dialect boundaries or emphasize the superiority of one's own dialect to neighbouring dialects occur in some regions (e.g., Bavarian and Franconian, Alemannic and Badian) but not in others (e.g., Berlin), for reasons that are historical in nature. Discourses of dialect maintenance and decline are characteristic for Low German, an endangered regional language, which was also the subject of a few dialect-learning videos. Comments that voice tensions between newcomers and residents occurred in response to videos from Berlin, a city that has experienced a massive influx of German and international newcomers in recent years.

At the level of *genre*, the analytical focus shifts to the social activities in dialect-tagged videos and their comments. Questions for analysis include: What genres do dialect-tagged videos draw on, and how do these genres frame the representation of dialect in the video? What genres do comments draw on in engaging with a reference video? Common genre orientations of German dialect-tagged videos are: music, theatre and comedy, poetry, sermons, story- and joke-telling, media reports on dialect, documenting dialect, learning dialect, and dialect dubbing, to which we return below.

At the level of *style*, the focus turns to the social identities that video actors and commenters associate with dialect and the semiotic resources that are deployed to stylize these identities. In stylization, performers bring up images of socially typified dialect speakers, thereby relying on the cultural and sociolinguistic knowledge they assume they are sharing with their audiences

(Coupland 2001). We can ask how video characters are stylized, what dialect features are used for this purpose, and how commenters engage with dialect identities – for instance by identifying themselves as speakers of a particular dialect. For example, a video tagged as *Berlinerisch* shows a tourist-bus driver who talks about Berlin while driving by some of Berlin's iconic monuments. The driver's use of heavy Berlin dialect is part of his stylization as working-class Berliner, to which his visual appearance also contributes. YouTube videos feature both traditional and innovative stylizations of Berlin dialect speakers, the latter including characters such as nightclub girls and a computer tutor.

Finally, the analysis of *mode* examines the semiotic modes and technological resources that shape the representation of dialect in the videos. One genre of dialect videos that makes heavy use of remix techniques is the so-called 'synchros' (a clipping of *Synchronisation*, the German term for dubbing), i.e. videos that appropriate pre-existing video material and (re)dub it in a German dialect. Synchros typically appropriate excerpts of movies, pop music or broadcast shows and substitute their audio track with a dialect voice that may or may not be semantically equivalent to the original. Hollywood movie excerpts and American pop music are particularly popular targets for synchros. Hollywood movies are by default dubbed in Standard German, and YouTubers re-dub them in dialect. For example, clips from the movie *Star Wars* are re-dubbed again and again in several German dialects, taking the form of a viral series (Shifman 2012). The propositional content of synchros is sometimes nonsensical or takes up local issues whose contrast to the original content generates humor or parody. In the dialect remix of a clip from the movie *Full Metal Jacket*, the re-dubbed movie dialogue is made to voice the old-standing conflict between the neighbouring regions of Baden and Swabia. This is a good example of how the analysis levels of discourse, mode and genre interact. Another example for such interaction is a remix of *Umbrella*, a pop hit by Rihanna, in the Bavarian dialect. The new audio and visual collage celebrates practices of binge-drinking in Bavaria, Germany (Androutsopoulos 2010). Such remixes that appropriate global material in order to comment on local practices are often applauded by commenters.

Participatory discourse on climate change: a corpus-assisted multimodal discourse analysis

The second case study takes its cues from discourse theory and critical discourse analysis, whose research interests are epitomized by Foucault's question: How are 'truth-effects produced inside discourses?' (Foucault 1980: 118). In the case of climate change, a discourse–analytic approach asks how knowledge about climate change is produced and reproduced, how different discourse positions are negotiated, which structures of power are reproduced, and which linguistic and semiotic means – including lexis, metaphors and argumentation patterns – are being used by discourse actors in order to make sense of climate change. As we aim to show below, YouTube offers the possibility of studying such negotiations in depth, because its participatory culture allows for a broad range of opinions to be articulated.

Traditional discourse analysis was developed for quite small samples of texts, which most commonly came from print media. However, discourses in the digital age are far-reaching, multi-layered and profoundly visual, leading to a need for new methods. One such methodological innovation has been the addition of corpus linguistic methods to discourse–analytic frameworks, thus enabling researchers to analyse large amounts of data (see Abdullah, this volume; Baker 2006; Hardt-Mautner 1995). These approaches, however, are generally limited to written (mostly printed) texts. The analysis of discourse in a complex multimodal environment such as YouTube is therefore still in need of adequate methodologies. This section therefore presents several methodological considerations.

The challenges of YouTube are apparent at the very start of data collection. There are thousands of videos on climate change on YouTube, and due to the site's dynamic character, videos and comments are added and/or deleted all the time. Using YouTube's web interface for data collection necessitates the problem that the research object is constantly changing, and no clear segmentation of the discourse is possible. Collecting large quantities of YouTube data by hand is hardly feasible, and the process of doing so leads to the researcher constantly influencing the data set, because clicking on a video always leads to a change of the view count. A comprehensive and representative study of discourse on YouTube creates a serious challenge that can be broken down into two components. The first is a technical one: how can comprehensive and representative data be collected from YouTube? Can it be collected at all? How can that chaos be converted into data? The second is a methodological one: how can the data be analysed? Integrating quantitative methods in order to study a large data set is limited by the fact that corpus–linguistic analysis is not yet capable of accommodating audio-visual material.

Fortunately, there is a technical solution to this technical challenge: with the aid of YouTube's *Application Programming Interface*, downloading the 1,000 most-viewed German-language videos on climate change together with meta-data such as video duration and description was an easy task. As in the first case study, a set of search terms was used to contextualize the selection in the first place. Saving this meta-data into a database creates a 'snapshot' of the discourse under consideration (Tereick 2012).

Regarding the methodological issue, the most common solution regarding the discourse analysis of the videos would be to transcribe the spoken language data in order to make it accessible to a corpus–linguistic analysis. But this is time-consuming and raises a number of problems associated with transcription. However, an alternative solution that is tailored to the specific discourse context of YouTube is to access the videos through their comments. Comments can also be downloaded via Google's YouTube *Application Programming Interface*; in Tereick's study, all comments – about 45,000 in total – that were posted to the 1,000 most-viewed videos on climate change were downloaded and made accessible to corpus–lingustic analysis. The two corpora, i.e. videos and comments, allow for a combination of two methodological approaches: a qualitative analysis of videos and comment threads, and a quantitative, corpus-linguistic analysis of comments. The analysis then oscillates between videos and comments in a circular manner, taking either a particular video or the entire corpus of comments as starting points. In the following, we will give examples for both directions.

An example of taking a video as the starting point is the second most-popular video in the corpus, called 'Climate change from an optimistic point of view'.[7] This video draws on an argument that is quite popular in climate change discourse and can be formalized like this:

(Premise 1)	As a consequence of climate change, the average temperature in Germany is rising.
(Premise 2)	It is desirable that the average temperature in Germany rises.
(Conclusion)	Therefore: Climate change is desirable.

This argument can be deployed in both an ironic and non-ironic way (Tereick 2011: 65). At 0:49, the video celebrates the future imaginary 'vibrant sea resort of Osnabrück' (a provincial North-German town far away from the sea), showing a set of palm trees (see Figure 22.3). Starting from this observation, a concordance search of 'palm' in the comment corpus turns up a number of results, which deploy palm trees as a metonym for the supposedly positive aspects of climate change. From these comments, the analysis can go back to the respective videos, thus tracking an argumentative pattern and its metonymic illustrations across different contributions and semiotic modes.

Figure 22.3   Frame from the 'Climate change from an optimistic point of view' video.

In the opposite direction, taking the comments as a starting point into the analysis can precede either a 'corpus-based' concordance search or a 'corpus-driven' calculation (Tognini-Bonelli 2001: 84). For example, an analysis of tri-grams (i.e., three-word combinations) in the comment corpus yields the pattern 'is not responsible', which is part of an argument in support of the discourse position that 'humankind *is not responsible* for climate change'. This indexes one of the most important debates in the German climate change discourse on YouTube, i.e. the 'climate change hoax' debate, which divides YouTube users sharply into two parties: one that thinks climate change is man-made and another that contests this view. Similar to other cases of conflict among YouTube commenters reported in the literature (see Bou-Franch & Garcés-Conejos Blitvich 2014; Bou-Franch *et al.* 2012; Pihlaja 2014), each party in this debate challenges the other's concepts. For example, both parties conceptualize each other as 'conspiracy theorists' (Tereick 2011), and tracking the term 'conspiracy' across the entire corpus helps the analyst to reconstruct a struggle over discourse hegemony whose diversity and depth is quite unique to YouTube.

The participatory culture (Jenkins 2006) that shapes YouTube allows for the expression of very different opinions while also confronting proponents of different 'regimes of truth' (Jenkins 2009: 122) with each other and facilitating collective norm-building. While German mass media display a de facto consensus in that man-made climate change exists (Weingart, Engels, & Pansegrau 2000), this is still heavily debated among YouTube users. Thus, YouTube offers the unique opportunity to study (counter)-hegemonic discourse positions, the process of their negotiation, and practices of creative discourse subversion (see Jones 2010).

Recommendations for practice

Among the various challenges that research on language and discourse practices in YouTube is likely to face, we limit our recommendations to issues of data collection and tailoring a research question.

As far as data collection is concerned, our survey clearly shows the importance of defining the snapshot of the discourse under consideration as precisely as possible. If you want to use a large corpus, we recommend data collection via the *Application Programming Interface* (*API*) through which YouTube data can be accessed via third-party programmes[8] (similar interfaces are available for Facebook, Twitter, Wikipedia and other social media platforms). A Google Developer Account and basic programming skills are required. Based on the API, you can write a short script in order to download a defined section of YouTube data, e.g., a set of videos whose title and/or tags contain certain search terms, or all comments for a specific video. You can also download meta-information of all videos relating to a set of search terms and then use, e.g., the Firefox-Add-on 'VideoDownloadHelper' to batch download the videos. To avoid scripting, a web data scraper might be of use as well. An important caveat to these techniques is the need to be aware of country-specific copyright laws. Usually, saving data on your local computer for a short period of time for academic purposes should be legal. However, you must not make these data available to others (even research colleagues or fellow students).

In terms of tailoring a research question, the literature survey in this chapter shows that it is common practice not to separate videos and comments as objects of inquiry, but to examine sets of videos and associated comments (Androutsopoulos 2013; Chun & Walters 2011; Sharma 2014; Tereick 2012). This is particularly the case for projects in discourse analysis which seek to examine how participants engage with an array of discourses on politics, culture, arts, language and so on. More specific questions for analysis can also be nested within this combined focus on videos and comments, dealing with linguistic and visual/multimodal resources in both modes. If your interests are specifically geared towards multimodality and visual semiotics, then focusing on videos only is a justified choice, and the opposite holds true for research interested in digitally mediated interaction or in linguistic issues appearing across a corpus.

Future directions

As our discussion suggests, there are manifold opportunities for future research on YouTube, including comment interaction, remix and multimodality, discourse participation, performance and stylization of linguistic variability, and others. A promising area of future research concerns the interrelation of YouTube to traditional mass media. On the one hand, mass media material is appropriated and remixed by YouTube users. On the other hand, media corporations themselves become increasingly active on YouTube, and at the same time YouTube videos are increasingly reproduced and discussed in traditional mass media, ranging from funny viral videos shown on entertainment programmes to war footage by amateur filmmakers that finds its way into prime time news. Determining the authenticity of such material is likely to become an increasingly important issue, as is the way in which YouTube footage is recontextualized in mainstream media programmes.

One of the discourses that has been and will remain central to YouTube concerns issues of piracy. Since part of YouTube's appeal has always consisted of the uploading of copyrighted material – a tolerated but nevertheless 'illegal' practice – the site owners and copyright holders have had to navigate a grey legal area. Whether something is considered 'piracy', 'creative adaption', or 'positive PR' is more often a question of power than of clear legal definitions. This discourse practice, too, can be studied, particularly in cases where users debate the removal of videos; in addition, a whole range of editing practices that try to avoid copyright charges (such as switching videos left to right) has emerged.

Jannis Androutsopoulos and Jana Tereick

Related topics

- Chapter 4 Multimodal analysis (Jewitt)
- Chapter 7 Multilingual resources and practices in digital communication (Lee)
- Chapter 15 Twitter: design, discourse, and the implications of public text (Squires)
- Chapter 21 Facebook and the discursive construction of the social network (Tagg & Seargeant)

Notes

The video IDs referenced below must be added to the URL: https://www.youtube.com/watch?v=

1 Ranking based on Alexa Traffic Rank, URL: http://www.alexa.com/siteinfo/youtube.com.
2 See http://en.wikipedia.org/wiki/YouTube#Localization.
3 See https://www.youtube.com/yt/press/en-GB/statistics.html.
4 'Do the Harlem shake (original)', Video ID: 8vJiSSAMNWw. 'Rewind YouTube Style 2012' Video ID: iCkYw3cRwLo. Both view counts on 13 October 2014.
5 Video ID: eIfzgBmcFlU.
6 The examples discussed here are: 'Energieriesen-Lüge' (translatable as 'energy giant lie' or 'giant energy lie', YouTube video ID: aTjHASBVA0Y; 'Atom-Energieriese' ('nuclear energy giant', video ID: 1kXE1672i1s); and 'RWE Energieriese – Director's Cut' (video ID: eQfr_ZH_Pj0).
7 Video ID: d1CRv-qghZg.
8 See http://code.google.com/apis/youtube/overview.html.

References

Androutsopoulos, J. 2013, 'Participatory culture and metalinguistic discourse: performing and negotiating German dialects on YouTube', in D. Tannen & A. M. Trester (eds.), *Discourse 2.0: language and new media*, Georgetown University Press: Washington, DC, pp. 47–71.

Androutsopoulos, J. 2010, 'Localizing the global on the participatory web', in N. Coupland (ed.), *The handbook of language and globalisation*, Wiley-Blackwell: Malden, MA, pp. 203–231.

Baker, P. 2006, *Using corpora in discourse analysis*, Continuum: London.

Bauman, R. 1992, 'Performance', in R. Bauman (ed.), *Folklore, cultural performances, and popular entertainments*, Oxford University Press: New York, NY, pp. 41–49.

Bauman, R. & Briggs, C. L. 1990, 'Poetics and performance as critical perspectives on language and social life', *Annual Review of Anthropology*, vol. 19, pp. 59–88.

Bell, A. & Gibson, A. 2011, 'Staging language: an introduction to the sociolinguistics of performance', *Journal of Sociolinguistics*, vol. 15, no. 5, pp. 555–572.

Bou-Franch, P. & Garcés-Conejos Blitvich, P. 2014, 'Conflict management in massive polylogues: a case study from YouTube', *Journal of Pragmatics*, vol. 73, pp. 1–82.

Bou-Franch, P., Lorenzo-Dus, N. & Garcés-Conejos Blitvich, P. 2012, 'Social interaction in YouTube text-based polylogues: a study of coherence', *Journal of Computer Mediated Communication*, vol. 17, no. 4, pp. 501–521.

Burgess, J. & Green, J. 2009, *YouTube: online video and participatory culture*, Polity Press: Malden, MA.

Chun, E. & Walters, K. 2011, 'Orienting to Arab orientalisms: language, race, and humor in a YouTube video', in C. Thurlow & K. Mroczek (eds.), *Digital discourse: language in the new media*, Oxford University Press: Oxford, pp. 251–273.

Coupland, N. 2001, 'Dialect stylization in radio talk', *Language in Society*, vol. 3, no. 3, pp. 345–375.

Dynel, M. 2014, 'Participation framework underlying YouTube interaction', *Journal of Pragmatics*, vol. 73, pp. 37–52.

Firat, B. Ö. & Kuryel, A. 2011, *Cultural activism: practices, dilemmas, and possibilities*, Rodopi: Amsterdam.

Foucault, M. 1980, *Power/knowledge: selected interviews and other writings, 1972–1977*, C. Gordon (ed. and trans.), Pantheon: New York, NY.

Georgakopoulou, A. 2013, 'Small stories research and social media practices: narrative stancetaking and circulation in a Greek news story', *Sociolinguistica*, vol. 27, pp. 19–36.

Goffman, E. 1986, *Frame analysis: an essay on the organization of experience*, Northeastern University Press: Boston, MA.

Hardt-Mautner, G. 1995, '"Only connect": critical discourse analysis and corpus linguistics', *UCREL Technical Papers*, vol. 6, pp. 1–31.

Herring, S. C. 2013, 'Discourse in Web 2.0: familiar, reconfigured, and emergent', in D. Tannen & A. M. Trester (eds.), *Discourse 2.0: language and new media*, Georgetown University Press: Washington, DC, pp. 1–29.

Herring, S. C. 2004, 'Computer-mediated discourse analysis: an approach to researching online communities', in S. A. Barab, R. Kling, & J. H. Gray (eds.), *Designing for virtual communities in the service of learning*, Cambridge University Press: New York, NY, pp. 338–376.

Jenkins, H. 2009, 'What happened before YouTube', in J. Burgess & J. Green (eds.), *YouTube: online video and participatory culture*, Polity Press: Malden, MA, pp. 109–125.

Jenkins, H. 2006, *Convergence culture: where old and new media collide*, New York University Press: New York, NY.

Jones, G. M. & Schieffelin, B. B. 2009, 'Talking text and talking back: "my BFF Jill" from boob tube to YouTube', *Journal of Computer Mediated Communication*, vol. 14, no. 4, pp. 1050–1079.

Jones, R. H. 2010, 'Creativity and discourse', *World Englishes*, vol. 29, no. 4, pp. 467–480.

Knobel, M. & Lankshear, C. 2008, 'Remix: the art and craft of endless hybridization', *Journal of Adolescent & Adult Literacy*, vol. 52, no. 1, pp. 22–33.

Kress, G. & van Leeuwen, T. 2006, *Reading images: the grammar of visual design*, 2nd edn., Routledge: London.

Lakoff, G. & Johnson, M. 2003, *Metaphors we live by*, University of Chicago Press: Chicago, IL.

van Leeuwen, T. 2005, *Introducing social semiotics*, Routledge: London.

Leppänen, S. & Häkkinen, A. 2012, 'Buffalaxed superdiversity: representations of the other on YouTube', *Diversities*, vol. 14, no. 2, pp. 17–33.

Lovink, G. & Niederer, S. (eds.) 2008, *Video vortex reader: responses to YouTube*, Institute of Network Cultures: Amsterdam.

Pihlaja, S. 2014, '"Christians" and "bad Christians": categorization in atheist user talk on YouTube', *Text & Talk*, vol. 34, no. 5, pp. 623–639.

Pihlaja, S. 2011, 'Cops, popes, and garbage collectors: metaphor and antagonism in an atheist/Christian YouTube video thread', *Language@Internet*, vol. 8, article 1, available at: http://www.languageatinternet.org/articles/2011/Pihlaja/.

Sharma, B. K. 2014, '"Some people should stop speaking English": transnational Nepalese and language ideologies in YouTube discourse', *Discourse, Context and Media 2014*, available at: http://dx.doi.org/10.1016/j.dcm.2014.04.001.

Shifman, L. 2012, 'An anatomy of a YouTube meme', *New Media & Society*, vol. 14, no. 2, pp. 187–203.

Sundararajan, A. 2008, 'Local network effects and complex network structure', *The BE. Journal of Theoretical Economics*, vol. 7, no. 1, doi: 10.2202/1935-1704.1319.

Tereick, J. 2012, 'Die „Klimalüge" auf YouTube: eine korpusgestützte Diskursanalyse der Aushandlung subversiver Positionen in der partizipatorischen Kultur', in C. Fraas, S. Meier & C. Pentzold (eds.), *Online-Diskurse: Theorien und Methoden transmedialer Online-Diskursforschung*, Halem: Köln, pp. 226–257.

Tereick, J. 2011, 'YouTube als Diskurs-Plattform: Herausforderungen an die Diskurslinguistik am Beispiel „Klimawandel"', in J. Schumacher & A. Stuhlmann (eds.), *Videoportale: broadcast yourself? Versprechen und Enttäuschung*, Universität Hamburg, Institut für Medien und Kommunikation: Hamburg, pp. 59–68.

Tognini-Bonelli, E. 2001, *Corpus linguistics at work*, John Benjamins: Amsterdam.

Weingart, P., Engels, A. & Pansegrau, P. 2000, 'Risks of communication: discourses on climate change in science, politics, and the mass media', *Public Understanding of Science*, vol. 9, no. 3, pp. 261–283.

Further reading

Burgess, J. & Green, J. 2009, *YouTube: online video and participatory culture*, Polity Press: Malden, MA.

The book offers insightful observations on YouTube as a space of activism, subculture and fan culture, and social norm-building in participatory culture. It offers in-depth analyses of many video examples.

Jones, R. H. & Hafner, C. A. 2012, *Understanding digital literacies: a practical introduction*, Routledge: London.

From a sociolinguistic perspective, the book gives an overview of digital language practices on a general level.

Lovink, G. & Niederer, S. (eds.) 2008, *Video vortex reader: responses to YouTube*, Institute of Network Cultures: Amsterdam.

An edited volume with articles by media studies scholars.

Snickars, P. & Vonderau, P. (eds.) 2009, *The YouTube reader*, National Library of Sweden: Stockholm.

This edited volume looks at YouTube from different angles: mediality, aesthetics, usage, economic issues and its function as a cultural archive. Available for free under a Creative Commons license (http://pellesnickars.se/index.php?s=file_download&id=34).

23

Translocality

Samu Kytölä

Introduction

Translocality is a key concept in the investigation of the complex forms of interplay of the local and the global in multi-semiotic digital communication. The goal of this chapter[1] is to discuss the notion of translocality from the point of view of language in digital communication. To this end, I will review the history and current usages of translocality *vis-à-vis* related concepts that have arisen from the need to describe the complex tensions between the local and the global in an era of growing globalization. After a more general review, the discussion turns to the relevance of translocality to today's digital communication in particular. Finally, I will outline certain future directions for research and practice.

Translocality can be defined, first, as a sense of *connectedness* between locales where both the local and the global are meaningful parameters for social and cultural activities and, second, as a fluid understanding of *culture* as outward-looking or exogenous, characterized by hybridity, translation, and identification (Hepp 2009a, 2009b; Nederveen Pieterse 1995). In the domain of digital communication, translocality is manifest in the enhanced connectivity afforded by burgeoning digital technologies and the semiotic (often linguistic, multilingual) choices that people make to identify themselves and to orient to their audiences ranging in the continuum between local and global (Leppänen, Pitkänen-Huhta, Piirainen-Marsh, Nikula, & Peuronen 2009).

Current applications of translocality in digital communication are discussed and illustrated below with an emphasis on contributions from sociolinguistics, linguistic anthropology and cultural studies. An overarching theme in this discussion is the dynamic and dialectical interplay of the local and global, as translocality is a bidirectional process in which local and global discourses impact and shape each other. Methodologically, the study of translocality points to a multidisciplinary approach, in which insights provided by ethnography, linguistics, discourse studies, cultural studies and social semiotics can be combined for detailed investigations of the forms, functions and meanings of translocal processes and practices in digital communication (Leppänen 2012). As an example of a recommendation for practice, I suggest the potential of translocality as a parameter in teaching language(s), (digital) literacy and communication. As future directions in this field, I briefly outline the growing importance of multisemioticity and resemiotization in translocal communication, and the need to look holistically into digitally mediated practices in relation to other (offline, face-to-face) practices.

Samu Kytölä

Historical perspectives

In this section, I will review the key contributions to the development of translocality, covering the notions of *connectivity* and *transcultural(ity)*, as well as the related concepts of *glocalization* and *cosmopolitanism*. This is done first on a more general level before turning specifically to digital communication in later sections of the chapter.

Translocality

I start with two particular aspects of translocality anchored in the foundational research of Nederveen Pieterse (1995). One is *connectivity* (see also Leppänen *et al.* 2009: 1081–1082; Giulianotti & Robertson 2007: 62–63): earlier work on translocality was influenced by cultural geography and paid due attention to the connectedness of physical and cultural spaces (e.g., countries, continents) via means of transport, migration, trade and 'old media' (newspapers, mail, telephone, radio, television). Our current era of increased digital communication adds an important accelerating element to this, as the affordances and means of computer (and mobile device) mediated interactions become available to a growing number of people and communities around the world.

Another crucial aspect is the hybridization of *culture(s)* in a broad sense. Nederveen Pieterse (1995) outlines two assumptions about culture which were prevalent in the social sciences up to the 1990s, with important repercussions for present-day understandings of culture(s), political ideologies, and conflict rooted in cultural issues. For him, the assumption of the more static 'territorial culture' was clashing with the assumption of 'translocal culture'; to the latter he ascribed attributes such as diasporas and migrations (instead of, e.g., societies, nations), crossroads and interstices (in lieu of locales, regions), or diffusion and heterogeneity (rather than being organic or unitary). In terms of cultural relations, translocal cultures involve hybridity, flows, pluralism and 'melting pots', in contrast to the more static metaphors of multiculturalism such as 'global mosaic' or 'clash of civilizations'. Following Nederveen Pieterse (and Hepp 2009a, 2009b), we can see 'culture(s)' as partly territorial, tied to a (habitable or occupiable) space, and partly de-territorial, finding dimensions and meanings from spaces and locales beyond our daily habitats. This is at the heart of the idea of translocality. Cultures have an almost infinite capacity for hybridization; considering the cultural transformations of the present day, this capacity is greatly enhanced by the exponential growth of digital communication.

These views are shared and complemented by Hepp (2009a), who suggests a shift of perspective from 'national–territorial' media cultures to a more *transcultural* view, acknowledging and analytically scrutinizing translocal processes of meaning making via the diverse media available to our contemporaries. In another article, where the empirical focus is on migrant communities' diasporas, Hepp (2009b) suggests the term 'translocal mediated networking' for analytically describing present-day communicative spaces, which are increasingly characterized by simultaneous orientations to what Hepp calls the 'domestic world', 'elsewhere' and 'somewhere'. 'The domestic world', in Hepp's framework, is 'the locality of the private life; the home in the closer sense of the word', while the 'elsewhere' comprises 'other localities of regular everyday media appropriation like, for example, shops or Internet cafés'. The 'somewhere', in turn, 'grasps all localities that are not habitual places of everyday media use but are produced situatively as localities of media appropriation' (Hepp 2009b: 333–334). All of these can be socially meaningful and collapse together in everyday interactions, particularly when we consider diasporic communities, Hepp argues. For him, the core of their translocality lies in the ways in which 'media are defined by their potential to constitute communicative relations across certain localities' (2009b: 330). However, Hepp also argues that 'migrants live their lives first and foremost locally and at the different localities of their everyday world' (2009b: 345). While studies of national–territorial media cultures, including comparatively oriented approaches, are still relevant (insofar as the division of physical land and material and non-material goods continues to operate on relatively firm nation state bases), the notion of translocality adds an important dimension to analyses and understandings based on, and fixed in, concrete and imaginary nation state boundaries. Moreover, a growing body of complex cultural phenomena *emerge as translocal and transcultural* in the first place, never 'produced' or 'consumed' – or meant to be consumed – in a national or local social context. In this cultural development, digital communication has played and continues to play a key role.

Alim (2009) addresses the translocal style communities of global hip hop youth, arguing that the translocal mediated connections between sites of hip hop practices serve to create 'the Global Hip Hop Nation/Culture' (2009: 103–107). For him, hip hop is essentially a globalized cultural form, creating multiple, renewed opportunities for its social actors to 'rework, reinvent, and recreate identities through the remixing of styles . . . more globally available than ever before' (2009: 105). As a research methodology and agenda, he proposes a multi-sited linguistic anthropology of globalization (pp. 122–124; see also Blommaert 2010; Blommaert & Rampton 2011) in order to tap into the multisemioticity and complexity of the processes of identification, hybridity, and connectivity of hip-hop youth. These connections and intersections Alim labels 'mobile matrices' – 'sets of styles, aesthetics, knowledges, and ideologies that move in and out of localities and cross-cut modalities' (2009: 123). Alim's piece does not, strictly speaking, focus empirically on digital communication, but arguably a great part of the global/translocal hip hop culture is digitally mediated in the twenty-first century, which further adds to the relevance of his research here.

Related concepts

In this section, I briefly review the history and current usages of the most central concepts related to translocality vis-à-vis globalization, along with their implications and applications for digital communication.

Glocalization

The notion of translocality is closely related to the idea of *glocalization*. A portmanteau of 'global' and 'local', it originates from the 1980s' business parlance, particularly in Japan (Robertson 1995: 28). Robertson argued for its usefulness when much of the discourse on globalization in the 1990s overrode issues of locality, although it still remained salient and meaningful to communities around the world in the face of globalization (see also Hepp 2009b). Robertson further pointed out that 'local' is constructed 'on a trans- or super-local basis' . . . 'expressed in terms of generalized recipes of locality' (1995: 26). In doing so, he echoed what Giddens (1991: 21) had suggested a few years earlier at a time of radical shifts and reorganizations of the European socio-political map: 'Globalization concerns the intersection of presence and absence, the interlacing of social events and social relations "at distance" with local contextualities'. For Ritzer (2003: 193), glocalization can be defined as 'the interpenetration of the global and the local, resulting in unique outcomes in different geographic areas', but he (like Andrews & Ritzer 2007) places a caveat on the assumed heterogeneity, stressing the overpowering, imperializing cultural and economic hegemony of 'the West' in glocalization processes. Similarly, Giulianotti and Robertson (2007: 60) suggest that glocalization involves the recontextualization of 'global phenomena or macroscopic processes with respect to local cultures, . . . societal *co-presence* of sameness and difference, and the intensified *interpenetration* of the local and the global, the universal and the particular, and homogeneity and heterogeneity' (italics original). Another critique of over-enthusiasm in glocalization is offered by Blommaert (2010), who highlights the resilience of the local in the face of the global, as 'local criteria and norms define the processes of change' (p. 23). To support this claim, Blommaert (2010) presents analyses of diverse contexts: a Tanzanian novel (in Swahili) and its reception, writing assignments from a Cape Town elementary school, and fragmentary linguistic repertoires of mobile African-background asylum seekers in the EU. These examples illustrate the diversity and, to an extent, unpredictability of translocal processes – for instance, Swahili (in lieu of English) can become the most appropriate cultural code for globalized cultural production; and constant life on the move can place asylum seekers outside the presupposed sociolinguistic orders of any nation states in their life trajectories. Moreover, Blommaert draws our attention to the social-semiotic facet of mobility and globalization: communication between and across locales involves the transportation of multimodal constellations of signs and messages prone to reinterpretation and further recirculation. This insight is particularly important in the study of digital communication, as pieces of multisemiotic discourses circulate in rapid flows and circles across the digitally connected parts of our globe (see also Kytölä 2012).

Transculturalism, transnationalism, cosmopolitanism

The literature on translocality often quotes the related concept of *transnationalism*, which emphasizes relationships and activities across nations, usually independent countries and their citizens. Like translocality, the idea of transnationalism draws heightened attention to the fuzziness and ambiguity of social life across and between relatively clear-cut national borders and citizenships (see e.g., Androutsopoulos 2007; Appadurai 1996; Jacquemet 2005). Focusing on a variety of youth language contexts, Bucholtz and Skapoulli (2009) point out the importance of researching transnational, transcultural and other mobile processes 'through the lens of interactional and sociolinguistic analysis, for language, as a primary interactional resource for the construction of flexible and shifting identities, mediates both local and translocal social experience' (p. 2). They further advocate for conducting such research locally and ethnographically to 'ensure that accounts of migration, globalization, and similar phenomena are empirically grounded in the everyday lives of those who experience them' (p. 12), while keeping a simultaneous focus on broader socio-political and sociocultural contexts. On a more macro level, Giulianotti and Robertson's (2007b) discussion of football (soccer) understands transnationalism as 'a processual sociological term . . . applied in regard to processes of migration and mediatization . . . referring to processes that interconnect individuals and social groups across specific geo-political borders' (p. 62). Similarly, Roudometof (2005) discusses glocalization through the concepts of transnationalism and *cosmopolitanism*. He argues that the reality of glocalization 'is responsible for the transformation of people's everyday lives irrespective of whether they are transnational or not' (p. 113). While the notion of 'transnationalism' originally helped conceptualize mass migration between countries as well as in various kinds of 'activities across borders' (p. 113), Roudometof further suggests that transnationalism is a property borne out of the emerging reality of social life under conditions of 'internal globalisation' – in other words, transnational social spaces, fields and networks are consequences of glocalization.

Another closely related notion of relevance here is *transcultural(/-ism/-ity/-ation)* (see Bucholtz & Skapoulli 2009; Pennycook 2007). This term refers, on the one hand, to the cosmopolitization (Roudometof 2005; Giulianotti & Robertson 2007) of cultures and identities, and, on the other, to cultural exchange between boundaries of nationality, ethnicity and the like. Pennycook's (2007) contribution is particularly relevant to language in digital communication, defining *transcultural flows* as ways in which 'cultural forms move, change and are reused to fashion new identities in diverse contexts' by way of 'take-up, appropriation [and] refashioning' (p. 6). While he acknowledges the 'detrimental effects of globalization on economies and ecologies' (p. 6), he draws our attention to the change and spread of cultural forms as they are received, adopted, reworked and recirculated locally and globally – translocally. For Pennycook, translocality is in essence a processual phenomenon of 'borrowing, blending, remaking and returning . . . alternative cultural production' (p. 6), while *fluidity* and *fixity* are key dimensions along which to interpret contemporary socio-cultural life (such as global Englishes and translocal hip hop; see Alim 2009). In his treatment of a range of background literature, Pennycook proposes and recommends a more comprehensive analytical vocabulary for analyses of language and contemporary culture based on the prefix *trans-*, which highlights the innate complexity of societal structures and divisions, the relationships between them, and processes of hybridization and mixing – key features of contemporary societies, communities, and their cultural, semiotic-linguistic interchanges. This complexity can also manifest as *translingualism* in diverse social processes of cultural and linguistic translation (Pennycook 2007).

Critical issues and topics

Of all the concepts reviewed in the previous section, it is perhaps the notion of translocality, with its roots firmly in cultural geography – a field fundamentally concerned with questions of 'place' – that has the strongest connotation of place ('locale'). Considering different contexts and settings of digital communication, the idea of *physical* place may often be undermined by ideas of *cultural or social* space; yet any participant in a digital community or 'affinity space' (see below) is always writing from a particular location, which may have significant repercussions for how digitally mediated interaction chains and discourses emerge. Even when the affordances of digital communication surpass the constraints of physical space, activities in digitally mediated contexts can be experienced by participants as both highly 'local' and connected to other locales.

Digital communication – predated by technologies such as letters, radio, or telephone – is thus by definition *always* translocal, comprising a variety of mediating means and technologies enabling individuals and communities to interact from a distance. Digital communication is also to a great extent a globalized domain of life: digital technologies, software, practices and discourses have the potential to circulate worldwide, to any digitally networked corner of the globe. However, there are remarkable differences and distinct nuances in the manifestations of translocality and globalization in different, deeply situated and context-bound manifestations of digital communication, a vastly diverse, hybrid and multisemiotic domain. Some of these will be discussed further in later sections.

Common to the notion of translocality and all the related concepts reviewed above is that points and axes of identification cut across more traditional boundary markers such as nationality, ethnicity or language. In contrast, digital communities and activities can be based on shared opinions, interests, styles and lifestyles (see chapters by Angouri, and Tagg & Seargeant, this volume). Drawing on a body of literature on translocality (and related notions) in general, and in digital communication in particular, three key issues can be identified:

1   Characteristics of various *digital technologies*. These include the affordances and constraints of:

 - digital devices (computers, smartphones);
 - mediating technologies (the Internet, digital TV); and

- various software and applications (e.g., email, text messaging, blogging, file sharing sites, social networking sites), as well as the ways in which they are adopted, applied, appropriated and extended by people.

Two key issues under this rubric are:

- how different digital technologies enable or constrain translocal processes and practices; and
- how people use various digital means for co-constructing and maintaining translocality, and with whom.

2   *Translocal communities* employing digital communication means. These include:

- old and new diasporic (mostly ethno-cultural or linguistic) communities shaped by migration and mobility patterns;
- other types of *communities of practice*, i.e. groups of people sharing common goals and acting together towards them (Wenger 1998); and
- digital *affinity spaces*, where people gather because they share interests, causes, lifestyles, activities or cultural products with short life spans or passing popularity (Gee 2004).

The lines between the different abovementioned types can be blurred and they can change over time.

3   *Translocal cultural phenomena* and their digital mediation and distribution. These include:

- production (writing, composing, performing, crafting, remixing, compiling) of cultural products that have a translocal orientation or a translocal trajectory;
- the consumption (reading, listening, attending, experiencing) of such cultural products; and, increasingly,
- 'prosuming' (Burgess & Green 2009) translocal culture, i.e. the blurring of divisions between creators and consumers, the constant interplay between them, and the co-construction of culture, particularly via diverse digital platforms (e.g., YouTube, blogging, image sharing platforms, meme generators).

Key issues within this 'cultural dimension' of translocality are design, choice and alternation of semiotic means, as well as linguistic and stylistic diversity.

Current contributions and research

This section reviews some of the current contributions on translocality in various types of digital communication. Some of these studies do not use the notion of translocality per se, but approach similar phenomena from different perspectives. In spite of the rapidly growing role of multimodality (see Herring, this volume), verbal (mainly written) language continues to have a key role in digital communication and the negotiation of the local and the global in people's life-worlds (Leppänen *et al.* 2009). My focus here, therefore, is on sociolinguistic and ethnographically framed studies and conceptualizations. In several of them, *heteroglossia* (Bakhtin 1981) is invoked as a key notion for the description of the availability and deployment of linguistic and discursive resources for identification and self-expression. In addition to shorter reviews of current research articles, I will include here a slightly longer preview of my work-in-progress (Kytölä & Westinen 2015) dealing with the transcultural online activity of the Finnish footballer Mikael Forssell and his multiple online audiences.

Echoing the critical issues and topics identified above, translocality in digital communication can manifest in several dimensions, including:

- *translocality of individuals*, who move and navigate across different physical, socio-cultural and virtual locales;
- *translocality of communities*, who occupy and inhabit several physical, socio-cultural and virtual spaces;
- *translocality of communication*, which takes place simultaneously in different parts of the physical world, enhanced by forms of digital communication;
- *translocality of culture(s), cultural expression and cultural products*, which are produced and consumed, as well as given significance, various meta-readings and evaluations across and between locales;
- *translocality of experience and social meaning*, which arise from processes where individuals and communities across several locales have common interests, values, affiliations and identifications, and share these through digitally mediated means.

Next, I turn to recent studies of digital communication contexts that draw on the analytical concept of translocality, particularly in connection with globalization. The following examples from the literature on translocality reflect the different dimensions outlined above. They show a degree of contextual diversity: the geographical contexts range from Tanzania to Finland, the domains explored reach from hip hop culture to photograph sharing, and the technologies in focus vary from web discussion forums to YouTube.

Jacquemet (2005) integrates observations of digital communication with other forms of interactions in his treatment of communicative 'mutations' in the Adriatic region (especially Albania–Italy) influenced by factors of current globalization. Like Blommaert (2010) and Pennycook (2007), Jacquemet argues for a reconceptualization of communicative contexts, with a focus on mediation via technologies and the reterritorialization of members of communities (i.e., the 'translocalization' of those communities). He suggests the term *transidiomatic practices* to cover translocal communicative phenomena involving diasporic and mobile communities and what he calls 'recombinant identities'. These practices are co-constructed via multiple channels, online and offline, with fluid participation frameworks; Jacquemet illustrates this through an ethnographic study of the ways in which Italian soap operas and English-language cinema acquired a salient position in the daily practices of a diasporic Albanian family, and in the city of Tirana more broadly. Compared to the already established understandings of linguistic borrowing, pidgins, and lingua francas, Jacquemet argues, there is now 'the extraordinary simultaneity and co-presence of . . . languages produced through a multiplicity of communicative channels, from face-to-face to mass media' (2005: 271). He further proposes that we ought to reconsider the very concept of communication, not necessarily in established national (or international) languages, but in the multiple practices of global cultural flows (p. 274). For Jacquemet, these 'transidiomatic practices' of transcultural social actors illustrate how new discourses and modes of representation are reterritorialized within the local environment (p. 267), and they should be a key focus in studies of language and globalization.

Uimonen (2009) explores translocal and transnational linkages facilitated by the introduction of the Internet at an arts college in Tanzania. Based on her ethnographic research, she stresses the persistence of the local in the face of increasing translocal interchange, noting that the mobility afforded by the adoption of the Internet in Tanzanian arts studies is not necessarily enacted much in the everyday practices of the same students, but nevertheless 'their social relations and cultural imaginaries' reach beyond their local site of engagement (2009: 289). For key social actors in Uimonen's study, the Internet showed – and fulfilled – a promise of connectivity and access to information resources as well as transnational (and translocal) connections. She proceeds to describe the launching of the arts college's own website and the everyday personal digital activities of her key informants, emphasizing the 'embeddedness' of the Internet in the imageries, relationships and practices of the Tanzanian students. For them, the affordances of the Internet brought along not only facilitated social relations with geographically dispersed social networks in rural Tanzania, urban Tanzania and outside Tanzania, but also cultural ideas of modernity, progress and social upward mobility.

Androutsopoulos (2007) analyses language choice and alternation in websites and web forums for German-based diasporic communities, particularly Persian, Indian and Greek ones. He outlines quantitative distributions of language choice vis-à-vis discussion topics on a Persian site and suggests that translocal links or their manifestations in digital diasporic discourse are stronger in certain topic domains (e.g., entertainment, picture posts, greetings, cuisine) than in others (e.g., technology, history, sports, health). Moreover, he covers the micro-sociolinguistic pragmatics of language alternation in sequences of (Greek) web forum interaction, suggesting a degree of compatibility with spoken code-switching frameworks, including participant-related, preference-related and discourse-related code-switching. For Androutsopoulos, interactive diasporic websites are a key empirical context for the study of 'how the Internet is appropriated for the construction of diasporic identities and how it reflects the diversity of societal bilingualism' (2007: 357).

More recently, Androutsopoulos (2013b) explores German-based, Greek-heritage secondary students' 'networked multilingualism' via practices on their Facebook 'walls' (later called 'timelines'), arguing that the heteroglossia (Bakhtin 1981; see also below) of their everyday discourse is constructed by means of self-presentation, genre, repertoires, dialogicality, and performance. His 'networked' practices, therefore, refer both to 'being networked, i.e. digitally connected to other individuals and groups' and 'being in the network, i.e. embedded in the global digital mediascape of the web' (2013b: 4). The parameters of his analysis are 'constraints of digital writtenness, access to the global mediascape of the web, and orientation to networked audiences' (p. 17). Androutsopoulos sees these three in a dialogical, mutual interrelation, with his young informants displaying fuzziness, flexibility and great diversity in their multilingual performance. In another recent article, Androutsopoulos (2013a) does not explicitly use translocality as a theoretical ingredient, but its exploration of the representations of German dialects on YouTube videos and their commentary sections is a highly relevant example for our present purposes. He highlights aspects of performance, stylization and multimodality, showing how dialect uses are elevated via media representations from local contexts and statuses into a target of metalinguistic discourse and 'spectacles' in wider circulation. While he rightly emphasizes the earlier (stigmatized and non-stigmatized) presence of German dialects in pre-digital media, Androutsopoulos shows that participatory web cultures enhance and complicate the interplay of the stable/local and mobile/global. While the YouTube stylizations and meta-commentary on German dialects have German speakers as their primary audience, they are globally available to (and searchable by) transnational audiences not constrained by national boundaries or identifications.

Leppänen et al. (2009) focus on the new media practices of Finnish youth, highlighting the intricate connections between young people's translocal affiliations and their language choice and language alternation between Finnish and English. Finnish youth in their focus access and engage in highly global(ized) cultural practices and processes, and, at the same time, localization and appropriation of those processes are at work. Moreover, Leppänen et al. argue that linguistic and stylistic heteroglossia, which constitute a range of 'linguistic and discursive resources available for self-expression, communication and identification' (p. 236), are key means of translocality. This is a point stressed in sociolinguistics, but often ignored in sociological or cultural studies of translocality. As examples, Leppänen et al. investigate four different contexts where both digital technologies and uses of varieties of English (alongside or instead of Finnish) enable Finnish youth to access wide and diversified translocal cultural spaces, activities and communities. Their ethnographic inquiries range from everyday media usage and online gaming activities to fan fiction and web forums of Christians engaging in extreme sports. All of these contexts have a strong local component (e.g., connection to Finland or Finnish-ness), while simultaneously aspiring to, and succeeding in, engagement with communities and cultures spread across the online world. Furthermore, Leppänen *et al.* stress the personal and affective dimension of these contexts: they show how such translocal engagements have profound social meanings for the young, multilingual, multi-skilled Finnish participants.

Leppänen later elaborates on the topic of Finnish fan fiction writers, arguing that, for fan fiction communities and other translocal communities online, 'the Internet can function as a space . . . for sharing, discussing, acting upon and critiquing images of globalization' (2012: 233). Here, too, she highlights the role of linguistic resources and language choice in translocal practices online: for example, writing fan fiction in certain styles and registers of English, and mixing them with certain styles and registers of Finnish, is a tool for connecting the fan fiction writers as well as their cultural products (the fan fiction pieces) to diverse audiences that can read and respond to texts in English and/or Finnish. Leppänen expands the notion of bilingualism to the more versatile and inclusive concept of heteroglossia. The heteroglossic practices of fan fiction writers range from media technological realms (gaming and computing terminology) and popular culture (novels, television series) to reaching out for diverse audiences from across linguistic boundaries.

Comparable to the diverse contexts of cultural production reviewed above, Kytölä (2012, 2014) has studied digital football (soccer) discourses, particularly web forum discussions, from the perspective of multilingual language use. Football is a fruitful domain for the study of language, globalization and translocality, since it is a form of culture, social activity and entertainment that is present in nearly all parts of the globe, and involves a high degree of mobility across nations and social spaces. While not using translocality as a theoretical concept, Kytölä (2012) is an account of how linguistic features of varying kinds of non-standard English travel from context to context in digitally mediated ways with varying and ambivalent indexical values and loads. Elsewhere, Kytölä (2014) shows how members on major Finland-based football web forums deploy the affordances of heteroglossic pseudonyms and other features in personal member profiles in order to create hybrid, globally oriented but locally meaningful blends of identification, stylization and performance. These articles, together with Kytölä and Westinen (2015) portray a picture of digital football discourse, football supportership and fandom as highly globalized and, arguably, translocal sites of engagement.

I turn now to an illustrative example. The activity by the Finnish professional player Mikael Forssell (b. 1981) on the micro-blog platform Twitter is a case of transnational, transcultural and translingual social activity. By the age of around thirty, Forssell's career had spanned several clubs and locations in Finland, England and Germany. His family background is bilingually Finnish–Swedish, and he has acquired fans and followers throughout his professional career. When he launched his public Twitter account,[2] he began to address multiple audiences from several cultures and language backgrounds; his updates, along with the responses they elicit, are highly multilingual, appearing in alternations and mixtures of English, Finnish, Swedish and German, with significant 'intralinguistic' and stylistic variation within these languages. A particular feature of interest in his tweets is his use of non-standard features, often borrowed from African–American vernacular English. While his physical life trajectory involves British connections (London, Birmingham, Leeds) rather than North American ones, Forssell makes himself publicly known as a fan of hip hop and rap from the USA, particularly of certain relatively mainstream 'Gangsta Rap' artists. This cultural feature is frequently shown in his writing, which turns into a jocular, highly stylized performance.

Figure 23.1 shows a tweet by Forssell. The simultaneous 'offline' context is a meet-up of the Finland men's national team; Forssell is directly addressing his fellow Finland player Tim Sparv

Figure 23.1 A jocular update ('tweet') from Mikael Forssell's public Twitter feed.

(a similarly active tweeter); here, he is discursively constructing one recurring jocular aspect of Forssell's Twitter presence – his addiction to chocolate.

At that point (March 2011) there had been, for at least 16 months, parallel discussion threads on the largest Finnish football discussion forum, Futisforum2.org (see Kytölä 2012, 2014), which had fluctuated between Forssell's turbulent career turns and his multilingual, hetero-glossic Twitter usage.[3] Forssell's tweets – or even shorter excerpts from them – had frequently been copy-and-pasted and embedded in these Futisforum2 discussions. This time, the chocolate tweet (shown above) is accompanied by another tweet with yet more heavily stylized, jocular and overdone wordings (particularly the epithet 'Timsta da pimpsta'), as well as an emoticon presumably expressing the writer's sadness or disappointment at such performance. The first part of Figure 23.2 below shows how Forssell's tweet becomes copied to Futisforum2 and accompanied with a meta-reading (the sad face emoticon).

When we look at Forssell's public Twitter writing, his Twitter contacts' publicly displayed responses, and the consequently emerging pieces of interaction together with the meta-discussion going on simultaneously on the Finnish football fans' Futisforum2.org, we see an intermingling of translocality at work. The cosmopolitan, transnationally wired Forssell adopts elements of the 'Gangsta' style for his tweets; his usages of African–American vernacular features elicit indexical links and social meanings which are vastly different from similar usages by African–Americans, for instance, or by hip hop artists around the world. This is followed by further appropriation and recirculation of Forssell's 'Gangsta' style for the Futisforum2.org community's jocular in-group usages. While these translocal, digitally mediated discourses show orientations to multiple centres and audiences, we found a great deal of conventionality, purism or normativity in the responses of Forssell's followers across several online sites. However, in this 'purist' discourse, we were also able to distinguish the simultaneous communal awareness and acceptance of such (socio)linguistic variation and playfulness (Kytölä & Westinen 2015).

In a similar vein, Peuronen (2011) explores the translocal identities of Christian extreme sports cultures. While her target community is also based in Finland, where members engage in social activities offline, the members 'orient themselves to global contexts, cultures and lifestyles by engaging in processes' of adaptation and appropriation (2011: 155). The members of Finnish Christian extreme sports communities display heteroglossic linguistic and discursive repertoires, co-constructing hybrid, translocal identities. Peuronen analyses these identities from the point of view of stylization, playfulness, online–offline relations and the co-construction of expertize.

In turn, Jousmäki (2014; forthcoming) investigates Christian metal youth cultures as a translocal phenomenon geographically and culturally set in specific localities, but interlinked

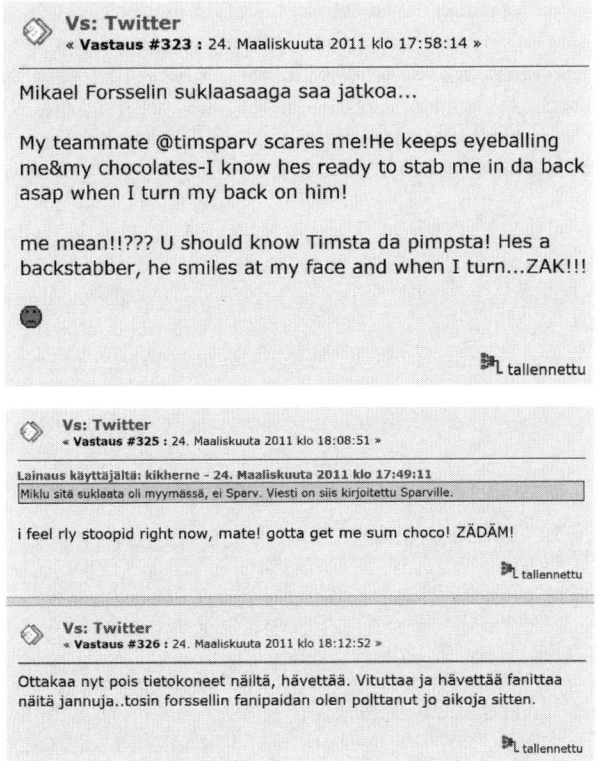

English translations (by SK)

1 (the first row of the upper posting) 'Mikael Forssel's [sic] chocolate saga is continued . . . '
2 (the embedded quote in the second posting) 'It was Miklu [Forssell] who was selling the chocolate, not Sparv. So the message was written to Sparv.' ('ZÄDÄM' appears to me just an onomatopoetic exclamation with no particular meaning).
3 (the last posting) 'Now take their computers away from them, I feel ashamed. I am pissed off and ashamed of being a fan of these guys . . . actually I have burnt forssell's fan shirt a long time ago.'

Figure 23.2 Responses by members of Futisforum2 to Mikael Forssell's Twitter language use.

through virtual communication technologies. Both religion and music have been previously understood in translocal terms within cultural studies, and translocality offers a valid perspective on Christian music, in this case heavy metal. Jousmäki suggests that translocality can simultaneously denote the 'local relevance of Christian metal bands' and 'their potential for mobility [making it] possible for the bands to become, again, locally relevant *elsewhere*' (forthcoming). The same applies for the global and translocal audiences of this musical genre; like Christianity or heavy metal per se, the fans and consumers of Christian metal are transnationally and translocally connected, particularly via the affordances of digital media such as YouTube. As a third parameter for translocality in Christian metal, Jousmäki suggests that 'Christian metal provides its audiences with an experience of translocal religiosity, leading many to find the Nordic region as a particularly suitable place for practicing (evangelical) belief through the type of music one enjoys'. She concludes that, in this social activity, a translocal space is created where spirituality, music, language, and place become points of (dis)identification for the participants.

Finally, a currently emergent topic of research is online photo-sharing sites. Studies of these sites have adopted the perspectives of new literacies (Lee & Barton 2012; see Knobel & Lankshear, this volume) and multimodality (Thurlow & Jaworski 2011; see chapters by Jewitt and Keating, this volume). For Thurlow and Jaworski, the sharing of travel photos via the online site Flickr is a telling example of language and globalization at work in the context of tourism, a key domain of social activity in current globalization. Their empirical analysis concerns the practice of taking 'Pisa Pushers' photographs with a forced perspective; this practice is by definition locally bound to Pisa's famous tower, but it finds increasingly global distribution channels via mobile people (tourists) and the file sharing sites of the Internet. Lee and Barton's (2012) research also concerns Flickr, but their focus is on multilingual practices and digital literacy. They conclude that while the multilingual uses of photo-sharing sites are by no means static or fully patterned, at least four factors affect language choice: the users' available linguistic resources, their purposes and reasons for being Flickr users in the first place, their imagined audience(s), and the contents and origins of the photos themselves.

Common to all these current research contributions on translocality in digital discourses is that participants have (and display) access not only to local but also to global discourses, points of identification, or means of meaning making. As Leppänen et al. (2009) and Leppänen, Kytölä, Jousmäki, Peuronen, and Westinen (2014) point out, new constellations of communality and identifications may not have national or local bases; rather, inquiries of digital language in globalization show that affinities and communities are being created on a more complex constellation of identificational axes. Through their locally situated, digitally mediated social activity, users form translocal communities or affinity spaces, which may go far beyond their locally bound networks (Leppänen 2012; Leppänen et al. 2009). Online participants may have strong orientations to the globally occurring and globally meaningful aspects of their point of interest. At the same time, they may adopt, appropriate and reformulate global discourses into locally meaningful and organized experiences. Computer-age participants carve out their 'translocal social and cultural realities' (Leppänen et al. 2009: 1102) in digitally mediated forms of culture; processes of identification and community construction play a key role in this cultural development. Recent research demonstrates that creativity, playfulness (see Nishimura, this volume) and, often, a sense of ambivalence are central ingredients in this process. All in all, translocality is a multi-directional process by which local and global discourses shape each other through varying networks of dissemination and different types of interactional set-ups. The current phase of globalization is neither 'finished', nor completely new, nor previously unattested; but it arguably accelerates and facilitates such practices in new combinations.

Main research methods

Echoing the empirical contexts and approaches reviewed in the previous section, I briefly revisit here the main methodological choices that researchers in the field of translocality have deployed.

Many scholars of translocality have utilized demographic or sociological information, either as a backdrop for qualitative, relatively synchronic case studies, or part of more historical, diachronic analyses. This seems particularly suited to research into the translocality of migrant and diaspora groups, although the importance of sufficient historical and sociological contextualization of studies on other kinds of digitally connected communities should also be stressed. For example, Jacquemet (2005) backs up his study of 'transidiomatic practices' in the Adriatic geopolitical region with brief information about the history of Albania, along with statistics on the electronic media consumption and exposure to different languages in Albania. Alternatively, on a more micro-level, Blommaert (2010) introduces his discussion of a Cape Town second-ary school with a compilation of relevant history and demographic information on the district where the school was located.

A number of studies on translocality have utilized ethnographic perspectives, mostly in the form of extended immersion and observation in the researched target group, with the aim of a holistic understanding of the groups and communities in focus. Examples of on-site ethno-graphic studies of digital media usages include Uimonen's (2009) study of Internet usage at an Tanzanian Arts College, Lee and Barton's (2012) studies on online photo sharing, Alim's (2009) multi-sited linguistic ethnography of hip hop youth, Jacquemet's (2005) examination of the multilingual, transcultural television watching practices of a big diasporic Albanian family, and Leppänen et al.'s (2009) investigations of the everyday life of young Finnish users of digital media (e.g., websites, online games). Of these, Lee and Barton (2012) include the most com-prehensive account of the different stages of the collection and sampling of online and interview data (for more on sampling and selection, see also Kytölä 2014).

On the (socio)linguistic side, scholars have been interested in the emergence and distribu-tion of novel, translocal ways and styles of speaking and writing. Examples of this in digitally mediated communication include Jacquemet's (2005) study of mixed-language idioms used by Albanians and Italians, Kytölä's studies (2012; Kytölä & Westinen 2015) of 'deliberately bad English' idioms across and beyond Finnish online football sites, and Androutsopoulos's (2013a) research on German dialects in YouTube videos and meta-comments. Androutsopoulos's stud-ies (2007, 2013a, 2013b) mainly deploy qualitative analyses of systematic and ethnographically motivated selections of data from digital contexts ranging from websites and web forums to social networking and video sharing sites. This approach is also shared by Leppänen (2012; Leppänen et al. 2009, 2014), who adds the elements of discourse and genre analysis to her work on digital writing of fan fiction communities of practices. Leppänen (2012) argues that in translocal online fan fiction writing practices, in addition to language and stylistic choices, the awareness of genre differences is one key tool fan fiction writers use to orient to their translocal contact zones.

Similarly, Thurlow and Jaworski (2011) narrow down their data selection to a very spe-cific subgenre of tourism photos, coupled with the particular phenomenon of stance-taking. Furthermore, the majority of the studies reviewed in this chapter highlight the importance of multimodal perspectives (e.g., Jousmäki 2014; Lee & Barton 2012; Leppänen et al. 2014; Thurlow & Jaworski 2011) in accordance with the well-documented increase in the complex-ity of the multimodal digital communication over the past two decades. Thurlow and Jaworski (2011) describe the remediation process of photos that 'travel' from a 'staged performance' at a famous tourist site (such as the Tower of Pisa) to a tourist's Flickr profile, accompanied with titles, descriptions, tags, and verbal commentaries between posters and their followers. They rightly argue that tourism is fundamentally a semiotic, mediated activity.

Quantitative methods have been used variably in translocality research; examples include Androutsopoulos's (2007, 2013) and Kytölä's (2014) analyses of the distributions of languages or linguistic varieties in diasporic (e.g., Greek in Germany) or otherwise translocal communities (e.g., Finnish football fans drawing influence from football cultures across the globe). Moreover, quantitative insights can be crucial for obtaining more accurate descriptions of target groups; this can be a key component of demographical and sociological dimensions of translocality research.

In sum, the investigation of translocality in all its complexity seems to call for a multidisci-plinary approach in which insights from ethnography, linguistics, discourse studies, sociology, social semiotics, cultural studies and communication studies (and others) can be combined to provide detailed information on the forms, patterns, functions and meanings of translocal processes and practices in digital communication.

Recommendations for practice

As we have just seen, current literature on translocality and globalization suggests a heightened awareness of the fuzziness of traditional, essentialist categories based on clear-cut divisions between classic sociological, demographic and sociolinguistic categories such as nationality, ethnicity, mother tongue, or country of origin. The accumulated understanding of translocal (transcultural, transnational) connections and activities in the context of globalization, then, suggests a critique concerning those essentialist categories.

As possible recommendations for practice, we might suggest the importance of translocality as a parameter in teaching language(s) and culture(s), communication and digital literacy. In the crafting of digital discourse with diverse, transcultural audiences, it is important to learn to design and interpret messages translocally – to address audiences both 'here and elsewhere'. One broad field of practice where the notion of translocality could gain more currency is in education, and in language (and culture) teaching in particular. In most (nationally delineated) education systems, language subjects are itemized, niched and essentialized, and while there is a growing tendency for school curricula to accept the diversity that speakers of target languages represent, these curricula can still lack a sense of translocality and transculturality, or complexities brought about by globalization. Digital communication – in its all richness, complexity and contradiction – is one key domain that could be harnessed to a greater extent in order to teach aspects of translocality and globalization, and ultimately to illuminate the complexity and richness of human culture and experience, at all levels of education. Another possible field of application is statistical demographics, along with applied social science, public policy, and politics traditionally based on demographic information with clear-cut, niched categories. While media and popular discourses on communities and ethno-cultural groups within societies and nation states often draw on simplified and uniform relationships between variables such as country of origin, country of residence, ethnicity, or mother tongue, scholars and professionals working on demographics should ideally reconsider (and advocate) the idea of translocality as an antidote to those popular, reductive discourses (see Vertovec's 2007 call for *superdiversity*).

Future directions

In this section, I suggest current developments that seem promising for the study of language in translocal digital communication. These include the notions of *superdiversity*, *multisemioticity*, and *resemiotization*, as well as a fuller integration of the study of online activities with 'the offline'.

Superdiversity

A recent perspective on issues of translocality and globalization in language use is offered by the notion of *superdiversity*. Originally coined by Vertovec (2007) in order to denote the growing complexity of sociological and demographical diversity in multicultural spaces such as Greater London, the concept of superdiversity has been adopted by critical sociolinguists and linguistic anthropologists (Creese & Blackledge 2010; Blommaert & Rampton 2011) to conceptualize the growing complexity of current linguistic diversity. Both of these studies identify digital communication as one definite key domain where the superdiversity of language is produced and enacted, but a more detailed, ethnographic understanding of 'digital superdiversity' is only now emerging (Androutsopoulos 2013b; Leppänen *et al.* 2014). In empirical work based on multicultural classrooms in the UK, Creese and Blackledge (2010: 569) point out the complexity of the questions of locality 'as digital communication made available resources which superseded territorial boundaries, offering linguistic resources' which reside in none of the localities attributable to pupils on the basis of their origins and life trajectories. Blommaert and Rampton complement this insight by suggesting that 'emigrants and dispersed communities now have the potential to retain an active connection by means of an elaborate set of long-distance communication technologies' (2011: 3), and, importantly, that these technologies also have an influence on the host communities.

Multisemioticity and resemiotization

Translocal digital communication in the age of enhanced globalization and (super)diversity is also increasingly multisemiotic in nature. While early digital communication (through Usenet, websites, or SMS, for example) was largely based on the mode of written language ('text' in a more restricted sense), currently popular formats of digital discourse are more and more based on complex combinations of visual and audio, verbal scripted language and still or moving images (Blommaert & Rampton 2011; Iedema 2003; Jacquemet 2005; Kytölä 2014; Leppänen *et al.* 2014). These come together in sociocultural and socio-historical discourses, which are 'socially significant and culturally valuable' (Leppänen *et al.* 2014: 113) to today's digital individuals, who further deploy them for the construction of their translocal and hybrid identities. Leppänen *et al.* (2014) incorporate the notion of resemiotization (Iedema 2003) into their analysis of complex identification processes in a variety of Finland-based online contexts. They argue that semiotic resources available to individuals in online communities can provide new opportunities for multiple identifications. Participants' abilities to produce and interpret multimodal discourses play a key role in such a process, while new hierarchies and divisions may develop based on varying degrees of participants' digital literacies (see Lee & Barton 2012).

What is new? Translocal processes online vs offline

A key question among researchers of digital communication has been how digitally mediated processes and practices relate to processes and practices offline, in the 'face-to-face' experience of the world. Indeed, the 'first wave' of studies in computer-mediated communication was largely concerned with the novelty of the new digital technologies and the impact they were having on human communication and language use. In contrast, the 'second wave' added a more cultural–relativistic approach investigating online cultural processes as 'real life' in their own right, while the 'third wave' has again begun to emphasize the complexity, interdependency and dialectics of online and offline contexts (Androutsopoulos 2007, 2013b; Kytölä 2012; Leppänen 2012; Leppänen *et al.* 2014; Peuronen 2011; Thurlow & Mroczek 2011). As a historical caveat, we ought to remember that translocal activities and communities existed before the current era of the digitalization of communication. In parallel with the broad concept of globalization, it is the scope and volume of the translocality – as we currently experience and observe it – that seems unprecedented in history. The question of whether the ways of digital writing in an online community are similar (or different) compared to their offline ways of speaking has preoccupied scholars of computer-mediated communication for quite a while now; yet studies that attempt to understand holistically translocal connections offline vis-à-vis translocal connections online are still relatively few. This seems a promising near-future research strand (see Androutsopoulos 2013a, 2013b; Blommaert & Rampton 2011; Jacquemet 2005; Leppänen

Samu Kytölä

2012; Peuronen 2011; Uimonen 2009); and these problems will be addressed further in the last part of this volume (see Part VII, 'New debates and further directions').

Related topics

- Chapter 3 Digital ethnography (Varis)
- Chapter 4 Multimodal analysis (Jewitt)
- Chapter 6 Style, creativity and play (Nishimura)
- Chapter 10 Vernacular literacy: orthography and literacy practices (Iorio)
- Chapter 20 Online communities and communities of practice (Angouri)

Notes

1 I am thankful to Sirpa Leppänen and the editors of this Handbook for their critical and constructive comments on an earlier draft of this chapter.
2 Currently available at <twitter.com/MikaelForssell> [Accessed 11 June 2015]. He started his Twitter account in October 2009, and it was in November 2009 that Futisforum2.org's metapragmatic commentaries on Forssell's Twitter begin.
3 The forum can be found at <futisforum2.org>. One discussion thread devoted to talk about Forssell is at <futisforum2.org/index.php?topic=83064.0>, while a thread specifically dedicated to discussion on Finnish footballers' Twitter usage is at <futisforum2.org/index.php?topic=107799.0> [all three accessed 11 June 2015].

References

Alim, H. S. 2009, 'Translocal style communities: hip-hop youth as cultural theorists of style, language, and globalization', *Pragmatics*, vol. 19, no. 1, pp. 103–127.
Andrews, D. L. & Ritzer, G. 2007, 'The grobal in the sporting glocal', in R. Giulianotti & R. Robertson (eds.), *Globalization and sport*, Blackwell: Oxford, pp. 28–45.
Androutsopoulos, J. 2013a, 'Participatory culture and metalinguistic discourse: performing and negotiating German dialects on YouTube', in D. Tannen & A. M. Trester (eds.), *Discourse 2.0: language and new media*, Georgetown University Press: Washington, DC, pp. 47–71.
Androutsopoulos, J. 2013b, 'Networked multilingualism: some language practices on Facebook and their implications', *International Journal of Bilingualism*, vol. 19, no. 2 (April 2015) pp. 185–205.
Androutsopoulos, J. 2007, 'Language choice and code-switching in German-based diasporic web forums', in B. Danet and S. C. Herring (eds.), *The multilingual Internet: language, culture, and communication online*, Oxford University Press: Oxford, pp. 340–361.
Appadurai, A. 1996, *Modernity at large: cultural dimensions of globalization*, University of Minnesota Press: Minneapolis, MN.
Bakhtin, M. 1981, *The dialogic imagination: four essays*, M. Holquist (ed.), University of Texas Press: Austin, TX.
Blommaert, J. 2010, *The sociolinguistics of globalization*, Cambridge University Press: Cambridge.
Blommaert, J. & Rampton, B. 2011, 'Language and superdiversity', *Diversities*, vol. 13, no. 2, pp. 1–20.
Bucholtz, M. & Skapoulli, E. 2009, 'Introduction: youth language at the intersection: from migration to globalization', *Pragmatics*, vol. 19, no. 1, pp. 1–16.
Burgess, J. & Green, J. 2009, *YouTube: online video and participatory culture*, Polity Press: Cambridge, UK.
Creese, A. & Blackledge, A. 2010, 'Towards a sociolinguistics of superdiversity', *Zeitschrift für Erziehungswissenschaft*, vol. 13, no. 4, pp. 549–572.
Featherstone, M., Lash, S. & Robertson, R. (eds.) 1995, *Global modernities*, Sage: London.
Gee, J. P. 2004, *Situated language and learning: a critique of traditional schooling*, Routledge: New York, NY.
Giddens, A. 1991, *Modernity and self-identity*, Polity Press: Oxford.
Giulianotti, R. & Robertson, R. 2007, 'Recovering the social: globalization, football and transnationalism', in R. Giulianotti & R. Robertson (eds.), *Globalization and sport*, Blackwell: Oxford, pp. 58–78.

Hepp, A. 2009a, 'Transculturality as a perspective: researching media cultures comparatively', *Forum: Qualitative Social Research*, vol. 10, no. 1, article 26.

Hepp, A. 2009b, 'Localities of diasporic communicative spaces: material aspects of translocal mediated networking', *The Communication Review*, vol. 12, no. 4, pp. 327–348.

Iedema, R. 2003, 'Multimodality, resemiotization: extending the analysis of discourse as multi-semiotic practice', *Visual Communication*, vol. 2, no. 1, pp. 29–57.

Jacquemet, M. 2005, 'Transidiomatic practices: Language and power in the age of globalization', *Language & Communication*, vol. 25, no. 3, pp. 257–277.

Jousmäki, H. forthcoming, 'Translocal Christian metal: the young, social media and religious identity', in F. Holt & A-V. Kärjä (eds.), *Popular music in the Nordic countries*. Oxford University Press: Oxford.

Jousmäki, H. 2014, 'Translocal religious identification in Christian metal music videos and discussion on *YouTube*', in L. Kaunonen (ed.), *Cosmopolitanism and transnationalism: visions, ethics and practices*, Helsinki Collegium for Advanced Studies: Helsinki, pp. 138–158.

Kytölä, S. 2014, 'Polylingual language use, framing and entextualization in digital discourse: pseudonyms, "locations", "favourite teams" and "signatures" on two Finnish online football forums', in J. Tyrkkö & S Leppänen (eds.), *Texts and discourses of new media*, Varieng: Helsinki, np.

Kytölä, S. 2012, 'Peer normativity and sanctioning of linguistic resources-in-use: on non-Standard Englishes in Finnish football forums online', in J. Blommaert, S. Leppänen, P. Pahta & T. Räisänen (eds.), *Dangerous multilingualism: northern perspectives on order, purity and normality*, Palgrave Macmillan: Basingstoke, pp. 228–260.

Kytölä, S. & Westinen, E. 2015, '"I be da reel gansta"—A Finnish footballer's Twitter writing and metapragmatic evaluations of authenticity', *Discourse, Context & Media*, vol. 8.

Lee, C. & Barton, D. 2012, 'Multilingual texts on Web 2.0: the case of Flickr.com', in M. Sebba, S. Mahootian, & C. Jonsson (eds.), *Language mixing and code-switching in writing: approaches to mixed-language written discourse*, Routledge: New York, NY, pp. 128–145.

Leppänen, S. 2012, 'Linguistic and generic hybridity in web writing: the case of fan fiction', in M. Sebba, S. Mahootian, & C. Jonsson (eds.), *Language mixing and code-switching in writing: approaches to mixed-language written discourse*, Routledge: New York, NY, pp. 233–254.

Leppänen, S., Kytölä, S., Jousmäki, H., Peuronen, S. & Westinen, E. 2014, 'Entextualization and resemiotization as resources for identification in social media', in P. Seargeant & C. Tagg (eds.), *The Language of social media: identity and community on the Internet*, Palgrave Macmillan: Basingstoke, pp. 112–136.

Leppänen, S., Pitkänen-Huhta, A., Piirainen-Marsh, A., Nikula, T. & Peuronen S. 2009, 'Young people's translocal new media uses: a multiperspective analysis of language choice and heteroglossia', *Journal of Computer-Mediated Communication*, vol. 14, no. 4, pp. 1080–1107.

Nederveen Pieterse, J. 1995, 'Globalization as hybridization', in M. Featherstone, S. Lash, & R. Robertson (eds.), *Global modernities*, Sage: London, pp. 45–69.

Pennycook, A. 2007, *Global Englishes and transcultural flows*, Routledge: New York, NY.

Peuronen, S. 2011, '"Ride hard, live forever": Translocal identities in an online community of extreme sports Christians', in C. Thurlow & K. Mroczek (eds.), *Digital discourse: language in the new media*, Oxford University Press: New York, NY, pp. 154–176.

Ritzer, G. 2003, 'Rethinking globalization: glocalization/grobalization and something/nothing', *Sociological Theory*, vol. 21, no. 3, pp. 193–209.

Robertson, R. 1995, 'Glocalization: time-space and homogeneity-heterogeneity', in M. Featherstone, S. Lash, & R. Robertson (eds.), *Global modernities*, Sage: London, pp. 25–44.

Roudometof, V. 2005, 'Transnationalism, cosmopolitanism and glocalization', *Current Sociology*, vol. 53, no. 1, pp. 113–135.

Sebba, M., Mahootian, S. & Jonsson, C. (eds.) 2012, *Language mixing and code-switching in writing: approaches to mixed-language written discourse*, Routledge: New York, NY.

Thurlow, C. & Jaworski, A. 2011, 'Banal globalization? Embodied actions and mediated practices in tourists' online photo sharing', in C. Thurlow & K. Mroczek (eds.), *Digital discourse: language in the new media*, Oxford University Press: New York, NY, pp. 220–250.

Thurlow, C. & Mroczek, K. (eds.) 2011, *Digital discourse: language in the new media*, Oxford University Press: New York, NY.

Uimonen, P. 2009, 'Internet, arts and translocality in Tanzania', *Social Anthropology*, vol. 17, no. 3, pp. 276–290.

Vertovec, S. 2007, 'Super-diversity and its implications', *Ethnic and Racial Studies*, vol. 30, no. 6, pp. 1024–1054.

Wenger, E. 1998, *Communities of practice: learning, meaning, and identity*, Cambridge University Press: Cambridge.

Samu Kytölä

Further reading

Alim, H. S. 2009, 'Translocal style communities: hip-hop youth as cultural theorists of style, language, and globalization', *Pragmatics*, vol. 19, no. 1, pp. 103–127.

> This article discusses hip-hop youth's metapragmatic theorizing about their own style and social activities from the point of view of translocality, with no explicit focus on digital communication.

Androutsopoulos, J. 2015, 'Networked multilingualism: some language practices on Facebook and their implications', *International Journal of Bilingualism*, vol. 19, no. 2, pp. 185–205 (First published 11 June 2013.)

> This article discusses the heterogeneous language use of Greek-heritage secondary school pupils in a German city on Facebook profile 'walls' (later changed to and renamed 'time-lines') from the point of view of self-presentation, genre, repertoires, dialogicality and performance.

Leppänen, S., Pitkänen-Huhta, A., Piirainen-Marsh, A., Nikula, T. & Peuronen, S. 2009, 'Young people's translocal new media uses: a multiperspective analysis of language choice and heteroglossia', *Journal of Computer-Mediated Communication*, vol. 14, no. 4, pp. 1080–1107.

> This article explores young Finnish people's linguistic, social and cultural activities and practices in a variety of online sites, including online gaming, fan fiction and Christian web forums on extreme sports, with a specific focus on multilingualism and heteroglossia.

Nederveen Pieterse, J. 1995, 'Globalization as hybridization', in M. Featherstone, S. Lash, & R. Robertson, (eds.) *Global modernities*, Sage: London, pp. 45–69.

> This canonical piece argues for the benefits of seeing globalization(s) as multiple processes of hybridization, and culture(s) as translocal, exogenous, heterogenetic and moving towards 'global mélange'.

Part VII

New debates and further directions

24

Social reading in a digital world[1]

Naomi S. Baron

According to author Henry Hitchings, the Internet "erodes, slowly, one's sense of self, one's capacity for the kind of pleasure in isolation that has, since printed books became common, been readers' standard experience" (quoted in Kingsley 2010). Otis Chandler, founder of the online social reading platform Goodreads, declares books to be "one of the strongest social objects that exist" (Chandler 2013a). Who is right? This chapter examines the interplay between individual versus social reading, including the role of digital media.

In earlier centuries, relatively few people were literate, so "reading" commonly meant listening to others read aloud (Darnton 1991: 150). A social activity? Yes—but a unidirectional one. Today, online social reading tools invite "conversation" with other readers. Amazon Kindle's "Popular Highlights" shares what other readers of the same eBook have chosen to annotate. Media guru Steven Johnson captures the essence of digital social reading: "even when we manage to turn off Twitter and the television and sit down to read a good book, there will be a chorus of readers turning the pages along with us, pointing out the good bits" (Johnson 2010).

Technology shifts the balance between solitude and social in the world of reading. During the heyday of print culture (from about 1700 to the dawn of the Internet), the growing literate (and increasingly affluent) population of the West largely did their reading in private. Now, in a world with more than a billion Facebook users, the pendulum has swung to reading as a public act. In the words of novelist Cynthia Ozick, "the Gutenberg era moved human awareness from the collective to the reflective. Electronic devices promote the collective, the touted 'global community'—again the crowd" (Ozick 2000).

In the company of others

What does it mean to say reading is social? Does mental conversation with the author count? What about reading someone else's annotations, browsing a friend's bookshelf, or discussions at a book club?

Between reader and author

Marcel Proust's *On Reading* (*Sur la Lecture*) is an eloquent discussion of the relationship between author and reader. For Proust, the reader's conversation with the author is conducted in solitude.

When we allow another person into the discussion, our dialogue with the author "dissipates immediately" (Proust 1971: 31). Proust's notion of reading is highly active: "we can receive the truth from nobody . . . we must create it ourselves" (p. 35). Reading, says Proust, entails a friendship—but with a person dead or otherwise absent.

Annotation as conversation

Another form of social reading stems from the markings we leave. Sometimes we ourselves are the interlocutors. Ten years ago, we read a book and made copious notes in the margins. Returning to that book today, our conversation is with our younger selves. Anyone getting hold of our marginalia (say, by purchasing the book used) can enter into discussion with us as well, though at one remove.

Books on display

Leah Price, a professor of English, candidly describes some of her early reading habits: "In my college dorm, a volume of Sartre was spread-eagled across the futon when I expected callers" (Price 2011: 1). She goes on to observe, "We display books that we'll never crack; we hide books that we thumb to death." Think of those "beach books" we judge will look impressive on our towels. Bookshelves also provide opportunities for a version of social reading. When we visit homes or offices, we scan the shelves and, in the process, construct a mental profile of the books' owner, maybe seeding conversation.

Authors on display

Authors themselves are sometimes on display. Take Charles Dickens, a master of public readings (Ferguson 2001). Between 1853 and 1870, the year he died, Dickens packed in 472 readings in Britain and the US. Author book tours have become standard fare for writers (and their publishers). These events are social in the manner of Dickens' readings, but also in that, now, audience participation in the form of questions or discussion is usually welcomed.

Literary events, like so much of contemporary living, are becoming more casual. Writers are reading—and competing—in book slams that might combine "cabaret, comedy and club nights" (Clark 2010). There are also virtual solutions for putting authors on display. One model is the blog book tour. Instead of traveling to physical locations, the author makes "stops" at a number of websites (typically blogs). At each, authors might be interviewed, make guest blog posts, upload new material, or answer questions. A newer alternative is essentially a live video conference. Video chat providers like Shindig enable authors (or anyone else, such as musical groups or press events) to "give an online reading, talk, or interview in front of an online group of 50 to 1000" (Shindig nd.).

Gathering together

What about discussions readers have with one another? Sometimes we might chat with a stranger on the bus who is holding a book we just finished, or check in with the friend to whom we gave a favorite book for Christmas. If two people listen in the car to an audiobook as they drive cross-country, it's natural to share reactions when they stop for dinner. Teachers structure book discussions on works they have assigned their students. And then there are book clubs—formal or casual, face-to-face or virtual.

Social reading evolves

It is hard to date the earliest organized gatherings of readers talking about printed works. A reasonable guess might be by the late seventeenth century. No guessing is needed about the participants, who would have been overwhelmingly men.

In the company of men: modern roots of social reading

The first coffee house opened in London in 1652. Over time, coffee houses became gathering places to hear the latest news. Initially the news was read aloud, but by the early-eighteenth century, men congregated to drink coffee, read newspapers themselves, and discuss (among other things) their contents (Desmond 1978: 27).

One motivation for readers coming together was financial, with monetary interests cutting two ways. For readers, the high costs of books or periodical literature (newspapers, and later magazines) sometimes led readers to share copies (Barzun 2001: 49). For eighteenth-century booksellers, setting up book clubs in their stores could lead to subsequent business:

> Provincial booksellers often turned their stock into a library and charged dues for the right to frequent it. Good light, some comfortable chairs, a few pictures on the wall, and subscriptions to a half-dozen newspapers were enough to make a club out of almost any bookstore.
>
> *(Darnton 1991: 151)*

Some of these clubs focused more on socializing, smoking, and drinking than intellectual activity (Kaufman 1964); and of course this social dimension continues in many reading groups to this day (Heller 2011). By contrast, other early groups took their reading quite seriously. The goal was generally self-improvement, with reading playing a role in the enterprise. Benjamin Franklin founded the Junto Society in 1727 in Philadelphia to talk about issues ranging from morals to politics or natural philosophy. To help structure the society's discussions, Franklin devised a list of twenty-four questions, the first of which was: "Have you met with any thing in the author you last read, remarkable, or suitable to be communicated to the Junto? Particularly in history, morality, physics, travels, mechanic arts, or other parts of knowledge?" (Franklin 2004: 48–49).

On both sides of the Atlantic, workingmen's associations and mechanics' institutes sprang up to help improve the working conditions—and education—of laborers. Group meetings often took the form of lectures, and many of the organizations had libraries attached to them (Harrison 1961; Rice 2004). The Lyceum, Chautauqua, and especially Atheneum movements all provided opportunities for reading and discussion (Gould 1961; Ray 2005; Story 1975). Both genders were welcome in some of these later self-improvement programs; it was largely women, however, who created the modern book club (Long 2003: 31).

Broadening the base: women and book clubs

By the late 1700s, young women had begun informally meeting in New England (and later elsewhere, as the US grew) to "improve their minds," as well as promote cultural fellowship. Such early reading clubs were for women only. Today, reading groups continue to meet, though much has changed. The self-development theme is largely gone. While many groups end up predominantly (often wholly) female, gender composition tends to result from affinity, not fiat.

The usual model we think of for book clubs is face-to-face conversation in the company of others. But there are other options. Radio and television provide opportunities for what we might call "armchair" book clubs: You listen to an author and interviewer, sometimes having the opportunity to call in or text comments or questions.

And then, of course, there's Oprah.

The mother of all book clubs

In September 1996, Oprah Winfrey announced she was starting a book club. Face-to-face reading groups were going strong in America. However, the people attending them tended to be college-educated and often upper middle-class. Oprah's audience did not neatly fit the profile. They were less likely to have completed higher education, less likely to be frequenting bookstores, and less likely to be reading mainstream book reviews (Farr 2005).

Can we call Oprah's Book Club "social reading," when most readers were at home in front of their television sets, watching Oprah interview an author on-camera, and seeing pan shots of the studio audience? Indeed, we probably can. Oprah carefully laid the groundwork to help viewers feel part of the conversation. The show's website offered advance questions for readers to think about. There were opportunities for online discussion, both before and after the show. Readers could write in (Oprah read some letters on-air), and studio audience members participated in the live conversation.

Oprah's TV Book Club redefined what a book club might look like. But yet another redefinition of reading in the company of others was waiting in the wings, enabled this time by the virtually networked connections of the Internet.

Join the crowd: online social reading

Digital communication technology has profoundly expanded possibilities for sharing books and reading experiences with others. Besides the profusion of private "Bookshelf Tours" found on blogs and YouTube, online sites invite users to catalogue their collection and share it with others.

One of the earliest entries was LibraryThing, an online site for creating and sharing book collections (Met 2006). Besides giving users a speedy way of tracking their own collection (automatically filling in a picture of the book cover, date of publication, ISBN number, and list of alternative editions), the site encourages interaction. Among the options are joining book groups, getting book recommendations, accessing early reviews of new books, and linking directly with Twitter to tweet reviews. Another early cataloguing entry was Shelfari (Shelfari nd). But the real game-changer came in early 2007.

Goodreads

Like their predecessors, Otis and Elizabeth Chandler wanted to build an online tool through which readers could share their common love of books. And so Goodreads was born. By 2013, there were 20 million members (Chandler 2013b; Greenfield 2012). Readers can post reviews of books, create catalogues of their own bookshelves (real or virtual), and form virtual groups. On Goodreads, there are thousands of book groups—plus very many reviews. The review counts for *Twilight*, *The Hunger Games*, and *Harry Potter and the Sorcerer's Stone* are each around two million.

There is also the author component. Authors (and publishers) are invited to give away free books and blog with Goodreads members. By the end of 2013, over 96,000 authors were part of the Goodreads authors' program.

Other social reading options

Scores of other social reading platforms have appeared. One of the newest is Zola. Unlike Amazon, which has driven hundreds of brick-and-mortar bookstores out of business, Zola is designed to support publishers, authors, and independent bookstores through member discussion, professional reviews, and profit-sharing.

A more radical option is futurist Bob Stein's Institute for the Future of the Book. Viewing books not as closed, completed physical things, but rather as places "where people congregate to hash out their thoughts and ideas," Stein argues that

> the reification of ideas into printed, persistent objects obscures the social aspect of both reading and writing, so much so, that our culture portrays them as among the most solitary of behaviours. This is because the social aspect traditionally takes place outside pages.
>
> *(2013)*

One of Stein's ventures is Social Book (Open Utopia, nd). As Stein said in an interview with the Canadian Broadcasting Corporation (CBC), "This idea that we read by ourselves is a relatively recent idea and is going to go away" (quoted in Prpick 2013).

Is Stein's prediction realistic? Not if you listen to some of those posting comments on the CBC's web site for their documentary *Opening the Book*. As one wrote, "We can only read by ourselves. sharing the experience (as with discussing stories with others) is an event that happens after the fact."

Assessing social reading in a digital world

How do we evaluate the growing social aspect of reading, as books and reading activities increasingly go online? The answer entails a blend of personal taste, genre, motivation for reading socially, custom, and business practice.

Writer Judith Shulevitz pithily summed up her preference for individual reading: "You read your book and I'll read mine" (2002). Others advise that reading socially is fine, but only after we have seriously encountered a book on our own. Even builders of online social reading sites acknowledge the need to distinguish between individual and social reading experiences (Alber & Miller 2012).

Literature professor Patricia Spacks reminds us that if we have read a book in a social context (a book group, a college course), it is valuable to reread the work for ourselves to formulate our own perspectives (Spacks 2011). It's all too easy to assume we agree with the interpretations of whoever was dominating the earlier conversation. Only by returning to the book in solitude can we hold our own conversation with the author.

Solitary reading is more relevant for some books than others, at least the first time around. If you're reading *Twilight*, you might not be particularly distracted by other readers' annotations showing up on your eBook. An online social reading tool like Kobo's "Pulse Indicator," which gets larger and brighter as you reach pages with more comments and reader activity (Kobo nd), surely favors the social over the individual. But one can hope that readers initially discovering Sherlock Holmes might be left in peace to experience for themselves the language, the characters, the story line, and the way Arthur Conan Doyle builds suspense.

There is also the issue of custom. We have noted the practice of putting books on display. This practice has its counterexample in Japan: upon entering a Japanese bookstore and selecting the volume you wish to buy, the clerk checking you out will invariably offer you a plain white cover, effectively camouflaging title and author. When you are sitting on the subway or bus, no one can see what you're reading.

If you use an eReader, your privacy is compromised at the corporate level. Companies can track every time you open an eBook, every page turn, every annotation. Here the social reading relationship is not one you requested but part of the Faustian bargain for reading onscreen (see also Jones, this volume).

As reading on digital screens with Internet connections expands, the idea of "reading social" is likely to proliferate. While talking about books with other readers (even virtually) can enrich both our intellectual and interpersonal lives, it behooves us not to lose our private conversations about books with their authors—and with ourselves.

Note

1   This contribution is based on Chapter 5 of Naomi S. Baron, 2015, *Words onscreen: the fate of reading in a digital world*, Oxford University Press: New York, NY.

References

Alber, T. & Miller, A. 2012, "Above the silos: social reading in the age of mechanical barriers," in H. McGuire & B. O'Leary (eds.), *Book: a futurist's manifesto*, O'Reilly Media: Boston, MA, pp. 153–175.

Barzun, J. 2001, "Three men and a book," *The American Scholar*, vol. 70, no. 3, pp. 49–57.

Chandler, O. 2013a, "What's going on with readers today? Goodreads finds out," 25 February, available at: http://www.goodreads.com/blog/show/410-what-s-going-on-with-readers-today-goodreads-finds-out [accessed 3 April 2015].

Chandler, O. 2013b, "Goodreads grows to 20 million readers," available at: http://www.goodreads.com/blog/show/425-goodreads-grows-to-20-million-readers [accessed 3 April 2015].

Clark, A. 2010, "The new wave of literary events," *The Guardian*, 30 July.

Darnton, R. 1991, "History of reading," in P. Burke (ed.), *New perspectives on historical writing*, Polity Press: Cambridge, pp. 140–167.

Desmond, R. W. 1978, *The information process: world news reporting to the twentieth century*, University of Iowa Press: Iowa City, IA.

Farr, C. K. 2005, *Reading Oprah: how Oprah's book club changed the way America reads*, State University of New York Press: Albany, NY.

Ferguson, S. 2001, "Dickens's public readings and the Victorian author," *Studies in English literature 1500–1900*, vol. 41, no. 4, pp. 729–749.

Franklin, B. 2004, *Franklin: the autobiography and other writings on politics, economics, and virtue*, edited by A. Houston, Cambridge University Press: New York, NY.

Gould, J. 1961, *The Chautauqua movement: an episode in the continuing American revolution*, State University of New York Press: Albany, NY.

Greenfield, J. 2012, "Goodreads CEO Otis Chandler on the future of discoverability and social reading," *Digital Book World*, 8 November.

Harrison, J. F. C. 1961, *Learning and living, 1790–1960: a study in the history of the English adult education movement*, Routledge & Paul: London.

Heller, N. 2011, "Book clubs: Why do we love them so much? Is it the zucchini bread?," *Slate*, 29 July.

Johnson, S. 2010, "Yes, people still read, but now it's social," *New York Times*, 19 June.

Kaufman, P. 1964, "English book clubs and their role in social history," *Libri*, vol. 14, no. 1, pp. 1–31.

Kingsley, P. 2010, "The art of slow reading," *The Guardian*, 14 July.

Kobo nd., "A new world of social reading," available at: http://www.kobobooks.com/stats [accessed 3 April 2015].

Long, E. 2003, *Book clubs: women and the uses of reading in everyday life*, University of Chicago Press: Chicago, IL.

Met, C. 2006, "LibraryThing," *PC Magazine*, 21 July.

Open Utopia nd., "Social book," available at: http://theopenutopia.org/social-book/ [accessed 3 April 2015].

Ozick, C. 2000, "Where to connect to the inner hum," *New York Times Magazine*, 7 May.

Price, L. (ed.) 2011, *Unpacking my library: writers and their books*, Yale University Press: New Haven, CT.

Proust, M. 1905/1971, *On reading*, trans. and edited by J. Autret & W. Burford, The Macmillan Company: New York, NY.

Prpick, S. 2013, "'Social reading': the next phase of e-book revolution," CBC News Documentary, *Opening the book*, 25 February.

Ray, A. G. 2005, *The Lyceum and public culture in the nineteenth-century United States*, Michigan State University Press: East Lansing, MI.

Rice, S. P. 2004, *Minding the machine: languages of class in early industrial America*, University of California Press: Berkeley, CA.

Shelfari nd., available at: http://www.shelfari.com [accessed 3 April 2015].

Shindig nd., available at: http://shindigevents.com [accessed 3 April 2015].

Shulevitz, J. 2002, "The close reader: You read your book and I'll read mine," *New York Times Book Review,* 19 May.

Spacks, P. M. 2011, *On rereading*, Belknap Press: Cambridge, MA.

Stein, B. 2013, "The future of the book is the future of society," available at: http://futureofthebook.org/blog/ ("Archives," March 2013) [accessed 3 April 2015].

Story, R. 1975, "Class and culture in Boston: The Athenaeum, 1807–1860," *American Quarterly*, vol. 27, no. 2, pp. 178–199.

Further reading

Adler, M. 1940, *How to read a book*, Simon & Schuster: New York, NY.

> Adler's classic discussion of how to be an engaged reader has guided several generations of students and adults alike.

Darnton, R. 1991, "History of reading," in P. Burke (ed.), *New perspectives on historical writing*, Polity Press: Cambridge, pp. 140–167.

> Historian Robert Darnton's article provides an incisive summary of the modern history of reading.

Farr, C. K. 2005, *Reading Oprah: how Oprah's book club changed the way America reads*, State University of New York Press: Albany, NY.

> Farr's lively *Reading Oprah* offers an in-depth look at how Oprah Winfrey convinced millions of women that serious reading was within their reach.

Proust, M. 1905/1971, *On reading*, trans. and edited by J. Autret & W. Burford, The Macmillan Company: New York, NY.

> Proust's essay makes a convincing case for the importance of dialogue between reader and author.

25

New frontiers in interactive multimodal communication

Susan C. Herring

Introduction

This chapter describes two emergent phenomena related to multimodality in digital communications. The first phenomenon is *interactive multimodal platforms*—Web 2.0 platforms that support a convergence of channels or "modes" (text, audio, video, images) for user-to-user communication. The second is *robot-mediated communication*—human–human communication in which at least one party is telepresent through voice, video, and motion in physical space via a remotely controlled robot. At first blush, these two phenomena may appear unrelated: Websites are on the Internet, whereas robots are physical, mechanical objects; web interaction is persistent and often asynchronous, whereas robot-mediated interaction takes place in real time and does not leave a verbal trace; and so forth. At the same time, both technologies mediate human-to-human communication, support social as well as task-related interaction, and involve multiple modes or channels. More generally, both can be situated under the broad rubric of multimodal computer-mediated communication (CMC), as represented in Figure 25.1.

In what follows, I discuss each phenomenon in turn. I also identify research opportunities and challenges raised by each phenomenon for scholars of multimodal discourse, and conclude by considering their future outlook.

Interactive multimodal platforms

Interactive multimodal platforms (IMPs) allow social media users to comment on multimodal content via multiple channels on a single website, and even within a single thread or conversation. An IMP minimally involves text plus one other mode (audio, video, and/or graphics); the modes may be synchronous or asynchronous. While IMPs are Web 2.0 sites, in that they are web-based platforms that incorporate user-generated content and social interaction, not all Web 2.0 sites are IMPs: Sites on which messages are mainly textual (excluding multimedia attachments), such as Wikipedia and Twitter, are not IMPs in their current form. One of the first IMPs was YouTube, which allowed users to comment on a shared video asynchronously, either via text or video. Facebook became an IMP when it added video chat to its suite of textual communication options. Another example is the multiplayer online game World of Warcraft,

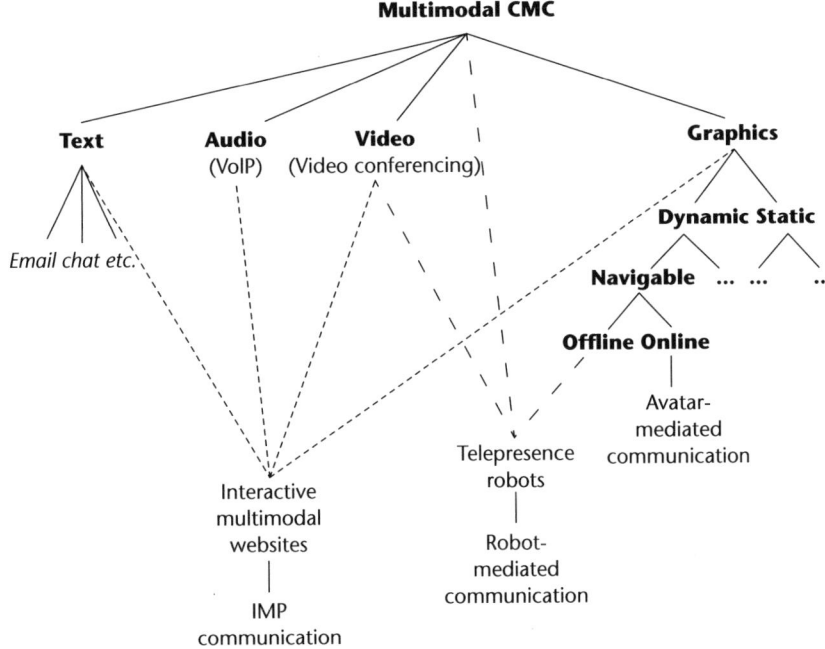

Multimodal CMC

Text

Audio
(VoIP)

Video
(Video conferencing)

Graphics

Email chat etc.

Dynamic Static

Navigable ... ...

Offline Online

Avatar-
mediated
communication

Interactive
multimodal
websites

Telepresence
robots

IMP
communication

Robot-
mediated
communication

Figure 25.1 Multimodal computer-mediated communication.

which for several years incorporated synchronous audio chat (Voice-over-IP) in addition to text chat. The messaging service WhatsApp is arguably an example of an IMP on a mobile device: In addition to text messaging, it enables smart phone users to exchange images, video, and audio media messages in a single "conversation."

Multimodal commenting environments raise theoretical and practical questions about why and how people communicate in a given mode. To what extent does the choice of text, audio, video, and/or images affect the nature of users' communication? Which is most efficient, most positive in tone, most social? What impressions do messages in each mode make on their recipients? Does communication in one mode influence communication in other modes? From a practical perspective, can knowledge of mode differences be leveraged to engineer more pro-social outcomes through the design of multimodal web environments?

IMP research is starting to be conducted, and its early findings suggest that mode choice makes a communicative difference. In her study of World of Warcraft, Newon (2011) found that voice chat was dominated by a few individuals, whereas text chat favored more democratic participation. Sindoni (2014) researched a one-on-one communication environment similar to Skype, observing that interlocutors were more self-conscious in video chat than in typed exchanges. Moreover, seeing themselves in the feedback image "produce[d] psychological effects influencing the verbal and nonverbal features of the online exchange" (p. 333). Relatedly, in discussions on Voicethread.com, a website that supports asynchronous commenting in text, audio, and video, Herring and Demarest (2011) found that audio and video comments were more self-conscious and ego-focused than text comments, as well as being more positive in tone. As regards tone or sentiment, Bourlai and Herring (2014) found that emotions expressed in animated GIFs in Tumblr posts were more positive than emotions expressed in text comments. Text, in addition to being more negative, was more sarcastic.

Although the latter two studies are based on limited data and their results should therefore be considered preliminary, the finding that text was more negative than the non-textual modes in both Voicethread and Tumblr is intriguing. Following early CMC theorists such as Daft and Lengel (1984), Bourlai and Herring (2014) propose that the relative paucity of paralinguistic and social cues in textual CMC creates a distancing effect between interlocutors; it also lends itself to ambiguity, a prerequisite for sarcasm. Thus IMP research can help evaluate claims of technological determinism, which in its strong form holds that features of a technological medium determine user behavior through that medium.

Robot-mediated communication

Telepresence robotics is a sophisticated form of robotic remote control in which a human operator has a sense of being on location. Telepresence robots are distinct from autonomous robots, which depend on artificial intelligence; they are mainly used to facilitate geographically distributed communication, e.g., for teleworkers, academics, and medical professionals, and in security/high-risk operations. Because of the embodiment and enhanced control that they offer, particularly in terms of mobility, telepresence robots provide a richer sense of "being there" than online videoconferencing technologies such as Skype (e.g., Rae, Mutlu, & Takayama 2014).[1]

Telepresence robots are giving rise to a new form of CMC: robot-mediated communication (RMC), human–human communication mediated by one or more telepresence robots. How to classify RMC in relation to CMC is not yet clear. On one hand, RMC is a type of videoconferencing supplemented by movement. On the other hand, it can be considered a type of avatar-mediated communication (like graphical avatars in virtual worlds such as Second Life) in which the user's avatar is a robot that moves around in physical space. The telepresence robot could also be considered a mediating technology in and of itself—a mode, on a par with text, audio, and video. These conceptual relationships are represented schematically in Figure 25.1.

RMC constitutes a potentially rich domain of analysis for scholars of discourse and social interaction. How is interaction management affected when human–human communication is mediated by a robot avatar? How does the limited mobility and range of visibility of persons piloting robots affect their ability to attract attention, gain and hold the conversational floor, and time turn-taking appropriately? What is their social and hierarchical status: Are they taken seriously when they are in positions of leadership? Do they receive politeness and deference the same as if they were physically present, and to what extent does this vary by gender—theirs and that of their interlocutors? How do others refer to the person-in-the-robot—as "you," "s/he," or "it"—and what factors condition variation in reference?

RMC has only been investigated by one research group so far, to the best of my knowledge, and its studies are based on laboratory experiments. One study, for example, found that subjects rated "leaders" interacting through taller robots as more persuasive than "leaders" interacting through shorter robots (Rae, Takayama, & Mutlu 2013a). Another found that persons communicating through a telepresence robot were trusted more than those using a tablet computer (Rae, Takayama, & Mutlu 2013b). While such experimental findings are valuable, they do not necessarily translate to naturalistic contexts of RMC use.

Future outlook

As the trend towards media convergence continues, more IMPs will emerge. Along with the new communicative possibilities that they open up, IMPs are a rich source of data for multimodal discourse analysis. However, most discourse analysis methods (including the approach to computer-mediated discourse analysis put forth in Herring 2004) were devised for spoken or written/typed language, but not for nonverbal communication in video, graphics, music, etc. The challenges are compounded by the practical reality that different modes or channels of communication often co-occur (and co-construct meaning) on the same platform, in the same interaction, and even in the same message. An approach needs to be developed that analyzes disparate modes in relation to one another, ideally with a common set of research questions, methods, and so forth, to permit meaningful comparisons across modes and across platforms. In-depth studies of individual IMPs are also needed. The findings of such research raise the practical possibility of engineering web platforms to optimize the use of modes that produce specific outcomes—for example, platforms with audio and video commenting to reduce negativity in political forums, which tend to be contentious and polarized.

As for RMC, it is still in its infancy: telepresence robots are just starting to be commercially produced and employed. However, RMC will probably never completely supplant videoconferencing—for one thing, it would hardly make sense for *all* participants in remote gatherings to use robots. If there is no reason to be in a particular physical location, virtual presence is simpler and more economical. But telepresence robots are already coming into greater use for remote participation in classrooms and conferences, instruction, and collaborative physical tasks (see, e.g., Herring 2013), and their use produces RMC. Researching RMC is arguably even more challenging than researching IMPs. There are ethical issues associated with collecting data from naturally-occurring robot-mediated interactions, which could be misconstrued as mobile surveillance. Unlike web communication, RMC is not self-archiving; the researcher needs to devise methods of recording, transcription, and presentation for information not normally found in CMC: movement, gaze direction, etc. To address these challenges, RMC analysts could usefully borrow from the ethnographer's methodological toolkit. And as with IMP research, RMC research has implications for designers: It can inform telepresence robot designs that better support natural interaction and communication.

Finally, these emergent technologies can change the way we understand multimodal CMC. Multimodality in CMC is not new, of course. But IMPs are new in that they enable the use of multiple channels in the same conversation. And RMC is new in that it extends video avatars offline, enabling physical movement and navigation (and potentially, gestures) as part of mediated interaction. They both enrich multimodal CMC, according to Information Richness Theory as laid out by Daft and Lengel (1984): They add channels of communication. But in contrast to Daft and Lengel's assumption that the more channels, the more the communication will resemble face-to-face communication (the richest, ideal mode), in the case of both IMP-mediated and robot-mediated communication, forms of communication distinct from face-to-face communication are emerging, with their own unique affordances, which are both less than and more than face-to-face interactions. In this sense, IMPs and RMC promise to provide fertile ground for both empirical exploration and theorizing about language in digital interaction.

Note

1 Examples of telepresence robots that are currently commercially available in the US include the Beam and the Beam+ (Suitable Technologies), the VGo (VGo Robotics), and the Double (Double Robotics).

References

Bourlai, E. & Herring, S. C. 2014, "Multimodal communication on Tumblr: 'I have so many feels!'," *Proceedings of WebSci 2014*, ACM, New York, NY, available at: http://www.sheridanprinting.com/14-websci4chRV610jmp/docs/p171.pdf.

Daft, R. & Lengel, R. H. 1984, "Information richness: a new approach to managerial behavior and organizational design," in B. M. Staw & L. L. Cummings (eds.), *Research in organizational behavior,* JAI Press: Greenwich, CT, pp. 191–233.

Herring, S. C. 2013, "Telepresence robots for academics," *Proceedings of ASIST 2013,* November 1-6, 2013, Montreal, Canada, prepublication version available at: http://ella.slis.indiana.edu/~herring/AM13.telepresence.robots.pdf.

Herring, S. C. 2004, "Computer-mediated discourse analysis: an approach to researching online behavior," in S. A. Barab, R. Kling, & J. H. Gray (eds,), *Designing for virtual communities in the service of learning,* Cambridge University Press: New York, NY, pp. 338–376.

Herring, S. C. & Demarest, B. 2011, "Mode choice in multimodal comment threads: effects on participation and language use," Unpublished manuscript.

Newon, L. 2011, "Multimodal creativity and identities of expertise in the digital ecology of a World of Warcraft guild," in C. Thurlow & K. Mroczek (eds.), *Digital discourse: language in the new media,* Oxford University Press: Oxford, pp. 203–231.

Rae, I., Takayama, L., & Mutlu, B. 2014, "Bodies in motion: mobility, presence, and task awareness in telepresence," *Proceedings of CHI 2014,* ACM, New York, NY, pp. 2153–2162.

Rae, I., Takayama, L., & Mutlu, B. 2013a, "The influence of height in robot-mediated communication," *Proceedings of the 8th ACM/IEEE international conference on human-robot interaction (HRI '13),* IEEE Press: Piscataway, NJ, pp. 1–8.

Rae, I., Takayama, L., & Mutlu, B. 2013b, "In-body experiences: embodiment, control, and trust in robot-mediated communication," *Proceedings of the SIGCHI conference on human factors in computing systems (CHI '13),* ACM, New York, NY, pp. 1921–1930.

Sindoni, M. G. 2014, "Through the looking glass: a social semiotic and linguistic perspective on the study of video chats," *Text & Talk,* vol. 34, no. 3, pp. 325–347.

26

Moving between the big and the small

Identity and interaction in digital contexts

Ruth Page

The question of how people construct their identities through their interactions with each other has been and remains central in the study of digital communication. In part, the ongoing centrality of this concern is an outworking of the discursive turn in the social sciences, which framed identity as a fluid, plural accomplishment that is constantly under negotiation rather than a single, stable and essentialist entity. The focus on the discursive construction of identity was particularly well suited to the forms of digital communication emerging in the 1990s, where the text-based (written) interactions in online contexts could be taken as examples of disembodied identity play through the use of anonymity or pseudonyms (Turkle 1995), and interpreted as yielding democratic potential which allowed for greater articulation of previously marginalized identities. But over the last two decades, a more complex picture has emerged in which the contexts of interaction where identities are played out are no longer polarized in simplistic, binary contrasts as online or offline, text-based or embodied, playful or authentic. The use of digital communication is embedded in day-to-day interactions in physical locations (Jones 2005) and the identities which are constructed offline are also multiple, shifting and unstable. There is also recognition that the participatory culture associated with social media has not done away with existing hierarchies – indeed, they are often reproduced rather than eradicated in online contexts. (See Herring's (2003) early critique of gender hierarchies in forums and Marwick and boyd's (2011) observations on the hierarchies of celebrity and fame; see also Graham, this volume).

These contexts for interaction have flourished in the first decades of the twenty-first century, where social network services and sites are listed among the most visited websites globally on analytics sites such as Alexa (www.Alexa.com). The immense archives of social networks contain the accrued interactions of many millions of members. The available source material for exploring identity practices played out through online interaction is thus immensely rich, but also messy, vast and in many respects difficult to probe. Here I highlight two aspects of complexity which raise questions about the methods we might use to analyse the online production of identity. First, the identities constructed online make use of a multimodal range of semiotic resources that are recombined and transposed from one mode to another. Although this multimodality is now broadly recognized (see Herring, this volume), the analysis of semiotic systems outside verbal content is relatively less developed, and the tools for extracting and processing image and sound are separate from those developed to analyse language. Second, the digital medium means that the contexts of interaction also include additional information in the form of meta-data appended to the content published online. This meta-data may be more or less visible (for example, the location of the other person and the device they are using to create a post may not be seen from the perspective of the participants looking at a post reading it on a screen, but these facts may be embedded in the post's code as it is built into the site's databases). Knowing how to access, analyse and interpret this metadata requires specific tools and skills. Both the multimodal nature of online interactions and the meta-data available as contextualizing information about that content point to the diverse range of phenomena which are included alongside more traditional objects for linguistic scrutiny, such as the written text itself.

It would be untenable to suggest that there could be any single approach, method or framework that could deal with all the different aspects of the interactional contexts that frame how identities are constructed. Indeed, the methodological breadth of Internet studies across different disciplines is a positive attribute. We need diverse approaches to examine the highly varied aspects of online communication. But within that methodological diversity, there remains much unrealized potential for integrating approaches to expand our understanding of how interactional contexts operate. A priority for future research lies not in polarising these methods, but in testing and refining them by developing new combined mixed methods. In particular, there is a need for approaches that link the methods used to probe 'big' data with the close micro-analytic reading of 'small' features of interaction.

Focusing on the small: positioning in talk

The analysis of identity developed within interactional sociolinguistics focuses on the 'small' details of the interaction, particularly the turn-by-turn negotiation of identities, which can be inscribed (stated explicitly by the participants) or more or less inferred through stylistic features within the interaction. Analysis of these micro-analytic features of lexico-grammar and interactional patterns of (mis)alignment have been applied effectively in positioning theory (Davies & Harré 1990), where 'micro-' interactional features are interpreted in terms of 'macro-' social meanings (Bamberg & Georgakopoulou 2008) relating to the participants' personal and social identities. Although this approach was developed in relation to face-to-face conversation, it has been applied with relative ease to online 'talk,' such as posts to a discussion thread within a forum or a social networking site (Georgakopoulou 2014). Within this paradigm, the contexts of interaction consist of the immediate co-text – the turn-by-turn unfolding discourse itself. This methodological premise, founded on the empirical emphasis of conversation-analytic research, is a salient reminder of just how far analysis can go even with relatively small-scale data samples and a fairly narrow view of what might constitute 'context'.

Focusing on the big: mapping meta-data

At the other extreme, large data sets can be searched and visualized using computer-assisted methods of analysis, such as employing network analysis tools to understand how participants are connected through their interactions. Unlike the text-immanent approach to interaction typical of conversation analysis, the analysis of 'big' data from a network perspective is interested in how tools can process the meta-data to provide additional information about the context, such as when the post was published and from which location, and whether and how the post was redistributed in the network elsewhere (for example, how often a post was shared within

Facebook or retweeted within Twitter). These interactional characteristics can be modelled as visualizations, which have been able to show how particular collective identities (such as viewers of television shows) are modelled as 'publics' (Highfield *et al.* 2013). From this methodological perspective, the contextual picture is derived from the meta-data appended to the posts, and the interpretation of constructed identities emphasizes the interactions rather than the content of the individual posts. Although there are great strengths to this kind of analysis, like other quantitative methods which survey large bodies of data, network analysis tends to focus on high-frequency items (such as nodes connecting a large number of interactions), while lower-frequency items can be relatively less scrutinized. Finally, because social network analysis is (as the name suggests) interested in the network, it is difficult for this kind of analysis to address the multimodal content within individual posts and to account for ways in which identities are constructed through audio-visual as well as verbal material.

The 'big' and 'small' interactional foci of these two approaches might be regarded as complementary perspectives which together could yield a more nuanced picture of how localized exchanges are embedded in much larger interactional networks. Yet despite this complementarity, it is rare to find the two approaches combined within the same project or applied to the same data (but see Caulfield 2013). In part, this exposes the interdisciplinary gaps which hinder collaborative enterprises. Social network analysis has currency among media scholars and those working within computer science, while interactional sociolinguistics is within the purview of humanities and social sciences. We still have much work to do to bridge disciplines and combine our methods and insights. But to illustrate the potential of combining these approaches, I present a brief analysis which moves between the 'big' and 'small' details of analysis to interpret the ambiguous identity construction that took place on a public Facebook page set up in response to the death of former British Prime Minister, Margaret Thatcher.

Combining the 'big' and the 'small': interpreting the interactions of a troll

As the scale of online interactions has increased, so have incivility (Suler 2004) and 'e-bile' (Jane 2014), for example in forms of trolling. The actions of a troll can involve 'luring others into a pointless discussion' (Herring *et al.* 2002) in order to disrupt interactions, or acting as a trickster and using disruptions as a form of cultural critique (Phillips 2011). The interactions associated with troll-like behaviour exploit the discursive nature of identity enabled through online contexts. Trolls can hide behind anonymous or pseudonymous representation, and the contextual details which might reveal their offline behaviour are often quickly deleted. As Herring's description suggests, the interactions of a troll can also be ambiguous and it is only over time as the interactions unfold that the troll's presence is suspected. Small-scale observations of localized interactional patterns thus need to be set within the wider, longitudinal contexts found across a larger dataset.

The example here was taken from a public Facebook group page, 'RIP Margaret Thatcher'. Margaret Thatcher was and remains a polarizing figure for the public, and the interactional context of a public Facebook group responding to her death provides a window on the clash between her supporters and critics. In such a space, we can also expect interactions and negotiated identities to be less than straightforward. Indeed, the Facebook page brought into sharp focus the contrast between those who wished to pay tribute to her and those who celebrated her death. The group page appeared superficially as a tribute to Margaret Thatcher and garnered over 15,000 'likes'. Its timeline includes nine images within 11 posts made by the page owner, which suggest respect for the former Prime Minister. The posts were published between 18 and 27 April, 2013 and attracted 31,424 comments, which, unlike the stance in the original posts, included highly negative critiques of Margaret Thatcher; in their wake, aggravated arguments ensued. These interactions are more akin to the overt incivility of 'flaming' found in other online contexts (such as discussion forums) than to trolling. The suspicions that a troll might be involved in the interactions are prompted not so much by the incivility within the comments as by the multimodal content of a post made one day after Margaret Thatcher's funeral.

The post read, 'Lovely funeral yesterday, please take a second of your time to like this page to show your respect. RIP The Iron Lady' and was accompanied by an image showing Meryl Streep playing Margaret Thatcher in the 2011 film. The visual content is crucially ambiguous and many of the 280 responses to that post suggested that use of this image was inappropriate – 'Get Meryl Streep off and put the REAL Margaret Thatcher on out of respect!' – and eventually concluded that the page itself was 'fake and has been set up by the opposition'. The participants' interpretation of Streep's image as inappropriate thus repositioned the page creator as a trickster-like troll, who had lured the commenters into making tributes that only resulted in spurious arguments. But in order to test whether the 'page-creator-as-troll' interpretation could be sustained, further analysis was required. Given that the page contained a large number of comments, manual coding of individual contributions was impractical. The anonymous nature of the page also meant that analysing the participants' behaviour was problematic. The Facebook page information gave no details about the person who created it, and the page profile used only generic images of Margaret Thatcher in its representation. It was thus very difficult to tell who exactly was interacting with whom on the basis of a qualitative analysis of the posts alone.

A network analysis using Gephi[1] enabled an examination of the interactional context across the page as a whole. The metadata embedded in the posts and comments could be used to identify which participants were interacting most frequently across the posts. The network analysis showed that one participant posted more than any other and interacted across multiple posts, posting comments that were both supportive and critical of Margaret Thatcher. This participant used an IP address located outside the UK, and the Facebook account associated with the post has since been deleted. It is impossible to tell if this participant was also the person who created the page but it does suggest that the interactions that appear between posts and comments cannot be taken at face value. This participant took several measures to obscure his or her offline identity – behaviour that might be considered in line with a trickster-type troll wishing to critique Margaret Thatcher and her supporters.

Together, the qualitative analysis of an individual comment thread and the wider interactional context as indicated by the quantitative network analysis provide complementary perspectives that suggest 'big' and 'small' analytic foci can be combined usefully. Without close attention to the individual thread, the ambiguity created by the visual content and the participants' perceptions of this inappropriate interaction would not have been observed. But without the network analysis using the meta-data in the posts and comments, it would have been extremely difficult to see the wider interactional picture and the steps certain participants had taken to obscure their identity.

As we strive for a fuller picture of how interactions are used to negotiate ambiguous and elusive identities, no doubt we will find many further ways of integrating methods associated with probing 'big' data and those used for scrutinizing localized contexts. Even more certain is that our efforts to explore the intricacies of identity work will benefit from cross-disciplinary and cross-methodological collaborations. Through a diversity of lenses, we can examine 'big' pictures without overlooking the 'small' features embedded within them.

Note

1   http://gephi.github.io/.

References

Bamberg, M. & Georgakopoulou, A. 2008, 'Small stories as a new perspective in narrative and identity analysis', *Text and Talk*, vol. 28, no. 3, pp. 377–396.

Caulfield, J. 2013, 'A social network analysis of Irish language use in social media', Unpublished PhD Thesis, Cardiff University.

Davies, B. & Harré R. 1990, 'Positioning: the discursive construction of selves', *Journal for the Theory of Social Behaviour*, vol. 20, no. 1, pp. 43–63.

Georgakopoulou, A. 2014, 'Small stories transposition and social media: a micro-perspective on the "Greek Crisis"', *Discourse and Society*, vol. 25, no. 4, pp. 510–539.

Herring, S. C. 2003, 'Gender and power in online communication', in J. Holmes & M. Meyerhoff (eds.), *The handbook of language and gender*, Blackwell: Oxford, pp. 202–228.

Herring, S. C., Job-Sluder, K., Scheckler, R. & Barab, S. 2002, 'Searching for safety online: managing "trolling" in a feminist forum', *The Information Society*, vol. 18, no. 5, pp. 371–383.

Highfield, T., Harrington, S. & Bruns, A. 2013, 'Twitter as a technology of audiencing and fandom', *Information, Communication and Society*, vol. 16, no. 3, pp. 315–339.

Jane, E. A. 2014, 'Beyond antifandom: cheerleading, textual hate and new media ethics', *International Journal of Cultural Studies*, vol. 17, no. 2, pp. 175–190.

Jones, R. H. 2005, 'Sites of engagement as sites of attention: time, space and culture in electronic discourse', in S. Norris & R. H. Jones (eds.), *Discourse in action: mediated discourse analysis*, Routledge: New York, NY, pp. 141–154.

Marwick, A. & boyd, d 2011, 'To see and be seen: celebrity practice on Twitter', *Convergence,* vol. 17, no. 2, pp. 139–158.

Phillips, W. 2011, 'Facebook trolls, memorial pages and resistance to grief online', *First Monday*, vol. 16, no. 12, available at: http://firstmonday.org/ojs/index.php/fm/article/view/3168/3115 [accessed 15/10/2014].

'RIP Margaret Thatcher', available at https://www.facebook.com/pages/RIP-Margaret-Thatcher/2686 77236599745 [accessed 16/10/2014].

Suler, J. 2004, 'The disinhibition effect', *Cyberpsychology and Behavior*, vol. 7, no. 3, pp. 321–326.

Turkle, S. 1995, *Life on the screen: identity in the age of the Internet*, Simon & Schuster: New York, NY.

27

Surveillance

Rodney H. Jones

Perhaps the most conspicuous consequence of the rise of digital technologies over the past few years is not how they have facilitated new forms of communication, but how they have facilitated new forms of *surveillance*, allowing governments, corporations and even individuals unprecedented access to information from people who do *not* intend to communicate it. Thus far, issues of Internet privacy and security have been the purview of legal scholars, political scientists, systems engineers, and sociologists in the burgeoning field of "surveillance studies." In this short comment, I would like to argue that scholars of language have a particularly important role to play in discussions of digital surveillance, and, more than that, that understanding practices of surveillance is increasingly central to understanding digital language.

For scholars in other fields, debates about digital surveillance often focus on questions about technical systems, laws, rights and ethics. For linguists, they cut to the heart of the most fundamental definitions in our field: what it actually means to "read," to "write," to "speak," and to "listen." Even answering the questions posed by ethicists and technicians often depends on how these basic linguistic processes are understood. In the recent debate over NSA spying, for example, the augments of both the agency and its critics hinged on questions such as whether or not collecting "metadata" about communication is the same as "listening" to someone's phone calls or "reading" their emails.

This is no surprise. Digital technologies have been confounding the neat categories of language scholars for a long time. In the 1990s, hypertext disturbed traditional understandings of reading, and asynchronous chat blurred the boundaries between spoken and written language. Later, the rise of Web 2.0 and social networking further confused the relationship between reader and author and threw into question what actually constitutes a "conversation" or a "social interaction."

Digital surveillance represents a further challenge, one in which we must adjust the way we conceive of "texts." In the past, applied linguists and discourse analysts have been accustomed to regarding texts primarily as information delivery devices, focusing on how they communicate meaning. The primary function of many texts we encounter nowadays, however, is not so much information delivery as information gathering.

A good example is my Amazon.com homepage, which carefully monitors my behavior as I search, click and purchase products and then changes its content accordingly. Texts on commercial sites like Amazon, search engines like Google, and social networking sites like Facebook have essentially morphed into cybernetic feedback mechanisms that not only "read" their readers, but also "write" them, constructing discourse positions and social identities for them based on the history of their interactions with the system. Such texts are increasingly the rule rather than the exception. Most of the pages we visit on the Internet, as well as most of the apps we have installed on our smartphones, not to mention the web browsers and smartphones themselves, have built into them sophisticated information gathering capabilities, of which most of us are entirely unaware.

Addressing the analytical challenges posed by this transformation will require increased attention by language scholars to three basic aspects of discourse, which I call *subtexts, pretexts* and *contexts*.

Subtexts

Of course the information gathering function of texts is not entirely new. Many "old media" texts also have this function: think of things like application forms. And when it comes to interaction, scholars such as Goffman (1959) pointed out long ago that all social interaction involves a kind of "information game" in which participants constantly try to extract as much information as they can from their interlocutors while maintaining as much control as possible over their own information. Digital technologies, however, have brought this information game to a whole new level.

One key difference is that the data gathering function of digital texts is more effectively hidden from readers, existing underneath the surface of the text in what I am calling the *subtext*. For most linguists and literary scholars, the subtext has always had a virtual existence in the intersubjective space between the reader and the writer, or the speaker and listener, and has played out in negotiative processes of implicature and inference—processes that, while not always immediately visible, have nevertheless proven amenable to analysis using principles formulated in such fields as pragmatics.

For digital texts, on the other hand, subtexts exist in a more literal way in the form of *algorithms*, strings of computer code that determine our experience of interacting with the texts. Much of the discourse we find online, in fact, is not produced by humans at all, but by algorithms. At the same time, the intentions and agendas behind these texts are becoming less and less legible. Algorithms are often much more difficult to figure out than people, not subject in the same way humans are to quaint conventions like felicity conditions and the cooperative principle. As Wendy Chun (2011: 17) puts it, "as our machines increasingly read and write without us, as our machines themselves become more and more unreadable . . . every act of reading (becomes) an act of faith."

Furthermore, what constitutes the act of writing for human agents has also become ambiguous. Nowadays, simple actions like clicking a hyperlink, choosing an item from a drop-down menu, making a purchase, or "checking in" at your favorite restaurant is likely to produce some sort of text—texts that are often broadcast or archived in ways that their authors cannot control.

Nevertheless, humans continue to actively form inferences about the protocols that lurk beneath digital texts, and often adjust their online actions and utterances based on how they think the algorithms of Facebook or Google might entextualize them. As they do so, they build up new sets of assumptions and inferential processes that are different from those they have developed for communicating with humans. A key challenge for scholars of language will be to develop analytical tools to address these new forms of reading, writing, speaking and listening, and to cultivate an "algorithmic pragmatics" that can explain how implicature is created and inferences formed in these new communication environments.

Rodney H. Jones

Pretexts

One common rejoinder to privacy advocates who object to the constant harvesting of information by digital texts is that users of these texts more often than not "share" their information willingly and that, in any case, they have relinquished their rights to privacy through agreeing to the "terms and conditions" governing these texts. What I mean by *pretexts* are the semiotic processes that contribute to situations in which people become willing to offer themselves up as objects of surveillance.

One good place to start to appreciate how pretexts are created is in existing discourse analytical work on "phishing," the rhetorical strategies used in emails and websites that attempt to lure users into giving up valuable personal data (see, for example, Blommaert & Omoniyi 2006). Such research points to two basic linguistic mechanisms that help to create pretexts: *framing*—creating credible activities for readers and writers to engage in that make the exchange of information seem "normal" (activities like playing games, searching for information, and, of course, "sharing"), and *positioning*—creating credible identities of people with whom one might want to engage in these activities (identities like "friends" and "followers").

Other useful concepts in language studies that can help us understand how people online sometimes feel strangely compelled to disclose come from studies of the structure of interaction from fields such as conversation analysis. Internet companies have become adept at exploiting the pairwise, reciprocal structure of talk and the momentum it creates that makes people respond almost automatically to certain conversational stimuli. It is this momentum that makes it so easy to be tricked by the predictable responses of "bots" or makes people so ready to click "agree" when prompted to by pop-up windows that appear at strategic moments in online interactions.

The task for language scholars in this regard is to thoroughly examine the role of language and other semiotic resources in the formation of pretexts, to explore how "trust" is discursively constructed in digital environments, and to propose strategies for interrupting the discursive "funnels of commitment" (Scollon 2001) that lure people deeper and deeper into acts of disclosure.

Contexts

The final set of challenges for applied linguists and discourse analysts in confronting practices of digital surveillance involves understanding the ways digital media change our sense of the *context* in which communication takes place. According to philosopher Helen Nissenbaum (2009), privacy is not so much a matter of how much information people are willing to communicate as it is about the degree of control they have in creating and managing the contexts in which that information is communicated—what she calls "contextual integrity."

The notion of "contextual integrity" explains why, as danah boyd (2011) points out, teenagers object when their parents look at their Facebook pages, even when those pages are "public." When adults think about privacy, boyd explains, they often imagine the home as a private space. Yet for many teens, the home is about the least private place they can think of, and so they escape into the privacy of "public" spaces like shopping malls and social networking sites. Insights such as this remind us of something that scholars of language, from conversation analysts to ethnographers of communication, have known for a long time: context is not something "out there," independent from what people say or write. It is *brought about* through discourse and enforced through social norms and competencies like those described by Hymes and other linguistic anthropologists.

The problem with much digital media is that they have the tendency to disrupt these delicately negotiated social norms, altering traditional expectations not just about time and space

410

but also about boundaries to participation and barriers to monitoring (Jones 2004). In fact, the whole discursive environment of the Internet seems to be about *decontextualization*: hyperlinks propel us from one textual environment to another, blogs and social media sites curate content from across the web and combine it in ways the content creators never imagined, and the actions that we take of reading and writing, searching and clicking, and purchasing and "liking" are wrested from the contexts in which they occur and converted into "big data," which is used to create profiles of us to be sold to advertisers.

Perhaps the biggest challenge for understanding surveillance is coming to terms with the larger socio-economic context of digital communication, a context in which the value of texts and utterances is ultimately reduced to their *commercial* value, which usually depends on the degree to which they can be removed from their original contexts and turned into "data." In this new political economy of discourse, communication contexts are designed not to facilitate deliberative debate or deep relationships, but to encourage forms of communication that can be most easily directed towards commerce. What will the consequences of this be, we must ask, on our communication and our relationships?

Digital literacies and surveillance

The upshot of this argument is that language scholars have a responsibility not just to describe and analyze these new forms of surveillance, but also to help people to formulate ways around them, to advocate for the privacy rights of individuals and actively resist the colonization of communication by governments and commercial interests. Part of this will involve helping people to develop the literacies necessary to confront the issues I outlined above.

What I mean by digital literacies are skills whereby users of digital media can begin to uncover the algorithmic *subtexts* that govern their interactions and experiences of reading online, become better players of the "information game" by interrupting the sophisticated *pretexts* governments and corporations use to get information from them, and exercise increased agency in managing the *contexts* in which they exchange information, deciding where, when and how they wish to be visible to others. Finally, it means helping them to engage critically with the broader political and economic contexts in which communication takes place, and to work out how they can play a role not just as potential customers, but as digital citizens.

References

Blommaert, J. & Omoniyi, T. 2006, "Email fraud: language, technology, and the indexicals of globalisation," *Social Semiotics*, vol. 16, no. 4, pp. 573–605.

boyd, d 2011, "Dear voyeur, meet flâneur . . . sincerely, social media," *Surveillance & Society*, vol. 8, no. 4, pp. 505–507.

Chun, W. H. K. 2011, *Programmed visions: software and memory*, MIT Press: Cambridge, MA.

Goffman, E. 1959, *The presentation of self in everyday life*, Doubleday: New York.

Jones, R. 2004, "The problem of context in computer mediated communication," in P. LeVine & R. Scollon (eds.), *Discourse and technology: multimodal discourse analysis,* Georgetown University Press: Washington DC, pp. 20–33.

Nissenbaum, H. 2009, *Privacy in context: technology, policy, and the integrity of social life,* Stanford University Press: Palo Alto, CA.

Scollon, R. 2001, "Action and text," in R. Wodak & M. Meyer (eds.), *Methods for critical discourse analysis,* Sage: London, pp. 139–183.

28

Choose now!

Media, literacies, identities, politics

Charles M. Ess

I begin with virtue ethics and its view that the vast majority of human beings seek to pursue lives that are marked by a sense of deep contentment or well-being (*eudaimonia*). Virtue ethics further articulates this human impulse as one towards a good life, a life of *flourishing* that includes fostering and expanding those talents and abilities that both result in our own sense of accomplishment and pleasure (e.g., as musicians, as artists, as athletes, as skilled workers, etc.) and help us engage with those around us in harmonious and constructive ways (e.g., as we learn the basic virtues or habits of excellence such as patience, perseverance, empathy, and trust (Vallor 2011)).

Virtue ethics recommends itself as our starting point here for five reasons. First, virtue ethics is a strong candidate for a global ethics: virtue ethics emerges in the large majority of both ancient and modern societies and traditions, including the ancient western ethics of Socrates and Aristotle, and in eastern traditions such as Confucian thought and Buddhism, as well as in the Abrahamic traditions of Judaism, Christianity, and Islam (Ess 2013: 238–244). Second, virtue ethics is embedded in the foundations of Information and Computing Ethics (ICE)—namely, in the first book on computer ethics by Norbert Wiener, father of cybernetics (1950/1954). Third, virtue ethics has undergone an extraordinary renaissance over the past several decades, beginning within the domains of ICE. Fourth, an increasing number of individuals, projects, and even entire disciplines *outside* of academic philosophy and philosophical ethics—beginning precisely with media and communication studies—are taking up virtue ethics as offering us a primary way of thinking about "the good life" that might be possible for us in the contemporary world (e.g., Couldry 2013)[1]. Last, we will see that a primary virtue of virtue ethics is that it foregrounds central questions of what habits and practices of excellence we must cultivate in order to achieve contentment and flourishing. I thus use virtue ethics here to bring these questions into focus vis-à-vis the sorts of communicative *literacies*—as I will argue, *both* digital and analogue—that are essential workings out of such virtues and of our potential contentment and flourishing.

Applied ethics further reminds us that our ethical norms and frameworks depend on two additional concepts: first, what is the *self*—the human being as an identity and an agent—and, second, what are the *realities* within which such a self must take up and resolve the ethical challenges that arise before it? Most briefly, virtue ethics is enjoying a renaissance in part because, especially in more "Western" societies, it is arguable on a number of grounds that our sense of selfhood is shifting from a strongly *individual* conception of the self as a moral–rational *autonomy* towards a more *relational* sense of self whose identity and agency are inextricably interwoven with those of the multiple Others whose relationships increasingly define such a self. This shift towards more relational selfhood, moreover, seems strongly driven by the changing realities of contemporary life—realities increasingly defined precisely by the multiple networks and networked communications technologies that suffuse and interweave with more or less every aspect of our contemporary existence (e.g., Ess & Fossheim 2013).

In particular, a recent European Commission initiative has produced an "Onlife Manifesto" that seeks to address precisely the questions of how we may conceive and move towards a good life in what we characterized as a "hyperconnected era," i.e., one increasingly defined by these digital networks (Broadbent *et al.* 2013: 1). In this Manifesto, for example, we highlight the importance of protecting our attentional capabilities, including the capabilities of *shared* attention, as critical components of the good life (Broadbent *et al.* 2013: 6f.). In addition, the Manifesto calls for new approaches towards a "digitally literate society," including the observation that "Endorsing responsibility in a hyperconnected reality requires acknowledging how our actions, perceptions, intentions, morality, even corporality are interwoven with technologies in general, and ICTs in particular" (Broadbent *et al.* 2013: 6).

In the following, I would like to elaborate on this analysis and thus this call. I elaborate on the analysis in two ways. First, I argue that we must not let our focus on "the digital" blind us to the many ways in which we remain resolutely *analogue* beings first and foremost, as our relational selves are precisely *embodied* beings. Certainly, "the digital" has become the defining commonplace of our day for many important and well-known reasons. Three of these are perhaps worth noting. To begin with, the ability to capture a seemingly endless range and kinds of "information" makes possible the well-known phenomenon of *convergence*. For example, what were once the separate technologies of photography, sound recording, and text production are now seamlessly interwoven with one another through the common denominator of digital information. Secondly, as the philosopher James Moor (2000) aptly noted, once information is digitized, it is "greased"—it slips easily (and oftentimes more easily than we would like or need) from one source across a global Internet to potentially billions of sites and receivers ("users"). Finally, we in the developed world find ourselves increasingly surrounded and saturated by the various networks and communication technologies that more or less ensure that we are "always on" (Baron 2008), constantly "on the grid" as producers and consumers of digital information— and more and more to the exclusion of older, non-digital technologies. To speak of our time as a "digital age" is not without grounding.

But even in such a digital age, to focus on "the digital" alone risks blinding us to important and, I argue, critical and essential facts of our human condition. To begin with, our commonplace digital technologies remain inevitably analogue when it comes to our *inputs* and their *outputs*. The microphone in my computer or mobile takes in my voice as an analogue signal, just as the speaker or earphone transforms a digital signal into an analogue one for my ear. All of this is because, more fundamentally, despite certain enthusiastic dreams to the contrary, we remain steadfastly *embodied* creatures—ones whose consciousness, reflections, ethical sensibilities, etc. are inextricably interwoven with our bodies. Phenomenologically, our bodies define first of all our experience of the world from a first-person perspective: as Albert Borgmann (1999) put it, the body is the pivot or anchor point from which I experience the world (p. 190). Indeed, as neuroscience reveals in striking ways—e.g., in terms of embodied cognition (Wilson & Foglia 2011)—our experiential abilities to know and navigate the world utterly depend on a range of *analogue* processes that, as almost entirely tacit and prereflective, both escape consciousness and simultaneously make consciousness possible. Our engagement with the world thus remains profoundly embodied and fundamentally analogue (Massumi 2002).

All of this means that just as we are to be alive and responsive to the various impacts, affordances, and possibilities (for good and for ill) of *digital* technologies and communication networks, so we must not neglect the impacts, affordances, and possibilities of our embodiment as analogue beings. To say this differently: if we take "digital" to mean *only* "the digital," we thereby neglect a very large and essential proportion of how we experience, reflect upon, and navigate our world.

As a second elaboration: before our focus on "digital literacy" there were, of course, other kinds of literacies. To be more precise, Medium Theory highlights the rise of writing as the emergence of literacy as a technology of communication. To be sure, in its beginnings, the art and technologies of writing served the strongly instrumental ends of administering city-states and then empires. But as both Medium Theory and the late works of Foucault foreground, the rise of literacy facilitates the emergence of a novel sense of selfhood and identity—namely, the self as a primarily *individual* self, in contrast with the strongly *relational* selves that correlate with pre-literate (oral) peoples (Foucault 1988). Literacy enables the (then utterly novel) Socratic and Stoic injunctions to "know thyself"; this becomes radicalized in the Protestant Reformation, as the rise of the printing press and gradually expanding literacy makes sensible the Lutheran insistence of *sola scriptura*—"only the Scripture": meaning that it is the *individual*—a *literate* individual with access to the Bible as a standardized text—who, relying solely on Scripture, is now responsible for his or her understanding of and relationship with the Divine (Ess 2014 : 624).

This insistence on the ultimate importance of the self qua individual becomes both secularized and amplified even more dramatically with the spread of literacy and print (*literacy-print,* in Medium Theory terms), culminating in modern philosophical accounts of the self as a rational autonomy (Kant 1785/2012) and what Charles Taylor has characterized as the "punctual" or disengaged self (Taylor 1989: 167). Such a self—echoing its Protestant forebear—is emancipated from the constraints of earlier traditions, practices, and norms, and is thus free to determine for itself its own conception of "the good life." Such a self both requires and justifies the liberal-democratic state—at first, precisely as a minimal state, one that relegates the determination of the good life to the individual first, rather than to the Church (of whatever denomination), the community, or even the State.

In numerous ways, Medium Theory associates this sort of self with the skills of (what we should now call analogue-embodied) *literacy*, as practiced especially vis-à-vis the products of print technologies and the art of writing as what Foucault has called a "technology of the self." To be sure, some Medium Theorists, most notably McLuhan, celebrate the loss of such an individual in the emerging "electric age," as literacy-print shifts toward what Walter Ong (1988) has characterized as a "secondary orality"—one that likewise (re)turns us to more relational understandings of selfhood. Others, such as Neil Postman, have argued that a thoughtless embrace of electric media (initially, television) as it works to replace the skills of literacy-print threatens to undermine the sense of individual autonomy and critical reflection necessary for democratic polity (1985). Instead, we busy ourselves with "amusing ourselves to death"—immersing ourselves more and more in the immediate pleasures of entertainment, shopping, and the thousand other distractions of electric media. Postman recalls the dystopia of *Brave New World* as the best descriptor here—a world in which we fall in love with the technologies of our enslavement. As I have argued, the Internet—what someone has aptly called a weapon of mass distraction—only amplifies these risks (Ess 2014).

Such comments risk being mistaken for a technological Luddite's Jeremiad—in part precisely because of our largely enthusiastic embrace of and immersion in "the digital" and secondary orality. But there is some evidence and argument that as we increasingly submerge ourselves in the pleasures of electric media, including the more relational forms of selfhood that correlate with secondary orality, we risk a move away from high modern conceptions of individual autonomy and its correlative emancipatory politics marked by expanding democratic processes and rights, including rights to privacy, and norms, including norms of equality and gender equality (Ess 2014).

Finally, insofar as these concerns are well grounded, they justify an elaboration of the call of the Manifesto. We are not simply in need of *digital* literacies focusing exclusively on whatever skills and abilities are needed to produce, distribute, navigate, and make meaning out of digitally based information and communication. As the Manifesto quietly hints with its reference to "corporeality" (Broadbent *et al.* 2013: 6), we are in need of sustained attention to the skills and abilities affiliated with *analogue* literacy-print, as these strongly correlate with the sorts of selves required for liberal-democratic states, emancipatory politics, democratic processes, and norms of equality, including gender equality. To state this differently: just as the focus on "the digital" risks blinding us to the extensive—if not vital—role and importance of embodiment and the analogue in our knowledge and navigation of the world, so an exclusive focus on "digital literacies" risks the loss of skills and abilities that may well prove crucial to democratic processes, norms of equality, and, most fundamentally, the strongly autonomous selves that undergird these.

If this is correct, then now would be a good time to consciously choose just how we can take up both analogue and digital literacies in some sort of balanced way. Indeed, there is some reason to be hopeful that we may do so. To return to the beginning: the virtue of virtue ethics is that it brings to our consideration the point that if we are to enjoy good lives, lives of contentment, flourishing, and harmony, we will do so only if we consciously *cultivate* the virtues—the practices and habits of excellence—that these require. Virtue ethics, that is, is exactly suited to bringing our habits and practices—including those entangled with our diverse uses of media and communication technologies—to the foreground as matters of conscious and informed reflection and decision, as focused by a single and more or less universal human concern with contentment and well-being.

And so it is heartening—and perhaps not accidental—that virtue ethics is now indeed emerging as an ethical sensibility and approach in domains beyond philosophy, first and foremost in media and communication studies (e.g., Couldry 2013). The truth of the digital era is that we are indeed surrounded and permeated by digitally based communication technologies. The truth of virtue ethics is that we must choose carefully the blend and balances of literacies—both digital *and* analogue—that will play such a central role in our shared pursuit of contentment and flourishing as embodied and analogue, not simply digital, beings.

I hope this chapter will provide at least some of the reflection needed to help us, both individually and collectively, consider and make such choices.

Note

1 It may also be worth noting here that the International Communication Association, the largest such association in the world, chose the theme of "Communication and 'the good life'" to define its 2014 annual conference.

References

Baron, N. 2008, *Always on: language in an online and mobile world,* Oxford University Press: Oxford.
Borgmann, A. 1999, *Holding on to reality: the nature of information at the turn of the millennium,* University of Chicago Press: Chicago, IL.

Broadbent, S., Dewandre, N., Ess, C., Floridi, L., Ganascia, J-G., Hildebrandt, M., Laouris, Y., Lobet-Maris, C., Oates, S., Pagallo, U., Simon, J., Thorseth, M., & Verbeek, P-P. 2013, *The onlife initiative*, European Commission, Brussels, available at: https://ec.europa.eu/digital-agenda/sites/digital-agenda/files/Onlife_Initiative.pdf.

Couldry, N. 2013, "Why media ethics still matters," in S. J. Ward (ed.), *Global media ethics: problems and perspectives*, Blackwell: Oxford, 13–29.

Ess, C. 2014, "Selfhood, moral agency, and the good life in mediatized worlds? Perspectives from Medium Theory and philosophy." in K. Lundby (ed.), *Mediatization of communication,* Mouton De Gruyter: Berlin, pp. 617–640.

Ess, C. 2013, *Digital media ethics,* 2nd edn., Polity: Oxford.

Ess, C. & Fossheim, H. 2013, "Personal data: changing selves, changing privacy expectations," in M. Hildebrandt, K. O'Hara & M. Waidner (eds.), *Digital enlightenment forum yearbook 2013: the value of personal data*, IOS: Amsterdam, pp. 40–55.

Foucault, M. 1988, "Technologies of the self," in L. H. Martin, H. Gutman, & P. Hutton (eds.), *Technologies of the self: a seminar with Michel Foucault,* University of Massachusetts Press: Amherst, MA, pp. 16–49.

Kant, I. (1785) 2012, *Groundwork of the metaphysics of morals,* M. Gregor & J. Timmermans, (eds., trans.), Cambridge University Press: Cambridge.

Massumi, B. 2002, *Parables for the virtual: movement, affect, sensation*, Duke University Press: Durham, NC.

Moor, J. 2000, "Toward a theory of privacy in the information age," in R. M. Baird, R. Ramsower, & S. E. Rosenbaum (eds.), *Cyberethics: social & moral issues in the computer age,* Prometheus Books: Amherst, NY, pp. 200–212.

Ong, W. 1988, *Orality and literacy: the technologizing of the word*, Routledge: London.

Postman, N. 1985, *Amusing ourselves to death: public discourse in the age of show business*, Penguin: New York, NY.

Taylor, C. 1989. *Sources of the self: the making of the modern identity*, Harvard University Press: Cambridge, MA.

Vallor, S. 2011, "Flourishing on Facebook: virtue friendship & new social media," *Ethics and Information Technology,* vol. 14, no. 3, pp. 185–199.

Wiener, N. 1950/1954, *The human use of human beings: cybernetics and society*, 2nd edn., Doubleday Anchor: New York, NY.

Wilson, R. A. & Foglia, L. 2011, "Embodied cognition," in E. N. Zalta (ed.), *The Stanford encyclopedia of philosophy* (Fall 2011 edition), available at: http://plato.stanford.edu/archives/fall2011/entries/embodied-cognition/.

Index

For Product Safety Concerns and Information please contact our EU
representative GPSR@taylorandfrancis.com Taylor & Francis Verlag GmbH,
Kaufingerstraße 24, 80331 München, Germany

Printed and bound by CPI Group (UK) Ltd, Croydon, CR0 4YY
04/05/2025
01860529-0001